W9-CCX-222

TOMBEE

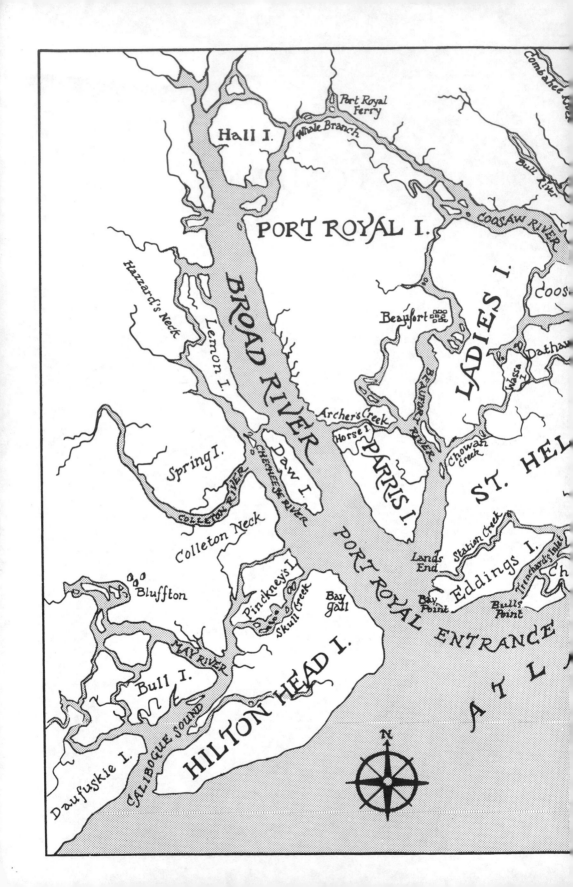

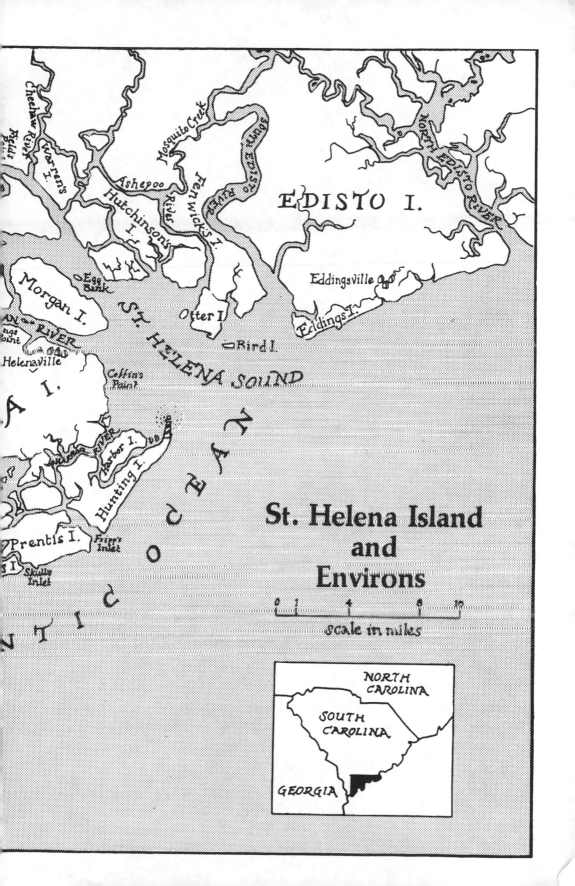

Chechaw River
Fields Point
Warren's I.
Mosquito Creek
South Edisto River
NORTH EDISTO RIVER
EDISTO I.
Ashepoo River
Hutchinson's I.
Fenwicks I.
Egg Bank
Eddingsville
Morgan I.
Otter I.
Eddings I.
ST. HELENA
Bird I.
Helenaville
RIVER
Coffin's Point
ST. HELENA SOUND
A I.
RIVER
Harbor I.
Hunting I.
OCEAN
Prentis I.
Fripp's Inlet
Skull Inlet
ATLANTIC

St. Helena Island and Environs

0   1   4   6   10
scale in miles

NORTH CAROLINA
SOUTH CAROLINA
GEORGIA

ALSO BY THEODORE ROSENGARTEN:

All God's Dangers: The Life of Nate Shaw

TOMBEE

PORTRAIT OF A
COTTON PLANTER

Theodore Rosengarten

---

with
THE JOURNAL OF
THOMAS B. CHAPLIN
(1822–1890)

Edited and Annotated with the
Assistance of Susan W. Walker

QUILL
WILLIAM MORROW
NEW YORK

Copyright © 1986 by Theodore Rosengarten

All rights reserved. No part of this book may be reproduced or utilized in any form or by any means, electronic or mechanical, including photocopying, recording, or by any information storage or retrieval system, without permission in writing from the Publisher. Inquiries should be addressed to Permissions Department, William Morrow and Company, Inc., 1350 Avenue of the Americas, New York, N.Y. 10019.

It is the policy of William Morrow and Company, Inc., and its imprints and affiliates, recognizing the importance of preserving what has been written, to print the books we publish on acid-free paper, and we exert our best efforts to that end.

Library of Congress Cataloging-in-Publication Data

Rosengarten, Theodore.
    Tombee : portrait of a cotton planter / Theodore Rosengarten : with the plantation journal of Thomas B. Chaplin (1822-1890), edited and annotated with the assistance of Susan W. Walker.
      p. cm.
    Includes bibliographical references and index.
    ISBN 0-688-11609-4
    1. Chaplin, Thomas, Benjamin, 1822-1890—Diaries. 2. Slaveholders—South Carolina—Saint Helena Island—Diaries 3. Plantation life—South Carolina—Saint Helena Island—History—19th century. 4. Cotton trade—South Carolina—Saint Helena Island—History—19th century. 5. Saint Helena Island (S.C.)—Biography. I. Chaplin, Thomas Benjamin, 1822-1890. II. Walker, Susan W. III. Title.
    F277.B3C487 1992
    975.7'9903'092—dc20   92-1292
    [B]   CIP

Printed in the United States of America

First Quill Edition

1 2 3 4 5 6 7 8 9 10

TO JAY AND MARTHA

The plowers plowed upon my back:
They made long their furrows.
—Psalms 129:3

PREFACE

One of the vexing problems about studying the southern plantation is that you come to know the masters better than you know the
slaves. The masters left a wealth of writing from which, and from
which alone, it is possible to recover the history of the Old South.
Only the masters kept diaries and account books. "I know of not a
single slave diary," remarked historian Kenneth Stampp, in 1971.[1]
And to my knowledge, none has surfaced since. Only the masters
wrote wills, deeds, and mortgages; the slaves were prevented from
learning to read and write. Besides, they could own nothing, so
they had nothing to convey. Only the masters were heard in civil
court, and transcripts of their abundant lawsuits have been saved.
The names of slaves appear in many of these papers, as it was often
the Negroes themselves who were seized, sold, taxed, pledged, and
fought over like so many candlesticks or cows.

Having said this, I propose to introduce a slaveholder and his
journal. I will relate the life story of a cotton planter which, in its
range of subjects, its rootedness in cultural tradition, and its evoca-
tion of group and individual psychology, reveals the larger character of Sea Island society in the prosperous decade and a half before
the Civil War.

Thomas Benjamin Chaplin owned Tombee Plantation, on St.
Helena Island, in Beaufort District, South Carolina. From his birth
in April, 1822, a month before the discovery of plans for a massive
slave uprising in Charleston, to his unnoticed death in December,
1890, Chaplin's story is a gold mine for the historian. He was heir
to a fortune consisting of rice lands and slaves on his mother's side,
cotton lands and slaves on his father's; at home and in school he
received an aristocratic education that was supposed to prepare

him to rule his Negroes; he grew up in the tumultuous decades when the white South was coming to see itself as a distinct cultural and political entity; he married a rich city girl, fatherless like himself, who brought to the match a dowry of stocks and bonds; he held numerous offices in local institutions charged with keeping the peace and providing public works; he cheered the war with Mexico, in 1846, shuddered at the revolutions in Europe, and stayed home to oversee his crops; in 1850, and again in 1860, he sat at the head banquet table with honored guests and speakers promoting secession; he hobnobbed with R. B. Rhett and Richard DeTreville, important separatist leaders, and with William Elliott, Captain John Fripp, and William Grayson, Jr., outspoken unionists; he never wondered about slavery, never found it odd or interesting or controversial; he fought in the Civil War, at times gallantly, always obscurely, and he crossed paths with Lee and Sherman; when peace returned he tried with bitter results to reassert control over his family and free black workers; his last living son, Daniel, rejected him while wrapping himself in the myth of the plantation past.

My major source of information about Chaplin is the journal he kept from 1845 through 1858. It is a lengthy manuscript, penned in a flowery, sometimes hieroglyphic hand, especially unsteady when its author had been drinking. I was shown the journal in 1979 by David Moltke-Hansen, then archivist and now director of the South Carolina Historical Society. At the time, I was studying agricultural slavery in the profitable 1850s. I had found that in spite of the economic boom, something was amiss. Planters in the coastal districts of South Carolina were making more money than at any other time in their lives; yet they were increasingly at odds with social currents in the rest of the Americas and Europe. They craved a literary and a technical culture worthy of their status, but they imported their books, tools, and simple machines from people hostile to their ideals. They wanted to modernize their industry, improve roads and waterways, and develop communications, but they were ideologically opposed to a strong central government with the means and authority to carry out the program. To tamper with the apparatus of government was to let in the worm of political democracy and increase the leverage of the state's majority of whites who owned no slaves and whose interests frequently clashed with slavery. These serious strains were glossed over or held in abeyance by the need to show unity in the face of an increasingly coherent threat from the North. And because the War was such a profoundly transforming event, they have been overlooked ever since. Nowhere was the transformation more acute, and the mythology of a prewar paradise quicker to take root, than in the tidewater region, or lowcountry, of South Carolina. I was going to write about these issues at length when Chaplin interrupted me.

Mr. Moltke-Hansen thought I would find support for my hypotheses in Chaplin's journal. I felt, as I read it, that it not only substantiated my ideas—it was already a book. What I found distinctive about the journal was its picture of ordinary life—the naming of things and the ebb and flow of relationships, the diminution of experience by monotony and its elevation by passion. Great events loom behind the scenes, but in the visible world people are eating, working, sleeping, falling ill, and dying.

I received permission from the Historical Society to prepare the journal for publication and hired a friend, Beverly Leichtman, to transcribe the manuscript. A year later I hired another friend, Susan Walker, to help me with the research. I estimated it would take six months, or a year at most.

Upon reading the journal a second time I realized the inadequacy of my plan. I had to admit that many of the entries which seemed clear and insightful to me would be gibberish to the nonspecialist. The first reading had given me a tactile understanding of life on a Sea Island plantation, but I had not reckoned with how idiosyncratic and difficult the text could be, and how very much was obscure to me, too. Moved by my intrinsic interest in Chaplin's story, and encouraged by finding some spectacular sources of information, I decided to search for the fullest possible context for the "items" he recorded in his journal. For four years, Susan Walker and I stalked Chaplin in public and private archives, reconstructing the world he took for granted, filling in the gaps in his story, trying to fathom his personality and its role in guiding the impact of impersonal forces.

The results of this investigation are the biography of Chaplin and his annotated journal. The two pieces can be read in any order. In no way does the biography exhaust the material in the journal or make the journal redundant. Rather, the biography provides a key for gaining entrance to a distant world and a framework for organizing the seemingly random notations. It allows the journal to yield its meanings less hesitantly, even to those who will disagree with my interpretation.

On the other hand, one may want to go directly to the journal and get the story in the protagonist's own voice. The reader who chooses this path will find that the problem of the journal's discontinuous style gives way to the excitement of exploring an original source, a product of human workmanship written for specific purposes by someone who lived long ago.

The journal has survived because Chaplin took steps to save it. He carried it off St. Helena Island, with precious little else, in the panic which followed the rout of Confederate forces at Port Royal, in November, 1861. Other St. Helena planters kept journals, but except for the diary of John E. Fripp, which records the progress of crops, and the account books of Thomas Aston Coffin, we will never know what they were like. Two journals were taken from plantation "Big Houses" by liberated slaves and given to William F. Allen, a Wisconsin schoolteacher and song collector who arrived on the Island in 1862. These manuscripts have disappeared.

Survivability, however, is not sufficient grounds for publication. Many private papers are pertinent to specialists only and are properly at home in an archive. Other documents, once polished and placed in a setting, can make a contribution to questions of general interest. Chaplin's journal belongs to this second group of sources. Its milieu is a single, well-defined plantation society set apart from the rest of the South by the sea and by a special staple crop. Hardly had the ink dried on Chaplin's final entry than conditions for perpetuating the old regime were struck off at the root. His journal offers rewarding reading into the last years of planter sovereignty, recorded without a glimmer of the changes ahead. It chronicles the young adult years of a discrete life which may be compared to popular images of plantation society. It contains a social history of the Sea Islands during the second "golden age of cotton." It furnishes an extensive account of the Sea Island cotton industry and a relentless, if inadvertent, study of the dull horror of plantation slavery.

Chaplin put his "other" self, the one he did not show in public, into his journal. Therefore, the journal is a subject as well as a source of his biography. Chapter 1 lays out the narrative sequence of his story, based primarily on what he himself has written. For the years before 1845 and after 1858, and for the historical setting, other sources are paramount, including histories of colonial Carolina, the *Official Records* of the Union and Confederate armies, and my correspondence with Chaplin's descendants and relatives.* Chapters 2 through 9 are organized by topics, each discussion moving chronologically. Chapter 10 rounds out Part I of the biography, exploring the journal's significance to Chaplin, his motives for writing it, and the mind and personality it projects. Part II follows Chaplin through the Civil War, Reconstruction, and the restoration of white rule. These last four chapters take leave of the journal, but not entirely. Chaplin's notes, added after 1865, are nuggets of information about the postwar period and Chaplin's personal evolution. Moreover, having formed a picture of the man from his journal, we can visualize him protesting and sighing and wishing he had a change of fresh linen as the prospects for repairing his fortunes dimmed forever.

*See the Note on Selected Sources, following the journal, for a discussion of outstanding source materials.

ACKNOWLEDGMENTS

I thank my friends for making this a more orderly and accurate book. Conscientious as a medieval copyist, Beverly Leichtman transcribed Chaplin's handwritten journal. Susan Walker, a gifted researcher, tracked Chaplin through the archives for four impecunious years. Jay Shuler, Billy Baldwin, Jon Wiener, David Moltke-Hansen, and Jane Raley strengthened the book with their astute criticisms. Jay alerted me to the ecological dimension of Sea Island life; Billy insisted that I tell a story and let my analysis issue out of the narrative; Jon urged me to balance the personal history with the history of local planter society; David demonstrated to me that the study of an individual is a study of values; Jane supplied evocative details and deterred me from imposing patterns on my subject.

I thank the descendants of the Chaplins and people who knew the family for opening their homes and libraries to me. Ann Fripp Hampton, Ethel Fripp Jones, Juddie K. Fortsen, Ellen P. Chaplin, Harriet Underwood, Cray Fripp, Saxby Chaplin Davis, C. E. Hickman, and the Reverend Dr. Robert E. E. Peeples generously shared their knowledge. History, they quite rightly believe, is something that happened to them.

For their informed and amiable assistance, I thank Wylma Wates and Robert McIntosh, at the South Carolina Department of Archives and History; Allen Stokes, at the South Caroliniana Library; William F. Sherman, at the Fiscal Branch of the National Archives; Julie Zachowski, at the Beaufort County Public Library; and the entire staff at the South Carolina Historical Society. The courtesies extended to me by Gene Waddell, former director of the Society, set my project in motion and assured its completion.

On St. Helena Island, Alexander and Betsy Yearley graciously welcomed my family to Tombee. Their neighbor, Fred Chaplin, the grandson of Tombee slaves, described to Susan Walker and me the antebellum layout of the plantation and post–Civil War visits by the former master's son. Emory S. Campbell, executive director of Penn Community Services, gave me access to the Penn School's distinguished archive.

Other individuals contributed materially to the Chaplin work. My thanks go to Edith Dabbs, Leah Wise, Peter Wood, George Geer, Joel Patrick, Joseph Holleman, Alice Quinn, Gerhard Spieler, Beulah Glover, the Reverend Peter Larsen, Craig M. Bennett, Carol Craw, and Debbie Thames. I am indebted to Joseph Duffey, past chairman of the National Endowment for the Humanities, for his support and encouragement, and to the Lyndhurst Foundation and its president, Deaderick Montague, for awarding me a prize in 1982 which enabled me to devote my time to this book.

I am grateful to Harvey Ginsberg, senior editor at William Morrow, for his patience and loyalty. Bruce Giffords did an awesome job of copyediting, creatively dealing with many thorny problems of usage and style. Kerry O'Connor Hood drew the exquisite maps which evoke the character of the Sea Islands as nature and human occupation have shaped and altered them. My deepest appreciation goes to my wife, Dale, for criticizing each draft of this work and helping me to think through and write the revisions. Her comradery was most important of all.

AUTHOR'S NOTE

In the biography of Thomas B. Chaplin, historical and explanatory notes appear at the bottom of the page. Numbered references to source material may be found on pages 300–317. Annotation has been limited to direct quotations, borrowed ideas, and novel or disputed points. Quotations from the journal of Thomas B. Chaplin are not footnoted. The spelling, grammar, and punctuation of old documents have been left unaltered. All italics within quotations belong to the original sources.

Contents

PART II

THE JOURNAL OF THOMAS B. CHAPLIN

MAPS

A map of "St. Helena Island and Environs" appears on pages 2–3.

TOMBEE

PART I

1. The Drift of Life

The Biographical Problem

The world should have been his oyster. Thomas B. Chaplin's fortune was made before he ever lifted a hand. Chaplin inherited a good name, a productive plantation with a large force of skilled workers, a virtual village of outbuildings, and all the tools, vehicles, and livestock necessary to raise and transport a crop of Sea Island cotton. He carried forward the wealth of five generations. At the least, he should have lived his days in comfort, and with only moderate exertion he should have added to his estate.

Yet the theme of his life was loss and disappointment. He lost the people he loved, or he lost their love. Much of his property he squandered through extravagance and reckless business habits. The rest was swept away by "that great blast of ruin and destruction," the Civil War.

For the white people of St. Helena Island, this calamity had a special bite—they lost their land as well as their slaves. Following the invasion of Port Royal, in November, 1861, the Federal Government confiscated and sold their plantations. "A planter paradise was almost wholly turned over to negroes," recalled an unrepentant Confederate.[1] "An old established civilization was replaced by an experiment," declared another.[2] The War leveled all differences among the competitive planters of St. Helena. The effort to appear richer than one's neighbor, to set a heavier table, to drive a fancier carriage, to sail a larger boat—all were so much water through a sieve. Nowhere else in the Old South was the system of landed wealth and power so resolutely dismantled.

Even in his heyday Chaplin never had much cash. He was land-rich and slave-rich, but he seldom had ten dollars in his pocket, and he would resort to selling fish for pin money. Compared to his neighbors, he was a moderate- to large-scale planter at the start of his career. By 1850, his fortunes had fallen while theirs had begun to rise. On paper his assets still put him in the top two percent of wealth in America. But by the standards of St. Helena he had become a small planter. The contrast to his former condition, his painful sense of loss and humiliation, and a rash of troubles at home mortally undermined his self-esteem.

By his own account, Chaplin did not stand out from the crowd. He wanted to be liked and included. He excelled at the manly pastimes approved by his group and he had no pursuits or interests that were uniquely his. He was a crack shot, a fine horse breeder, a good sailor, a decent billiards player. Away from society he was easily bored. He worried that people did not appreciate him for his company, but only wanted him along because he would supply the champagne for dinner, the dogs for hunting, or the Negroes for rowing.

As a cotton producer, he lagged behind his neighbors and friends. His crops were small overall, though not bad when figured by the bales produced per worker. He simply did not, or could not, put enough hands into the fields at the right times. Furthermore, the fertility of his cotton land was apparently declining.[3] While fertilizer for rejuvenating the soil was his for the taking, other tasks always seemed to come first. His corn crops were decidedly good, however, and improved steadily. He got great satisfaction from selecting and perfecting his own corn seed and watching it outbear standard varieties. He was also fond of fruit trees, and he always planted a diversity of vegetables.

In his life's work, his goals, his methods, his ideals, and his associations, Chaplin was a typical Sea Island planter—though unlike his friends, he was more often a debtor seeking to borrow than a capitalist wanting to invest. The most remarkable fact about him is that nearly every day for thirteen years, he sat at his desk and wrote in his journal. He recorded the weather and tallied his crops; he itemized the tasks performed by his slaves; he put down his comings and goings and anything unusual he happened to see or hear about; he complained about his wife, children, aunts and uncles, neighbors, creditors, friends, slaves, and enemies; he fretted over the impressions he had made on other people; he rehearsed attitudes he intended to adopt in the future.

In its form and features, Chaplin's journal shows that its author was aware of the genre. Perhaps he had read Pepys's journal in school. His father or one of his uncles might have kept a journal. Possibly he took to heart the advice of agricultural writers who urged young men to build self-discipline and sharpen their powers of observation by keeping a daily record of plantation affairs.

Much in Chaplin's development can be traced to growing up without a father and to being shunted around by his mother, Isabella, who was occupied in wooing men and spending her money. She married him off just before his seventeenth birthday—very early for a young man of his background to be pushed out of the parental nest. His marriage might have been a solution to one of her problems, for she had too many plantations and no one to manage them.

We know from Chaplin's circumstances why he became a planter. The biographical problem he presents is to understand how he both typified his social class and was simultaneously a full-blown individual. His own endeavor to understand himself was sporadic and flawed; still, it was one of the endearing things about him. He knew he was ill-tempered, that he drank too much and wasted his time; he was an example, he believed, of a person spoiled by money. He wished he could be different, and though he did not work very hard to change, he lamented his failure. Looking back from 1875, he described himself as a "sufferer"—a characterization confirmed by his acquaintances. Colonel Ambrose Gonzales, chief of Confederate artillery at Charleston, identified him, in 1863, as "a high-toned gentleman and a great sufferer."[4] Gonzales emphasized Chaplin's losses since the occupation of St. Helena by "abolitionists," yet suffering was a part of Chaplin's demeanor even before the War. Insofar as it gave him stature, suffering was its own strange consolation.

"A high-toned gentleman," in the usage of the mid-nineteenth century, was a man who carried himself with a vivid sense of role, who affected a distance between himself and people of lower birth, servants, and strangers. This posture was cultivated to show off wealth, breeding, and authority, and to offset the physical closeness of cramped living quarters. Chaplin's life was filled with contrasts. Perhaps the most striking disparity was between his great wealth and his perennial struggle to feed his dependents, or between his capital and his income. He fluctuated between periods of morbid self-consciousness and obliviousness; he thought of virtue, but he practiced vice; he was a man of the clubhouse and the dinner party, but he felt lonesome in company. Each family and seignorial role he filled required a different balance of assertion and subordination—as husband, father, master, brother, son, nephew, cousin. He is most involved, and most himself, as a son, when we meet him in 1845. The journal follows his progress away from being his mother's child, toward becoming his children's father.

Our interest in Chaplin as a man, as well as a type of man, a planter, grows out of a paradox. While he felt his life was an exercise in futility, the telling of it was a great accomplishment. Whatever happened to him, for gain or for loss, the diarist took pleasure in writing it down. Part of him lived close to the soil, close—if cool—to his slaves, and part was absorbed in society; but he withheld another part for the world of letters. Chaplin the man lived at a safe distance from us, where the gross problems of human inequity seem comfortably in the past; but Chaplin the diarist is immediately present, in an ethical world where people's capacity for good and evil is only superficially different from ours.

Chaplin's Journal: Its Nature and Scope

Chaplin began his journal in 1845. He was twenty-two years old and the master of between sixty and seventy slaves. He lived with his wife Mary, their four children, and her half-sister Sophy, at Tombee Plantation—376 acres of fields, pastures, and woods bordering the marshes of Station Creek, in the southwest corner of St. Helena Island, near Lands End. The census of 1840 does not show him on the Island. Sometime in the early 1840s he produced his first cotton crop at Tombee.

Page one of the journal is missing. The first entry we have, dated January 13, reports bad news: the sheriff has seized twenty-seven Negroes belonging to Chaplin's mother, under a mortgage to Charleston merchants. It appears that her disgruntled husband—husband number four—was behind the move. Thus, the first extant words of the diary introduce Robert Little Baker, Chaplin's nemesis and chief rival for his mother's wealth and affection. From this day through May, 1858, with a few lengthy interruptions, Chaplin wrote almost daily in his journal. He stopped writing several pages from the end of the volume, adding irregular entries over the next three years.

Then the War came to St. Helena with its surprising results. Chaplin was cut adrift from his plantation forever. For thirteen years he had kept faith with his journal; for thirty years more he lugged it around in exile, periodically reading it and penciling in afterthoughts. Often he dated his notes—'68, '74, '76, '77, '84. On January 1, 1886, he wrote a three-page epilogue and stuck it at the back of the book. Here he brought his life up to date from the war years, made a final wish—and it is the last we know of him until his death, in 1890. So, while the consecutive entries cover a little more than thirteen years, the journal spans a story of forty years. After 1866, Chaplin was continually filling in the fates of his characters, contrasting his hand-to-mouth existence with the affluence of former days, deploring his many unpaid kindnesses, and congratulating himself on being alive.

The method of the journal is like a slow meander along a tidal creek, with long portages between stretches of navigable water, and detours ending nowhere as often as not. Topics are introduced and dropped; characters show up when they have not yet arrived, or they have gone when we think they are still in the picture. We don't learn the outcome of situations for days, or even years, if at all. In contrast, Chaplin's notes offer quick resolution. What was the result of storing potatoes under pine straw? The experiment failed and the potatoes rotted, a note tells us. How did the marriage of John H. Webb and Emma Jenkins turn out? Very well, they lived happily, although their friends all had opposed the match. What became of the slave Mary's baby, Amy, at whose birth Mary made such a fuss? The girl died at age two or three.

Thus the notes impose a consciousness of the end in the midst of life. For example, at the very moment that Dr. William Jenkins is building a mansion or showing off his new horses, he is the ruined man eking out a living in his son's liquor shop in Beaufort, after the War. No contrast so forcibly colors our reading as that of the 1845 entry describing the birth of Eugene, Chaplin's third son, and the note inserted thirty years later. Mary Chaplin was "taken sick" late in the evening of September 26. Since she was prone to long labors, her husband settled down in the hall, "very quietly reading the newspaper, expecting to keep awake nearly all night." This time he did not have to wait long. In about two hours, "I heard something like a young child cry. Could hardly believe it was over so soon, but Lo it was. A little boy was born." Chaplin peeked in the room as the midwife washed and dressed the baby, then fed him some butter and sugar. "Left the mother & child doing well," exulted the happy father. "Good God, the changes since then," opens the note. "And that boy—fell, a victim to cruel war, his bones molder in an unknown grave in North Carolina. He died from war, pestilence & famine, & cruelty while prisoner in the Yankee army, in 1864. Who dreamed of the end when this page was written. . . ." There is the life. From butter and sugar to moldering bones in the space of ten lines. Thereafter, when we see Eugene—at his christening, traveling to school, fishing with his father, eating a sheepshead on his eighth birthday—it is as if we are watching his spirit, and the body is already in the grave.

Chaplin's journal spans seven years of decline and dissipation followed by six years of comparative recovery. Shortly after the cotton was sown in 1845, he was forced to sell off "ten prime Negroes" to meet his creditors' demands. "I never thought that I would be driven to this very unpleasant extremity," he wrote, unaware that his troubles were only beginning. Outwardly he appeared optimistic, planting a fruit orchard and shade trees. But he was not destined to enjoy them. First, astronomical debts overtook him, though how he came to owe large sums of money is a mystery. Nobody could, or would, come to his aid. His mother was prevented from helping him by the outcome of a notorious legal battle over her rights as a married woman to dispose of her property as she wished. Chaplin's ruin followed immediately. Forty to fifty slaves, more than two-thirds of his labor force, were seized and sold at auction. He lost woodlands, a summer house, a plantation boat, furniture, horses, and all his livestock except for two cows which he was allowed by law to keep. "I am compelled to begin in the world again," he announced, in April, 1848. But he was held back by troubles at home—sickness in his family, the deaths of three of his daughters, and the lingering death of his wife. With Mary dying, he could not think of his crops. At the same time, he was stung by a series of social humiliations: he got drunk and was made a fool of at a militia meeting; friends engineered his removal from the post of road commissioner; he was deceived out of a chance of renting a house in St. Helenaville, a refuge from the sickly plantation environment; no one would put up security for him to hire some Negroes; his Uncle Ben died without heirs but left him nothing.

Meanwhile his capital was rapidly depreciating. "My horse-cart is broken, my ox is dead, and God knows how I will get along."

Mary died at last on November 4, 1851. Life went on—Chaplin killed a beef cow for a planters' market; his slaves dug potatoes and cleaned the cotton. Now he could think about his estate, and indeed his prospects were good. He was twenty-nine years old, father of four living children, master of twenty-five slaves, and owner of hundreds of acres of choice land. Cotton prices were climbing—already they were the highest he had ever known—and though he no longer had the labor to produce a large crop, he could improve the quality of his staple and take advantage of the widening price differential between the common and finer grades of Sea Island cotton. Chaplin approached spring planting in 1852 with enthusiasm. Even recurrent bouts of fever did not discourage him. His nagging food problem was relieved by substantial gifts of meat from his mother, who had regained some power over her property. But his chief source of happiness was Sophy, his deceased wife's half-sister. Five months after Mary died, Chaplin and Sophy were engaged to be married.

Chaplin got up from the ground but he never thoroughly dusted himself off. His slow, undramatic rise allowed him to replenish only a small part of his estate in the time that was left to plantation slavery. His mother's subsidies were the hidden hand behind his modest recovery. Doubtless her most important gift was the slave Robert, who came to live at Tombee in 1852. Robert quickly became Chaplin's mainstay. He understood the planter's directions and he was a natural leader. With Robert installed as his slave driver, Chaplin was freed from having to personally oversee the work in his fields. This development had two notable consequences. On the positive side, Chaplin could devote himself to improving his seeds: his burgeoning yields of corn and the steady refinement of his cotton showed that he was succeeding at it.

The second consequence tended to neutralize the benefits of the first. As Robert's influence quietly spread, Chaplin had less to do, and grew restless. Just when his cotton could have used his supervision most, he left for the mainland to visit his mother and brother. His cotton output fell, even while the quality of the fiber improved. In 1856, his corn production fell, too, because of sickness among the slaves and unfavorable weather. This put him in a hole. He tried selling fruit, vegetables, and meat to get money for corn.

To cut back on expenses, he kept his family at Tombee for the summer, warding off fever with quinine and ice. Ernest, Chaplin's oldest boy, nearly died. The slave Nelly lost her third baby in as many years. But the new corn crop was a good one. Chaplin's yield in 1857 was his best ever, some thirty-two bushels to the acre, topping by four bushels Edgar Fripp's crop that had won the Agricultural Society's premium for corn only five years before.

In the spring of 1858, Chaplin found the money to send his four children to school. Daniel, the second oldest, was preparing for the military academy. On the twelfth of April, Chaplin finished planting cotton, all except a patch, and observed that his earlier sowings of cotton and corn were "up very prettily." He put down the number of acres planted in cotton, corn, and potatoes, and expressed hope for good results. Then, declaring that the journal was about to end, he dedicated it to his children. A week later he reported the burning of one of the Island's two general stores. A week after that he acknowledged his thirty-sixth birthday. "Thought I was older, but I am not." Over the next two pages he scattered news from the following months and years—the death of a favorite horse, the marriage of the belle of St. Helena to a stranger from the mainland, and the births of seven Negroes, starting with "a girl name Grace," born to Peg's daughter Mary, and ending, on July 6, 1861, three months after the Confederates captured a Federal fort in Charleston Harbor, with the birth of Nelly's boy Sumter.

Methods and Meanings

Readers of Chaplin's journal have the advantage of knowing the outcome of events. In a sense, we start with a picture of the complete vessel and work backward to the shards, finding in every fragment the unmistakable imprint of the whole. With hindsight, a wisp of conversation tells us which way things were heading, which ideas were pivotal and which people were instrumental in bringing about a result, and how things might have gone differently. We may tend to read too much into a clue, where the diarist invariably did not read enough. But with an informed grasp of the setting, we can translate mundane and sometimes absurd details into significant historical evidence.

In 1850—to give an example of a small, local commotion that signals a deep disturbance in the social order—we hear of "a little jarring" among members of the Agricultural Society over "the proper time and place of holding a parish meeting for the purpose of expressing our feelings upon the death of John C. Calhoun, senator from this state." Well, what is "a little jarring" among quarrelsome men? Nothing out of the ordinary, yet a sign of greater dissension ahead. For nearly twenty years, Calhoun had suppressed political factions in South Carolina and united a wide range of views behind his leadership. Now, on the occasion of organizing his memorial service, a schism breaks into the open. New leaders, more radical and less popular men, would propel the state toward confrontation with the Federal Government. Two months after Calhoun's death, his successor in the Senate, the zealous separatist R. B. Rhett, delivered his "I am born of Traitors" speech at Hibernian Hall, in Charleston, proclaiming the time had come to leave the Union.* Three weeks later, Rhett was honored at a fête in St. Helenaville, under a "handsome flag . . . bearing on its silken folds" nine silver stars and the motto "Oh, that we were all such traitors" on one side, and on the other side, "Southern Rights and Southern Wrongs, we will maintain the one and resist the other."[5] Chaplin was there. But not for a moment in his journal does he step aside and let a more "historical" figure address us. We learn only that the "appearance of champagne" was the cue for speaking. Of all he might have chosen to write about, he described at length the stand "erected for the invited guests of distinction, entwined with evergreens and covered with a canopy" that won praise for the "Committee on Arrangements" on which he served.

Chaplin never dreamed where this excitement was leading. At the time he gave up writing daily in his journal, secession fever had subsided; people were talking about the cheerful outlook for cotton, high prices for slaves, improved communications with Charleston and Savannah, and a new railroad that would surely transform the sleepy harbor at Port Royal into a bustling commercial center. In 1858, you could not attract an audience to a political speech on St. Helena. That would change by the time of the presidential election of 1860. South Carolina would take the lead in declaring independence from the Union, and St. Helena planters would

*"I am born of Traitors—Traitors in England, in the Revolution, in the middle of the seventeenth century, Traitors again in the Revolution of 1720, when under the lead of an ancestor, South Carolina was rescued from the capricious rule of the Lords Proprietors, and Traitors again in the Revolution of 1776. I have been born of Traitors, but thank God, they have been Traitors in the just cause of liberty, fighting against tyranny and oppression." (Charleston *Mercury*, July 20, 1850.)

spearhead the movement to secede. Even then, they did not believe that war was imminent. In ten years, or five years, perhaps, but not soon. After the Confederate victory at Manassas, Virginia, in July, 1861, they did not imagine that when the War resumed, it would be within sight of their homes. And when the planters learned that the enemy armada out of Hampton Roads was steaming for Port Royal, they forgot the lesson learned by Scottish settlers at the hands of the Spanish, in 1686, and by the American rebels at the hands of the British, in 1779—that the islands could not be defended against attack from the sea.

Most unimaginable of all were the consequences of defeat. For the planters of St. Helena, there would be no coming home from the War and rebuilding a life with elements of the past. Home belonged to strangers. The Episcopal Church, the militia, the Agricultural Society, and the other institutions which had serviced the plantations were "all gone to rats." Property extinct, people lost the incentive to keep up old alliances, to choose spouses from the same select few families, or, as Chaplin sadly learned, to oblige and comfort their parents in anticipation of an inheritance.

"That horrid war," Chaplin called it. All he tells us about having been a soldier is contained in two little notes: that he rode in the cavalry, and that a cheap saddle he had bought in 1853 "galled every horse" he put it on. Yet the War hovers over the journal like a low dark sky. One cannot think of Chaplin, or Dr. Jenkins, or Ned Capers, or Captain John Fripp, or Ann Minott, without thinking of what the War did to them. They lived long lives, with as much intensity and singularity as anyone. But they happened to live in the last years of the slavery epoch, in the only country where it took a civil war to throw off slavery, and their distinction lies in relation to these facts.

A Lost World

Chaplin went to war at the age of thirty-eight. He came back an old man, shorn of his powers and fortune. In appearance and convictions he was firmly tied to the fashions of the fifth and sixth decades of the century. While a planter, he seldom left the Island. Once he went two years without going to Beaufort, his trading town, only twelve miles from home. Now, for the remainder of his life, he was a vagabond, drifting and bereaved. He did not return to live on St. Helena until 1872, after losing the last of his mother's old plantations, in St. Bartholomew's Parish. For the next twelve years, he and Sophy "thumped and bumped" around the east side of the Island, near Coffin's Point and the ruins of St. Helenaville. All the while he kept his eye on Tombee, which he had reason to hope he might yet recover. By a stroke of good luck, his old plantation had been designated by Treasury Department officials in 1862 to become a "school farm" and, consequently, it had not been carved up and sold. Shortly after his return to St. Helena, the Federal Government began allowing former landowners to sue to redeem property still in its hands. Chaplin applied, not suspecting he was falling into a bureaucratic snare that would entangle him for the rest of his life.

To support himself and Sophy, Chaplin took a job teaching at "a large school for Negro children," a post he held, with some pride, until 1877, when he became a trial justice. "Beaufort County is rich in trial justices," the town newspaper reported, "Governor Hampton having appointed fifteen just before the adjournment of the legislature."[6] Chaplin was among this bunch. Over in Colleton County, his brother, Saxby, was appointed to the same office. There were not enough trials to go around, however, and Chaplin had to seek additional work—anything "I could pick up." For one season he was "the custodian of government property" at the site of a new lighthouse on Hunting Island. In 1880, he took the census on St. Helena, and his candid reflections on the changes he had witnessed are part of the public record.

Throughout these years, Chaplin was addicted to opium. Before the War he had taken opiates for medicinal purposes. Mixed with alcohol, sweetened with molasses, and flavored with aromatic barks, opiates were administered to adults and children for bronchitis, "breast complaint," diarrhea, cancer, hysteria, and many other ailments. In large concentrations, opium was supposed to depress the appetite for alcohol. Chaplin may have become addicted during the War, when morphine, the major opium alkaloid, was given routinely by hypodermic needle to fight pain and nervous disorders.

Between 1876 and 1880, Chaplin wrote at least fourteen letters to Dr. G. W. Aimar, a Charleston pharmacist, begging for opium and apologizing for not paying his bill.[7] A letter dated September 3, 1878, begins, "I am doomed to disappointment"—the judgment of a life. The letter explains that a man to whom he had sold a cow was able to pay him only one-third in cash, not enough to permit Chaplin to forward a remittance. Four months later, Chaplin asked Aimar to recommend a book "on the cure of my curse." In May, 1879, he wrote that he was "going through a process . . . to break the habit." The "process" left him "unable to do anything"—that is, he could not work and so could not pay his bill—and he was "doubtful" the cure would work.

When he left St. Helena for the mainland, on October 11, 1884, he knew he was leaving for the last time. The voyage began ominously, as the boat "grounded on the marsh in the mouth of Coffin's Creek." Unable to float free, the party could do nothing but wait for the tide to rise. With Chaplin were his wife Sophy and his old friend and most valued possession, his journal. By his own admission, the volume is full of nonsense and repetitions. Whatever is shrewd, or eloquent, or original about it is at odds with the artlessness of the writer. The record shows he was vain, obtuse, abrasive. It also shows he had the qualities of an ordinary, decent person, including a mature yearning for peace, although his mental life was full of conflict.

What could he have done differently to avert his fate? Everything seemed to have happened against his choosing. If his father had lived to instruct him; if his mother had not remarried but had retained power over her property; if Uncle Ben had left him something; if his wives had been more active in the management of his plantation; if he had kept better accounts; if he had gotten rain when he needed it; if all these things had come to pass he still would have been there in the boat, waiting for high water. Luck, genius, capital, did not matter—an observation that gave Chaplin passing consolation. "Where are they now, that were so particular and saving back then," he asked, late in life, "—no better off today than I & some dead & gone, & their leavings belong to strangers. They saved, saved, for strangers."

2. Settings and Backgrounds

The Sea Islands: A Natural History

St. Helena Island is situated off the Atlantic coast, about fifty miles southwest of Charleston, South Carolina, and forty miles northeast of Savannah, Georgia. It belongs to a fertile chain of islands separated from one another and from the mainland by rivers and creeks, as they are called, according to their width and depth. Many of these streams might better be described as "arms of the sea" because they bring the salt water inland to a pine belt and carry it out again without meeting significant sources of fresh water; or else they wash parallel to the mainland through narrow depressions which drain the edge of the coastal plain. Twice each lunar day the tide flows toward the land, then ebbs back toward the sea. When the moon is in the first and third quarters, the tides rise six to eight feet around St. Helena—these are neap tides. At the new moon and the full moon, the waters rise eight to ten feet— these are spring tides. As the tides ebb, the islands appear to draw close together. Marshes and mud flats, submerged only a few hours before, emerge between the hills or high grounds. As the lower land disappears beneath the flooding tides, the islands appear to shrink and grow more distant from each other. Yet, it is at these high tides that travel between the islands is easiest. For the water is a road that connects human habitations, while the flats exposed at low tide are mud-filled moats, friendly only to oyster catchers and armies of hungry crabs.

St. Helena Island is an erosion-remnant island—one of three kinds of islands which shelter the mainland from the sea. The other two are marsh islands and beach-ridge, or barrier, islands. Erosion-remnant islands lie closest to the main. At one time they were part of the main, but were detached after the last glacial period when tributaries of large streams looking for new routes to the ocean eroded paths through unresistant soils. Sediments of clay and organic matter settled into the valleys which formed on all sides of the new islands, particularly on the ocean side. As the sea level rose and the tides moved in and out in their regular rhythm, grasses grew on the higher, wind-blown areas. These places became marsh islands.

From his second-story veranda, Thomas Chaplin could look south at low tide across three miles of marsh islands and mud flats to Bay Point, at the tip of Eddings Island, the most westerly of the four barrier islands which fence St. Helena from the ocean. The back, or landside, of these outer islands rises almost imperceptibly from the marsh. Behind the expanse of spartina grass looms a forest of massive live oaks, twisted cedars, crooked pines, and upright palmettos with spongy, branchless trunks and crowns of fan-shaped leaves which rattle like bones in the wind. Under a dark canopy, red-berried cassenas compete for sunlight with myrtle and holly and prickly pear, themselves swaddled by catbrier and jasmine. Approached from the ocean, the outer islands appear to be terraced. A hard white line of sand, capped by a dark green stripe, stops the sea at the horizon; feathery pinetops dust the sky. As you come near shore, the bright beaches command the view, while the "seaside jungles" fall back behind the dunes.

St. Helena is the largest island in its old political division, St. Helena Parish, which is entirely "a parish of islands."[1] At fifteen miles long and three to five miles wide, St. Helena is larger by half than Ladies Island, its neighbor to the west, across Chowan Creek (now Johnson River), a narrow tidal slough, and larger by a third than Port Royal Island, farther west along Port Royal River. To the northeast, St. Helena Island is bounded by St. Helena Sound, the widest opening on the Atlantic seaboard between Chesapeake Bay and the Gulf of Mexico. And to the southwest, the Island meets Port Royal Sound, a bay into which several large saltwater streams empty. The largest of these are Broad River and Port Royal River. Neither flows far inland, so neither could bring settlers or commerce into the back country or carry out the produce of the west to a waiting port. The bar, or entrance, to Port Royal Harbor is one of the deepest on the Atlantic coast—eighteen to twenty feet at low tide, exceeding the bar at Charleston by nine feet—deep enough to accommodate the largest commercial and military vessels afloat in 1860. Yet, because there is no easy passage to the interior, the harbor never realized the dreams of its promoters. Schemes to divert the water and trade of the Savannah River date from 1800. A year before the Civil War, a railroad came to the head of the Sound, and a small port prospered in the 1870s and '80s, to service the phosphate and lumber industries. But these activities were purely extractive: very little cargo came into the port, and when the phosphate trade turned to cheaper sources elsewhere, the port sank back into dormancy.

Discovery and Settlement

Impressions about geography and topography are impressions about productive capabilities. Not all people at all times look to the land and water to yield up the same things. The Spanish came in 1521, in search of Indians to work in the mines and on the sugar plantations of Santo Domingo. Sailing coastwise north of the Florida peninsula, Pedro de Quexós, an experienced seaman in the service of court justice and sugar planter Lucas Vásquez de Ayllón, sighted a cape and named it Santa Elena, for the saint's day. This may or may not have been the place which later bore the English name St. Helena. The Spanish returned to the coast of Carolina, which they called Chicora, in 1526, hoping to found a colony on the West Indian model. They had long-range plans to grow crops and raise livestock for the mother country, but for the present they needed a base for expeditions to the interior where, they had been told, they would find gold mines, caches of pearls, domesticated deer, and men with inflexible tails which they used as seats.[2] The large party of Spaniards—larger than the crew Cortés had taken to Mexico—landed at Cape Fear, then moved south to the Pee Dee River, near present-day Georgetown, South Carolina. Running low on food, they raided the Indians' corn; the Indians retaliated and destroyed the settlement. Ayllón, who had come in person to lead the hunt for riches, caught a fever and died, and the survivors embarked for Santo Domingo.

A colony of French Protestants, led by Jean Ribaut, made contact with Santa Elena in 1562. Also sailing north along the semitropical coast, the Huguenots came to "a mightie river" and named it Port Royal.[3] Impressed with the abundance of fish and the friendliness of the Indians, who hated the Spanish, the Huguenots built a fort, called Charlesfort, on what is now Parris Island. A group stayed to defend this eccentric outpost of French Protestantism, while Ribaut went home for reinforcements. France, meanwhile, had plunged into the Protestant and Catholic Wars. Ribaut immediately entered the fight on the side of his religion, and dropped the project at Port Royal. Restless and demoralized, the colonists abandoned Charlesfort in 1564. Sailing in a leaky ship they had built with the help of the Indians, only a handful of settlers survived the harrowing passage to Europe. They had left Port Royal none too soon, for the Spanish had sent an expedition to remove them. On the ruins of Charlesfort, the Spanish built a fort of their own. For twenty-one years, "Santa Elena was Philip II's northernmost outpost on the Atlantic coast."[4]

Thus Spain and France carried the fight for supremacy of Europe into the New World. Neither nation was able to build a lasting settlement in Carolina, each butchering the colonies of the other—to the astonishment of the Indians and to the good fortune, ultimately, of England.

The Spanish King had warned the English that he would "cut off their heads" as he had done to the French,* if they tried to settle in Florida—the Spanish name for southeastern North America. Encouraged by successes in Virginia and New England, and aware that Spanish military power was in decline, Charles I defied King Philip and granted a charter, in 1629, to Sir Robert Heath, giving Heath the right to settle Englishmen in a territory called "Carolana," just south of Virginia and overlapping the Spanish claim. Heath failed to act on the opportunity and in 1663, Charles II granted to eight "right trusty and right beloved cousins and counselers"[†] the territory lying between the 31st and 36th parallels of north latitude and extending from the Atlantic Ocean to the South Seas, a portion of America "only inhabited by some barbarous people who have no knowledge of Almighty God."

At the same time, planters on Barbados were looking for new lands to cultivate. The West Indian island was overcrowded and its

---

*A reference to the slaughter, by Pedro Menéndez de Marqués, of Jean Ribaut and another party of Huguenots, in 1565, near the River May.

†Sir John Colleton; Anthony, Lord Ashley (who later became Earl of Shaftesbury); Edward Hyde, Earl of Clarendon; George Monck, Duke of Albemarle; William, Lord Craven; John, Lord Berkeley; Sir George Carteret; Sir William Berkeley. Known collectively as the Lords Proprietors, these eight men had raised money and soldiers for Charles II in the English Civil War. They were investors who had their hands in many pots. Lord Ashley, for example, was a shareholder in the Royal African Company, procurers of slaves, and in the Hudson Bay Company, which monopolized the fur trade in eastern Canada. At one time he considered selling Africans to the Spanish in Florida and the Indies.

soil overtaxed. To counter the falling agricultural yield, planters enlarged their operations by gobbling up smaller estates. But they needed to expand still further. Seeking "fresh avenues for their children,"[5] "Several Gentlemen and Merchants of the Island of Barbados" sent William Hilton, aboard the ship *Adventure,* to explore the Carolina seaboard. Hilton crossed the bar at Port Royal Sound, probed the land and cataloged its plants and animals, found a small company of Spanish soldiers from St. Augustine, with whom he exchanged letters and gifts, and picked up a party of shipwrecked Englishmen. He befriended the Indians and concluded a peace. Returning to Barbados he reported on "the good soyl, covered with black mold, in some places a foot, in some a half a foot," which, he was certain, would produce as much as the best land of the Indies. "The ayr is clear and sweet," he praised, advising "all they that want a happy settlement of our English nation" to come quickly to Port Royal.[6]

Hilton's auspicious report was followed up in 1666 by Robert Sandford. Prospecting for a place to plant after his settlement had failed at Cape Fear, Sandford cast an envious eye on "the fields of maiz of a very large growth" which surrounded the Indian town at Port Royal. He was confident that the English could get along with the Indians, who received him "with such high testimonies of joy and thankfulness as hugely confirmed to mee their great desire of our friendship and society."[7]

The English "planted" a permanent colony in 1670. William Sayle, a former governor of Bermuda and now an old man of eighty, led 148 English settlers to Port Royal, via the Bahamas. Finding the ground very low and fearing the proximity of the Spanish, the company moved to a safer haven on the Ashley River, at a place they called Albemarle Point, after the eldest of the Lords Proprietors, and later renamed Charles Towne, after the King.

The next settlers to reach Port Royal sailed from Scotland in 1684, under the command of Lord Cardross, who hoped to found a refuge for Covenanters.* At "a verie convenient place" midway between the present-day towns of Beaufort and Port Royal, they built Stuart Town. "It shall be a port toun for ever," predicted Cardross.[8] Spain still regarded the territory south of the Ashley River as its possession, but the Spanish tolerated the Scots until the

---

*Members of the Reformed Presbyterian Church whose forerunners in 1638 had entered into a "Solemn League and Covenant for the Reformation and Defense of Religion" against the influence of the papacy.

Scots induced the Yamassee Indians to cross the Savannah River and attack Spanish missions in Guale, the seacoast of Georgia. These flimsy missions could not have threatened Stuart Town, and attacks against them were reckless. The Spanish retaliated in 1686, sending three shiploads of soldiers from St. Augustine who burned the settlement and chased the survivors into the woods. Not everyone in Charles Towne was unhappy with the fate of the Scots, because Cardross had cut into the English monopoly on the lucrative Indian trade.

In 1698, after a twelve-year hiatus, the Lords Proprietors began issuing land grants in the area of Port Royal, this time to individuals. Among the first was a warrant to Mr. John Stewart for one thousand acres on St. Helena Island, "being a neck of land formerly inhabited by the Pocatalagoes. . . ."[9]

Destruction of the Indians

The Indians who welcomed the English claimed to be recent arrivals on the coast themselves, having been driven "to the salt water" by more powerful tribes to the west.[10] The small coastal tribes, such as the Edistos, Escamacus, Ashepoos, Bohicketts, Kiawahs, and Stonos, were segments of the weak Cusabo group. Barred from their traditional upland hunting grounds, they now lived year-round along the tidal streams and rivers which they used to visit seasonally. Their villages had taken on a look of permanence; they built durable houses, painted them, and even laid down floors. Fishing and agriculture had increased in importance, and the Cusabos built granaries and cribs to store their harvests.

Yet their survival was threatened by belligerent, well-armed enemies. Disunited by waterways, feuds, and by the decentralized character of a fishing economy, the Cusabos had difficulty defending themselves. Hence they wanted the English for allies, and each tribe made a plea for the newcomers to settle near its towns. The main enemy of the tribes living near Port Royal was the Westoes, a people either of Iroquoian or Uchean stock—the Cusabos were of the Muskhogean stock*—living on the south bank of the Savannah

---

*The fifty or so tribes which inhabited present-day South Carolina when the Europeans made contact belonged to five distinct linguistic stocks—Iroquoian, Muskhogean, Siouan, Uchean, and Algonquian. The first three "are the richest of all the stocks north of Mexico in literary and historical records, and are also the largest and strongest." (David Duncan Wallace, *The History of South Carolina* [New York, 1934], 11.)

River. The Westoes had been lately joined by a band of Ricohi-crans, who may have been Iroquoian refugees from New York. Possibly they were renegade Cherokees—also an Iroquoian peo-ple—from the southern mountains. Whatever their origin, the Ri-cohicrans had lived briefly in Virginia, where they had established a trade in firearms with Jamestown and won a reputation for feroc-ity. The Westo-Ricohicran axis terrorized many southeastern tribes, not only the weak Cusabos but the Yamassees, Creeks, Cherokees, and Catawbas—a Siouan remnant that had held on along the present-day border of North Carolina, while the rest of this once populous southern people had migrated west, in pursuit of the retreating buffalo, across country through which they had once walked east.

English policy was to ally with the strong and make vassals of the weak. Only the Westoes could provide the skins and furs which were the country's major source of wealth. Yet the security and food supply of the colony depended on good relations with the Cu-sabos, the enemies of the Westoes. The situation was complicated by the slave trade. Soon after settling at Charles Towne, the English began subsidizing Westo attacks on other tribes in order to procure slaves. What had formerly been raids for corn became pri-marily raids for slaves. Many a Cusabo captured by the Westoes and sold to the English at Charles Towne was resold in the slave marts of New York, New England, and the West Indies.[11]

But the slave trade was fickle, and turned against its function-aries. Ten years after the founding of Charles Towne, the Westoes themselves became targets for the trade. Commerce in firearms, cloth, and rum had indebted them deeply to Charles Towne mer-chants. Dealers in Indian goods wanted to do more business directly with the Cherokees and Creeks to the west, rather than appease the mercenary Westoes. Employing a newly arrived band of Shawnees, of Algonquian stock, the English waged war on two fronts against their recent allies. The Westoes were ruined. Cap-tives were brought to the slave market in Charleston, and escapees fled north, perhaps to the Iroquois Confederation. By 1683, fewer than fifty Westoes were left on the seaboard.[12]

For about a decade, the Shawnees occupied the old Westo home on the Savannah River, taking up the vocation of kidnap-ping other Indians—fugitive Westoes, Winyahs from the future border with North Carolina, Cherokees from the highlands, Appomattox from Virginia—and selling them to the English.[13] But the Shawnees never became the power that the Westoes once had been. The continued decline of the Cusabos and the elimination of the Westoes left the southern flank of the colony exposed to Spanish Florida and disrupted the Indian trade. More important than the disruption was the opening of a golden opportunity to expand trade with the large, industrious tribes of the interior.*

During the first generation of English settlement, at Charles Towne and at Port Royal, the Indians kept the white people alive. They fed them produce from their gardens and corn from their fields; they traded fish and game for trinkets; they gave the English land to till and taught them to cultivate corn, beans, melons, squash, tobacco; and they showed them how to navigate the inland waterways. As the English poured in with their African slaves, the presence of the Indians became a problem. They were a hindrance to extending settlement, enclosing plantations, and exercising rights of ownership over the land. To the Indians, of course, the problem was the English. As the settlers began to feel confident in their hold on the soil, and as their crops and naval stores became more prominent in imperial commerce, they demanded territorial and economic concessions from the native inhabitants.

While Carolina's traders prospered hugely, the Indians grew poorer. Tribes like the Yamassees had become dependent on European goods and their economies were distorted from trying to meet the demand for deerskins. The Yamassees had been in the colony since 1685. They had lived previously on the Guale coast of Spanish Florida but abandoned the area after the Spanish attempted to enslave and carry some of them to the West Indies. Moreover, the Spanish were unable or unwilling to protect them from Indians allied with the English. After killing and driving away the Westoes, the English had permitted the Yamassees to move into the southeastern corner of Carolina. At Port Royal, they became neighbors and accomplices of the ill-fated Scots, who had just arrived there themselves. Lord Cardross settled the Yamassees on St. Helena Is-

---

*The inland trade would feature all the vices of the coastal trade, including "Small-Pox and Rum" and the instigation of wars for the purpose of capturing slaves. In 1697 and again after 1700, smallpox desolated piedmont, mountain, and southern valley cultures, such as the Creeks, Cherokees, and Choctaws. (Peter Wood, "Circles in the Sand: The Southern Frontier at the Arrival of James Oglethorpe," unpublished paper, February, 1985, 14.)

land and then on Hilton Head, as a kind of first line of defense. After the Spanish destroyed Stuart Town, the Yamassees moved to the mainland where, joined by Indian refugees from St. Augustine, they dispersed in villages between the Combahee and Savannah rivers.[14]

By the end of the century, the English had begun moving in again, pushing the frontier southward and westward from Charles Towne. Ostensibly to prevent friction between Indians and Europeans, the provincial government set aside a reservation of land in 1707 for ten Yamassee towns—the first Indian reservation in America. Whites observed the boundaries for a few years; infrequent violations involved mainly incursions of cattle onto Indian land. In 1711, the English ordered a highway built from the Edisto River to Port Royal and St. Helena islands, and the Lords Proprietors described plans for a seaport on Port Royal to be called Beaufort Town. The creation of an administrative division called St. Helena Parish was announced in 1712. These signs of settlement frightened the Yamassees, despite English assurances that Indian lands would not be touched.

Pressures on the land contributed to Indian discontent. More important were the accumulated abuses of the Carolina trading regime. The Indians accused the traders of taking Indian food without paying for it, killing Indian livestock, and beating anyone who protested. They accused the English of drenching the Indians in rum to beat them in bargaining, enslaving Indians for debt, and forcing Indian men to serve as bearers, beasts of burden. By 1711, the Indian debt to the traders was one hundred thousand skins, the equivalent of a whole year's kill.[15]

Feeling cheated, humiliated, and desperate, the Indians struck a blow to turn back the English. On April 11, 1715, the Yamassees and Creeks killed all the white traders in their territories. Attacks followed against white settlements on a 120-mile front from the Savannah to the Santee River. The siege was well planned—probably by the Creeks—and not without hope. An English counterattack, led by Governor Charles Craven, was nearly overwhelmed at the head of the Combahee River. In the end the colonists prevailed and the Indians were vanquished. Effective leadership by seasoned Indian fighters, assistance in men and arms from other provinces, the conversion of the Cherokees to the colonists' side, and the arming of Negro slaves to defend the colony determined the outcome. Blacks may have outnumbered whites in the hastily raised provincial army. "In simple proportional terms," one historian has suggested, "Negroes may never have played such a major role in an earlier or later American conflict as they did in the Yamassee War of 1715."[16]

Yamassee survivors took refuge in Florida with the Seminoles, a society of refugees largely of Muskhogean stock. Only the Cherokees remained strong in Carolina after the Yamassee War, and they were summarily crushed "as soon as they really stood in the way."[17] The Cusabos withered into a few wretched towns, or migrated north or west to live with the small Siouan tribes who have given their names to the major rivers of South Carolina—the Pee Dees, Waccamaws, Santees, Congarees, Waterees. By 1740, the once plentiful coastal peoples had disappeared.

Now rid of the Indians,* the colonists sought to remove a second obstacle to the settlement of the lower Carolina coast. In 1719, the provincial Council and Assembly petitioned King George to depose the Lords Proprietors. The patrons were charged with failing to defend the province, falsely claiming to have sent money and supplies during the Yamassee War, neglecting to build Anglican churches, and violating the rights of Dissenters. Behind the colonists' charges lay fifty years of grievances against the Proprietors—disgust with their aristocratic arrogance and ignorance of conditions on the Carolina frontier, with their agents and rent collectors who funneled the profits of the colony to the shareholders in England, and with the heirs and trustees of the original investors who had multiplied like fleas and had declined to take risks to develop the province. To revive trade and immigration, the colonists begged the King to assume administration of Carolina personally. He agreed, and the rule of the Proprietors came to an end.

Plantations, Populations, and Early Crops

Before 1695, the labor force of Carolina was predominantly white. Blacks made up about a quarter of the population, many having

---

*Looked back upon from the mid-nineteenth century, the removal of the Indians and the settling of Africans appeared to have followed the laws of progress. "Upon the lands which [the white men] took from the savage whom they could not tame," remarked Charleston's William Henry Trescot, the "father" of American diplomatic history, "they placed the savage whom they could tame." (September 8, 1866, quoted in Katherine M. Jones, *Port Royal Under Six Flags* [New York, 1960], 97.)

come from Barbados. From the very start, the Proprietors had hoped to settle the colony with experienced planters and seasoned slaves, by relocating people from the Indies. All that was wanting was a crop that could be sold for a profit in Europe. Just before 1700, rice from Madagascar was successfully introduced on the mainland. Quickly, large estates were enclosed and shiploads of slaves were removed to Carolina. By 1708, the majority of settlers in the province were black.

The characteristic institution of the young colony was the plantation. In its outlines, the plantation was a system of forced labor directed by men who had invested their own money, and other people's money, in workers and land, to produce a crop that was sold through agents and consumed elsewhere. Planters contracted heavy debts and made large profits, which they used to buy more Africans. The sharp increase in the black population frightened many of the whites, but the demand for cheap labor prevailed.

We can say, therefore, that the plantation was a stage in the migration of people and capital from the Old World to the New.[18] A white man of little wealth could obtain a large acreage through a "headright"—an allotment of land based on the number of people in his household, including servants and slaves. In 1670, the headright for a free white man was 150 acres; this was reduced in 1672 to 100 acres, and in 1682 to 50 acres. Each Negro man brought his owner 20 acres in 1670, and each Negro woman brought 10. Not all white people who came to Carolina received land as soon as they got off the boat. Many whites came as indentured servants, bound to other white men or families for a fixed number of years—usually six—at the end of which, if they had fulfilled their obligations, they were eligible for land. Other whites came as hunters, traders, and agents for commodity dealers. Still others came to live in white townships set aside by the Proprietors and later by the Crown for white farmers and artisans who had no slaves. These immigrants were given transport to the townships and provisions for up to twenty months. But this settlement scheme was never adequately supported, and its lapse encouraged slaveholding on an even broader scale.

Grantees with experience in working both white hands and black came to prefer the blacks. It was easier to discipline Africans, to force them to accept the frightful labor and meager rewards of breaking new ground and building homesteads in a hostile environment. Black women could be yoked to field work alongside the men, while white servant women, though they labored prodigiously in the fields, demanded time for homemaking. The term of servitude for Negroes was life, their fertility compared favorably to the whites', and black children who survived were a permanent addition to the master's estate. Blacks were less likely than whites to complain. Whites could send home word about living conditions to deter other Europeans from coming, while blacks could not deter other Africans. White servants shared their masters' traditions and motivations: they wanted land, rights, status. They were potential competitors, which the blacks could never be. Resources in Carolina may have seemed unlimited in 1663, but by the early 1700s the forests were receding, game in many areas was growing scarce, and the choicest lands were occupied.

Contact between masters and servants was closer in the settlement years than at any later time. Whites and blacks together cleared land, hewed ship timbers, distilled tar and pitch from pine sap, and planted subsistence farms. It was rough, humble work. Masters and servants ate the same foods, wore similar clothing, and lived in houses which differed in roominess, perhaps, but not significantly in materials or refinements.

When the first Chaplins appeared on St. Helena Island, around 1720, the sparsely populated parish was overwhelmingly white. This is because commercial quantities of rice were not grown on the Sea Islands. There was no way to impound the fresh water necessary for flooding rice fields. Cattle grazing and mixed farming were the major agricultural activities, neither of which called for large numbers of field hands. With the introduction of indigo to the Sea Islands in the mid-1740s, the ratio of blacks to whites shifted drastically. In indigo, the Sea Islanders found a staple crop suitable to the plantation organization of labor. The leaves of the indigo plant contain a substance that makes a fine lasting blue dye for which there was an eager market in England. To suppress the indigo industry in the French West Indies, Parliament set a bounty of seven pence a pound above the price manufacturers were willing to pay for Carolina indigo, and cultivation spread rapidly. For thirty years, indigo was the major money crop on St. Helena Island. At one time, prices were said to be so good that a planter could fill his saddle bags, "ride to Charleston and buy a Negro with the contents, exchanging indigo pound for pound of Negro weighed naked."[19] England reduced the bounty on indigo to four pence in 1770, revoked it during the Revolution, and declined to renew it afterward, turning instead to the East Indies for its supply. Furthermore, a "destructive caterpillar" invaded the indigo fields around 1780.[20] The crop became unprofitable and commercial production of indigo on the Sea Islands ceased. But indigo left behind a social structure and a labor routine perfectly adaptable to the next great staple crop.*

The white people of St. Helena Parish were not eager to fight England. From England came the ministers for their churches, and to England their sons went to be educated. Independence was a distant cause—"the cause of New England," as it was sardonically remembered, a hundred years later.[21] War would remove the bounty on indigo and might destroy the market for the staple entirely. Shipbuilding, the chief industrial activity on the islands, was financed wholly by English capital.† And from a military point of view, the islands were at the mercy of British sea power.

The British and Continental armies took turns occupying the town of Beaufort and traipsing over St. Helena. Both sides found the Sea Islanders fickle and untrustworthy. The American "Swamp Fox," General Francis Marion, remarked that Beaufort's local militia was "completely useless."[22] When the British took possession of the islands in March, 1780, American Colonel Daniel Horry asked the whites to evacuate, but they chose to stay and look after their property.[23]

After the Revolution, damage to the plantations inflicted by the contending forces was quickly repaired, and supplies of livestock and slaves were replenished—some slaves had run off to the British, some had been killed fighting with the Americans. But the bounty on indigo was lost and shipbuilding never revived. The ani-

*One vestige of indigo culture has come down to the present day—blue-painted door and window frames in the homes of lowcountry blacks. Believed to keep out "hants" or ghosts, the blue residue used to be skimmed from indigo pots.
†In the decade before the Revolution, at least thirty ships were built on the Sea Islands, some over one hundred tons and ten over two hundred tons, larger by a third than the size of the average merchant vessels that sailed between England and Charleston. The shipbuilders were itinerant craftsmen who pitched camp near their sources of wood and moved on when their work was done. Shipbuilding did indeed decline after the Revolution. By 1860, no state on the Atlantic seaboard was building fewer ocean-going vessels than South Carolina.

bivalence of white Sea Islanders toward the American cause was not soon forgotten in other parts of South Carolina. In defense of fleeing their homes in 1861, the Sea Islanders themselves alluded to the contrast between their conservatism in 1776 and their current devotion to the cause of southern rights that had led them to abandon everything to the enemy rather than submit to Yankee rule.

Long-Staple Cotton: The First Golden Age

The search for a new cash crop intensified after 1786. Planters in the southern states and Louisiana began experimenting with varieties of cotton. An international traffic in seeds broadcast strains of cotton from Siam, Egypt, Malta, Cuba. The cotton that first took hold in South Carolina was a long-staple, black-seed variety that migrated to the Sea Islands from Georgia, which had received it from the Bahamas, where it had drifted from Anguilla, in the Leeward Islands. Nor was it native to the West Indies, but had journeyed there from the Near East, possibly from Persia.[24] William Elliott, of Hilton Head Island, raised the first successful crop of long-staple cotton in South Carolina, in 1790. Great fortunes awaited those who followed his example. Thomas B. Chaplin's grandfather probably built the Big House at Tombee with the profits from his first Sea Island cotton crops.

Cotton is a soft, white, downy substance made of the hairs or fibers attached to the seeds of plants of the genus *Gossypium*. When carded or combed to its full length, the fiber of Sea Island cotton measures one and a half to two inches long, compared to a range of five-eighths to one inch for common upland or short-staple cotton. The fineness of cotton is reckoned by the number of hanks that can be spun from one pound—a hank is a length of yarn 840 yards long. Sea Island cotton normally spun about three hundred hanks to the pound, versus half that number for short-staple cotton. The longest and finest of the long staples was said to have spun five hundred hanks.[25] Because of its superior strength, long-staple cotton was used for making the warp, or longitudinal threads, of many woven fabrics. It went into the finer cloths which adorned the wealthy classes of Europe. The entire Sea Island crop was shipped abroad, most of it to the mills of Lancashire, none to the mills of New England.

Only the Sea Islands of South Carolina and the northernmost

islands of Georgia produced the finer varieties of Sea Island cotton.* The same seeds planted on the mainland near the coast yielded a less fine but still valuable cotton called Mains, or Santees, depending on the location. Sea Island seeds sown inland yielded a coarser fiber, less profitable than the short-staple cotton that could be raised in the same place. A variety of long-staple cotton grown on the islands off the lower coast of Georgia and northern Florida passed for Sea Island, but it was an inferior fiber and brought less than Mains or Santees.

Though Sea Island cotton commanded at least twice the price of upland cotton, and usually much more, it bore considerably less fruit and produced only about half as much lint to the acre. A great deal more labor went into a pound of Sea Island cotton. Sea Island fields needed heavy manuring, the plants needed many hoeings, and the lint needed special handling during its preparation for market. The bolls opened slowly and the picking season could last six months. Being so long in the field, the fiber was vulnerable to bad weather, though to the planter's advantage, slow ripening allowed time for all of it to be picked, and once picked the cotton did not rot.

Before 1805, Sea Island cotton fields were fertilized lightly or not at all. Barn manures simply were not plentiful. In the absence of an efficient fertilizer, the crop was sown in a different field each spring. This "absurd doctrine" of resting arable land[26] ended with the discovery of a cheap, abundant fertilizer—salt-marsh mud, the sediment-rich peat that lay at the doorstep of every Sea Island plantation. Salt marshes are the most productive parts of the earth. They sustain more organic matter per square foot and are capable of nourishing more herbivores by weight than any other soil. Marsh mud enriched the sandy cotton fields and supplied vital elements like phosphorus and magnesium. It made the cotton hearty, less susceptible to disease. Salt-marsh grass was good for littering stables and stockpens; its judicious use could double the quantity

*Long-staple cotton prefers a mean maximum temperature of sixty-eight degrees and a mean minimum of forty-nine degrees—essentially the range on the Sea Islands, with their three-hundred-day growing season. The forty-five inches of annual rainfall on the Sea Islands exceeds the requirements of long-staple cotton by more than ten inches—though *when* the rain comes is as important as how much—so that maintaining ditches to assure the swift run-off of water is essential to the success of the crop. (Sir George Watt, *The Wild and Cultivated Cotton Plants of the World* [London, 1907], 288–299.)

of barn manure. Or the grass could be mulched directly into the fields.

In effect, the planters solved the problem of adapting their salty islands to a staple crop by tapping into an ecology whose primary plant, spartina grass, had solved for itself the problems of growing in salt. Spartina has no competition for sunlight or for the nutrients brought in twice a day by the tides. It grows on level ground, or flats, which hold water a long time, allowing the finest sediments to drop. The close-growing blades screen in decayed organisms, which settle slowly into the mud. These deposits constitute its richness. Planters experimented by mixing marsh mud with barn manures and vegetable composts. Each man carefully guarded his formula for the most efficacious concoction. During the first golden age of cotton, which ended in 1819, many Sea Island fortunes were built on foundations of mud and manure.

Once it was proved that the long-staple cotton could be grown economically in the warm sandy soil, its cultivation spread swiftly along the coasts of Beaufort, Colleton, and Charleston districts. In 1790, the Sea Island cotton crop of the United States was under ten thousand pounds, or just about thirty bales. By 1801, it had soared to 8.5 million pounds, or about twenty-two thousand bales. In the space of eleven years—three or four years, really, once the knowledge caught on—thousands of laborers had learned to make a new staple crop, an active market of buyers and sellers had sprung into operation, and a vast exchange of money, seeds, and information had thrust some fallow islands off the malarial coast of South Carolina into prominence as producers of the world's finest cotton.

The Sea Island crop of 1805 rose to twenty-six thousand bales. Twenty-five years later, the size of the crop was about the same. While the upland output increased phenomenally right up until the Civil War—with the exception of two brief recessions in the 1840s—Sea Island cotton approached a limit early in the century. It was restricted to the soil and climate of the Sea Islands, and the crop could expand only if more acres on the islands were planted. For this to happen, profits would have had to justify the expense of preparing the less accessible and weaker lands or impounding the few small interior marshes. Such enterprises generally were not attempted between 1819 and the late 1840s, the era of the Sea Island cotton depression. As a proportion of the total American crop, Sea Island declined steadily. It accounted for twenty percent of the

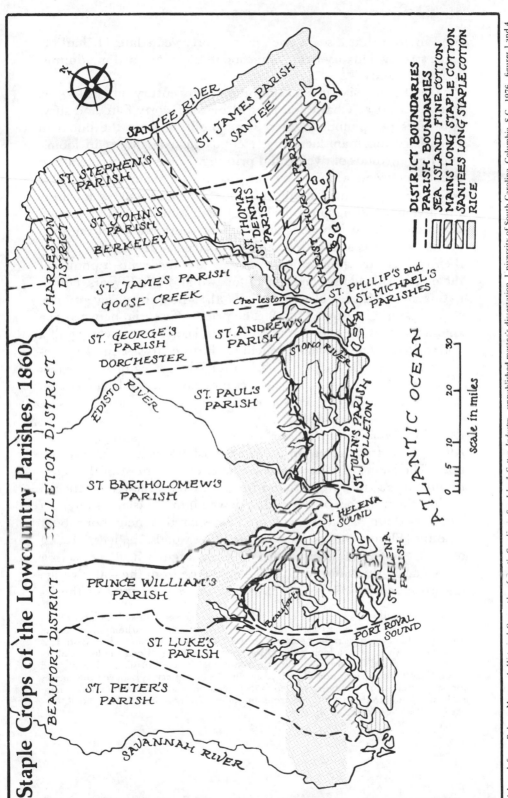

Staple Crops of the Lowcountry Parishes, 1860

N

SANTEE RIVER

ST. JAMES PARISH SANTEE

ST. STEPHEN'S PARISH

ST. JOHN'S PARISH BERKELEY

CHARLESTON DISTRICT

ST. THOMAS & ST. DENNIS PARISH

CHRIST CHURCH PARISH

ST. JAMES PARISH GOOSE CREEK

Charleston

ST. PHILIP'S and ST. MICHAEL'S PARISHES

ST. GEORGE'S PARISH DORCHESTER

ST. ANDREW'S PARISH

STONO RIVER

COLLETON DISTRICT

EDISTO RIVER

ST. PAUL'S PARISH

ST. JOHN'S PARISH COLLETON

ATLANTIC OCEAN

ST. BARTHOLOMEW'S PARISH

ST. HELENA SOUND

ST. HELENA PARISH

BEAUFORT DISTRICT

PRINCE WILLIAM'S PARISH

Beaufort

PORT ROYAL SOUND

ST. LUKE'S PARISH

ST. PETER'S PARISH

SAVANNAH RIVER

scale in miles

0 5 10   20   30

DISTRICT BOUNDARIES
PARISH BOUNDARIES
SEA ISLAND FINE COTTON
MAINS LONG STAPLE COTTON
SANTEES LONG STAPLE COTTON
RICE

Adapted from Robert Mason, *A Historical Geography of South Carolina's Sea Island Cotton Industry*, unpublished master's dissertation, University of South Carolina, Columbia, S.C., 1976, figures 1 and 4.

total in 1801, but a scant one percent forty years later. It had become strictly a luxury item, "almost entirely consumed in administering to vanity."[27]

For the first six years of the nineteenth century, prices for Sea Island cotton at Charleston ranged between forty-four and fifty-two cents per pound. Planters were profiting from the boom in English cotton manufacturing, technological advances in looms, and new methods of dyeing and printing. Prices slumped to about twenty-five cents a pound by 1809, then rose again the next year when, perhaps coincidentally, a labor-saving lace-making machine was invented in England. The War of 1812 stimulated construction of cotton mills in New England, but for short-staple cotton only. Prices for Sea Island cotton sank to thirteen cents in April, 1813, then revived, reaching a heady fifty to fifty-five cents a pound at the end of 1815. High prices held for two and a half years, culminating in a "frenzy of speculation" that peaked at seventy-five cents a pound in August, 1818. The price differential between Sea Island fine and the better grades of upland cotton was nearly half a dollar. Prices fell suddenly, touching thirty cents a pound in December, 1819. They kept falling,* and in the spring of 1822, when Thomas B. Chaplin was born, prices for common Sea Island cotton hovered at twenty-five cents a pound.[28]

Land Use and the Intensification of Cotton

All of the cotton raised on St. Helena Island went to market by boat. The Island is shaped like a blue crab, and most of the plantations were distributed around the perimeter. A few were tucked against the branches of creeks that flowed into the Island's interior. Three or four landlocked plantations shared a neighbor's boat landing. Plantations were separated by woods, hedges, creeks, ditches, and fences. They tended to be rectangular in shape, with a short side on the water, stretching lengthwise from the water's edge toward a belt of woods that extended across the center of the Is-

---

*Observers could not agree what caused the depression. Some linked the abrupt decline to the passage of Sir Robert Peel's Act of 1819, by which Parliament set a date for requiring England's trading partners to pay for manufactured goods in cash. It is not clear, however, if a sudden demand for precious metals strained the financial resources of England's customers, or if "the contraction of enterprise, confidence, and credits" led to the resumption of cash payments. Many observers believed that prices for Sea Island cotton had been inflated for a generation, and were settling into a more realistic relation to the cost of food crops and other commodities. (E. J. Donnell, *History of Cotton* [New York, 1872], 79.)

land. Fields were in the shape of large squares intersected by cart paths and drainage ditches. Costly rail-and-pole fences or natural divides protected cropland from livestock. By and large, the plantations were rectangular and open; the fields were square and closed. Tombee's outline was exceptional—a crown-shaped tract, looking at it from the northeast, bisected by a branch of Station Creek.

Tombee contained 376 acres of improved and unimproved land. It was larger, in 1860, than thirty-three plantations on St. Helena Island, and smaller than twenty-one others. More than half the plantations contained between 100 and 300 acres. Eighteen plantations had 500 acres or more, and two had more than 1,000 acres—Coffin's Point, on St. Helena Sound, and Frogmore, on the Seaside, both belonging to Thomas A. Coffin. St. Helena Parish had the lowest ratio of improved to unimproved acres—about seven to five—of any parish in the lowcountry. Though the Sea Island cotton industry was limited to the acreage on the Sea Islands, individual planters did not feel pinched, insofar as most owned more land suitable for planting than they had the labor, or the incentive, to work.

Two roads traversed the Island, one running southwesterly from St. Helenaville on a pine bluff overlooking St. Helena Sound, the other running more westerly from Coffin's Point, about two miles below the village. A fork of Lands End Road, or Church Road, as the upper, more northerly road was called, led west to the Ladies Island Ferry. The lower road, called Seaside Road, crossed the rich Coffin, Fripp, and Jenkins lands before reaching Tombee and Lands End. These sand roads with intervals of wooden causeways over tidal drains and marshes connected the plantations to one another and to the institutions which serviced white society— the churches, general stores, Agricultural Society lodge, muster house, and village of St. Helenaville, with its wharf, sand beach, summer mansions, parsonage, and small boarding schools.

There were no farms on St. Helena Island worked by free labor, and no cotton that was not produced by slaves. Many plantations bore the names of their owners, but not necessarily their current owners. Some plantation names suggested a location or some physical feature—Riverside, Corner Farm, Pine Grove, Mulberry Hill. Every name had a history and a reputation, in Equity Court as well as in public opinion. A name signified a house and a lineage, a collection of assets and the means of producing more wealth, a credit rating and an appraised value. Once a name became attached to a tract of land, it took more than a change in ownership to pry them apart.

What will the land produce? How much to the acre? This is what people who looked to the land for a living wanted to know. Utility mattered most. Every part of the land—and water—contributed to the plantation economy. The sea and tidal streams provided fish and shellfish at all seasons. The barrier islands yielded deer and duck for the master's larder, and wood for a great variety of uses—for heating and cooking; for Negro houses, outbuildings, and fences; for wagon parts, tool handles, and crude furniture. From the marshes came the fertilizer for the cotton fields, without which a different agriculture would have evolved.

The plantation grounds produced the money crop and most of the food. But the pattern of land use was not static; the land was put to many different uses over time.[29]

In 1795, a typical St. Helena planter was sowing the new long-staple cotton in an old indigo patch where root crops had been growing since the indigo market's collapse. Young woods had grown up on fields which had been cultivated twenty years before. The human settlement was compact and centralized on a piece of high ground toward the interior of the plantation. The planter's family lived in an old, plain, low house, a sprawling assemblage of rooms added on to the basic dwelling over the years. A porchless front façade looked out on an irregular row of Negro houses, stables, and provisions grounds, including a piece set aside for a house garden. A road ran from the front door of the house half the distance across the plantation to a small boat landing on the creek. Behind the house, in a small crowded cemetery, might rest the remains of the planter's father and mother, his stepmother, several of his father's brothers, and numerous children.

Fifteen years later, fattened by fabulous prices for his cotton, the typical planter would have moved into a mansion, or Big House—a house about the size of a large New England or Ohio farmhouse—on the creekside of his plantation. From the front veranda, he could look out over water and marshes to neighboring islands. It was a short walk from the front steps of the house to a new dock and boathouse. Beyond the back door extended the larger part of the plantation. Nearest to the Big House was a separate kitchen building with a small garden beside it; beyond that lay the fields. New Negro cabins and stables sat farther from the planter's new residence than they had from his old one, which was now in ruins, pilfered for firewood. There were more Negro cabins—more Negroes—more cotton, and relatively less land in grain and vegetables. Cotton was selling so well that the planter did not try to grow a surplus of food; if he fell short he could afford to buy what he needed. Cotton occupied all the highest ground and was moving into the lower. The woods that had sprouted over old indigo fields were cut to make room for more.

Although by 1830 prices for Sea Island cotton had been depressed for a decade, effects of the large profits made before 1819 were still visible from the dock. Where a flood tide used to creep freely up a gentle incline toward the Big House, leaving lines of debris to mark its advances, the tide was frustrated now by a levee that gave to the landscaped yard behind it the appearance of added elevation. The typical planter had set out shade trees and fruit trees. His wife had planted a flower garden and had rooted such strangers as crested irises and mayapples at the edge of the salt marsh. A cluster of outbuildings—a dairy, a smokehouse, a fowl house with a coop for exotic birds—seemed to have risen out of the ground. In the fields, cotton was firmly established in the low ground as well as the high, though neither area was planted to capacity. More land was in corn and potatoes because it cost more to buy food relative to the income from cotton. One sign of tight economic times was the dilapidation of the Negro cabins, now shielded by bushes and trees from sight of the Big House.

Between 1830 and 1845, the outward appearance of the typical Sea Island plantation deteriorated slowly. Cotton prices stayed low and the planter hesitated to make capital improvements. Fences rotted, the Negro houses became mildewed and worm-eaten, and even the Big House lost its luster. The roof leaked and the exterior stairs needed patching. On the remains of an old generation of outbuildings, new, frugal structures were rising. Crop acreage and the ratio of cotton to corn, peas, and potatoes were about what they had been in 1830, but distribution of the crops had changed. Cotton now filled the lowest arable land, thanks to the recent introduction of oxen to haul manure through damp ground. More corn was planted through the cotton rows, and in the cornfields the rows were longer, narrower, and higher—a sign that the plow had come back into favor. In cotton, however, the plow was still used sparingly and did not challenge the system of raised beds worked entirely with hoes. Orchards were numerous but run down. Pastures were kept up and fine horses prospered. But stock raised for the table, left to forage on their own most of the year, looked thin and poor.

Land use changed conspicuously between 1845 and 1860. Pastures and livestock declined, cotton spilled over into acres previously planted in grains and vegetables, and more land than ever, including recent impoundments of salt marsh, was in production. The impetus for change was higher cotton prices. Once again, it was more profitable to grow cotton to the doorsteps of the Negro cabins than to set aside land for food crops. "Now plantations are cotton fields rearing a crop for foreign markets and little more," lamented Beaufort's William Grayson, at the close of the era. The effect of raising one great money crop, he wrote, was "to starve everything else." Fruit orchards had "almost disappeared. Oranges are rare, pomegranates formerly seen everywhere are seldom met with, figs are scarce and small. Few planters have a good peach or strawberry. . . ."[30] Even the fish and game had mysteriously fallen off.

One effect of specialization was to deliver the profits of Sea Island commerce—the brokering, freighting, insuring, and financing of cotton—to middlemen in New York and Liverpool. A handsome part of the receipts that made it back to the Sea Islands was taken North and trifled away at watering holes, instead of being spent at home. It was objectionable, in Grayson's view, for planters to purchase their pianos and pineapples from northern merchants, but unforgivable for them to buy cider pressed in Vermont, butter churned in New York, corn grown in Pennsylvania, and hogs raised in Tennessee, any of which could be produced at home. Even oysters from the North found a market in Charleston, though the salt waters of South Carolina teemed with shellfish.

We might view the intensification of cotton planting in a different light than Grayson. Where he saw change, we might remark on the persistence of Sea Island cotton over a period of eighty years— far longer than the age of cotton in such Deep South states as Alabama or Mississippi. Grayson stressed the departure from traditions of mixed farming and conservation of natural resources. We might point to the plantation's capacity to retain its economic function and social character from decade to decade. To Grayson, taking refuge in the upcountry after Beaufort was abandoned by whites in 1861, the question of specialization was a question of life and death, settled on the side of death. Moreover, it had been settled at least a generation before when, in 1841, at the depth of the agricultural depression, planters began stepping up production of Sea Island cotton. As specialists, they grew the old staple to the exclusion of almost everything else. Once prices recovered, they grew as much of it as they could. Grayson suggests that they extended this strategy to hunting and fishing, exploiting resources with no thought to posterity. The tragedy, he felt, was not simply in the passing of a happy, harmonious way of life, but in the prospect that planting for a maximum yield would destroy the fabric of society. In Grayson's thinking, the modern concepts of maximum and sustained yield were powerful social concepts. Maximizing production would necessarily weaken the land; weakening the land would devitalize the link between generations. Strained to produce the most it could year after year, the land would produce progressively less. It would lose its steady, sustainable, Sea Island character. When cotton prices fell, the land would hardly be worth handing down to one's children—or waiting around to inherit.

Twenty years of agitation for crop diversification by the agricultural press and the State Agricultural Society had fallen on deaf ears. Planters might set aside a sandy hill for grapes, or import a bull to improve their milch stock, but they never considered an alternative to cotton. There were numerous practical difficulties, of course, in switching from an established staple to a new one. Not the least of these was marketing. Then, too, memories of old fortunes built on cotton in two or three wildly prosperous years made men reluctant to try something else. They may not have been growing richer with cotton, but neither were Sea Island planters faced with out-of-pocket losses.[31] They stuck with what they knew because it had been good to them or to their fathers before them, it was not currently bankrupting them, and it held out the dream of immense wealth quickly earned. Until that dream came true they could live comfortably, if fretfully, off the fat of old harvests.

Then, in the late 1840s, commenced a new era of high prices for cotton which shored up their attachment to the old staple, if indeed it had ever eroded. Had they turned to sugar beets or millet or hemp or any of the other foods and fibers proposed as substitutes for cotton—had history gone in the direction Grayson would have preferred—Sea Island planters still would have been susceptible to secession hysteria, so long as they worked their crops with slaves. But if their major crop had not been cotton they might have been less prone to the catastrophic illusion of their importance to the rest of the South and to England. Less cotton would have made them a less inviting target. The great cotton crop of 1861, some of it already ginned and baled, and the balance of it waiting to be picked, inclined Union military planners and their friends at the Treasury Department to aim for Port Royal, of all the likely places on the South Atlantic coast.

Sea Island cotton in 1860 had brought upward of sixty cents a pound for medium-fine varieties. Planters were expecting even better returns in 1861. In October, the Charleston *Mercury* reported that bales of the new cotton, received at the market but kept in port by the Union naval blockade, compared "most favorably with the growth of former years, in bright appearance, strength, and length of staple." Following the invasion of Port Royal in November, the crop of St. Helena Parish was confiscated and shipped to New York, where it was ginned and sold, contributing $675,000 to the United States Treasury. Thus, the proceeds from one of the largest and finest Sea Island crops ever produced—including from St. Helena Island, 20 bales from Thomas B. Chaplin, 45 bales from T. G. White, 85 bales from Dr. William J. Jenkins, and 110 bales from J. J. Pope—were used to finance the war against the planters.

3. The Chaplin Family

Generations and Connections
The John Chaplin who arrived in Carolina in 1672 sailed from Barbados as an indentured servant of the Colleton family. He was not a wealthy man. In 1678, "John Chaplin and his wife Ann" were granted 140 acres of land "on the north side of the Stono River,"[1] which would have placed them on James Island, just below the peninsula that became the city of Charleston. Under the headright system of 1672, a man who completed a six-year term of servitude was entitled to 70 acres, as was a free female, while a woman who completed her servitude was entitled to 50 acres. John and Ann Chaplin's 140 acres may have represented 70 acres he earned by fulfilling his servant's contract plus 70 acres she had coming as a free woman. They could have been married before they emigrated. It was not unusual for a husband to come first, serve his six years, then send for his wife to join him.

In 1684, we find John Chaplin testifying before the provincial Grand Council that he had observed the Spanish delivering arms to Yamassee Indians. The next year, Chaplin sold part of his tract on James Island—he identified himself in this transaction as a carpenter—and lost the rest of it for nonpayment of a debt. He, his wife, and their young son John, Jr., joined the march of failed and disgruntled settlers away from Charles Towne, south to the Combahee River, two-thirds of the way to Port Royal.

John Chaplin, Jr., was raised in St. Helena Parish. He married Phoebe Ladson, the widow of Caleb Toomer, and together they had eight children. Parish records show that John and Phoebe were the progenitors of all the Chaplins in the lower part of the state. Their fifth child, William, married Sarah Saxby, the widow of James Reynolds. William and Sarah had five children including a son, Thomas Benjamin, born in 1742, who became the grandfather and namesake of Thomas B. Chaplin.

Indeed, the major white kin groups on St. Helena Island in the middle of the nineteenth century—the Chaplins, Jenkinses, Fripps—stemmed from common roots and continued to intermarry. One of Sarah Saxby's daughters by her first husband married Benjamin Chaplin, the brother of Sarah's second husband, William. William's sister Phoebe married Joseph Jenkins. All the Jenkinses on St. Helena were descended from Phoebe and Joseph's son John and his wife Mary Fripp. John and Mary were also the parents of Chaplin's mother's first husband, Daniel.

Chaplin's grandfather Thomas married a Fripp—Elizabeth, one of fourteen children of John Fripp and Elizabeth Hann. Two of Elizabeth's siblings also married Chaplins, three married Jenkinses, three married Scotts, one married a Fripp, and one married a Pope. Thomas and Elizabeth had ten children, five of whom married Fripps and Jenkinses. Their seventh child, Saxby, was Thomas B.'s father. Saxby married his second cousin Isabella Field, widow of her first cousin Daniel Jenkins, and daughter of John Cato Field and Elizabeth Perry. Saxby's great-grandparents on his father's side, and Isabella's great-grandparents on her mother's side, were John Chaplin, Jr., and Phoebe Ladson, the first Chaplin settlers in St. Helena Parish.

Isabella had a son, John, by her first husband, but the boy died at the age of twelve. She had four children with Saxby, two daughters and two sons. Elizabeth Isabella died in 1840, at the age of twenty-three, unmarried. Mary Louisa died in 1828, at nine years old, while attending boarding school in Pleasant Valley, New York.* Thomas Benjamin, born in 1822, and Saxby, Jr., born in 1825, survived to become fathers and planters on their own, fought in the Civil War, and lived to old age.

When the children were young, the family stayed at Tombee Plantation, in Thomas's father's house. They moved away after Saxby, Sr., died, in the late '20s. Thomas inherited half the plantation, which was held in trust for him and continued to go by the name Tombee; the other half went to his mother, Isabella, with the understanding that Saxby, Jr., would inherit it one day. The

*One source indicates that she died in 1836, at seventeen—a more likely age to be in boarding school. But this later date cannot be confirmed.

Chaplins called this plantation Riverside, though after Isabella's marriage to R. L. Baker it was known in the courts as the Baker Place.

Young Thomas B. Chaplin

Thomas was six or seven years old when his father died. He mentions him only four times in his journal: once for having planted an Asiaberry tree which Thomas cut down to make a gunstock, once in connection with some Revolutionary War paintings that had hung in the house, and twice as the source of contested property.

Within twelve months of Saxby's death Isabella had married John S. Fields, an Episcopal clergyman whom she and Saxby had hired to tutor Thomas. Fields owned considerable property near Greenville, in the northwestern part of the state. He took his new family up there while he bought and sold some land and looked after his affairs. Then he died. Widowed for the third time, Isabella carried her boys to her Fields Point Plantation—which had devolved to her through her father, John Cato Field, not through her late husband Fields—on the Combahee River, in St. Bartholomew's Parish, Colleton District.

How long Thomas lived there and who looked after him are not clear. In December, 1830, we find Thomas B. Chaplin, of St. Helena Island, enrolled at "The Richland School for Classical, Scientific and Practical Education," near Rice Creek Springs, between Columbia and Camden, South Carolina. Perhaps his mother patronized "the salubrious spring" and found the location of the school convenient. Or she might have been attracted by advertisements in the Charleston newspapers, boasting that Richland was organized "on the plan of the most improved gymnasia in Europe and America." Or a school catalog may have fallen into her hands by way of the Webbs, or Guerards, or some other lowcountry family that sent one of its sons to Richland. In any case, before he was eight years old, Thomas was packed off to a school about 150 miles from home.

Richland offered young men three curricula "designed for the practical life." The commercial-minded could take courses in mathematics, penmanship, bookkeeping, "and all forms of business." Would-be engineers studied surveying, navigation, civil engineering, and geology. Future planters were taught chemistry, botany, mineralogy, and "the application of Science to the Arts of

Agriculture." Although Richland offered no sustained program leading to the "literary or professional life," students might sample courses in Greek, Latin, oratory, and belles-lettres. Younger scholars took such primary subjects as spelling, grammar, "mental arithmetic," and geography. Older boys learned infantry tactics and artillery procedure. While not designed as a military school, Richland was "formed into military corps for drill and discipline." All students drilled one hour a day, before breakfast. Morning and evening prayers were mandatory, as was public worship on Sunday. Religion according to sect was "disregarded," but school authorities sought to impress upon their charges an awe of God and a "living conviction of Moral Accountability."[2]

It cost $250 to send a boy ten years old or under to Richland, and $275 for a boy over ten. The fee included tuition, board, room, bed and bedding, washing, mending, firewood, lights, and the services of two resident physicians. Parents were promised that younger boys would receive "the added supervision of a matron" who supplied "the personal attentions which belong to the duties of a mother."[3]

Was Richland a good school? Were the quality of instruction and the effort demanded of the students high? Was "government" of the school "parental, kind, and liberal but firm," as advertised; or was Richland a typical American "boarding school for adolescent rioters?*[4] Evidently, there had been a major disturbance at Richland just about the time Chaplin went there. "Very little order is kept at school," wrote eighteen-year-old Thomas G. Law, a Richland student, in a letter to his mother, in August, 1830.[5] Several troublemakers had to be flogged or expelled, Law explained. He hoped that a "general reformation" would remedy the situation soon, so that his parents could think their money was well spent.

How long Chaplin stayed at Richland we cannot say. The next we hear of him is in April, 1839, eleven days before his seventeenth birthday, when he married young Mary McDowell, of Charleston, the granddaughter of a wealthy Scots-born merchant. Her father,

---

*Good schools were few and far between, and the South had no monopoly on the bad ones. William Grayson recalled that "the art of keeping a school at the North," attended by large numbers of southern students, consisted in "making the most money with the least annoyance to teacher and scholar. The great and important inquiry was, are the bills regularly paid. . . ." English boarding schools at the time were also notorious for student riots. (*The Autobiography of William J. Grayson*, ed. Samuel Gaillard Stoney, *South Carolina Historical and Genealogical Magazine*, vol. 48, 1947, 126.)

like Chaplin's, had died when she was a child. It was not unusual for a girl to marry at fifteen or sixteen, but it was rare for a young man of Chaplin's social class to marry before eighteen or nineteen. Also, unlike most young men of his parish, Chaplin married someone outside of his social circle. How did he meet Mary McDowell, who had grown up in a world apart? Perhaps through a friend or adviser of his mother who had heard about the girl and her handsome legacy. Isabella Fields would have welcomed the Charleston connection. There were also McDowells in Greenville from whom she might have learned about Mary. Once Thomas and Mary were introduced, a romance blossomed. Upon her death in 1851, Chaplin reread love letters they had written to each other before their wedding—letters that were stored in his desk and lost in the War.

First Days at Tombee

Sometime after 1840, young Chaplin and his wife moved into the old family house at Tombee. At once he began directing the work on the cotton crop, taking over, possibly, from one of his father's brothers, or from an overseer hired by his Uncle Ben. Until he was twenty-one, in 1843, the income from his inheritance was held in trust by Ben Chaplin, who was required to advance only as much as it took to maintain the heir and his family. By the time Thomas reached his majority, his wife had borne four children.

Tombee was a two-story clapboard house on a high tabby* foundation. It was laid out in a modified cruciform, or T, so that all six rooms had windows on three sides, to catch as much breeze as possible. The house had high ceilings, tall sashes, narrow halls, and two exterior chimneys venting four fireplaces, two on each floor. In winter the rooms were difficult to heat, but in summer they stayed cool. A two-story porch, with six square columns on each story, faced Station Creek. On the landside, or back, was a single-story portico.

The house was not luxurious. Its floors were heart pine and the lower portions of the walls were covered in wainscotting, but this was customary even in modest dwellings. Until Chaplin's children went off to school, the Big House felt crowded. When his journal opens, in 1845, there are seven white people living there—Chaplin,

*Tabby is a cementlike substance made from sand, lime, oyster shell, and water. It was first used on the Sea Islands by the Spanish for ramparts, seawalls, cisterns, and foundations.

his wife Mary, their four children, and Mary's half-sister Sophy—
plus five or six black people waiting on them. Mary's invalidism
and the sickness that frequently kept the children indoors made the
place feel claustrophobic. "The children making a great noise, &
wife sleeping in the drawing room," wrote Chaplin, pining for soli-
tude, one desultory day in July, 1848.

Still, the house was stately, straightforward in design, and
sturdy enough to withstand nearly two centuries of storms and neglect. Its strength derived, in part, from its magnificent foundation—broad tabby piers rising eight feet out of a subterranean slab
that prevented the house from settling unevenly—and, in part,
from its peg-and-beam construction. It stands today, immaculately
restored, the oldest dwelling house on St. Helena Island. In Chaplin's day it was not in such prime condition. He complained of its
leaky, "miserably constructed roof," and was never able to keep
panes of glass in all the windows. What is today a faultlessly maintained lawn was a dirt yard harrowed by the heavy traffic of people
and animals. Only the Big House remains. No one can say with
certainty where the Negro houses used to stand—wood-frame
cabins about sixteen feet by twelve, with shingle roofs, rough board
siding, wood chimneys, and floors of sand and lime. Gone are all
traces of the outbuildings—stables and barns; the fowl house,
smokehouse, and dairy; the provisions and tool houses; the gin and
the cotton houses; and a boathouse that jutted into the silent creek.

Whites and Blacks in St. Helena Parish

The census of 1830 counted 1,063 whites and 7,725 blacks in St.
Helena Parish. Sixty-five of the blacks were free people. In 1860,
there were 1,062 whites and 7,673 blacks in the Parish; the number
of free blacks, mainly people who had been manumitted in their
old age, had dwindled to 29. Though the death rate was high, the
birth rate was higher; population stability.meant that people were
leaving. Yet, the land never supported as many people as it could.
At no time was all the available land, or even all the improved
land, tilled.

Planters who found better opportunities on the main moved off
the islands, usually taking their slaves with them. The removal of
whole plantation communities was offset over the long run by the
natural increase in the black population, and by slaves brought in
or purchased from other sections in flush times. Plantations and

slaves left behind by the emigrants were generally bought up by neighbors, not by strangers. While some wealthy planters kept putting money into land and slaves, ever enlarging their estates, others were dividing their property into parcels for their sons and daughters. The division of plantations was not an endless or irreversible process; rather, it was restrained by personal ideals and practicality. Large holdings conferred status. Moreover, the planter who farmed under fifty acres with ten hands or less was at a serious disadvantage: a small work force could not be deployed effectively to meet the seasonal demands of the crop or the crises caused by a capricious climate and the health problems of the hands.

In 1845, about 250 whites and 2,000 blacks were living on St. Helena Island—1 white person for every 8 slaves, and 1 slave for every 8 acres of arable land. Field hands accounted for between one-third and one-half of the Negroes; house servants, old people, and children made up the rest. The census of 1860 found Chaplin with 30 slaves, up by 5 since 1850, but less than half the number he had inherited. Over the same period, many of his friends and neighbors were acquiring great numbers of laborers. Dr. William Jenkins's work force increased from 42 to 148, Major Daniel P. Jenkins's from 16 to 50, and Thomas A. Coffin's from 133 to 253, making him the largest slaveholder on the Island. In 1845, Chaplin owned more slaves than did two-thirds of the planters on St. Helena; in 1860, he was in the bottom third of slaveholders.

4. Agriculture

The Sea Island Harvest

One cotton crop, two potato crops, and three or four corn crops made up the significant agricultural product of the Sea Islands. Potatoes could be dug and eaten as needed, from late summer on, or left to fill out and be picked in the fall, between other tasks, but before the first hard frost. Monthly plantings of corn in the spring yielded an early crop of "roastin ears" and later harvests for food and fodder. Chaplin grew many other foods, mainly for his table. In his journal he mentions more than forty different vegetables, herbs, nuts, and fruits, not all reaped every year, but many planted regularly.

The climate of St. Helena was hospitable to temperate as well as tropical plants and animals. Apples grew near oranges, wheat next to sugarcane, flax in sight of cotton. Sheep grazed in pastures drained by ditches where alligators might lurk. In general, St. Helena planters kept about half as many sheep as cattle. Chaplin, however, preferred the taste of mutton to beef and had more sheep than cattle in 1860. He sold cowhides to a saddler in Beaufort, slaughtered veal for a planters' market, and gave rations of beef to his slaves. He kept chickens, turkeys, ducks, and geese to eat, sell, barter, and give as gifts. At various times he tried selling beef, fish, and fowl, watermelons, tomatoes, and other garden vegetables for quick cash. The potatoes stolen from his potato banks and the sheep abducted from his pen circulated in still another far-reaching, underground economy.

Field hands raised small crops of their own on quarter-acre plots. Chaplin gave his laborers occasional days and half-days off to work for themselves. He encouraged them to grow corn. They got the ears and he got the blades, the leaves of the corn plant, which were dried and used for fodder. Often he bought the ears from them, paying with store-bought molasses. He was not out to make a profit in these transactions, but it was definitely a buyer's market. A statute from 1751 prohibited slaves from selling corn to anyone but their master, and though the law had been modified since colonial days, slaves still could not sell their produce to a white man without their master's permission. And if their master wanted to buy it, they had to sell to him. Slaves kept chickens and ducks, but planters reserved for themselves the right to raise turkeys and geese. Pigs provided the major cash income for slaves; the money was used to buy sugar, coffee, wheat flour, tobacco, and other small luxuries. Chaplin occasionally rewarded his slaves with meat—payment, actually, for working quickly when the seasonal demands of his different crops overlapped. But he paid them cash for their garden produce, such as pumpkins, which he fed to his horses. Once he paid a hired slave carpenter with a beef cow; the man turned around and sold the cow to his master for cash.

Chaplin did not buy any slaves in the thirteen years he kept his journal. He was forced to sell slaves, however, forty or so, in 1845 and 1847. Some he consigned to dealers in Charleston; the others were seized under court judgments for nonpayment of debts, and auctioned off. One planter's calamity was another planter's boon. Foreclosure of a white man's property, or its sale upon his death to satisfy creditors, opened the way for others to add to their estates. Since the prohibition of the slave trade in 1808, the supply of Negroes had to come from existing plantations, either directly or through the medium of the slave market. Prime field hands were always in short supply, if not in St. Helena Parish, then in districts and states to the west, where slaves from the seaboard brought excellent prices.* We know that not all of the slaves Chaplin sold stayed in the lowcountry. But our information is sparse because he made no effort to follow them after he picked them out for sale, declining even to accompany them to the boat landing. He was embarrassed, of course; he did not want to face either the people he was selling off or the relatives they were leaving behind. He eased

*The average price in Charleston for a prime field hand in 1845 was $550—the lowest price of the decade. Eight years later, a similarly rated slave would bring $900, and by 1860, $1,200.

his conscience with the lame conjecture that the black parents "may see their children again in time." Yet he knew it was not likely. For years, factions in the Baptist and Episcopal churches had been debating whether to forbid their members from selling wives and husbands away from each other, as well as children from parents. The Savannah River Baptist Association went so far as to call separation "the civil equivalent of death."[1]

After Chaplin lost the first group of slaves, he went on living as extravagantly as before. A child of a great agricultural depression, he inherited its fatalism but not its parsimony. That was his undoing. Several times whole chunks of his estate fell by the wayside, like the bluff at St. Helenaville washing into the sea. Still, he was able to live richly by the standards of any other Americans of his time, with the exception, perhaps, of the men he looked up to, the "large" planters of the Sea Islands who prospered like Midas in the second golden age of cotton.

Cotton: From Planting to Packing

From field to market, the requirements of Sea Island cotton were so different from those of upland cotton as to constitute a separate industry. Sea Island was a year-round crop needing intensive labor at every stage of production. It took heavy manuring, careful bedding, and numerous hoeings before being thinned to a final stand. The long picking season began in August and could run past the first of January. Once picked, the cotton was carried to the gin house, where it was cleaned and packed for market. Pains were taken to remove the seeds, crushed leaves, and dirt without disturbing the long silky fiber so prized in Europe. This laborious process took up most of the late fall and winter. Many of the operations overlapped. Hands might pick, then gin, then haul out manure for the next year's crop, then go back to picking.

The production of a crop took eighteen months, from the first manuring through the final baling and shipping, so work on one year's crop overlapped with work on the next. Soon after the last picking of cotton, the vegetation in the fields was hoed under. This was called *listing*.[2] *Tracking* the land came next—laying out the beds so that water would flow into the ditches that interlaced the fields. Some planters used the same beds year after year, but Chaplin rotated his. "Where the alley now is, is where the bed will be for the coming crop," he wrote, in January, 1846. Breaking up the alleys had formerly been done with the hoe, but when Chaplin began his career the plow was taking over the job. In combination with tracking, two men—the planter or overseer and a field hand—would set out wood stakes to mark the tasks, or work assignments, for the hands. Called *running out* the land, this tedious job made it possible to manage field work afterward with a minimum of supervision.

When the soil began to warm, around the first of March, the hands would hoe the earth into high oval beds, called ridges, spaced five feet apart from center to center. *Planting* was done by teams of drillers, planters, and coverers—one person to drill a hole, one to drop in a handful of seeds, and one to cover the hole, forty to eighty holes to the bed, "depending on the strength of the land." Early in the century, people commonly planted during the second and third weeks in March. By Chaplin's generation, the climate had changed, and out of respect for late frosts and the high winds of March, planting dates had been moved to between the fifth and twentieth of April.

Hoeing began when the young plants put out their fourth or fifth leaf. Sea Island cotton took five to eight hoeings over the growing season, compared to two or three hoeings for short-staple cotton. At the first hoeing, the ground was loosened and the tenacious grasses were chopped away. By the third hoeing, the cotton was thinned so that no plant stood closer than twenty-four inches to its neighbor. At the last hoeing, in mid-July if everything was on schedule, the cotton was thinned down "to a stand," with the remaining plants about five feet apart. Chaplin called this last operation *regulating* the cotton. The task for hoeing was half an acre, two times the task for planting.

A few weeks after the last hoeing, the first cotton flowers bloomed. Within a day, the petals turned from ivory to pink, and in two or three days they fell. Behind them bulged the cotton pods or bolls. Once the bolls started opening, cotton would clothe the fields for the better part of half a year.

Between the last hoeing and the first picking, the hands were assigned to digging marsh mud and hauling it either directly to the fields, at the rate of forty ox-cart loads to the acre, where it would sit until it was turned under in winter, or to a yard where it was mixed with stable manures and left to compost. Digging marsh mud was heavy, dirty work, made especially hateful in summer by heat and mosquitoes, and in winter by cold.

As soon as there was a "good blow" of open cotton, the hands began *picking*. Cotton was removed from the bolls, taking care to strike out leaves and pieces of the pods. Each picker was equipped with a bag and a sheet. When the bag was filled it was emptied onto the sheet and the cotton was either left to dry in the sun or else shaded at once and taken to the cotton house to dry *out* of the sun. Both methods of drying had their proponents. There was no set task for picking. Twenty-five pounds of raw cotton per hand per day was a low average for a fair blow. Thirty-five to fifty pounds was good picking. Sea Island cotton might require as many as a dozen pickings. With every heavy opening of bolls, the planter was advised to drop what he was doing and put all available hands into the field.

After picking, the cotton underwent five or six operations which transformed it into a semifinished product ready to be spun into yarn. First came *assorting,* the "grand secret" of cleaning cotton. This was the job of separating white cotton from yellow or stained cotton, and picking out leaves and trash. Clean cotton ginned easier and cooler than dirty cotton and kept a higher shine after ginning. One person could "assort" sixty pounds of seed cotton in a day.

Next came *whipping,* a technique adopted in the 1820s for brightening the cotton and throwing out more trash before ginning. It was done by feeding the seed cotton through a simple hand machine called a whipper, or by thrashing it with sticks.

After assorting and whipping came *ginning,* a machine process that extracted the sticky seeds from the lint. Three-quarters of the weight of freshly picked cotton was in the seeds, and it took about fourteen hundred pounds of cotton from the field to make one 350-pound bale for market. The ratio differed slightly from one variety of cotton to another and was an aspect the planter considered in selecting seed for the future.

When cotton first was cultivated in North Africa and the Near East, the seeds generally were separated from the lint by the fingers. The Sea Islanders used roller gins—devices resembling a turner's lathe,[3] employing two short oak rollers stacked horizontally in a frame and made to revolve in opposite directions by a hand crank or foot pedal. The rollers had to be replaced frequently and the tension on them adjusted, or the gins would cut and heat the lint. Foot gins were particularly popular on the Sea Islands.* Working steadily, one person at one foot gin could generate twenty-five to thirty pounds of "freed cotton" in a day. It was slow, dusty, dreary work, often performed in numbing cold weather when the cotton ginned best. The slaves hated it almost as much as they hated digging mud; negligence at ginning was common grounds for punishment.

After ginning, Sea Island cotton was laid out in a frame for *moting,* the removal by hand of all specks, cracked seeds, and yellow cotton trapped in the lint. These bits of refuse, or "motes," were set aside and processed with the yellow cotton. Motes were also used for stuffing mattresses and cushions, and for littering animal pens. One person could mote about forty pounds of ginned cotton in a day. Care had to be taken to handle the lint lightly, to avoid a pressed or smudged appearance.

Now the cotton was ready for *packing* into "old fashioned round bales" of about 350 pounds apiece. Short-staple cotton was generally packed with a screw press into five-hundred-pound rectangular bales called square bales. The St. Helena Agricultural Society tested this method and found that the pressure of the screw injured the looks of the long staple, if not the fiber itself.[4] Sea Island planters preferred to pack their bales with an iron pestle, or by having the packer stomp down the cotton with his feet. Still, after packing by the Sea Island method, the bales felt as dense as wood. Once baled, the cotton was stacked in the cotton house until the planter was ready to send it by flatboat to Beaufort, where it was loaded onto a schooner or steamboat which took it to market in Charleston or Savannah.

These were the steps in the production of a single crop of Sea Island cotton—a semifinished commodity traded on a world mar-

---

*Eli Whitney's saw gin was five times as efficient as the roller gin, but it was never used in the Sea Islands. It was strictly a short-staple tool because its teeth would tear up the long fiber. Dr. C. W. Capers, of St. Helena Island, wrote in the *Southern Agriculturist* (August 19, 1833) that Whitney had invented another gin "which could clean the seeds from the long staple" cotton as ably as the saw gin cleaned the seeds from the short staple, but because he had been so badly abused by the southern states, the Connecticut genius refused "to make this great discovery known," so "that the secret should die with him." Dr. Capers reported that the foot gin used on St. Helena had originated in the Bahamas. The Bahamian machine was actually adapted from a Moorish device which itself was based on a roller-type foot gin in use in India for two thousand years before the settlement of America.

ket. There were variations, of course, from plantation to plantation. Shorthanded planters might eliminate one or two hoeings and pray that a dry spell would keep down the grass. Some omitted the step of whipping the assorted cotton, and some juggled the steps and whipped their cotton *before* assorting it. Chaplin tried this "by way of experiment" in 1854. "I think it makes the cotton look better," he reported, "at least it serves to show the specks better, to be picked out." The next year he tried whipping his cotton after ginning it. "I know that if the factors & buyers knew of it, they would say the cotton is too much handled," he conceded, "but not knowing it, that the cotton is beautifully prepared." Once, in 1851, a very bad year for him, he put his cotton bales out in the yard "thinking to improve the weight, by the action of the dews and perhaps a little rain." The trick backfired, and his cotton sold for below-average prices.

Risks

It cost the planter between $75 and $150 to produce one bale of Sea Island cotton, or between 22 and 42 cents a pound, depending on the quality of the fiber. A bale of very fine cotton took more than fifty "hand days" to prepare, after picking. On top of this had to be added the time and costs of transporting the crop to market and other expenses incurred after the cotton left the planter's boat landing; among these were storage and insurance fees and commissions to the cotton broker. Cotton in transit could be ruined by rain, or the flatboat might capsize. Fires were always a threat to the cotton warehouses in Charleston, and several of Chaplin's acquaintances lost crops in warehouse fires.

The weather posed many dangers. Too little or too much rain at planting time and the crop might have to be planted again. Too much or too little rain when the cotton was fruiting could cause it to open too quickly or too slowly. A storm on the heels of a drought was particularly harmful, blowing down cotton, corn, and fences, and carrying away the topsoil. A late spring frost would kill the young cotton plants. A hard frost in the fall could arrest the opening of the cotton bolls and wipe out the precious potato crop still in the ground. But the very conditions that threatened the cotton in the field made the unsold portion of the previous year's crop more valuable. Heavy rains in the fall of 1847, frosts in the fall of 1850, drought in 1855, all drove up prices and touched off waves of buying by English manufacturers worried about future shortages.

Rain and drought both were blamed for causing *rust* in cotton. Genuine rust comes from a parasitic fungus that attaches itself to the plants and turns the leaves brown or black. Plants hit by rust early in their growth fruit prematurely and thinly. Plants hit while they are fruiting drop their pods shortly after they open. Rust was also the name given to any number of nonparasitic diseases which produced similar symptoms, and to *blight*, which killed the plants suddenly without any sign of rot, as if someone had cut off their roots with a hoe. St. Helena planters occasionally suffered the ravages of cotton caterpillars which would devour the leaves, then go for the bolls. Chaplin fought caterpillars by sending turkeys into the fields to stuff themselves with the small green larvae. Yet the depredations of insects and diseases combined were nothing next to the dangers that awaited planters at the market.

Crop Yields and the Secrets of Seed Selection

Chaplin's cotton yields were consistently low. A study of his crops from 1845 through 1858 reveals a pattern of diminishing productivity, with a slight turnaround at the end of the period. The crop harvested and sold in 1845 averaged 80½ pounds of ginned cotton, or about 380 pounds of raw cotton, to the acre. This was a third under the average for all Sea Island plantations, and a quarter under the average for plantations in St. Helena Parish. By 1856, Chaplin's yield had slumped to a miserable 60 pounds of ginned cotton to the acre. What caused this decline? Foremost, it seems, a lack of manpower. After his work force was reduced by two-thirds, in 1847, Chaplin did not have enough hands to fertilize his land sufficiently or to hoe the crop thoroughly.

Yet even before he lost forty slaves his yields were not good. A clue to his low productivity might be found in the ratio of his white cotton to stained or yellow cotton. Seven or eight bales to one, white to stained, was a fair average for the Sea Island staple, and ten to twelve bales to one was not unusual among careful growers. Stained Sea Island brought a fraction of the price of white Sea Island; still, it brought as much as a fair-to-middling grade of upland white cotton, and could be sent off and sold any time of year. In 1845, Chaplin produced fourteen bales of white and three bales of stained cotton, or under five to one, a poor though not disastrous crop. There were no reports of untimely rains during the picking season which might have yellowed the lint, and no reason to suppose that the cotton had opened too quickly. Most likely, Chaplin's own bad management was to blame. The cotton could have been stained by the oil of cracked seeds left in the lint after slipshod ginning and moting. Or perhaps it was carelessness at some earlier stage showing up now in the bale. He may have neglected to clean his drainage ditches, for example, or he may have allowed his seeds to degenerate. Sea Island cotton demanded close and steady attention. Young Chaplin, by his own accounts, was caught up in the distractions of the billiards table and the racing skiff. He stayed home mornings long enough to give orders but was not around to see them carried out. Without his supervision, or that of a competent overseer, his fields could not be kept "in good heart." As the old saw put it, "a planter's footsteps are manure to his land."[5]

Of all the components of the crop under the planter's control, selecting a good seed was the most important. Seed varieties bore the names of the men who developed them—Seadings, Grayson, Edings, Owen, Godly, Fraser, and Fripp seeds made the rounds on St. Helena Island in the 1840s and '50s. Some were fine varieties; others were common cottons bred from the finer strains of coarse stocks.

Seed selection began when the planter went into his fields and marked his best plants. The bolls nearest the stalks were later picked and ginned separately; the weight of the seeds and lint was recorded, and the fiber was tested for uniformity. Next spring, the seeds would be planted off to themselves on well-drained, well-manured ground. As the new plants grew, departures from the desired type would be removed. The next year—into the third crop year now—cotton from the seeds of the selected plants would yield enough seeds to sow the next general crop. Meanwhile, the finer plants would be marked, and the process of selection would begin again. The planter who selected his seed with the aim of improving his common crop could not hope to do so in a single crop year, or even two or three years.

Thomas Chaplin's aptitude for seed selection was more the side effect of his long acquaintance with cotton than the result of systematic study or a passion for science. He used to advantage the knowledge of his slaves. Isaac, for example, is credited with doing the actual selecting in the field, in the mid-'50s. Without the field hand's eye for a superior stand, the ginner's judgment on the adhesiveness of the seeds, and the moter's opinion of the texture of the lint, there would have been no basis for improvement. Chaplin achieved less than some of his neighbors, but the seeds he produced after 1853 were in the mainstream of Sea Island commerce. His coarse or crop seeds became accepted even-up in trades, and his fine cotton began bringing a high enough price over his crop cotton to justify the expense of producing it.

Corn

Cotton was king, but corn ruled Chaplin's imagination. The whole corn plant was useful—ears, leaves, stalks, and stubble. Corn grew quickly and returned hundreds of grains for every grain sown. It made bread, pone, hominy, mush, or it could be eaten before it ripened right off the ear with a minimum of preparation. Hogs fattened on corn and it kept well.

Chaplin made a notable success with corn. He more than doubled his yield in twelve years—from fifteen to thirty-two bushels to the acre—in contrast to his decline in cotton. By 1857, he was growing more corn on less land with fewer hands to tend it. He went from buying corn to growing a surplus and selling some himself. He was beholden then to no one for food and fodder.

Why did Chaplin's corn crop improve so dramatically? He pointed to seed selection, which no doubt accounted for part of his higher yields. "I believe in selecting," he declared, as he chose the "Ward" seed to plant on eleven acres in March, 1856. From this crop he selected grains or seeds which "beat" the yield of the parent stock by several bushels to the acre. Apparently he was fertilizing his corn land heavily, too. What seems decisive is that he was able to adapt his small work force to the cultivation of corn. Corn took less exertion than cotton and it thrived on plowing, where one person could do the work of four with hoes.

Preparation for the corn crop started late in February when the fields were listed and the ground laid off in rows. Toward the end of March, the furrows or alleys between the rows were filled with stable manure or crushed cotton seeds, then covered with earth and built up in hills or ridges. Three or four grains of corn were dropped in holes every two or three feet; within six weeks the plants were thinned to one every three or four feet. March corn, or early corn, was sown more thickly than later corn. But if the corn was left to mature in a thick stand, it produced heavy fodder and little grain.

Grass was the nemesis of corn. After a wet spring, it was difficult to keep the grass down. Chopping it out from around the tender stalks was delicate work for a heavy hoe. In July—June, if the season was favorable—the corn was *laid by,* or cultivated with the hoe or plow for the last time. Then peas were sown between the rows. After the corn was picked and the leaves stripped, the dying stalks hosted the running pea vines, "which when in blossom, and with full pods pendant from every stalk, present the field in an aspect rich and abundant in promise."[6]

Chaplin's yield in 1857 put him at or near the top of St. Helena corn growers. But despite this, he could not count on making money from corn. Prices fluctuated with the supply of a better grade of corn raised for market in Pennsylvania, Maryland, and North Carolina. Coastal corn produced more stalk and leaf to the quantity of grain than corn grown inland, and Sea Island yields could not compete with yields elsewhere. Furthermore, the soft and sweeter corns preferred by many buyers became "flinty" when planted by the coast—the layer of soft starch, which had the texture of snow, did not rise to the top of the grain but was covered by a layer of translucent, hard starch, which had the texture of ice.[7]

Potatoes

Chaplin's third great agricultural product was sweet potatoes—called simply potatoes in the southern states—an "essential article of sustenance" for half the year or more.[8] Two potato crops were harvested annually, one ready to dig in September and the other left to fill out until frost. The first was the root crop, planted in early spring from seed potatoes; the second and heavier-bearing crop was planted in June with slips, or vines, cut from the growing plants. After digging, the tuberous roots were divided into seed potatoes and eating potatoes. The larger eating potatoes were set aside for the planter's family and house servants; the rest were stored and rationed to the field hands.

One-sixth of the cultivated land on the Sea Islands was devoted to sweet potatoes. Potato land was prepared much the same as corn land except that it was manured before planting by movable cow pens—fenced enclosures where cows were herded for the night. Composted marsh sedge made a good fertilizer for potatoes, and marsh mud was used with some success in very sandy soils.

Grass was as much a menace to potatoes as it was to corn. Hoeing cleaned the stubborn "jointer" from the furrows, but it had to be removed by hand from around the young plants. In rich land kept clean by hoeing, the potatoes shot out vines which were cut off and immediately replanted, preferably in ground enriched by a winter crop of oats or peas. Vines were also used to "supply over" the root crop—which meant setting them out where the seed potatoes had failed to sprout.

Sweet potatoes were stored in banks made of earth and straw, with from ten to thirty baskets in a bank. A few planters kept their potatoes in wood buildings similar to corn houses, but this method was not widespread. Once the potatoes were safely put up, sheltered from rain and frost, hogs were turned loose in the field to dig for roots while they incidentally tilled the soil.

Some varieties of sweet potato were heavier bearers than others. Some were grown for their keeping qualities, some for their flavor, some because they matured early, and some because they thrived in a particular soil. Chaplin grew several kinds at the same time. He grew the common yam, or Spanish potato, a late, heavy-bearing, long-keeping root; leathercoats, which were larger and more mealy than yams but were rated best for table use; brimstones, early bearers but poor keepers; red-skinned potatoes with white hearts, early, heavy-bearing roots that kept well and were said to be "preferred by the Negroes."[9]

While counting his potatoes in bushels and banks, Chaplin was mentally converting the yield to allowances. A good potato crop was one that would feed all the people on the plantation for six months. In 1852, a very good year for potatoes, Chaplin's crop came close to the mark. In fact, had he not had to "feed out to horses, hogs &c," the potatoes would have lasted from January through June, when, if conditions were favorable, a new harvest of potatoes and all kinds of vegetables and fruit would have begun.

From seven and a half acres of slips, his workers dug twenty-eight banks of eating potatoes in 1852. Each bank held twenty-eight baskets, or fourteen bushels. At 80 pounds to the bushel, each bank stored about 1,120 pounds. Thus, his per-acre yield of eating potatoes was close to 4,200 pounds, and his total yield, about 31,360 pounds of solid food.

The Task System

On plantations throughout the cotton belt, field hands were organized into gangs of men and women who worked together under close supervision—except in the lowcountry. On the Sea Islands and nearby mainland the task system was universally employed. Each hand was assigned a specific quantity of work to do in a day, the equivalent of hoeing one "task" of ground. The basic task measured 105 feet square—a quarter-acre—and contained twenty-one or twenty-two beds, taking cotton as the standard.[10] Nearly every job had a set task which was the same from one plantation to the next and was known to masters and slaves alike. The task for listing, for example, was "a task and a half," or a quarter-acre plus ten or eleven beds. A man plowing was expected to complete four tasks a day—that is, to till as much ground as four men or women could turn with hoes in the same time. Tasks were intended to leave no room for misunderstanding. The worker needed only to locate the task stakes in the field. The assorter, the ginner, and the moter knew just how much cotton they were supposed to process in a day. There was no set task for picking or harvesting, however, because the daily yield would vary with the blow of cotton or the size of the potatoes.

Under the task system, the workday was effectively divided into two parts—the master's time, which the slaves spent toiling on the white man's crops, and the slaves' time, which they spent working for themselves. Though the master could move his hands to other jobs once the day's crop task was finished, normally he did not. Time off, which had originated as a reward for diligence, had become by Chaplin's day an expectation tied to completing a standard quantity of work.[11] To revise the standard upward was to take from the slaves something they thought was theirs and to invite discontent.

Slave garden produce was a species of property as well as food.[12] The corn, vegetables, and meat raised by the slaves on their own time belonged to them—except for the blades from their corn, which the master took for fodder. Growers could keep their produce, swap it, or sell it. Chaplin recognized his slaves' rights to their small property and even encouraged them to be acquisitive. Once, when he learned that Perry's man Peter who had sold him a hog was about to be sold himself, Chaplin hurried to find the Negro because he owed him ten dollars and wanted to pay him before he was removed from the Island.

The task was the measure of the slave. A full hand or prime hand was one who could complete the standard task day after day. A half-hand could do half a task; a quarter-hand could do a quarter. The task was identical for men and women working at the same job. Certain jobs were reserved for each sex. Plowing, cutting wood, and hauling mud and manure to the fields were men's work. Cutting marsh grass and digging stable manure generally were done by women. Men and women planted, hoed, harvested, and dug marsh mud together. Men handled all the loading and transport, by boat, wagon, cart, and beast. Some planters experimented with putting women behind their horses and oxen, speculating that the women would treat the animals more gently than men did, but the practice never caught on.

Visitors to the Sea Islands were surprised by the paltry use made of the plow. In its place, men and women wielded "great big heavy" hoes which, in the view of a soldier from Pennsylvania, were "as big as three of our own."[13] The plow had nearly vanished from the Sea Islands during the reign of indigo, and the prejudice against it was as hard to root out as the joint grass of the fields. Why this aversion to a tool that had been tilling the soils of Europe for centuries prior to the settlement of America? Planters shrugged off the plow as unnecessary in the light island soil, a soil without stones. They believed that plowing ruined fertility by mixing the weak substrata with the rich upper crust. Using plows meant providing pasture and upkeep for plow beasts, and threatened to disrupt the task system. The many drainage ditches which laced the fields made plowing "inconvenient" by stopping the horse or ox and forcing the plowman to lift the plow. A man who broke his land with a plow might open more ground than his hands could manure or plant more cotton than his workers could pick and clean.

In Chaplin's day, there was renewed excitement over the plow, particularly among smaller planters looking for ways to increase their ratio of cultivated acres per hand. Chaplin liked the plow because it made it easy for hoes to come behind and "haul" or throw up the loosened earth around the cotton and corn, and because it freed workers for manuring. Though uninventive in his approach to planting, Chaplin welcomed the changes promised by the plow. Larger planters, on the other hand, insisted that the plow would never be more than "an assistant" in their operations.[14]

Cotton: Selling the Crop
Just after the first of the year, or earlier if the season was advanced and buyers were active, bales of Sea Island cotton were carted from the plantation cotton house, loaded onto a flatboat, and sent off to

Beaufort on a rising tide. As many as seven or eight hands would accompany a large shipment. The men poled and rowed the bargelike crafts, and sometimes hung a sail. The flats were slow moving and unstable in rough seas, but they managed heavy loads and their shallow drafts suited them for tidal creeks. By the late 1850s, St. Helenaville had become a port of call, and cotton was loaded there. Chaplin, living at the opposite end of the Island and disaffected from the village, continued shipping his crop via Beaufort, an easy voyage on a favorable tide, through the southwest outlet of Station Creek, and up Broad River.

Once the cotton arrived in Charleston or Savannah, buyers for English and Continental spinning mills declared what they were willing to pay for the various "descriptions" of the long staple. White Sea Island was known by informal grades based on the relative fineness of one planter's cotton to another's. The larger part of every Sea Island crop was called common, coarse, or crop cotton. Of greater value were the fine, very fine, and finer cottons, which brought stunning premiums. But these grades were inexact and undependable—unlike the classification of upland cotton into definite grades corresponding to published prices. Buyers exploited this ambiguous situation by paying "a special and individual, rather than a general market, price."[15] Each planter was led to believe it was in his interest to keep his transactions secret. William Elliott noted in 1829 "a growing inequality in price among Sea Island cotton originally of the same market value."[16] Some price adjustments were based on real differences in the cleaning and preparation of the lint. But others were based solely on the planter's name. He who was known for fine, carefully handled crops in the past received a fair market value, while his less notable neighbors received less than what their cotton was worth. One's name, therefore, could be an asset or a liability at the marketplace, especially when sales were slow. Chaplin tried selling his cotton with Captain Daniel T. Jenkins, and with his cousin Ben Chaplin, hoping that his small crop would bring a better price as part of a larger shipment under another man's name. His mother's cotton, produced at Fields Point and sold together with his, brought less than it would have brought on its own.

Cotton sales were made by agents of the planters, called cotton factors, who took commissions of about four percent. Factors also wrote mortgages and loaned money to planters at rates of eight to twelve percent.[17] Planters could pay their bills and taxes by writing drafts against their accounts with their factors. These drafts were like checks, except that the income they drew upon was not yet earned or deposited, and was secured to the factors by the crop in the field or by the land itself. Besides furnishing planters with money, factors sold them nearly everything which the plantation did not produce—groceries such as wheat flour, coffee, granulated sugar, and salt; clothing; tools; luxury items; and sometimes slaves. The factors had interests of their own to protect, and took their time selling the planters' cotton. They waited for the market to rise, they held out for pennies, but they had no appreciable impact on prices, which were subject to England's money supply, itself a hostage to wars, grain shortages, stock speculations, and bank failures.

Chaplin was represented in Charleston by the firm of Ingraham & Webb. George A. Ingraham, a scrupulous accountant, had built a reputation for caution and reserve; he was well known for avoiding risks. Thomas L. Webb was more outgoing and adventuresome. While his partner stayed in the office with the books, Webb enjoyed socializing with the customers, to the point of insinuating himself in their affairs and exercising a mild form of surveillance through his network of relatives. In terms of their functions, Ingraham was the pen and Webb was the gun. Chaplin seemed pleased enough with them, before 1847, and he even sent Webb a gift of a horse. But his feelings changed when his finances collapsed. He complained in his journal that Ingraham & Webb did not work hard enough in his behalf, and that they delayed sending him his money. He fumed when the corn or ice he had ordered from them did not arrive. His factors got annoyed with *him* for sending his cotton late—*their* notes had come due—and for shipping a crop that was "badly prepared, too much handled."

In spite of their mutual discontents, Chaplin and Ingraham & Webb stuck with each other for as long as he planted. They had been his mother's factors before they were his, and family intrigues wound them all in a tight net. Chaplin sent some fine cotton to another Charleston factor, but he preferred to have the greater part of his crop sold by people who knew him well and identified with the well-being of his estate. From the factors' point of view, it might seem that Chaplin hardly produced enough cotton to make dealing with him worth their trouble. But he was a good customer on the mercantile side of the business. He never had fewer than thirty people to feed and clothe. Besides, he owned a valuable tract of land and had a life interest in his mother's property. At a crucial moment in Isabella Fields's premarital negotiations with R. L. Baker, Webb advised her to insert into her marriage contract a clause that retained for her the right to dispose of her property after the wedding and denied that power to Baker—a client, incidentally, of a competing factorage firm, James H. Ladson & Company. Webb was no doubt urged on by Chaplin's attorney, and he certainly wanted to protect his company's influence with Mrs. Fields's estate. Mrs. Fields, soon to be Mrs. Baker, accepted Webb's advice, the consequences of which reverberated for thirty years.

By family and occupation, Webb belonged to Charleston's commercial elite. James H. Ladson, the partner of William C. Bee, was his first cousin, and Ladson was Webb's middle name. Ladson & Company held mortgages on property belonging to Chaplin's brother Saxby and to Chaplin's mother, *after* her marriage to Baker. Both Webb and Ladson were third cousins to Chaplin. Between them, they had a lock on the mortgageable property of the Chaplin and Baker families.

For several years, Chaplin sent a few bales of cotton to P. H. Behn, in Savannah. Each time he was disappointed; the same cotton in Charleston brought four cents more a pound. Yet he kept trying Savannah, perhaps to secure more places from which to *buy*. But the difference in cotton prices was so great—about one-sixth the total value of his crop—he finally stopped sending to Savannah. After 1854, all his business went to Charleston.

Once his cotton was sold, Chaplin did not ask what became of it. Events outside his locality affected him indirectly but quickly. The slightest rifts in the diplomatic relations of remote countries, or rumors of crop failures and stock frauds, registered at once at the cotton market. Wars tied up money and disturbed commerce, though the demand for goods and the money to pay for them returned with peace, and the wars themselves often were wedges to open trade. "There is not a battle that England has fought in India, Afghanistan, or China," noted *DeBow's Review,* "nor that France has fought in Africa, or that the United States fought on the plains of Mexico, that did not extend the consumption of cotton."[18] Visions of millions of Chinese buying cotton cloth from Manchester fueled speculations right up to 1861.

The Decline and Rise of Prices

The giddy rise of the market on the eve of the Civil War contrasted with the gloom at the start of Chaplin's career. The crop year ending September, 1845, "was one of unmitigated dullness and depression," observed the cotton historian E. J. Donnell, "prices touching lower points than ever before, or since, in the annals of trade."[19] Profits were so small in the mid-'40s, wrote Whitemarsh B. Seabrook, an authority on coastal crops, that "legal interest on the capital of the grower is rarely ever realized."[20] In 1846, Ireland's potato crop failed. Unprecedented expenditures for foodstuffs by Britain drained money from all other commodities. Purchases of cotton picked up in 1847, and prices rose accordingly, but they fell again in 1848 when several English brokerage houses collapsed and the Royal Bank of London suspended payment. Reports of bad weather and the chance of a short crop revived prices, but they were prostrated again by the startling news of the abdication of Louis Philippe and the revolution in France. The movement for popular rights "rapidly spread to other countries of Europe, and . . . commercial credit was completely overthrown and trade in a measure annihilated." Fears spread that the war between Denmark and Prussia would engulf all of Europe. Cotton prices, already flattened, received still another blow from "the unruly spirit manifested by the population of Ireland."[21] Notwithstanding this catalog of turmoil, the cotton market recovered rapidly, and by the end of 1848 prices had begun an upward climb that would last thirteen years. Denmark and Prussia made peace. In France, "quiet" was restored through the liberal use of the guillotine. The Mexican War, touched off by the admission of Texas to the United States in 1846, ended with the country's acquisition of California. After a thinning of the ranks, confidence was restored to English commerce and cotton buyers showed "a more cheerful feeling" than they had in years.[22]

Chaplin did not partake of the general prosperity until the mid-'50s. Even then his profits could not be called great, but they were large enough so he could plant without fear of losing his property. By 1855, he was producing three grades of cotton—a coarse grade from Fripp seed that brought thirty-one cents a pound; a finer crop cotton that brought a solid thirty-five cents a pound; and a true fine variety by the name of Seadings that brought forty-five cents a pound. His fine cotton in 1856 fetched fifty-three cents a pound, as the disparity between his coarse and fine cottons widened; yet his coarse variety of 1857, the last year for which we have a record, brought a hefty forty cents a pound.

The world depression of 1857 brushed Liverpool lightly. Cotton was considered "an exception to the general rottenness."[23] Boosted by three very profitable years following the settlement of strikes in the mills in 1854, manufacturers continued to pay high prices for all grades of cotton, and this in turn stimulated large plantings. Between 1857 and 1860, the cotton crop of the southern states increased by more than twenty percent per year, while the number of spindles in English mills grew by forty thousand per week. Sea Island cotton shared in the general expansion, though as the cultivation of upland cotton intensified, Sea Island necessarily declined as a portion of the total crop. The demand for the long staple was never greater, however. While prices for upland cotton rose by pennies a pound every year, prices for Sea Island gained by nickels and dimes. In January and February, 1861, the market waxed "buoyant, notwithstanding the Southern states were passing ordinances of secession."[24] Following the bombardment of Fort Sumter in April, prices rose stupendously. But planters could not take advantage of the rise because by ginning time in autumn, a Union naval blockade had sealed off Charleston Harbor, and the cotton could not get out.

Profits

From Chaplin's figures and the observations of his contemporaries it is possible to calculate roughly the profits he made from his cotton in various years. Take his crop of 1852, which was sold in January, 1853. Hearing that his neighbors' cotton was bringing better than 50 cents a pound, Chaplin hurried to get his to market. But he was too late. Prices had fallen by the time his crop reached Charleston. Still, at 41 cents a pound, his ten bales of coarse cotton brought him $1,374.37 after commissions. "Bad sales," he grumbled, though he had never received a better price. Only his fine cottons, later in the decade, brought more.

How much of this was profit—the net proceeds left after deducting his expenses and outlays? We might make the following simple and approximate computation.

Of Chaplin's thirty slaves, about twelve were taskable hands, each of whom, by 1853 prices, produced $120 worth of clean lint. It took one hundred days of labor to plant, cultivate, and pick enough seed cotton to make a 350-pound bale; and it took fifty days more to sort, gin, clean, and pack it. Thus, a bale of Sea Island cotton represented a half-year's work for a full hand. Counting the hands who worked cotton and the hands who did not—including house and yard slaves, the very young, the very old, and the infirm—the cash value per slave of cotton produced at Tombee in 1853 was $46. About $10 went for clothing, shoes, blankets, medical care, and a property tax on the person of the slave. It would have cost about $60 in food, at mercantile prices, to maintain a slave for one year; but Chaplin fed his people largely on the corn and potatoes they raised, and on hogs supplied by his mother from her Fields Point plantation. He probably did not buy more than $5 worth of food for each of his Negroes annually. He would have been left, then, with a net profit of $31 per slave. Since his slaves were worth an average of $350 apiece—$10,500 for the thirty of them—and the crop he sold in 1853 netted $924—$1,374 minus a cash outlay of $450—he earned roughly nine percent on his investment in slaves.

Nothing has been said yet about the land, Chaplin's other major capital asset. Based on figures from the agricultural census of 1850, and allowing five percent appreciation per year, farmland along the Seaside of St. Helena Island sold in 1853 for about seventeen dollars per acre. At this rate, Tombee Plantation was worth sixty-four hundred dollars. Adding this value to his money tied up in slaves, Chaplin's return from cotton in the excellent year of 1853 falls to about five and a half percent of his agricultural capital.[25]

Chaplin reported his profits in absolute dollars—the amount he received from his factor after the sale of his cotton. Like most planters, he did not stop to calculate the cost of keeping up his plantation.[26] A profit that preserved his standard of living and allowed him to curb his borrowing was his goal. Sufficiency on a grand scale, and not efficiency, was his guiding economic principle. Behavior which on its face was economically irrational—such as taking some of his best workers fishing during cotton-planting time—enhanced his social standing and enjoyment of life.

Spending the Income
Before Chaplin saw a single dollar of profit, Ingraham & Webb subtracted payment for all the goods and any cash they had ad-

vanced to him during the crop year. These included necessities such as foods he did not raise on the plantation; supplies for his slaves; iron tools, like hoes and spades, to which he attached his own handles; gin frames and horse harnesses; crockery, candles, and sewing thread. Chaplin had no idea how much he owed until his factors sent him the balance. He tried to set aside some money for doctor bills, taxes, and his children's education. The rest he took to Beaufort, where he would settle accounts with shopkeepers, artisans, and lawyers, and spend a little on himself. While his friends were buying slaves and horses, carriages and boats, pianos and books, and taking costly trips to the North, he was limited to a few modest luxuries. From his profits in 1853, Chaplin bought two metal ovens, a tin roaster, and a steel grist mill—small items, but symbolic of modern living and a craving for gustatory pleasures. He also bought a ten-gallon can of coal gas, possibly to fire his new ovens, and he began buying ice. By 1855 he could not do without it. While other families spent summers migrating in search of health and pleasure,[27] or camped at their hot-weather retreats, the Chaplins stayed home and fought the heat with ice, going through 125 pounds every week.

The list of "things from town" that made their way to Tombee reflects a hierarchical view of the world—"molasses & salt for the Negroes, white sugar and 1M cigars for self"; whiskey, brandy, wine, ale, and soda water; opium, quinine, vitriol, and castor oil; ready-made coats and curtains; a thermometer, a whip, and a signet ring. Each group of items catered to a specific hunger—for caste, sociability, stimulation and sedation, fashion, and prestige. No item added anything of lasting value to his estate. Like the ice that melted quickly on a hot day, the liquors and opiates were soon gone, leaving only the desire for more.

Towns

Traveling was one luxury Chaplin did not indulge in. He lacked the inclination, time, and resources to gad about like his mother. And even local trips could be physically grueling. In dry weather, horses and carriages bogged in the deep sand roads; in wet seasons they sank in mud. Riders and passengers arrived at their destinations jostled, dirty, and usually late. The ferries which linked the islands to each other and to the main were hazardous and unreliable. No one knew when a storm would blow up or when the wind would rise or die or change direction. A boat that "missed the tide" would have to wait until the tide turned, and then might lose what light was left in the day. Chaplin spent many anxious hours waiting for overdue boats.

The trek from Beaufort to Charleston, today a pleasant hour-and-a-half drive, could be made in twelve hours on a fast horse. By carriage and ferry it could take up to three days, with stops for lodging at night. Once steamboats began calling at St. Helenaville, one could leave the Island in the morning and arrive in Charleston before shops and offices closed for the day.

Between 1845 and 1858 Chaplin went only once to Charleston, on a desperate errand to convert part of his wife's legacy to cash. Mary Chaplin and Sophy, though raised in the old city, did not go back at all. Yet they affectionately referred to Charleston as their "town." There the Chaplins sold their cotton and their slaves, purchased most of their merchandise, and retained lawyers to defend their property. The Charleston of their youth was economically stagnant. Its foreign commerce had fallen off, many of its more ambitious residents had moved west, and the city had failed altogether to keep pace with its northern port rivals and with the newer southern ports on the Gulf coast. "The grass grows uninterruptedly in some of her chief business streets," reported the City Chamber of Commerce, in 1827.[28] As cotton prices revived in the late 1840s, prosperity returned, and by the mid-'50s Charleston could fairly be called a boomtown.

Beaufort was close as the crow flies, but it took an effort to get there. What is today a twenty-minute drive from Lands End to Beaufort, on paved highways crossing two bridges and several causeways, was in Chaplin's era a two- to three-hour row with six oars, or a three-hour ride by horse and wagon. A round-trip could take a day and part of the next, depending on the tides. Until he switched to the St. Helena company, Chaplin went regularly to Beaufort to attend militia meetings. His principal lawyer lived in Beaufort, and also his saddler, painter, cabinetmaker, and gunsmith. The town's leading manufacturers in 1850 included two bakers who turned out one hundred fifty thousand loaves of bread, cakes, and confections a year; a leatherworker who made four hundred pairs of boots and shoes; and a blacksmith who fabricated ironwork. Imported goods cost more in Beaufort than in Charleston, and Chaplin tried to avoid the local shops. Week in and week out, Chaplin would send a man to Beaufort to get the mail, carry messages, and pick up things that were waiting on the wharf for him—dropped off by a schooner or steamship from Charleston.

Northerners compared Beaufort to Newport and Saratoga.[29] Beaufort was smaller—the "picturesque" seat of Sea Island society had a permanent population of about eight hundred—but the villas were grand, the views were stunning, and the obvious purpose of the place was to serve the wealthy. Prosperous planters from the outlying islands built second or even third homes in Beaufort, and restored the dwellings of the postrevolutionary generation. Beaufort appeared "almost wholly exempt from the poorer classes"[30]—except, of course, for the ubiquitous black servants whose living quarters behind the mansions were shielded from the streets.

The white people of Beaufort were exceptionally well educated. Virtually every native-born white adult could read and write, and many of the men had been to college. George P. Elliott, the town's leading antebellum propagandist, boasted in 1857 that the Beaufort Post Office distributed annually some sixty-five thousand newspapers and periodicals to the twelve hundred white residents of St. Helena Parish.[31] "Woe to the man who had no books," wrote the Reverend Robert W. Barnwell, recalling the Beaufort of his father's youth. And woe to the man who "chanced to have no boat." Young men of Beaufort were taught to use their leisure seriously and to take their learning in a spirit of sport. "Each lad was taught to sail and row/But also how to quote."[32]

Not every man had a library, but the many who did counted their books among their most bitter losses, after the War. As for a boat, a man might live better without a horse, or even a pair of shoes, than without a boat. Boating was Beaufort's chief recreation. Situated on Port Royal Island, "at the upper end of a tongue of land which extends itself down toward the sea,"[33] Beaufort drew summer vacationers from the sickly plantations who raced their sailboats in sight of crowds on the long wharf or down river into the Sound. Chaplin, who was stripped of his favorite boat in 1847 and lived to watch other men sail it, lost the means and then the urge to mix with this group. Developments in Beaufort influenced his political behavior and his agricultural thinking, but when he came out of his shell in the mid-'50s and began looking for companionship, he gravitated toward the society of Combahee and Ashepoo River planters—rice growers as well as cotton growers, friends of his mother and brother and kin to his brother's wife—whose seat was Walterboro, an affluent piney-woods town removed from the sea.

5. Estates

The Family as a Corporate Property Group

On a map of the lower Carolina coast just before 1840, the Chaplin name swept northerly like a brushstroke from its center on the Port Royal side of St. Helena. Wherever Chaplins lived, Fripps were living nearby, on the islands and the main. On St. Helena Island, plantations originating in the estate of John Fripp, father of Captain John and Good Billy Fripp, along with plantations the sons acquired on their own, filled the eastern half of the Island. Other Fripp lands adjoined Jenkins, Chaplin, and Capers places, along the Seaside, Port Royal River, and Chowan Creek. Roughly speaking, when Thomas B. Chaplin started planting, there was a Fripp territory on the east of St. Helena and a Chaplin territory on the west, touching Jenkins lands; after 1850, a belt of Jenkins plantations was forming at the heart of the Island.

The geographical range of family property tells us where brothers and male cousins of past generations settled, and which staple crops they grew. If a man owned several plantations, the extent of lands identified by his name expressed the breadth of a single influence and authority. When he died, his estate and all its powers lived on. Until his holdings were divided among his heirs and beneficiaries, certain of his property rights continued to be exercised in his name by relatives, executors, and court-appointed guardians and trustees—the right to receive the income from a plantation, for example, but not the right to sell the place. During the settlement of an estate, creditors of the deceased could assert claims which conflicted with the pleadings of the heirs. Not surprisingly, estate settlements invited litigation. Chaplin was party to numerous suits over his whole adult life, involving both his father's and his mother's estates. His father had left him a plantation to live on and several more to inherit upon the death of his mother. Isabella was young when Saxby died, and likely to live a long time. Chaplin could not hope to benefit from the wealth he had coming unless his mother made some provision to give it to him while she was living. Her effort to do so touched off the long and rancorous dispute between Chaplin and her fourth husband, R. L. Baker, who also wanted the property.

An estate consisted of whatever could be owned. The main objects of value were land and slaves. With land went dwelling houses, outbuildings, fences, drainage works. Slaves, in law, bore qualities of both personal and real property. They could be attached to the land by a mortgage, and they could be sold one at a time to pay a master's debts. When a property owner died, or put his or her estate in trust, as Isabella Fields did before she married Baker, the slaves stayed bound to the estate, its executors, and trustees. In effect, the estate, and not the master, was the final authority over the slaves. The woman Daphne, for example, moved back and forth between Tombee and Fields Point, with stops in between at Isabella's house in Beaufort. That was Daphne's territory, the old estate of Saxby Chaplin, and none of the masters of any particular piece of it could decide where she should stay; that power belonged to the trustees of Isabella's marriage contract.

Though Chaplin did not get all he wanted, property that once had belonged to his father buffered him in daily crises. From his brother's plantation at Green Pond, and more importantly from his mother's plantation at Fields Point, Chaplin enlisted hands to work when he was pressed for labor, and received food, seeds, and building supplies. Chaplin knew he was not expected to return the gift of a bacon hog in kind. Not only his mother, but his uncles and aunts tolerated an imbalance in giving. Getting more from his kin than he gave was one of his major modes of acquiring things. These one-sided exchanges embarrassed him but also made him feel that he was part of something greater than himself—a bloodline and a clan.

The Importance of Uncles
Because many living people had the same name, it may seem difficult on first reading Chaplin's journal to affix personality to a character. One Daniel Jenkins seems to merge with another, though it

soon becomes apparent that they are different people. The same can be said for the several Ben Chaplins, Caroline Fripps, and John Webbs. To further complicate matters, many Fripps and Jenkinses were Chaplins, and vice versa. Not only was the choice of spouses limited by demography and the rigors of travel; plantation whites chose to marry their cousins, even first cousins, to keep property in the bloodline. The persistence of surnames attests to this pattern, while the small variety of Christian names reflects the practice of naming children after close relatives, where mothers and fathers have common ancestors.

The practical problem of telling apart people who had the same name was solved by the use of titles. Relatives were addressed as "Uncle," "Aunt," and the highly adaptable "Cousin," a term of endearment that selected out of the mass of first, second, and third cousins a few well-liked or important individuals. Three of Chaplin's best friends were his cousins, but he called them by other titles. Daniel T. Jenkins, a first cousin to Chaplin on his father's side, was called Captain. Daniel T.'s first cousin, and Chaplin's second cousin on his mother's side, was Daniel P. Jenkins, Cousin Betsy's son, called Major. Neither the Captain nor the Major acquired his title on the battlefield, but rather by making the drinking, eating, and parading rounds with the local militia. Chaplin's mother's first husband was also a Daniel Jenkins, an uncle to these two Daniels. Daniel P.'s brother, William, was known as Dr. Jenkins. He was indeed a medical doctor, but he made his mark by skillfully using his network of relatives and positioning himself to inherit their wealth. When citing the Jenkins men, Chaplin used their initials, or their titles, or their Christian names, depending on how he felt about them at the moment. When talking to them directly, he called the Daniels "Dan," and William "Bill."

Chaplin's plantation was bounded on three sides by land owned by his father's brothers—Tom and Paul, both bachelors, and Ben, who was married to Elizabeth Hann Jenkins. Her mother was a Fripp, and she was a former sister-in-law of Chaplin's mother. Aunt Betsy and Uncle Ben had no children, and Tom and Paul had no heirs, either. Though not directly in line to inherit his uncles' property, Chaplin was as familiar with them as was anyone else, and his need and physical proximity should have favored him. He had the usual complaints against his uncles that he had against other neighbors—they did not mind their share of common fences and ditches, they allowed their livestock to tramp on his crops—

but he held his tongue because the "old folks" were "too useful." They kept him going with gifts and loans just when it seemed he would "give out." They also paid his bills and taxes by letting him write drafts against their names. Uncle Ben once stood his security so he could hire three slaves, though he refused to do it a second time. Aunt Betsy—Ben's wife—sent Chaplin ducks, fish, bacon, lard. When he sent her a quarter of beef, she kept the loin and generously returned the leg. Without being asked, she once sent him eleven field hands to help dig his potato slips. Next to his mother, Aunt Betsy contributed most to his day-to-day support. To the women in his household she also gave pretty things such as caps, collars, and lace.

But when it came to Uncle Ben's substantial wealth, Chaplin was shut out of his will. The property went instead to Ben's brother Paul and to another nephew and niece, Dr. and Mrs. William Jenkins. Dr. Jenkins was also a nephew of Aunt Betsy, giving him additional leverage in the contest for Ben's estate. Chaplin was dejected but not surprised to get nothing, considering the lengths that Jenkins's wife, Eliza, had gone to drive a wedge between Chaplin and Uncle Ben and to discourage Aunt Betsy from helping him.

It was not the first time Uncle Ben let Chaplin down. In 1847, when Chaplin's creditors foreclosed, Ben had watched with his hands in his pockets. He had the funds to rescue his nephew, but he chose not to. Of course, even if the property had been saved, there was every chance that Chaplin would lose it the next time his notes came due. Young Chaplin was intemperate and cocky, and Ben may have hoped the setback would teach him a lesson. Or withholding help may have been Ben's way of repaying an insult arising out of Ben's management of Chaplin's father's estate—in particular, that part of the estate held in trust for Chaplin and Saxby, Jr. It had been Ben's duty, as trustee, to account for the income earned by the property and hold it for the Chaplin boys. Young Thomas had reason to feel he was being shortchanged. When he came of age he promptly sued his uncle to recover the interest due on the rents and profits from Hickory Hill Plantation, at Green Pond.

Hickory Hill became the property of Chaplin's younger brother, Saxby, Jr., when *he* reached twenty-one, and Saxby immediately sued Thomas for taking more than his share of the Hickory Hill receipts. The brothers stayed cool to each other for ten years.

Chaplin rarely visited Saxby and Saxby visited him once—Saxby had come to St. Helena to go hunting with friends, and the brothers saw each other only in passing. Though allied against their stepfather, Baker, they were rivals for the very same property which they were trying to keep *him* from having. Once Chaplin dreamed that Saxby was dead—which, had it been true, would have made him the sole heir—and by midmorning people were coming to his house to offer condolences. Chaplin must have told the dream to his wife in the presence of a servant who spread the story as fact. The news traveled off Tombee and reached white ears. Afterward, Chaplin scolded himself for talking out of turn and exposing his private thoughts to scrutiny.

Isabella Chaplin Baker: Mother and Provider
Chaplin's mother remained the most influential person in his life for at least twenty years after he moved out of her house. He wanted her love and her property, and she wanted to give them to him, but their transactions were never smooth. Chaplin, for his part, held out the carrot of his affections in return for deeds to her lands and slaves—which she had set aside in her marriage contract for the support of her new husband, Baker. Isabella helped feed her son and provision him until 1858, at least, and while her gifts were always appreciated, they were but crumbs of the wealth she might have settled on him had she refrained from marrying for a fourth time, and kept unequivocal control of her estate.

What an estate it was! From her father, John Cato Field, she had inherited Fields Point Plantation, also called Laurel Bower, the last plantation on the Combahee River, next to St. Helena Sound, and Walnut Hill Plantation, which backed against Fields Point and faced the Chehaw. She also owned Dunham Plantation, on the Ashepoo River. From her first husband, Daniel Jenkins, she acquired Riverside Plantation on St. Helena Island, along Broad River, which her second husband, Saxby Chaplin, united with Tombee. Riverside and Tombee may have made up a single plantation in earlier times, too. Isabella's third husband, the Reverend John Fields, left her Chestnut Hill, a plantation near Greenville, in the upper part of the state. With these productive lands went about 250 Negroes. In 1843, when R. L. Baker married her, Mrs. Fields was an extraordinarily wealthy woman.

Her wealth inspired a family myth. In the luckless years following Reconstruction, Saxby, Jr.'s daughter Emma recalled that "before the Confederate War," Grandmother Isabella had traveled "in *style."* She drove "four black horses in her carriage, had a white Irish coachman in livery and a footman sat beside the coachman to wait on them." If that was not enough, she had " 'outriders' to help in time of need." The horses' harness was "silver mounted" and harness and carriage bore the Chaplin coat of arms.[1]

So Emma was told, and so she told others, in turn. In reality, there had been no white coachman, no silver in the harness, no coat of arms. Yet the spirit of the tale was true. Isabella had a surplus of servants; her plantations were undercultivated and some of her people were idle. They ministered to her physical comfort and spared her all exertion. They were available to travel with her, and it seems she was always on the move. Epicureanism prompted her to keep "a floating capital of labor unemployment—a boat's crew for a pleasure excursion. . . ."[2] Her slaves had it easy, it may seem, but they were not secure. Because she lived off her capital and not her income, and because she did not like to pay her bills, the courts would make her cash in slaves, with whom she parted as if they were so much loose change.

She visited Tombee often through the mid-'50s, when she cut back on her visits and Thomas began making the trip to the main to see her. Whenever she came she brought a crowd of servants. "Such ruined Negroes I never heard of," exclaimed Chaplin, unable to get them to work in the cold, or to work at all if they felt a job was beneath them. Isabella was spoiled herself. If she did not get her way she would fly off "into one of her tantrums." In October, 1852, while she was on a camping trip to Chaplin's Island, the mosquitoes made her lose her temper, though of all the company she, "of course, was made the most comfortably off." She carried her displeasure back to Tombee and left the next day without saying goodbye, snubbing Sophy, who had gotten up to fix her breakfast. "This manner of *marked* insolence that Mother has treated *both* my *wives* in succession is beyond endurance," protested Chaplin; "it *ought,* it *must* and it *shall be resented,"* he promised, harmlessly venting his indignation in his journal. But mother and son did not stay estranged very long. Soon the flow of bacon hogs from Fields Point to Tombee resumed. "Mother came over with plenty of nice things as usual," he noted happily, two months later. And the "nice things" kept coming—ice, poultry, oats, rice, peas, corn, cooks, and carpenters.

She was a valuable grandmother, too, helping care for the children during Mary Chaplin's long illness and Thomas's financial and emotional depression. She was on especially good terms with Ernest, the oldest boy, and Virginia, the surviving daughter, who both begged to stay with her. Some seasons she boarded several of the children with her in St. Helenaville so they could attend school, relieving Chaplin of having to pay strangers to keep them. But the village was a dull place in winter, a haven for widows and clergymen. It certainly was no place for pleasure-seekers. Her element was the mineral springs, the mountain resorts, and the city. She was a vigorous woman who had outlived three husbands and three of five children, and still she had a craving for life. As she approached sixty years old, in 1850, she was healthy and passionate, and as independent as the law permitted a married woman to be.

Robert Little Baker: Stepfather and Rival

The man Isabella chose for her fourth husband was a bankrupt pharmacist and portrait painter, a widower eighteen years her junior and but fifteen years older than her son Thomas. Robert Little Baker ran a "Druggist and Soda Water Establishment" at the corner of East Bay and Broad streets, in Charleston, until about 1840. He sold "Drugs, Chemicals, and every article usually kept in the Medical Department." In addition, he imported "choice English and French seeds," exotic plants, and fruit trees for nurseries and orchards.[3] Both his lines of business, the pharmaceutical and the botanical, were fiercely competitive.

Bold advertisements for drugstores and bottled remedies occupied the classified pages of Charleston's newspapers. Different pharmacies promoted cure-alls for which they were "exclusive agents." At Baker's shop, and there only, one could buy "J. Crosby's Compound Bitters," a spirituous liquor with a macerated root or herb, warranted to cure "dyspepsia, colic, cholera morbus, bowel complaints, biliousness, ague, fever, headache, irregularity of circulation." Baker also carried a line of "highly medicinal renovating bitters" for people afflicted with "a derangement of the liver and nervous debility." For sufferers of syphilis and gonorrhea, he offered "Dr. Cullum's Celebrated Red Pill," "a general antidote to the venereal virus." These extravagant claims were corroborated by testimonials from consumers who gave a graphic picture of the physical miseries on lowcountry plantations.

Baker's debts piled up and his business failed. Looking for a quick source of money and the chance of a lifetime income, he courted Chaplin's mother, or returned her advances, to a successful conclusion. In June, 1843, less than a month after he married Mrs. Fields, he pledged a portion of her estate to J. Ladson & Company, for eight thousand dollars. In the language of the mortgage papers, Ladson had him firmly bound. The factor advanced to him "divers large sums of money," and expected "from time to time to make other advances." Part of the first installment Baker put toward reviving his wife's cotton and rice operations, and part he used to pay old debts.

Chaplin hated him. He was a stranger and a latecomer, a known defaulter and quack who had taken advantage of Isabella's loneliness and vanity. He had fooled her into marrying him and now he was trampling on the Chaplin name and devouring the family wealth. Baker, in turn, loathed Chaplin for prejudicing Isabella against him. Stepfather and stepson went out of their way to harass and humiliate each other, each more eager to defame his enemy than to protect his own reputation. They exchanged verbal blasts, and took potshots with loaded guns; their friends nearly came to blows. They never talked to each other, but they could talk about nothing else. Chaplin felt it "very provoking" to hear that Baker had mentioned him and to "appear to be of so much importance to so low & vile an insect as that thing that crawls about and calls himself R. L. Baker."

Chaplin's opinion of Baker endured in the family lore. Emma Chaplin's sister Florence remembered sticking pins into a portrait of her grandmother, not out of disrespect for Isabella, who belonged to the golden age, but because it had been painted by that scoundrel Baker.[4] The painting was down at Hickory Hill, Chaplin's brother's old place, which Saxby lost to foreclosure in 1868.

We meet a very different Baker in the transcripts of his court battles with the Chaplin brothers. He paints himself as a devoted husband, heroic in the face of his wife's irrationality, a man unmoved by flattery and disinclined to flatter, yet innocent enough to be fooled by Isabella's unprincipled sons and their diabolic lawyers. It was Thomas and Saxby, Jr., who had seduced their mother out of her property, thereby depriving him, Baker, of the means to support *her*. Several prominent Charleston gentlemen supported Baker's claims and testified to his character. Isabella herself was persuaded before she married him that despite "his pecuniary condition and the disparity in their ages," her property was not "his main object."

Was Baker the villain Chaplin said he was? Or was he the honest defender of a woman who, like himself, had fallen victim to her sons' avarice?

Chaplin Versus Baker, Act I

One week before she married Baker, Isabella Fields had a marriage contract drawn up in which, by a first clause, she deeded her entire estate to two trustees who were to turn over the profits from her plantations to her husband-to-be, for the "joint use of himself and his wife during their joint lives."[5] By a second clause, Isabella reserved for herself the power to dispose of any part of the same property, either by deed while she lived, or by her will upon her death. In effect, one clause was gunpowder and the other was fire. Opposing claims about Mrs. Baker's right to use her wealth for anything but the pleasure of Mr. Baker generated four cases in Equity Court and an armed struggle marked by kidnappings, ambushes, and the pirating of plantation provisions. On one side were Thomas and Saxby Chaplin, Jr., insisting that their mother could do whatever she wished with her property at any time. On the other side was R. L. Baker, maintaining that his new wife was prevented by her marriage treaty from deeding away her property.

The war against his stepfather gave Chaplin an outlet for ambitions blocked by his failures at planting. There are at least fifty direct references to the struggle, and many more oblique ones, in his journal. It troubled him day and night, for twenty-two years. The strain of contention fed his short temper and inspired a morbid anxiety over his health. After his defeat at the bench of the State Appeals Court in 1847, he had to live with the thought of his enemy gnawing away at the Chaplin family fortune and intermittently sharing a bed with his mother. Not that he was offended for his father's sake. Old Saxby Chaplin had been dead for twenty years. This new husband was Thomas's rival, not his father's. Thomas forced his mother to choose between him and Baker, all the while working frantically to expose his stepfather as an impostor.

"They were married, and it was all well for a time," until Baker discovered that his wife was obligated for debts incurred by her sons, and was using property from her settled estate to pay them. "This produced some remonstrance," testified Francis L. Roux, a Charleston accountant and close friend of Baker who was serving as one of the settlement trustees. Without Baker's consent, "and for no sufficient cause," Mrs. Baker "withdrew from the society of her husband" to a house in St. Helenaville, where she lived by herself, "under the influence and persuasions of her sons, who used every means to excite her against her husband."

Roux wondered what he should do. Both Isabella and Baker were demanding the income from her plantations. Roux received a letter from Thomas B. Chaplin that made the problem "insurmountable." Chaplin confirmed the rumor that Mrs. Baker had deeded her property to him and Saxby. He ordered Roux to start sending the rents and profits from his mother's estate to them, not to Baker and not to his mother. Roux believed the deeds were invalid. Baker called them "improvident," "unconscionable," "the act of a married woman calculated to impair the marital right of her husband, against public policy, and void." Having planted a crop on her lands, he felt entitled under the law to reap it.

The Chaplins tried to take what Baker would not surrender. "Using forcible and illegal means," Baker testified, "they went upon the plantations ... entered the buildings and attempted to dispossess" the agent, Roux. They enticed the Negroes "to quit work" and encouraged "insubordination" by interrupting the overseers "in their management."

Fearing he might lose the crop and be liable to lawsuits from both sides, Roux filed a bill in the Beaufort District Court, on August 7, 1845, seeking to enjoin Isabella's sons from meddling with the Negroes "and other personables," and from disturbing him in his duties as trustee. "The prayer of the bill" was that the deeds to Thomas and Saxby be set aside; or if left to stand and "it be adjudged that Baker has no further interest in this estate," that he, Roux, be allowed to quit his trust. Also named in the bill were Mrs. Baker and Daniel T. Jenkins, Roux's co-trustee.

This was the first of four cases heard together at Gillisonville, in February, 1846. When it appeared that "nothing effectual" would come from the bill, Thomas and Saxby filed one of their own against Baker and Roux. They recited in detail the contents of five deeds their mother had drawn up in their favor through June, 1845, embracing all of her property, every last teacup, except for "a family of Negroes" she held back for herself. They asked the court to stop Baker from receiving the income from the deeded property or from interfering with it—he had been seen talking with the slaves and Chaplin heard he was scheming to transport them out of the state. They wanted Roux removed from his trust and Jenkins named sole trustee.

Baker countered with a bill against his wife, her sons, Jenkins, and a new party, Richard DeTreville, attorney for the Chaplin clan. He claimed that the first of his wife's contested deeds, which singled out Negroes to be sold in order to pay debts in her name and Thomas's, was an invasion of his right to select property for conversion to cash. He accused his stepsons of pressuring their mother to draw up the deeds, just as they had unduly influenced her to sneak the pernicious second clause into the marriage contract hours before the wedding. Yes, he had been told that a clause had been added, but one that had no bearing on his interests and concerned only the division of Isabella's estate after her death. He argued that Jenkins and DeTreville had "tampered" with his wife to defeat "the main objects" of the marriage treaty, and he begged the court's relief.

The defendants denied his charges. Mrs. Baker swore she had not surprised him or added anything to their agreement surreptitiously. She had in her possession, she said, a statement written by Baker eighteen months after their wedding to the effect that he had read the "settlement as it now stands" and "approved and willingly accepted it." She would never have married him had he not "repeatedly assured her" that her right "to do as she be minded, from time to time, and always, with every part of her property, after marriage, should be carefully reserved to her, and should always be acknowledged and held sacred by him." She admitted that she had hoped her reserved power would act as a means "of attaching her intended husband to her, and of securing, to some extent, his consideration and respect." No one had persuaded her to leave Baker—she left because he had threatened to kill her. No one had talked her into deeding her property to her sons—it was her idea, and perfectly consistent with her powers. The authority to decide which property to sell when the couple needed money belonged to her; she had never contemplated giving him the authority. His claims were "untrue in every particular."

DeTreville told the court that Mrs. Baker owed him $485 in legal fees, for advising her since her marriage. The figure seemed high, he confessed, but he had worked hard for it, and he stood willing to let a tribunal pass on its fairness. He had composed a last will for Mrs. Baker, "an instrument . . . of great length and difficulty," and he had drawn up the five deeds in question, on instructions from Thomas B. Chaplin. He anticipated recovering his fees from the sale of slaves named in one of the deeds.

Chaplin denied ever exciting his mother against Baker, before or after the marriage. He said he knew nothing about the circumstances "attending" her marriage settlement, and had not even known of the wedding "till he saw it announced in the newspaper." He was on St. Helena and she was in Charleston when all this was happening. The charge of persuading his mother to draw up the deeds was false, he said. In fact, she had executed the first deed in Greenville. It was true, he had gone upon one of the deeded plantations "to exercise certain acts of ownership." But beyond this single act, "the charge of his pursuing a system of annoyance to the estate's property, &c, has not the slightest foundation."

Then came the fourth case, a bill filed by Roux making DeTreville a party to his earlier bill, and complaining of two more deeds executed in favor of the Chaplins. The defendants answered as they had before, denying undue influence and defending Mrs. Baker's powers.

At the initial hearing in Beaufort, the presiding justice rejoiced "unfeignedly" at getting through the long statement of charges, countercharges, and denials. After all of that, the points to be decided were "very few, and not difficult."

The deeds Mrs. Baker signed after her marriage might be evidence of "imbecility" and "egregious folly," as her husband alleged, but that was not cause for voiding them. Whether the deeds prevailed would depend on the answers to two questions: first, whether the clause in the marriage contract reserving Mrs. Baker's power over her property was "rightly" installed. Second, whether the deeds fell within the limits of her power.

The question of undue influence brought to bear against her to execute the deeds was swiftly disposed of. Daniel P. Jenkins, Chaplin's second cousin on his mother's side and first cousin to co-trustee Daniel T. Jenkins, gave the only testimony. He said that he and his brother, Dr. William Jenkins, had witnessed the signing of three deeds to Thomas and Saxby Chaplin, and one deed to Daniel T. Jenkins—a deed naming Negroes to be sold—at Mrs. Baker's house in St. Helenaville. Thomas was in the room, "ten or fifteen feet from her" when she signed. From what Jenkins could see, Mrs. Baker acted "of her own free will."

Under cross-examination, however, Jenkins described a coercive situation. Thomas B. Chaplin and his mother had houses in the village a half-mile apart, and he visited her once a week. The implication was not that Chaplin had persuaded her to do what he wanted by coming to see her, but that he had let her know he was angry by not coming more often. Besides her son, Isabella's most constant visitors were the witness's mother, Cousin Betsy Jenkins, and Uncle Ben's wife, Aunt Betsy Chaplin, "and their visits were about once a month"—the equivalent, to these social-minded people, of banishing her from society. All her other relatives disapproved of her marriage and had entirely "cast her off." After signing the deeds, "she removed to the house of her son," Thomas, where she stayed through the winter of 1846.

The court found nothing extreme in Thomas's behavior, only reasonable inducement applied against an impetuous woman. Evidence about the origins of the marriage contract was "more voluminous" but equally decisive. The court agreed with the Chaplins: the clause reserving Mrs. Baker's power over her property had not found its way into the treaty by fraud or mistake.

Baker's sister, Mrs. Elizabeth Toomer, of St. Helena Parish, testified in her brother's behalf that she had been staying at the Charleston Hotel where Baker and Mrs. Fields also had rooms, just prior to the wedding. Mrs. Toomer said Isabella had told her she intended to make Baker "comfortable," and had instructed her attorney, C. G. Memminger, to draw up a contract reflecting her desire. Soon afterward, she was visited at the hotel by Thomas L. Webb, her cotton factor; when Webb had gone, Isabella "seemed troubled" and said she would call for Mr. Memminger and have him insert a clause giving her the power "to dispose of her property as she might think proper, independently of the marriage settlement." That was all Mrs. Toomer knew of the matter until after the wedding, when she heard Isabella say that "had she known that Baker's indebtedness was so small, she would not have bothered with lawyers and marriage settlements."

Mrs. Toomer could not say if her brother had been informed of any change in the contract before he signed it. Mr. Memminger testified that he could not recall reading the entire draft to Baker, though Baker was in his office "from time to time, as the papers were progressing." Memminger did not think it necessary to read them, because Baker "completely filled my mind with the belief that he had no desire to interfere with Mrs. Fields's wishes, be they what they might." It was Baker who had approached Memminger on Mrs. Fields's behalf and asked him to meet with her, not as Baker's adviser, but as her own. "Any settlement she desired" was all right with him. "I distinctly remember the impression left on my mind," Memminger related, "that I had never seen an occasion where a man, marrying a fortune, had acted so handsomely, in waiving all interference with the lady's wishes and control over her fortune."

Baker had indeed introduced Memminger to Isabella and left them to confer. She gave the attorney a description of her wealth and "an outline of her family concerns." "The leading idea in her mind, seemed to be, the preservation of power over her property," Memminger recalled. She asked him how to achieve it. He tried to talk her out of the idea, saying "that it was proper, in a lady who was to surrender control in her person, to give the husband a large participation in control of her property." Mrs. Fields listened coldly, and Memminger offered no further advice.

The first draft of the settlement was "engrossed" but not executed when Mrs. Fields directed Memminger to make a change reducing Baker's share of her estate in the event he outlived her. That was the only last-minute change Memminger recalled. Baker knew of it, and suspected Webb, the factor, of "prejudicing" Isabella's mind against him. Memminger, too, believed that Webb had authored the change, but he did not say that to Baker. However, he advised Baker to pay off Mrs. Fields's debt to Webb "and recommended him to see the house of Ladson & Company on the subject."

The proviso spelled out by Mrs. Toomer was *not* the one Memminger said he had added to the settlement. Mrs. Fields's power over her property was written into the first draft—it had been there from the beginning and had remained unchanged, according to the man who wrote it. Memminger had "no doubt all the terms of the settlement were well-known to Mr. Baker." At two P.M. on the day of the wedding, a few hours before the ceremony, Memminger's partner William Jervey read the complete settlement to Baker and Mrs. Fields, who put their signatures to it. Perhaps Baker did not comprehend its meaning. But neither did Memminger. Mrs. Fields's instructions, he said, "never contemplated the disposal of the whole, or even the greater part of the property." Memminger himself "never contemplated any case, but the exercise, in good faith, of the power, for the proper advancement of the usual arrangements of a family." Had such deeds as Mrs. Baker subsequently executed been considered within the scope of her reserved power, he acknowledged, "I would have felt bound to limit its words." Here, Memminger came close to admitting he had made a mistake, by failing to foresee what the woman could do if she took her power literally. But he argued that the oversight should not be allowed to have such dire consequences, because the deeds were out of sympathy with the leading and customary intention of a marriage contract. In his opinion, Mrs. Baker's deeds "conveying away every cent of the property" were "a fraud upon the rights of Mr. Baker."

Memminger's testimony doomed his friend—in the lower court. There was no proof whatsoever of any contract other than the one which had been made and executed. The evidence was "too clear to admit of discussion, that there was no fraud in the case." The "unfortunate husband" pitched his claim on the "hopeless" ground that the settlement "as it now stands was imposed on him." How could it have been? Baker had told Mrs. Fields to select any terms she pleased. "There could be no surprise upon him, because his mind had not resolved upon anything that could be disappointed." Nor could he prove he had been mistaken, "which means misled." He had relied upon his own judgment. Memminger may have given him bad advice, but Memminger was Mrs. Fields's lawyer at the time, not his. As if it were defending a local principle against an alien code, the Beaufort court dismissed the Charleston attorney's thoughts about the contract. The extent of the power reserved to Mrs. Fields, now Mrs. Baker, "must depend altogether upon what appears on the face of the settlement" and not on "extrinsic" evidence. "We are not to be guided by explanations given even by the draftsman." Memminger was doubly embarrassed. His memorial to Baker's "fairness, liberality, and confidence in the integrity and justice of a lady" had the effect of painting Baker as a liar. The contract he had framed to accommodate the wishes of a wealthy, headstrong woman nullified the rights of her husband, contrary to the attorney's idea of the public good.

Baker's ignorance was difficult to accept. Was it possible, mused the court, that he had hoped his wife might indulge *him* with the power she reserved "in all its plenitude"? True, events had gone against him. "But who knows what hopes he may have entertained" that Isabella would deed her wealth to him, as a reward for his kindness and companionship. If any part of his sister's—Mrs. Toomer's—testimony invited belief, it was her remark that Mrs. Fields had been fighting with her son Thomas just before the wedding—a state of affairs that favored Baker's chances. Baker probably knew what he was doing and what he was signing all along; if not, said the court, it was because he did not ask. He gave his intended wife leave to do as she wished, gambling that as her relationships with her sons deteriorated, his standing would improve. It was not the court that gave "or now gives, license to Mrs. Baker; it is Baker who does it. And if she is allowed to act capriciously, it is not by leave of the Court, but by his."

The court declared Mrs. Baker's deeds to her sons and to Jenkins "sustained by the marriage settlement." It "perpetually" enjoined Baker, Roux, and their agents from interfering with the "appointed estates," and dissolved the injunctions against Thomas and Saxby Chaplin, and Daniel T. Jenkins. Roux got his wish and was discharged from his trust.

But Baker appealed and won on the important question. The Appeals Court, consisting of the state's four Circuit Court judges, including Chancellor David Johnson who had heard the cases in Beaufort, agreed with Johnson's ruling that Baker's charges of fraud and mistake were "without foundation." But where the lower court found the wife's power unlimited, subject only to her discretion, the Appeals Court held the husband's interest in the couple's joint estate paramount. Where the lower court accepted the "tendency" of the second clause of the marriage contract to "destroy" the first, the Appeals Court felt obliged to give each clause "its appropriate effect." Where the lower court declared that "Courts do not sit to make bargains," or to reform them, or to set them aside just because a deal does not work out to someone's liking, the Appeals Court "inclines against any construction which would operate in an unusual manner, harshly, and injuriously to any party." Where the lower court found the meaning of the marriage settlement in a literal reading of its clauses, the Appeals Court looked to the "general" object of such contracts, which was "to provide for the support of the parties" who signed them. Where the lower court did not question Isabella's competency to contract as a *femme sole*, while she was yet Mrs. Fields, or later Mrs. Baker, the Appeals Court sided with her husband's objection: that the reservation of "so ample" a power by a married woman "is against public policy, by furnishing her the power to predominate over her husband, who, by law, should be the master and not the slave of the wife." If the lower court's construction was allowed to stand, "the husband might be left in utter poverty, while he would still be liable for the wife's debts and maintenance." Not only could an "indiscrete wife"—like the woman "in the present instance"—deprive herself of support, but "children of the marriage (always considered possible) might be left unprovided for." In the view of the Appeals Court, the Chaplin brothers were simply "children of a former marriage" whose claims to their mother's wealth were no more urgent than the claims of her unborn dependents.

Ultimately, the Appeals Court adopted a construction of Isabella's marriage contract that restored "the natural and reasonable restraint on the wife's power of disposition"—stating a rule that in the future would make it impossible for a woman of property to leave her husband destitute, lest she "run the risk of leaving herself so." Mrs. Baker might use her reserved power to deed her land and slaves to her sons, agreed the court, but the deeds could not take effect so long as both she and her husband were alive. This was a great triumph for Baker, and the ruling would stand for eighteen years. The Appeals Court ordered Roux reinstated as trustee. Baker was ordered to pay the costs of Roux's suit out of the profits of the joint estate. The trustees were instructed to turn over to Baker the rents and income from Mrs. Baker's estate. Thomas B. and Saxby Chaplin were enjoined from interfering with Baker's possession and management of the property "during the continuance of said joint lives."

The Rights of a Married Woman

An attractive, well-to-do widow, two covetous sons, and a young fortune hunter of a husband whose luck had run out in the city; partisan trustees and corruptible overseers; the most expensive lawyers in the lowcountry—the case must have been the talk of

Charleston. Even the justices were titillated by these *"odia conjuga-lia."* "Having separated from her husband in some resentment or disgust," they volunteered, "it is probable" that Mrs. Baker executed the deeds "more to annoy and injure him, than out of kindness to her children."

Four years later, in January, 1851, the Appeals Court heard another case involving these same combatants, grouped together this time as defendants in a suit brought by the Charleston merchants Hastie & Nichols, suppliers of "goods, wares, and merchandise" to the plantation trade, who were seeking to recover three old debts from Mrs. Baker's estate.[6] In each instance the Appeals Court was asked to determine if her property was liable. What make the case memorable to a modern reader, however, are its implications for the integrity of slave families and for the rights of married white women.

The first debt, which Isabella contracted while she was Mrs. Fields, had touched off the quarrel that led to her separation from Baker, not long after their marriage, in 1843. With a delicacy that indicated family peace was shaky, the court ordered the debt paid without disturbing "unnecessarily, any of the family arrangments," by selling "the negroes assigned for that purpose, by the deed of June, 1845," which had never been carried into effect. Writing for the court, Justice George W. Dargan tried to put himself in the shoes of both the plaintiffs and the defendants. He felt he had arrived at a compassionate remedy "respecting the rights of all parties."

Yet it is precisely the narrow scope of the court's concern that reveals the defectiveness of the law. Justice Dargan did not consider how his decision would affect the intimate arrangements and peace of mind of the *Negroes* whom he was directing to be sold. Lucy, Flora, Clarinda, Kit, Cretia, Agrippa, Jackson, Beck, June, Dee, Dick, August, Elcy, Thomas, Peggy, Daphne, and Daphne's child—"name unknown"—could be plucked from their homes at any moment and sold to strangers. Their marriages would be snuffed out; their family bonds and friendships would be permanently severed.* Indeed, all of Mrs. Baker's slaves had reason to feel in jeopardy. Her husband had mortgaged ninety of them to

---

*Ironically, Mrs. Baker's former attorney, C. G. Memminger, had for years campaigned to get the Episcopal Church to recognize the sanctity of slave marriages. (Nicholas Olsberg, *Desolate Places: The South Carolina Chivalry at the Time of the Civil War*, unpublished doctoral dissertation, University of South Carolina, Columbia, S.C., 1970, 155.)

Ladson & Bee within a month after he married her. He soon would enlarge his reputation for misapplying and wasting money, but enough was already known about him to fear that he might lose the security he pledged for a loan. Chaplin warned his mother's slaves about him—and Baker told some tales on Chaplin. Their fight for the slaves' allegiance had no effect whatsoever on the court's deliberations. But it indicates that the blacks were made to ask themselves: with which white man and which piece of paper do my best interests lie? The struggle for supremacy over Mrs. Baker and her property involved the fortunes not merely of the twelve or so people who pleaded in court, but of twenty times that number who toiled in rice and cotton fields to pay the court fees.

A second debt that Hastie & Nichols sued to recover had been partially paid by the sale of ten of Chaplin's slaves, in May, 1845. The debt was in Chaplin's name, but his mother had stood security. In estimating the amount due on the note, the merchants had made an error in Chaplin's favor, and consequently, they had applied to the lower court for less than the actual amount due. They had since discovered their mistake and were appealing to make up the difference. The justices were ready to throw out the claim, since the failure to collect the full amount was not Chaplin's fault, and the lower court's judgment had been satisfied. But Mrs. Baker waived the objection and offered to pay the remainder out of her settled estate, "provided it was paid out of the Negroes assigned for the payment of debt by the deed of June, 1845." As her power to dispose of her property was "unlimited," and she was willing to dispose of it, the court felt "indisposed" to contradict her.

The court went out of its way, however, to distinguish between her power to enter into a contract *before* and *after* her marriage. The issue involved a store account run up by Baker—also at Hastie & Nichols. Neither Mrs. Baker nor the trustees of her estate had asked for or been given credit. The court ruled that her estate was not liable for this debt, since by a third clause of the marriage contract her property reverted to her use alone if her husband was sued for debts he made on his own. "But I will go farther," declared Justice Dargan. Supposing the debt had been contracted personally by Mrs. Baker—the complainants still would be prevented from recouping their money from her settled estate. It was the rule that "a married woman is incapable of binding herself by contracts." Her "legal existence" was considered to be "so blended with that of her husband as to place her under the most perfect disability of entering into contracts." Even if the husband and wife were living apart, and the wife had her own income, her contracts would be "null and void." "Such a thing" as a court decree against a married woman founded on contracts she made during her marriage "is unknown to the law" of South Carolina.

On these points the law of South Carolina and the common law of England agreed. But the law of South Carolina was "essentially different" in regard to a wife's power to dispose of her separate estate. Mrs. Baker had the power because it was written into her marriage treaty. She had no powers other than those reserved for her by the provisions of the settlement, whereas in England, a wife had all the powers to dispose of her property which any person might have, except for ones she explicitly renounced. Marriage contracts in South Carolina could give some powers to an otherwise powerless woman; in England, such contracts restricted the unlimited powers which were her natural right.[7] The husband's supremacy had been shaken in old England, and now the northern states were fooling with it. Even some of the southern states had lately "adapted to a fearful extent, the Northern idea on the subject of divorce and the independency of married women." South Carolina was the "honorable exception" where the doctrine of a married woman's subjection flourished "in all its pristine vigor."[8]

6. Social Life

Relatives and Friends

At twenty-two and twenty-three years old, Thomas B. Chaplin was busy trying to make himself felt in society. He and his friends, the younger planters of St. Helena, seemed to be in perpetual motion. They gave themselves up to sport and play, to carousing and to conspicuous consumption. No one would guess from their excessive sociability that agriculture was deeply depressed and cotton prices were at a twenty-five-year low. Every day, Chaplin dined somewhere else or had guests at home to dine with him. The Big House at Tombee was the center of a dense social life. Friends, relatives, and slaves, all with strangers in tow, invaded the house by night and day, making privacy impossible. One lived in public and earned a good name by knowing how to get along with people of different social standings and of varying emotional closeness. Status among whites was measured in capital goods—in the number of acres and slaves a white person owned. A friend described Chaplin, in 1846, as "a man worth sixty negroes and a plantation."[1] He also owned a house in St. Helenaville, the summer resort on a pine bluff at the eastern end of the Island. A house in Beaufort would have counted for more.

Planters were obsessed with the problems of transmitting property. Not without reason did they attach importance to the concept of the family line. Knowing how one was descended in a society so intricately interrelated was a person's surest claim to a just inheritance. Knowing the lineage of other people meant knowing how one was related to them, a knowledge that was useful in choosing wives and husbands, guardians and trustees, executors and appraisers. Because society was small, people commonly occupied a wide variety of relations to each other. Imagine the emotions that Chaplin and Daniel T. Jenkins had to manage whenever they met. Jenkins was a close friend of Chaplin's, a cousin on both Chaplin's mother's and his father's sides, godfather to Chaplin's son Daniel, a trustee of Chaplin's mother's immense estate, and the executor of the estate of Uncle Ben, Chaplin's father's brother who died without heirs. Jenkins also held a controlling interest in Lands End Plantation, just southwest of Tombee, and could make its resources available to Chaplin or to anyone he pleased. Here was a source of persistent tension in society, and of drama in Chaplin's journal: that a man with whom Chaplin shot ducks and shared his liquor, a bachelor cousin whom Chaplin felt obliged to nurse when he was ill, filled many important roles in Chaplin's life, some of which could have drastically affected Chaplin's fortunes, and all of which contained seeds of intimacy and conflict.

Chaplin's best friends were unified by common descent and had known each other since they were boys. They shared occupations and traditions that were already old when they were born. They agreed broadly on what constituted success and how a man should spend his money. They had an overriding interest in maintaining the peace and profitability of their plantations. They were men of capital competing against each other to get the best price for their crops—competing, too, to acquire more fertile land and disciplined workers, and to tilt the institutional wealth of society in their direction. They minded each other's business as closely as they minded their own. They built very little that was new, and while they talked about progress, they were fond of the social code and virtues of the past. They were inventive, however, in the area of political thought, and the consequences of their inventiveness cost them their fortunes.

Chaplin's intimates included his cousins the three Jenkinses; his three uncles; and Ned Capers, the third son of Charles Gabriel Capers, a wealthy old man who kept close watch over his estate while his sons killed time waiting to inherit plantations of their own. Unlucky in love and too fond of his liquor, Ned roamed between his father's plantation on St. Helena and one on the outskirts of Charleston. When he was on the Island, he visited Chaplin nearly every day. They were drinking buddies, and when Chaplin's other friends deserted him, Ned Capers stayed true, though in the late '50s, he may have had another reason for coming by—Chaplin's daughter Virginia. After the War, of all the men Chaplin called friends, only Ned returned to St. Helena, where he ran a little store and managed elections for the Democratic party.

Chaplin and Major Daniel P. Jenkins drifted apart after the Major married. Chaplin's friendship with Captain Daniel T. Jenkins was injured by the Baker fiasco and the scramble for Uncle Ben's estate. In his time of adversity Chaplin sulked as his friends grew rich. The Captain sported a new thousand-dollar boat while Dr. William Jenkins, the Major's brother, acquired a string of superior horses and three plantations, built a mansion on St. Helena, and bought another one in Beaufort. Chaplin continued to play billiards with the Doctor, when he could make room for himself among Jenkins's other guests. "He can get any quantity of these with the amusements & refreshments he can offer," sighed Chaplin, in 1856.

How different from the youthful days of the '40s, when none of them had money. They had enjoyed an equality, floating along at low water, but the rising economic tide did not treat them equally. Chaplin made other friends—J. H. Webb, a brother of Thomas L. Webb, the cotton factor, and second husband of Emma Jenkins, the Captain's sister; William J. Grayson, Jr., the merry-making son of the man who wrote *The Hireling and the Slave,* the planters' answer to *Uncle Tom's Cabin;* William W., Alviro, and Clarence A. Fripp, the late-maturing sons of the Baptist champion Good Billy Fripp. None of these friendships, however, engaged him as deeply as his relationships with the Jenkinses and Caperses, whose opinions of him and whose twists of fortune weighed heavily in how he thought of himself.

The Agricultural Society

In the absence of a strong central authority, planter institutions were the principal self-regulating mechanisms. Though separate institutions had distinct functions with respect to the morals, safety, and prosperity of the white people, in everyday life their operations overlapped. Thus, the Agricultural Society organized police patrols, while at militia meetings planters set up meat markets and swapped seeds. Some institutions were voluntary, like the Agricultural Society and the Episcopal Church. Some were compulsory, like the militia and road committees. All provided occa-

sions, mainly for white men, to offset the loneliness of the plantation. They channeled aggression into target shooting and agricultural competitions. They added duties toward neighbors to the
obligations people already felt toward kin. They honored generosity and public-spiritedness, but they also bred bitter disputes which
shook the morale of the Island and permanently divided families—disputes over dereliction of duty or the location of a ferry
crossing or rules for judging watermelons. In reality, the identity of
goals was never as conscious or complete as a structural analysis
would make it seem.

Chaplin showed the finest melons and vegetables of the season at
the August, 1851, meeting of the Agricultural Society. Yet he seldom competed for premiums; his interest in the Society was primarily social. He went to monthly meetings to meet friends, and to
be received as a colleague and good citizen. And he liked the dinners, gossip, and frequent show of tempers. Other members came
and went but his attendance never flagged. Participation in the
Agricultural Society helped him maintain his sense of who and
what he was. In turn, he felt obliged to the Society and dedicated
himself to keeping alive its name and the record of its accomplish-
ments. At the annual election of officers, in April, 1853, Chaplin
accepted the post of secretary, out of a desire to see its business
more accurately recorded.

The St. Helena Agricultural Society was an autonomous organization, neither chartered nor governed by the State Agricultural
Society. It was in existence as early as 1826, and it may have
evolved from a hunting or dinner club, or some other "convivial"
society. Or, it may have begun in response to the great agricultural
depression. Though members paid lip service to belonging to the
larger agricultural community, the Society's major concerns were
intensely local and dominated by "the principal and most important business" of eating and drinking. Over the many courses of the
monthly banquet, the men discussed "agriculture, politics, and
wine," as Chaplin succinctly put it.

Before 1846, the Society communicated with its "sister societies" in other parishes through the pages of the *Southern Agriculturist*,
a regional planters' magazine. Published in Charleston and dedicated to "change and improvement" in the countryside, the *Southern Agriculturist* put planters in touch with the latest ideas in

political economy, chemistry and botany, and the science of managing Negroes. The magazine printed orations delivered at various local societies and at annual meetings of the State Society. Planters submitted accounts of experiments with different crops and techniques; urban gardeners reported their latest hothouse discoveries; agricultural and horticultural societies sent along the results of crop and flower contests. The *Southern Agriculturist* announced that Benjamin Chaplin—probably Chaplin's Uncle Ben—won the St. Helena premium for corn in 1829 and 1830, with yields of fifty-four and seventy-three bushels to the acre. These remarkable figures represented the harvest of one acre only; they were not a typical yield, which was less than twenty bushels. By Chaplin's day, the Society was offering its prize for the best *average* yield—a more reliable measure of progress.

As associations for the common defense of the white minority, agricultural societies recruited posses to hunt runaways and put down disturbances in the slave quarters. The lodge hall of the St. Helena Agricultural Society doubled as a courtroom for trying and punishing slaves. The planters' organization of St. John's Parish, Berkeley District, incorporated its security function in its name—Black Oak Agricultural and Police Society—and offered rewards to slaves for spying and informing on their fellows. It was under a resolution of the State Agricultural Society that a collection called *The Negro Law of South Carolina* was published, in 1848.

The spirits of science, scholarship, and public safety were not the only spirits active at Agricultural Society meetings. "As the hour for dinner comes on," wrote Joseph E. Jenkins, of Colleton District, "the countenances which before were heavy and dull become bright and radiant with expectation."[2] Members took turns "finding" dinner and drink, from which it was considered impolite to go home sober. Some providers took the opportunity to show off. Edgar Fripp, a colossal egoist whom Chaplin had the pleasure of beating in a horse race, would serve four times more food than could be eaten. Reminding members that excessive generosity was a breach of manners, and that it was their duty to bear wealth as gracefully as they endured debts, the Society resolved to fine a man fifty cents if he brought more than six dishes of meat.

"Finding" dinner was costly and troublesome for Chaplin, who was hard pressed to put food on his own table. The days before his turn were filled with "the bustle of great preparations." "Everybody in the yard busy preparing for my Agricultural dinner to-morrow," he wrote, on October 5, 1853. Wine, whiskey, and champagne had to be sent for. Meat had to be slaughtered out of the pen or hunted in the wild. Sometimes the hands were sent fishing. Often his mother would help out with a gift of meat and the loan of a cook. Once the dinner was fixed, it had to be carted across the Island to the Society lodge. A cart or two had to be cleaned, repaired, built new, or borrowed. En route to the lodge one day in December, 1855, Chaplin's black mare kicked off the front of her cart, "fortunately spilling only some sauce." His trial ended when his friends sampled his spread and pronounced it "very good."

In spite of its members' convivial intentions, meetings of the Agricultural Society were regularly marred by quarrels. A dozen masters, each used to having his own way, found it difficult to agree. Men hotly disputed whose turn it was to find the next dinner—a duty some wished to avoid. They also argued over principles, such as whether to add "Horticultural" to the name of the Society. A majority, including Chaplin, voted in 1845 to include it, but not because the group had decided to mend their ways. Indeed, it was "horticulture" whose meaning had changed. The cotton men were readmitting a wayward member to their club, a branch of botanical science that had broken from agriculture and set itself up as a rival. Now the two were compatible again. In the early years of the economic depression, "horticulture" had been the code word for cutting back on cotton and diversifying crops. Horticulture, the art of growing fruits, vegetables, and ornamental plants, had been the rallying cry for a generation of reformers. In the new situation, it took on a double meaning. First, it stood for applying to *cotton* the techniques of seed selection associated with hothouse science and small-scale gardening. Second, it expressed the old ideal of self-sufficiency in food, but without promoting food crops as an alternative to cotton. By advocating horticulture, Chaplin was indicating how he wanted the collective agricultural resources of his neighborhood to be used. He wanted men who grew the finer varieties of cotton to share their secrets; and he wanted to learn how to break out of the impoverishing pattern of buying provisions.

But the glimmer of prosperity dulled interest in the kind of co-operation Chaplin was looking for. Men took more seriously their role as aristocrats, while the increased money supply sharpened social gradations. Naturally, men of new wealth wanted to be recognized. Edgar Fripp is an example of a person suddenly making big money and "showing for rich," or competing for attention, with men of old money. "Edgar Fripp is an ass," ventured Chaplin in his journal, while other members of the Agricultural Society, also offended by his pretensions, challenged Fripp in the open.

Fripp once provoked a row so serious it nearly broke up the Society. The details are obscure, but at a meeting in February, 1857, Fripp evidently remarked that some members were trading illicitly with Negroes, perhaps by buying forbidden items, such as meat, from the slaves of other planters, or by bartering whiskey for corn. A fracas ensued and Chaplin expressed doubt that the Society would meet again. It did meet, several months later, and then regularly until 1861, when it abruptly ceased to exist.

One detail of its demise continued to rankle Chaplin. Twice in later years he noted that when the War had broken out, Ned Capers's brother William, the treasurer, "had all the valuables of the Society in his hands, silver spoons & forks & money, & never accounted for any of it." Although the loss was small next to the destruction of all private property, it symbolized for Chaplin the eclipse of values and customs he held dear. The silver had embodied the wealth of the Island and reflected the eminence of the planters. The spoons and forks were the very tools with which the Agricultural Society accomplished its mission. If only the Yankees had been the ones who had taken the stuff. But "Puritan avarice" was not to blame. St. Helena had been violated from within.

Self-defense: Militia and Patrol

When he was sixteen years old, in 1804, William J. Grayson "happened to be near the scene of a negro conspiracy," while on a visit to the plantation of his cousin, Major Hazzard, on the Euhaw River, in St. Peter's Parish.[3] There was "a rumor afloat" that slaves in the neighborhood were plotting to revolt, and the white people started taking guns to bed. The rumor was true, but the rebellion fizzled when a slave tipped off his master, only hours before "the time appointed for the outbreak." Forewarned, the whites surprised and seized the ringleaders, and tried them "without delay," condemning "ten or a dozen" to be hanged. Sentence was carried out swiftly. "Their heads were cut off, stuck on poles, and set up along the highway leading from Purrysburg, the place of the trial, to Coosawhatchie," the old judicial seat of Beaufort District.[4]

By these lights, Chaplin's era was tranquil. No slave plots were uncovered and only once in his vicinity was a black person charged with killing a white. There were no mass uprisings or retaliations, though Chaplin reported several isolated slayings of blacks. The possiblity of slave insurrection seemed as remote as the chance of an Indian uprising. Militiamen took their slave patrol duties lightly, often adjourning early to drink and play. By the mid-'40s, muster days were as notorious for drunkenness as political barbecues.

Yet the lull in apprehension was merely a break between sieges of fear. In 1818, the Combahee area northeast of St. Helena had been thrown into "a state of alarm in consequence of the depredations of runaway negroes."[5] Denmark Vesey's aborted insurrection, at Charleston, in 1822, was answered with reprisals against troublemakers and a wave of armed vigilance up and down the seaboard. Nine years later, word of Nat Turner's rebellion in tidewater Virginia revived patrol activity in the Sea Islands and inspired South Carolina lawmakers to tighten restrictions on blacks. Between this most famous of all American slave uprisings and John Brown's raid on the Federal armory at Harpers Ferry, Virginia, twenty-seven years later, Sea Island planters experienced comparatively little anxiety over their personal safety. They felt more threatened by abolitionists in the North than by the slaves in whose midst they lived and who vastly outnumbered them. But they had not lost their habitual defensiveness. When it was learned in October, 1859, that John Brown had targeted Gillisonville, in Beaufort District, on his ambitious map of rebellion, the white people of the town formed five new vigilance committees to enforce patrol laws.[6]

Patrols were gangs of white men who were empowered to "correct" any slave "met beyond his master's plantation" without a pass. Twenty lashes inflicted on the spot was the normal penalty for a first offense. Patrols were authorized to break up all assemblies of Negroes "held for mental instruction" or for worship after certain hours. They were supposed to search the slave quarters regularly for arms and ammunition, but this rule was ignored. When they bothered to search, it was for stolen food and runaways.

Patrol districts were the smallest units in the military organization of the state. From the top down, the militia consisted of five divisions corresponding to five administrative regions.[7] Each division was made up of two brigades; each brigade, four regiments; each regiment, two battalions; each battalion, four beat companies;

each beat company, four patrol districts. Each division had to maintain a troop of cavalry, and a battalion might include a company of riflemen. Patrol captains were appointed by beat captains. Every white man between the ages of eighteen and forty-five was subject to service in the militia, and every member of the militia had to ride patrol or hire a man to take his place. Physicians were exempt from military service, except in times of alarm. So were ferrymen, judges, bank clerks, schoolmasters with more than fifteen students, and keepers of the lunatic asylum.[8]

During the first few years he kept his journal, Chaplin looked forward to militia meetings in Beaufort—to parading, eating, target shooting, and horse racing. His attention waned as his troubles mounted, and in June, 1847, he even forgot the anniversary of his company. "Don't give a damn," he barked, as if by staying home and reserving a part of himself from the clutches of public life, he had found a new way to assert himself. In 1849, he quit the Beaufort company and turned out for muster with the St. Helena Mounted Riflemen. The secession crisis of 1850 quickened his interest in military affairs and he accepted the post of clerk of the company. His first job was to summon defaulters from meetings and patrol duty to court-martial in Gillisonville. In 1854, Chaplin was elected orderly sergeant, an office he held for at least two years.

The political urgency passed like a comet. As cotton prices rallied in the early '50s, enthusiasm for marching and drilling declined. Yet Chaplin kept faith with his company, not because he feared the slaves or anticipated a war, but because he felt he belonged to a tradition worth perpetuating.

The St. Helena Mounted Riflemen were a company of about forty rank and file, descended from a home defense band organized after 1690 to keep the Indians "in awe and subjection," to repel French and Spanish adventurers, and to chase pirates who raided Port Royal en route to better pickings at Cape Fear.[9] In October, 1775, the South Carolina Council of Safety signed commissions for Captain John Jenkins (grandfather of Dr. William, Captain Daniel T., and Major Daniel P. Jenkins), Lieutenant William Fripp, Jr. (great-uncle of Captain John and Good Billy Fripp), and Lieutenant Benjamin Reynolds (great-great-uncle of Thomas B. Chaplin), to form the St. Helena Volunteers, a band of irregulars that harassed the British and guarded against slave defections during the Revolution. A contingent of St. Helena Volunteers fought in the Seminole War of the mid- and late 1830s, a long, episodic campaign to remove or exterminate an Indian remnant in Florida whose numbers were swelled by free and fugitive Negroes. Another contingent went to war against Mexico in 1846, helping to push United States sovereignty west and south, along the northern rim of the Gulf of Mexico, which southern congressmen were claiming as a southern sea. The St. Helena fighters' greatest glory came on November 8, 1861, however, when they guarded the successful retreat of Confederate soldiers from Fort Beauregard, at Bay Point, on the eastern shore of Port Royal Sound, across the Hunting Islands and marsh expanses to St. Helena Island, then to safety on the main.

The Scales of Justice

To correct a Negro charged with a crime against the property of a white person other than his master, someone had to call a trial. Prosecutor, jurors, judge, and executioner were drawn from planters in the neighborhood. Chaplin, for example, prosecuted an old slave doctor and fortune-teller for assaulting another slave, in 1845. And he whipped two slaves convicted of stealing cattle at a trial he attended in 1858 as a "favor" to Dr. John Scott.

Black defendants were not free to defend themselves. They could not hire lawyers or take time out from work to gather evidence and prepare a case. They could testify against one another, but not in cases to which whites were a party. Thus, their hands were tied and their mouths were closed. Slaves could "invoke neither magna charta nor common law. . . . In the very nature of things [they are] subject to despotism."[10] They had hardly more status in the legal process than livestock. Slave trials sometimes became forums for conflicts between whites who accused one another of using their Negroes as pawns or proxies. A slave might pay for his offense with a whipping, and his master could be made to pay cash to the injured party.

Slaves who repeatedly violated local laws could be locked up or sentenced to leave the Parish—a punishment called transportation. To fine slaves was futile, and since they already were in lifetime custody, time could not be added to their term. They could be whipped or paddled or deprived of privileges—forbidden, say, to go off the plantation—but deprivations were shunned because they demoralized innocent slaves and were difficult to enforce.

One particular crime and one hearing moved Chaplin to write his most eloquent narration. The case concerned the murder of a black man by a white and, although not typical, therefore, of most criminal proceedings, it forcefully illustrates how the legal system apportioned justice to each race.

On Monday, February 19, 1849, while eating breakfast, Chaplin was summoned to go to James H. Sandiford's plantation, on the Seaside about two miles from Tombee, "and sit on a jury of inquest on the body of Roger, a Negro man belonging to Sandiford." The purpose of the inquest was to determine if there was sufficient evidence to make Sandiford stand trial for killing Roger, a cripple, who had choked to death on a chain his master put around his neck, after he was shackled and bolted to the floor of an outbuilding. Who informed on Sandiford? Chaplin does not say. One of Sandiford's slaves may have reported the killing to a white man or passed word to a friend on another plantation who went and told his master. Somehow the magistrate learned about Roger's death and decided it was a matter of public concern.

The evidence heard at the inquest convinced Chaplin of Sandiford's guilt, but the jury declared that Roger had died accidentally, *"having slipped from the position"* Sandiford had placed him in. "The verdict should have been that Roger came to his death by inhumane treatment to him by his master," dissented Chaplin. He felt confused and ashamed. How was a man supposed to discharge his duty if not by drawing reasonable conclusions from the facts and obeying his conscience? If right and wrong were not relevant to the case, then what rule was a thinking man to follow?

Chaplin recounted the hearing in detail. The whole twelve-man jury—about one-sixth of the adult white males on the Island—examined Roger's body. "Such a shocking sight never before met my eyes," exclaimed Chaplin. The "poor Negro," who all his life had walked on his knees "more than his feet," was found "in the most shocking situation, but *stiff dead,"* having been "placed in this situation by his *master,* to punish him, as he says, *for impertinence."* Sandiford had sent Roger into the creek to get oysters on Saturday morning, "cold & bitter weather, as everyone knows, though Sandiford says, 'It was *not very* cold.' " He ordered the man to return before high tide and to bring back a bundle of marsh grass. Roger did not return until "ebb tide"—six hours later than he was due—but he brought with him "7 baskets of oysters & a small bundle of marsh." Chaplin was impressed. "More than the primest of my fellows would have done," he digressed. "Anthony never brought me more than 3 baskets of oysters & took the whole day."

Sandiford asked Roger "why he did not return sooner & cut more marsh. He said that the wind was too high. His master said he would whip him for it, & set to work with a cowhide to do the same. The fellow hollered & when told to stop, said he would not, as long as he was being whipped, for which impertinence he received 30 cuts." Sandiford walked away and Roger went into the kitchen and began talking "to another Negro when Sandiford slipped up & overheard this confab, heard Roger, as he says, say, that if he had sound limbs, he would not take a flogging from any white man, but would shoot them down, and turn his back on them." The person Roger was talking to—whether a man or woman we are not told—reported that Roger did not say this, but rather "that he would turn his back on them if they shot him down," which, to Chaplin, was "much the most probable of the two speeches."* Sandiford then had Roger "confined, or I should say, murdered, in the manner I will describe. . . ."

From Sandiford's point of view, Roger had committed at least three offenses: he had not done all the work he had been ordered to in the time allotted; he had answered his master rudely; and he had threatened to kill his master—"if it can be called" a threat, scoffed Chaplin. "For these *crimes,* this man, this demon in human shape, this pretended Christian, member of the Baptist Church, had this poor Negro placed in an open outhouse, the wind blowing through a hundred cracks, his clothes wet to the waist, without a single blanket & in freezing weather." Then he left him for the night at the end of a chain, "a position that none but the 'most *bloodthirsty* tyrant' could have placed a human being. . . . The wretch [Sandiford] returned to his victim about daylight the next morning & found him, as anyone might expect, dead, *choked, strangled,* frozen to death, *murdered.*"

---

*This person's testimony could have been heard in court had Sandiford been brought to trial, because it bore on the Negro's behavior, not the white man's. "The words of a negro are at least as significant as the cry of a brute animal . . . and if any sound whatever, contemporaneous with an act, might serve to give meaning to an act, it would be admissible." (*Parris* v. *Jenkins,* 2 Richardson 106, December, 1845, in Helen T. Catterall, *Judicial Cases Concerning American Slavery and the Negro* [Washington, D.C., 1929], vol. II, "South Carolina Cases," 396.)

If the truth was so plain to Chaplin, why didn't the others see it? Why wasn't Sandiford made to stand trial? Didn't the law forbid a master from chastising a slave "with unusual vigor" so as "to maim or mutilate him, or to cause his death"? The statute seemed written for this atrocity.* Why didn't the planters apply it?

Sandiford was related through marriage to at least four of the jurors, but it is unlikely that this is what saved him. The Perrys, the Fripps, and the other men on the jury may have felt to a man that they would never do what Sandiford did, but to overrule him could set an unwelcome precedent for community interference in their private affairs. Perhaps they believed they were defending the sanctity of property rights, including the right to destroy one's own property. Some may have found the murder repulsive, as Chaplin did, but wanted it to pass unpunished in the hope that it would scare their slaves into deeper subjection. But to Chaplin, the jury's verdict compounded the original crime; it was a new wrong to be accounted for. Yet he carried his protest no further than his journal, and he never referred to the incident again.

Within a year, Sandiford sold his plantation to Dr. William Jenkins and left the Island. He had been thoroughly disliked, by whites and blacks, and no one lamented his departure. In retrospect, the legacy of his crime was to reduce the area of life regulated by conscience and morality.[11] In five years' time, Chaplin himself was defending an overseer who had killed a runaway slave for stealing watermelons. His youthful sympathies had been worn away by personal calamity, and while his friendships had weakened, his loyalty to the institutions of his class was as strong as ever.

Roads and Fences

In May, 1848, the South Carolina legislature appointed Chaplin to the Board of Road Commissioners for St. Helena Parish. He had held the office for three years when, to his surprise, he failed to be reappointed and Captain Daniel T. Jenkins was named in his place. "I have very strong suspicions that some of my friends have

*An act of 1821 declared the murder of a slave to be a felony. On commission from the South Carolina State Agricultural Society, John Belton O'Neall compiled the state laws regulating Negro behavior and relationships between whites and blacks, in *The Negro Law of South Carolina* (Columbia, S.C., 1848). The Agricultural Society rejected the work, which included O'Neall's suggestions for modifying slavery by taking measures to increase the slaves' well-being. For example, O'Neall contemplated attaching the Negroes to the land, in the manner of Russian and Italian serfs, rather than to individual owners whose personal fortunes jeopardized the family security of the slaves.

been officiously busying themselves to get me out," he confided to his journal. He had served diligently and for no monetary reward. It hurt to think that people were "displeased" with him and "wished for a change," but he was relieved to give up the head-aches and expense of the office. So he said. "They did not dream they were doing me a favor instead of an injury," he crowed, find-ing some satisfaction for his wounded pride.

The job of road commissioner required the skills of a peace-maker, slave driver, quartermaster, and general. The commissioner took petitions and complaints from the planters in his division. He met in Beaufort with the other commissioners to lay out new roads and schedule maintenance of old ones. He directed his neighbors to provide hands and material several times a year, on schedule and in emergencies. He rounded up horses and wagons, allowing plant-ers to deduct so many slaves from their quota for each contribu-tion. He made out "returns"—reporting delinquent planters to the Board, which might decide to fine them. He procured lumber for bridge planking and bulkheads and arranged to have materials de-livered at the right moment, so that workers would not stand idle. He appointed a white man to oversee the hands, and rode back and forth to the job sites to see how work was progressing. And he made sure that an ample dinner was served, at some stopping point along the road, to the overseer and any planters who might show up. In essence, he had to coax private men who were rivals for the collective resources of the Parish to work as a team. It was a ticklish business, with many opportunities for offense. Planters worried that they were asked to give more than their share; that their slaves were worked harder than the next man's; that their neighbors would benefit more from the project than they would.

In no endeavor was mutual assistance more crucial or more pronounced than in working the roads. Yet, in no other public set-ting was the habit of sovereignty more divisive. The roads were hotbeds of contention. "Long wrangling between several of the men over how the work should be done, everyone differing as usual," began Chaplin's journal entry for November 30, 1846. Two days later the work was set back when a pier head floated away, a blunder Chaplin attributed to "there being too many directors on the work." On December 3, Edgar Fripp and J. W. Pope "had a few harsh words." The next day, Fripp got into it with his cousin Oliver Fripp. "Whose turn will it be tomorrow," Chaplin wondered. During his tenure as commissioner, Oliver Fripp fell out with C. G. Capers, his neighbor on Chowan Creek; and Capers locked horns with Henry McKee in a notorious squabble over the placement of a new road.* Chaplin was sensitive to the injury a man could suffer from having a road run across his land, and to the hard feelings which could arise from placing a road too far from where it could do a particular planter any good. He tried to be fair and to set an example of public-spiritedness, but no one seemed to notice or reciprocate. "I claim no hands for my boat & flat which the public have been using all week," he offered, in August, 1848. "Yes, & ditto, horse." Being commissioner did not excuse a man from road duty. If anything it put his performance in the spotlight without even affording him the privilege of working the roads at his convenience, "that is, when he can best spare his own hands from home. . . ."

A planter who was short of labor had trouble keeping up his fences. It was an endless job, especially taxing in late winter when new fences had to be raised. These post-and-rail structures rotted from the moisture, blew down in high winds, and burned in fires which were set to clean the stubble off the fields. During cold snaps, fences would mysteriously disappear, piece by piece, picked apart at night for firewood. To mend and build his fences, Chaplin had to take his hands away from other important work, such as manuring. After he lost his carpenters in the foreclosures of 1845 and 1847, he had to trust the cutting and notching of fence timber to less skilled workers.

Fencing a forty-acre field on four sides took more than a mile of fence, an investment of about one hundred dollars. Fencing several smaller fields, as was commonly the practice, instead of one larger one, took more miles and more dollars. Fence timber was plentiful enough on St. Helena, but difficult to transport. Planters particularly resented the time spent repairing fences. Like road work, fence work was habitual and mandatory. The law required planters to enclose their fields to avoid lawsuits caused by the depredations of cattle and hogs. But there was no Board of Commissioners

---

*Capers and McKee had been fighting with each other for years. In 1840, McKee dug a ditch to drain a roadway he owned that crossed Capers's property and intersected with the main road leading to Capers's house. At the junction of the two roads, McKee severed Capers's road with his ditch, making it impossible for Capers to pass without constructing a bridge. Capers sued McKee and won, but the case was not settled until 1847. (*C. G. Capers* v. *H. McKee,* 1 Strob. 164, 32 S.C.)

to organize the tasks and compel cooperation. A planter who was negligent about his fences might earn a bad name or even get sued if his inattention brought harm to his neighbors' crops or livestock, but no other sanctions could be brought to bear on him.

Chaplin complained continually that his neighbors ignored their common fences and looked out only for themselves. Once, when a swamp fire approached a fence that ran along a boundary of Uncle Ben's place and continued along a boundary of Tombee, Ben quenched only as much of the fire as threatened his part. Chaplin singled out Major Daniel P. Jenkins as "a bad neighbor" for neglecting his fences. Jenkins, in turn, criticized Uncle Tom, and once ordered his slaves to shoot Tom's cattle when they got into his fields. Chaplin thought of following Jenkins's example after the Major's hogs got into his corn. Indeed, he did shoot two cows belonging to his cousin Ben Chaplin when they broke into his cotton, on December 2, 1853. Ben acted as though he didn't care if Chaplin shot all his cattle, "for he knows the most of them will die this winter." Stock was usually turned loose in the swamps and woods at the end of November and driven up again in May. Left to their own devices, cattle would test the fences until they pushed an opening into the fields. Many did not find enough food to survive, and many others were surreptitiously slaughtered by the slaves. On December 3, Chaplin resolved not to kill any more of his cousin's cattle lest, despite Ben Chaplin's show of indifference, he be made to pay for them, "& they are not worth 1 dollar pr. head."

Hunting and Fishing

Free to do what he wanted most of the time, Chaplin liked to hunt and fish. Except for chasing wildcats to keep his dogs in shape for running deer, he did not hunt on St. Helena. Game had long been scarce on the Island, either killed off or driven across the marshes to the sandy outer islands, which were maintained as hunting reserves. Wildcats—medium-sized, yellow-gray cats, twenty-five pounds on the average, with blunt tails and appetites for domestic poultry—had managed to survive because they had a strong sense of smell to help them locate food and to warn them of danger, they were fleet-footed, they traveled over large territories, and they did not stay long in one spot. But deer, whose territory was more restricted, had no place to hide around the plantations. Woods which might have afforded cover were burned to clean out the undergrowth and make pasture for cattle and hogs.

Chaplin never hunted alone. In his early twenties, he often would go with a favorite slave, who had the privilege of using a gun. When he got older he hunted more frequently in large groups of white people. Sometimes women would go along, not to shoot but to civilize the camp. Neither Mary nor Sophy ever went hunting with Chaplin. When he went off, he emphatically left his wife behind. Negroes, however, were an essential part of any expedition, providing knowledge of the environment as well as labor. They rowed the boats, cared for the horses, carried the gear, drove the deer, cleaned the kill. Whites seemed to enjoy their company— their songs and their gaiety. The blacks, too, were glad to be away from the plantation.

Of all the reasons people hunted, food gathering was especially important to Chaplin. He counted on putting venison on the table in winter. The prospect of cavorting, drinking, and shooting with his friends exerted a strong pull on him as well. Hunting provided opportunities for broadening one's social contacts, as when Chaplin would go down with his brother's friends to Chehaw, the game-rich peninsula formed by the Ashepoo and Combahee rivers, where his mother had three plantations. A large party of hunters increased each man's chances for success. Hunting was far from a meditative or contemplative activity; it was extremely sociable, gregarious.

Chaplin's favorite hunting grounds, the "Hunting Islands," on the ocean side of St. Helena, are composed of sand ridges that run parallel to the sea. In the mode of hunting designed to triumph over this topography, men were stationed at intervals along two ridges while the driver, a black man, ran the dogs in the valley between them.[12] Pursued, the quarry would break up the side of one of the ridges, trying to cross to cover. The men would ride or run along as the deer and the dogs went by, and shoot at the deer as it ran up or down the ridge. This moment was a high point in the life of a Sea Island planter. He had to remember not to shoot while the deer was on the ridge itself, or he would jeopardize other hunters. Indeed, the danger of being shot by a member of the party or by one's own gun was the major risk of the hunt.

Once detected by the dogs, the deer's chance of getting away was slim. The ridges were walls which cut off its retreat. If the deer made it to the sea, the dogs would chase it into the surf where it would drown, or else double it back onto the beach where it would be an easy mark. Its only hope was to make it into the tangle of vegetation in the Island's interior where neither fire nor axe had thinned the natural refuge.

The hunter's odds were improved by the limitations of the reserve and by his enlistment of help. Instead of having to seek out his prey, he knew just where to find it—on a tract of land surrounded by deep water. And instead of stalking the creature himself, he employed his slaves, horses, and dogs. In effect, he put several other hunters between himself and the game. By utilizing the black driver's knowledge of animals and terrain, the horse's speed and maneuverability, and the dog's instinct to sniff out and give chase, the hunter did not have to study the habits of the deer. These conditions gave rise to new pleasures, such as pride in the performance of domesticated animals, and maximized the time that could be spent in camp.

Chaplin was perfectly at ease killing animals for food or sport. Yet, his attitude was not aggressive, because the chase in essence involved a contest between other animals. His role was to finish off the catch after his "hunters" had exhausted it, then to oversee the butchering and distribution of the meat. Once, for good luck, he daubed his slave Ben with the blood of Ben's first deer—the vestige of an ancient rite for initiating novices that is still practiced among southern deer and fox hunters. Chaplin was troubled that he did not get an opportunity for anointing or "blooding" his son Ernest, who had no luck hunting. And though Ernest grew up to be a great "shooter" of birds, Chaplin read the boy's future in his failure to bag a deer.

Chaplin enjoyed hunting birds, too. Some he shot for food, such as wild ducks and turkeys, doves and plover—wading birds which were not to everyone's taste. He shot birds which pestered his corn, and he shot other birds simply because they were abundant—robins, for example, which he destroyed by the hundreds. Robins are reputed to be very good eating, but Chaplin apparently just killed them for sport. Shooting birds was a common pastime. Even the great naturalist and bird-painter John Audubon, a contemporary of Chaplin who did some of his most important work in Charleston, indulged in it.* As plentiful as were certain species,

---

*"How we rejoiced when, after taking so wide a tour over the 'Charleston Bridge,' we at last found out where the 'White Cranes' fed; how you cheated me out of a shot; and

Chaplin realized that life was a struggle for birds, as it was for every creature. He sympathized with crows which a drought had obliged to pull up his potato vines in search of food. Crows were pests, but they also were ingenious adversaries. He had had to take a woman off her tasks for days and weeks at a stretch to "mind" the crows off his crops. Scarecrows did not fool them, and they seemed to alight from nowhere when the "crow-minder" turned her back.

In mid-April, while the field hands were planting cotton, Chaplin and his friends would drop what they were doing and go fishing. Drum fish were running. These large, edible game fish came into Port Royal to drop their spawn.[13] Named for the drumming sound which they make only when they are spawning, drum fish were a significant source of food. They weighed between thirty and forty pounds on the average. Everyone prized them for eating. Chaplin was glad for a change from mullet and trout, which were bountiful the year round in Station Creek. A "side of drum" made a welcome gift. Some men sold drum fish, the only fish that had any local market value. But men went after them mainly because they gave tremendous sport. Drum attacked the hooks and fought frantically until pulled on the boat.

Like hunting, drum fishing had an important place in social life. No one wanted to miss the action. At the first rumor of drum fish, planters would slip their boats—recently caulked and painted for the season—into the water and row, sometimes with the aid of a sail, to their favorite spots off the banks in Broad River, in sight of land, as always. Rowers chanted "their native songs" to the quizzical delight of their masters. Though the songs underlined the different cultural origins of the whites and blacks, the outing inspired an unusual forgetfulness of race and status. For a moment, all in the boat were fishermen, united in purpose and free from the cares and distinctions of shore. "Imagine yourself afloat on our beautiful day," wrote Beaufort's most famous sportsman, William Elliott, "the ocean before you—the islands encircling you—and a great fleet of forty or fifty fishing boats (their awnings glistening in the sun) riding sociably around."[14]

---

how we hung up the fellows by their long necks on the bushes." (John Bachman, reminiscing to John James Audubon, January 23, 1833, in Catherine L. Bachman, *John Bachman, the Pastor of St. John's Lutheran Church, Charleston* [Charleston, 1888], 129–130.)

Success at drum fishing depended more on imitation than on cooperation, and the sport tended to be very competitive. Each man had his eye on how the boat next to him was doing. When the drum struck at a particular boat, the boats nearest it would quickly run up alongside, thus indicating to everyone the direction of the school. Boats lying out of the run would pull up anchor and join "the boat line." With five fishing lines—one for the master and each of his four oarsmen—a boat "may count on fifteen to twenty fish."[15] Chaplin kept a running tally of his personal catch and the total for his boat. "Caught 11 fish," he reported, on April 10, 1845, "took 5 on my own line—making 7 I have taken myself & 21 in the boat this year." If the fishing was bad, the crew could at least enjoy a sail, or even a race; but when Chaplin was needing the food, he could hardly contain his anger if the fish were not biting.

Drum fish in the spring, sheepshead in the summer, and bass in the fall gave three seasons of sport. Sheepshead are deep-bodied, spiny-finned relatives of porgies, equipped with broad incisor teeth for crushing mollusks. They are outstanding when eaten fresh. Lands End planters constructed feeding grounds for sheepshead by sinking wooden arbors in Broad River, near shore, to which barnacles and oysters could attach. Other favored species of fish taken on hook and line included whiting, blackfish, and cavally. Cavally are narrow-bodied, fork-tailed relatives of pompano, visitors from tropical waters. They were esteemed the tastiest of all game fish.

Shellfish were abundant and easy to harvest. Oysters and clams could be picked, scratched, and raked in the creeks and mudflats at low tide. Shrimp could be caught in seine nets pulled along the creek bottoms, or by cast nets, thrown from a boat or a creek bank. Gathering shellfish was work for blacks, in general, and not recreation for whites. Chaplin, for one, hated to get down in the mud. But he did like to comb the sand for turtle eggs. Once, in a single afternoon, he robbed more than four hundred eggs from their nests on the beach.

Rules of Exchange

Lending and borrowing, gift giving and trading, were the gears that moved society. Even the most self-reliant planter would occasionally run short of corn or meat and want to avoid buying. Or he might want to try out his neighbor's cotton or corn seed. To protect his honor while engaging in a loan or a trade, a man would adhere scrupulously to a code of behavior and expect the same from his trading partner. Violating the delicate, unwritten rules of exchange could lead to embarrassments and grudges. Conversely, the man who upheld his end of a bargain might feel a degree of pride that seems excessive to us, perhaps because the planter's morality was more clearly defined than ours, not least in the area of economic behavior.

Exchanges with his neighbors were a constant source of shame to Chaplin. In straight swaps he normally felt he got the worst of a deal. His problem was that he could never afford to trade for the future, but had to settle for what he needed at once. As a lender, he felt that people repaid him with inferior goods. As a borrower, which was more often the case, he would come on hands and knees, expressing his desperation and failure. And as a gift giver, he felt his gifts were unappreciated and misconstrued. Conscience and religion moved him to be charitable. He would give expecting to receive periodically, not necessarily from the person he had helped but from the general pool of charity. Every time he loaned a cow or made a gift of meat he thought he was building capital to see him through future shortages. He received most gifts amiably, especially fish and game. Anything sent over from Fields Point by R. L. Baker, however, he would not accept.

Chaplin regularly borrowed seeds and slips from his neighbors, either to upgrade his crops or because he had run out of his own. He would pay back in kind or with the standard equivalent of another item—so many bushels of corn for so many hundreds of potato slips. He also swapped seeds to be sociable, to stay in the flow of goods and sympathy, to act neighborly. After 1847, he had to borrow horses and wagons to move his family, oxen and carts to carry his furniture to the village or to haul manure, flats and boats to ship his cotton to market. Chaplin preferred to ask favors of his uncles, his father's brothers, who were more likely to lend to him and with less publicity than other men.

In Chaplin's case, misunderstandings were more likely to occur when he was on the giving end. After he loaned a cow to Dr. Jenkins for the summer of 1848, the Doctor's "fellow Toby" hit her with a stick and broke off one of her horns. The cow died, and Jenkins never acknowledged the incident. In 1850, Chaplin loaned another cow, this time to John L. Chaplin, so that his poor cousin could have some cream for his coffee. "Bad off as I was then, I helped that man," Chaplin noted, long after his cousin had died. How did the man show his gratitude? By turning around and claiming the cow had been a gift.

"I never did get any good for my kindness," Chaplin bitterly recalled. Not that he expected people to put his interest ahead of theirs, but he did expect them to deal fairly and honestly and to accord him the courtesy and consideration due to a gentleman, a white man. He was deeply insulted when Uncle Paul refused to lend him corn because Chaplin did not grow the variety that Paul's Negroes liked to eat, and when Dr. Scott denied him the use of his summer house because he was saving it for his Negroes who were not used to spending the summer on the plantation. "This is real St. Helena friendship," moaned Chaplin. As it turned out, the insult was more serious even than it appeared, because Scott had lied. He was holding his summer house for another white man and had made up the story about the Negroes to put off Chaplin until the deal was sealed.

A leading motive to trade was to avoid having to borrow. So that his wife and daughter would have something to ride in without his going to beg one of his uncles for a carriage, Chaplin swapped a favorite mare for Thomas J. Fripp's buggy. The buggy he was replacing he had acquired in a swap with C. G. Capers for a colt and forty dollars—due when he sold his crop that year. Dealing with rich men was risky, he learned, because they treated trading as a sport, and their object was to come out ahead. Chaplin had high hopes for Capers's buggy. It appeared to be "a very strong, serviceable, and convenient article with seats for four," stout enough to "carry all my family as well as a carriage." After the trade was consummated, Chaplin felt taken. "The old man rather stuck me," he confessed, "the hiding being rather motheaten, no pole or harness, or wrench to take off the wheels."

One basis of prestige, in and out of the household, was a man's ability to provide. Another was his ability to give gifts. A planter needed to produce a surplus so he would have something to give. When W.O.P. Fripp returned ten bushels of corn to Chaplin on the day they were due, Chaplin sent him a gift of a pair of geese. Fripp did not know it, but the gift cleaned him out. Two days later, Chaplin had great difficulty coming up with enough food to feed the Agricultural Society. Worse, he reported, "we can hardly find enough to eat at home."

Opening one's home to guests and strangers was also a kind of gift giving. Anyone might drop in at any time, with a friend or a servant or several of each. A good host would serve food and drink to the white people, send the blacks to eat in the kitchen, and have hay or oats put out for the horses. Visiting and playing the host might take up five or six afternoons a week, in addition to evenings spent at parties or entertaining overnight guests. An increase in the use of written invitations in the mid-1850s indicates that the etiquette of hospitality was becoming more formal, and the planter community more stratified, as the profits earned in the booming cotton market created opportunities for making distinctions.

Before he suffered his great losses in the late 1840s, Chaplin was a busy visitor and host. When he rebounded, his desire to socialize was rekindled. But the flame never burned as hot again. He looked forward more to being invited than to actually attending events. After the War, when his social life was dead, he condemned his old sociability as wasteful and pointless. Most sternly he remembered the effort he had made to keep up appearances so that visitors would take home the right impression, and the distress he had felt knowing that his cotton and corn were weak looking and spotty along the road that led up to his house.

All this had made him painfully nervous, and at the end of his trials he had found no reward. He shared only marginally in the economic recovery of the 1850s, unable to put any money aside or to lessen his dependence on his neighbors. They were not as forthcoming as they used to be, he felt. Something had changed. Charity and cooperation had declined—a cost of the recovery, Chaplin conjectured. While he deplored the resurgence of selfishness, his personal solution would have been to join the ranks of the very rich. Like his mother, he was inclined to show off, but circumstances constrained him. Hence, he became a critic of vanity, noting that history had saved the harshest fates for the most puffed-up individuals. Protest as he did that he was not to blame for his miseries, he did not allow other people to get away with such humbug. Yet neither did he get away with it himself. The price of denying responsibility was "mortification"—the painful thought that people perceived him as foolish, loud, awkward. Thus he felt his unconscious critique of himself, but in an alienated form, as something emanating from others.

The problems of self-presentation were more acute away from home. Imagine the covert smiles and icy looks which greeted

Chaplin when he approached his uncles and friends for money, after he had squandered his own. "I suffered much mortification in those things," Chaplin noted, pondering the many times he had felt degraded. His self-perception had alternated between two extremes: he worried that he stuck out in public as if he were painted red, and he feared that no one saw him at all. When, for example, he had had too much to drink and became loud and boisterous at a dinner he had helped to organize for St. Helena volunteers to the Mexican War, his enemy in disguise, Dr. William Jenkins, tried to "expose" him and make his situation more "conspicuous." Jenkins succeeded, too, by proposing that Chaplin be put out of the building. Chaplin took the bait and aggravated his dilemma by attempting to throw Dr. Jenkins out the window. At this point Captain Daniel T. Jenkins stepped in and stopped him—an act that was friendly on the surface, Chaplin believed, but calculated to ridicule him. After the incident, Chaplin stayed indoors for a week, nursing his pride and hiding from view. He even lost touch with what his slaves were doing, though he assumed they were shirking.

In a different era, the incident might have ended in a duel.[16] Certainly Jenkins and Chaplin were as quick as their ancestors to give and take insults, but remedies had moderated.* No longer was it necessary to exchange pistol shots. The delivery and acceptance of a challenge was sufficient to give satisfaction. By issuing a challenge, the injured party got to publicize his grievance and show his allegiance to a ritual code. He showed that he belonged. And by accepting the challenge, the offender restored the social balance upset by the original insult. He might firmly believe the man he insulted was a scoundrel or a snake, but his acceptance was tantamount to admitting the man was his equal in society.

At least four times in thirteen years, acquaintances of Chaplin went through the motions of preparing to duel. Significantly, none of the duels came off. Once, Captain Jenkins asked Chaplin to act as his second in a duel against John H. Webb. Chaplin thought dueling was barbaric but he could not turn his cousin down. The quarrel had arisen evidently over Webb's intentions toward the Captain's sister, Emma Jenkins. To Chaplin's relief, everyone's

*The "evil custom" of dueling was especially popular after the Revolution, wrote Grayson. "Seven years of war and license" had left an appetite for homicide. Church attendance declined, men spent the Sabbath at quarter-races and cockfights, and drinking and swearing became the marks of a gentleman. (Grayson, *SCHM*, vol. 49, 1948, 28–29.)

honor was restored without bloodshed. Webb later married Emma, and he and the Captain became good friends.

Elections

"A stranger may live among us for years and see no traces of government," remarked the New Orleans publisher J.D.B. DeBow, recalling life in the lowcountry.[17] Yet the stranger would see many traces of democracy—the kind of government practiced by slaveholders in the small republics of antiquity—particularly in the large number of elections. Planters voted for sheriff and tax collector, legislators and congressmen, militia officers below the rank of colonel, commissioners on the Board of Roads, delegates to church and political conventions, and officials of their clubs and societies. Each election might be held on a different day, creating many election days.

Chaplin worked at the polls in several capacities—as a poll watcher, ballot carrier, and vote counter. He believed in elections. He liked the egalitarian feeling that election day conferred on the voters. Granted that only adult white males could vote, and that voting eligibility was based on "the immutable fact of human inequality," the few who enjoyed democracy got to practice it often. As important to voters as the views of a candidate was how he fit into the social structure. Did his family have ties to the neighborhood? Was his first loyalty to Beaufort or to St. Helena Island? A serious quarrel disturbed an election managed by Chaplin in 1856. Three Beaufort men cast ballots on the Island on the basis of lots they owned in St. Helenaville. They also happened to be relatives of one of the candidates for Congress, Joseph D. Pope. Several Fripps challenged their right to vote and turned against Pope. Chaplin thought the incident would "greatly injure" Pope's future. "Several that had already voted for him regretted it," he reported. The only issue that ever raised as much excitement was whether delegates to political conventions should be made to commit themselves to positions on issues before the election.

Though lowcountry planters were a small minority of the voting population of the state, the parish system gave them a working majority in the upper house and accounted for their political supremacy over the more numerous small planters and slaveless white farmers in the interior. Each lowcountry parish was allotted a seat in the State Senate equal to a seat from a whole upcountry district. Beaufort District, with four parishes, had four seats in the Senate while each upcountry district had only one. Since appointments to major offices were decided by a joint ballot of both legislative houses—the Governor was appointed, for example—the parishes could block office seekers who did not champion the rights of property. "The whole system of slavery is class legislation," remarked a candid seaboard planter. The parish system was abolished by the State Constitution of 1865, a victim not of Yankee conquest, but of the upcountry's repudiation of lowcountry rule.

The Politics of Separation

After his defeat at Waterloo, in June, 1815, Napoleon Bonaparte was exiled to an island called St. Helena in the South Atlantic Ocean, about a thousand miles off the western coast of Africa. Learning of his sentence, the citizens of Beaufort District, South Carolina, made preparations for his arrival. According to an old story, Charles B. Capers, father of C. G. Capers, and grandfather of Chaplin's close friend Ned, was chosen to greet the Emperor and offer him hospitality. The meeting never came off, of course. Whether or not the Sea Islanders really expected to see Napoleon, the story expresses their provincialism as well as their yearning for nobility and their capacity for self-delusion. It gave mythic proportion to their feelings of remoteness—a physical separation from the main that would be conquered in time by steamboats, bridges, and telegraph lines, and an emotional separation that would never be spanned.

The white people of St. Helena felt like a people apart. They lived in the southern section of a young country whose population was moving inland from the seaboard, and for the first two decades of the nineteenth century they did not think of themselves as belonging to a distinct cultural territory called the South. After the second war with England, however, their attachments to their section and to their nation developed simultaneously. At an 1819 rally celebrating American independence, a Beaufort man raised his glass to "the Federal Union—may it receive daily strength by an increasing unanimity of sentiment and feeling." Another man toasted "the Constitution of the United States—embodying the accumulated wisdom of the ages," and added, "may it become the creed of every American."[18] The South Carolina legislature added its collective voice to the Federal ideal when, in 1820, it suppressed a motion to condemn a new law imposing duties on goods imported from Europe. Hinting at an undercurrent of dissension, however, the lawmakers denounced the practice of individual states "arraying upon questions of national policy" as if they were "distinct and independent sovereignties."[19]

But as New England and the mid-Atlantic states pressed for higher tariffs to boost their infant industries, South Carolina's national feelings quickly dissipated. Northerners could easily maintain simultaneous allegiances—to state, section, and country—because national policy reflected their economic interests. But southerners found it increasingly difficult to balance their loyalties. Only four years after proclaiming her fealty to Federal rule, South Carolina was leading the fight against the tariff, in the name of the purely agricultural southern states. "The power to protect manufactures is nowhere granted to Congress," South Carolina objected. The higher the tariff, the more that southerners would have to pay for finished goods, European or American. The lower the tariff, the more they could buy with their cotton dollars.

But what could the southern states do about the tariff? What could South Carolina do alone? When Congress passed the tariff of 1828, dubbed the "Bill of Abominations," South Carolina declared that states had the right to nullify Federal laws they considered unconstitutional. This was Calhoun's idea, the cornerstone of his "Exposition."

The issue came to a head in 1832. Congress renewed the tariff, and when President Jackson would not give relief, South Carolina adopted an "Ordinance of Nullification," a bill "to nullify certain acts by the Congress of the United States purporting to be laws, laying duties and imposts on the importation of foreign commodities." But the states she thought she was leading were not ready to follow. Virginia, Georgia, Alabama, and North Carolina all repudiated nullification. Mississippi, sounding like South Carolina ten years earlier, stood "firmly resolved . . . in all events and at every hazard" to preserve "the integrity of the Union—that Union whose value we will never stop to calculate, holding it, as our fathers did, precious above all price."[20]

Congress came back with a compromise tariff in 1833. Isolated from her friends and disarmed by the compromise, South Carolina repealed the nullification ordinance. But the state continued to oppose Federal trade policies and passed a new law repudiating the

Force Bill, an act for collecting customs. The rule of the state was in the hands of the "nullifiers" and the "nullifiers" were "under the spell of Calhoun."[21] South Carolina stayed in the forefront of the antitariff struggle through the 1830s and '40s, when other issues, such as the right to bring slaves into the western territories and the reluctance of the free states to return fugitive slaves, clarified the nature of the conflict between the South and the North.

At the start of the period covered by Chaplin's journal, no Fourth of July celebration on the Sea Islands was considered complete without a recitation of the history of the War of Independence, calculated to make men feel "the friendship of the Revolution."[22] By the summer of 1850, "the gentle bond of old associations" was broken, and the more outspoken Sea Island planters saw themselves as the vanguard of a separate, southern nation. John C. Calhoun, who had suppressed the voices for disunion for almost a generation, had died in April. His successor in the U.S. Senate, the original secessionist R. B. Rhett, was a much more provincial man whose strength lay in his hometown of Beaufort. His ideas were well established on the neighboring Sea Islands and, though cropped back repeatedly, they kept reappearing. Rhett's success in spreading the gospel of secession had brought him to the pinnacle of his career. By 1850, a majority of whites in South Carolina would have supported secession had there been a chance that other states would follow.

Independence Day orations reflected the new political orientation. Instead of emphasizing the ties that bound the American people, speakers dwelt on the things that divided them. William Trescot explained in Beaufort why the South would dissolve the Union before it would give up slavery. "Slavery," he said, "informs all our modes of life, all our habits of thought, lies at the basis of our social existence, and of our political faith."[23] Slavery was much more than a system for growing cotton. The South was wholly dependent on forced labor; without it the white planter class would not have the life it loved.

Beaufort's crusade to protect slavery developed a serious fissure in 1851 when, on the first anniversary of the Southern Rights Association of St. Helena Parish, thirty members—a quarter of the total—resigned to protest the strategy of disunion. The day they announced they were pulling out, Chaplin joined the organization.

He had gone to Beaufort not for political reasons but to buy medicine for his wife, who had been sick a long time and now was "worse than ever." He found "quite a busy day there," and was relieved to immerse himself in the crowd and activities. "In the first place," there was an election of delegates to "a Southern Congress"—a convention planned for Nashville to discuss secession. Second, it was Muster Day for his old company, the Beaufort Volunteer Artillery. And third, the Southern Rights Association was meeting. After the company's parade, he was invited to a sumptuous dinner, "a good one with champagne & other liquors & wines, over which there were five fiery secession addresses delivered by Messrs. DeTreville, E. Rhett, Trescot, J. D. Pope, & G. P. Elliott, all of which were loudly cheered."

Chaplin probably would have joined the Association the year before but the day it met not only was his wife sick, but two of his sons as well. Mary Chaplin was dying and excitement over states' rights coincided with her decline. Not surprisingly, Chaplin paid only scattered attention to politics. Still, he lent his name to the cause and on occasion took a more active role. He helped to arrange the dinner in honor of R. B. Rhett, in St. Helenaville, on July 24, 1850, at which he "offered a few remarks in my own way & style." On September 28, three weeks before the Southern Rights Association convened, he and seventy other "citizens of St. Helena Parish" pledged "never to employ any 'coaster' owned by a citizen of the North or manned by a northern crew, to take part of our products to the city of Charleston or elsewhere." In a notice that ran in the Charleston *Mercury,* on November 4, the group vowed to broaden its boycott. No longer would signers "buy goods of non-slaveholding states, transact business with any merchant or factor who was a freesoiler, countenance school teachers or patronize schools not wholly southern in feeling & opinion. . . ."

Though Chaplin was not there to tell about it, the first meeting of the Southern Rights Association can be reconstructed from minutes found "among other papers" by officers of a Union Navy gunboat in Beaufort, on November 20, 1861.[24] The meeting in 1850 had been chaired by Edmund Rhett, Representative to the state legislature from St. Helena Parish and brother of R. B. Rhett. Richard DeTreville, Chaplin's attorney in his suit against R. L. Baker, had chaired the Committee on Resolutions, and while it was no secret that he "embraced the doctrine of secession to its full-

est extent," he had drawn up a compromise statement that secessionists and unionists alike could sign. "The Federal Government,"
he had written, "was controlled by a fanatical minority" that was
inciting attacks against the Constitution and "upon the property
and feelings" of the slaveholding states. "Conscious of the necessity
of resistance," he had continued, the citizens of St. Helena Parish
"have determined to form ourselves into an Association for the
protection and defense of our rights, honor, and institutions."
They, the resisters, were the true constitutionalists, whose aim was
to restore the Federal compact to "its original purity and simplicity, as the only means of preserving the Union."

The Association had elected officers and formed an executive
committee called the Council of Safety, made up of fifteen men including, from St. Helena Island, Daniel P. Jenkins, Edgar Fripp,
W.O.P. Fripp, Dr. J.A.P. Scott, J. S. Pope, and Joseph D. Edings.
It had been agreed to hold meetings quarterly "until the wrongs of
the South are redressed."

The papers found by the Federal invaders in Beaufort describe
meetings through the end of October, 1851, by which time the secessionist faction had driven out the unionists and was nakedly advocating withdrawal from the United States. At the regular
meeting on January 13, 1851, the Association denounced the Compromise of 1850—the Senate's bitterly negotiated formula for extending slavery to the western territories, toughening fugitive slave
laws, and ending the slave trade in the District of Columbia—as
"unjust, unconstitutional, and degrading to the South." To accept
the "disastrous" compromise was to accept, in principle, the
North's right to tell southerners what they could and could not do
with their property, and to make the slaveholding states permanently subordinate. The majority declared that only immediate action on the part of the state would save them all from personal
catastrophe. A minority of members protested that the call for separate action was "subversive of the main object of the Association"—the vindication of southern rights *within* the Union. The
South's situation was desperate, they agreed, but it could not be
improved by one small state acting alone. They wanted South
Carolina to cooperate with other southern states, at least with other
cotton states.

The first defection came in September, 1851: R. W. Barnwell
resigned as president of the Association.[25] At the October 13 meet-

ing, delegates chosen to attend a convention of like-minded associations in Walterboro were instructed to recommend "the early withdrawal of the State from the Federal Union, as the only practicable remedy for our wrongs." But the two delegates appointed by the Council of Safety, Daniel P. Jenkins and John M. Fripp, declined to go and were replaced by men who favored immediate secession. Then a letter was read announcing the resignation of the thirty "cooperationists." The majority was unhappy to see them go. Its leaders rejected the charge that states' rights was a foil for secession, or that secession was "inconsistent with the original purpose of our organization." "Let us secede at once," counseled De-Treville,[26] before words of caution could blunt the collective will.

The split was not over first principles. The cooperationists quit the Association with an "unabated devotion to the cause of Southern rights" on their lips. Slavery was as dear to one side as it was to the other, and faced with the choice of giving up slavery or leaving the Union, the cooperationists would have left, with deep regrets but no hesitation. But they did not believe that events compelled them to make that choice, and they repudiated leaders whom they regarded as hotheads and opportunists. While the cooperationists were clearly in a minority in the Parish, their views were in tune with the voting majority in South Carolina. In statewide elections held on October 13 and 14 for delegates to what Chaplin called "a Southern Congress," the cooperationist slate defeated the separatists everywhere but in the coastal parishes. Several days later, the St. Helena Association held an "extra" meeting to express its "deep mortification" at the results.[27]

For all the outcry and excitement, October, 1851, was a month of deceleration in South Carolina's course to secession. Once the anticipation of great events passed, people stopped attending political meetings. They turned their attention back to their crops and left the business of making a revolution to specialists like the Rhetts. The southern rights movement of 1850 and '51 produced a blossom but no fruit. Yet the scent of the blossom lingered through the decade, preparing society for the upheaval of 1860 and '61. The movement had given shape and voice to amorphous feelings of separateness and injury. It spread the view of the United States as an incompatible union of "two popular wills—a northern and a southern";[28] two moral cultures—a Puritan and a cavalier; two economic communities—an industrial and an agricultural; two classes of working people—hirelings and slaves, "an indolent, vicious, and unthrifty species of Lazaroni"* and "the best agrricultural population in the world." These dichotomies dramatized the sectional conflict in terms which convinced many slaveholders that no policy could reconcile the two regimes.[†]

Chaplin was well placed to hear propaganda from all sides. He was in daily contact with separatists, cooperationists, and outright unionists. He went along with the separatists, but not from any coherent philosophy or hatred of the North—upon which DeTreville, for example, based his fight. He was attracted to the mood of resistance and the fellowship of the resisters. He grasped the economic aspect of the South's conflict with the North, as it was portrayed in the tariff debates, and he identified deeply with the feeling of being taken advantage of. He was always moved by an eloquent speech, political or otherwise. Style meant as much to him as doctrine, images as much as ideas, emotion as much as logic.

Beset by problems at home, Chaplin's heart was not with politics. When the tempest was over, he expressed no disappointment but merely noticed that times were duller. In thirteen years of keeping a journal only once did he remark directly about a sectional issue. On May 6, 1846, he was visited by "a gentleman of Georgia, near Augusta," who owned "a large cotton manufactory" and was "traveling about the country with samples of his Geo. plains," a cloth he was trying to sell to planters "for their Negro clothing, instead of their buying Northern goods." Chaplin placed an order with him. "I hope he may succeed," he wrote. "It would relieve us a great deal from the heavy tariff on that article."

"At a later day, we find we were mistaken," he commented, after thirty years. "Not about that cry of 'Tariff,' " but in failing to keep the promises which he and his friends had made to themselves. "We ought to have supported Southern enterprise," he re-

---

*Homeless idlers and beggars, named for their place of refuge, the Hospital of St. Lazarus, in Naples, Italy. The currency of this phrase in South Carolina's political dialogue was a sign of the slaveholders' sensitivity to industrial trouble in Europe and of a hardening attitude toward manumission. It was also a statement that slavery was preferable to class struggle. The South Carolina Equity Court applied "Lazaroni" to the "free African population," which it called "a curse on any civilized country," "a dead weight to progress," a class of "consumers without being producers." (*Morton* v. *Thompson,* May, 1854, 6 Rich. Eq. 370, in Catterall, 441.)

†"Let some bard prepare the requiem of the Republic," declared a defender of states' rights (Charleston *Mercury,* June 28, 1852), on the first anniversary of the Palmetto Guard, a Charleston militia unit organized in preparation for secession, after the crisis of 1850. Compare this toast with the toasts of 1819.

flected, implying that the pledge of 1850 to boycott northern manufacturers had never been carried out, and that too few of its signers had followed his example. If the truth be told, the Georgia cloth
cost more than cloth from New England and abroad, and planters
were unwilling to pay the difference, even for better quality. They
grasped at the short-term gain, lamented Chaplin, instead of trying
to build an economic base for independence.

True Religion

"In Beaufort you are all trying to become every day more religious
and more States Rights," observed a friend of William Grayson, in
1831.[29] The town, Grayson recalled, had become a "great congregation of Christians," swept up by a "fervor of devotional feeling"
in which political and religious piety mingled as one. Earlier revivals had succeeded in stopping horse racing on Sundays and in getting men to accompany their wives to church, but this revival was
different. Coming at a moment when the adherents to nullification
were huddled in the lowcountry in need of reinforcements, it signaled religion's new defensiveness over slavery. While northern
churches were denouncing slavery as a violation of God's law,
southern churches were justifying it on the basis of passages from
the very same Bible. No longer was slavery an evil that had to be
tolerated; it was a positive good, a divine gift to the African and the
Anglo-Saxon alike. The struggle against northern capitalists, congressional compromisers, and other disguised abolitionists was ultimately warranted not by political theory, but by the word of God.
When the fervor died down, a religious assurance remained—the
conviction that God was pleased with slavery and the identification of true religion with the defense of southern institutions.
Chaplin's generation assumed that slavery was providential.
"Hence it is the Negro came, by God's command/For wiser teaching in a foreign land," expounded Grayson.[30] If the kidnapper of
Africans were "by Mammon driven/Still have they served, blind
instruments of Heaven." Why the deity had chosen this method to
elevate a barbaric race, and picked the sons of the British Isles to
uplift them, was beyond knowing. "The ways of Providence are not
to be scrutinized" was, in fact, a motto of Chaplin's, which he varied to suit the occasion.

Revivals reached out to blacks, too. They had souls in need of
salvation and minds capable of understanding the Word. The

same teachings which absolved slaveholders obliged them to provide religious instruction for their Negroes. But the notion that God valued the souls of black people as much as he valued the souls of white people was hard for planters to swallow. Many of them— Chaplin included—did nothing to spread Christianity among their slaves. Others hired religious instructors who drilled the blacks in a simple catechism and taught them that after life on earth they would have a better one in heaven. Missionaries fought against idolatry and tried to undermine the authority of slave doctors, conjurers, fortune-tellers, and other fomenters of spiritual resistance.

In material terms, a Christian slave was worth more at the market than a heathen. Many ministers, however, were moved by purely religious incentives. The Reverend Stephen Elliott, later to become bishop of the Episcopal Diocese of Georgia, and no friend to abolition, gave communion to blacks and whites together at the same altar. The practice was not widely imitated. Nor was it intended to change social relationships outside the church building. But alongside the broad movement to stave off northern interference with slavery, it revealed a frame of mind congenial to radical ideas about the unity of the human species, ideas which traced racial differences to culture and history, not biology. These ideas left "the slavery principle" intact. In the short run, they had the ironic effect of encouraging some thinkers, aroused by news of industrial strife outside the South, to abandon race as the sole grounds for slavery. In the long run, just as a dying pine tree bursts forth with a multitude of cones, so the slavery establishment produced a flurry of defenses containing seeds for the reconstruction of social thinking after the southern defeat.

The Chaplin family attended the Protestant Episcopal Church, the dominant white congregation on St. Helena Island.* The graves of several of Thomas Chaplin's uncles can still be distinguished in the yard of the ruined chapel. Three of his children and their mother, Mary, were also buried there, but their graves cannot be found.

The church began as a chapel of ease—a small sanctuary and altar for worshipers who lived at a distance from the parish church

*Wilbur J. Cash compared the Episcopal Church in the South to an "exotic" plant that "established itself only under royal patronage." (Quoted in Francis Butler Simkins, *The South Old and New* [New York, 1947], 75ff.) In 1860, the church had sixty thousand southern members, most of them in the tidewater region of Virginia and the lowcountry of South Carolina.

in Beaufort. The Reverend John S. Fields, Chaplin's first stepfather and second rector of the chapel, reported "the church very
much depleted, the [white] population of the island decreasing," in
1827. Church attendance improved under the ministry of David
McElheran, who succeeded Fields in 1831 and served for twenty-
five years. An epidemic in the summer of 1841 reduced the congregation; but afterward, except for a rash of deaths in the summer of
1853, the number of communicants increased slowly until McElheran departed.

Chaplin went to church to hear the sermons, news, and gossip;
to see people he did not see the rest of the week, including, sometimes, his children; to be perceived as a good man, a churchgoer;
and to help keep up the congregation so that in his time of need the
church would be there to help him. The question of salvation did
not trouble him. Neither did he engage in religious speculation.
The articles of faith were well established and he never doubted
them nor sought to improve them. He was disturbed, however, by
mysteries and contradictions in the gospels, and he turned to
David McElheran for light. But light was not generally forthcoming. McElheran was long-winded and dull; and he could not stick
to a text. At length, Chaplin grew "nauseated" with McElheran
and contrived a legion of reasons to stay home. His neck hurt or his
tooth ached, his horse broke the trace lines or his saddle girth
popped, he lost a glove or, on a day he planned to take his wife
with him, the driver of the buggy could not find a clean shirt to
wear. Even before McElheran was forced to quit his pulpit, Chaplin had begun dropping in at the Baptist Church.

"Chief mover and supporter" of the Baptists was William
Fripp, Sr., patriarch of the Baptist line of Fripps. The white part of
the Baptist congregation was smaller than the Episcopal, but the
black part was much larger, numbering many more souls than the
white. The races prayed together at the Baptist Church, whites occupying the pews and rows at front center, and blacks filling the
sides and galleries. Fripp was proud of the Baptists' mission to the
blacks. "The gospel has been preached for many years to our Negroes on St. Helena Island," he reported, in 1845, "and many are
leading honest and upright and Christian lives."[31] The same man,
known to all as "Good Billy" Fripp, was remembered by his former
slaves for bringing the Bible to the field, reading "Moses' law" and
flogging them "accordin'."[32]

Besides meeting at the Baptist Church on Sundays, Baptist slaves met two or three times a week at "praise houses" on the plantations, where they united in "singing, praying, and reading the word of God, when one is present who can read, and in exhortation."[33] Black readers taught the catechism "as put out by our Methodist brethren." There was no Methodist church on the Island, but itinerant Methodist preachers led revivals and hired themselves to groups of planters for the purpose of instructing the blacks. Apparently they also visited whites who were unable to get to church and desired religious companionship. Mary Chaplin, for example, exchanged visits with a Methodist friend in Beaufort, the wife of a teetotaling minister who bored Chaplin to tears.

The Episcopal Church hired a catechist in 1846 to go out among the blacks, and McElheran's wife "superintended the instruction of Negroes" at her Sunday school,[34] but it was the Baptists who appealed to them on a sustained basis. In turn, the blacks were drawn by the Baptists' passionate style of worship, by the rite of baptism which admitted all believers into a spiritual community, and by doctrinal emphasis on the sufferings of Christ and the open ear of the Father. In one season, Chaplin witnessed the baptisms of at least thirty-six Negroes at the Baptist Church. He gave permission to his man Isaac and Isaac's wife, Amy, to join the Baptists.

But he appears to have invested nothing in the spiritual welfare of his slaves. He did not worry about their souls or inquire into their devout thoughts and feelings, and he seriously doubted that they were equipped with the same emotions and susceptibilities as he was. He always seemed surprised, for example, when they demonstrated grief just like white people. He preferred not to have to think about them, and to encourage peace he tolerated their doctors and conjurers, so long as they did not interfere with work on the plantation or use his horses.

In his own life, the influence of religion showed up in a heightened sense of duty toward white institutions; in an ethic of charity and helpfulness that he looked for in others; and in the resignation with which he bore the sufferings and deaths of his first wife and six of their seven children. None of these tragedies made him feel that God was abandoning or punishing him. To the contrary, after each death he praised God's secret purposes. Nothing happened accidentally, everything was in God's hands—the weather, life and death, the course of history. Chaplin's few articulated beliefs boiled down to disavowing responsibility for the existing state of things— an outlook consistent with a deep faith in fixed social positions. Change was God's business, not his.

Changes came, and with awful abruptness. The finely rifled artillery of the Union Navy sounded "the death-knell" of his church. Before the northern invaders set foot on St. Helena Island, the planters had fled, "most of them never to return." Certainly, the invasion signaled the end of one era and the beginning of another in the history of society and religion on St. Helena Island. Yet, in a terse comment added two or three decades after the event, Chaplin dated the decline of the Island from the hasty departure of David McElheran, in June, 1856. It had been difficult to find a replacement for him; several ministers came and went in the five years between his removal and the start of the War. The church met infrequently and members grew estranged from each other. Looking back on these times, Chaplin discerned in the loss of communion the beginning of the end.

"His health failing, Mr. McElheran resigned . . . and removed to Mt. Pleasant," reads the official church history.[35] What really happened was that McElheran was accused of molesting a student in his wife's school, who had come into his study to get a book. Though the girl contradicted herself and was reputed to be "imprudent & forward," the charge against the minister produced "a most abominable scandal." McElheran left "in consequence." Chaplin felt "truly sorry for him" at the time, but later envied McElheran's luck for having escaped the Island "with all his family & effects" before the War drove off everyone else with nothing but the clothes on their backs.

In the late '60s, an Episcopal "Committee on the Destruction of Churches and Church Property" reported that the parish church in Beaufort had been converted to a Federal hospital. The pews and galleries had been removed and a second floor hung beneath the high ceiling. The church on St. Helena Island had also been stripped of pews and furniture, and "is now in the hands of the Methodists." It was "used by freedmen, who constitute the sole population of the Island, as a place for their meetings. It may be considered dead."[36]

7. Slavery

A Problem of Human Relations

"Slavery," wrote Beaufort's William J. Grayson, "is the negro system of labor."[1] It was also the white system of command. Ordering Jim to go and watching him move, making Helen take up her hoe—telling his slaves what to do gave Chaplin a purpose. Telling them was what *he* had to do; it was how he conceived of his vocation. In essence, *his* daily task was to distribute the work force, apportioning slaves to a variety of competing jobs. "I am head over heels in work," Chaplin reported in July, 1848, endeavoring to make ten people do the work of twenty. "Blades to strip, peas to plant & my cotton getting very grassy." Meanwhile, the work of maintaining the plantation grounds could not be put off. Fences had to be mended, ditches had to be cleaned, dikes around the lowlands had to be repaired. Then, too, the Big House was dilapidated and needed fixing. Wood had to be cut and put up to keep the kitchen going year-round and to feed four fireplaces in winter. The hands had no time to lose. *He* could not relax, thinking of all *they* had to do.

Every Christmas Chaplin would sit around in bad humor waiting for the three-day respite to end. "Last day of the holidays & I am glad," he sighed, on December 27, 1848, "for then the Negroes will go to work & something for me to do." Wanting to take full advantage of record cotton prices in the late '50s by exploiting to the hilt their labor as well as their land, planters tried adjusting the task load, lengthening the workday, and cutting back on holidays. "The day is fast approaching," Chaplin had written in December, 1857, "when Negroes will only be allowed Christmas Day alone, instead of three days."* That would have pleased him mightily, for he lost his sense of himself when the Negroes were not working.

He was never satisfied with their output, however, and he always suspected that they were deceiving him. In spite of his troubles, he thought of himself as an above-average provider, and he resented his slaves for not acknowledging the sacrifices he made to keep them in corn and bacon and "Negro cloth." He attributed their ingratitude to racial behavior; it was innate, he believed, like the tendency to exaggerate, and could not be expunged by contact with a higher civilization. Nevertheless, he was plagued by the thought that the problem was not *in them,* but between him and them, a problem of human relations and feelings no different, at bottom, from the problem of his friends' failure to show him respect.

In rare, lighthearted moments, Chaplin seemed struck by how little reason and how much luck lay behind the racial division of earthly rewards. A small anecdote nicely illustrates his insight into the gratuitous nature of the hierarchy.

Captain Daniel T. Jenkins came to dinner one Wednesday in July, 1857. Sophy Chaplin fixed "a pudding made of starch, & extras which was considered fine by all hands. Listed pea land," the entry continues, "with all the hands (not those that eat the pudding)." While the white folks were eating, the black folks were working. Nothing unusual there; it happened every day. But struck by the several meanings of "hands" and by the possibility of confusion, the diarist was moved to make a joke.

When his troubles turned him inward, however, Chaplin's sensitivity to his slaves diminished. While experience should have revealed to him a community of diverse individuals, he saw a school of fish. Persons who earned his attention were the mischievous and the ill—Jim, a runaway; young William, a watermelon thief; Peg and Helen, sickhouse recidivists. Their opposition could take the form of a grinding day-to-day struggle or a sudden squall. The frequency and duration of slave resistance show that "absolute power

---

*Ironically, the renewed profitability of Sea Island cotton resulted in tighter controls over the slaves, or at least in an increased workload, while the rosy outlook for the staple depended on the destruction of serfdom in Europe and on the enhanced buying power of the working classes. William Elliott counted on the "tendency of modern equality" and the authority of fashion to do for long-staple cotton what they had done for tobacco and sugar—transform them from luxuries for the wealthy to necessities for everyone. (*DeBow's Review,* July, 1858, 182.)

did not rest with one side and helplessness on the other." Rather, relationships between the master and his slaves were characterized by "everlasting tensions."[2]

Because Chaplin had very little to do with his slaves outside of work, we seldom see them in their quarters, and then only when the peace is disturbed. Periodically, Chaplin searched for stolen food and runaway Negroes from other plantations. He knew that thefts were generally the work of organized gangs, and that fugitives were assured of finding shelter and aid with his Negroes.

But the intricacy and extent of slave networks apparently escaped his observation. He was startled, for example, at the speed with which news, rumors, and secrets flew from one plantation to another across the islands. Word traveled remarkable distances in short periods of time by relays of boat, horse, and foot.* A favorite topic of reports was the movements of the master, where he was spotted coming from and going to—news of interest to everyone on the plantation. Imagine the communication labyrinth that brought out a huge congregation of mourners to the funeral of Chaplin's man Anthony. Anthony died on Sunday, May 5, 1850. Monday morning his body began to smell, and Monday night he was in his grave. Despite the hasty burial word had gotten around. "I attended the funeral," wrote Chaplin. "There were a large number of Negroes from all directions present, I suppose over two hundred."

Chaplin did not inquire who they were or where they came from, so we do not find out. We can say, however, that the black community appears to have had a high degree of autonomy. This should not be taken to mean that St. Helena slaves had a firm hold on their homes. The lesson of Chaplin's journal, illustrated time after time, is that nothing but a white man's conflicting claim could limit a master's property rights in a Negro—not the immunities given to slaves by law, nor the sentiments of kind owners, nor the powers of independent black institutions. Chief of all property rights was the right to transfer ownership—to sell, deed, or be-

---

*And perhaps by drum, though this possibility must be inferred from sources other than Chaplin. Drums were important instruments on the Sea Islands of South Carolina and Georgia, and while periodically outlawed for fear they would be used to signal rebellion, they were employed by slaves throughout the antebellum era to beat out rhythms for dancing, to communicate with spirits, to announce funerals and assist the spiritual migration of the dead. (See *Drums and Shadows: Survival Studies Among the Georgia Coastal Negroes,* collected by the Savannah Unit of the Georgia Writers' Project, Work Projects Administration [Athens, Georgia, 1940].)

queathe title in a Negro to another white person. Removal from
one's relations and familiar surroundings was a permanent prospect for every slave. A death or marriage in the master's family, a
foreclosure or court judgment for debt, an acquisition or disposal of
land, was invariably an event in the formation, erosion, or breakup
of the black community. Whether the cause brought joy or sorrow
to the whites, its frequent consequence was a measure of pain to the
blacks. One did not have to be a troublemaker to face removal,
which, among punishments meted out to felons and chronic mal-
contents, was second in severity to death; one only had to be a
chattel owned by a mortal master.

The People at Tombee

The census of 1850 listed twenty-five slaves at Tombee. By his
count, Chaplin was feeding thirty. Some of the five missing people
may have belonged to his mother; perhaps they had lived at Riverside Plantation, Tombee's neighbor to the west, which lay fallow
during the Baker years. Chaplin's occasion for counting was a dismal day in February when he could muster only eight healthy men
and women, equal to seven full hands, into the field. "God knows
when I will get all of my small force at work," he moaned, falling
behind in manuring his land. "So many mouths to feed & so few to
work that it is *impossible* for me to get along." The obvious solution
was "to have fewer Negroes about the yard and more in the field."
But it seemed "that not one of those about the house & yard can be
done without."

If everyone was healthy, Chaplin could put the following people in the field: "Isaac 1, Peg 2, Jim 3, Sancho 4, Judge 5, Moll 6,
Helen 7 and Amy, Mary and Summer equal to 2 hands, making in
all that I plant for"—all those fed with field hand allowances—"9
hands." To these should be added the "stable boy, Frank," who did
the carting and the plowing but received his food from the house
supply. "Now, those about the yard, and those that eat & do nothing in the world for me," Chaplin continued, "Mary, seamstress, 1;
Judy, washer, 2; Suky, cook, 3; Charles, dairy, 4; Nelly, nurse, 5;
Eliza, house, 6; Jack, ditto, 7; Sam, ditto, 8; Nelly,* nurse 9; Anthony, garden 10; May, hogs, 11; Old Nelly, nothing, 12; Judy,
ditto, 13. Not counting the children & Old Sam, who can't do any-

*Chaplin apparently counted Nelly twice.

thing, but make 9 mouths more to feed." Chaplin was appalled. Out of "30 head to feed, only 9 to work and make feed for them," he figured, knowing the imbalance could lead to ruin; "then they expect clothes & shoes regularly."

The census reports the slave population by age. Comparison from one census to the next shows that the given ages of adult Negroes were approximations. The information is useful however, in plotting family configurations and in understanding how Chaplin might have estimated the value of individuals and planned to employ them. Of the twenty-five slaves officially counted in 1850, thirteen were females and twelve were males. Nine slaves were under sixteen years old, nine were between sixteen and thirty-three, and seven were in their forties, fifties, or just sixty. Five women were of childbearing age, and six children were under four years old. By 1860, the slave community at Tombee had grown younger. The census counted thirty slaves this time, though Chaplin may have been working as many as thirty-eight, the number he claimed was living on the plantation when the War broke out. Fourteen people, or forty-six percent of the number officially counted, were under sixteen years old, compared to thirty-six percent in 1850. Eight people were between sixteen and thirty-three, and eight were older. Only one of the thirty was over sixty. At least seven, and perhaps nine, of the women were of childbearing age. From the planter's point of view, the life stages of a slave were correlated to the person's strength and usefulness—from a child who did no work to a quarter-hand, half-hand, three-quarter hand, full hand, and back down the ladder in the older years. Applying this measure to his work force in 1860, Chaplin's future looked bright because his hands were advancing into their prime.

The census did not name slaves or place them into family units. Chaplin, too, was indifferent to their family arrangements. In his journal he registered the births of black children as he did those of his colts, except that he named the horses' sires but omitted the names of slave fathers. Yet there is plenty of evidence that black men demonstrated fidelity to their children at great personal risk. Isaac, for example, may have lost his job as driver because he showed preferential treatment toward his offspring. He balked at whipping the hands to make them work, but "as soon as one of his family was molested"—by another black—"he could directly *feel* it his *duty* to *inflict punishment.*"

Robert repeatedly went off the Island to visit his wife, after extracting permission which Chaplin dared not refuse. When old Charles came back from a twelve-day junket to his wife, Phoebe, who had been sold off of St. Helena in the disposal of Chaplin's property four years before, he reported that her master had moved to Texas leaving Phoebe behind; he had sold her to a man who in turn "wishes to sell her, & asks $150." Charles was obviously asking Chaplin to buy her. "Wish I could," Chaplin told his journal, but he couldn't. He did not allow himself to believe that the loss of a spouse could hurt a black person as much as it could hurt a white. It was as if, to him, the blacks only played at being married. They were too selfish, he thought, to know real intimacy. When Amy went to church instead of coming to him for quinine for her sick husband Isaac "as she was directed," Chaplin supposed she cared little about her husband's health. In fact, Isaac may have wanted her to go to church. They were devout Christians and prayer certainly was the less bitter medicine. What Chaplin perceived as indifference and insubordination may actually have been the result of a slave woman's devotion to her husband and her faith.

Chaplin avoided Negro wedding ceremonies. He felt debased by the "great doings" which violated his worldly possessions as well as his religious sense.* He was off hunting with friends when, on the evening of December 26, 1849, his maids Eliza and Nelly "took to themselves husbands." He had caught "a good chance of fish" and killed a deer, but his pleasure was spoiled thinking about the wedding. From his hunting camp, Chaplin envied the good time his slaves were having at home. Still, he was glad that he had stayed away. "I did not wish to be here to see the tomfoolery that was going on about it, as if they were ladies of quality." A social rule and a law of nature were being broken in his living room, with the encouragement of his wife, "their mistress," who gave them a "grand supper," putting out, "very foolishly, my crockery, tables, chairs, candlesticks, & I suppose everything else they wanted." As late as 1876, he was still peeved at Mary for having made "some of my good liquor into a bowl of punch for the company."

His mother's man Robert performed the ceremony. Eliza married Uncle Paul's June; Nelly married Uncle Ben's Taffy. Thus, the

---

*Contrast Kenneth Stampp's picture of the typical planter who "found it a pure delight to watch a Negro bride and groom move awkwardly through the wedding ceremony." (*The Peculiar Institution* [New York, 1956], 329.)

slaves of three different masters were joined in matrimony by a slave belonging to a fourth. The couples would not live under the same roofs. There would be constant visits, Chaplin knew, adding to the movement of Negroes on and off the plantation. And now Chaplin's women would have somewhere to run to.

Slaves had many good reasons for choosing husbands and wives from different plantations. The breakdown of Tombee's black population by sex and age shows there was a very small pool of eligible mates at any one time. Even a population twice as large would not have satisfied the matrimonial demands of the people. Age, of course, is not the only ground of compatibility, and almost any other requirement is sure to have reduced the pool even further. A young man commonly went off the plantation in search of a wife, and though a woman had less opportunity to leave home, if a man from the outside found her she could request, and expect periodically to receive, permission to travel to him.

"Don't like it at all," grumbled Chaplin. But the movement of husbands and wives across plantation lines could not be stopped. Custom had long permitted it, and while masters begrudged the slaves' show of independence and lost time, they wanted their Negroes to marry and reproduce. For the blacks, marrying off the plantation had one outstanding disadvantage—the family was not able to live together. But other considerations prevailed. Having a spouse abroad helped a slave to escape the encompassing tendency of the plantation. It freed the visitor, for a day or two or more, from the surveillance of his or her master. It joined a person to new social networks, promoting commerce in news and material goods. It spread a person's influence beyond the confines of home and, to the chagrin of the master, introduced outside influences in the persons of unknown men and women onto his plantation.

Though Chaplin's record of Negro relationships at Tombee is fragmented and unsystematic, one can piece together a few scant histories highlighting the formation, size, and longevity of a number of black families. Following up on the marriages of Eliza and Nelly, for example, Chaplin noted at Christmas, 1876, that both "girls" were alive and staying "on my old place"—which, of course, was their old place, too. Even "stranger," Chaplin found, they "have the very same husbands." One of the women, he did not know which, "has a married daughter I believe." A check through his journal reveals that by 1859, Eliza had given birth to four children, and by 1861, Nelly had had five, three of whom died as infants in three consecutive years.

Poor Nelly! But Chaplin felt no pity. He was looking to an increase in "the people" to make up for his small crops. He took the deaths of Negro children as a personal affront. "My luck with little niggers," he raved, after one of Nelly's babies was born dead, in June, 1856. Though he had suffered the loss of three babies of his own, and had waxed eloquent over their mother's grief, he had no words of compassion for black mothers. Rather, he accused them of killing their babies. How else could he account for the high infant mortality rate and for the suddenness of death? How can we account for it?

Today we have the advantage of medical knowledge which was not available to Chaplin. We might look for a connection, therefore, between the hurricane of 1854, which submerged St. Helena Island, and the deaths a few months later of four black children. Our idea of contamination inclines us to hunt for the causes of disease and debility in places Chaplin did not think of looking. It did not occur to him that heavy rains and flood tides could defile his shallow wells and spread contagion from open toilets. Going barefoot was an invitation to worms, but Chaplin did not know it. Neither did he know that herding the sick with the injured in one room by day, then sending them back to their cabins at night, helped to spread disease.

We should also observe what Chaplin's biases caused him to miss, that black babies died from the same causes as white babies—dysentery, pneumonia, lockjaw, worms, fever.* Their chances of contracting disease were enhanced by the squalor of the slave quarters and by simple exposure inside their leaky cabins. Furthermore, medical researchers speculate that sudden infant deaths on antebellum plantations might have been the same thing we know as crib death, or sudden infant death syndrome.[3] The causes of this phenomenon remain baffling but almost certainly they are related to conditions in the mother's prenatal environment. Poor nutrition and physical strain are two leading suspects.

---

*Children of both races ten years old and under accounted for more than half the deaths in the Parish, in the census years 1850 and 1860. Forty-seven of the fifty-six children who died in 1860 were three years old or under.

Daily Resistance

Slaves had several ways of getting around a master's wishes without being openly rebellious. A person who felt too ill to work or who had another motive for "laying up" might report to the sickhouse. Stays of twenty, fifty, and even a hundred days were not unheard of, especially by women during difficult pregnancies. Peg, like Helen, "never knows when to come out once she goes in." Chaplin vowed "to look more closely into their complaints, and not allow anyone to shirk from their work and sham sickness." He would follow up by raiding the sickhouse and forcing people out. Then his determination would slacken and things would go back to normal. He would continue to imagine that individuals were playing possum, and even coordinating their time off, but if a man or a woman who worked hard generally took a day in the sickhouse for no perceptible cause, he would look the other way.

One did not have to report to the sickhouse to absent oneself from work. A person could show up in the morning for his or her task assignment and refuse to participate mentally. Withholding one's mind from the task and willfully misunderstanding an order were the most common and inventive methods of resisting compulsion. For example, Chaplin might tell the hands to *hoe* and instead they would *haul*, covering the grass with dirt when he wanted them to chop it out. Or he would send them for fence rails and they would bring back poles. At the end of May, 1851, following a drought that had decimated the cotton, Chaplin pondered from inside his house the work that needed to be done. "I have not been out to see what the hands are doing," he admitted, having left it up to them to size up the situation. Later he learned they were hauling cotton "when their own sense should tell them they ought to be supplying"; that is, they were throwing dirt around the remaining stunted plants when they should have been replanting the spotty rows. Meanwhile, he noticed, just to the east of his own fields, Uncle Paul's hands were supplying cotton on Carter's Hill.

He could not punish them for defying orders that he had failed to give, but he let them know they would be flogged for disobeying a direct command. Yet the situation was seldom so clear-cut, and Chaplin was often at a loss about how to respond. What should he do when his hands worked diligently enough but not at the task he had assigned? Surely they did not intend to sabotage the cotton. It was in their interest as well as his to produce a crop large enough and clean enough so that he could pay his bills without having to sell any of *them*. But above this minimal aim masters and slaves had few economic motives in common. A windfall one year might enable a planter to visit Niagara Falls or to sit home and smoke Spanish cigars while nothing would change in the slave quarters.

We know woefully little about the blacks' understanding of the economic situation. Did they put special effort into corn and potatoes, knowing that their master could ill afford, or was reluctant to buy, provisions? Did they follow prices at the cotton market? Did they know how much money the planter had to earn to show a profit? Could they translate that into bales of cotton and would they work toward that goal? We cannot say. What we can do is see if their habitual misinterpretation of the planter's orders achieved any other identifiable goal. We find that just as the planter was perpetually exercising some means of surveillance or control, either through his formal institutions or in mundane contact with his slaves, so the slaves, by the various ways of physically and mentally withdrawing from the field, were forever creating elbow room to rest, pray, plot, love, heal, or for no other reason than to remain human. When the master told them to hoe, they might have had their own opinion about whether the order made sense, especially if it was the fourth or fifth hoeing and there was a prospect of rain which would make the grass sprout again. Or they might be wholly indifferent to the job they were told to do that morning, and might react instead to their master's tone of voice. At night, when they were back in their quarters and he was back in his, the planter would curse his luck at being saddled with such trifling Negroes— in contrast to the proof offered up at the end of every crop year.

Runaways and Theft

Slaves who ran off usually did not run far or stay away long. It was a common occurrence for people to take off to see their loved ones on nearby plantations. Some people ran to the woods and marshes to avoid punishment. Others ran because they were tired or fed up. A few ran hoping to find new masters. One runaway, a man whom Chaplin had previously owned, accosted him from across a fence, and asked him to buy him back. Chaplin declined to do so, but neither did he try to catch the fellow or report him to the patrol leader, which was his duty. Very rarely did a Sea Island slave set out with the goal of reaching the free states, which were far away and hard to get to. No slave of Chaplin's and none belonging to his close acquaintances escaped to the North during the years Chaplin kept a journal. Uncle Paul's Sambo, an infamous troublemaker, was caught once without a pass in Savannah, but he apparently was just taking a breather. For persistently running away, Sambo was later sold out of the District.

Runaways were always a nuisance, but only in extraordinary times did they excite alarm. Sometimes they banded together, set up camps, or hideouts, and sustained themselves by stealing corn and potatoes and preying on livestock. Inevitably they involved "good" slaves in their conspiracies. Not every slave had a history of running, but most conspired at some time by harboring or feeding a fugitive, sharing his spoils, or feigning ignorance about him.

From the master's point of view, this was, perhaps, the chief danger of runaways: they demoralized others by their example and encouraged secrecy and deceit. Yet, unless the master was tipped off to the runaway's plans, or knew that the person had relatives in other districts to whom he might run, no rush was made to apprehend him. Once a slave had been out for two or three weeks, his master might place a notice in one of the Charleston newspapers, offering a reward for his or her return. The advertisement would reach subscribers, like Chaplin, deep in the countryside, but it was meant for city readers, too. Runaways who were intending not to return might head for the city, where they could more easily conceal their identities or fabricate new ones, acquire forged permission slips, and find casual employment with white people who did not ask questions.

Thinking he would be held accountable for the disappearance of a hen, Chaplin's man Jim ran off on the morning of July 14, 1856. He had gone to work "as usual," but before his master got to the field, he "pretended to go to the well to get water, & did not return."

Chaplin could not believe the man would run. Jim had worked under him for thirteen years, and they had known each other longer than that. Only the drivers at Tombee had more privileges than Jim, and not even they were so thoroughly trusted. Jim was a first-class plow hand, and could be counted on to work well without supervision, in and out of the field. He had traveled to Beaufort countless times, sometimes staying overnight. He had carried let-

ters and things to Chaplin's mother, on the main, taking three days
to make the round trip. If Chaplin needed his cotton ginned
quickly, or if he wanted to be certain the staple was packed satis-
factorily, he turned to Jim. Once he had flogged Jim for poor ginning, but that had happened five years before, and there were no
hard feelings so far as Chaplin knew. He had favored Jim for special jobs and worked alongside him in making a fence gate and
digging a new well. In fact, Jim had become a fair carpenter. He
fashioned shafts for the oxcarts, put up hog pens and a poultry
house, and built the crucial trunks for the dams that protected the
fields from flooding.

What was Jim's motive for running? The night the hen was
taken—the culprit turned out to be a bobcat—was not even Jim's
night on watch. It was Frank's. "The act was on the impulse of the
moment with him," concluded Chaplin. Chaplin went straight to
Jim's wife's cabin next door on Uncle Paul's plantation and removed Jim's clothes, as if to say, "If you run from me I take away
my protection and cease to provide for you." On the fourth day of
Jim's "new career," Chaplin vowed to "keep a regular account of
the rascal's time & make him pay dearly for it whenever I get hold
of him." "No Jim." "No Jim yet," noted Chaplin, with each passing day. Twelve days passed and Chaplin announced, "I will have
to catch him." Finally, on the night of the fourteenth day, before
Chaplin had got around to hunting him up, Jim "made his appearance." The next morning Chaplin squared accounts. "Gave Jim a
very moderate punishment, say about 60 paddles, put on his bare
hide, with my own hands." Soon after, he restored Jim's privileges
and possessions.

Chaplin's rewards and punishments were meant to remind his
slaves that everything they had, they had through his benevolence.
But while he thought of himself as a great provider, they saw him
as a rival for the things he was providing. They felt they were not
getting enough—as indicated by their unauthorized consumption
of food. The theft of meat, grain, fruits, and vegetables was particularly prevalent in the summers of 1848, '52, and '55, which were,
respectively, a tight-money year, a year of mediocre profits, and a
lucrative year. Theft apparently was not a response to shortages
brought about by hard times. Rather, the slaves' need and desire to

supplement their standard food allowances was constant. Thievery was most rampant when it was most likely to succeed; that is, when the slaves were organized to pull it off and the planters were unprepared to catch them.

Everyone knew that food thieves acted with the close cooperation of slaves living on different plantations, yet Chaplin paradoxically insisted the criminals were out for themselves. "Here is a whole barrel of meat," he blustered, when a load of store-bought rump pork was filched from the corn house, "the very best stolen by perhaps *one* or *two* Negroes, depriving the others of getting any atall, but such is their character & nature." Not hunger or dissatisfaction or vengeance drove them to steal, in his opinion, but selfishness. But when it came to exposing the thief or thieves, the people would not tell what they knew. "Heard nothing of thief or meat," wrote Chaplin, a week after the break-in. The contradiction between the Negroes' inborn selfishness and their tendency to stand up for one another was explained, in Chaplin's theory, by still another Negro quality—contradictoriness, which was perhaps the most predictable thing about them.

"Some black rascally rogue killed a sheep yesterday evening in my pasture," he announced, on May 23, 1850. "I would give $5 to know who was the sheep stealer." But all he did was ruminate. Once, when his potato banks were broken into, he tracked the thieves to Major Daniel P. Jenkins's plantation and searched the Major's Negro houses without success. Later he learned it was another man's slaves who had stolen his potatoes. "Now the proof falls on Isaac K. Fripp," he intoned, laying the blame on the white man. It was not the last time Fripp's slaves bothered him. In July, 1855, some runaways from Fripp stole several of his sheep, and it was they, Chaplin found out, not his own hands, who had broken into his corn house and taken the infamous barrel of meat. In cases where evidence pointed conclusively to a person or persons on his own plantation he set up a guard, but the cure cost more than it saved because he lost the labor of the man on watch and because the watchman often connived with the thieves or walked off with what he was supposed to be guarding.

Why didn't Chaplin take firm steps to stop the pilfering? He could have whipped the hide off suspected thieves to deter others; or he and his neighbors could have tightened their patrols and made more regular inspections of the slave quarters. But he preferred to wink at the problem. What was the advantage of letting it go on? For one thing, the losses were light compared to the total value of the crops and stock. For another, they were not really losses. Better to let the hands have the outside acre whether they picked it in the field or stole it from the provisions house than to discourage them from working. "Commenced digging slips," Chaplin noted punctually, on November 21, 1853. "The acre near Ben Chaplin's line has little or nothing left—has been dug for me." This was the literal truth. By digging the potatoes and feeding themselves, the hands saved him the responsibility. Much as a regime may tolerate a black market that distributes goods in violation of official prices, priorities, and ration restrictions, so the planters of St. Helena countenanced food theft in the interest of tranquillity and to avert open discussion of the human wants of their slaves.

Slave Drivers: The Case of Robert

Next to the planter, and in the absence of an overseer, the most powerful person in the field was the "driver," a field hand chosen to lead because of his superior knowledge of the crops, his ability to motivate others, and his rapport with his master.* The driver held the keys to the tool house and the provisions house. He received daily orders from the planter and transmitted them to the hands, then made sure they complied. He whipped offenders, either on the planter's initiative or on his own. While the planter used him to carry out his wishes, the driver also had the planter's ear, and could take up the request or grievance of a slave less able to command a hearing. Between 1845 and 1861, Chaplin employed three drivers—Anthony, an expert butcher; Isaac, an alert and crop-wise man but a fickle disciplinarian; and Robert, the most worldly of the three, exceptionally well informed and respected by everyone. Since Chaplin communicated with the driver every day, inspected the fields and the outbuildings with him, and charged him with the most sensitive tasks, the two formed a close, if functional, relationship.

*Depending on the locality, the term "slave driver" could apply to a slave trader, a white overseer, or a black supervisor of field labor. Moreover, "titles such as foreman, overlooker, leading man, headman, boss, whipping boss, crew leader, overdriver, underdriver, and straw boss were also used to describe the slave who possessed supervisory and police authority over the field hands." (William L. Van Deberg, *The Slave Drivers: Black Agricultural Field Supervisors in the Antebellum South* [Westport, Conn., 1979] 3-4.)

Isabella Baker left Robert to live at Tombee after a New Year's visit in 1852. Chaplin employed him at once, sending him to Beaufort by land and by water. Robert knew the way. He may have lived previously at Mrs. Baker's Riverside Plantation—his wife lived at Jericho Plantation north of Riverside, across Chowan Creek on Ladies Island. After just three weeks, Isabella sent for Robert to return to the main. "He was of much use to me," muttered Chaplin, upset over the loss of a competent servant and hurt by the thought that R. L. Baker was behind the move. But on March 23, Isabella brought Robert back to Tombee. "He is now to stay with me," exulted Chaplin, "*I hope* always." Again, Robert was put right to work—whitewashing Chaplin's bedroom, and running errands to Beaufort as if he was on display. Sometimes he went alone and sometimes he was put in charge of other hands. The next March, Chaplin had him in the field helping Isaac straighten the rows and set out new task stakes. A month later he was installed as driver, completing his extraordinary rise.

"He did very well," confided Chaplin, in a postwar note. No one, in fact, ever got more work out of the hands than Robert. Robert already enjoyed wide prestige when Chaplin elevated him. He was a religious authority and a seer, a giant of learning among the Negroes. He could talk to white people without losing his dignity. He had practical skills which other slaves had not been fortunate enough to acquire. He could count and figure—Chaplin complained that he tracked rows inaccurately and misweighed the cotton, but his errors were insignificant next to the miscalculations of other drivers and overseers. Furthermore, Robert could read. How useful this made him to his master! It meant Chaplin did not have to be there to give orders. He could leave written instructions with Robert while he went off the plantation. "Found everything going on well & all hands well," wrote Chaplin, with an air of surprise, upon returning to Tombee from a two-week visit to his mother and brother in October, 1856. "A very good blow of cotton in the field & the peas have been picked through once, & the first time, during my absence. . . ."

As Robert strengthened his position as headman and go-between, the other hands grew less visible. "Sent 3 hands & Robert," Chaplin would say, in his later style, without naming the three. Robert's personality perplexed him. Robert had a defiant streak which he kept under perfect control. He was friendly yet cool, obedient yet irreverent, servile yet self-possessed. Chaplin didn't know what to do about his stubborn independence, so he did nothing. An incident that occurred two months after he appointed Robert driver typified his quandary. Chaplin gave Robert permission to go to the main. Robert went, accompanied by six other slaves who did not have permission. "I blame Robert for their going," declared Chaplin. "He 'knew of it,' & the thing has been planned for more than a fortnight, & he told me nothing of it, which a driver, he should have done." Chaplin determined to punish them all, "but I have not decided how." What could he do? He did not want to appear indecisive, but his arsenal of punishments seemed inappropriate for the offense. "The *runaway* Negroes" got back in time to go to work on Monday. To all but Robert, the master "gave . . . a good flogging." But Robert did not get away scot-free. Chaplin made *him* inflict the beatings. "He seems to be well punished in seeing this done & doing it with his own hands," said Chaplin, putting on a good face. "Unjust," he reconsidered, many years later. Robert "alone should have been punished." But the act was done; it could not be undone. Reading about it gave Chaplin a moment's discomfort. Yet, in admitting his mistake, he sought only to pin the guilt more firmly on Robert.

Robert stayed at Tombee until his death, sometime before 1876. Until November, 1861, he was Chaplin's slave driver, the best driver Chaplin ever had. "But," Chaplin demurred, "he was not faithful to his trust when the war broke out. . . . I left everything in his hands, & he never saved a single thing for me." Other people let him down—Isaac, the former driver, who divided up his master's oak chairs with Robert; Jack, Chaplin's coachman, the man he had instructed to lock up the Big House and who moved his relatives in instead—but Robert affected him most. He "got all he could for himself," fretted Chaplin, as if they were scavengers at a shipwreck. The former master did not seem to realize that what was disaster for him was the chance of a lifetime for his slaves. After the War, many blacks resumed relationships with the white people they had known for so long. Robert did not. He "has always kept out of my way since peace," wrote Chaplin, pained by the rejection. A critical gate to the past was closed.

Slavemasters Remembered

Chaplin was remembered neither for great kindness nor outstanding cruelty. By his own recollection, he was given to cursing, but—

he says—he went very light with the whip. Several times he made up his mind "to whip all around," or to "flog every Negro in the field," but did not carry out the threat. "Cowhide was all talk with me," he avowed. Because he had his drivers do his whipping for him he forgot just how frequently the whip had been used at Tombee. Whippings were routine for common misdemeanors—doing bad work or going off the plantation without permission—though less often for social infractions such as insolence or rudeness, which the master tended to answer in kind.

How were Chaplin's friends and colleagues remembered? In answer to the inquiries of the abolitionists who occupied St. Helena after 1862, the freedmen told how their former masters had treated them. Proud Edgar Fripp "would whip any Negro who upon meeting him did not remove his hat at once."[4] It was also said that he had made his hands pick cotton by the full moon, that the moon made him mean, and that it was safer to be around him when there was no moon. Old man Gabriel Capers and Good Billy Fripp's son Alviro were reputed to be "devils in cruelty."[5] Thomas G. White, Joseph D. Edings, and Daniel Pope were held to be less cruel but still "very tight"—the term used to describe a hard master. There seemed to be a consensus that among those regarded as vicious Joseph Pritchard had been the worst white man on the Island.

On the other side of the ledger, Thomas B. Fripp, Thomas A. Coffin, and Ben Chaplin were "all well-spoken of by their former slaves." Fripp, who was killed at Pocataligo in 1862, had been especially well liked. So was his uncle, Captain John Fripp. "All the people unite in praising his kindness." Fripp's Negroes were "almost the only ones on the island who did not plunder their master's house . . . in part from their affection for him." Captain John never let anyone whip his slaves but himself, and "whenever he flogged he never licked the same place twice."[6] His wife was less esteemed. It was said that she used to stand at the window and watch the slaves receive their stripes against a leafless chinaberry tree. She had been a poor woman before Captain John married her, but she came home from the wedding "just as much a lady as anybody else," entirely incapable of getting a "drink of water for herself."[7]

The freedmen's sentiments toward their ex-masters were not always understood or accurately rendered by the people who solicited the information. Two abolitionists, hearing the identical stories about a planter, would arrive at totally different conclusions. For example, everything that William F. Allen heard about Dr. Clarence Fripp, a brother of wicked Alviro, made him think that Clarence had been "the most of a man around here." His father, Good Billy Fripp, "couldn't make him drive the colored people"—it felt too much like driving cattle. But in the opinion of Laura Towne, a teacher who came to St. Helena Island from Philadelphia in 1862 and devoted herself to educating the freedmen, Fripp "led an infamous life, too bad to write of, too vile to speak of."[8] What had Fripp done to earn Towne's disgust? He had had sexual relations with his slave Rachel. To Allen, who marveled at how few mulattoes there were on the Island, Fripp's affair had little bearing on the question of how the man had treated the blacks. If anything, it put Fripp in a favorable light. Fripp and Rachel did not go sneaking around the outbuildings at night or running to the bushes. They lived together in his plantation house—Fripp had never married—and they had at least two children.* Miscegenation was unusual on St. Helena, and Fripp's arrangement was typical of the few cases. Sexual relations between the races generally involved white men and black women living in quasi-family arrangements acknowledged by the white man and disdained by his white kin.

Unlike his compatriots who came to St. Helena convinced that all planters had been monsters, Allen came with an open mind. Slaveowners may indeed have been tyrants in other parts of the South, he reasoned, where traditions were not old enough to smooth the rough edges of slavery and where the mode of agriculture was more like mining—looting the soil until it gave out, then moving on. But here in the cradle of slavery, where the fertility of the land was constantly being renewed, he expected to learn that slavery was what Grayson and its other muses had said it was—an amicable exchange of "life-maintenance for life-labor,"[9] an unspo-

---

*At the outbreak of the War, Fripp transferred title to his house and furniture to Rachel. Then he ran off to Confederate lines, sneaking back to St. Helena to see her until a strengthened Federal guard made such adventures impossible. One night, pickets ran him off into the woods, and Rachel had to pay a black man two hundred dollars to row him to safety. She left the Island herself shortly after and became a cook for United States General Rufus B. Saxton, commander of the occupying forces in Beaufort. She put her furniture in the hands of a carpenter named Edward who sold a sideboard and two pine tables to Miss Towne. Clarence Fripp served as a surgeon in the Confederate Army. He returned to St. Helena after the War, moved into a house next door to Miss Towne, and practiced medicine among the blacks.

ken agreement sanctioned by family feelings and policed by controls located deep in the psyches of the slaves. On these fundamental points he was disillusioned. "I find the people so much less degraded than I expected," he wrote, "and the barbarism [of their former masters] so much greater."[10] Cruelty, he learned, was a fact of life not only in the distant past or farther west. There was a frontier in the life of every white man on St. Helena, a time when he became the enslaver of his Negroes and not merely their inheritor. From the freedmen's close studies of their masters, Allen learned that planters of each generation had perfected their own controls, whether by making consistent shows of kindness or by resorting to the ancient, proven methods of compelling work and keeping order. All might have wished to be loved for their generosity, but most settled for being feared for their power to inflict pain.

8. The Household

Mary McDowell: A Young Bride

Mary Chaplin had four children before she was twenty-one years old. By the time she was twenty-seven she had had three more—seven altogether, more than any other woman that we know of, on the plantation. She lived for a little more than two years after the birth of her last child and died an agonizing death at age twenty-nine. Of her seven children, four lived to be adults and were alive when their father reached forty, but only one, Daniel, the second son, was alive ten years later.

When Mary McDowell married Thomas Chaplin she moved from Charleston to a faraway island of strangers and never went back, at least not after the sixth year of her marriage, when her husband took up his diary. Sickness, pregnancy, and babies to care for confined her to the plantation and the house, and for long periods to her bedroom. When her strength allowed, which was not often, she went to church or on a visit to a neighbor. For company, and for help with the children and with her responsibilities around the house and yard, she had her half-sister Sophy. Sophy was an essential part of the Chaplin household. She moved to Tombee with Mary and after Mary died she married Thomas and completed the job of raising her sister's children. Mary had kin in Ohio, Tennessee, Georgia, and upcountry Carolina, but in the years Chaplin kept his journal none of them was ever heard from. No one who had known her before she was Mrs. Chaplin came to see her, and she never visited a blood relative. Sophy once received a letter from her full sister Sarah—Mary's half-sister; that was the sum of Mary's communication with her family of origin, that we know of.[1] Her husband was her link to wider society. He went off into the world, beyond the plantation, and she stayed put. They lived surrounded by his kin and in daily contact with them. Marriage gave Mary a place in a large, deep-rooted family. But her husband's strong blood ties also had the effect of cutting him off from her.

Mary's chronic suffering forced Chaplin to keep a lid on his feelings. "I must hold my peace," he told his journal, reflecting that while he did indeed give her cause to scold him, it was her condition that led him to drink. In March, 1851, eight months before Mary's death, wife and husband took turns writing in his journal what they could not bear to say face to face. "I opened your book to put a little extract in it," she wrote, on Monday, the seventeenth, referring to a homily on the evils of alcohol. She happened to read his "last items" in which he anxiously noted that the firm which supplied the opiates she depended on would no longer sell to him on credit. "Don't give yourself uneasiness for *me*," Mary offered. "I have always endeavored to spare you any trouble I could, in this case I only reap punishment due to my own weakness, believe me, *you* are one of the best husbands. I can only hope you will not long be troubled with a wife so frail, weak, and suffering."

The next evening, when Chaplin settled down at his desk after a day spent fixing the yard fence, he found "that my dear wife has again, very contrary to my wishes, written some of her ideas in this foolish journal." To which he replied, ". . . you may write till doomsday and never *then* can you express what I feel." His command of language was sufficient, he felt, for keeping to the surface of things, but he was "not given to *manly words*" befitting strong emotions. Yet he made his feelings known. "*I know* what you *feel* & *suffer* & the inability to relieve is death *to me.*"

Why did Mary keep having babies in her weakened condition? She already had a large family. Each new birth shortened her life and reduced her capacity to care for her children. Birth control was primitive and cumbersome, but not unknown. Mary and Thomas could have taken steps to keep her from getting pregnant, but they wanted the children. As feared as childbirth was, the babies were eagerly welcomed. Had she lived, there is no reason to believe she would not have had more children. Many of her contemporaries had more than she did. Dr. Jenkins's wife, Eliza, had nine children in sixteen years. Mary's sister-in-law, Ann O'Hear Witsell, Saxby Chaplin's wife, had twelve children. Ann Rebecca Fripp, wife of Chaplin's first cousin John F. Chaplin, had fourteen. Catherine

Toomer and Harriet Martinangel, the first and second wives of Chaplin's second cousin William Fripp Chaplin, had a total of eighteen children between them.

A Lingering Death

The first four months of 1845 give a picture of the good times Thomas and Mary Chaplin might have had, if she had stayed healthy. The couple went out horseback riding, visiting, camping, and partying in Beaufort, while the children remained home with Sophy. But after April, the fun stopped. Mary felt "unwell" past the third month of her pregnancy with Eugene. Her labor was quick and the delivery was easy when the time came, but she was slow to recover. In fact, thereafter she was an invalid. She stopped going riding with her husband and nearly stopped going out altogether. What little traveling she did, by wagon or boat, was to benefit her health—leaving sickly places for safe ones, or simply going to see new sights, in the hope that a change of scenery would work a cure.

Eugene was a month old when his sister Maria died. She had been sick with fever "occasioned by worms," Chaplin thought, but she appeared to be recovering, and her death was a shock. Named for one of her father's deceased sisters, Maria was the second-oldest child and the first to die. Mary, her mother, was in "such wretched health" there could be little time for mourning or for seeing after the cotton that was opening fast in the field. Mary's breast had "risen very large and almost black," causing her excruciating pain and preventing her from feeding Eugene. No sooner did the abscess abate than she was struck with violent pains in her left side and stomach. Calomel, cupping,* and the application of hot flannels gave some relief, but the pains soon became chronic and she needed narcotics.

Mary was in no shape to help her husband run the plantation. Besides, she was a city girl and knew nothing about making a crop. Thus, Chaplin lacked an advantage many of his neighbors had—a wife who was a business partner, or who at least could give an informed opinion on matters relating to work going on outside the house. Chaplin never mentions talking with Mary about plantation affairs or involving her in making decisions, though his moods,

---

*Drawing blood by scarifying the skin and applying a "cup" or cupping glass in which the air is rarefied by heating.

if not his conversations, must have kept her apprised of developments. As a gift, and perhaps also as an attempt to interest her in the crop, Chaplin announced in the spring of 1848 that he was going to give Mary the proceeds from five acres of fine cotton. Chaplin once had the field hands plant a crop of peanuts near the house and Mary promised to have them harvested by the yard hands, who were nominally under her authority. That was the extent of her involvement in farming.

Before she became an invalid, Chaplin had hoped she would be more of a help. He even asked her to keep up his journal while he went hunting for a few days at Christmas, 1845, a far cry from the annoyance he would show when she wrote in it during her dying days. So she knew he was keeping a journal and what he was writing in it. They had different ideas, however, about how the book should be used. He wanted it to be a record of daily events which he could read for entertainment and practical guidance from one season to the next. She wanted it to be a self-correcting device, a record of spiritual experience, and an instrument of moral reform. In April of the same year, she had her husband write down a gentle warning to resist temptation—inspired by a Methodist temperance tract. It was her duty as a wife, she felt, to help him subdue his passions as she had subdued her own, and otherwise to stay out of his way. She would watch over his morals, not his business. On May 31, 1846, she inserted a long article on the "common ways in which drunkards make their exit." The piece was morbid and severe; gone were the lightheartedness and playful indirection she had shown the year before. As her physical strength declined, she brought her attack into the open. Silent in response, Chaplin had the last word in his journal: "those who live in glass houses should not throw stones." He was alluding to her habit of taking snuff— pulverized tobacco mixed with an aromatic such as cognac or rose leaves by the mouthful. On November 5, 1850, almost a year to the day before her death, he described in grisly detail the "demoralizing and injurious" ritual that "entirely destroys all social and domestic enjoyments & comforts and prevents all chances of prosperity." He scratched out the entry afterward, but most of it can still be discerned. Snuff made Mary vomit and prevented her from speaking, but it numbed her stomach and diverted her mind. Her personality was inclined to be retiring; the snuff habit shut her away altogether.

When she emerged from her bedroom to take meals with the family, she found the food unappealing and the quantity insufficient. She complained about the tiresome diet of hominy and bacon, and she attacked the problem herself by "making havoc with the breeding poultry," until Chaplin was shamed into killing a calf. Then, she and Sophy, who was better able to make the sacrifice, refused to eat, leaving the small dishes of meat on the table for Chaplin and the children. Stabbed by this example of self-renunciation, Chaplin promised to shoot "the last cow, sheep, or hog that I have on the place . . . so there shall be no stinting." He began by killing a veal, which may have been what the women were hoping to make him do. Soon Mary was refusing food because she could not hold it down, and refusing medicine because she had had enough of her ordeal. On October 31, 1851, two days before she died, Chaplin killed a yearling steer "as much to get the feet to make jelly for wife as to get something to eat." It was too warm for the meat to stay fresh very long, but right after Mary's funeral the weather turned cold, and with his mother's help he did not run so perilously short of meat again.

Boys and Girls

The boys were interesting to Chaplin as soon as they could hold a fishing rod or sit up in a saddle. He enjoyed their company, though he did not involve them in the day-to-day operation of the plantation. He does not say whether he tried to instruct them methodically in making a crop or managing slaves. They would ride with him around the fields, but if he taught them to know what constituted a day's labor, how to select seeds and when to plant them, or how often to sharpen the hoes and change the rollers in the gins, he did not mention it in his journal. During the growing months, the boys generally were kept away from the plantation, and the rest of the year they were busy at school. Before they went off, their closest companions were the black children at Tombee. Apparently they taught each other what they knew. "The little Negroes are ruining the children," Mary warned her husband. "I couldn't tell you half the badness they learn them"—bad manners, crossing swollen creeks, eating green fruit. Chaplin had to keep his boys at home for semesters at a time in the late '50s when he ran short of money, and he says he taught them himself, but what they learned he does not say.

Ernest, the oldest boy, was prone to mishaps and bad luck. The fish wouldn't bite for him, boating made him seasick, and the deer eluded him when he went out on a hunt. Once he had "a providential and narrow escape" when powder from a flask he had carelessly rested on the muzzle of his shotgun ran down the barrel and exploded. When he was eleven he was sent to school in Bluffton, St. Luke's Parish, across Port Royal Sound. "Ernest is rather young to be sent away from home," mulled his father, who had been sent to Richland at age eight. "I can't help my thoughts wandering constantly to Ernest," he sighed. "It seems to me he is now cast upon the waters of life, for weal or woe, to sink or swim." If it were Daniel, instead of Ernest, Chaplin would not have been so worried—or he would have worried for different reasons. Ernest was shy, immature, depressed—"dull," in Chaplin's usage. He had no confidence in his abilities. Nothing could lift his spirits except cake—he was very fond of cake. Mary had accused her husband of stifling him, but Chaplin felt blameless. At thirteen Ernest still could not write a letter home. "It is so distressing to think he is so very backward," wrote his father. But his social skills improved and by September, 1857, he was making the circuit of parties in St. Helenaville. A fever brought a halt to his socializing, and for almost a week his survival was in doubt. He lived for fifteen years more and died, in 1872, at thirty-two, in the overseer's house at Coffin's Point, twelve miles east of Tombee on the shore of St. Helena Sound, where his father and stepmother had found an anchorage after losing the last of Chaplin's mother's plantations on the main.

That left only Daniel, Chaplin's fourth child and second son, and he was deeply estranged from his father. It would be twelve years before he "redeemed himself" by taking Chaplin and Sophy under his wing. He and his father had never gotten along well. He had screaming fits before he could talk and, afterward, whenever he was frightened or displeased, he would throw a tantrum. He repeatedly protested against the family environment—his mother's slow death, his father's moodiness, the air of gloom and confusion in the house. Chaplin believed he was born spoiled: it was in the blood and it showed up in the volcanic-tempered Daniel more than in the others. Eugene had fits, too, alarming ones, but Chaplin attributed them to a child's normal tendency to mental instability. It is difficult to imagine Eugene ever abusing the horses as Daniel did. Young Daniel was as high-strung as his father, and in adulthood he moved with the same air of sufferance. People who knew him in his forties and fifties recalled that he was deliberately unfashionable. He liked to dance the old plantation dances and he was inordinately proud of his small feet. Every afternoon, he and his wife, "Aunt Lou," would change into formal clothes to receive guests who seldom stopped by.[2] He was living out the myth his father had believed, but which his father's life had not borne out. Still Daniel went on impersonating the planter type of old, with its legendary charm, solemnity, refinement, and posturing. But he had no plantation to go along with the role, no wealth or source of income other than his own labor. The War had disinherited him and neither his father nor his father-in-law had a dollar to help him get started. After 1875 he ran a teamster business, hiring wagons and hauling supplies to the phosphate mines, and well into the 1900s he bought and sold real estate around Walterboro.

Daniel's father-in-law was his father's brother, Saxby—Daniel had married Saxby's daughter Maria Louisa, named for the same aunt as his dead sister. Both sets of parents had vigorously opposed the match. The children of Daniel and Maria Louisa were Chaplin's only grandchildren. His daughter Virginia had died in childbirth in 1867, and the baby had died, too. Ernest never married, and Eugene had died before he could marry.

When Ernest died, Chaplin was comforted by the thought that he had made his son's last days more restful. But no consolation could be drawn from the deaths of Eugene and Virginia, the one "sacrificed to his country," the other, "to her love or perceived love for a worthless object"—the man she had married. Chaplin never saw enough of Virginia, his only daughter to live past two, especially after her tenth birthday. He had kept her on the move between home, school, church, her grandmother Isabella, and her great-aunt Betsy, a step ahead of the dreaded fever. Their encounters at church and at Tombee the few times Aunt Betsy brought her home were loving and demonstrative. To keep up family feelings, Chaplin would send her brothers to St. Helenaville to see her. The plantation was a dangerous place, he believed, especially for his daughters. Three of them had died there—Maria Louisa, in 1845; baby Isabella, in 1847; and little Missy—Mary Frances—in 1851. Virginia must not be allowed to stay at home. "Poor Virginia," he wrote, on September 2, 1852, the day he married Sophy. "She cried bitterly to return with us, but that of course was not to be thought of for a moment." Then she grew up and caught the eye of the young men, and some of the older men, too. In 1866 she married Wilson Glover, of St. Bartholomew's Parish, an ill-starred fellow who named a child by his next wife after her, and was struck dead by lightning in 1882.

Education

While their black playmates were maturing into full hands on the plantation, Chaplin's boys were going to school, before settling on their own plantations. Chaplin was not nearly ready to part with his land and slaves or to divide them up to make room for his off-spring. He was a young man himself when they were ready for college. His mother had enough plantations to take care of his sons, but while she—and Baker—lived, her property was out of reach, and even in the event of her death he would have to share her estate with his brother, Saxby, who had children of his own to provide for.

Education was expensive. The state set aside a small sum annually for public schools, but these were urban institutions that catered to the poor, in the spirit of charity.[3] The District and the Parish did not subsidize education at all. School, to Chaplin, meant private school. Several small academies opened and folded on St. Helena—Mrs. McElheran's was the longest running and for four years Virginia attended it regularly. The other schools consisted of a single teacher hired by a "company" of three or four planters who provided a house in the village or a room in a building on one of their plantations. It was a costly way to improvise an education, and it could not be paid for in peas.

The expense of educating his children staggered Chaplin. To send Daniel, Eugene, and Virginia to a village school run by the couple who replaced the McElherans cost ninety dollars for two-thirds of a quarter, including board for the boys, a price he considered "unconscionably high." At that rate it would have taken more than four hundred dollars—the gross receipts from three bales of cotton, or a third of his income—to send his children to school for three-quarters of the year. And that fee was low compared to charges at more prestigious schools in Beaufort and on the main.[4] Room and board off the Island were difficult to find, and school-masters were notoriously unreliable. "In this state," grumbled Chaplin, at the start of the prosperous year of 1856, "it seems that all rules & regulations of schools are opposed to the diffusion of learning among those not rich." Not that he had in mind any significant reform. He simply wished he were richer. Nevertheless, his complaint reflected the heated debate about the state's responsibility to educate its people that had been going on in leading journals and intellectual circles for decades.

Educational theory was entwined with the philosophy of slavery. A writer in *DeBow's Review,* the South's most important political magazine, outlined the two leading principles of the southern system of education. Neither addressed the question of *what* should be taught, only *who* should not be educated and *who* should be. The first principle excluded slaves from state-supported instruction: a state "is not required to provide education for the great bulk of its laboring class."[5] The second principle recognized that since enlightened people must rule, the chief function of education must be to teach them *how* to rule: the state *"is* required to afford the degree of education to every one of its white citizens which will enable him intelligently and actively to control the slave labor of the State."[6]

Why was it so important to keep the slaves ignorant? By the late 1850s, many justifications had evolved. William Trescot and William Grayson argued on the basis of the different levels of culture achieved by the African and European races at the time of enslavement. "The only school/Barbarians ever know," wrote Grayson, is "a master's rule."[7] But barbarians might one day become civilized, in which case discrimination in education, as well as in everything else, would persist merely as a right of conquest. This would never happen, some propagandists maintained, because the Negro's position was fixed by Nature, not history. By this theory Negroes were biologically incapable "of that mental improvement which is generally understood by the term education."[8] Other apologists cited the right to forestall revolt. Didn't Nat Turner's rebellion in Virginia, in 1831, demonstrate that a slave who could read was a danger to society? Education made slaves dissatisfied; it encouraged them to expect things from life which were not forthcoming under slavery. Some white Christians worried that forbidding slaves to read was tantamount to excluding them from "the religion of the Bible." But the opinion prevailed that reading was not essential to salvation, and that learning from books was the wrong preparation for a life of menial labor.

To talk about the degree of education that qualified white people to direct the labor of blacks was not necessarily to talk about schools, either. The cause of public education for whites was slow to advance in a society that regarded learning as a dangerous thing in the hands of the wrong people. There were also practical obstacles to operating public schools in sections where the labor force was nearly all black and the white population was widely dispersed.[9] Legislators held to the belief that the state should play a minimal role, in contrast to the situation in the northern states, where a vigorous public-school movement had mobilized government support. Thus, slavery not only required masters to arrest the intellectual development of the blacks, it severely limited educational opportunities for most whites, as well.

Those who lost out were those who could not pay. The cotton planters of St. Helena and neighboring parishes had money to spend on education, however, and the schools they patronized were more than equal to their needs. Chaplin's financial troubles were not typical of his group—not in the lucrative '50s. Individually and as a class, Sea Island planters were thriving in the decade before the Civil War. Their children were learning what they had to know to maintain their numbers in a high standard of living. The value of their capital assets was growing, and so were their incomes. They took for granted that women should be educated, though not trained for the professions, if they were going to be the companions of educated men. Their institutions were turning out a steady stream of accomplished individuals—doctors, lawyers, clerics, orators—and people who made a pastime of reading.

Sophy Creighton: A New Wife

In the opening pages of Chaplin's journal, one might mistake Sophy, Mary's half-sister, for Chaplin's wife. Sophy accompanied Chaplin more often than Mary to church and on trips to Beaufort and St. Helenaville. She called on other households as the representative of the Chaplin family, and she paid visits to Chaplin's mother, Isabella, in place of Mary. Adding to the reader's confusion is Chaplin's practice of referring to his wife as "Mrs. C" or "my dear wife" but never calling her Mary, so that it is not immediately apparent that there are two white women living in his house. Sophy had her own bedroom—leaving two bedrooms for everyone else—but no one begrudged her presence. On the contrary, neither the master nor the mistress could do without her. Healthier and livelier than Mary, and without the burden of childbearing, she exerted a cheerful influence on the family. Given the pall of sickness and death that hung over the house, and the endless worries over food and money, Chaplin and Sophy got along very well. At bottom there was strong sexual feeling between them. They would occasionally quarrel over trifles and stop speaking to each other, then walk around the house tingling with rage until the other would break down and speak. Sophy infuriated her brother-in-law with periodic "coldness" and he would resolve, in turn, "to have little to do with her in the future."

What happened was completely different, however. Sophia Creighton, of Scotch-Irish stock, married Chaplin ten months after the death of her sister and remained his wife for almost forty years. During the eleven years of married life allotted to Chaplin and Mary, Sophy had no suitors. As sister of the wife, escort of the husband, aunt to the needy children, and delegate of the household, she had carved out an acceptable social role outside of marriage. Had Mary lived, Sophy might never have married. By 1851, she had no other family to return to and she was already as devoted as a mother to her sister's children. When Mary died, the mantle of responsibility passed smoothly to her. She simply took over in name the job she had been doing in fact. At the close of the entry marking "the saddest day of my life," the day "my poor, poor wife breathed her last," Chaplin acknowledged the "debt of gratitude & love" he owed to Sophy. Five weeks later, he put away his sorrow and went out horseback riding with her—a pleasure that Mary's condition had forbidden. By March of the new year, Chaplin and Sophy declared their love. Not mere duty to the children or respect for the wishes of the dead brought them together, but long-standing desire. Before the month ended, Chaplin announced, "The secret is out. Sophy, dearest Sophy will be mine." Chaplin's mother gave her consent to the match and the couple made plans to marry, intending to wait until Mary had been dead a year. But they wound up getting married sooner because, Chaplin said, he wanted "free access" to his children who stayed in Sophy's room when they were sick.

Happier times followed—months of visiting and seeking out entertainment. Chaplin stepped into society again, with a wife by his side for the first time in six or seven years. He was not as wealthy or brash as he once had been, but neither was he troubled by the sickness of his loved ones or threatened by financial embarrassment. Sophy was sturdy. She beat off fevers and although Chaplin reports that she once experimented with a galvanic belt—a contraption alleged to relieve stomach and intestinal pains—it was not a sign of a lasting disorder. They had no children of their own, but she loved Mary's children, and they loved her, as a mother.

Quietly and for obscure reasons, they stopped going out in public together and settled into a pattern of obligatory affection and indifference. Sophy withdrew more and more, as Mary had, until she was nearly a recluse herself. Once the children were off at school and she was left alone in the house with the servants, she suffered from cabin fever, a kind of depression. Like Mary before her, she developed a hair-trigger temper which became the bane of Chaplin's existence. But they supported each other through terrible times. Twenty-five years after they were married, when they had nothing in the world but each other, Chaplin praised Sophy for being "a most excellent wife to me & mother to my children." "Everybody has faults," he observed with compassion; "hers are few, & circumstance, trouble, disappointments of many kinds have somewhat soured her." She outlived him by a year and died at the last Chaplin stronghold, near Walterboro, in 1891.

9. Sickness and Healing

The Racial Bias of Medical Knowledge
Next to the weather, itself an important influence on hygiene, the awesome problems of maintaining bodily health and strength were more frequently noted in the journal than any other subjects. Disease spread rapidly, mysteriously, from island to island, striking at one plantation and skipping another. A history of good health and quick recoveries did not guarantee long life. Someone might come down with indigestion in the morning, or wake up in a sweat; by afternoon nausea or delirium would have set in; and by night the victim, who had appeared as fresh as April the day before, would be dying or dead.

Sickness and death tormented all classes of people. Childhood was the risky season of life. A woman's childbearing years were a perilous time. Women commonly died or were permanently disabled from childbearing. Prolapsus, or falling of the womb, was routinely experienced by both black and white women who had had many children. Drastic treatments for the pain of prolapsus, breast tumors, urinary disorders, and other "women's complaints" created numerous invalids. Individuals of both sexes, of both races, endured months and years of debilitating illnesses and grueling remedies. Though able to predict the occurrence of certain endemic diseases, planters were limited in their abilities to prevent them. Respiratory diseases flourished in winter; in summer, it was gastrointestinal disorders accompanied by high fevers.

Disease ate away at the social fabric, depleting the small white community through death, enervation, and forced absenteeism. The absence or loss of a handful of people was enough to disrupt institutions like the church and the Agricultural Society. Disease threatened the very persistence of what could be called a community.

Blacks suffered the same ailments as whites, with varying incidence and severity, depending on individual genetic features and hygienic conditions in the slave quarters. Their masters provided doctors and medicine, which they submitted to and supplemented with their own medical resources. The "great object" of health care, as one writer bluntly put it, was "to prolong the useful laboring period of a Negro's life."[1] This was Chaplin's view, too. In entry after entry in his journal, he represents the health problems of his slaves in terms of his own economic well-being. "This sickness is bad for me in getting out my crop," he griped, one bitter-cold day in January, 1849, when he could call out only enough hands to keep three cotton gins going.

White people correctly observed differences in how blacks and whites reacted to specific diseases. Blacks tolerated malarial fevers better than whites, but they succumbed in greater numbers to pneumonia and pleurisy.* Medical science was not interested in whether other racial and ethnic groups also experienced different degrees of vulnerability;[†] blacks were "the only group whose medical differences mattered."[2] Practitioners believed that Negroes were inherently susceptible to worms and dysentery; we know today that this notion is false. The effort to account for the medical distinctiveness of the Negro was complicated by the desire to place the defense of slavery on a scientific foundation. Peculiarities of Negro physiology not only defined a range of diagnoses and treatments, but were used to justify the Negro's status. "Feeble heat generating powers" justified a "heat-producing" diet of bacon, corn, and peas.[3] Negroes were said to breathe less air and to dissipate a greater amount of animal heat through their skins. Their lungs were different from white people's lungs, in theory, and

*The "major reason for black immunity" to malaria, writes medical historian Todd L. Savitt, "is not acquired resistance, but . . . selective genetic factors" including the abnormal hemoglobic condition called sickle-cell anemia. But regarding Negroes' susceptibility to pulmonary infections, "even today there is some confusion. . . . Some claim a racial or genetic predisposition, others deny it." (Todd L. Savitt, *Medicine and Slavery* [Chicago, 1978] 34–41.)
†Modern research has determined, for example, that "Jews are less prone to contract tuberculosis, but more subject to Neimann-Pick Disease and Gaucher's Disease. Other vulnerabilities exist among Swedes (sarcoidosis, porphyria, and pernicious anemia), South Africans of Dutch descent (porphyria cutanea tarda hereditaria), Ulster Scotsmen (nephrogenic diabetes insipidus), and Italians, Greeks, Syrians, and Armenians (thalassemia)." (Savitt, 47.)

worked best in high humidity. Negroes were designed, it was said, to live in low altitudes and swamps.[4] Medical writers fortified the planters' claim that only blacks could stand to work in the tropical southern summer. They ignored the fact that many white people became acclimated to the environment and worked as well as blacks. Whites "only needed a bit more salt."[5]

Health Hazards

The land yielded everything but health. A lowcountry planter told the Yankee traveler Frederick Law Olmsted that he would "as soon stand fifty feet from the best Kentucky rifleman as to spend a night on his plantation" during the hot months.[6] What made the countryside so dangerous in summer? Some blamed the "noxious miasmata" given off in the "copious evaporation" of brackish water left behind by the tides.[7] Others, observing the rapid growth of fungi on food, clothing, eating utensils, tools, harnesses, and leather goods, blamed the "putrescent effluvia" produced by rotting "vegetable and animal substances." John Drayton conjectured that summer fevers were caused by the prevailing "southwardly winds" and the vapors "exhaled" by the earth "as a consequence of freeing new lands." He expected the "evil" to end once "the earth recovered from its sourness to a proper state of cultivation."[8] Drayton was on the right track when he observed that a major source of trouble was the "multitudes of mosquitoes" which bred in stagnant water. He did not know that they did their damage by injecting parasites into the bloodstream, or that other common pests such as fleas and lice also transmitted febrile diseases.

White people had not always abandoned their plantations in summer. Before 1790, the custom was to stay. The towns and cities were considered unhealthy. From June through October, public offices in Charleston shut down and many people went into the country. By the turn of the century, the direction of the summer migration had reversed. Epidemics chased people out of the towns periodically, but after 1800 the fear of fever drove the whites off their plantations every summer.[9] In Chaplin's era, the sickly season occupied almost half the year, from the middle of May until the first hard frost in November.

The whites were fleeing from the mosquito-borne disease we call malaria, which they knew as "remittent fever," "intermittent fever," "country fever," "marsh fever," "summer fever," "autumnal fever," and just plain "fever." Malaria killed fewer people than typhoid or cholera, but it left its victims weak and at the mercy of other diseases. As a result it caused tremendous economic damage, measured by days of labor lost and tasks left undone. The first symptoms were chills and flushes of heat, followed by high fever, nausea, and headache. Cathartic medicines such as castor oil, calomel (mercurous chloride), and jalap (a powder ground from the tuberous root of a Mexican plant of the morning glory family) were taken in huge doses, one after the other, to purge the bowels and purge them again. Quinine was used to bring down the fever— Chaplin gave it as a preventive, as well. Quinine is an alkaloid extract from the bark of the cinchona tree native to the Andes. It was introduced in the lowcountry in the early 1830s and its success as a febrifuge earned it the title "Samson of Materia Medica."[10] Quinine was as effective against fever as opiates were against pain, but its side effects could be deadly.

Pneumonia was the "Great Killer of Negroes."[11] Planters were warned to keep their slaves warm and dry, but this advice was impractical. Outdoor work could not all be saved for sunny days. And though staying indoors would have protected slaves from rain, it would have exposed them to other dangers. Their cabins had window openings and shutters but no glass, and between letting in the mosquitoes in summer and letting out the heat in winter or closing off the air, they preferred to shut themselves in the dark and smoky rooms. Because sunlight seldom penetrated the cabins, and the earthen floors stayed damp, food spoiled quickly. Poor ventilation, crowding, contaminated food and water, crude toilet facilities, and the indiscriminate heaping of garbage all encouraged parasites. Dysentery was rampant in summer and many people harbored worms in their bodies sometime during their lives.[12] The human body can support some parasites, such as tapeworms, for years, but a person has to eat more to keep up with them. In times of stress, parasites may get out of hand and overwhelm the host. Planters did not understand that a nutritionally adequate diet could become dangerously inadequate once worms invaded the body.

While Chaplin's slaves showed signs of dissatisfaction with their rations, they did not show symptoms of malnutrition, such as sore eyes and mouths, skin ulcers and lesions. Infections, however, afflicted everyone. Infections were lanced and drained, but not in a sterile setting. Warm flannels were applied and opiates taken for pain. Antibiotics, of course, were unknown. Chaplin himself suffered painful boils and toothaches which prevented him from thinking about anything else. Just as diverse diseases were grouped together as fevers, two classes of ailments called inflammations and obstructions described various disorders of the vital organs.* Inflamed or tender stomachs, livers, and wombs were treated with compresses and bleeding. Obstructed bowels were violently purged, and powerful emetics were taken to "assist in producing the monthly courses in women." Cuts from the sharp tools handled daily and strains from heavy labor were the most common work-related traumas. Chaplin lost one man from strangulated hernia. Another man drowned—many of the boat hands could not swim—and several were shaken up and bruised in mishaps with horses.

Whooping cough, measles, mumps, scarlet fever, and smallpox all visited St. Helena, between 1845 and 1858, and they found an ideal environment in which to spread. Since whites and blacks communicated with each other every day, and the children in particular came in close and continuous contact, disease passed swiftly between the races. Knowledge of the causes and treatments of disease progressed through isolated breakthroughs—such as the discovery in the late eighteenth century that inoculations of benign cowpox could protect against smallpox, and the introduction of quinine in the 1830s. Medicine's capacity to help women through childbearing had advanced very little since the invention of the forceps. Forceps were called upon as often to destroy and extract the unborn baby in an attempt to save the mother's life, as to ease the baby's delivery. The wives of at least four of Chaplin's friends died in childbirth; so did his daughter. His wife Mary survived seven deliveries, but she was disabled by the aftereffects—puerperal fever, an infection of the reproductive organs, and prolapsus, the protrusion of the uterus through the vagina, resulting from the weakening of pelvic support tissue. Plantation medical guides blamed women for bringing these afflictions on themselves by getting out of bed too soon or by talking too much after delivery.

Slaves faced one medical risk which their masters did not—the effects of punishment, most commonly whipping.[13] Whipping

---

*Savitt suggests that if hypertension was as prevalent among slaves as it is among blacks today, stroke and heart disease might have caused many deaths that were attributed to other conditions.

caused unspeakable pain and often resulted in loss of blood, as well as shock and infection. Paddles did not lacerate the skin as whips did, but they raised large blisters. Which was more painful, whipping or paddling? We cannot say because the degree of suffering depended, in part, on the strength of the man wielding the instrument. Nor is it easy to assess the impact of punishment and deprivation on mental health; but it seems reasonable to infer that the systematic attempt to keep black people fearful and to impress upon them their inferiority and dependence was fertile breeding ground for personality disorders, psychoses, depression, aggression, and anxiety.

The Age of "Heroic" Medicine

It was an age of "heroic" medication, of dangerous drugs taken in large doses, of cathartics strong enough to purge a horse yet given freely to children, of bloodletting and blistering which weakened the already feeble but satisfied the requirement that healing be painful. Drugs were intended to suppress symptoms and forcibly clean out the stomach and bowels, rather than to attack disease-causing microorganisms, which were largely unknown to medicine. Six or seven favorite drugs were prescribed in varying quantities and sequences for entirely different diseases. Opium, for example, as a powder, in pills, and mixed with alcohol in the popular tincture laudanum, was taken to ease cramps and convulsions; to fight scurvy, skin ulcers, and other kinds of putrefaction; to relieve pain and nervousness and to produce deep sleep; to constipate and to stimulate, according to the dosage. An overdose could bring on convulsions and death. Because each drug had multiple uses, and any one use or purpose was served by several drugs, patients were commonly treated with a diversity of medicines. When Chaplin's son Ernest went "down with hot fever," in September, 1857, Chaplin gave him twenty grains of "blue pill," or powdered mercury, a promiscuously prescribed drug now recognized as a poison, said "to increase or improve the secretions of the body." The fever stayed on, and Dr. Clarence Fripp diagnosed it as "remittent fever with a touch of pneumonia"—a severe case of malaria. He put blistering ointment on Ernest's chest and gave him a draft of calomel to flush his bowels. The treatment was repeated but the fever continued and the boy could not hold down food. After staying up with him two nights in a row, Chaplin gave Ernest laudanum and brandy "to keep life in him." When, on the seventh day, Ernest began to show improvement, Chaplin began administering quinine "in large doses," followed by paregoric, a camphorated tincture of opium, taken to relieve stomach acid and soothe tender bowels, and preceded by a purge.

Similar scenes were enacted at the bedsides of other family members, who sometimes survived and sometimes did not. By the late 1850s, medical opinion was turning against "heroic" therapy. "To bleed, purge, blister, and calomelize is to kill," declared Dr. Robert Ward of Georgia.[14] But medical practice lagged behind, and plantation physicians continued to battle over the size of doses and the appropriate areas of the body to cut and singe.

In 1850, about one in every eight planters on St. Helena Island had a degree from the state medical college. For some, this represented merely a "polite accomplishment." But many doctors had active practices and supplemented their cotton revenues by providing medical care for their neighbors' slaves. Planters either contracted annually with a doctor, for a lump sum, or else, like Chaplin, they paid for the doctor's services as they needed them. At one time or another, Chaplin employed Drs. Jenkins, Fripp, Scott, Croft, and Sams—Melvin Melius Sams, son of Dr. Melvin Melius Sams and Elizabeth Ann Fripp. Though they did not grow rich from medicine alone, these doctors all had money, and they went off the Island to spend it. Chaplin relied mainly on Dr. Jenkins, until Jenkins began splitting his time between his St. Helena plantations and his new home in Beaufort.

Chaplin contended that Jenkins overcharged him—after the War, Jenkins spread the story that Chaplin had never paid his bills—and he expressed a general disesteem for the medical profession. "Who is it that cannot get a diploma from the state medical college?" he asked sarcastically, upon learning that two of R. L. Baker's nephews had graduated. Yet he usually sent for a doctor whenever anyone on the plantation was sick or injured. His efforts to minister to the health of his slaves were inconsistent, however. He tried to purge disease while doing nothing to change the physical milieu in which disease-causing microbes throve. In part, he was ignorant of what to do; in part, he did not want to make the investment. Whitewash for walls, lime for floors, shingles for roofs, extra blankets and shoes for the people, all required an outlay of money or time or both. He did take one outstanding preventive measure: In February, 1854, he had his young slaves vaccinated against smallpox.

Medical relations were relations of force. The threat of calling the doctor was enough to drive some hands out of the sickhouse and into the fields, because they feared the doctor would find nothing wrong with them or because they feared his treatment. Blacks tried first to cure themselves, with teas, powders, and salves made from local plants and animals; with charms, prayer, and conjuration—magic. Drugs alone, they believed, could not restore good health. Only by conciliating an evil spirit loosed by an enemy, living or dead, could a person overcome illness. If herbal remedies and magic failed, the patient's condition might be desperate by the time the master was notified. Once seen by a doctor, the patient had to be closely watched if he or she was to follow the doctor's instructions. Planters wanted to think of their slaves as unwilling children who had to be made to take their castor oil. The slaves wanted to control their own bodies and souls. Their attitude suggests the existence of an alternative theory of disease. But whites in general showed no interest in the blacks' ideas of causation, which Chaplin typically dismissed as "foolishness."

Despite many basic differences, the medical thinking of the two peoples was not entirely dissimilar. In both, the fight against disease occurred at the level of the organism, not the cell. The whole body was treated, not merely the seat of disturbance. Just as disease delivered punishing blows to people, so people fought back as if disease had a spirit, by purging, pummeling, and driving it out of the body. Both whites and blacks obtained their drugs from plants. During the eighteenth and early nineteenth centuries they relied on many of the same local roots and herbs. After 1830, the white pharmacopocia turned to plants found mainly outside the United States—quinine from Peru; opium from the Orient; the flower heads of European chamomile, the roots of ipecac and jalap, essential purges on Chaplin's shelf, from Mexico and South America. Although blacks had access to white medicines through their masters, they resorted first to remedies made from plants found in nearby yards, woods, and margins of fields. It is difficult to identify the plants precisely because different plants went by the same popular name, and the same plant was known by different names within a single neighborhood. What was called feverroot by some people was called wild coffee by others. More than one plant was known as the feverbush. Furthermore, identification is hindered since conditions favoring the abundance of certain useful plants have changed, coinciding with the loss of status for homegrown remedies. With the passing of dirt roads and the horse carts that traveled them, for example, an important medium that supported a plant called the cross-root, whose bark was boiled into a froth and applied to painful parts of the body with a woolen cloth, has disappeared.

When the Federal blockade of the southern coast, in 1861, made the supply of drugs uncertain, whites were encouraged to follow the Negroes' example and find substitutes within their reach. As part of the war effort, Francis Peyre Porcher, a Charleston physician and a surgeon in the Confederate Army, published a guide to the medicinal properties of southern flora. *Resources of the Southern Fields and Forests* was an expansion of his earlier "Sketch of the Medical Botany of South Carolina," and drew heavily on sources from the lowcountry. Porcher identified more than four hundred substances which might serve in place of scarce and costly imported drugs. Some of them were known to have been used by the Indians, and many were tested and refined by slaves. In place of calomel, Porcher's informants suggested using the milky juice from the leaves and roots of dandelion; for quinine, a decoction from common knotgrass, thoroughwort, or any of four or five other grasses and herbs; for opium, the powdered rind of the fruit of the horse chestnut. Apart from its medicinal uses, a paste made from mashing the fresh horse chestnut kernels with water and wheat flour was said to intoxicate fish, "so that they float on the surface and may be taken."[15]

Chaplin as Doctor and Patient

Chaplin was the practitioner of first call on his plantation. Upon learning that someone was ill, he made an initial diagnosis and decided whether to send for a doctor or to treat the person himself. He may have sought opinions from one of several popular medical handbooks, just as he referred to Holmes's manual for help with planting. *The Planter's Guide and Family Book of Medicine* (Charleston, 1849) instructed planters "who may be out of reach of physicians" in the art of making pills, plasters, and poultices, and in the skills of lancing, cupping, and bloodletting. It offered general advice on raising Negroes, emphasizing the need to punish those who did not keep their bodies and their cabins clean. Agricultural journals offered medical tips and the Charleston newspapers ran lavish advertisements for prepared medicines alleged to work wonders on the Negro constitution.* Chaplin preferred to roll his own pills and dispense a few trusted generic drugs.

He was never dangerously ill himself. He had several bouts of dysentery and many minor bouts of fever, from which he rebounded quickly. When fevers laid him up, his chief concern was that his mother take notice, send a servant to learn how he was doing, and come herself if the report was bad. Once, an overdose of quinine, administered by Dr. Jenkins, left him temporarily "as deaf as a teaspoon." He had his share of corns, piles, boils, and toothaches, but all in all he was healthy and whole, in contrast to a great many people around him. He claimed several permanent disabilities—a ringing in his ears, from a bad case of the mumps; weak vision in one eye, from a rocket burst at a Fourth of July celebration; "shortness of breath," brought on by exposure to cold and wet weather; and pains in his joints, which he called "inflammatory or flying rheumatism." But his significant health problems were emotional—fits of depression and a confirmed persecution complex.

*"10,000 Negroes/Saved Annually/Planters Take Notice," proclaimed an advertisement for "Jacob's Cordial," a sweetened alcoholic beverage given for dysentery, diarrhea, and flux; in the Charleston *Mercury,* during the winter of 1849.

10. The Journal

Motives and Purposes

At Christmas, 1845, Chaplin asked his wife to "continue my journal" for a few days while he went off hunting. His candid instructions disclose the purposes he had in mind in starting the journal a year before. He wanted Mary to write down what he had been writing—"thoughts and observations, also any little occurrences that may take place . . . whether concerning the family or the plantation." He claimed no aesthetic intention, only the aim of holding up a mirror to life, just as a gentleman might examine his appearance both before *and* after going out in society. The habit of writing grew more elaborate and tyrannical over the years, and his reasons for keeping a journal changed. From what he said and what he did, his overt motivations may be divided into three phases: first, 1845 through the summer of 1847, the mirror-of-life phase, in which he exposed his reckless disregard for consequences and the adolescent illusion that a wealthy mother could take care of everything; second, October, 1847, through the autumn of 1852, a period of grave losses and defeats, when he turned inward and tried by writing to subordinate the impact of the world rather than to reflect it; third, from his marriage to Sophy and the brightening skies of 1853, to the day he announced his journal was finished, in May, 1858, years when he thought he was writing for his children as well as for himself, and began to look upon his journal as a book he was creating for future readers, an heirloom. In the postwar years he would renew his interest in the journal as a literary work by contemplating its structure and veracity, and attempting to tie up loose threads, bring matters up to date, and write an ending.

* * *

When he lost his property in the mid-'40s, he lost his friends, or so he believed. They stopped coming around to see him and, in truth, he was no longer fun to be with. His confidence and humor had been shattered. He tried to protect himself against his friends' rejection by spurning them first and vowing "to keep them at a proper distance." One attachment after another seemed lost to him: to his mother, whom Baker had won; to his wife, whom sickness was carrying away; to his daughters, who lived for a while and died; to his brother, disaffected by their rivalry over the family wealth; to his uncles and aunts, who were leaning toward other nieces and nephews; and now to his friends. Quietly isolated, he found time weighing heavily. He wrote not only to account for how he spent his days but to help the days pass. His writing became infused by his sadness but also by an uplifting, if unreasoned, devotion to the task. No matter that he wrote in order to justify himself and damn his enemies; writing every day, in the same room at the same hour, was a kind of good conduct in itself, an orderly procedure like prayer that was sanctioned by tradition and recommended by reformers. Days he had trouble "getting on with my journal" were days of deep despair when he scarcely made it to night without "giving way." Yet he always resumed writing after a catastrophe, and if writing was one of his trials, it was one that gave him pleasure during years when little else did. It was the pleasure of giving order to arbitrary events, not a way of understanding why things happened, and even less a path to avoiding trouble in the future, but a means of strengthening belief in some hidden meaning behind events from which, against all appearances, some good might come.

Chaplin felt there was little he himself could do to repair his fortunes. Foreclosure had deprived him of the large slave force necessary to make big crops. He could not expect much help from his mother, and his wife had nothing to offer. Neither was he running a family farm where his sons might contribute to his prosperity by going to work as they became able. Progress in his life was reduced to filling his book. Resigned to recovering very slowly, if at all, he dutifully kept up his diary and matured with it, as beans fill a pod. There was no unfolding of talents and sympathies as he grew older, only an accumulation of incident and a narrowed field of concern. Yet nearly every day he wrote something, even if it read like the day before, so that there are stretches in his journal where all that is expressed is the habit of writing.

Exactly a month after Mary died, Chaplin inserted in his journal "a record of births, deaths & marriages in my own immediate family & in those connected to it in any way. . . ." This was serious business. "I do not *intend* to *be* or to state anything but what may be relied on by *future generations* as *strictly correct,* for it is for this purpose that *it* is recorded, that they may be informed how their ancestors went and came." He made a start on the record—forty-one lines— then crossed it out at a later date. It amounts to an inkblot in the long manuscript, but it was the first of several indications that he hoped his journal would survive him, that he was not writing for himself only. He thought the book might induce his children to think kindly of him when he was gone. Little did he imagine in the 1850s that he himself was the future reader he was writing for, or that he would become the journal's protector against the staunch indifference of his intended audience.

Models and Influences

Once Chaplin decided to keep a journal, what models did he follow to express himself and to dramatize his role? What literary influences shaped his style, molded his opinions, and suggested topics to write about? Compared to his more affluent and better-educated colleagues, he was not a widely read man. His personal library was small and he did not borrow books. But we know that he did read. He named some of his beloved horses after characters in British fiction: Becky Sharp, Tom Jones, Humphrey Clinker, Little Dorrit. He enjoyed battening down on a rainy day with a novel; he read the Bible, consulted an agricultural manual, and probably a home medical guide, too; he subscribed to the Charleston *Mercury* and to the *Southern Literary Gazette,* just before it folded; he ordered books from Samuel Hart, Charleston's leading bookseller. Twice Chaplin mentioned books he was reading, both novels—*Les Amours du Cheva- lier de Faublas,* an erotic romance from the late eighteenth century, by Louvet de Couvray, and *David Copperfield,* by Charles Dickens. In Chaplin's farewell to Mary, ". . . *she* is *gone, gone*—Oh! The golden opportunity that I have let escape me of rendering *her happy,*" we hear an echo of Copperfield's parting homage to Agnes: "Oh Agnes, Oh my soul, so may thy face be by me when I close my life indeed." Not that Chaplin learned how to express his feelings by reading Dickens; rather, he had imbibed the same conventions which Dickens so faithfully reproduced. On the other hand, Chaplin's narrative style is spare and breathless—nothing like Dickens's. He tells few whole stories at one sitting, which is unfortunate because his few tries at unified narrative are moving indeed.

The *Southern Literary Gazette* was serializing Dickens's *Bleak House* when Chaplin took out a subscription, in April, 1852. A mix of book excerpts, reviews, and editorials, the *Gazette* was anti-Catholic, anti-French, anti–women's rights, anti–working class; it embraced slavery as the universal solution to capital's grievance with labor, and not merely as a local expedient. France, once the paragon of gentility, had sunk to "a nation of revolutions, of civil commotions, of kindred strifes, and barbarous massacres. No other nation," remarked the *Gazette,* calling for unity of the civilized classes, "has so cruelly pierced its own bosom with the sword."[1] In spite of the torrent of class conflict around the world, the *Gazette* advocated industrialization and called itself a "friend of southern enterprise." It condemned the simplicities of country life glorified in such contemporary pastoral novels as William Mountford's *Thorpe: A Quiet English Country Town and Human Life Therein.* It preferred "the sound of the steam whistle" to the song of the mockingbird.[2] It applauded paper mills and textile factories, while it wanted to suppress the influence of the people who worked in them. It raised questions being asked in high political and financial circles: should the South employ Negro slaves in industry? Could it afford not to? In the *Gazette*'s vision of the future, the social order stood still while accommodating immense economic changes. Negroes would remain slaves and wives would continue to observe "the antique virtues" such as "patient devotion," "self-sacrifice," and "sublime endurance."[3]

The agricultural orations Chaplin heard before and after the political flurry of 1850 and '51 should be counted, along with the sermons he analyzed, among his literary influences. By and large they contained a point of view contrary to the *Gazette*'s. Instead of foreseeing the reduced importance of agriculture, they looked forward to larger and more profitable harvests. Agriculture was the South's natural enterprise, they argued. Plantations needed only to be made more efficient and experimental to ensure their prosperity. Profits were but one part of the rewards. Planting ennobled men by giving them the duty and the luxury to do good. Living in the country offered outlets for charity, hospitality, and friendliness that were lacking in cities and towns. The propagandists of agriculture painted a gloomy picture of factory life, comparing the miseries of wage workers to the comforts of slaves. They distrusted the political thrust of industrialism and questioned whether planters and factory owners could agree on the allocation of public resources, trade legislation, and the nature of the compact between the states and the Federal Government.

Reporting on what he had heard, Chaplin had more to say about the delivery of a speech or a sermon than about its content. If arguments varied from speaker to speaker, or from what was published in the *Gazette* to what was spoken from the podium of the Agricultural Society, he nevertheless felt at home within the framework of the debate. He did not wrestle with ideas. Classical rhetoric and talk of his "homeland" meant something to him, regardless of what he thought about steam-driven cotton gins or who should govern the western territories. In any case, to the planters of St. Helena Island, the question of the economic development of their region seemed settled. A railroad and a port might bring commerce, but traffic would be in the service of intensified agriculture. Most planters owned enough good land to employ the natural increase in their work force for many years to come. Their consuming passion, as it had been for their fathers, was to acquire as many slaves as they could.

Intellectual ferment over such issues as building up industry in the South, organizing planters into economic cooperatives, spending cotton profits at home, developing a southern literature and school curriculum to combat the cultural threat of abolitionism— all touched Chaplin lightly, like vapors from a glass of brandy. His mind was engaged in outwitting his adversaries and making ends meet. Though as opinionated as the next man, he seldom spoke up at public events. He was pleased to listen, to be seen among the listeners, and to record his thoughts in private. For six years, at least, he also recorded the minutes and handled the correspondence for the local Agricultural Society. Once he had exchanged letters with Mary, but after they married he had no personal correspondents except his creditors, to whom he sent many artful letters begging for time to pay his bills. He rattled off messages to his mother and his lawyer, and he kept a memorandum book in which he left orders for his overseer or driver and jotted down notes on pur-

chases, sales, and loans. His major literary product was the journal—a paragraph or two a day for the better part of thirteen years,
which entries he read to himself again and again over the next
three decades as if they were parts of a long letter from a friend
leading a more authentic life than his own.

The Writer's Routine

Between five and six P.M., while the hands who had finished their
tasks were at work in their gardens, Chaplin secluded himself at his
desk in one of the upstairs rooms and wrote his daily entry. If he
was separated from his journal for days at a stretch he would save
up his thoughts and write them down later, backdating the items.
During the summers he spent at St. Helenaville, he left his journal
at Tombee and would make perfunctory additions on his trips
home. His entries for the hot months reflect the slow pace of
work—though there might be a great deal to do—and the tedium
of life centered around the billiards table. Other seasons he sometimes wrote twice a day, laying out what he hoped to get done and
following up with the results. "John is to be sold today in Beaufort
at public sale," he put down on the morning of February 9, 1846.
"John was bought by J.J.T. Pope for $300," he reported in the eve-
ning.

Chaplin took a special interest in John's fate. He felt sorry for
the man, who, if sold off the Island, would be parted from everything he held dear. Chaplin may also have felt responsible for his
distress. Captain Daniel T. Jenkins had given John "a ticket to go
& look for a master," indicating that John was one of Mrs. Baker's
slaves whom the court had ordered sold to pay a debt. The debt
may have been Chaplin's, one that his mother had countersigned.
A casualty of debt—to the slave, it did not matter whose—John
could not find anyone "that would or could buy him" at private
sale. Subsequently, Pope bought him cheap at auction, intending
to use him "for a house servant or a driver, neither of which he is
capable of being," remarked Chaplin, who knew John very well
and would have bought him himself if he had had the money.
After the sale, Dr. Jenkins offered to buy John from Pope for $350,
but Pope turned him down. John was disappointed. While the results of the sale meant he would stay on St. Helena, John did "not
at all wish to belong to Pope." So Chaplin offered to hire John and
John went to "ask Pope to hire him to me."

A modern reader winces at the pathos of the situation—the slave desperately trying to sell himself, his preference for one master over another and his poor means of influencing a sale, his blameless condition and the white man's sterile sympathy. Reading over the page in 1876, Chaplin had a different reaction. He noted that Dr. Jenkins's offer to buy John "was all sham . . . & only offered because he knew Pope would not sell." Jenkins had done "all he could to keep Uncle Ben from lending me the money to buy him." As usual, Chaplin viewed the slave's dilemma through the lens of his own preoccupations. He saw only that something was happening to *him*. At least four times over the years he reported a slave hunting for someone to buy him, but the diarist was unwilling or unable to make a general statement.

Chaplin was unhappy with some of the things he wrote, and at a later date he scratched out or cut out several entries. Two of the crossed-out passages can be deciphered—Chaplin's account of Mary's snuff addiction, and his abortive attempt to compose a genealogy. The others are unreadable. Much more frustrating for the reader are topics he glossed over or omitted altogether. Since he was not writing for outsiders, he had no reason to describe what he took for granted, such as the view from his bedroom window or the interior of a Negro cabin. That readers in the next century might want to know at what point his wife weaned her babies or how his slaves named their children was no concern of his.

Nearly every entry begins with a report on the weather. Nothing may seem more tedious than to read about yesterday's drizzle, or to know that on June 17, 1851, it rained all day. To Chaplin, the information was enormously important. In a situation where the weather had a critical impact on daily life, and scientific forecasts did not exist, his carefully recorded observations provided his most reliable basis for making predictions. As a farmer, he worried about sufficient rain for his crops, about frosts, winds, sandstorms, hurricanes. The intensity of rain determined if his hands would work "out of doors" that day. A darkening sky in December could postpone shipping the cotton to market, at the risk of missing out on the most recently quoted prices. Falling temperatures in early spring might mean a delay in planting and a backlog of work later on.

Sometimes the face of the sky was symbolic of how Chaplin was feeling; other times he saw in "auspicious" sunsets and thickening clouds the signs of God's attitude toward him. He felt that the weather discriminated against him, and that he lived on an unlucky part of St. Helena. "It is a singular fact," he observed, with restrained indignation, that if it rained on his end of the Island, "that is, the southwest end," it always rained "at the other or northeast end." But it might rain there, "even as far down as the Episcopal Church & farther & we have not a drop here. Certainly there is a much better chance of making a crop there than here," he concluded, "for they get the rain, when we see the cloud, expect it, and are disappointed."

The rains that he longed for, and the spring tides, which came on schedule, brought out great droves of mosquitoes and polluted his wells. In time of drought, his wells dried up, his crops baked, and his livestock died. The cold of winter was less extreme than the heat of summer and did not last as long. Chaplin, who had a good supply of underwear and a gentleman's outer coat, suffered more in winter from the effect of the cold on his slaves' productivity than from physical discomfort.

Chaplin tried to spot trends in the weather from one year to the next, and to apply the information to his agricultural practice. He learned, for example, that he could plant sugar cane a month earlier than was commonly done, but that corn benefited from later planting. He did not measure the rainfall and he had no barometer. But after considerable yearning, he went to Beaufort on August 25, 1856, and bought a thermometer—as well as an umbrella and a whip—and began taking temperature readings several times a day. His excitement over being able to measure the degree of warmth was out of proportion to its practical significance, but it was not a trifling activity. At last he could say something about the weather with scientific certainty. Though isolated from other observers, he was caught up in the current of thought that would lead in the 1870s to the establishment of the first permanent meteorological stations in South Carolina and to a system of interpreting climatic observations made simultaneously at different points in the country.

First Ending
The major breaks in Chaplin's journal correspond to disruptions in his life, some of them calamitous. Besides the summers of 1846 and

1854, when he left the book at home while he stewed at St. Helenaville, sickness in his family and financial reverses distracted him from writing for periods totaling ten months. He stopped writing in July, 1847; wrote a single despondent entry in October, announcing the death of "the fairest and loveliest of my flock," his daughter Isabella; and was silent until the next April, having been "sold out of land and Negroes, furniture, stock, possessions & everything I was worth in the world," in the interim. Following the hurricane of September, 1854, it was four months before he wrote again. From January, 1855, through his thirty-sixth birthday, in April, 1858, he kept up his journal steadfastly, though his style, which had never been expansive, grew more concise. As he approached the six hundredth and final page of the bound volume—he misnumbered the pages, counting a hundred more than there actually were—he announced, "This is about to be the end of my journal. Let me then conclude"—later he wrote in the word "dedicate"—"thus, to my children Ernest A. Chaplin, Virginia S. Chaplin, Daniel J. Chaplin, & Eugene L. Chaplin, to you all."

Why did Chaplin stop writing? If keeping a journal gave him a sanctuary and a friend, what had he gained to take its place? He did not have to stop writing when he came to the end of the book; he could easily have bought a second volume. But he did not. The various purposes for which he had undertaken and kept up the journal were fulfilled. No one, not even he, would want it longer than it is. He had wondered on several occasions why he kept it at all, calling it nonsense; but this was just a rhetorical concession to its deficiencies that was swallowed up in his overwhelming devotion to it. By the spring of 1858, he felt he had accomplished his self-imposed tasks. He had written a comprehensive record for his children, who were beginning to leave his fold. He had made peace with his neighbors and friends. He enjoyed a growing intimacy with Captain Daniel T. Jenkins, and Ned Capers was steadier than ever. Dr. Jenkins was socializing with the rich families of Beaufort and was only a small irritant to him now. Chaplin's burdens felt lighter and events seemed altogether less haphazard as he advanced into the second half of his life. He had cut back on his appetites, so his debts were smaller and his property was out of jeopardy. Cotton had become fantastically profitable again. He was planting large acres with a labor force that was healthy, young, and increasing. Progress no longer meant filling a book. Objective reality had changed and he was in a position to take advantage of it.

When he was ready to hand down his journal, all of his children were dead "but one," and *he* did not want it. Whether Daniel flat out refused the book or just took it without thanking his father, or whether it was silently understood that he did not care to have it, is unimportant. What matters is that Chaplin felt rejected by the only person obliged by blood to shelter him in his old age. Ever since Dan was a baby, scaring his parents with hysterical fits, he had made the cost of loving him high. Now he was his father's last hope, and he disappointed him once more. He was just like all the others who had paid back Chaplin's kindnesses with unkindness. But Daniel was his own seed. In no other person had Chaplin seen so much of himself as in Daniel. It was cruel, felt Chaplin, to punish a father who through no fault of his own was unable to keep the promises of high birth.

Second Thoughts: Chaplin's Use of Irony
As he closed his journal in the spring of 1858, Chaplin had no reason to suppose that the way of life it chronicled would not continue for another fifty years. All economic indicators pointed to an intensification of Sea Island cotton culture. Cotton prices were climbing to their highest levels in thirty-five years. Land values were soaring, and while there was land for lease on St. Helena, there was none for sale. Slave property was keeping pace with the new valuations and planters could make back their investment in slaves two or three years sooner than they could a decade before. St. Helenaville had become a port of call for coastwise schooners and steamers, and a railroad was coming to Port Royal.

Reading over his journal in 1866, when the familiar and richly promising world had only just vanished; in 1876 and '77 when nothing had yet risen from the ruins; and in 1884 and '85, when he was failing physically and locked in battle against a coldhearted bureaucracy for the return of some of his land, Chaplin's attitude was ironical. What had happened to him and his people was "unjust, unprecedented, unbelievable."[4] Their fall was made especially conspicuous by the radiant outlook of the late '50s, and by the thoroughness of their defeat. Chaplin had no house of his own after the War, no horse or carriage, and only infrequently a cow. Lands that had belonged to his mother and his first wife fell into his hands and out again—lands which once had produced great crops of fiber and food and now lay under a tangle of weeds for want of capital, labor, and organization. He, who had been a superior producer of corn, was "not worth shucks, much less 50 lbs corn," in 1876. Dr. Jenkins was making enough to feed himself by selling whiskey. Old Ned Capers, once the dashing young suitor of St. Helena, was living "with a colored woman, the only wife he'll ever know." Ned's sister Ann, who had married into the Minotts, a wealthy Combahee River family that was allied with the Chaplins, turned up in a room in the old cotton house at Tombee. She had been a friend of Isabella Baker when they both had fortunes. Chaplin found her "very bad off indeed, quite thin," in 1877, an observation he penciled in under an account of the hearty Christmas dinner his mother had served them all in 1853.

The War scattered Chaplin's friends and relatives like chaff in the wind. Some landed close to where they had started from; others landed far away; still others were threshed out entirely. Survivors had to concentrate on staying alive. With their wealth and institutions destroyed, and their needs so great, they had not means to help any but their closest connections. Chaplin could not see how the war had benefited anyone. He believed it meant catastrophe for black people as well as white. Yes, the War gave blacks freedom, but it removed them from the protective care that had given them life. Take the case of "Old Sam" and Sam's wife. Sam died the day after Christmas, 1850, following a long illness. "There was an instance out of many," argued Chaplin, many years later, "—an old man had to be fed, clothed & a woman did nothing else than attend to him for 3 years before he died & he wanted for nothing." How did Sam's wife die, Chaplin went on, since she was "made free"? "Why she died of smallpox, in the most wretched manner, not even her children would go near her." Under slavery, as Chaplin recalled it, a person died contentedly and in the presence of loved ones; while under freedom, death was miserable and lonely.

Already conversant with death and a massive loss of property, Chaplin had begun cultivating a kind of gallows humor long before 1861; afterward, it cushioned the impact of seeing his friends and himself reduced to rubble. His laugh was angry, ambivalent, with a touch of both triumph and empathy, as if, having once fallen from great heights himself, he were watching a man rapt in thought about to step off a cliff. Not just one person met this fate, or a few, but a whole class of people who thought they were heading into green pastures. Where had the "splendid" secession speech from Colonel DeTreville led? To "a devil of an end," Chaplin noted, to death, poverty, and heartache.

Proud old Edgar Fripp died in 1860, yet his dignity still suffered in the War. Fripp, who had triggered many explosions by trying to outspend and outswagger his colleagues at the Agricultural Society and at church, imported a stonecutter from Charleston in 1852 to built him a vault in the graveyard. "Said vault was a fine affair," Chaplin recalled, in 1876, "& did not have to wait very long for its occupants, Edgar & wife. The Yankees broke it open during the war, hoping for treasure. It is somewhat out of order now."

The moral of the story is that ostentation brings misfortune, a moral that had made sense in Edgar's day but was ridiculous in the postwar years when a man would be well off when he died to have even a humble headstone. Everything was "somewhat out of order" in 1876, and Edgar's large, vandalized tomb had become a symbol of the universal disarray. Chaplin's intricate joke draws on everything we know about Fripp—his self-love, gravity, and pathos. What gives it power and distinguishes it from a young man's humor is its knifelike clarity of perception, honed on the experiences of war. Edgar Fripp, as everyone knew, would have liked to take his wealth with him, like the Pharaohs, and he did take part of it by building such a fancy resting place. There was contentious Fripp, peacefully removed from the hostilities, when the Yankees, that gang of grave robbers dressed as soldiers, disturbed his tomb. Lucky for him that his money was not buried with him, or the enemy would have gotten it. In any case, they took all his worldly estate, as they stole even the organ he had given to the church in 1846.

PART II

11. War

The Imminent Invasion

On Sunday, November 4, 1861, morning service at St. Helena Island's chapel of ease was interrupted by a courier bearing a dispatch for W.O.P. Fripp, captain of the St. Helena Mounted Volunteer Riflemen. The paper was handed to the pastor, who read it from the pulpit. It announced that a great Yankee armada out of Hampton Roads, Virginia, had steamed past Charleston, bound for Port Royal. The news was received "without apprehension or any real appreciation of its significance."[1] Captain Fripp came to the front and requested that members of the St. Helena company "appear properly armed and accoutered at Dr. Jenkins' house at Seaside, prepared to meet the dastardly foe." The Doctor—Private William Jenkins—was ordered "to have a good and substantial dinner provided for the Company." Lieutenants Thomas G. White, Alviro Fripp, and Young Gabe Capers, "who live at conveniently different sections of the island," were told "to impress all boats, flats, and means of transportation, and congregate them at Dr. Jenkins' place on Station Creek," in case it became necessary to abandon St. Helena.[2] The congregation was eager to provide an armed response, and the thought of making ready to flee aroused "indignation." Fripp apologized that he was merely conveying orders. Still, leaving was unthinkable. There was so much to be done, and prospects for prosperity were exceedingly bright. No man in the prime of life had ever known cotton prices so high. If it hadn't been Sunday, the hands would have been in the fields picking the fast-opening bolls, as fine a crop as anyone could remember. The potatoes were safe in the ground until frost, yet growing conditions had been so favorable that if digging did not commence at once the whole crop would never be harvested. Worshipers left the chapel intending to convene there next Sunday. Subsequent events, however, would make this their last service in the ancestral church.

A Besieged Minority

Having for a very long time felt separate and different from their countrymen, St. Helena planters had instinctively understood what outspoken secessionists meant by the phrase a "besieged minority." They sympathized generally with the campaign to spread slavery to the western territories, although they themselves were not about to go; neither were the new lands suitable for long-staple cotton, the only money crop they knew. In fact, the climate, soil, and economies of the territories were not conducive to slavery at all. Yet, St. Helena planters wanted parity for southern interests in populating and governing the new parts of the country. Their desire to see slavery established in the West was as chauvinistic as the North's resolve to keep all Negroes, slave and free, out of the territories. The question of settlement boiled down to what form racial subordination should take, slavery or exclusion. The Sea Islanders were for slavery, and for parity with the North.*

Because they were large consumers, St. Helena planters were sensitive to the South's commercial and cultural dependence on the North. They had vowed in 1850 to stop buying from northerners, but they could not resist modernizing their homes with the latest gadgets, comforts, and luxuries available only through northern outlets. As late as 1861, J.D.B. DeBow was urging his readers to boycott the North and shun, if not expel, northern teachers and peddlers, while his magazine was running columns of advertisements for books, tools, clothing, paper goods, and delicacies from Philadelphia, Boston, and New York. The reality was that the South did not manufacture or import directly enough of the right

---

*Not all white southerners favored spreading slavery and American sovereignty to the West. Edmund Ruffin, the popular agricultural writer from Virginia, represented the antiexpansion point of view. He regarded the large Catholic population of the territories targeted for expansion as dangerous and unassimilable. Who would speak for a larger, more diverse South? he asked. It was not self-evident to him that cotton planters on the Texas frontier were the natural political allies of the tidewater elites. Moreover, since the climate and topography of much of the West were not hospitable to slavery, "the territorial question could be viewed as an abstraction—a contest over 'an imaginary Negro in an impossible place' . . ." (David M. Potter, The South and the Sectional Conflict [Baton Rouge, La., 1968], 98.)

things to satisfy the buying power and tastes of its upper class. From a radical perspective, however, the campaign against buying from the North was successful. It heightened local allegiances at the expense of allegiance to the United States. Taking a step, even a rhetorical one, toward self-sufficiency transformed the guilt of dependence into aggression. While their political representatives continued to press for concessions from the Federal Government, the Sea Islanders had become southern nationalists. Their loyalties were to home, state, and the South as a nation, not as a section of some other nation. For all its explosiveness and posturing, party politics lagged behind the people. In their churches, schools, Agricultural Society, and militia, the white people of St. Helena were creating an institutional reality to embody their subjective allegiances.

Almost a year to the day before the war alarm was sounded, and just one month before South Carolina seceded, St. Helena planters hosted a banquet at their muster house to honor their old friend DeBow.[3] An ardent secessionist and proslavery man who had used his magazine as a platform for the most up-to-date and obscene racial theories, DeBow had come home to the lowcountry to savor the political climate and to do his part, in his scholarly manner, to push his comrades over the brink. Lincoln had just been elected President, giving South Carolina the provocation it was seeking to leave the Union; DeBow's visit gave the St. Helena crowd an occasion to endorse secession before the event, thus taking a place in the forefront of history. On stage with DeBow, at the head table, sat a distinguished group of politicians and planters including Joseph D. Pope, the inveterate vote-getter; William DeTreville, a former schoolmaster and uncompromising southern nationalist, son of Richard DeTreville; Dr. William Jenkins, Alviro Fripp, Young Gabe Capers, William Chisolm, and Thomas B. Chaplin—the last five men composing the Committee on Arrangements.

Alviro Fripp offered several resolutions, all heartily adopted, to the effect that the citizens of St. Helena Parish regarded the state's pending resolution to secede "as a second Declaration of Independence, equal in significance and as pregnant in results as that adopted by our fathers in 1776."[4] Though the original Declaration had been followed by a large number of slave manumissions and a momentary expansion of black liberty, its meaning to white southerners had come to lie elsewhere. Independence meant the power to regulate the black population without interference from outsiders. Annual recitations of the Declaration had drilled home the point that independence was a right of a "people"—not of mere dissidents or political minorities, but of persons united by common institutions and devotions—"to dissolve the political bonds" which connected them to another people. Fripp's analogy implied that the Union had fractured into two nationalities with a common British inheritance modified by different immigrant groups, different forms of agriculture and industry, different systems of labor.[5]

Following "sustained" applause, Dr. Jenkins introduced DeBow, who spoke for more than two hours, "enchanting" his audience with "facts illustrative of our wrongs" and "copious statistics exhibiting our wealth and resources, and our ability to make our enemies feel our power." After DeBow, but still in the first half of the program, came Joseph D. Pope. Known for his "Court House" style, refined over a relentless political career, Pope "excelled himself" by incorporating "the stirring appeals and burning eloquence" of the genuine orator. In ability to excite an audience, "he equalled anything we have ever heard," remarked a satisfied listener. When Pope finished, the "company sat down to a sumptuous dinner," the serving table "literally groan[ing] under the weight of the savory dishes." After relieving the table's suffering, the crowd heard William DeTreville implore South Carolina to take "immediate action." Appealing to "the honor of the State in the present crisis," he was "exceedingly happy in his language," and was received "with the most enthusiastic applause."[6]

More "brief but happy addresses" followed, including one by Captain John Fripp's son-in-law, William Chisolm, and one by Thomas G. White. Dr. John A. P. Scott, Chaplin's first cousin and one of the wealthiest men in the Parish, closed the meeting by extending the company's thanks to the Honorable John F. Townsend, of St. John's Parish, Colleton District, a frequent visitor to St. Helena and author of "The South Alone Should Govern the South," which, in Scott's words, "has done more good in the cause of the South than any other publication that has ever appeared."[7]

The Negro Threat

The full title of Townsend's work was "The South Alone Should Govern the South and African Slavery Should Be Controlled by

Those Only Who Are Friendly to It." A dense, sixty-three-page po-
lemic with four appendixes, it was the first of four tracts published
by a Charleston secessionist group known as The 1860 Association.
Townsend also wrote the fourth tract in the series, entitled "The
Doom of Slavery in the Union: Its Safety Out of It." Both tracts
combined emotional calls for "manly RESISTANCE" with low-
pitched, well-documented arguments proving that the South's vital
interests were jeopardized by staying in the Union. Motivated by
jealousy over the South's wealth, the North had broken the rules
which the Founding Fathers had laid down. There was no turning
back; the political deck was stacked irrevocably against the South.
"Like practical and sensible men, who have to deal with a great
Reality," argued Townsend, "let us realize to ourselves . . . that the
Union is lost; that its spirit has departed from it." Townsend was a
latecomer to the southern cause. He had opposed nullification in
1832 and separate state action in 1851. Like many a convert, he
proselytized with more vigor and less tolerance than a born be-
liever. In "The South Alone Should Govern the South," he recounted the ways that the South had been wronged, starting with
the dismal history of protective tariffs.[8] He accused the North of
inciting slaves to rebel, stealing slaves and refusing to return fugitives, denying southern rights in the territories, invading the South
and butchering its citizens, rejecting the right of a state to secede,
and governing the country through "irresponsible majorities." "In
the name of a God of Justice," he exclaimed, "what more or greater
wrongs are wanting, to Justify a Revolution."

His appendixes were more stimulating than his text. One described the horrors which followed emancipation in Santo Domingo and the British West Indies, and another reported a Republican party plan to unleash the same havoc on the South. A third
described in detail John Brown's plot for a South-wide slave rebellion. Another appendix itemized and condemned the North's economic mastery of the South. Townsend was chiefly concerned,
however, with the problem of race. Slavery was the South's particular form of Negro subordination. Since the North was determined
to end slavery throughout the country, and the North dominated
national policy, it was only a matter of time until the Negro would
be free. The essential threat of the Republican party, indeed, of a
republican form of government in which slaveholders were in a minority, was that it would take away slavery but leave the blacks.[9]

What would this mean for the South? "The end of all negro labor," prophesied Townsend, "a jubilee of idleness, and a reign of sloth; until famine shall drive them to robbery or scourge them with pestilence: nine thousand millions of property destroyed . . . in return for negro equality conferred upon the black race: a war of races, the subjugation of one to the other, certain poverty to the whites; degradation, want, expatriation."*

Who believed this propaganda? Did the planters as a group subscribe to beliefs which as individuals they would have dismissed as rubbish? Were their critical faculties overwhelmed by the sensation of power? Or were they simply "buckling on their armor"[10] and steeling themselves to fight a battle they could no longer put off? Did Dr. Scott believe that the people who over the past generation had produced more than a thousand bales of cotton for him and doubled his worldly estate, would not work if they were free, and that only slavery stood between the white race and the plunge of civilization? Or was he afraid he would have to scale down his standard of living?

By praising Townsend's work at the end of a festive rally, Dr. Scott was reminding his audience of the one issue which begat all others. Negroes, as field workers and servants, were the source of everything good and tasty and fine. Allowed to follow their own impulses, however, or governed by people who did not "understand" them, they were enemies of the planters' happiness. If they did not destroy with their own hands the wealth they had built, they were, by racist lights, cultural enemies, and would destroy it through passivity and parasitism.† Normally, Negroes were "harmless, peaceful, and contented," but like other creatures of meager intelligence, they were highly suggestible. If the Yankees incited them, there was no telling what they would do. "The old cooks, maumas, house servants and negro eavesdroppers" knew that a "great measure" was afoot. "Our negroes are being enlisted

---

*As figurative speech, Townsend's imagery matched in malevolence the imagery of abolitionist propaganda, or at least of abolitionist intentions as they were represented to the South. For example, Townsend quoted Charles Sumner, the radical Republican Senator from Massachusetts, as gloating that the free states carved out of the territories would form a "belt of fire" around the old slave states, and that slavery would die, in Sumner's words, as "a poisoned rat dies, of rage in its hole."

†Proslavery writing turned deeply racist in the 1840s. Black inferiority—not merely a doctrine of backwardness or unattainment, but a conviction of ineradicable differences—became a staple of southern political philosophy. It was rampant, too, in northern and European intellectual circles, where it existed side by side with a sentiment for abolition.

in politics," charged the old Yankee-hater Lawrence M. Keitt, during the presidential campaign of 1860. "I confess, this feature alarms me, more even, than everything else in the past."[11]

The Nonslaveholding Majority

On the eve of secession, the great majority of white people in South Carolina did not own any slaves. Slaveholding was a minority interest, and the proportion of slaveholders to the total number of whites in the state was declining. Lowcountry planters, and all planters who owned more than twenty slaves, were a minority of a minority. Secession, for them, was a program for survival. But they had to convince the nonslaveholding majority that leaving the Union was in the interest of all white people. This was not easy to do. White farmers in the midlands and piedmont sections of the state resented the aristocrats' wealth and pretensions. White farmers knew that slavery monopolized the most fertile soils. Matthew C. Butler, who won fame as a Confederate cavalry commander, told a congressional committee five years after the War that "most of South Carolina did not believe in slavery and great estates, but looked forward to the day when substantial white farmers would people the land, from the mountains to the sea."[12] Like northerners who dreamed of keeping the western territories white, the poor white farmers of South Carolina imagined a state from which the blacks, along with the plantations, would disappear. Their vision was neutralized, however, by propaganda about dangers from the North, and by pressure to prove their loyalties to powers closest to home. They could not be forced to like slavery, but they agreed with planters on the need for racial safety. They battled planters along solid class lines in the state legislature over such issues as judicial and electoral reform, but they closed ranks in blaming the northern middle classes for the economic troubles of the state.

White farmers' support for secession could never be taken for granted. It was kept up by the continuing political excitement, which extremists knew must not be allowed to wane. The radicals were able to make a flamboyant case at the level of state politics, where their consistent promoters, the parish planters, were overrepresented. "When you find that the property in a community consists of large estates and in the hands of a few persons," explained a lowcountry representative, justifying the state's undemocratic political system, "it becomes necessary for the security of that property ... that it should be largely represented."[13] All six South Carolina governors during the 1850s owned more than one hundred slaves, and major offices were "crowded with members of the master class" who used the power of their positions to advance the interests of property, specifically slave property. Politics, to them, meant class politics, and they expected that if men of a different class held power, those men would work in behalf of different interests. They feared what might happen if the moment to leave the Union were lost. Every planter on the seaboard, whether he called himself a secessionist or a unionist, knew that his political privilege was threatened by the growth of the nonslaveholding class. Planters did not anticipate a violent revolt, but they did foresee a new political equation that would be much less favorable to them than the old one. Just as Lawrence Keitt shuddered over the political awakening of the blacks, so planters of more moderate views grew alarmed at the slumbering power of the state's free white majority.

Secession

Each slave state had its own "storm center" of secession.[14] In South Carolina, the movement was traditionally strongest in the low-country, while pro-Union sentiment pervaded the upcountry. At least seven other slave states were similarly split. Secession was clearly a strategy to save property, yet the largest property owners were not in all cases its leaders. In states to the west, militant expansionists were in the forefront. In Virginia and the border states, planters did not call disunion by name, but spoke euphemistically about forming a southern federation and reworking the South's compact with the Union. After the secessionists' defeat in 1852, no serious candidate for public office anywhere in the South openly called for single-state secession. In South Carolina, contenders for power inclined toward one of two general opinions: first, that the antislavery party, the Republican party, was destined to rule the country, and that the South should prepare to resist. Second, that antislavery would burn itself out, and that safety for the South lay in an alliance between southern and northern Democrats in a viable national party. Year by year the first group grew stronger until, by 1859, it made up a majority in the state legislature.[15] Before then, successful candidates for statewide offices drew support from both camps. Of the state's six congressional districts, no more than two at any time sent so-called fire-eaters to Washington. By the fall of 1860, after the national political conventions nominated candidates for President, the pro-Union men realized that antislavery would rule, and except for a few undying unionists, they came over to secession. Even then, secession did not mean the same thing to everyone. Some, like Richard DeTreville and Joseph D. Pope, believed that leaving the Union would put an end to the tensions and controversy they had grown up with.* Others, like William Elliott and C. G. Memminger, resorted to secession to *save* the Union, hoping to force Lincoln's party "to come to terms." Counting people who favored secession does not accurately measure the breadth or intensity of anti-Union feeling; rather, it shows how widespread was the conclusion, often reluctantly reached, that the antislavery powers were about to move against the South.[16]

Lincoln hoped secession would pass. As late as July 4, 1861, less than three weeks before "First Bull Run," he found "reason to believe that the Union men are in a majority in many, if not in every one, of the so-called seceded states."[17] Leave the rebels alone, advised Horace Greeley's *New York Tribune,* and they would "wear out" their "military ardor" in "fruitless drilling and marches" and tax themselves out of favor. Lincoln waited. But the strategy failed because it was based on the delusion that secession was intended as political blackmail, and not as an earnest rejection of the Union.[18] Neither side could assimilate the truth about the other. The North believed that southern dirt farmers would not fight for the slaveholders. The South had been taught that "the rank and file of the

---

*Chaplin noted that the men who clamored loudest for secession insisted the revolution would be peaceful. R. B. Rhett promised fifty years of peace and prosperity. While the North and South were frantically arming, DeBow coolly maintained there would be no war, because the South's trading partners—especially England and France—would not allow it. Lawrence Keitt quipped that a small silk handkerchief was all one would need to mop up the blood that would be spilled in a war over secession. South Carolina poet Henry Timrod believed secession would be an instant cure for the South's insecurities:

> The snows of southern summers! Let the earth
> Rejoice! beneath those fleeces soft and warm
> Our happy land shall sleep
> In a repose as deep
> As if we lay entrenched behind
> Whole leagues of Russian ice and Arctic storm!

(From "Ethnogenesis," written during the meeting of the first Southern Congress, at Montgomery, Alabama, in February, 1861; quoted in Olsberg, 184.)

North" were foreign born, "or a mixture of foreign blood, would not remain loyal to the Union ... and would not fight." When Lincoln called for troops, the southern press jeered: "Who will he get to fight and how will he pay them?"—unconsciously echoing what northerners were saying about the secessionists. Mutual bitterness, the feeling that all the stakes were on the table, and the impetus of aggressive military preparations made it difficult for the two sides to retreat from a collision course. The North was determined to stop appeasing the disunionists; the South had resolved to stop asking the abolitionists for concessions. But the North would not let the "seceders" go, as some abolitionists wished, because it viewed a breakup of the Union as fatal to American civil institutions and personal liberties, as well as a national disgrace.

Preparing to Fight

On January 21, 1861, a month after South Carolina declared its independence, "the entire fighting population of St. Helena Island, numbering thirty-two," met at the Agricultural Society lodge to ratify secession and reorganize their military company.[19] After eating another big meal, and pledging allegiance to the Confederate States of America, they elected officers and, in keeping with club tradition, divided the company into messes, rivaling one another for the best cooks. Each man was required to "provide himself with a horse, sabre, pair of Colt's revolvers, Maynard rifle,* trappings and uniform." Rules were devised to govern the use of servants. A soldier could bring any number of blacks with him to the front, but only one in battle "to carry extra weapons and reload them when discharged." Whites only were to shoot: "under no circumstances was a Negro to fire a shot. Obnoxious as the Yankees were, they were to be fought as gentlemen by gentlemen," decreed the Riflemen,[20] in the sporting spirit, as if the imminent War would follow the kind of rules which regulated target shooting and horse racing.

Looking ahead with minimal realism, planters offered to contribute the labor of their slaves for building earthworks at the approaches to harbors and railroads, if the state would supply the cannon. Small fortifications were built at Beaufort, Pocotaligo, and Coosawhatchie; embankments were thrown up on several islands; and two large forts were constructed at the entrance to Port Royal Harbor—Fort Beauregard, at Bay Point, an old summer

---

*A short, light breech-loading percussion rifle favored by the cavalry.

campground on the tip of Eddings Island, and Fort Walker on Hilton Head. Artillery was supplied, but of such small caliber and inferior quality that ships could move between the two forts yet stay out of range of both.

These bulwarks, whose flimsiness ought to have been cause for despair, actually inspired confidence. In the minds of the defenders, the justice and invincibility of their cause would prevail, whereas in fact the battle would be decided by superior manpower and gunpower. Ignorant of the destructive capacity of steam-driven warships fitted with rifled cannon, the St. Helena Volunteers "practiced tilting at rings, and gaily prepared for the coming conflict, to which they eagerly looked forward as did knights of old to the tournaments where they are to win their spurs."[21] Their optimism was fed by several streams: by a grandiose idea of their historical destiny, by early Confederate successes and the apparent demoralization of the North, and by promises of military assistance from their leaders.

The white women of the Parish also were deeply involved in the war effort. To the reorganized militia, they contributed a banner "of heavy blue silk," with a palmetto tree and crescent on one side, and on the other a single star, signifying state sovereignty, and the motto *"Vive Libertas in Patria,"* or *"Ubi Libertas Ibi Patria,"* as it was variously recalled.[22]* In August, at the urging of Edmund Rhett, R.B.'s brother, they formed a Soldiers' Relief Organization. Mrs. William Morcock, keeper of a boardinghouse in Beaufort and wife of a ferryman, was elected president. The women set to making uniforms but were hampered by a shortage of cloth. A Union blockade of the coast made raw cotton plentiful at home but finished goods scarce. So they used bed ticking to make pants, "all blue, except some which looked like peppermint candy and were reserved for noncommissioned officers."[23] Parlors in prominent homes were converted to "manufactories" which literally hummed with industry. "Fancy work and delicate stitches were things of the past, giving place to sewing machines and knitting needles."[24]

After First Bull Run, which campaign demonstrated that victories in this war would cost as many lives as defeats,† C. G. Mem-

*"Long Live Liberty in the Homeland," or "Where Liberty Is, There Is the Homeland."
†The war cost the life of one soldier, Rebel or Yankee, for every six slaves freed and for every ten white southerners saved for the Union. (Potter, 261.) The money spent to field the two armies would have purchased the liberty of the four million slaves five times over.

minger, architect of Isabella Baker's marriage contract and first Secretary of the Treasury of the Confederate States, wrote to Mrs. Joseph D. Pope, "describing the sufferings and dire needs of our sick and wounded."[25] Mrs. Pope organized a Hospital Committee to gather "lint, bandages, sheets, pillows, towels, and blankets," and arrange shipment to Virginia. Turning its attention nearer home, the committee set up a hospital for troops stationed at Bay Point and Hilton Head, and helped to outfit the St. Helena Riflemen.

When the enemy was reported but forty miles away and steaming for Port Royal, the white men and women of St. Helena Parish renewed their vow to meet force with force. The ensuing battle must be assessed, therefore, not only as the result of tactical error or miscalculation, but also as the fruit of the Sea Islanders' deep desires. They had campaigned long and hard for secession. They had disdained competing and bargaining with the North, convinced that it was futile to seek a better deal for the South because the North was irredeemably wicked. With patriotic fervor, they had upgraded their militia and mobilized other institutions. They were ready to strike a blow for their faith and prove their southern nationality. Unfortunately, the War came sooner than anyone had predicted, and instead of testing them on some faraway field such as the Valley of Virginia, it turned their beloved islands into a battleground.

The Yankee Enemy
Port Royal had been targeted early in the War, along with Bulls Bay, a spacious but comparatively shallow inlet above Charleston, and Fernandina, Florida, at the mouth of St. Marys River, on the Georgia line. The Federal fleet would have sailed in September, but after the fiasco at Bull Run, Lincoln ordered the support troops to Washington. On August 29, a small Federal force captured Forts Hatteras and Clark, at the entrance to Pamlico Sound, North Carolina, giving the Union its first naval victory, indeed its "first victory of any kind."[26] The Navy was eager to press its advantage before the Confederacy could mount a challenge at sea.

Finally, at the end of October, the largest fleet ever assembled to date under the American flag weighed anchor. The sailors and soldiers did not know their destination. In fact, their enemies learned before they did, thanks to spies in high places. The choice of Port Royal, however, surprised no one.* "Port Royal alone admits the large ships," wrote Admiral Samuel F. Du Pont, president of the Navy's War Planning Board and commander of the fleet. Port Royal would give the Union "such a naval position on the sea coast as our Army is holding across the Potomac."[27] Located halfway between Charleston and Savannah, within easy inland passage of both, the harbor would make an ideal coal depot for supplying coastal blockaders. Port Royal could be taken easily from the sea and held from the sea. It lay near a railroad that could bind the region to "the 'backbone of the Union,' extending from the Ohio to the falls of the Rivers in the Carolinas and Georgia."[28] It was as near to Havana as was the promising Gulf Coast harbor at Pensacola, Florida, and was ideally situated to command the Caribbean. Furthermore, the agricultural produce within range of the gunboats might be used for the benefit of the Union. Treasury Department agents greedily eyed the exceptional cotton crop of 1861, most of which was still in the fields. Cotton prices were "feverish," and Liverpool was showing "the wildest excitement" over rumors of shipments.[29]

The Federal fleet consisted of seventy-seven vessels, including seventeen warships and four small gunboats, thirty-one transports and supply ships, and twenty-five coal-laden schooners. The transports were bringing more than twelve thousand soldiers from Maine, New Hampshire, Rhode Island, New York, Pennsylvania, and Michigan, and a labor battalion of some one thousand Negro field hands and dock hands, former slaves recruited at Fortress Monroe, Virginia. On the supply ships were fifteen hundred horses, field ambulances and medical supplies, food and fresh water, powder and shot. "Gigantic preparations" and "enormous expenditures," marveled a Confederate defender, "the outfit of nothing less than an immense armada to rout a handful of men from their sand holes in the beach."[30]

The Battle of Port Royal

Late Sunday afternoon, the fourth of November, the Sea Islanders caught their first glimpses of the fleet. A Union survey ship crossed

---

*With unintended foresight, Beaufort's George P. Elliott had asserted in *DeBow's Review* ([September, 1856], 411): "As if preserved by Providence for some great purpose, this noble bay has been lost sight of almost entirely, and is now open to those who will go and possess it. . . ."

the bar at Port Royal to sound the channel and replace navigation markers removed by the Confederates. The ship was fired upon without effect by the Confederate naval guard—a paddle-wheel steamboat and three converted tugs, under the command of Josiah Tattnall, a veteran of forty years in the American Navy. Behind Tattnall, emerging from the mouth of Skull Creek at the north side of Hilton Head Island, sailed several pleasure boats from Savannah loaded with "bourbon boosted picnickers" who had come to witness the fireworks.[31]

Monday morning, the fifth, four Union warships "engaged and dispersed" Tattnall's "mosquito fleet" in Port Royal Sound, and fired a few testing rounds at Fort Walker and Fort Beauregard. Du Pont wanted to attack Fort Walker immediately, at close range, but the flagship *Wabash* grounded on a shoal and by the time the tide rose to free it, the better part of the day had passed, and Du Pont withdrew. By dark, sixty-four ships were counted at anchor. That evening, Confederate Brigadier General Thomas F. Drayton visited Bay Point and left a small number of reinforcements. Drayton, most recently president of the Charleston-Savannah Railroad, owned a plantation across the harbor on Hilton Head. His brother Percival, an officer in the United States Navy when the War broke out, had stayed with the Union and now commanded the gunship *Pocahontas,* anchored inside the bar and waiting for the order to attack.

Tuesday, a gale blew all day, and the fleet stayed at anchor. Tuesday night, cheers went up inside Fort Walker, upon the arrival of reinforcements: 500 men and two howitzers from Georgia and 650 men of the Fifteenth South Carolina Volunteers. One hundred twenty of the new support troops stayed in the fort, joining the 100 men already there, representing Companies A and B of the German Artillery from Charleston; the Charleston Artillery Battalion; Company C, Eleventh South Carolina Infantry; and three detachments from the Ninth South Carolina Volunteers. The rest dug in behind the beach to repulse an anticipated landing. Confederate strength at Fort Beauregard stood at 149 men from the Beaufort Volunteer Artillery, and Company D, Eleventh South Carolina Infantry. The St. Helena Mounted Volunteer Riflemen were poised at Dr. Jenkins's house, at Seaside, from which they could see and hear the action at Bay Point.

By Wednesday morning the winds had calmed. "Not a ripple

upon the broad expanse of water," wrote Confederate General Drayton, "to disturb the accuracy of fire" from the attacking fleet.[32] Just as calmly and serenely, the residents of Beaufort awaited "the sinking of every ship . . ."[33] At nine A.M. the battle began. Against 155 Yankee guns, 46 on the *Wabash* alone, the Rebels answered with 43 mounted cannon, of which only 20 faced the sea. The attackers had a number of 11-inch guns in their arsenal, large guns for the time, while the defenders had one 10-inch gun at Fort Walker, and no guns that large at Fort Beauregard.

Du Pont had planned to attack by sea and and land, but scrapped the idea because some of his disembarkment boats had been lost in a storm during the voyage south, and no safe place could be found to land troops on Hilton Head shore. The troop transports were anchored far out, the currents were strange, and Du Pont felt his sea power was all he would need to clean out the insurgents. Rather than attack only Fort Walker, as he had planned to do on Monday, Du Pont directed the squadron to steam by Fort Beauregard, at the east entrance to the harbor, bombarding it in passing, then turn west and south and approach Fort Walker from the inland side, raking the main battery before facing its fire.

The attack came off according to plan. To a roll of drums and the trill of fifes, fifteen warships moved up in line, pouring shells into Fort Beauregard at a distance of eight hundred yards. Four smaller gunboats joined them, and when all had passed well above Bay Point, they turned to attack Fort Walker. Commodore Tattnall's fleet plied out of Skull Creek to draw the Federals into range of Fort Walker's guns. Du Pont was concerned that in the "heat and smoke of battle," Tattnall would try to slip by the gunboats and fire on the troop transports lying at anchor like sitting ducks. But he was easily driven off and was not a factor in the battle.*

Three times the Federals circled inside the Sound, the second time at a distance of six hundred yards from the forts, the third

---

*Tattnall retreated by inland waters to Savannah. In March, 1862, he replaced Admiral Franklin Buchanan as commander of the *Merrimac*, after the ironclad's famous duel with the Union boat the *Monitor*. When the Confederates abandoned Norfolk, Virginia, in May, Tattnall sank the *Merrimac* to prevent its capture. He was court-martialed and acquitted, and spent the last thirty months of the War harassing the Federal blockade and defending the Savannah River. After the Confederate surrender, he moved to Nova Scotia, but returned to Georgia and was installed as inspector of the port of Savannah. (Mark M. Boatner III, *The Civil War Dictionary* [New York, 1959], 826.)

time even closer—close enough to be shot at by riflemen on shore. Then they pulled back, keeping up the shelling with their superior guns. "It was a most unequal conflict." Shells fell into the forts "with the regularity of machinery," reported one Federal observer; "as fast as a horse's feet beat the ground in a gallop," wrote another.[34] By two P.M. all but three of Fort Walker's guns were disabled. The ten-inch gun had bounded off its carriage in the morning and was useless through most of the fight. Some shells did not fit the guns, and the guns on the flanks never worked. As ammunition ran out, Colonel William C. Heyward ordered his men to abandon the fort. Across the harbor, at Fort Beauregard, Colonel R.G.M. Dunovant quickly followed suit.

As victory went to the fleet and strains of "Yankee Doodle" broke the air, St. Helena planters watching from the safety of Dr. Jenkins's porch "jumped on their horses and galloped off to their families to prepare for flight instantly."[35] Once they had piled their wives and children and a few possessions into wagons and carts, the members of the St. Helena company turned and advanced toward the sea. Their families went one way, toward Confederate lines on the main, and the Riflemen went the other, toward the retreating soldiers at Bay Point. Twelve flats, rowed and poled by slaves at gunpoint, removed the garrisons from Fort Beauregard, by way of Eddings Island and Station Creek. The Yankees failed to give chase, or even to detect the retreat.

On Hilton Head, the garrisons inside Fort Walker and behind the beach escaped across Skull Creek. Thus, the retreats were successful on both sides of the Sound. And despite the intensity of shelling during the fight, casualties were light: sixty-six Confederates killed or wounded, and thirty-one Federals. Fort Walker was reduced to rubble, but Fort Beauregard was only bruised. Every Yankee warship had been hit by Confederate fire, but none was sunk or put out of action.

Federal troops landed on Hilton Head late Wednesday afternoon. They occupied Fort Beauregard the next morning. Reconnaissance revealed that the entire coastal region, from the North Edisto River, twenty miles below Charleston, to Ossabaw Sound, south of Savannah, had been abandoned by the white population. On Friday, the ninth of November, the Federals entered Beaufort, where they found, besides the black residents, only one white man, "an infirm old Yankee shoemaker, who had been there for thirty-five years"[36]—not long enough, in the view of Beaufort attorney and now refugee Richard DeTreville, to purge the Yankee out of him.*

A Perfect Retreat

Eleven hundred white people fled St. Helena Parish, leaving behind seventy-eight hundred blacks. The Chaplin, Capers, Fripp, and Jenkins families had lived there 140 years. With the other whites, they uprooted themselves in a few frightful hours. Not everyone left willingly. The fear that spurred the majority to run froze other people in place. Captain John Fripp wanted to stay, but his children "over-persuaded" him, packed him and his wife in a boat with their favorite servants, and sent them to the main. Mrs. Fripp wanted to keep the blacks, but her husband made them go back, telling them to work so they would not starve. J.E.L. Fripp, a brother and neighbor of Captain W.O.P. Fripp, had to be led away by friends. So did the Massachusetts-born widow of Reverend Joseph Wallace. Only one white person was suspected of going over to the enemy. Chaplin's third cousin Ben Chaplin, Jr., was said to have "joined the fleet and turned Yankee."[37]

Some planters sneaked onto St. Helena in the early days of the occupation to save belongings and try to persuade their slaves to go off with them. By and large, the blacks did not cooperate, during or after the flight. They did not raise arms against the whites or impede them from leaving, but they "shrank" from executing orders, "and in many cases secreted themselves at the appointed time."[38] They told the missionaries who arrived on St. Helena in 1862 that their masters had threatened to shoot them down like dogs if they did not obey until the evacuation was completed. In their final capacity as slavemasters, however, different planters told their slaves different things. Captain John Fripp exhorted his Negroes to watch out for themselves and to obey the white strangers who would soon be telling them what to do. He wished them well when they parted.

---

*DeTreville maintained the white citizens were ordered to leave by Confederate military authorities. But other witnesses found "no evidence of any military order compelling evacuation of the place." Whether or not an order was issued, the people left "under the conviction that there was such an order." Union officers called the abandonment of Beaufort and the Sea Islands an "insane action" intended to "prevent any weakening of the feeling of intense bitterness." (Daniel Ammen, *The Navy in the Civil War* [New York, 1883], vol. II, 35.)

Alviro Fripp warned his people that the Yankees intended to put them in chains and sell them to Cuba. Thomas B. Chaplin told Robert, Isaac, and Jack to take care of the plantation in his absence, until normal life could resume.

Not one Confederate soldier or civilian was captured or detained on St. Helena Island. The weather, tides, and the temerity of the enemy contributed to the success of the retreat; but its orderliness was "entirely due to the exertions of the little band of men comprising the St. Helena Mounted Riflemen,"[39] whose achievement was made more remarkable, in their own eyes, by the fact that they had taken it upon themselves to act. "Our company were without orders," observed a disillusioned Lieutenant Thomas G. White. Deserving gratitude, they were bombarded instead by calumnies from their friends. Not quite a century earlier, during the Revolutionary War, their ancestors had been criticized for refusing to evacuate the islands and for fraternizing with the British. Now they themselves were assailed for leaving, and for allowing their wealth to fall into enemy hands. To correct the slanders which arose in lieu of reliable information, Lieutenant White defended the "apparently precipitate" retreat in a letter to the Charleston *Courier,* a month after the event. He focused on "a little incident" proving "the singleness of purpose" and "utter recklessness of themselves" which had characterized the defenders.

"At daylight upon the morning of the retreat," while Federal troops were entering Fort Beauregard, it was discovered that "twenty or thirty men and as many horses" had been left behind, to get away by their own devices. Two brave Confederates, "Sergeant T. B. Chaplin and Lieutenant J. A. Johnson, the former of the St. Helena Company and the latter of the Beaufort Volunteer Artillery, resolved not to quit Bay Point Island until every man was removed, and hunted up if they had lost their way." Chaplin and Johnson stayed "long into the morning, within hearing of the enemy's reveille drums, and within sight of their outpost sentinel." They succeeded in bringing out "every man and every horse," neglecting their own safety until they had matched the horses with their owners. Such "is the spirit which actuates" the Sea Islanders, wrote White. "Can such a people be reproached with not having done their duty?"[40]

Whether the St. Helena Riflemen should have stayed to resist the invaders and keep possession of their plantations was a question of deep personal significance. But from a military point of view, the battle of Port Royal was inconsequential. The Federals never used the port to stage a major offensive. Except for securing a harbor for the ships which captured Fort Pulaski at the mouth of the Savannah River and hammered with great noise but little consequence at Charleston and Fort Sumter, the victory went unexploited.[41] What was lost, therefore, in November, 1861, was not the strategic position both sides imagined it to be, but simply the homeland of the old Sea Island families.

After the battle was decided, in the course of a perfect retreat, Thomas B. Chaplin displayed exceptional devotion to duty. A quality of courage that had lain dormant in him was called to life by an extraordinary necessity. Normally, he reacted to adversity with a touch of hysteria, but "upon this memorable day" he was calmer than others, he could sense what had to be done. What glory there was to seize from defeat was the name of hero, and he took it.

Recriminations

In the wake of their retreat, white Sea Islanders felt betrayed. The fighting men believed they had been "sacrificed by the indifference or lukewarmness of those not far removed who could have rendered service by their presence."[42] Older noncombatants, like William Grayson and Richard DeTreville, blamed propagandists and incompetent generals for encouraging "the idle delusion" that Port Royal was defensible. Port Royal was proof, said Grayson, that the Confederacy did not learn from its mistakes—in particular, the losses of the two forts at Hatteras Inlet the previous August. It would have taken millions of dollars and years of labor to fortify the islands properly. The South had waited too long to build up its coastal defenses, and the little it had done proved counterproductive, because it duped people into thinking they were safe. In truth, their "very fine fortifications" were formidable only to "the inexperienced eye." Yet, they were the "best resistance which the Confederate Government could then present," DeTreville derisively remarked. "It ought, at this point, to have offered none."[43]

The loss was old news by the time the press reported it, and editors wanted to move on to more positive developments. "Thus ended the defense of Port Royal," the Charleston *Mercury* commented blandly, consigning Sea Island civilization to the "picturesque" past. "The mortification of the disaster is lessened by the consciousness that our troops deserved success."[44] As for the civilian population, or rather for the fighters in their civil capacity as planters, there was no mourning, only a pathetic description of "the heterogeneous throng of fugitives" that filled the roads and ferries leading out of St. Helena Parish. No call for aid was issued; to localize the panic and to dampen criticism of overall military strategy, the episode was dropped like hot lead. The "fugitives"— not the most sympathetic word, since it was also applied to deserters and runaway slaves—were an embarrassment to war planners who had been saying the state was impregnable.

Yet it was no secret that the Union had been planning an assault against South Carolina. And where else could it have been aimed except at the coast? The Union Army was bottled up at Washington, protecting the capital. Only the Navy was capable of waging an offensive. Aware of the danger to the seaboard, Confederate Secretary of War Judah P. Benjamin had persuaded President Jefferson Davis to transfer Lieutenant General Robert E. Lee from western Virginia, where his first field command had ended in failure, to South Carolina. Lee was told to organize the defenses of the South Atlantic coast. He arrived in Charleston on November 7 and reached Coosawhatchie later that day, in time to learn that Port Royal had fallen. To try to hold the islands would be futile, he felt. His troops were green, he was unfamiliar with his field commanders, and he had no guns to challenge Union artillery.

Lee settled in to defend the Charleston-Savannah Railroad. He wrote to Benjamin: "The enemy has complete possession of the water and inland navigation, commands all the islands on the coast and threatens both Savannah and Charleston and can come in his boats within four miles of this place."[45] On November 9, the *Mercury* reported that Lee "is said to be constructing fortifications at Beaufort." He was not. November 9 was the day Federal troops entered the town. Lee stayed at Coosawhatchie preparing to meet the Federals when they arrived on the mainland.

But the Federals did not take advantage of the opening. From his command post on Hilton Head, General Thomas W. Sherman— "the other General Sherman"—commander of the army that had sailed with Du Pont, debated sending his troops inland and turning "left or right to one of the cities." Deterred by "the winding and shallow creeks," and the inexperience of his men, Sherman chose to stand still.[46] Observers on both sides agreed he had missed a great opportunity. DeTreville contended that Du Pont had erred as well. Sherman, who had watched the battle of Port Royal from a troop transport ship, called the fleet's maneuvering a "masterpiece . . . that must have elicited the applause of the rebels themselves as a tactical operation."[47] DeTreville acknowledged the Federals' muscle but not their brains. He thought the attack had been a stupid display, as outrageous in exposing Union sailors to risk as Confederate strategy had been in endangering the defenders. Had Du Pont passed rapidly up the Sound, "in less than an hour, without firing a gun," he could have placed the fleet "beyond the very longest range of the guns of both batteries, reversed, and captured their garrisons, threatening Savannah by way of Calibogue Sound. . . ."[48] Instead, he stopped to preen like a peacock, showing off his "greater means and efficiency, by silencing these little forts." Yet it was "well known that a fleet moving with a strong flood tide under a good head of steam could receive no effectual check from these or even much larger batteries." Why make the ships into targets and pass up a chance to capture a bigger prize? Fear and lack of imagination, DeTreville concluded, and not some sinister purpose, explained the Federals' behavior. Tactically, he insinuated, the Union was as inept as the Confederacy.

What turned out to be an unimportant encounter at the start of a long war inflicted permanent injury on the "fugitives" from St. Helena. Despite all they had done to bring forth the Confederacy, they remained a people apart, deserted by their countrymen, made homeless by their enemies. Preparing to make war had brought them together with the rest of the South, but their first real skirmish destroyed that unity. Old feelings of separateness, repressed under the influence of sectional and Confederate pride, exerted new force over their self-conceptions. In their wartime and postwar writings, the Sea Islanders denounced the Confederate and United States governments from an emotional vantage point apart from both. Once the War was lost they signed loyalty oaths to the United States. But because their lands and personal property were not returned to them, they stayed alienated from, yet locked in battle with, authorities who apparently forgave everyone but them.

Private Thomas B. Chaplin

After reassembling at Coosawhatchie under Lee's command, Fripp's Company, the St. Helena Mounted Riflemen, engaged the enemy at Port Royal Ferry, on New Year's Day, 1862. The Federals were trying to capture or put out of action Confederate batteries on the east or mainland side of the Coosaw River, across from Brickyard Point, on Port Royal Island. The defenders, including units of the Twelfth and Fourteenth South Carolina Infantry, and a detachment of forty men from Martin's Mounted Regiment, of which Fripp's Company was a part, were forced to pull back under an artillery barrage, abandoning what gun emplacements they could not destroy. Martin's cavalry guarded the retreat and brushed with the enemy, but did not suffer any casualties.[49]

Though a minor loss, it was a loss nevertheless, and it raised suspicions that the Yankees were indeed preparing to attack the railroad and move against Charleston. Lee would have to stop them. But he found it impossible "to get an accurate report of the troops under my command."[50] Authority was fragmented, and small units like "Captain Fripp's," which reported "4 commissioned officers and 19 privates," were top heavy and expensive to maintain. "I think all had better be reorganized," wrote Lee.[51] Three days after the clash at Port Royal Ferry, the St. Helena Mounted Riflemen were "mustered out" of service, having completed just two months of their one-year term of enlistment. Sergeant Thomas B. Chaplin lost his rank; he and his three sons, Privates Ernest, Daniel, and Eugene Chaplin, suddenly were civilians again. The next month, in Charleston, the four men enrolled in Company D, Fifth South Carolina Cavalry, Ferguson's Regiment, each bringing a horse valued at $125. Apparently they served in the same unit for only two months. In April, 1862, the elder Chaplin—just turning forty—was detailed as a courier on extra duty with Colonel Ambrose Gonzales, chief of artillery for the Military Department of South Carolina, Georgia, and Florida.* Muster rolls, quartermaster receipts, and payroll returns in-

---

*Cuban-born Ambrosio José Gonzales "obtained a colonelcy" from General P.G.T. Beauregard, after Jefferson Davis refused to make him a general. Gonzales and Beauregard were former schoolmates and business partners; in 1860, they sold rifles and a grapeshot revolver, "a terrifying machine with nine chambers and two barrels," to southern legislatures. In the late 1840s, Gonzales tried to recruit American veterans of the Mexican War to invade Cuba and take it from Spain. He did not succeed, but John C. Calhoun consoled him by comparing Cuba to "a pear" that eventually "will drop into the lap of the Union." In 1856, Gonzales married Harriet Elliott, the fifteen-year-old daughter of Beaufort's William Elliott—to the dismay of her family. Mary Chesnut reported that he was handsome and courtly and "so like Beauregard as to be mistaken for him." (*A Diary from Dixie,* ed. Ben Ames Williams [Boston, 1949], 108, 205.)

dicate that he stayed with Gonzales at least until October, 1864, delivering messages between James and Morris islands, and Charleston.

It was extremely hazardous duty. In the summer of 1863, four of ten couriers detached from Chaplin's company to Morris Island had their horses shot out from under them. Morris Island is a small, low island on the south side of the mouth of Charleston Harbor, about a mile and a half from Fort Sumter; much of it falls under water at very high tides, and it had no permanent settlement. Because of its strategic location, however, the Federals planned to take it as a step toward capturing Charleston. Its only land defense was Fort Wagner, a hastily built redoubt that occupied all the high ground at the narrow south end of the island. By feinting with smaller operations on James Island and at the railroad bridge over the Edisto River, the Federals were able to land two thousand men on Morris Island without interception. Confederate troops pulled back into the fort. Twice—on July 11 and 18—the Federals tried to storm the redoubt, and both times they were repulsed with heavy casualties, losing nearly two thousand men to the Confederates' two hundred. Then the Federals changed tactics: they began shelling the fort while their land forces crept closer and closer. For Confederate couriers running between the defenders and their high command, reserves, and supply posts, the summer-long siege meant sleepless nights, constant danger, and intense activity. Surviving records do not locate Chaplin day to day, but from month to month they place him in close proximity to fierce, if inconclusive, fighting. After fifty-eight days of shelling, Fort Wagner was rendered defenseless; its guns were broken, food and ammunition could no longer be brought in. On the night of September 6, hours before the Federals would have stormed the ramparts again, Colonel Lawrence M. Keitt, the radical Congressman turned soldier, stealthily led his men out of the fort and off the island.[52]*

*Keitt was killed at the Battle of Cold Harbor, near Richmond, on June 1, 1864. Just arrived in Virginia at the head of the Twentieth South Carolina Infantry, Keitt was handling troops in the open field for the first time. Given the order to advance, "Keitt led his men like a knight of old—mounted upon his superb iron-gray, and looked the embodiment of the true chevalier he was." Never before had "the brigade been led in deliberate battle by its commander on horseback." As he charged across an opening toward a thick stand of oaks, "Colonel Keitt was a fine target for the sharpshooters." (Augustus D. Dickert, *History of Kershaw's Brigade* [Newberry, S.C., 1899], 370.)

Three Soldiers: Ernest, Daniel, and Eugene Chaplin

Chaplin's three sons served together in Fripp's Company, the St. Helena Mounted Riflemen, and afterward in Company D, Fifth South Carolina Cavalry. In the fall of 1864, Ernest and Eugene evidently switched to the infantry—to Company I, "the Palmetto Guard," Second South Carolina Volunteers. Daniel's records are the most complete but also the most ambiguous. He was reported wounded, captured, and "exchanged" at Fredericksburg, Virginia, in December, 1862. Apparently he had been serving in Colonel William D. De Saussure's Fifteenth Cavalry Regiment, which had been assigned to Kershaw's Brigade after the Seven Days' Battle near Richmond. Recuperating in South Carolina, Daniel may have joined his brothers' outfit, the Fifth Cavalry, engaged in defending the coast. He was captured again on June 11, 1864, in a bloody skirmish at Louisa Court House, Louisa County, Virginia, two months after returning to the major theater of the War. A "D. Chaplin" appears on an infantry muster roll later in 1864, but Daniel was already in prison.

Ernest Chaplin's records are also problematic. An unofficial compilation shows him "discharged on account of illness" in 1862. This seems plausible, since he was sickly before and after the War. But other documents show him "sick in camp" in 1864, and his horse was reported "killed in action" in June of that year. Furthermore, his name appears on an oath of allegiance to the United States "subscribed and sworn to" at Point Lookout, Maryland, on June 20, 1865, ten weeks after Lee's surrender. He had been captured, along with his brother Eugene, near Orangeburg, South Carolina, the previous February, during Sherman's sweep through the Carolinas. On his loyalty oath appears the following physical description, the only one we have for any of the Chaplins: height, five feet six and three-quarter inches; eyes, dark brown; light complexion; hair, dark.

Company D, Fifth South Carolina Cavalry, spent more than two years near Green Pond, on the Combahee River, where Saxby Chaplin had a plantation.* For the men of the company, drawn

---

*Saxby Chaplin was a first lieutenant in Company B, Third South Carolina Cavalry, Colcock's Regiment. In the early years of the War, his outfit was also stationed near his home. He moved his slaves across the railroad tracks to a plantation behind Confederate lines, where they raised provisions which he sold to his company.

from the coastal parishes, the War never lost the character of local defense. They gathered intelligence, raided Yankee bases on the islands, and occasionally attacked a lone gunboat. Ernest Chaplin was a member of a reconnaissance team that captured a Yankee soldier stranded near the mouth of the Ashepoo River—downstream from Ernest's grandmother's Dunham Plantation. In April, 1864, after General Lee, then commanding the Army of Northern Virginia, complained to President Davis that too many South Carolina soldiers had never served outside of the state, Company D and the full Fifth Regiment, along with the Second and Fourth South Carolina Cavalry regiments, were sent to Virginia where they constituted Butler's Brigade, named for its leader, Brigadier General Matthew C. Butler.*

This was not the first time that Lee had called Davis's attention to "the abuse of the right of volunteering."[53] South Carolina infantry regiments in Lee's army, such as the five which made up Kershaw's Brigade,† found it difficult to recruit, "principally, if not entirely," said Lee, because the military authorities in Charleston encouraged young men to volunteer for local service, and once enrolled, "they acquire the idea that they have a right to remain in such service and desert when ordered to other points."[54] Carefully choosing his words, Lee maintained "the right to volunteer ceases after enrollment, and I respectfully suggest that it be vigorously enforced." Lee recommended that no more men be accepted into "home" regiments, and that "some of the full regiments in the Department of South Carolina, etc., be ordered to the field, and that reduced regiments be sent to Charleston to recruit."[55]

By the third week in April, the three Chaplin boys were on their way to Virginia, land of "good fresh buttermilk and golden

---

*Matthew Calbraith Butler was born in Greenville, South Carolina, in 1836. His father had been a surgeon in the United States Army, and one of his grandfathers was a Revolutionary War hero. A secessionist Democrat, Butler married Maria Calhoun Pickens, daughter of Governor Francis W. Pickens. He was twenty-five when the War broke out and at twenty-seven he became a brigadier general, after losing a foot at Brandy Station, in June, 1863. Following the battles of Spotsylvania and The Wilderness, he was promoted to major general.

†Kershaw's Brigade and three others constituted the division of Major General Lafayette McLaws, "and that, with the divisions of Pickett and Hood, formed the First Corps of the Army of Virginia, known as Longstreet's." (Joseph B. Kershaw, "Kershaw's Brigade at Gettysburg," in *Battles and Leaders of the Civil War* [New York, 1887], vol. III, 331.) In 1862 and '63, before returning to Charleston to recruit, the brigade fought at First and Second Bull Run, Harpers Ferry, Sharpsburg, Antietam, Fredericksburg, Chancellorsville, Gettysburg, Chickamauga, and Knoxville.

butter,"[56] where they would face eight weeks of incessant fighting along Lee's line of defense, at Petersburg, twenty miles below Richmond; in the Rappahannock and Rapidan Basin, west of Fredericksburg; and north of the James River.

Daniel was captured while his company was repulsing General Philip Sheridan's cavalry. When Grant decided to cross the James River and make a direct assault on Petersburg, he sent Sheridan to join up with General David Hunter's forces at Charlottesville, to the west, and destroy a stretch of the Virginia Central Railroad. Lee learned of the plan, and sent General Wade Hampton's cavalry division, led by Butler's Brigade, and also General Fitz Lee's division, to check Sheridan. On June 11, four miles north of Louisa, Butler skirmished with Sheridan. While this was happening, Hampton was informed that General George A. Custer's* cavalry had surprised Fitz Lee and was closing in on Hampton from the rear. Hampton broke off action in front and turned to meet Custer, whom he hit hard, recovering some eight hundred horses and vehicles Custer had won early in the day, and taking many prisoners. But Custer held on to Trevilian Station, the site that gave the battle its name. The next day, Sheridan charged Hampton's entrenched troops, who tore his unit to pieces. The defeat ended his mission.[57] Sheridan's tactics had been discredited by previous experience, yet he foolishly hoped to gain the advantage of terror and surprise. Three years into the War, cavalry on both sides fought mainly dismounted. "Our cavalry were not cavalrymen *proper*," explained Confederate General John Bell Hood, "but were mounted riflemen, trained to dismount and hold in check or delay the advance of the enemy."[58] Cavalry units were assigned generally to cover the flanks of the infantry and to throw the enemy off balance. In dismounted action, every fourth cavalryman stayed in the rear holding the reins of his horse and of the horses of three other men who had places on the firing line. If the enemy got between the "horseholders" and the dismounted troops, the "horseholders" were helpless and might easily be captured.[59]

Each side at Trevilian Station suffered about one thousand casualties. The Fifth South Carolina Cavalry lost six men killed,

---

*George Armstrong Custer (1839,–1876) had been named a brigadier general, USA, at the age of twenty-three. Known as a brilliant cavalry tactician, Custer took part in every major battle of the Army of the Potomac from First Bull Run until Lee's surrender. He was killed in an ambush by Sioux Indians at the Little Bighorn in Montana, June 25, 1876.

forty-one wounded, and eight missing or captured, one of whom was Daniel Chaplin.[60]

Ernest and Eugene were captured eight months later with a remnant of Company I, Second South Carolina Infantry, that had returned to its home state in January, 1865, while Confederate positions were collapsing in almost every theater. Hood's Army of Tennessee had been routed and ruined. All southern ports, except Wilmington, North Carolina, and besieged Charleston, were in Federal hands. Lincoln had won reelection, squelching southern hopes for an armistice that might include compensation for the slaves who were certain to be freed. Some southern legislatures, with rebellious members declaring a preference for independence over slavery, were debating whether to arm the slaves.* And some were covertly exploring the possibility of making a separate peace with the Union. Lee was still unbeaten in Virginia, but Sherman's army of conquest had marched virtually unopposed through Georgia and was recuperating at Savannah, preparing to punish the Carolinas.

Eugene had returned to Charleston in September, 1864, and was hospitalized for three months. He was sick for much of the last year of the War. The previous June, while his company was fighting east of Richmond and concluding a campaign in which it suffered casualties of thirty-five percent, he was confined in Richmond with fever. He returned to duty in July before he had fully recovered; and when he left Charleston in January to try to stop Sherman at the Salkehatchie† crossing of the Charleston-Savannah Railroad, he was still in poor health. But every man was needed at the front. General P.G.T. Beauregard‡ could raise only

*C. G. Memminger urged the Confederacy to conscript slaves, reminding leaders that "Abraham's servants fought with him." (Olsberg, 188.) Jefferson Davis proposed purchasing forty thousand slaves from their owners, arming and training them, and giving them white officers, then setting them free after the War. Neither plan was carried out.
†The Salkehatchie is the major tributary of the Combahee River.
‡Pierre Gustave Toutant Beauregard, the "hero of Sumter," and a hero, as well, at First Bull Run, had been commander of the Military Department of South Carolina, Georgia, and Florida until his command was merged with the Army of Northern Virginia. An accomplished engineer—like Lee—who was wounded twice in the Mexican War, Beauregard was superintendent of West Point for five days in January, 1861; he was summarily transferred after telling a Louisiana cadet that "he would go with his state if it seceded." In the spring of 1864, he fought off Grant at Petersburg, then was sent to command the Division of the West. He returned to the Carolinas second-in-command to Joseph E. Johnston. After the War, he was a railroad president and supervisor of drawings for the Louisiana lottery.

fifteen to twenty thousand veterans, state troops, and last-call reserves to meet Sherman's sixty thousand sound and highly motivated soldiers. No help could be expected from Lee, whose lines were stretched to the limit in a losing war of attrition. The remainder of Hood's army was too small and too far away to make a difference.

Eugene's name appears on a list of Confederates taken prisoner by the Seventeenth Corps, United States Army, on February 13, 1865. The Seventeenth Corps, one of two units commanded by Sherman's brigadier general, O. O. Howard, had sailed from Savannah to Beaufort at the end of January, camped briefly on Port Royal Island, then crossed over to the main, marching east and north and brushing with Confederates at Pocotaligo and Combahee Ferry. Through heavy rains, the Federals advanced to the Salkehatchie and pushed the Confederates behind their next line of defense, the Edisto River. "The eighth [of February] was spent in destroying the railroad," wrote Howard.[61] So was the seventh, and the ninth, and the tenth. After crossing the south fork of the Edisto, and feinting toward Charleston, the Seventeenth Corps marched on Orangeburg, "a beautiful village of about 1000 inhabitants" and currently "a favorite retreat of refugees from Charleston."[62] "Local citizens" and a small number of Confederate regulars "had thrown up a slight breastworks" in front of the Orangeburg Bridge. The Federals swept this obstacle away "by a dash," and the Confederates retreated into the town.[63] The bridge, like all other bridges in the path of the advancing army, was burned, either by the Confederates before the Federals could cross, or by the Federals after crossing. By four P.M. on the twelfth, the Seventeenth Corps was inside Orangeburg. It spent the next day demolishing the railroad depot, burning cotton bales, and twisting miles of track into shapes called Sherman's neckties, as far as the State Road, a straight run to Columbia.* Near or on this road, on February 13,

---

*Asked after the War if he had been aware "of a spirit of vengeance—a desire of vengeance—animating your troops to be wreaked upon South Carolina," Sherman answered: "I was; the feeling was universal and pervaded all ranks.

"Q. Officers and all?
"A. Officers and all; we looked upon South Carolina as the cause of our woes.
"Q. And thought she thoroughly deserved strong treatment?
"A. Yes sir; that she thoroughly deserved extirpation."

(J. J. Browne v. the United States, quoted in The Diary of Emma Le Conte, ed. Earl Schenck Miers [New York, 1957] xii.)

exactly two months before all the shooting stopped, Ernest and Eugene Chaplin surrendered. Judged by the fruits of victory, their resistance was a failure, but they may have managed to slow the Federals by a few hours, giving residents and refugees a chance to flee to Columbia.

Surrender

Ernest and Daniel survived prison; Eugene did not. He was alive and unhurt when he was captured—though he probably was sick—and what happened to him afterward we cannot say, because his name disappears from the records. His father thought he was buried in North Carolina, but Virginia or Maryland is more likely. Ernest's late parole, at the end of June, may indicate that he, too, was sick at the time of his capture, or became sick shortly after, and that several months passed before he was well enough to travel home. Daniel, first of the three to be taken, was sent to Fortress Monroe, at the mouth of the James River. From there he was transferred to the huge Federal prison at Point Lookout, Maryland, where the Potomac River meets Chesapeake Bay. But the prison was crowded to suffocation—it had no barracks, only tents—and he was moved again, this time to Elmira Prison, in New York State, a facility for enlisted men which had barracks, but only enough for half the prisoners. About ten percent of the prisoners had no blankets, and the sick and death rates were very high. Daniel spent the winter of 1864–65 at Elmira and was paroled on March 2. He was supposed to be sent to Virginia, in an exchange of prisoners, but he was too sick to go. He left within a week, however, and on March 10 he was admitted to the "Receiving and Wayside Hospital, or General Hospital No. 9," in Richmond, where his illness was diagnosed as pneumonia.[64] He was discharged from the hospital on the twenty-first, and furloughed for sixty days, but the War ended before his leave was up. Lee surrendered to Grant on April 9; on the twenty-sixth, at Greensboro, North Carolina, General Joseph E. Johnston, commanding the balance of Hood's army and the irregular units which had made up Confederate resistance in the Carolinas, surrendered to Sherman—although Jefferson Davis had ordered him south to continue the War.*

*Johnston and Davis had been feuding since the start of the War—over rank, assignments, and strategy. In the Atlanta campaign of 1864, Johnston dropped back successfully before the powerful Sherman, contrary to Davis's wishes that he attack.

*   *   *

At Greensboro, while the details of Johnston's surrender were being worked out, railroad cars containing the Confederate archives were left unprotected on their way from Richmond to the emergency capital at Charlotte, ahead of the fleeing Davis and his cabinet. General Beauregard noticed papers from the cars "floating up and down the railroad track," and ordered the archives guarded until they reached their destination.[65] At Charlotte, the cars were again left unprotected. General Johnston learned of the situation and had their contents turned over to the Union Army for safekeeping. Incidents like these attending the hectic, demoralizing surrender explain, in part, why there are significant gaps in the Confederate records and why the personal histories of common soldiers like the Chaplins can never be fully told. Yet, the wonder is not that papers were lost, but that so many were saved. Immensely weary and troubled by what lay ahead, the generals might have let the papers fly and go to the devil. Instead, they quietly and heroically saved them. As a result, an accurate history can be written about any campaign in the War, drawing confidently on sources from both sides. Because neither side was embarrassed or confused as to why it had fought, neither had any need to manufacture lies or to destroy the truth. Where a skirmish was reported by any of the combatants, one can be certain it happened; very little that did happen was allowed to slip into silence.

Davis replaced Johnston with the offensive-minded Hood, who proceeded to lead the Army of Tennessee to its destruction. Johnston came out of retirement to salvage Hood's forces and to oversee their surrender. He died in 1891 "of pneumonia contracted by standing hatless in the rain at Sherman's funeral." (Boatner, 441.)

12. 1864

Chaplin Versus Baker, Act II

On June 23, 1864, twelve days after her grandson Daniel was captured in Virginia, Isabella Baker died near Green Pond, north of the tracks of the Charleston-Savannah Railroad, a line separating the rich coastal peninsulas from higher sandy ground considered safe from Federal raids. Chaplin wrote a poignant letter to his brother, Saxby, whose unit was on active duty in Georgia, telling him of their mother's last illness and death and of the difficulty finding horses and a carriage to carry her body down to Fields Point for burial.

The Combahee River was quiet at the time. Four months before, black troops organized in Beaufort had raided the riverine plantations, burning gins and barns and liberating hundreds of slaves. Mrs. Baker had managed to keep her slaves by sending them to Dunham Plantation, a rice-growing island in the Ashepoo River, east of the Combahee. She kept a retinue of twelve servants, who were with her when she died. Many of the people she sent to Dunham had returned to the Combahee, growing rice, cotton, and provisions for her husband's son-in-law, John Bennet Bissell, who was leasing William Heyward's former plantation, near Fields Point.* The entire Heyward work force had gone over to the Yankees, and Mrs. Baker's slaves were cultivating in their place.

Within three days of her death, her son Thomas and his attorney Richard DeTreville filed a bill of complaint in the Walterboro

---

*The same William Heyward who had commanded Confederate forces at Fort Walker. Heyward had graduated from West Point but gave up a military career for planting on the Combahee. He lost his command in the War after his first term of enlistment and served afterward as a private until he contracted yellow fever and died in Charleston, in 1863.

Court, Colleton District, demanding that her husband, Robert L. Baker, and his accomplices, turn over to the Chaplins all of her property. The bill had clearly been contemplated, if not actually written, while Isabella was alive—a space was provided to fill in the date of death. Baker was shocked by the suddenness and rapacity of the bill. Unnerved by the recent death of his attorney, the brilliant James L. Petigru, who had defended him against the Chaplins twenty years before, Baker searched for someone to take his case. He made up his mind not to do anything the court did not make him do and to bring a suit of his own against his dead wife's heirs and beneficiaries.

Many characters in the second act of this protracted drama had participated in the court battles of the 1840s, but everyone's position had changed. Three of the leading actors were dead—Mrs. Baker, Petigru, and Daniel T. Jenkins, Chaplin's first cousin and close friend, and a trustee of Mrs. Baker's estate. Jenkins had been replaced as trustee by his brother-in-law, John M. Webb, but Webb had died, too, and was succeeded by Dr. Joseph Johnson, of Beaufort. When the first suits were filed, in 1845, Thomas and Saxby had been twenty-three and twenty-one years old respectively. Now they were forty-three and forty-one, and they were joined in their bill by Thomas's four children and Saxby's nine.

Only Thomas actually appeared in court; the other men of fighting age were unable to come. Baker was confined to Charleston by the deteriorating military situation. He had been hawkish before the War and melodramatic in his repudiation of "the rotten, abominable Union." He had wanted to help arm the state for "the irresistible conflict." He thought about selling weapons himself, possibly rifles made in Scotland, and he sharply criticized the alternatives, such as Colt, Sharp, and Maynard breechloaders. "A spirit of true sportsmanship" moved him, he said, "to aid and advance all improvements in the firearm department." South Carolina will "require the most effective firearms and ordnance to defend and protect her institution of slavery," he wrote to a friend, getting to the heart of the matter.[1] The Union was through. "Black Republicans" had turned the Constitution into "a rope of laws." He, Baker, was for immediate "single state action and separation." He chided those "timid, non-fighting, non-committed, halfway, half-masculine men of the watch and wait, cooperation classification." Now was the time to act, he wrote. "As Othello said to Iago, 'Blood, Blood, Iago. If it is needed let blood be spilled.' "*

Now at fifty-seven, Baker was still strident but he had grown afraid. The War was going badly. He felt sick and suspected he might never get well. He leaned heavily on his friend Francis L. Roux, the second trustee, who in the first round of cases had passed himself off as a disinterested servant, but whose partisanship had deepened after twenty years of turning over the profits from Mrs. Baker's estate to Baker. He tried to lean on Bissell, too, but the young man was having troubles enough trying to operate a plantation in the war zone and wanted to be left alone. That was impossible, both Roux and DeTreville reminded him, because he possessed the main bones of contention—Mrs. Baker's slaves.

DeTreville had started out as an adviser to Isabella Baker when she left her husband shortly after their wedding, in 1843. He had drawn up the deeds by which she had conveyed all of her wealth to her sons, leaving nothing for her husband and herself, and he had represented the Chaplins against Baker in their attempt to make the deeds apply at once. He himself had been deeded several slaves as payment for his services, giving him a personal interest in the outcome of the case. Baker hated him intensely and regarded him as one of the two chief villains in his life. "He has been my enemy and persecutor for twenty years," declared Baker, plotting a sweet revenge. By "name and nature," DeTreville was the "De-Vil."[2] Baker's second villain was C. G. Memminger, who only days before Mrs. Baker's death had resigned as Confederate Secretary of the Treasury. Memminger and Baker used to be friends. Baker had introduced him to Mrs. Fields, and she, in turn, had instructed him to draw up a deed of marriage settlement. Baker accused Memminger of violating his trust and conspiring with T. L. Webb, the Chaplin family's cotton factor, to talk Mrs. Fields into reserving the power to dispose of her property. He "has done me injury beyond human endurance," Baker said of Memminger. "I shall yet hold him up to public scorn."[3] Memminger had testified for Baker in 1845, but his testimony made Baker look foolish. It had taken Petigru's expensive, convincing legalisms to save the day.

Baker chose James B. Campbell to represent him. Campbell specialized in estate and financial litigation, had been a friend of

*A paraphrase of *Othello,* Act III, Scene IV: "O, blood, Iago, blood!" Suspecting his wife of being unfaithful, Othello's feelings of love turned to a desire for vengeance.

Petigru, and, more important, had a reputation for winning. "I trust it will be in your power," Baker wrote to him, to hold DeTreville "entirely in check," as Petigru had done before.[4] Roux and Bissell also hired Campbell. Roux suggested that Campbell solicit help from Memminger; he had reason to believe that Memminger was sorry for the trouble he had caused and wanted to make amends. While he had scorn for Memminger's lapses, Roux took a softer line than Baker, out of deference perhaps to Campbell's personal feelings for Memminger.

Baker, meanwhile, may have been playing on Memminger's recent unpopularity. As Treasury Secretary, Memminger had failed to curb inflation and had initiated a series of odious taxes. Memminger and DeTreville, whom Baker regarded with equal abhorrence, stood in opposite political camps. Likewise, Petigru and DeTreville had been ideological enemies. Attorney Campbell was also unsympathetic to the Beaufort secessionist. Ironically, Baker and DeTreville shared an extremist political streak. Three years into the terrible War, however, these ideological alliances may have counted for very little. Certainly, agreement about northern tyranny and southern rights did not stop DeTreville and Baker from trying to annihilate each other in court.

At stake in the dispute was *part* of Mrs. Baker's estate. The Chaplins claimed all of it, while Baker claimed a third. Thomas and Saxby based their demand on the deeds she had made out to them in 1845, which, the Appeals Court had ruled, would take effect after the termination of the "joint life" of Mr. and Mrs. Baker. The husband alleged that by a clause in the first draft of her marriage settlement, Mrs. Baker had set aside a third of her estate for him in the event that he outlived her. The clause had been removed surreptitiously from the second and final draft, contended Baker, and he had signed it without knowing. This was all he had to go on, and he knew that his case was weak. In the first round of hearings, the court, speaking for the state, decided that a husband's power to dispose of his wife's property was inviolate while she lived, and superior therefore to the claims of her children by a previous marriage. Now her death made her sons' claims supreme.

Isabella Baker left four plantations and about 170 slaves—one plantation and 80 slaves fewer than she had owned in 1843, before she married Baker. Unlike her three previous husbands, Baker had no assets, only liabilities, and the combination of his debts, her debts, and the debts of her sons for which she had stood security had taken a large bite out of her wealth. She had sold her Greenville land and slaves outright, and the court had designated other properties for sale. Over the years, Thomas and Saxby each had acquired several slaves who originally were listed in her settled estate. At least nineteen of her slaves escaped to the Yankees before she died, and more ran off as opportunities presented themselves while her husband and sons contested the remainder.

The fight unfolds in some thirty documents written between the last week of June, 1864, and the third week of December, almost six months later. They include letters from Baker, Roux, and Bissell to Campbell, and court papers such as bills of complaint, injunctions, and subpoenas.[5] Baker's output was prodigious—an eight-thousand-word letter to Campbell rehashing the origins of the marriage settlement, and a four-thousand-word response to the Chaplins' charges that he had mismanaged their mother's plantations and abused her slaves. While Baker was writing to Campbell, Sherman was destroying the railroads that supplied Atlanta, Grant was tightening his chokehold on Petersburg, and Yankee artillery was pouring four hundred shells a day into Fort Sumter.

In 1845, the property dispute had made rich gossip, but in 1864 it would have held the interest of hardly a half-dozen people besides the contestants. The first time around, the Baker-Chaplin litigation had embodied a great public issue—a woman's right to control and convey her property, before and after marriage. Now the integrity of society depended on the outcome of a war that was going badly. The War overshadowed the case and made it difficult to proceed. First, not all parties were free to travel to court. Some were fighting in Virginia, one was impressed into local service in Georgia, and military restrictions impinged on everyone. Second, mail and messages were uncertain. The very character of "these troublous and disjointed times" made it "of moment to the parties" that the court move quickly, yet the course of the War made the court move slowly.[6] The stress of circumstances aggravated the stress inherent in the case. Baker came down with "nervous headaches" which delayed his answers to the court and impeded his mobility.

Whether the Chaplins retained title to all the Negroes, or Baker won his third, neither party could realistically have hoped to save them from the Yankees. The southern regime's capacity for waging an offensive war had ended. Did the litigants believe that slavery would outlast the War? Or were they fighting for title to the Negroes in the hope that an armistice would give them compensation for the slaves they could prove they had owned? Compensation may have been at the backs of their minds, but each side's effort to get the better of lifelong enemies, to drive the other side sick, broke, and crazy, had become an absolute goal.

"Dark Deeds"

Isabella Baker's last will and testament left the deeds of 1845 "in full force and unrevoked." Far from a defeat, the ruling that "deferred" their "operation" had affirmed Mrs. Baker's power to deed, making it "subject *only*" to the continued existence of both marriage partners.[7] Now that death had removed the wife, the Chaplins demanded what was theirs. Their bill of complaint opened with an inventory of what they believed they had coming: four plantations, all "settled with dwelling houses, outhouses, barns, Negro quarters and such other houses and outbuildings as are necessary on such plantations," and all "well stocked with horses, cattle, hogs, poultry, provisions, boats, flats, wagons, carts, plantation utensils, carpenters' tools and so forth. . . ." Forty to fifty slaves were living at each place in 1845, and the Chaplins had expected to reap a healthy increase.

But under the management of Baker and Roux, Isabella's estate had declined. Plantation buildings and fences "were neglected and became dilapidated," the Chaplins told the court, "so that at this time there is hardly a building of any kind which is habitable or capable of being made so." Many buildings "have fallen down, others have been pulled down or removed, & not the least effort has been made to replace them." Livestock, poultry, and provisions "have nearly all been either consumed in use, destroyed, *sold* or lost, so that very little remains but the land and negroes," who were left without houses or provisions "for their subsistence."

The bill further stated that Baker and Roux had shuffled around the slaves, "many whose names complainants have not yet learned," and refused to tell the Chaplins which people were where. Baker had hired out at least 150 slaves to his daughter's husband, Bissell, who "employs them" growing rice on a Combahee plantation "from whence, not very long since, the Enemy carried off the greater part of the negroes." Thus the Chaplins' chattel property was exposed to the twin risks of Yankee raids and "diseases incident to the cultivation of rice, and such as may be occasioned by the change from dry cotton lands, on which most of them have always lived, to reclaimed swamp lands."

Other deeded Negroes had been taken out of state. Roux recently had started to carry four of them to Georgia, but passing through Charleston he lost one, the man Thomas, who smuggled himself to "the Yankee fleet" outside the harbor. Ten years earlier, Baker had "clandestinely" taken seven or more Negroes to Georgia or Florida, including the well-regarded Binah. Roux had known about it, and as a trustee he should have tried to get them back, but he had not. Now he could not say where they were, "or what is the subsequent increase of the woman who was young and healthy when removed." His "breach of good faith and want of common honesty," and Baker's general failure to preserve the settled property, "indicate a determination to defraud and deprive complainants of as much of the said Estate as they can."

The Chaplins begged the court to stop "this wanton waste and destruction." They wanted their mother's property distributed "in exact conformity" with her deeds and will. Baker, Roux, and Bissell should be made to account for all the Negroes, together with their issue, named in the "deed of marriage settlement"; to turn over to Dr. Johnson all slaves not cultivating crops; and to post security for the Negroes carried to other states. Bissell should give security for Mrs. Baker's field hands and contract a reasonable sum for their hire until the end of the year. Baker and Roux should restore the deeded lands, at their own expense and not from the profits of the estate, to the condition they had been in when the deeds were drawn up, in 1845, and should replenish or pay cash for the stock and other property since consumed.

Baker refuted the charges and leveled some of his own. He contrasted his own humanity and patriotism with a pattern of meanness, disobedience, and selfishness on the part of the Chaplins. He recited their history of "interference" with their mother, of "annoyance" with his lawful administration of her property, and of "defiance and violation" of injunctions forbidding them from trespassing on Mrs. Baker's estate. To the charge that he had stood by while her plantation buildings fell to ruin, he answered that they had been in an advanced state of decay when he married her. The dwelling house at Walnut Hill was dilapidated and "long since converted to the use of a negro driver & family," and the Negro houses were "barely tenantable." He had paid for constant repairs and even added two rooms to the dwelling house at Fields Point, in spite of his limited rights. He would have spent more on the place had his wife's lands been more productive and had their small income not been diverted to pay her debts.[8]

The War completed what time and other people's negligence had begun, said Baker. Fields Point was periodically boarded up after 1861. In February, 1864, a Federal raiding party burned the dwelling house, Negro houses, and outbuildings. But the enemy failed to liberate the Negroes. Baker had moved them, not to frustrate the Chaplins, as they pretended, but to save the property from falling into Yankee hands. Everything the Chaplins insinuated about his treatment of the Negroes was false, he declared. He never ill-treated them, but had always been "a kind and humane master" who gave them "good clothing [and] good medical treatment." It was the Chaplins who were evil masters, not he. When Mrs. Baker's people learned they had been deeded to her sons, "they openly expressed and demonstrated . . . that they wished no more children as they did not choose to belong to them." Hence, explained Baker, "the increase was very limited."

On the face of it, Baker's countercharge seems fantastic, outrageous—but not impossible. The only evidence—the number of Negro births and the mortality rate of the children—could be used to corroborate either side's accusation. Each had tried to enlist the support of the slaves against his adversary. Baker had an advantage because he lived with them. With his tendency for hyperbole, he may indeed have made out the Chaplins to be monsters. Whether from genuine fear or to please and flatter him, some of Mrs. Baker's slaves may have said in his hearing that they did not want to live with her sons. But to attribute to them the refusal to bear children because they believed that living with the Chaplins would be more oppressive than living with him must have tested the court's credulity. The Chaplin brothers were too new to planting in 1845 to have had much of a reputation for anything. If young Thomas Chaplin deviated from the norm, it was probably on the side of indulgence. There was enough contact among slaves from the Chaplin and Baker plantations for the word to get around. Baker did not make his charge lightly, but he knew that he did not have to prove it, and that the Chaplins could not disprove it. The charge was a gamble. It was based on hearsay and it flew against common sense. It was a damning admission that something was terribly wrong on Mrs. Baker's plantations, that her Negroes were unhappy and were not reproducing.

Baker took the gamble because he had a lot to explain. He had not made a good living at Fields Point and the slaves had suffered. Slowed by "failing" health and discouraged by his annual "failure" to make enough corn and potatoes, he moved the bulk of field hands as early as 1848 to Dunham Plantation, where he planted rice for twelve years. Fields Point was exhausted by sixty years of steady cultivation and he did not have the capital to rest it, or to break new land. Yet his luck was no better with rice than with cotton. He made poor crops, he said, because he could not impound enough water to flood the fields in time of drought.

Done with planting but not with slaves, he asked his friends for advice. Roux told him to hire out the Negroes "to the highest wages." So he sent some to work in Charleston, and contracted with Bissell to take the rest. True, nineteen* of them had run away "to the Yankee foe," but not through any fault of his. "It was an occurrence unavoidable and almost daily transpiring along our coast and Sea Island plantations," wrote Baker. No man "had power to prevent it." He could not move all the Negroes inland, as the Chaplins said he should have, because "suitable lands" were hard to find. Besides, he could not take them away from Bissell without abandoning the provision crops which "have greatly benefited our brave soldiers." While the Chaplins worried only about saving their property, Baker implied he wanted to help the Confederacy.

Bissell was also raising rice, at Dunham, and having better luck than Baker had had. "It is only necessary to state," wrote Baker, denying that rice cultivation was bad for the slaves, "that the habit, health and labor of the 'negro' is universally adapted to labor and exposure to the swamps and lowlands of the southern shores." As proof of his argument, he noted that not one of the slaves hired to Bissell had died. The blacks liked Bissell, Baker claimed; they called him "a good humane master," and the thought of leaving his "protection" filled them with "distress."

---

*"1-Eliza 2-Lydia 3-Willy 4-Sabrena 5-Eve 6-Billy 7-Sander 8-Ben 9-Bob 10-Pompey 11-Lavinia 12-Joe 13-Ben 14-Brister 15-Cumsee 16-Sharper 17-Abram 18-Susan 19-Thomas."

Baker responded irately to "the grave and insidious charge" that he had taken slaves out of the state and hidden them. The charge was nothing but a "false and malicious slander" whipped up by the Chaplins and *their attorney in collusion.*" The Chaplins knew it was not so, because those were the very Negroes he had sold to pay debts Thomas and Saxby had incurred and had talked their mother into co-signing. How absurd for him to be accused of improprieties, he moralized, when *he* was the victim of "extraordinary and unjust conduct"—"to wit," the deprivation of his marital rights. By giving everything to her sons and nothing to him, Mrs. Baker had displayed "an ill feeling and malice" inconsistent with "the ordinary good will and affection of the female heart." Either Mrs. Baker was unduly influenced to do what she did, or she was no ordinary female. Her behavior was "especially" strange because, he swore, *she* had proposed marriage to *him* and he had agreed only after receiving "promises of deep love" and a life interest in her estate. Then, to his everlasting regret, he was "most grossly deceived by the dissemblages of the lawyer," C. G. Memminger, who "never communicated nor exposed . . . the injurious alterations" in the marriage deed, cutting him out of the one-third share he had been promised. After the wedding, Mrs. Baker "violently and maliciously exercised the change of powers" in favor of her sons. "Dark deeds do rise to overwhelm men's eyes," Baker ended, calling on Shakespeare to express his plight.*

The Husband's Case

Baker laid out his case in full to his lawyer, Campbell.[9] He painted his wife as vain, needy, and unstable, possibly a murderer. "O, Hamlet, it is given out, etc.," he harangued, in support of the theory that two of his wife's first three husbands had died by foul play.[†] His situation did not exactly follow the script of *Hamlet:* in the play, the Queen's current husband has killed her last one, and *she* gets poisoned in the end. But Baker was not trying to be literal.

---

*Baker had in mind Hamlet's monologue anticipating the course of events, at the end of Act I, Scene II: ". . . foul deeds will rise/Though all the earth o'erwhelm them, to men's eyes."

†The line comes from *Hamlet,* Act I, Scene V. Hamlet's father's ghost has just confided that he did not die accidentally, but was murdered by Hamlet's uncle, the present King: "Now, Hamlet,/'Tis given out that, sleeping in mine orchard/A serpent stung me . . . The serpent that did sting thy father's life/Now wears his crown." And sleeps with his wife, he added.

He wanted to establish a climate of intrigue and to suggest that the world is made up of dupes and deceivers, that his relationships with the Chaplins were poisonous, that Thomas and Saxby were motivated by "engendered hatred" and incestuous impulses, and that his tragedy could be compared to the downfall of an innocent king. He wrote his story in fine detail, recalling conversations that had taken place more than twenty years before; meanwhile outside his room the city of Charleston lay under siege.

The marriage had been Isabella's idea, he repeated. Through his widowed sister, Mary E. Toomer, she had learned about the "great loss" he had suffered when his "lovely charming wife" died, leaving him to care for an infant girl.* Soon after the women talked, Baker received "a most unlooked for letter" from Mrs. Fields: she offered to ease his burden and raise the child. Baker's "dear aged mother" opposed the idea, so he wrote back to Mrs. Fields, thanking her but rejecting "her noble generous offer." Then came a second "remarkable letter," containing money and a list of things Mrs. Fields wanted him to buy for her. Next she sent a message that she would be passing through Charleston on her way to Greenville and wanted to see him; she closed the note with a few amorous lines of poetry. "I was not so green that I could not fathom her intentions," Baker told Campbell.

Mrs. Fields arrived in the city and "begged" him to meet her in her hotel room at ten o'clock at night, promising to explain her reasons for secrecy. He went, as directed, and she told him that her son Thomas and "her beautiful, delightful daughter-in-law, Mrs. Thomas B. Chaplin (sister of those noted rowdies, Wm. & John McDowell)," had heard of her "attachment" to him "and did most shamefully abuse her and myself and threatened that they would shoot me if she married me." Baker was shocked; marriage was the farthest thing from his mind. But he liked Mrs. Fields's attitude. "She left them indignantly, saying she was her own mistress, etc." Now she had come to Charleston with her other son, Saxby, and his wife, and she did not want Saxby to know her business, so she scheduled her meeting with Baker at this late hour. He was charmed. Mrs. Fields behaved "as remarkable and romantic as though she was a young woman, over head, heart, and ears, in love." She confessed she had been enamored of him ever since she

*Sarah Ann Brow was Baker's first wife; Sarah Harriet was his daughter.

spotted him as a young man clerking in a pharmacy. One thought led to another, and although she had buried three husbands, she said, she was determined to marry again because she could not count on her sons. Without a pause, she asked if he would be willing to change his "situation" and accompany her to Greenville. Baker replied "frankly" that he had heard of her sons' "bitter feelings" and while he did not fear the Chaplins, he did not wish "to risk my happiness by coming in contact with them." Don't "regard" them, she said; they were "beneath" him. If he would marry her she would make him entirely independent of them. Baker went home and talked over her offer with his family and friends. Solely to benefit his daughter, he agreed to marry Mrs. Fields. She wanted to leave for Greenville at once and marry when they got there, but he protested. They should marry before traveling together; and before they married, she should draw up a marriage settlement.

Baker recited to Campbell the convoluted history of this document: how Mrs. Fields had assured him he would get a third of her estate, and how Memminger, Webb, and "the lady" had conspired to cheat him out of it. There was not "a nick of truth" in Memminger's assertion that Baker had known about the changes in the settlement when he signed it. Memminger had told the court that Baker had said a "bad word" about Webb to him before the wedding, indicating that Baker knew Webb had been talking to his intended wife. Not true, Baker told Campbell; had he known Webb had been sneaking around, Webb would not have been welcome at the wedding—Isabella had invited him. Memminger had commended Baker's "liberality," when actually he was covering his tracks by suggesting that Baker's generosity prevented him from comprehending the changes so clearly set out in front of him. The truth, said Baker, was that he did not realize he had been deceived because he had never been told that changes had been made. Memminger had slipped him a string of assurances—"specimens of his peculiar tact and silvery tongue." "Give me a list of the negroes and I will draw up the settlement," Memminger had declared, slapping him on the back, as if the matter were sealed.

Neither had Memminger told Baker that Webb had met secretly with him, too. Webb had a hand, and a foot, in everything. On the day of the wedding, Isabella disclosed to Baker that she had recently paid off a twenty-five-hundred-dollar note to Webb by having him sell some of her stock, at a heavy loss, and she had just learned that Webb had purchased the stock himself. "We better change our factor," she told her husband-to-be. Baker obliged her the next day. He borrowed money from Ladson & Bee—at the suggestion of Memminger, who was playing both ends of the deck—to close out her account with Webb and to pay for their trip to Greenville.

A month passed, however, before Baker discovered the extent of Webb's tinkering. One night, Isabella said, " 'Mr. Baker, I think Mr. Webb is an enemy to you.' " She swore Baker to secrecy and told him all about Webb's visit to her two days before the wedding. Webb had asked if it was true that she was going to marry. " 'Who is the fortunate man?' " " 'Dr. Baker.' " " 'Who? Baker the druggist? That man?' " (Baker explained to Campbell that "Mrs. Baker had been a belle in her early days, & much tainted with vanity.") Why did she want to marry again, Webb continued, after three marriages? (The remark "aroused her sparkling eyes," Baker interjected.) If Webb were a widower, she replied, " 'you would not think me too old to become your wife.' " Webb laughed and changed the subject. " 'Do you know that Baker is bankrupt, and is only marrying you for your property?' " Isabella was unmoved. Then Webb tried a different tack. He asked her if she was going to change her church. ("Mrs. Baker was attached to the Episcopal Church," wrote Baker, explaining the significance of the question, "and extremely bigoted.") Webb told her that Baker was a Unitarian. " 'You must be mistaken,' " she snapped. Webb kept up "his diabolical artifice," and though Mrs. Fields hotly defended the Unitarian faith, he had upset her. (The night before the wedding, recalled Baker, she had inquired into his religion. He told her he had attended the Unitarian Church three or four times but did not believe in their doctrine.) Webb wanted to know if she had drawn up a marriage settlement. He "very inquisitively asked how she had distributed her property." She told him, and not liking what he heard, he said he would speak to Memminger. She silently assented. ("Mark me," Baker told Campbell, this was the moment the plot to defraud him was hatched.)

As a result of this conversation with Isabella, wrote Baker, he had "lost all confidence and regard for her." He was furious that on the eve of their wedding she had allowed Webb to "assail" his character. How dare Memminger deny knowing it was Webb who had " 'poured a *leprous distilment* into Mrs. B.'s ears and caused her to change the deed.' "* Memminger as much as said so in his testimony. He said so many things, and he contradicted himself several times, but wisely he never took an oath. First, he claimed that he, or his partner, had told Baker about the changes in the marriage deed. Then, "shameful and barefaced," he had said, " 'I am sorry Baker, I thought Mrs. Baker had informed you.' " Still, he placed the burden of responsibility on Baker. " 'You have married into a hornet's nest,' " Memminger told him, in front of Roux. Scarcely able to control his "passions of resentment," Baker paid off Memminger—$465—wrote him a letter calling him "a liar," and hired Petigru to conduct his appeal. Memminger and Petigru were opposites. Memminger was "rascally" and "trickish." "Honest" Petigru "had a large noble heart, open to the appreciation of human rights and justice," and so forth. It was difficult to replace such a man. "Mr. Petigru made him [Memminger] suffer seriously before the chancellor and the Court," exulted Baker. He hoped Campbell would represent him and do as well "in this extraordinary item, which I am about to endeavor to reopen for the courts of justice."

Baker closed the letter with flowery regards and a pledge of humility; but as there was blank space left on the page, he filled it with a postscript, adding a final charge to his indictment of Memminger. Days after the wedding, he wrote, Memminger had taken "the liberty" of talking to Mrs. Baker without her husband's knowledge or consent, and had proposed that she separate from Baker—divorce was not permissible in South Carolina—giving him a third of the settled property for a send-off. There is no evidence she ever considered making such a deal. That a proposal was in the wind, however, may explain why Thomas and Saxby moved quickly and ruthlessly to secure deeds from their mother. Had Memminger kept quiet and not aroused their fears and jealousies, Baker might have waited for a favorable moment—one of the infrequent periods in their twenty-year marriage, for instance, when he and Isabella shared a bed—to press his claim.

Material Witnesses
Of the other parties to the case, John Bissell was the most reluctant. He had married Baker's daughter, Sarah, with the hope, perhaps,

---

*Hamlet's father's ghost tells him (Act I, Scene V): "Upon my secure hour thy uncle stole/With juice of cursed hebenon in a vial/And in the porches of mine ears did pour/The leprous distilment. . . . Thus was I, sleeping, by a brother's hand/Of life, of crown, of queen, at once despatch'd."

of eventually acquiring one of Mrs. Baker's plantations, if his father-in-law could win his third. In the meantime, he assisted Baker
and Roux in managing Isabella's estate, and when the War broke
out, he had sole control of most of her slaves. As soon as Isabella
died, DeTreville informed him that the Chaplins now owned all
the property, and proposed that in exchange for using *their* slaves to
finish making his crops, Bissell compile a list of Negroes in his possession, arranged by families and with their ages as near as he could
guess; that he deliver the house servants and mechanics immediately to Walterboro; that he give security to Thomas and Saxby
Chaplin for the field hands' wages through January 1, 1865, and
security to Thomas alone for rent "of so much of the land called
Dunham" as he had planted.[10]

Bissell cooperated at first. He sent along a list of slaves but put
off paying security until he talked to his lawyer. DeTreville wrote
back saying Bissell had confused the names of several house servants. Thomas B. Chaplin had taken mental notes on the Negroes
at his mother's funeral, and the one Bissell called Carly was Celia;
Sarah was Sarah Ann; Bissell forgot to identify Neptune, who had
been walking behind Bissell's sulky in the cortege; and the woman
he called Martha was someone else. DeTreville advised Bissell to
pay the war tax on the Negroes, to "clothe & shoe them," but to
deduct the costs equally from the "hire" due to Baker and the hire
due to *"us."* He "respectfully" asked Bissell to respond to the rest of
his proposition and to help close the matter quickly. Bissell did not
get back to him for a month. DeTreville grew impatient and offended, each week sending Bissell a curt reminder. "Time is slip-
ping by rapidly," he wrote, on September 24; "January is near at
hand"—referring to the expiration of Bissell's lease. "You have
kept me waiting for an answer or an interview much longer than I
expected," he wrote again, on September 30. "Do let there be no
further delay."

Ten days later, DeTreville received a disappointing fifty words
from Bissell, "in tone unlike anything" he had ever heard from
him. No longer cordial, or even neutral, Bissell had gone over to
Baker's camp. Apparently the envelope was addressed in Baker's
hand. "This at once explains the influence under which you
wrote," DeTreville replied. Your letter "has put an end to a nego-
tiation which only had for its object the extraction of yourself from
the consequences of a disagreeable litigation." DeTreville had been
candid and fair. The previous summer he had sent Bissell a list of

"certain requirements which a child could understand." Bissell had objected only to paying rent on Dunham—"so small a matter," DeTreville had assured him, that the Chaplins could be persuaded to forget it. Bissell had seemed pleased but strangely silent on the rest of DeTreville's terms. "You kept me under the delusion that you intended to accept them and even sent me a list of the negroes in your possession," grumbled DeTreville.[11]

Now Bissell had switched lawyers, taking on Baker's man Campbell, and telling DeTreville to go to *him* if he wanted to read Bissell's lease—which, DeTreville mocked, "I am not aware that I ever wanted to see." DeTreville had met with Bissell, at Bissell's request, and promised that "every and anything you might say to me should be sacred & never used against you in any way." He had assumed "the obligation would be *reciprocal*," but he was fooled: Bissell had repeated to Campbell what DeTreville had told him in confidence, "using what was intended by me as an act of kindness and courtesy to you to my disadvantage," and placing him in a "false position with my clients." DeTreville cautioned Bissell that he was being used by Baker, "who I know a great deal better than you do." "I beg you to bear in mind," he concluded, "that at the death of Mrs. Baker, our negroes were in your actual possession—not in Doct. Baker's." There was nothing more to discuss. "You have received notice that they are our negroes," he reiterated, "and we shall expect you to produce them when we call for them."[12]

DeTreville followed up this letter with a separate bill against Bissell. He obtained an affidavit from Saxby Chaplin's brother-in-law, Lawrence J. Witsell, stating that Bissell's position on the Combahee was "peculiarly exposed & a dangerous place of residence for negroes." If the Yankees came up the river, "it would be impossible to remove the negroes . . . in time, or to prevent them from going to the enemy."[13] Bissell wrote Campbell that the sheriff had delivered DeTreville's demands, but that he, Bissell, had refused to comply. "I would not give one cent security," he crowed. The sheriff left empty-handed and went back to the court for instructions. Savoring his triumph, Bissell asked Campbell if he might keep the Negroes past January 1, to give him additional time "to get my rice and cotton out."[14]

Roux had written to Bissell, half-warning and half-pleading with him not to give up *any* of the slaves because "such a proceeding would seriously compromise Mr. Baker's interest under the marriage settlement,"[15] which was Bissell's interest, too, indirectly.

Roux also wrote a long letter to Campbell, from the upcountry, at the end of October—while 120 miles to the west, Sherman was gearing up in Atlanta for his march to the sea. Making no mention of current events, Roux rehashed the origins of the marriage settlement, supporting Baker's version on all major points, and offering a few new facts. He confirmed that he had been in the room when Memminger told Baker that the first draft of the deed gave him "absolute privilege of the whole property" during his wife's life, "and absolute third at her death." Mrs. Baker had also been in the room, he added, and while "she was under some excitement, nothing unpleasant occurred." Memminger regretted past misunderstandings, but said he could do nothing to invalidate the settlement.

In the days and weeks that followed, Memminger "appeared to be put to his wits' end to arrange matters so that they should work smoothly"—a possible reference to his separation plan. Keeping up a positive front, Memminger vouched that Mrs. Baker could not execute the power she thought she had—she was *not* in the room for this discussion—because it went against tradition and the public interest. He advised Baker to press for his rights and to "resist & refuse to pay the debts of the Chaplins." At this time, Baker "was much annoyed by the trespasses of Thomas B. and Saxby Chaplin" on their mother's plantations. Memminger told him "to employ some bulldogs & double-fisted irishmen to keep them off the place"—a suggestion that Baker called "trashy gasconade." Yet Baker and Roux had stuck with Memminger through the lower-court hearing because "we presumed that he ought to know the nature of the deed." They turned to Petigru when the Chaplins and DeTreville filed a countersuit. Petigru convinced the court that the "smuggled clause" was " 'an innovation' " which should not "take precedence over the bona fide settlement." If justice was served, wrote Roux, "after all the litigation, provocation & heartburnings" Baker had suffered, he would again be rewarded "with a liberal construction of the first deed without regard to the objectionable clauses."[16]

Baker's Last Stand

Baker was first to show a willingness to compromise. Writing to Campbell on November 12, a day after DeTreville filed a second bill demanding security for the seven slaves Baker allegedly had sent or carried out of state, Baker accounted for each one and of-

fered to "give up and over to the legal claimants" the two he nominally controlled—Martha, his personal servant, and Hagar, an inveterate runaway he had hired out in Charleston. Violet was with
Roux, in Georgia, beyond his reach. Thomas had "gone over to the
enemy." Binah, the "healthy" young woman about whom the
Chaplins were so concerned, had been sold with her two children
during Mrs. Baker's lifetime, "to pay her individual debts and
those of her sons, Thomas B. and Saxby Chaplin." Thus, Baker was
not proposing to give up very much, and in no way was he abandoning his ultimate goals. He was "willing and ready" to relin-
quish two-sevenths of the property he was accused of abducting,
but only by "a proper and legal" order and not by a browbeating
bill written on official stationery.

On November 18, Baker, Roux, and Bissell were subpoenaed to
appear in court on the twenty-eighth. Roux's subpoena could not
be delivered, and while papers might reach Baker and Bissell,
fighting on the roads could bar them from traveling. To speed the
case along, the master in equity for Colleton District, C. B. Farmer,
wrote to Campbell stating how he was inclined to act on the
Chaplins' bills, and asking Campbell to write a response at once, so
that the case could be decided before the War encroached on any
more of the property. Farmer was leaning toward giving the Chaplins almost all that they asked for, but he insisted his mind was not
made up. "Your argument and authorities," he told Campbell,
"may dissipate entirely . . . my present inclination." (The issue of
Baker's inheritance was not raised.) If Campbell needed more time
to answer, Farmer would "accommodate" him. But if he heard
nothing before the court date, Farmer would conclude that Campbell "acquiesce[s] in what I have suggested as my course."[17]

Campbell's answer, if he wrote one, has not survived, but other
documents indicate that Baker wanted to go on fighting. On December 6, he and Bissell were enjoined from interfering with Mrs.
Baker's estate in any way. On the eleventh, Baker wrote to Campbell, cursing "the sneaking and malicious procedure" of DeTreville, who had gotten the injunction "through his 'chum,' "
Farmer, an old friend of Mrs. Baker and her son Saxby. Farmer
had also ordered Baker to post a five-thousand-dollar bond for the
seven outstanding Negroes.

Baker repeated his willingness to surrender Martha and Hagar
and to prove the whereabouts of the others. New worries, generated
by the other enemy, were eating at him. Roux had been forced into

the militia in Georgia and might be lost to him for the duration of the War. Bissell was trapped down on the Combahee by "the exciting and terrible fighting along the line of the Charleston & Savannah Railroad."[18] He was trying to remove his family—Baker's daughter and her children—as well as the 170 Negroes with whom he had been enjoined from interfering. Even if he got them all out of harm's way, the military authorities might not let him go to Charleston to borrow the money he needed for security. All white men capable of bearing arms were forbidden to leave their districts. Baker himself was refused a "passport" to go to Green Pond to help Bissell. "I was referred to General Ransom,"* he told Campbell, "and applied to leave on a freight train," but the "De-Vil" made him change his plans and stay in Charleston. Every way he turned he was pinned down by his two enemies—the slave-stealing Yankees and the thieving secessionist lawyer. Unable to do anything to check the military foe, then closing in from two directions, he marshaled his strength for one last fight against his old persecutor. "It is high time to end my sufferings and the *dark malice of his furious revenge,* etc., etc."[†] Though Baker would not have said so, he was in a race against Sherman to thwart DeTreville's desires.

The last part of Baker's letter was taken up with his tribulations over a cow. Bissell had been keeping a cow for Campbell down on the Combahee, and Campbell wanted it moved to Columbia, where he was retreating for safety. First the cow had to be sent to Charleston. But Baker could not get train passage for her. Space on trains was scarce, and the trains were not sticking to schedule. Friday's train for Savannah arrived in Charleston on Saturday. Saturday's train never came, "oweing to the destruction" of a railroad bridge. Baker had "heard personally from the Express Messenger Mr. Slatterly . . . that our forces had repulsed and driven off the enemy." Despite the good news, "matters look very gloomy . . . quite blue and in a bad state." Sherman was reported to be ten miles from Savannah—actually, he was inside the city when Baker

---

*Robert Ransom, Jr., former Indian fighter and cavalry teacher at West Point. He led the Confederate cavalry under Longstreet in the latter part of 1863 and the first half of 1864. He had recently assumed command at Charleston when Baker petitioned him.
†Shakespearean language, but not a quotation. See, for example, *Measure for Measure,* Act III, Scene II: Vincentio, Duke of Vienna, disguised as a friar, upon hearing himself described by Lucio as "a very superficial, ignorant, unweighing fellow," replies, "You speak unskilfully; or, if your knowledge be more, it is much darkened in your malice."

was writing—and when the Yankees got there train service would stop altogether.*

As the noose tightened around Baker, it loosened up around Roux. Augusta was safe for the moment, though there was no telling where Sherman would strike next. With single-minded belligerence toward DeTreville and the Chaplins, Roux wrote to Campbell, on December 15, telling him not to let Bissell give up any of the Negroes before the case was heard, since " 'possession is nine points in the law.' " Roux's letter did not contain a single reference to the War. If there was a sense of personal danger, the source was DeTreville, not the Yankees. Roux stuck doggedly to the case, taking sustenance from the events of 1845. DeTreville had filed injunctions against Baker and him before, but "as Mrs. B. had made over a part of her estate to DeTreville in one of her 'charitable' deeds under the contraband clause," Petigru had obtained a court order prohibiting Mrs. Baker, the Chaplins, *and* their attorney from visiting any of her plantations, except the one she lived on. The court had given Roux "supervision of the whole estate," and he in turn "had made Baker my agent to visit the places in my stead." Now, Roux heard from Baker, "DeTreville has commenced at his old tricks of injunctions, securities, etc., against us." With Petigru dead, Roux was taking no chances. He was staying put, not—as Baker contended—because the military situation compelled him to, but because he feared if he returned to Charleston, DeTreville would place him under an injunction. Thus, like an army unto himself, DeTreville had Roux and Baker pinned down in separate cities. Their fate was in Campbell's hands, said Roux. He was optimistic because the presiding judge in 1846 had "expressed a very favorable opinion to Mr. Petigru upon Baker's ultimate prospects." His dearest wish, like Baker's, was to stop DeTreville. "I trust, my dear sir," he implored, "that you will not let that archfiend have his way entirely in this matter, as he has heretofore hesitated at nothing which would enable him to accomplish his designs."[19]

A Sudden Resolution

The danger that Mrs. Baker's slaves would all be set free by force did not dampen the ardor of the disputants. If anything, the

---

*On December 22, 1864, Sherman sent a message to President Lincoln: "I beg to present to you, as a Christmas gift, the city of Savannah."

danger tended to strengthen their attachment to slavery. It high-lighted the fact that slaveholding was their means of obtaining an income. By pursuing title to the Negroes in the face of extraordinary obstacles, Baker and the Chaplins were not only defending their livelihood but, as they pointed out, their rights and honor as well.

No records survive to show whether Magistrate Farmer ever wrote his decision, or whether Baker countersued. Attorney Campbell may have advised Baker and Bissell to accept Farmer's preliminary terms, and persuaded Baker that the evidence would not support his claim of a third. In any case Baker probably would not have had time to sue before the conquering Union Army disbanded the court. It would be wrong to conclude, however, that the emancipation of Mrs. Baker's slaves ended the case.* Still unresolved was the division of Mrs. Baker's plantations—except for Riverside, on St. Helena Island, which had been confiscated by the Federal Government, under the Tax Act of 1862. Unless Bissell had already paid the Chaplins, he still would have owed them rent for planting at Dunham and for using *their* Negroes while they were yet slaves, having incurred these obligations under "the recognized and subsisting law." DeTreville could have demanded the cash value of the slaves Mrs. Baker had deeded to *him,* and the court would have had to decide whether Baker or the Chaplins were liable. All these claims are theoretical, but the State Appeals Court heard many cases after 1866 involving identical issues. A debt was a debt; neither emancipation nor any other "legal consequences of extraneous events" could change that.[†]

Mortgage papers signed at the beginning of 1866 confirm that Thomas, Saxby, and their children acquired all of Isabella's land. They would lose it all by 1872. Baker died intestate in Charleston in 1867. Thus, as Thomas Chaplin noted again and again, the land

---

*For the purpose of establishing a date when Negroes ceased to be property, the State Appeals Court in 1866 held that slaves "were not made free by the President's proclamation, in law, any more than they were in fact. . . . Emancipation was accomplished by the conquest of the country. Until that took place, slavery continued after the proclamation [signed January 1, 1863] just as it had existed before, and it ceased to exist in the different parts of the State as they fell into the hands of the conqueror." (*William L. Pickett* v. *John H. Williams,* December, 1867, 13 Rich E.Q. 366, in S.C. Reports, Book 29.)
†Exceptions to this rule were contracts for the purchase of slaves. The South Carolina State Constitution of 1868 declared such covenants "null and void" and unenforceable.

did none of them any good.* Stripped down to his own labor, Chaplin had one hope of rising above subsistence—to redeem his plantation on St. Helena Island. By luck, Tombee had been reserved for a school and hospital which never were built. Had it been divided into small parcels and sold, as were many St. Helena plantations, Chaplin would not have been allowed to sue for it. Had the place *not* been confiscated and kept out of his hands, he would have mortgaged and lost it when he first went back to planting.

*Bissell, however, continued to plant on the Combahee, through the 1870s, and vastly expanded his holdings. In 1873, he controlled thirty-five hundred acres and employed eight hundred wage laborers at harvest time. One man who worked for him declared that he had " 'bin a grate help to our poor colord people' " by advancing supplies and credit to them in hard times. Yet not everyone praised his generosity. Bissell maintained his own store and paid his workers in checks or scrip which only he could redeem. Bacon, for example, which generally sold for ten cents a pound, sold for twenty-five cents at his commissary; molasses, "regularly forty cents per gallon, was three times that price, 'and other articles in proportion.' " In 1876, his workers all walked off the job and joined in a general strike on the Combahee protesting low wages and the practice of payment by checks. Bissell tried to break the strike by recruiting members of a black Democratic club in Walterboro and calling "on the white Democratic rifle club to protect them." The tactic did not work. He found, as one journalist later recalled, that "politics and labor" were "oddly mixed." His striking workers were "Republican negroes." *Their* party, the party of Lincoln and the emancipators, was yet in power in the state. They regarded the black Democrats as traitors and forcibly stopped them from working. But their white Republican allies, worried about the upcoming election, failed to come to their aid. The strike collapsed, the Republicans were driven from office, and the planters breathed easier, knowing they could count thereafter on the state to crush any workers' resistance. (See Eric Foner, *Nothing But Freedom: Emancipation and Its Legacy* [Baton Rouge, La., 1983], 90–104.)

13. The Home Front

Northern Invaders

On November 8, 1861, the day he landed on Hilton Head, "the other General Sherman" issued a proclamation: "Citizens of South Carolina, the civilized world stands appalled at the course you are pursuing; appalled at the crime you are committing against your mother—the best, most enlightened, and heretofore most prosperous of nations. . . ." Federal aims were limited, Sherman declared, to suppressing the insurrection. If the Sea Islanders would lay down their arms, slavery would be left alone. "We have come amongst you with no feeling of personal animosity; no desire to harm your citizens, destroy your property or interfere with your lawful rights or your social and local institutions." But if "this fratricidal war" continued, the planters stood to lose their property, because rights protected by the state were "subordinate to military exigencies" created by rebellion.[1]

Despite its conciliatory language, Sherman's proclamation justified the seizure of civilian property—a new twist to the rules of warfare and a harbinger of things to come. This was the first of several important decrees addressed to people who had no way of hearing them. The planters had gone. Their property was already changing hands. The Negroes, reported Union officers, were "feasting upon the corn, cattle, and turkeys of their fugitive masters."[2] They were occupying the Big Houses, smoking cigars, and trying out the billiards tables. Clothes were the first items taken, and when the clothes gave out, women made dresses out of lace curtains and men cut suits from "gaudy carpeting just torn up from the floor." The very floors were ripped up, recut, and laid down in the Negro cabins.

From all reports, Union soldiers were making a beeline for the planters' wines and liquors. With the arrival of Treasury Department agents sent to gather the cotton, looting commenced on a grander scale. Furniture, books, paintings, vases, rugs, botanical collections—"every article which would command a price either on Broadway or Chatham Street"[3]—was packed up and shipped out. Cotton agents appropriated the finest horses and wagons on the islands. They would drive from plantation to plantation, swooping up the cotton as it was picked. Within a few months they shipped two and a half million pounds of raw fiber to New York. Some of the profits went to fund the War, but much of the money simply "melted away." A greater loss, one that would be felt for many years, was the cotton seed thrown away after ginning, seed that represented many generations of selection. Not until 1866 did the cotton planted in St. Helena Parish again approach "fair" quality.

On the heels of the soldiers and cotton agents came abolitionists. Three weeks after the military invasion, the Treasury Department sent Edward Pierce, a young lawyer from Massachusetts, to take charge of abandoned lands and to organize the blacks to work for wages. Pierce recruited about a dozen young white men to superintend the plantations. In general, they were the well-educated sons and relatives of old-time abolitionists. Some were medical or divinity students, and only one called himself a farmer. None had any experience raising cotton or managing field hands. To guide the black people's transition to freedom, Pierce mobilized teachers and missionaries from religious and charitable organizations in the North.[4] Most came South with the idea of doing "emancipation work"; some stayed to make money and some stayed out of satisfaction with their new lives. Laura M. Towne, who commented on Chaplin's political activities in the late '70s, exchanged a cosmopolitan existence in Philadelphia for a lifelong career of educating the freedmen. William F. Allen, the song collector, saw an opportunity to study a culture that had never been taken seriously. He stayed three years.* Allen made friends with the superintendents but kept his distance from the missionaries. The missionary societies, he complained, sent embezzlers and maniacs fit "for nothing" but living off charity, "hangers-on," and "scoundrels who came only to speculate for themselves and their sect."[5] These people went home when the novelty wore off. Sickness, heat, mosquitoes,

---

*The first fifty-seven songs in Allen's *Slave Songs of the United States* (New York, 1867) were collected at Captain John Fripp's Big House Plantation, on St. Helena Island.

and assorted hardships drove others away. Among those who stayed, many felt crossed by the Army, the Treasury Department, and other Federal agencies for whom the "great occasion of the War" was saving the Union, not freeing the Negro. "Anti-slavery is to be kept in the background for fear of exciting the animosity of the Army," wrote Towne, in April, 1862. "We have the odium of out and out abolitionists," she admitted; "why not take the credit?"[6]

Prominent in the flood of invaders were scores of merchants and tradesmen. The withdrawal of the old landowners and sudden freedom for the blacks turned the Sea Islands into an economic frontier. Now that black people were earning wages, they had money to spend, as well as the need and liberty to buy groceries and dry goods. Wheat bread, formerly reserved for white tables, became a universal favorite. The people craved underwear, colorful clothing, hats, shoes—anything but the yellow osnaburgs and russet-colored brogans of slavery. "All sorts of Yankee ventures" cropped up, some to serve and some to prey on the freedmen and soldiers. A Philadelphia aid society opened a store on St. Helena Island "for the purpose of maintaining reasonable prices." Its manager, "Friend Harris," once was "fined in Delaware three thousand dollars for harboring and assisting fugitive slaves," wrote Edward L. Pierce, paying Harris lighthearted respect, "but he now harbors and assists them at a much cheaper rate."[7] One enterprising individual began manufacturing pies "in the old Connecticut style,"* a Yankee lieutenant sardonically observed, and soon had "laid the foundation of an immense fortune."[8]

To the wealthy men who had been displaced, the Yankee occupation seemed an exercise in exploitation. Never at peace after the Confederate defeat, Richard DeTreville blasted the enemy: "The local citizens of Martha's Vineyard, Cape Cod, Boston, and Providence—descendants of the glorious Puritans—true and fervent worshippers of the *Almighty Dollar*—rushed in with their codfish and onions and molasses, to trade with the half-civilized negro, on the fairest and most honorable terms. Cuffee, in the hands of a real 'Downeaster' . . ."† [9]

---

*A deep-dish fruit pie sweetened with molasses.
†"Cuffee" was a common Negro name, from the Fanti (a West African language), given to a boy born on a Friday. DeTreville was using it generically, to stand for the typical slave. A "Downeaster" is a native of New England, particularly someone from Maine.

By 1863, the white population of St. Helena Island, bolstered by five thousand soldiers camped at Lands End, had increased twentyfold. Longtime black residents, used to being an overwhelming majority, were outnumbered by whites two to one, and by black outsiders, three to one. As word spread that St. Helena was free, the Parish became a haven for people running from slavery from as far away as Florida. Thousands of black refugees rowed and paddled to St. Helena from Edisto and other islands near Charleston.* Worried they might lose their places on the land, the native freedmen hemmed the new arrivals into St. Helenaville. By Christmas, 1864, refugees were going ashore on St. Helena in advance of William Tecumseh Sherman's army at the rate of one hundred a day.

The Port Royal Experiment
"Oh, but it is a great time to live in," exclaimed Arthur Sumner, one of Pierce's superintendents. "I am only in John Brown's Army," he wrote to a friend in the First Massachusetts Heavy Artillery, "but I feel I am doing something nevertheless."[10] Sumner eventually soured on the work, but early on he felt he was helping to change the world. To him, as to Allen and Towne, the "Port Royal Experiment" was primarily an educational movement. They found the black children "very teachable," "as bright as white children the same age," only held back by "bad habits." Towne's experience was discouraging at first. Her new students "had no idea of sitting still, of giving attention, of ceasing to talk aloud. They lay down and went to sleep, they scuffled and struck each other. They got up by the dozen, made their curtsies, and walked off to the neighboring field for black berries, coming back to their seats with a curtsey when they were ready. They evidently did not understand me and I could not understand them, and after two hours and a half of effort I was thoroughly exhausted."[11] But discipline could be taught, drilled. "Generations of mere animal life" had retarded cultural development but had not impaired people's minds.[12] The abolitionists took it upon themselves to conquer the "barbarous element" wherever it appeared—in song, dance, reli-

---

*Edisto residents tell a different story. They claim that hundreds of blacks from St. Helena sought refuge on Edisto because Federal authorities at Port Royal could not assure provisions and would not allow the people to grow food for themselves. Indeed, many freedmen did flee St. Helena to avoid conscription into the Union Army when they were guaranteed neither food nor wages.

gion, medicine. Sumner and Towne were repulsed, for example, by a form of religious devotion called the shout, a combined dance and chant decidedly not of European origin. Towne denounced it as "idol worship" and savagery. Allen was more analytic, but cold, dismissing the "shout" as a harmless curiosity that "arises from the strange connection between dancing and religious worship which was so frequent among the ancients."[13] He recognized the superiority of sonorous African spirituals to dull white hymn-singing, but he shrugged off the freedmen's patois as an example of "phonetic decay."

Notwithstanding their good intentions, the superintendents and teachers began mimicking the departed masters. They availed themselves of servants and settled into a pattern of afternoon visits and teas. "I have usurped the dominion of William A. Chisolm," wrote Arthur Sumner, from his quarters at Littlewood Plantation, "including his house, his ox, his ass, his manservant, his maid-servant, and everything else that was Chisolm's."[14] He also borrowed Chisolm's horse, Tom B. After a year of playing the part of Chisolm, Sumner had changed. "He is now a landed proprietor, or planter," observed Towne, "and takes a planter's view of all things."[15] Unhappy with himself and feeling unappreciated by the blacks, who, he believed, distrusted all white people indiscriminately, Sumner pulled out in a huff.*

To Edward Pierce and his boss, Treasury Secretary Salmon P. Chase, the great question of the Port Royal experiment was whether the freedmen would work without masters and "keep up the culture of cotton, an industry which was deemed essential to the national prosperity."[16] Pierce told a gathering of freedmen on St. Helena "that their masters had always told us, and had many people believe so, that they were lazy and would not work unless whipped to it. . . . Mr. Lincoln had sent us down here to see if it was so." They would have to work, he lectured, "if they were to be free . . . and would be shut up or deprived of privileges if they did not." The Government would pay them wages, not much at first, but if they proved willing, "by and by they would be as well off as white people."[17] The freedmen were dubious. They wanted assurances that the Government "would stand by them against their masters ever coming back."[18] They knew a good wage from a poor

*Sumner lived in Charleston after the War and found satisfaction working in schools for the freedmen.

wage and resented the idea of being underpaid. Who would own the land? the freedmen wanted to know, having heard from soldiers that Mr. Lincoln wanted them to have it. Such forwardness delighted Pierce. "Here is the solution to the vexed industrial question," he rejoiced. "The indisposition to labor is overcome by motives . . . such as the love of life, the desire to be well clothed and fed."[19]

Disappointed by the small, inferior cotton crop of 1862, the Treasury Department took steps to build a stable, conservative economy. The "great object" of the Government's experiment was redefined as "the proper, permanent, and efficient organization of a system of labor for the freed people," who were expected "to crowd upon" the Union Army as it advanced.[20] Tax commissioners, sent in 1862 ostensibly to collect a war tax, proposed selling the abandoned lands to loyal whites, thus returning agriculture to private enterprise and spreading northern managerial practices in the South.

If the plan worked in St. Helena Parish, it could be tried wherever the Government took control of the land; it might even evolve into a system of rewarding white southerners for staying loyal to the Union. The plan was hatched, however, without consulting the freedmen, who were growing bolder in expressing their hopes for the future. Short of demanding title to the land, they asserted the right to decide what to grow. Just as Pierce had feared, they wanted to concentrate on food crops and minimize their dependence on the market. They refused to dig marsh mud, without which they could not grow as large a crop or fine a staple as they used to. Laura Towne found it "very touching" to hear freedmen beg the superintendents "to let them plant and tend corn, not cotton."[21] The Yankees were adamant: they "preach nothing but cotton, cotton." In secret, the blacks sowed corn in the cotton rows; when the corn sprouted, they were told to dig it up or face expulsion themselves.

Thus, newcomers and natives all had plans for the land. The missionaries envisaged a commonwealth of independent farmers, a replica of mythic New England, complete with public schools and neatly painted towns. The Treasury Department wanted to maximize revenues and production by selling property in large geometric tracts—disregarding topography, history, and the wishes of the freedmen. Military authorities wanted to break up the large estates which had conferred such unreasonable powers on a small proprietary group. They also wanted to punish the "high-blooded hidalgos"[22] who had started the War, and to keep the blacks from moving anywhere else. "Nearly all conceivable social problems are involved . . . in the fundamental distribution of the land," declared the soldiers' newspaper, *Free South*.[23] Though the generals disdained the abolitionists, they backed the idea of conveying the land to the freedmen—with one stipulation, harking back to the military incentives of the ancient Roman Empire: if the conquered lands were to be sold, Union soldiers and sailors should be allowed to bid for them.

The "essential pre-requisite" for carrying out any of these schemes was that the Federal Government obtain legal possession of the soil, so it could give clear title to whoever came next. Months before the theories justifying confiscation were articulated, the machinery for seizing the plantations was in place.

Land Confiscation and Redistribution

On August 5, 1861, Congress levied a tax on all the states, including the eleven which had seceded, to raise money for the War. South Carolina's share was computed at $363,570.66. Once Federal authority was reestablished on the Sea Islands, the Government could begin collecting. On June 7, 1862, Congress passed "an Act for the collection of taxes in insurrectionary districts within the United States," appointing three commissioners to determine the amounts owed by St. Helena planters, according to prewar property valuations. The rebels were to be given sixty days to pay, or forfeit their lands to the United States. Plantations thus acquired by the Government would be offered at public sale in lots not exceeding 320 acres. Only "loyal citizens" and freedmen would be allowed to bid. Since the freedmen had no money to make large purchases, they were effectively barred from buying. The first sale was set for February 11, 1863—in time for planting the cotton crop.

Though called a tax act, the Act of 1862 was, in Richard De-Treville's words, "simply an act of confiscation . . . a bill of attainder, intended to punish, without trial all who owned property in an insurrectionary district. . . ."[24] Ironically, the abolitionists, Union generals, and freedmen were also outraged, because the Act foreclosed against the blacks. "The Negro of the South owns the soil of the South by virtue of his long labor upon it, as the only cultivator," protested the *Free South*.[25] On February 7, four days before the scheduled sale, General David Hunter, commander of the Military District of South Carolina, canceled it. The tax commissioners complained to President Lincoln. Their job was to get the best price for the lands, not to give them away. On February 11, they sold a plantation, against Hunter's orders. Hunter promised to have them arrested if they tried to sell another. Congress stepped into the dispute, postponing the auction and authorizing the commissioners to strike off at least two-thirds of the property in the name of the United States, for military, educational, and charitable purposes. Lands in the latter category would be held for resale at a later date.

Meanwhile, work on the new crop had come to a standstill, "because nobody knows whom it is for or who is going to pay for it."[26] Anxious to resume preparations for planting, the commissioners accepted the compromise, thus putting off for a year the question of who ultimately would acquire the land. On March 9, the sale got under way. By the evening of the tenth, ninety percent of the high land in St. Helena Parish, a total of 76,755 acres, had been sold. Most of it, 60,296 acres, was struck off to the United States, at fifteen to seventy-five cents an acre. Private white investors bought another 14,479 acres, including forty-one plantations, at a dollar to a dollar and a quarter an acre—about one-fifteenth the prewar value. Freedmen on six plantations pooled their money and bought 2,000 acres. Edward S. Philbrick, a New Englander who had superintended a plantation for a year, led a syndicate that purchased 6,795 acres on St. Helena Island, for seven thousand dollars. At the close of the sale, Philbrick and friends owned one-third of the Island, home to one thousand black people. Philbrick bought heavily into Fripp properties, including Captain John Fripp's Big House and Mulberry plantations, and William Fripp's Point Place. In two days, twenty Fripp plantations, covering 11,000 acres, passed forever out of Fripp hands. Plantations belonging to Daniel P. Jenkins, Dr. William Jenkins, and Paul Chaplin also were sold to private parties on March 9 and 10. Isabella Baker's Riverside Plantation, which was deeded to Saxby, Jr., and Thomas B. Chaplin's Tombee, were sold to the United States for fifty and a hundred dollars apiece.

Six months later, Lincoln announced his plan for disposing of the Government's land. The terms could not have made the tax commissioners happier if they had written them. Some acreage would remain with the military. Thirteen school farms, not to exceed 160 acres each, would be leased to white growers. Seventeen selected plantations would be opened to "heads of families of the African race" in lots not larger than 20 acres, and at a minimum price of $1.25 an acre. The great bulk of land would be auctioned to private bidders in tracts as large as 320 acres—a move implicitly designed to perpetuate the plantation organization of labor. The sale was scheduled for early February, 1864.

Again, the abolitionists and generals objected, and the freedmen threatened to stop working. They felt they had a right to live on their old plantations. Some said that to have to buy land away from home "was as bad as to be sold" themselves.[27] Brigadier General Rufus B. Saxton, who had come to Port Royal in November, 1861, as chief quartermaster to General T. W. Sherman and had risen to command all coastal territory under Federal jurisdiction, advised the blacks to pitch their property stakes and build cabins where they wanted to, so long as it was not on lands reserved for the military or for school farms. He took refuge in a clause of the Tax Act of 1862 which gave freedmen the right to preempt or settle on public lands with a privilege to buy before others. Saxton, whom the black people affectionately dubbed General Saxby, was responsible only to the War Department and to General Quincy A. Gillmore, commander of the Department of the South, at Charleston, and architect of the sieges of Fort Wagner and Fort Sumter, a man not known for his sympathy for the freedmen. For a moment, the preemptors appeared to be winning. On December 31, 1863, the Treasury Department changed course and instructed the tax commissioners to respect squatter's rights and honor the preemptions. The tax commissioners were promptly swamped with applications and down payments. But they refused to process the claims and continued advertising the sale. Ever looking to maximize revenues, the commissioners maintained that "improved" agricultural lands were too good for preemption. They hammered away at Treasury Secretary Chase until he gave in. Early in November, ignoring pleas from the Army, Congress, and other members of Lincoln's cabinet, Chase withdrew his preemption directive and ordered the sale to go forward. Freedmen would still be able to buy land, but only on selected plantations.

To everyone's astonishment, the lands sold for an average of eleven dollars an acre. "What an imposition upon the government it would have been," the commissioners taunted, "to have had these lands preempted at $1.25 an acre."*[28] The black people felt betrayed. "A crowd of women from a plantation near Lands End" surrounded a superintendent, complaining that land "they had pre-empted had been sold away from them and declaring they wouldn't work for the purchaser."[29] The sale had been advertised only in Beaufort, and that "was as good as no advertisement at all."[30] The women declared "they would have given as much as anyone for their plantation" remarked Allen, "but I suppose they didn't combine." Only on Marion T. Chaplin's place at the east end of St. Helena Island had the people "clubbed together and bought their plantation." Elsewhere, preemptors refused to budge until General Gillmore threatened to move them by force.† They went back to work without enthusiasm, and the small crop of 1864 reflected their disillusionment. In the coming year, the men vigorously resisted conscription into the Army—because, among other reasons, their wages were not guaranteed and the Government had gone back on its word too many times. More and more the freedmen showed their independence, determined now to establish churches without white people and to have their own political organizations. New religious sects sprang up, and the freedmen began claiming the right to vote.

By 1865, 347 black people, nearly all of them heads of families, mainly men but some women, too, had purchased land on St. Helena Island. A number of plantations which had been sold almost intact in 1863 or 1864 were later subdivided and sold again. Phil-

*One of the commissioners, Dr. William Brisbane, was a third cousin to Chaplin John Chaplin and Phoebe Ladson were their common progenitors. Once a planter himself, Brisbane had sold his land and Negroes and moved North, returning to St. Helena Parish as a Federal official during the War. His behavior was highly contradictory. On the one hand he was an unabashed abolitionist—on January 1, 1863, he read the Emancipation Proclamation to a holiday gathering at Port Royal. On the other hand, in his official capacity, he disapproved of selling land to the freedmen and he worked to block preemption. Brisbane wrote two books, one proving that the Bible justified slavery, the other proving the opposite. He remained in the Parish after the War, and in 1876 he backed the Redemption Democrats against the incumbent Reconstruction Republicans.

†Relics of preemption, hundreds of unopened and unfulfilled claims, have been preserved in the records of the tax commission at the National Archives, in Washington. Few hands have touched them. Willie Lee Rose looked into "packet after packet of these musty papers . . . brittle and dry as the broken hopes to which they are the mute witnesses." (*Rehearsal for Reconstruction* [New York, 1964], 287.)

brick disposed of Fripp's Big House Plantation and Thomas Coffin's Cherry Hill, in 1866, for five dollars an acre, five times what he had paid for them. Postwar litigation challenging the Government's administration of the Tax Act, and testing the legality of the new titles, kept old and new owners on edge for many years, and also resulted in some surprising alliances of freedmen and their former masters, alliances founded less on familiarity or past obligations than on mutual fatigue with uncertainty and strife.

A Speculator

Philbrick thought selling small farms to the freedmen was a mistake. "After a few generations," he reasoned, they would find themselves reduced like French peasants "with not enough land to live on or work economically."[31] He flirted with several plans of his own, and even people who disapproved of his love for money recognized his managerial genius. Once he bought land he abandoned gang labor and instituted a mixed system of tenant farming and wage work, allotting cotton ground to individual families and paying twenty-five cents a task, by old measures, and two and a half cents a pound for picking. Each family raised its own meat and provisions. Under this system, Philbrick tripled his crop in a year. William Allen, who taught the black children on Philbrick's plantations and sided with him against his critics, thought his crop of 1863 was "about as large as in old times, the price of Sea Island about double the old price." He was right about the price but wrong about the yield. Philbrick's workers averaged seventy-five pounds of ginned cotton to the acre—better than Chaplin was making in the late '50s, but fifty pounds shy of Captain John Fripp's standard.

Because he was contentious and ambitious, controlled vast acreage and many workers, and made no move to transfer his easily acquired wealth to the freedmen, Philbrick was accused of "aristocracy." But he did not care what was said about him: he was on St. Helena to grow cotton cheaply and to make money for his partners. Guided by the philosophy that "high wages" were "a bounty on the idleness" of the black family, Philbrick justified paying low rates as a way of teaching thrift and restraint and keeping everyone in the family working. "It will not be well with them," he expounded, "to make money so fast on their cotton and land" as they would if they had their own places. "I wonder," retorted Laura Towne, "whether it is good for *him* to be getting rich so fast."[32]

In the fall of 1865, with the country at peace, Captain John Fripp's lawyer, Henry Seabrook, wrote to Philbrick, appealing to his "sense of justice and generosity," in the hope that they could work out an "arrangement."[33] "An old man, sixty-eight years of age, Mr. Fripp was residing on one of his plantations, with his three daughters" when the Yankees bombarded Port Royal. "They were strangers to the experiences of war," Seabrook explained, "& imagined a thousand horrors as the consequence ... of being in the power of an enemy and at the mercy of their own liberated slaves." Surely Philbrick could appreciate "the force of the impulse" which made his clients flee "their happy home in terrified fright."

The story contradicted witnesses who swore that Fripp had had to be physically led off St. Helena. Hints of the special danger to white women passed right over Philbrick. The New Englander felt solidarity, not with white people in general, but with his business partners. What could Fripp have to give "except his old title, which he probably values a good deal higher than I do?" Nor was Philbrick in a position to bargain. "I was hampered in acts of 'generosity' by the fact that the present title was not in me alone, but that a dozen other gentlemen were interested...." Let Fripp "make a definite proposition" and Philbrick would submit it to his friends[34]—submit it, too, to the law of supply and demand and see how Fripp's offer compared to the price the lands might bring in open bidding. Let the market be the arbiter; then justice would be done.

The Land Takes Shape

Before land could be sold it had to be surveyed. In the months leading up to each public sale, teams of Federal surveyors walked and paddled the length and breadth of St. Helena Parish, cutting straight lines across the islands and waterways, and dividing the high ground into a system of townships, sections, and lots. "It was the intention to ignore all plantation lines and divide the land up *de novo*," reported William Allen, "just as France was into departments—and I suppose with the same political purpose."[35] The purpose *was* political, or partisan, insofar as the surveys were part of the scheme to resettle the Parish with "loyal citizens." Thinking they were bringing the Sea Islands into harmony with the modern world, the tax commissioners went about their work in smug ignorance of the origins and continuing importance of the old land lines. Here was "a Parish comprising islands of irregular form, and

of various size, serrated by firths and coves, occupied with plantations of every conceivable shape, with landmarks obliterated and
boundaries obscured, if not entirely demolished."[36] Out of this
"*chaos* and confusion," which had seemed perfectly workable in the
past, the commissioners endeavored "to bring order, distinctness,
definiteness, valuation, assessment and adequate certainty of description."[37] Deprived by the Confederates of all maps, charts,
plats, and other reliable data, the commissioners overstated the ir-
regularities—plantation lines were quite regular, in fact—and regarded topographical features such as creeks and marshes as
"impediments" to describing the Parish's resources.

"As a specimen of the absurd way in which they have gone to
work to cut up these islands," reported Allen, from the porch of
Edgar Fripp's house at Seaside, "this lot of land . . . including the
house, is described as Section 5 Town 2, South; Range 1 East."[38]
Needless to say, the nomenclature was difficult for the freedmen to
follow, and they resisted the new land lines by pulling up the survey markers and withholding their help and knowledge from the
surveyors. The commissioners' layout was a hindrance to preemption. It disoriented the people by violating old task divisions and
ignoring established uses of the land. "The people to whom plantation lines have a historical value, observe them religiously,"
noted Allen.[39] They knew the fields by the old names, knew which
soils were fertile and which worn out, which were suited for cotton
and which for provisions, and which should be left alone.

Shrewd self-interest, not backwardness or sentimentality, motivated the freedmen to insist on the old boundaries. They did not
want to exchange land they knew for land they did not know. Furthermore, the boundaries were meaningful in ways the tax commissioners could not fathom. Allen, who learned from collecting songs
that plantation lines were invariably cultural borders, understood
their importance in defining communities of kin. Even on the largest St. Helena plantations, he found, three or four black families
"pretty much exhaust the people."[40] The destruction of boundaries
would undermine social organization. It would weaken institutions
and leaders whose sphere of influence coincided with the plantation. A sense of peril, an amorphous fear of being cut off from one's
relatives and from the past, was felt by all.

The freedmen's objections confounded the commissioners.
Shouldn't the blacks be grateful to see the old laws and institutions

follow their oppressors into oblivion? Yet the freedmen interpreted the changes as an attack against *them,* part of a policy that included an obsession with cotton, the denial of preemption, slow payment of wages, and forced conscription. The new land lines were laid down as if the land were virgin, unpopulated, free for the taking. When the freedmen saw this, they felt uprooted, alienated from their rights. Once more they had been disregarded. Now they were caught, it seemed, between two terrible choices: accept the exploitation of new masters or leave. They stayed, and with the help of friendly whites who translated the Government's terms into a familiar idiom, they adapted to the scheme and adapted *it* to their aspirations. They bought the rectangular strips of land set aside for them, combined with their neighbors, usually relatives, to settle, build, and farm in patterns to their liking, and resumed the practice of designating pastures and woodlands as commons—a practice dating from slavery, when the hogs belonging to everyone on the plantation foraged on the loose. The geometric result of unequal sales—large estates to whites, small lots to blacks—and of subdivision and resale was, as Allen had predicted, "a queer patchwork ... of oblique patches, little three-cornered lots, and every now and then a plantation sold whole carried on still by the old land lines."[11]

A Planned City

On January 16, 1865, while waiting for the rain to slacken before ordering his troops into South Carolina, General W. T. Sherman issued Special Field Order Number 15 reserving all newly abandoned and confiscated lands along the Georgia and lower Carolina coasts for the settlement of freedmen. Families were to be given "possessory" titles until Congress could regulate their property rights.* The order made no pretense of collecting delinquent taxes, and it specifically excluded white settlers and investors. It did not apply to Port Royal, however, where property rights had already been established through the operation of the Direct Tax Laws. On the very day it was issued, the tax commissioners in Beaufort released for sale some three thousand lots comprising the "City of Port Royal," to be built at the southwest extremity of St. Helena

---

*After the War, Sherman would insist he meant the order to be temporary; that it was a military measure to relieve him of the burden of providing for the thousands of black civilians who trailed his army like the train of a gown.

Island. Anyone could buy, and the commissioners hoped to attract white capital to the waterfront. On paper, the city covered Lands End, the Ben Chaplin Place, Isaac Fripp's Orange Grove Plantation, Isabella Baker's Riverside, and the southwest corner of Tombee. The school farm section of Tombee lay just east of the city limits.

Port Royal was to be a planned city. At the time the plat was drawn, it included the most thinly populated part of the Island. Like the grids laid out on the western plains, perfectly square and rectangular lots were cut out of the brush. Indeed, the commissioners believed the city would come "under the influence of Northern men" and "flourish like the great West." "The city has a magnificent harbor," they marveled, as others had before, "and it will probably become in a few years only second to New Orleans as a Southern Commercial City."[42] But Port Royal never prospered. Though promoted by men driven by the profit motive, the plan bore the unmistakable stamp of a different class of visionaries— those New England reformers who had dabbled in experimental communities such as Brook Farm and Fruitlands, communities based on collectivist ethics and a hostility to commerce. There was a fanciful quality to the unbuilt city. No one wanted to live there; buyers stayed away from the sale in droves. And while planners were designing the city gardens, advance units of a great war machine were passing by on their way to devastating the midlands of the state.

Streets were named alphabetically. They ran as straight as stretched chains and were of unvarying width. The only angles were right angles—there was not a curve in the plan. Every ten-acre lot was made up of thirty-two "town lots," each 66 by 132 feet. The broad streets running east and west, from Broad River to the marshes of Station Creek, "have the names of distinguished men of the Revolution"—Adams, Hancock, Marion, Yates. The narrow streets or alleys running parallel to them "have the names of Trees and Fruit," some local and familiar, like Dogwood and Persimmon, some foreign and hard to roll off the tongue, like Xanthoxylum. The streets running north and south the length of the peninsula "have the names of Flowers and Ornamental Trees"—from Aster, Bumelia, and Clintonia, to Xanthium, Yaupon, and Zinnia. The piece taken from Tombee made up the neighborhood of "College Square" and included Adams through Franklin streets, crossed by Pink through Wistaria. On paper, the city boasted sixty acres of parks, two hospitals, a courthouse and a jail, a city hall and an arena, three marketplaces, and a customhouse, the key to its future.[43] The day that sales of lots commenced, the actual site of the city was a hodgepodge of scrubby fields and pinewoods, littered with the debris of prewar Negro cabins and outbuildings, and disfigured from several years' use as an army campground. About a fifth of the lots were periodically submerged under spring tides.

A few lots were sold, but as a site for urban development, the place remained a utopia. Laying out the peninsula in precisely measured lots and setting thousands of monuments to mark boundaries was a Herculean task. In the months between the survey and the sale, vegetation shrouded the markers and the land lines began to close. The problem of agriculture on the warm, moist, sandy loam had always been to beat back the natural growth rather than to force things to grow.

"The Spirit of New England"

As soon after the War as the former white residents of St. Helena Parish could assemble, they sent to Congress "a joint petition" asking to be allowed to redeem their homes and lands by paying the taxes imposed by the Act of June, 1862. They did not dispute the Government's right to levy a war tax. Instead, led by Richard De-Treville, who had lost thousands of dollars of property in Beaufort, they challenged "the infamous and fradulent manner in which the tax was collected."[44] The Act of 1862 had made no provision for "informing the unfortunate owner[s]" of their obligations. It had been impossible "to comply with a law of which they were not and could not be presumed to have been informed."[45] Furthermore, the Act contradicted an earlier measure which would have subjected land for sale "*only* in case sufficient personal property could not be found" to pay the tax. Yet the commissioners had swept up everything in a heap. Large tracts of land were sold when a small piece would have realized the debt. Two, three, four tracts belonging to the same person were sold when one tract would have paid the tax many times over. "With the land went the houses and barns, the family heirloom furniture, costly books in leather bindings, pianos, rugs, chandeliers, china; all were sold with the plantations"—all, that is, except "those items already appropriated by the former slaves and invading soldiers."[46]

No other group of white southerners lost as much. The Government's confiscation and resettlement scheme was confined to St.

Helena Parish. Shortly after the War, President Johnson rescinded Sherman's Special Order setting aside abandoned coastal lands for the freedmen—a cruel blow to the Government's allies, a stroke of luck for its recent enemies. If only St. Helena had been overrun by the second General Sherman and not the first, Chaplin and his friends would have had their lands returned to them when they laid down their arms. No wonder they felt they had been singled out for punishment. "What have these people done, more than their fellow citizens who lived out of the Parish of St. Helena?" asked Richard DeTreville, forgetting how hard he and his neighbors had worked for secession. "Are the people of the United States aware of the position of poverty and want into which this once opulent and thriving people have been reduced, by no fault of their own?"[47]*

Congress ignored the petition, leaving to the courts the job of deciding between the old and new titles. "The spirit of New England, ever hostile to South Carolina, was dominant," explained DeTreville. South Carolina's old landed class, once hugely powerful in national affairs, was without a voice, "represented as the poor State now is, in both houses of Congress, by New England men, or men whose sympathies are with New England or Africa."[48]

Starting Over: Chaplin Breaks Old Ground

Thomas B. Chaplin's family reunited in Walterboro in the summer of 1865. Barred from their home on St. Helena Island, they nevertheless were better off than most of their old friends because they still had land. Chaplin persuaded the Freedmen's Bureau, which had authority over "abandoned and confiscated lands" outside of St. Helena Parish, that because he had never actually possessed his mother's plantations on the Combahee and Ashepoo rivers, he could not have abandoned them and hence they should be returned to him.† He intended to revive Fields Point, consisting of

---

*The readiness with which DeTreville—and the South—embraced the Union after the Confederate defeat "will defy explanation unless it is recognized that southern loyalties to the Union were never really obliterated, but rather were eclipsed by other loyalties with which, for a time, they conflicted." (Potter, 78.)

†On August 3, 1865, in the office of the assistant U.S. provost marshal in Walterboro, Chaplin took the following oath: "I, Thomas B. Chaplin, do solemnly swear, in presence of Almighty God, that I will henceforth faithfully support and defend the Constitution of the United States and the Union of the States thereunder, and that I will, in like manner, abide by and faithfully support all Laws and Proclamations which have been made during the existing Rebellion with reference to the Emancipation of

the Point Place and Walnut Hill, but because neither had a house fit to live in, he leased a nearby plantation from Oliver Middleton. There, in 1866, he planted his first postwar crop, hoping to save enough money to build a dwelling house and outbuildings on the Point Place before the next crop year.

Chaplin was forty-three years old, healthy and able, when he took up his old profession. Sophy, his wife, had become an out-and-out partner, groomed by the War to the full load of domestic jobs, all that her servants used to do and some of her husband's duties as well. She was cook and housekeeper, nurse and tailor, trader and accountant. Ernest, Daniel, and Virginia, not having places of their own, lived at first with their father and stepmother. The boys were grown men now; they had seen something of the world. St. Bartholomew's Parish, to which they had returned, was their grandmother's home, and their claim to it was as strong as their father's. The War had made them more independent in some ways and less in others. Now its consequences—the short supply of houses, farm tools, and livestock; the high cost of credit and stiff competition for labor—forced them to stay with their father past the age when, in the old days, they would have left. Just at the time of life when they would have expected him to give them land or money to start out, he was needing *their* help, in particular their signatures on notes and mortgages. For one year, until the first of these loans came due, the Chaplins seem to have pulled together. Then, as indicated both in Chaplin's notes to his journal and in his sons' statements in court, family unity shattered.

From 1866 through 1872, when they were evicted from Fields Point, the Chaplins endeavored to plant large crops with free black laborers working under contract. Their experiences were typical of seaboard planters in the early years of Reconstruction—coping with the loss of wealth, status, and authority; trying to remake their fortunes by cultivating the trusted old staple on a new basis of shares; accepting the fact that black people were free while preserving ideals founded on slavery; riding out a period of high interest rates and low agricultural returns with faith in the land and in a Providence that one day would admit they had suffered unjustly.

Slaves—So Help me God." (Oath repeated in connection with Chaplin's petition for restoration of lands from the estate of Isabella C. Baker, in *Papers of the Bureau of Refugees, Freedmen, and Abandoned Lands,* War Records Office, National Archives, Washington, D.C., microcopy 869, roll 30.)

Chaplin recounted these years in the epilogue to his journal, written when he was sixty-three and aspiring only to avoid hunger and cold, and to die before Sophy. His notes, inserted from time to time through 1884, dwell on his losses and impoverishment. Chaplin's point of reference is the past, his method, comparative and ironical. While his current condition comes across vividly, details of his new life are sparse. Rather than discuss day-to-day events, the notes observe changes over intervals of time.

A more complete source of information are the records of four postwar suits filed against Chaplin for nonpayment of debt.[49] Chaplin progressed from one financial disaster to another, like a ship listing from storm to storm in open seas, losing the bowsprit here, the stern sheets there. In every case the outcome was the same: the court ruled against Chaplin and in favor of his creditor. With each continuance, however, and each delaying tactic, ultimate disaster was averted. Even when judgment came, the sun still rose the next day. Having mortgaged all of his land at once, Chaplin resumed borrowing on the strength of his name. Thus, when he failed to pay, his creditors could find nothing to attach. In one such instance, he countersigned a note for Daniel, whom he had sent to buy cotton seed from E. J. Fishburne, in Walterboro, to plant in the spring of 1866. The sixty-five-dollar note came due in July, and when the Chaplins refused to pay, Fishburne sued. Chaplin testified that the seed had been unsound; it had germinated poorly and he was forced to replant. Therefore, he felt justified in not paying. The court disagreed and ordered him to pay in full. But he had no money, and a "diligent search" of his quarters on Middleton's plantation turned up "no property . . . on which a levy can be made." Fishburne did not give up, and the case spun into the early 1870s, gathering costs and fees greater than the value of the suit.

The courts were clogged with cases, so defendants could look forward to long periods of grace between each step in the legal process: the filing of a complaint and the arrival of a subpoena, trial, judgment, and execution. Now that black people could own property and sign contracts, they, too, were bringing suits and getting taken to court. With little money in circulation and people of both races struggling to subsist, defaulting on a debt was no cause for shame. Chaplin's only income was the lump sum he received when he sold his cotton. If the crop was short, and invariably it fell below expectations, he felt justified in putting off his creditors, as if it were only right that the drought parch everyone alike.

*   *   *

By the terms of his lease for the Middleton place, Chaplin agreed
to pay the owner one-sixth of the cotton crop—one-third of Chaplin's half, the other half going to the workers as wages. In December, 1866, Middleton wrote to Chaplin, inquiring about the crop.
Chaplin wrote a long, somber reply in the form of a narrative of his
first year's experiences planting under the new regime.[50] "It is my
melancholy duty," he began, "to inform you of my almost entire
failure in making a crop this past year." Not only would the yield
be less than a quarter of what he had projected, but after piling up
reasons for having done so poorly, Chaplin asked Middleton to let
him try again. He was not ready to move onto his own place, he
explained, and it had taken all his "exertions of last year" to put
Middleton's fields into shape for making a decent crop. Also, he
had had to learn to manage within the new system—to draw up
and enforce a contract with free laborers. Nor were these the only
obstacles to success. As he named the others, Chaplin grew dazzled
by his skill at capturing a chaotic and rapidly changing situation.
At every point, his exhaustive letter invites comparison with the
life recorded in his journal. How alone the planter seemed in 1866.
His social network was fractured, while the blacks' network, largely
unobserved during slavery, had become conspicuous. The planters
were testing the freedmen, who were testing them in turn, each
group trying to learn how far it might push the other without disturbing the peace. In the shadows lurked the United States Army,
and no one could say for certain whom the troops were there to
protect.

    "It is a lamentable fact," wrote Chaplin, "that I will not pack
six 300 lb. bags to the crop." He felt "great mortification" in having to state the facts, but as always he did not "attribute even the
greater part of the blame to myself." Instead, he blamed everyone
and everything else, starting with "the climate & the half savage
beings around us." All the money he could scrape together or borrow he had used "to commence the struggle for existence" preparatory to planting. He had sunk a year into learning how to live with
the freedmen, providing a food supply, putting up outbuildings,
and managing Middleton's timber. "You might properly ask," he
wrote, anticipating an irritable response from his landlord, " 'What
have I to do with all this? It is nothing to me.' " On the contrary,
coaxed Chaplin, the moral burden was Middleton's. Unless he
gave Chaplin the chance "of benefitting by that experience & re-

trieving the past," Chaplin's future would be bleak. He was mired in debt and his workers owed him for all the food and store-bought goods he had furnished them. The "entire share" of each hand's cotton "will not be sufficient to repay me my advances." As he understood the law, he could "compell delinquents to work out" the balance of their obligations, "but only on the same place or plantation." Thus, if he was forced to move, he would lose valuable labor he had coming to him, no one else could collect it, and the Negroes would have gotten something for nothing. Moreover, since the workers used to belong to Middleton, or to Middleton's plantation—Chaplin was not sure which was technically correct—they could claim "to be hired by whosoever leases or plants this place."

Weighing on the planter's mind was the scarcity of labor. Because the freedmen were exercising their liberty to move about, and those who stayed on their old plantations were reluctant to devote full time to the white man's crops, or to tend as many acres as they had tended under their masters, landowners had difficulty finding enough workers to cultivate all the acreage they wanted to plant. An owner knew he was more likely to rent his land if people were living on it, even if they claimed rights which he thought were his. The workers knew they had leverage because other growers were trying to entice them away. Chaplin's request to stay on the land, polite and deferential as it was, contained an implicit threat: if Middleton did not extend his lease and allow him to make back what the Negroes owed him and also the money he had laid out for improvements, he might try to take the people with him, by offering, perhaps, certain benefits in the contract, such as the privilege of growing cotton on their provision plots, or time off to work on their own crops.

Chaplin apologized for having waited until December to "apply for the place" for the coming year. "But really," he insisted, only lately had he realized the extent of his calamity. He had had "a fair showing of fruit in the fields," but the weather ruined him. "My salvation depended on a late fall, whereas the first cold we had was a severe freeze, destroying and cutting off" half the bolls. Part of what remained to mature was stolen right off the stalks, he claimed, and disposed of at "the various shops" which had sprung up in the neighborhood, "the owners of which bought and sold indiscriminately." The shop nearest him was run "by four men— Gentlemen in the world's estimation," who also "contracted for & planted nearly every place around me." In the meteoric rise of the shopkeepers, Chaplin perceived the transforming potential of the War. The blacks had gone on working, under protest in some instances, but knowing they had to eat; they still were black, poor, and subordinate. Eminence had shifted from the planters to another class of white people who not only sold merchandise over the counter and bought up cotton without asking where it came from, but also leased and operated plantations. They raised prices on corn and meat when the planter needed them most—in July and August, as food stocks dwindled. Worst of all, the merchants talked against the old masters and "the negroes side & cooperate with them."* Much of Chaplin's cotton, he believed, wound up in the new shops, stolen from him sometimes "by night, but in many instances, by day light." One of his fields was "very accessible" to his landing on the river, and as it was "impossible to keep up an efficient guard," the cotton left by boat.

Chaplin accepted blame for two "egregious" mistakes. "Many of the hands who had agreed to sign my contract came suddenly to the conclusion that they could only perform half-hands work." He considered not hiring them, "but knowing there were still some planters about looking out for hands, I did not like to lose them." So he signed them, as half-hands. That was his first mistake. Then he thought he could "encourage them to work more faithfully" by allowing each hand "to plant for himself independently." That was his second mistake. Once the people signed contracts, "they would not & could not be induced to work." He sought "the assistance of the military" to make them work, but the Army would not come. Seeing his weakness, the workers "failed" him, "working their own crops & neglecting that of the contract."

After telling this tale of woe, Chaplin commented on the state of Middleton's land: it was "excellent," well rested, but there *was* a problem. With the exception of fields that had been planted "by the old people" who were "left on the place" when the War broke out, the ground was covered "with a dense second growth, the clearing off of which was equally as troublesome as new ground." He had lost at least a month at this unexpected task, and "did not strike a hoe towards listing before the 5th day of April." More "invaluable time was lost by having to replant" when Fishburne's seed

---

*Planters would soon challenge the merchants by setting up stores of their own and paying wages in scrip. The aim of this system, said Robert Smalls, a prominent black political leader, was to make it " 'impossible for the laborers to obtain any of the necessaries of life except through the planters.' " (Foner, 97.)

rotted. Consequently, "it was very late" before he "succeeded in getting a respectable stand." Even so, by late September, the crop looked promising and Chaplin had visions of making twenty-five bales.

It was more than he should have hoped for, considering the plagues that had visited him. "At a critical moment, my means began to fail me"—either the store cut off his credit or he refused to pay the high price of provisions. For "a month or so" his workers received no corn, potatoes, or meat. Standard supplementary fare was "made available"—"vegetables, fruit & early peas"—but the workers responded by walking off the job. "Not a days work could I get out of the hands," Chaplin fretted. "They moved about the country in idleness—the only work done being on their own crops."*

While the hired hands resisted Chaplin's control by walking off, the old people he found on the place opposed him by staying put. They "were a great source of trouble to me," Chaplin exclaimed. Toward old Negroes, as toward the young, his attitude had always been callous, impersonal: they were all a drag on his prosperity. The young might die before giving him a return on his investment, and the old might go on living without working. Of the old people on Middleton's place, "only one—old Joe, would contract." The rest would not sign an agreement. "In fact," wrote Chaplin, sounding suspiciously like the fox who could not reach the grapes, "there were very few worth contracting with." What had the old people done to provoke him? First, they "occupied many of the best houses," and with the exception of the family living in the overseer's house, which Chaplin wanted for *his* family, he did not dare disturb them. Second, when Chaplin got there they had "partly prepared to plant" wherever they wanted and by their own methods. Third, they insisted on growing a small cash crop of cotton for themselves, and he could "not prevent them from doing so." (Workers under contract generally were forbidden to plant cotton in their private garden plots.) "I am satisfied, though with-

---

*"The Combahee was the scene of labor troubles throughout Reconstruction." (Foner, 90.) Until 1876, when planters brought in workers from outside the area, freedmen on the Combahee successfully resisted attempts to turn them into wage workers wholly dependent on white employers. Even afterward, the pattern of labor organization remained complex, with blacks continuing to divide their time between securing a subsistence on their own small farms and working for wages or shares on the riverine rice and cotton plantations.

out positive proof," he declared, that "this left open a channel through which all hands could dispose of their pilferings." As evidence he cited the fact that "some decrepit old negroes made such very large crops of cotton off a few tasks of ground."

With the old people refusing to move, Chaplin had to quickly put up cabins for the workers under contract. Besides the overseer's house and what was left of the Negro quarters, "there was not a single outbuilding standing," when Chaplin took over. The old people had "pulled down" all the buildings that had not been burned, "saying that they were authorized to do so by the Yankees." Middleton was "probably ignorant" of these facts, and therefore he could have no idea how hard Chaplin had worked, and how much he had spent, to get the place in shape. "It was with difficulty that I could save the remnant of the frame of a barn," wrote Chaplin. "I have put up several outbuildings for immediate use"—conceding they were not much to look at—"without which no crops could have been housed or prepared." Having had all this to do on Middleton's estate, Chaplin had done "little toward settling my own places." He had cut and dressed some logs for a dwelling house, "but have not commenced putting it up. . . . Therefore," he repeated, "if you decline to renew my contract . . . I shall be homeless. At least allow me to occupy the house," he implored, referring to the overseer's house. "But I nevertheless entertain the hope that you will let me have the place another year." He had learned his lesson, so "sadly and dearly bought," and the workers had learned what to expect of him. They "are satisfied to work with me under more advantageous contracts on my part," he went on, almost cheerfully. "I would take pride . . . in showing that I am capable of doing better." As an afterthought, tucked at the bottom of the last page, he promised that as soon as he sent his small crop to market he would forward to Middleton "an order for one third of one half the proceeds."[51]

Middleton went along with him, renting him the house *and* land for one more year. But the crop money never arrived. Middleton wrote an angry note wanting to know why. Chaplin replied with a short list of excuses. He said he had not sent the crop to market because he thought if he waited the price would rise. The steam gin he had hired to clean his cotton broke down and he had to send for another. "And lastly the bales which were put under the house where I slept & I thought to be safe, were cut open and cotton extracted by some negroes. . . ." What was left he kept for evidence should someone be arrested for the theft. "Hoping this may prove satisfactory," he ended, without mentioning the money.[52]

His letter did not "prove satisfactory" and Middleton sued him for 250 pounds of long-staple cotton or the cash equivalent—about $150. Chaplin eventually lost the suit, but he gained a year of comparative comfort in the overseer's house on Middleton's place while he and his sons supervised the construction of a log house at Fields Point.

Debts and Losses

Chaplin's indebtedness was evidence not of fiscal mismanagement but of his success at finding credit in a tight money market. Most of his debts were small and reasonable; one was so large, however, and the date of maturity so near, Chaplin could not have hoped to repay it. Either he calculated recklessly when he mortgaged Fields Point and Dunham, or he gambled that the man he borrowed from could not win a judgment against him. On February 8, 1866, two weeks before he rented Oliver Middleton's place for the first year, Chaplin mortgaged his mother's former plantations to William H. Cowl, "of the city of Brooklyn, County of Kings, and State of New York." Appearing before Magistrate C. B. Farmer, in Walterboro, Thomas and his three children signed the note—after Sophy renounced her "right and claim of dower" in the property—agreeing that Thomas would "hold and enjoy said premises until default of payment shall be made." Cowl loaned the Chaplins eight thousand dollars at seven percent interest, due in full in eleven months.

It was a huge sum to raise in less than a year—the cash value of forty-five bales of long-staple cotton. Since the planter's share was one-half the crop, Chaplin would have had to sell ninety bales to earn eight thousand dollars—a remote possibility for someone who at the height of his career produced ninety bales in a decade. At most he could hope for twenty-five bales from Middleton's land, and a modest income from rice production at Dunham under Daniel's guidance. At two hands to a bale of cotton, and with enough workers to grow rice competitively, the Chaplins would have had to employ nearly a hundred people, who would have come with the same number of dependents. Besides laying out advances for these people, the Chaplins faced the costs of restoring dikes, ditches, and fences, and of clearing ground for planting. This time Chaplin could not be reproached for spending wildly or pampering himself. He simply tried to do too much. The idea that he might start a *small* farm did not occur to him until much later, when he had no choice in the matter.

Cowl foreclosed on the Chaplins, though not as soon as he might have. In a hearing to obtain a bill of foreclosure, he stated that when he "applied to the said defendants" for the money "long since due and owing," he offered them more time.[53] But the Chaplins would not talk about it. Sometime between eleven months and three years after the Chaplins defaulted, Cowl was granted the bill—it was not dated. During this period and after, Thomas and Sophy stayed at Fields Point with Ernest, who had become an invalid. Daniel married his Uncle Saxby's daughter, Maria Louisa, and brought her to Dunham in 1867. Virginia married and moved away in April of the same year. She died the following October and was replaced on the list of defendants by her husband, Wilson Glover.

In February, 1870, Chaplin, his two sons, and his son-in-law, Glover, were summoned to appear in court and explain why they should not be "forever barred and foreclosed from their equity of redemption, of and in the mortgaged premises." Chaplin did not dispute Cowl's right to the property, and he was ready to give the man most of what he wanted—but not all. Chaplin claimed "a right of homestead" under the State Constitution, entitling him, as the head of a family and a state resident, to exempt from seizure "a reasonable amount of property," including "a dwelling house, outbuildings, and lands appurtenant, not to exceed the value of one thousand dollars." Ernest and Daniel declared they had signed the mortgage without looking at the deeds and were informed afterward by Richard DeTreville that legal rights to the property were vested in a trustee named many years ago by their grandmother. Therefore, their signatures were null and void, and they prayed that the court dismiss them from Cowl's demands.[54] At this time, the debt, with interest, stood at $10,827.53.

The court listened but did nothing. Six months passed and the Chaplins went on the offensive, pressing their hometown advantage and retracting the concessions they had made to Cowl. On a motion by the defendants, Farmer ordered the complainant, "a non-resident of this state, to wit, a resident of the State of New York," to post bond to cover court costs, or the "cause" would be "struck from the docket."[55]

Then Farmer left the bench. His long tenure as magistrate

ended and he was replaced by William M. Thomas. But his involvement with the case did not cease. It went back a long way, too. Farmer had been a lifelong friend of Isabella Baker. He had decreed her entire estate for her sons in the last days of the War, thus completing the disinheritance of her husband initiated by the infamous deeds of 1844 and 1845. No one was better versed than Farmer in the sordid struggle over Isabella's property. Most recently he had used his office to help her son Thomas and *his* children hold on to it by stalling their mortgagee and tolerating their outrageous explanations—perhaps having a hand in contriving them. A few weeks after he stepped down, the Chaplins put Isabella's old plantations in trust and named him sole trustee.

Appearing in his old court before the new magistrate, Farmer argued that title to Fields Point and Dunham was vested in Thomas B. Chaplin and "cannot be reached by mortgages." As he read it, the contract between the Chaplins and Cowl "provided that . . . the mortgaged premises should in no wise be responsible for any debts."[56] Only a refusal to read the words on the paper, knowledge of some hidden covenant, or faith in the local allegiance and mercy of the court can explain Farmer's interpretation. In essence, he was asking the court to believe that Cowl had loaned thousands of dollars to strangers without asking for security, or to rule on the principle that it was all right to steal Yankee money.

By June, 1871, the debt had grown to $11,128.13. The Chaplins remained in possession of the lands, but the court was stirring. Magistrate Thomas agreed with Farmer that title belonged to Chaplin—rejecting by implication Daniel and Ernest's claim that title was vested in their grandmother's trustee. All that the Chaplins had to pledge was their land, and they thought they had pledged it. Magistrate Thomas thought so, too, and after adding Farmer's name to the list of defendants, he ordered them to pay Cowl by August 1 or be forever barred and foreclosed from repaying. He further directed the sheriff to sell the mortgaged plantations, or as much of them as it would take to meet the debt. In September, after failing to come up with the money, Thomas and Daniel Chaplin filed a "Petition for Homestead," seeking to block Cowl from selling their "interests" in Fields Point and Dunham.

But to no avail. On the first Monday in October, 1871, on the steps of the courthouse in Walterboro, the two plantations were sold at public auction. No one bid for the Chaplins, although the selling price was a mere fifteen hundred dollars. The buyer was William H. Cowl. A month after the sale, Farmer demanded that the sheriff show why he "has failed to set out a Homestead in this case to petitioners Thomas B. and Daniel Chaplin."[57] The court excused the sheriff, and though its ruling has been lost, we can venture a guess as to what it might have said. The homestead exemption for debtors, created by the state legislature in 1851, did not become a *right* until included in the constitution of 1868. A homestead exemption from a sale to satisfy a mortgage was not valid if the mortgage had been executed before 1868, and the Chaplins' mortgage dated from 1866. Furthermore, while a landowner could claim a homestead exemption against debts incurred for goods and services, he could not claim one against a mortgage on his land. A homestead would be allowed, however, if the sale of *part* of the land satisfied the mortgage. Nothing was left over from the sale of Fields Point and Dunham.* For a pittance, the maternal plantations at the heart of a grandiose estate were absorbed into the world of strangers.

Made homeless by the loss of his legacy, Chaplin returned to St. Helena Island. In January, 1872, he accepted a job teaching in a school for black children at Coffin's Point. He, Sophy, and Ernest moved into the overseer's house, about a half-mile from the plantation Big House, then owned and occupied by New Englanders. Since he last had lived on the Island, he had lost one son in war and a daughter in childbirth; a second son now despised and neglected him; a third son, his oldest, was chronically ill and living with him from necessity.

Seven months after the gavel came down on his hopes in Colleton County, an opportunity opened on St. Helena for Chaplin to

---

*What was lost was a remarkably wild, fertile, and scenic landscape. After rice and cotton had waned, the timber was cut and the plantation lands sold to outsiders for hunting preserves. Yet the country still was awesome. "The bold bluff, from Fields Point to Old Combahee, is without parallel in the entire South. It is crowned with magnolias, palmettoes, giant live oaks, and with a few large pines that the vandals have not cut yet. At intervals sharp and deep ravines cut through it, just as they do in the mountains, the sides of which would keep a botanist, mycologist, and musicologist busy for months. Far away, to the southeast, the smoke of Beaufort's factories may be seen and, in the immediate foreground, lines of palmettoes look so much like date palms that one fancies the Nile just above Cairo, when looking toward Ghizeh." (James Henry Rice, Jr., quoted in Harriette Kershaw Leiding, *Historic Houses of South Carolina* [New York, 1921], 235.)

redeem part of Tombee Plantation. An act of Congress of May 9, 1872, provided for refunding to purchasers of lands sold for direct taxes the amount they had paid, should the lands be recovered by the original owners. An act of June 8 provided for the redemption and sale of lands still held by the United States, especially the school farms. Chaplin looked into it, consulted with friends and lawyers, and decided to apply.

14. Redemption

St. Helena Island, 1872

Seen from the boat landing of a typical Seaside plantation, in 1872, the Big House was as imposing as ever, if a little frayed around the stairs and chimneys. Yet it seemed desolate, strangely alone, without its retinue of outbuildings. Behind the house, cotton was growing close to the yard, but in patches, not great fields. The higher cotton land and the old provision grounds were parceled into small, black-owned farms. The lower lands, wetter and harder to work, were uncultivated; the impoundments had reverted to marsh. The man-made dikes had been allowed to erode, like old teeth, and only the remains of fences were visible. Livestock were tethered, a practice unheard of before 1861. The number of property owners on the plantation had increased tenfold, while the size of the average holding had shrunk accordingly.

More acres were planted in corn and potatoes than in cotton, but the cultivation of cotton appeared to be spreading. Very little marsh mud was dug, but using garden forks introduced by the Yankees, the people cured spartina grass in salt water before mulching it into the fields. The industrial age was represented on the plantations by steam-driven cotton gins. The countryside, however, was purely agricultural. Beaufort had become a modern town, replacing Charleston as the service center of the new rural neighborhood. It had a bank, an insurance agent, a real estate agent, a newspaper, and many small shops. The realtor was offering some of the fine old plantations which the Yankees, who had bought them for a dollar an acre, were selling off. Professional people were less conspicuous than before the War; their numbers had declined by half, and the survivors, or successors, wore inexpensive clothing and drove plain horses. A music teacher, two artists, and thirty-seven "students" counted in the 1860 census were gone. A sculptor remained, probably a man who carved headstones.[1]

The white population of the Parish had fallen from 1,062 to about 600. Meanwhile the black population had grown by forty percent. On St. Helena Island, there still was an abundance of Fripps, Jenkinses, and Chaplins, but the bearers of the old surnames were black. In place of Captain John, William P., and J.E.L. Fripp, one might meet Prince Fripp, Scipio Fripp, Ishmael, Simeon, and January Fripp. The white Jenkinses had not returned to the Island—Dr. William Jenkins lay in wait in Beaufort—yet there were many Jenkinses: Ephraim, Binah, July, August. And until Thomas B. Chaplin returned, the only Chaplins on the Island were freedmen—Cyrus, Enoch, Abram, and their families.

While many former slaves took the names of their most recent owners, the majority did not. How and when these people chose surnames is a mystery. What can be said for certain is that the distribution of names across the islands did not match the old pattern of slaveholding, and the variance cannot be explained by the freedmen's mobility after emancipation. Among themselves, the slaves had used surnames they called titles in addition to the Christian names by which they were known to their masters. They may have inherited these titles from their mothers or fathers, or else derived them from the surnames of the white families which had owned their maternal or paternal ancestors. Some people apparently rejected the surnames of all the owners in their line, inventing names instead, or selecting from the growing lexicon with which they were acquainted.[2]

Petitioning for Tombee

Tombee Plantation had been occupied by a string of government superintendents. John Thorpe, of Providence, Rhode Island, lived there in 1863. A Mr. Waters, "from Salem, class of '63," shared the Big House with a Mr. Morrison, in 1864.[3] Between them, they managed five plantations near Lands End. Freedmen were living on only two of them, however, the others being occupied by soldiers. In 1865, the Government leased 80 acres of Tombee to Marcus L. Penniman. The next year, Penniman rented 160 acres and all the buildings "except for the east room and the north room of the second story" of the Big House, "and so much of the yard, garden, barn, and stable room as may be necessary for the use of a teacher or teachers on said place." Penniman agreed to cultivate only one-half the arable land; to employ each black resident capable of labor "for the exclusive benefit of the lessee at least one half his or her time"; to compensate them under terms "agreed upon in writing by the lessee and the laborer, to be approved by the tax commissioners"; and to prevent black people from living in or otherwise occupying the "mansion house or houses."[4]

In 1870, the Department of Internal Revenue succeeded the Direct Tax Commission as steward of the "Education Lands" still owned by the United States, and extended the practice of renting them out. Now a more experienced landlord, the Government demanded a quarter of the rent in advance and put a lien on the crop to secure final payment. The renter would forfeit his lease if he sold or allowed others to sell intoxicating liquor to the blacks. If the school farm was sold during the rental period, as the Government kept anticipating, the renter agreed to give up the dwelling house, yard buildings, "and all the unplanted portion of the place" to the buyer. The contract for Tombee stipulated that the orange trees— a grove set out by Chaplin—would go with the house. For years the school farms remained unsold, however, because the Government needed places to settle freedmen who were still wandering in search of better economic opportunities. Finally, Congress announced its intention to dispose of the properties and allow the former owners to redeem them. In June, 1873, Chaplin wrote to the Commissioner of Internal Revenue, in Washington, asking what steps he should take to redeem School Farm Number 33, "known by the local name of 'the T. B. Chaplin place.' "[5] He carefully described the boundaries, identified himself as the former owner, and declared that he had "abandoned" the plantation on November 7, 1861, at which time "all plats, titles, deeds, etc., pertaining to the same were lost." The place contained "six hundred acres, more or less," he claimed, making a curious error of more than two hundred acres, perhaps taking a deliberate bite out of the Baker Place, his mother's former plantation to the north, which she had deeded and willed to his brother, Saxby.

In July, Chaplin sent two affidavits to the commissioner, his own and that of William Washington Fripp, one of the four sons of Good Billy Fripp, the Baptist stalwart who had died in 1861.[6] Chaplin said simply that he had "inherited the said land from my father, the late Saxby Chaplin, and they were well known as lands of his Estate during my minority." Fripp said he had known Chaplin since they were boys—they were first cousins, once removed; there was three years' difference in their ages—and he could vouch that Chaplin had inherited the land from Saxby, Sr., "previous to 1845 and remained in possession of the same until the War."

Action on Chaplin's application was deferred almost two years, while the Government undertook a new survey of the school farms. In April, 1875, Chaplin's landlord at Coffin's Point, the Yankee settler S. W. Whitwell, offered to help him redeem his old place. Whitwell and his wife "were 'different from any people I had ever met with in my life,' " Chaplin wrote in his epilogue. "They appeared . . . to turn about, to be quite clever & obliging, & then quite mean & disagreeable, but the old man was by far the best of the two and often assisted us when assistance was really needed." Whitwell wrote to the commissioner on Chaplin's behalf, requesting a plat of Tombee, a statement of the taxes due, and an accounting of rents collected on the place since Chaplin had applied to redeem it. He asked "if some portion of the rents cannot be allowed to Mr. Chaplin," and offered to pay the taxes.[7] The commissioner wrote back that only 123 acres were redeemable at the present time. The war tax due on the place as of March 9, 1863, was $19.89, but twelve years' interest brought the figure to $43.90. Through Whitwell, Chaplin learned to his disappointment that he could recoup a part of his land, but not the house, because it apparently no longer belonged to the Government. The local internal revenue collector had told the commissioner that "the lot on which the old plantation house stands . . . was sold to the 'American Baptist Free Mission Society' . . . for $125, on 2 March, 1868." The Baptist group never took possession of the house, and the Government kept renting it, and even was prepared to sell it again, when the land certificate surfaced.[8]

Chaplin took what he could get, hoping to recover more of the property later on. Whitwell paid the redemption costs, and in August, 1875, Chaplin was mailed a "release" for 111 acres of "the Tom Chaplin place." Twelve acres stayed with the house, and 250 acres either remained with the Government or were permanently lost to him. In September, Chaplin was paid $16.25, or five-twelfths of the rents collected on his place for the current crop year. Twenty-two people were renting 61 acres at Tombee. Among the renters were three Jenkinses, three Browns, two Blues, and also a Baynard, a Beaufain, a Blake, a Bold, a Crawley, a Cuthbert, a Fripp, a Givens, a Grant, a Green, a Gridine, a Megget, a Reynolds, and a Young. Some names were native to the Island, and most names had belonged at one time to white people in the Parish; the variety reflected almost two centuries of migration and dispersion, changing fortunes and commerce in human beings.

Opium Years

Not having a house to move to, Chaplin stayed at Coffin's Point. The Whitwells persuaded him and Sophy—Ernest had just died— "to move up & occupy two or three rooms in their house," the former mansion of the Coffin family. Every summer when the Whitwells went North, the Chaplins had the whole house to themselves. Chaplin received no wages for looking after the place, but he was given as much land as he could cultivate and other considerations. He did not try to plant at Tombee, preferring to draw a small rent until he could recover the rest of the land. His income from teaching at the freedmen's school was sixty dollars a month, which would have kept him and Sophy in food and clothing if the school year had lasted twelve months, and if he had been paid in cash. Instead, he was compensated with "pay certificates" which he had to "dispose of at heavy loss." The certificates gave him credit at the store, and the Chaplins survived on "store provisions" and the food they raised for themselves. What little cash surplus they had went to pay for Chaplin's opium.

Opium was not a social drug, taken in company the way Chaplin used to consume liquor. To the contrary, he sequestered himself from white society, small as it was, while he rode the "up-hill and down-dale" of opium stimulation and "its antithesis, collapse."[9] He was not alone in his addiction, however. Newspaper testimonials and advertisements for cures indicate that opium was a problem for many people in the Beaufort area during the 1870s.[10] Opium was taken to relieve dejection, fear, nervous disorders, "the load of care" and "the tedium of life." At first, the opium dose produced the desired results. The user felt "exalted, serene, confident." His aches vanished, his burdens were "lifted from his shoulders, as the sun lifts the mist-clouds from the river." Soon, however, "a sickening, death-like sensation" wrapped around the heart; "a self-accusing sense of having committed some wrong—of being guilty before God" oppressed the mind. As the drug wore off, a depression deeper than anything experienced as normal gloom set in. The user craved another dose of opium.

In one story from the *Beaufort Tribune and Port Royal Commercial,* the "late Superintendent of the Soldiers Orphans Home" told how he became so despondent on opium he cut his own throat with a knife—but lived to warn others.[11] Pharmacists and mail-order sharks promised cures "at home" with "no publicity," "time short," and "moderate terms." Confessions of opium eaters became a literary vogue. Twenty years earlier, J.D.B. DeBow had been touting opium as the next wonder crop. He envisioned southern fields swathed in purple-flowered poppies yielding opium for medicine, for cattle feed, and for export to the masses of China. The dream never materialized. Small crops of opium were harvested for private use on the Sea Islands, but not for commerce.

Chaplin may have become addicted during the War. When he first knew he had a problem with opium we cannot say, but between the ages of fifty-five and sixty he was struggling to free himself, and he tried at least one store-bought cure. His need for opium kept him hustling, while the drug weakened and distracted him, making it difficult for him to work. As he became less able to make money, he grew frantic to assure his opium supply; for a short time, he cajoled his druggist into sending him the stuff when he could no longer pay for it.

Occupations

In the summer of 1875, Chaplin took a job as "custodian of government property on Hunting Island, North Point, where a new lighthouse was being built." His pay was "$50 pr. mo. & found, or $75 & find myself." He chose the latter, and though this meant he had to provide his own food, the Government "allowed" him a cook. He held the job until December when the "hands," having been away making their crops, "came back to work." Chaplin taught every winter up to 1877, when Governor Hampton appointed him to the slightly more lucrative office of trial justice. Around this time, Chaplin was active in the Democratic party, whose immediate goal was to wrest control of the state government "from the horde of blacks and vicious whites who controlled them."[12] In 1876, the Republicans, led by Massachusetts-born Governor David Chamberlain, were driven out, and the Democrats, riding a platform of white supremacy and led by Wade Hampton, were installed for the next hundred years. Chaplin's judgeship may have been his reward for loyalty. He did not march with the "redshirts"—the unofficial army of Hampton followers and bullies who paraded in the cause of white government. Rather, he worked quietly at the polls. In 1878, he was one of three men appointed by "the Democratic Commission of Elections" to supervise voting on St. Helena Island. "Mr. Chaplin takes opium," remarked Laura M. Towne, "and the other two"—Ned Capers and a man named Burton—"are drunken wretches."[13] The election came off without incident. The presence of white poll managers did not prevent a Republican landslide in the precinct. Only nine votes were cast for Democratic candidates, eight of the nine by white men, and half of those by Chaplin, Burton, Ned Capers, and Ned's brother Frank.

Suing the Government: The Necessity of Oral Evidence
Ned Capers was living in an outbuilding at Tombee when Chaplin returned to St. Helena Island in 1872. Four years later Capers bought a small lot that once had been part of his father's plantation and lived there with his black maid until he died, sometime after 1892. Each spring he would plant a garden and tend it until the hot weather set in; then he would sit on his porch sipping whiskey and watching the irrepressible "jointer" grass strangle his vegetables. Sedentary and glum, he nevertheless played an important part in the postwar lives of his old friends and neighbors. Time after time, when people sued to redeem their land or to recover the surplus proceeds from property sold for taxes, Ned Capers was called upon to tell what he knew. Because the land records for St. Helena Parish had been destroyed, as Dr. William Jenkins, one of the most active redeemers, repeatedly affirmed, one could prove ownership "by oral evidence only."[14] Capers testified, for example, that William A. Chisolm, former owner of Littlewood Plantation, had "got it through his wife," Caroline, daughter of Captain John Fripp, who had bought the place from Joseph J. Pope, after whom Fripp had named a son. Capers gave an affidavit for Edwin Chaplin, a nephew of Uncle Ben Chaplin and heir to Curlew Hill, next to Tombee, which Uncle Paul Chaplin had left to his brother Ben, who had left it to Edwin. When Oliver Pritchard, son of Ann Pritchard, petitioned to redeem "The Pritchard Place" on the Seaside, Capers was the chief witness. He recited in tortuous detail the his-

tory of the place since the time when his uncle Mr. Ladson had owned it.

These depositions show plainly how the exchange of land was bound up in social relationships. Land—and slaves—linked the generations of white people, vertically through a descent and horizontally through alliances. The War destroyed a century of land records and with them a history of estate formation and dissolution—a grievous loss to the planters, who felt their identities go up in smoke. But the redemption process enabled them to salvage the lost history by committing to paper the recollections of knowledgeable witnesses such as Ned Capers, Thomas G. White, William W. Fripp, and William J. Jenkins. The requirements of justice tended to reduce the past to mere chronology, however. All the contests of life, the personal drives and desires, were neglected. No one could glean from the testimonies the tale of Tom Pritchard's three wives, for example, or of Eliza Jenkins's sacrifices to feed her husband's ambition.

Before his death in 1884, Dr. Jenkins was a party to numerous suits against the Government—as a plaintiff in his own cause, as a claimant in the role of executor for such deceased friends as Chaplin's Uncle Paul, and as a witness for their children. Several times he attested "to the destruction of the land records for Beaufort County."[15] When John J. T. Pope's son Daniel sued to redeem his father's plantation, Dr. Jenkins stated that he had been "well acquainted" with the elder Pope *"and knew from his own lips* that he intended giving" the place to his son.[16] No will could be found— Pope had died in exile in 1864—and under these delicate circumstances, Jenkins's testimony was critical. Daniel Pope won his suit. He redeemed 235 acres, or half of the plantation, the rest having been divided and sold to freedmen. Years later he recovered the surplus proceeds from the sale of this second half. Dr. Jenkins was less fortunate. On the eve of the War he had owned six plantations. One he had inherited from his father's estate when he reached his maturity. Two he had acquired through his wife, Eliza, who had received them as gifts from her Uncle Ben Chaplin, but not before she beat back challenges from her cousins for the old man's wealth. Three he had purchased with the income from the others. Four of the plantations adjoined one another; a fifth, the Sandiford Place, was separated from the four by the Pritchard Place. The sixth was landlocked Indian Hills, where Uncle Ben's widow, Aunt Betsy, lived with the Doctor's bachelor cousin Captain Daniel T. Jenkins. In all, the Doctor had owned nearly 2,000 acres, making him the Island's third-largest landholder in 1860. In addition, there had been a house in St. Helenaville and a mansion in Beaufort. Who can doubt that had the War not intervened, he would have climbed higher? Of all he once had owned the only property he, Eliza, or their heirs ever recovered was 40 acres, or one-tenth, of Indian Hills, which had been set aside for a school farm. Shaped like a boot in prewar days, the plantation had been remolded by Federal authorities into "a perfectly rectangular tract."[*][17]

A Verdict for Chaplin
Some St. Helena exiles thought they saw in the Act of 1872 "signs of a returning sense of justice. . . ." It could be, they thought, "a first step to remuneration for losses suffered under the Tax Act." But they were not long deceived: "the more judicious and far see ing discovered, at once, that it was preliminary to abandoning property which 'did not pay.' In the parlance of the day," wrote Dr. John A. Johnson, Chaplin's comrade in heroism during the retreat from Bay Point, "it cost more to run the machine than it was worth." Endless and unexplained delays, astronomical legal costs, and "all manner of obstacles" put in the planters' path to redemption suggested "designs" to defeat the Act's "avowed purpose, and so impede its operation as, eventually, to render *a sale inevitable.*"[18]

"As everything has an end," observed Johnson, "so has the journey to Washington of one of these ill-fated applications." But

*A remarkable feature of the suit to redeem Indian Hills was the testimony in 1884 of ex-slave and Civil War hero Robert Smalls on behalf of Dr. Jenkins. Smalls had belonged to Jenkins's friends John and Henry McKee, of Beaufort, but at the time he testified he was a member of Congress—the last black Congressman from South Carolina in the Reconstruction era. "As to William Jenkins being the owner of the land known as the Dr. Jenkins place," Smalls told the District Court, he had "known the claimant all his life, and for many years prior to the fall of Port Royal, he exercised ownership of the said tract of land." Smalls himself had been sued after the War by William DeTreville, son of Richard DeTreville, for trespass on a lot in Beaufort that had belonged to the younger DeTreville—and before him to Henry McKee, Smalls's former owner—until the imposition of the direct tax and subsequent confiscations. Smalls had purchased the lot from the tax commissioners. DeTreville argued before the U.S. Supreme Court that the tax was unconstitutional. The justices decided it was not, and let stand the transfer of title. (*DeTreville* v. *Smalls*, 98 U.S. Supreme Court Reports, 174. On the incredible career of Robert Smalls, see Dorothy Sterling, *Captain of the Planter: The Story of Robert Smalls* [New York, 1958].)

the end was slow in coming. The courts were backed up. New surveys had to be commissioned. The plantations which had been so earnestly dissected had to be put back together again. "An application is sent in, setting forth the nature of tenure by which the claimant holds his lands, its names and boundaries are given, and every particular by which claimant and land could be identified." The claimant takes hope. His application "is verified and vouched by the clerk of a court of record and duly fortified by seal." Then the waiting begins. "Consigned to the charge of the Department Official, an interval of several months occurs, at the expiration of which, the expectant claimant receives by mail an immense, official document." Certificate of redemption? "No! Claimant is informed that no such tract is known to that office," because the tax commissioners had "changed the name at the time of sale." In the time it takes to undo the confusion, the old owners die, their heirs multiply; some of the heirs die and their beneficiaries are added to the list of claimants. Many shares are very small, as in cases where plantations had been owned by more than one person. Coffin's Point, for example, identified with Thomas Aston Coffin, had been owned jointly by him and his four brothers and sisters, whose descendants—seventeen in all—sued to recover the land and surplus proceeds. No one stood to get rich. "After exacting the tax, expenses of every conceivable kind, and the exorbitant interest of ten per cent per annum," Johnson calculated, "the question seriously presents itself . . . are our depreciated lands worth redeeming?"

Most people thought so. The economic benefits were doubtful, indeed, but the plaintiffs were suing for other reasons: to correct what they regarded as an unspeakable injustice and to end a war still being fought in their psyches.

An act of January 8, 1884, extended the time for redeeming the school farms and directed that monies collected from back taxes and interest be invested in government bonds to support public schools in the parishes of St. Helena and St. Luke. In July, 1885, after he had left St. Helena Island for good, Chaplin applied to redeem all of Tombee not previously released to him or sold to others. Nothing happened. He applied again in 1887. In March, 1888, the Commissioner of Internal Revenue, in Washington, asked the local collector, in Columbia, "to give your opinion and recommendation upon this application to redeem."[19] Seven months passed and Chaplin applied once more. This time, prodded by Chaplin's aggressive attorney, William Earle, a specialist in tax law and land confiscation cases, the Government's wheels turned.

In a letter of October 1, 1888, the commissioner asked the local collector to state all the "particulars" relating to School Farm Number 33—when it had been set aside, from which plantations it had been taken, why it was called a "Medical School Farm," and why it was so much larger than the other school farms. President Lincoln had instructed the tax commissioners, who had since disbanded, to incorporate no more than 160 acres in each. But School Farm Number 33 contained more than 700 acres. Before the collector had time to respond, the commissioner forwarded all that his office knew about Chaplin's plantation. He recited its boundaries, by the old names, and the history of its division and sale, by the new names. Already released to Chaplin, under the Act of June 8, 1872, were parts of Sections 14, 22, and 23, Township 2S 1W; held back were fifty-five town lots on Adams, Bartlett, Carroll, and De-Kalb streets, and the northwest quarter of Lot 5, Section 23, known on paper as College Square, in the dream city of Port Royal.

In answer to an inquiry from Chaplin about the status of two large neighboring lots in Section 14, the commissioner stated that they were not available for redemption, having been sold to "Isaac Jenkins, loyal citizen," and "Robert Lessington, loyal citizen"—Chaplin's two former slave drivers, known to him simply as Isaac and Robert. Chaplin also wanted to learn how much of the Baker Place was included in School Farm Number 33. Neither his brother, Saxby, nor Saxby's heirs had filed to redeem it. Possibly Chaplin was testing the waters for his son Dan, with whom he had reconciled and who, by his marriage to one of Saxby's daughters, was in line to inherit a share of Saxby's estate, or he may have been thinking of redeeming the place himself, since he had never recognized Saxby's claim to any part of their father's property.

Chaplin waited; his attorney grew restive. In January, 1889, a new acting commissioner told the collector to state the reason for the delay in processing Chaplin's application. The collector answered, in two separate letters, first that he did not have the plat book containing the site maps for the school farms and, second, having seen the book, that the plat for the Tom B. Chaplin place was "uncertain as to the original lines."[20] Consider, for example, the problem of the boundary between Tombee and Captain Daniel Jenkins's property at Lands End. Surveyors had discovered that the fence between them, which ran along an earthen dam, "was set without an attempt to make it strictly in line. The crook near the end of the dam was made to escape a bunch of roots."[21] Though the fence was a practical boundary, the law insisted on measuring the property to the middle of the dam. The commissioner authorized the collector to spend up to $10 for a new survey to determine the correct lines and the exact number of redeemable acres, and to take the money out of rents the Government had been collecting on the place, if he could lay his hands on them. For each of the past three years, Tombee had generated more than $130 in rents. But the place had become unmanageable, settled by squatters who were decimating the timber.

In May, 1889, a new commissioner—the third man to serve in that post in a year—ordered the collector "to report without unnecessary delay" on what could be holding up Chaplin's application. The collector responded with unusual haste. "I have the honor to state that the report has been delayed from the fact of the place, as to which much doubt existed about the location of the lines, is in a swamp and has been under three to four feet of water," he wrote.[22] Tree cutting and broken dikes had taken their toll. Consequently, "it was impossible to have the survey made." But thanks to the efforts of the collector, "this difficulty has ceased to exist," and a new survey "of the doubtful lines has been obtained." As soon as the plat was drawn, "which will be in a few days," he would forward the long-awaited report.

In his cover letter to the report, which duly followed, the collector addressed the old question about how the school farms originated. "These lots are the lands designated for the support of medical and other high branches of Education, more especially for the education of the freedmen," he offered. But as to the origin of School Farm Number 33, "when it was set aside and by whose authority," how it came to be a "Medical Farm" and why it was so large, the collector could "only state that I have been informed that it was set aside by an order of the President of the United States."[23] The questions held no fascination for him. The impetus for social reform, reflected in the idea of the school farms, was long since dead. Now the actual lands set aside for the experiment represented only a maintenance problem for an understaffed, indifferent bureaucracy.

The commissioner quickly computed the tax and interest owed on the unredeemed portion of Tombee. For $25.71, Chaplin could have the place back, including the Big House, which had inexplicably reverted to the Government. He paid the money but had to wait until the commissioner determined if the Government had made any improvements on the place. Eight months later, the collector—yet another new man—informed the commissioner that "no buildings on the school farm ever were erected for school purposes."[24] On March 4, 1890, twenty-eight and a quarter years after he had vacated his plantation, Chaplin was awarded "redemption and restoration of title."

He retrieved, in all, more than three hundred acres—a success none of his old associates could match. Because School Farm Number 33 was so large, it took in nearly all of Tombee, while most other school farms were smaller than any one plantation, and comprised parts of several. Fifteen school farms had been carved up and sold to "loyal citizens" and "Heads of Families" prior to 1872. By 1889, the Government was going out of its way to notify the "owners" of the school farms still held by the United States that they might yet redeem them. On February 27, 1890, three days before the deadline for applying, the ten living children of Saxby Chaplin, Jr., petitioned for the return of the Baker Place on St. Helena Island. In fifteen months the suit was settled and the land redeemed. Daniel Chaplin, Saxby's nephew *and* son-in-law, who at this time was approaching his fiftieth birthday, paid the collector of internal revenue $25.45 in taxes and interest—indicating, perhaps, that he had prompted the suit. Each heir recovered thirty-three acres and $3, or a tenth of the rents collected on the plantation for 1891. (Only twenty acres were in cultivation, half in cotton and half in vegetables.) Thomas Chaplin had always maintained his brother "had no right" to the place. Now Thomas's lone living son, Daniel, heir to Tombee and to a piece of the Baker Place, was in a position to unify the paternal side of the Chaplin estate and realize his father's claim.

Death in Walterboro

Chaplin was living outside of Walterboro, penniless and exhausted, but surrounded by family, in the house where his brother had died, when he learned that Tombee was his. But he never saw his old home again. Nine months after redeeming the place he was dead; the end came five days before Christmas, 1890. The register at St.

Jude's Episcopal Church noted that he had lived sixty-eight years, seven months, and twenty-three days. Whether the Walterboro *Press and Standard* carried an obituary we cannot say, because all copies of the newspaper from that period have vanished. In Beaufort, his death went unnoticed by the *Palmetto Post.*

At the time he died, the *Post* was conducting a vendetta against the railroad—which had been hailed as a savior in Chaplin's day—for intentionally underdeveloping the port to protect its monopoly on the phosphate trade. The recent inauguration of Governor Ben Tillman, an upcountry (Edgefield County) man suspected of "unfriendliness to the lowcountry,"[25] had aggravated Beaufort's ancient sense of vulnerability. The *Post* suggested that the legislature show its goodwill by reimbursing the Sea Islanders for the war taxes they had paid "for the entire state." The people "ask no interest," declared the editor. "They only ask that Trescot and Earle"—lawyers who had profited from land redemption—"be not allowed to dip their finger in the pudding."[26] Rather than recede into memory with the passing of time, the War loomed larger and larger, the way the bluff at Fields Point appears in all its immensity only when one rows out from the riverbank.

By redeeming Tombee, Chaplin had preserved a role for his grandsons. Thomas, the oldest of the four, was twenty-one and about to leave home; Daniel, Jr., Joseph, and Frederick were not far behind. Chaplin's legacy might do them some good—a consolation to him for his imminent disappearance. The land had always had the potential to provide security, dignity, and pleasure. Perhaps the boys could reap some of the fruits which for one reason or another had remained beyond his reach.

Great Losses and Small Things

Reflecting on the significance of Chaplin's life and character, the reader of his journal is drawn to a story from his early manhood that epitomizes the qualities which make him appealing and contemptible by turns.

On May 9, 1846, two weeks after his twenty-fourth birthday, Chaplin accepted an invitation to accompany John Webb and Charles Colcock to Webb's house on the main. Webb, a first cousin to Chaplin's cotton factor, T. L. Webb, and Colcock, a wealthy planter and himself a dealer in cotton, had just spent a convivial night at Tombee. Along with four black rowers belonging to

Webb, the party pulled out of Station Creek, hoisted sails, and rode a light south breeze to Parris Bank, in Broad River. Suddenly the wind fell and a "very black cloud" appeared in the northwest. It started raining and Chaplin proposed that they take down the sails and row. They made up the mainsail, brailed up the foresail, but before they could take down the foremast, "one of the most awful squalls struck us from the N.W., & in less than three minutes the boat was bottom up." Just as suddenly as the wind had risen it fell again, "almost to a calm," and the men could collect their thoughts. "We were in a horrid situation," Chaplin wrote later. Assisting one another, they all climbed on the bottom of the boat. Every movable object floated away except an oar and a knife. At once, the boat began rolling "over & over like a barrel," beating and dunking them with each roll. They pushed away from the boat, cut off their clothes and boots, and climbed back on when the bottom came up. "One poor fellow named Monday could not swim & though we got him on the boat twice the third time he went down, never to rise again, poor fellow, he was drowned without a struggle to save himself." The six remaining souls all were thinking the same thought: "which one of us would go next." The prospect of losing one's own life was terrifying, but "the idea was beyond description that one after the other we would drop off & the one that could hold on the longest would see the rest go. . . ." None had "the most distant idea of being saved, for nothing but the mercy of God could save us."

Twenty times the boat turned over. It would stay bottom down for a few minutes, but "her gunwales would be underwater & we could neither get the water out nor would she bear us inside." Then, "all at once, when it was perfectly dark & we had nearly given up all hope, she righted up, leaving about 2 inches of the gunwale" above the water. Hope revived. "We saw it was our only chance, & all with one feeling let go & supported ourselves in the water." Allowing the boat to rise as high as possible, each man grabbed with one hand "& reaching over with the other splashed out the water as well as we could, until we thought she would bear the weight of one person. One of the Negroes then got in, & with Webb's hat threw out water." As the boat lightened, the other five men climbed aboard one at a time. Using the oar and a piece of a seat they paddled for two hours against wind and tide before reaching shore.

After warming by a fire in "the cabin of two old Negroes belonging to Geo. Edwards," relaxing with "a piece of tobacco from the old fellows," and hewing "something to answer for oars," Chaplin, Colcock, and Webb got back in the boat and started for Webb's place. The black rowers apparently went by land—perhaps going to give the bad news to Monday's family—because the white men did the rowing. Webb and Colcock were so weak from exposure that Chaplin "had to row nearly the whole way. They were all astonished to see that I could stand so much," he boasted. Chaplin goes on to tell about his arrival at Webb's; his reunion with his wife, who alone on land had refused to stop hoping, and with his mother, who was "half crazy" thinking he had drowned; his welcome home—"it appeared like the house of death instead of life"—and the uplifting effect his deliverance had on everyone. Indeed, the point of the story becomes how much he is missed when people think he is dead, and how glad they are to find him alive.

Naturally, this knowledge makes him feel good. But the mood is soon subverted by the realities of life, and by the sense that something is missing. To Chaplin, that something is excitement. All too soon, after collecting his friends' congratulations, he returns to his mundane rounds: his potatoes have come up so badly he won't have enough vines to plant for slips; his sugarcane has rotted in the ground and his cotton, after sprouting nicely, has died off. The reader, too, after having shared in the general elation, misses the freedom, danger, and fellowship of the water. Something has not made it to land. The Negroes have disappeared from sight as if they had fallen off the end of the earth. On water, whites and blacks were of one mind, one feeling, equally human. Without thinking about it, Chaplin empathized indiscriminately with everyone. On land, however, the blacks become invisible drudges behind the ever rising and falling hoes.

A few days after his safe return, Chaplin went down to Lands End, "got a boat & rowed under the shore in search of things as far as Bay Point." Part of his gun case had washed up, also Colcock's walking stick and Webb's liquor case. Chaplin lost everything he had on board except his watch and pencil. "Lost my trunk with my best clothes, my gun & case, clock, saddle & bridle, shoes, coat I had on & shirt—gold sleeve buttons & studs." A rich man's paraphernalia—he must have been planning to go shooting and riding at Webb's, and to dine in company. He sent the watch to be cleaned in Charleston, but it was returned to him not worth fixing.

A broken watch is a small thing next to a life that's lost, but Chaplin did not see it that way. His self-indulgence, following a flash of empathy, suggests he had a large emotional capacity that was unnaturally stifled. Troublesome thoughts, such as the idea that Negroes are people, kept threatening to break into his consciousness, but he kept disowning them, from pride, lethargy, and the need to keep his world view intact.

Even so, his response to calamity was perfectly normal. Faced with great losses he clung to small things. Always aware of his class, the things he recalled when he had been stripped of everything were emblems of pleasure and ease. As unenviable as this conceit may seem, it had the virtue of protecting him from truly disabling emotions. Thus, we find him deploring the waste of his liquor when he should have been lamenting the death of his wife; missing his old oak chair when what had passed out of his hands were his house and land; and fretting over the loss of silver forks and spoons when what had perished was the social order.

NOTES

The following abbreviations appear in the notes:

JSH: Journal of Southern History

OR: War of the Rebellion: A Compilation of the Official Records of the Union and Confederate Armies

RG: Record Group #, United States Direct Tax Commission, Fiscal Branch of the United States Archives, Washington, D.C.

SCHM: South Carolina Historical Magazine (before 1952 called *South Carolina Historical and Genealogical Magazine*)

SCHS: South Carolina Historical Society, Charleston, South Carolina

Nineteenth-century periodicals are identified by their dates of publication, rather than by volume and issue numbers.

PREFACE
1. Kenneth M. Stampp, "Rebels and Sambos: The Search for the Negro's Personality in Slavery," *JSH,* vol. XXXVII, Aug. 1971, 367.

CHAPTER 1
1. James H. Rice, Jr., *The Aftermath of Glory* (Charleston, 1934), 291.

2. Thomas J. Woofter, *Black Yeomanry: Life on St. Helena Island* (New York, 1930), 5, quoted in the papers of the late William E. (Willy) Fripp, of Walterboro, S.C.

3. On the general problem of soil depletion on the Sea Islands, see Alfred Glaze Smith, Jr., *Economic Readjustment of an Old Cotton State: South Carolina, 1820–1860* (Columbia, S.C., 1958), chaps. I–III.

4. Col. Ambrose J. Gonzales, C.S.A., to Brig. Gen. Thomas Jordan, May 30, 1863, South Carolina Department of Archives and History, Columbia, S.C.

5. Charleston *Mercury*, Aug. 16, 1850.

6. *Beaufort Tribune and Port Royal Commercial*, June 14, 1877.

7. Chaplin-Aimar correspondence, SCHS.

CHAPTER 2

1. *The Autobiography of William J. Grayson*, ed. Samuel Gaillard Stoney, *SCHM*, vol. 48, 1947, 126.

2. Francis Butler Simkins, *A History of the South* (New York, 1953), 15.

3. René de Laudonièrre, chronicler of Jean Ribaut's expedition, *Histoire Notable de la Florida*, in Katherine M. Jones, *Port Royal Under Six Flags* (New York, 1960), 23.

4. K. Jones, 47.

5. Richard S. Dunn, *Sugar and Slavery: The Rise of the Planter Class in the English West Indies 1624–1713* (New York, 1972), 114.

6. K. Jones, 74.

7. *Ibid.*, 77.

8. Lord Cardross to Sir Peter Colleton, March 27, 1685, in *ibid.*, 87.

9. A. S. Salley, Jr., *Warrants for Land in South Carolina, 1692–1711* (Columbia, S.C., 1915), cited in Guion Griffis Johnson, *A Social History of the Sea Islands* (Durham, N.C., 1930), 10–11.

10. The following account of Indian-white relations along the lower Carolina coast is drawn primarily from Gene Waddell, *Indians of the South Carolina Lowcountry* (Columbia, S.C., 1980), 3–22, 169–198; David Duncan Wallace, *The History of South Carolina* (New York, 1934), 11–25; Verner W. Crane, *The Southern Frontier 1670–1732* (Durham, N.C., 1928), 3–46; Chapman J. Milling, *Red Carolinians* (Chapel Hill, N.C., 1940), 3–64, 73–112, 135–164.

11. David H. Corkran, *The Carolina Indian Frontier* (Columbia, S.C., 1970), 5.

12. Crane, 20.

13. *Ibid.*, 21.

14. *Ibid.*, 25–30; Wallace, 17.

15. Crane, 167.

16. Peter H. Wood, *Black Majority* (New York, 1974), 127.

17. Wallace, 23.

18. Edgar T. Thompson, *Plantation Societies, Race Relations, and the South: The Regimentation of Populations* (Durham, N.C., 1975), 1–40, 212–231.

19. Quoted in Lewis Cecil Gray, *History of Agriculture in the Southern United States to 1860* (Gloucester, Mass., 1958), vol. I, 120.

20. Ulrich B. Phillips, *The Slave Economy of the Old South*, ed. Eugene Genovese (Baton Rouge, La., 1968), 118–119. For a description of the steps in the production of indigo, see Chalmers S. Murray, *This Our Land: The Story of the Agricultural Society of South Carolina* (Charleston, S.C., 1949), 43–44; and G. G. Johnson, 21–23.

21. John Archibald Johnson, *Beaufort and the Sea Islands: Their History and Traditions,* published serially in the *Beaufort Republican,* Beaufort, S.C., Jan. 16–July 3, 1873, no. 17, 7.

22. Lawrence S. Rowland, *Eighteenth Century Beaufort: A Study of South Carolina's Southern Parishes to 1800,* unpublished doctoral dissertation, University of South Carolina, Columbia, S.C., 1978, 295.

23. *Ibid.*, 296.

24. Whitemarsh B. Seabrook, *A Memoir on the Origin, Cultivation, and Uses of Cotton* (Charleston, S.C., 1844), 18.

25. *Ibid,* 39.

26. *Southern Agriculturist,* Aug. 1844, 288.

27. *DeBow's Review,* Aug. 1858, 182.

28. Gray, vol. II, 738.

29. The following description of changing patterns of land use is adapted, in part, from charts and discussions in Robert Eugene Mason, *A Historical Geography of South Carolina's Cotton Industry,* unpublished master's thesis, University of South Carolina, Columbia, S.C., 1976, especially 126–136.

30. Grayson, *SCHM,* vol. 48, 1947, 131.

31. Smith, 60.

CHAPTER 3
1. Genealogical material in the private papers of William E. Fripp.

2. "Catalogue of the Officers and Students of the Richland School," Dec. 1, 1830, Special Collections, College of Charleston, Charleston, S.C.

3. *Ibid.*

4. Richard Hofstadter's characterization of antebellum academies, North and South, quoted in Geoffrey Hawthorn, *Enlightenment and Despair: A History of Sociology* (New York, 1976), 203.

5. Thomas C. Law Papers, The South Caroliniana Library, Columbia, S.C.

CHAPTER 4

1. Frederic Bancroft, *Slave Trading in the Old South* (Baltimore, 1931), 206.

2. The following discussion of cultivation techniques comes mainly from Seabrook, 22–24; William Henry Capers, "The Cultivation of Sea Island Cotton," *Southern Agriculturist*, Aug. 1835, 403–412; Robert F. W. Allston, *Essay on Sea Coast Crops* (Charleston, S.C., 1854), 13–16.

3. J. A. Turner, *Cotton Planter's Manual* (New York, 1857), 131, cited in G. G. Johnson, 49–50.

4. *Southern Agriculturist*, Feb. 1844, 42–43.

5. Quoted from the *Southern Cultivator*, in Gray, 547.

6. Allston, 20.

7. John Frederic Duggar, *Southern Field Crops* (New York, 1911), 112–117.

8. David Ramsay, *History of South Carolina* (Newberry, S.C., 1858), 289.

9. *DeBow's Review*, April 1846, 135.

10. G. G. Johnson, 82–83.

11. For a discussion of the origins and development of the task system, see Philip D. Morgan, "Work and Culture: The Task System and the World of Lowcountry Blacks, 1700–1880," *The William & Mary Quarterly*, vol. XXXIX, Oct., 1982, 563–599.

12. Gray (vol. 1, 150–156) suggests that the task system enabled slaves to acquire small property. Philip Morgan elaborates on this theme in "The Ownership of Property by Slaves in the Mid-nineteenth Century Lowcountry," *JSH*, vol. XLIX, Aug. 1983, 399–420.

13. *The William F. Allen Diary*, State Historical Society of Wisconsin, Madison, Wis., 21; also, anonymous letter, Union soldier to sister, March 3, 1863, South Caroliniana Library.

14. Seabrook, 23.

15. Gray, vol. II, 732.

16. *Southern Agriculturist,* Aug. 1829, 312.

17. A. H. Stone, "The Cotton Factorage System in the Southern States," *American Historical Review,* vol. 20, 1914, 561.

18. *DeBow's Review,* Aug. 1851, 307.

19. E. J. Donnell, *History of Cotton* (New York, 1872), 320.

20. Seabrook, 3–4.

21. Donnell, 358.

22. *Ibid.*

23. *Ibid.,* 465.

24. *Ibid.,* 511.

25. The question of profits is, in Harold Woodman's phrase, "A Historical Perennial" (*JSH,* vol. XXIX, Aug. 1963, 303–325). Woodman discusses some complexities of the problem and surveys the literature through 1963. For an earlier computation of a representative Sea Island profit, and a comparison of the *rate* of profit to returns from "free" farming, see Woofter, 32, and G. G. Johnson, 101–102. Chaplin's contemporary Robert F. W. Allston figured a Sea Island profit for the bright year of 1852, in Allston, 17–18. For a discussion of the social significance of profits and losses, see Kenneth M. Stampp, *The Peculiar Institution* (New York, 1956), 383–418.

26. "The idea never comes into their heads." William J. Russell, quoted in Nicholas Olsberg, *Desolate Places: The South Carolina Chivalry at the Time of the Civil War,* unpublished doctoral dissertation, University of South Carolina, Columbia, S.C., 1970, 151.

27. For a discussion of the migratory habits of the lowcountry elite, see Lawrence Fay Brewster, *Summer Migrations and Resorts of South Carolina Low-Country Planters* (Durham, N.C., 1947).

28. Smith, 9–10.

29. Hazard Stevens, *The Life of Isaac Ingalls Stevens* (Boston, 1900), vol. II, 353.

30. *Ibid.*

31. George P. Elliott, quoted in Nathaniel Berners Barnwell, "The Battles of Beaufort," Jan. 23, 1945, 18, Beaufort County Historical Society, Beaufort, S.C.

32. Rev. Robert Woodward Barnwell, "A Town's Peculiarity," in *Dawn at Daufuskie* (Florence, S.C., 1936), 52.

33. George P. Elliott, "Beaufort, South Carolina, as the Atlantic Terminus of the Pacific Railroad," *DeBow's Review,* June 1856, 713.

CHAPTER 5

1. Emma Chaplin to John Peto Chaplin, n.d., in the possession of Rev. Dr. Robert E. E. Peeples, Hilton Head, S.C.

2. *Southern Agriculturist,* July 1836, 346.

3. Announcement in the Charleston *Mercury,* throughout the fall, 1837.

4. Personal communication, Mrs. Jane Raley to Theodore Rosengarten, Aug. 14, 1981.

5. *F. I. Roux, trustee,* versus *T. B. Chaplin,* et al., Cases in Equity, Court of Appeals, Charleston, S.C., winter term, 1847. All quotations in this section, unless otherwise noted, appear in the transcript of *Roux v. Chaplin.*

6. *Hastie & Nichols* versus *R. L. Baker,* et al., Appeals in Equity, Charleston, S.C., Jan. 1851.

7. *Ibid.*

8. *DeBow's Review,* March 1857, 246.

CHAPTER 6

1. Testimony of Daniel P. Jenkins, in *Roux v. Chaplin.*

2. *Southern Agriculturist,* March 1835, 113.

3. Grayson, *SCHM,* vol. 49, 1948, 29.

4. *Ibid.,* 30.

5. *Witsell v. Ernest,* 1 N. and McC. 182, Jan. 1818, in Helen T. Catterall, *Judicial Cases Concerning American Slavery and the Negro* (Washington, D.C., 1929), 307.

6. Steven A. Channing, *Crisis of Fear: Secession in South Carolina* (New York, 1974), 27–28.

7. On the structure and duties of the state militia, see Benjamin Elliott and Martin Strobel, *The Militia System of South Carolina* (Charleston, S.C., 1835).

8. *Ibid.,* xxx.

9. Capt. Fitzhugh McMaster, U.S.N. ret., "St. Helena Volunteers, South Carolina Militia," *Military Collector and Historian,* vol. XVII, fall 1965, 92–93; J. A. Johnson, no. 16, 73.

10. *Ex parte Boylston,* 2 Strob. 41, Nov. 1847, in Catterall, 403. See also H. M. Henry, *The Police Control of the Slave in South Carolina* (Emory, Va., 1914), 6–17.

11. See Charles B. Sydnor, "The Southerner and the Law," *JSH,* vol. VI, Feb. 1940, 3–23.

12. J. A. Johnson, no. 9, 46.

13. William Elliott, *Carolina Sports by Land and Water* (Charleston, S.C., 1846), 61.

14. *Ibid.,* 65.

15. *Ibid.,* 64.

16. On dueling in South Carolina, see Jack Kenny Williams, "The Code of Honor in Ante-Bellum South Carolina," *SCHM,* vol. 54, 1953, 113–126; also Dickson D. Bruce, Jr., *Violence and Culture in the Antebellum South* (Austin, Tex., 1979), 21–43. For two opposing antebellum views, see S. H. Dickson, "Duelling," *Russell's Magazine,* May 1857, 132–142, and William J. Grayson, "The Duel," in *ibid.,* Aug. 1857, 439–454.

17. *DeBow's Review,* Jan. 1855, 129.

18. *Carolina Gazette,* Charleston, S.C., July 17, 1819, quoted in K. Jones, 158.

19. Arthur Meier Schlesinger, *New Viewpoints in American History* (New York, 1948), 229.

20. *Ibid.*

21. Harold S. Schultz, *Nationalism and Sectionalism in South Carolina 1852–1860* (Durham, N.C., 1950), 11.

22. Grayson, *SCHM,* vol. 48, 1947, 127.

23. William Henry Trescot, "Oration Delivered Before the Beaufort Volunteer Artillery," July 4, 1850, 14, SCHS.

24. "Document 31," *The Rebellion Record,* ed. Frank Moore (New York, 1866), Supplement, vol. 1, 197ff.

25. *Ibid.,* 200.

26. Richard DeTreville to Southern Rights Association, Oct. 1851, in *ibid.*

27. *Ibid.*, 201.

28. Trescot, 12.

29. Grayson, *SCHM,* vol. 51, 1950, 113.

30. William J. Grayson, *The Hireling and the Slave* (Charleston, S.C., 1856), 35.

31. "Findings of the Meeting in Charleston, S.C., May 13–15, 1845, on the Religious Instruction of the Negroes," 49, SCHS.

32. Allen, 83.

33. "Findings of the Meeting in Charleston . . . ," 49.

34. Albert Sidney Thomas, *A Historical Account of the Protestant Episcopal Church in South Carolina 1820–1957* (Columbia, S.C., 1957), 182.

35. *Ibid.*

36. *Ibid.*, 72.

CHAPTER 7
1. Grayson, *The Hireling and the Slave,* vii.

2. Stampp, "Rebels and Sambos," 384.

3. Michael P. Johnson, "Smothered Slave Infants: Were Slave Mothers at Fault?" *JSH,* vol. XLVII, Nov. 1981, 494; Todd L. Savitt, *Medicine and Slavery* (Chicago, 1978), 124.

4. Allen, 69.

5. Arthur Sumner Papers, May 25, 1862, Southern Historical Collection, Chapel Hill, N.C.

6. Allen, 83.

7. Laura M. Towne, quoted in the papers of Mrs. Robert F. Sams, Beaufort County Public Library, Beaufort, S.C.

8. Laura M. Towne Papers, Feb. 14, 1864, Penn Community Center, Frogmore, S.C.

9. Grayson, *The Hireling and the Slave,* vii.

10. Allen, 190.

CHAPTER 8

1. For a discussion of the separation of planters' wives from their families, and of the closeness of sisters, see Catherine Clinton, *The Plantation Mistress* (New York, 1982), 36–58.

2. Personal communication, Mrs. Jane Raley to Theodore Rosengarten, Jan. 5, 1981.

3. J. Perrin Anderson, "Public Education in Antebellum South Carolina," *Proceedings of the South Carolina Historical Association*, Charleston, S.C., 1933, 4.

4. On the superior educational opportunities available in Beaufort, see G. G. Johnson, 112–115.

5. *DeBow's Review*, Feb. 1856, 148.

6. *Ibid.*

7. Grayson, *The Hireling and the Slave*, 34.

8. *DeBow's Review*, Feb. 1856, 148.

9. On the practical difficulties of maintaining a public school system, see Lowell Harrison, "South Carolina's Educational System in 1822," *SCHM*, vol. 51, 1950, 1–9.

CHAPTER 9

1. *DeBow's Review*, May 1847, 420.

2. Savitt, 47.

3. *DeBow's Review*, July 1854, 281.

4. *Ibid.*

5. Savitt, 41.

6. Brewster, 6.

7. Ramsay, 282.

8. John Drayton, *A View of South Carolina* (Charleston, S.C., 1802), 27.

9. Brewster, 6–9.

10. *New Orleans Medical Journal*, vol. 1, 1844, 247, cited in John Duffy, "Medical Practices in the Ante-bellum South," *JSH*, vol. XXV, 1959, 58.

11. Dr. R. W. Gibbes to Robert F. W. Allston, quoted in Eugene Genovese, "The Medical and Insurance Costs of Slaveholding in the Cotton Belt," *Journal of Negro History*, vol. XLI, July 1960, 143.

12. Savitt, 64.

13. *Ibid.*, 112ff.

14. Quoted in Martha Carolyn Mitchell, "Health and the Medical Profession in the Lower South, 1845–1860," *JSH*, vol. X, Oct. 1944, 438.

15. Francis Peyre Porcher, *Resources of the Southern Fields and Forests,* (Charleston, S.C., 1863), 84.

CHAPTER 10
1. *Southern Literary Gazette,* May 22, 1852, 230.

2. *Ibid.,* 249.

3. *Ibid.*, June 12, 1852, 284.

4. Roger Pinckney, "Occupation of the Beaufort Area by Northern Forces During *The* War," April 15, 1975, 15, Beaufort County Historical Society.

CHAPTER 11
1. A. W. Dimock, "The Fleet Is Upon Us," in K. Jones, 204.

2. *Ibid.*

3. *Charleston Courier,* Nov. 29, 1860.

4. *Ibid.*

5. On the popularity of these dualisms, see David M. Potter, *The South and the Sectional Conflict* (Baton Rouge, La., 1968), 44.

6. *Charleston Courier,* Nov. 29, 1860.

7. *Ibid*

8. For a late-antebellum southern view of the tariff and its effects on cotton prices, see *DeBow's Review,* Aug. 1858, 131, and Nov. 1859, 703–705.

9. A retrospect of the Carolinians' fears is presented in Alice Huger Smith and Herbert Ravenel Sass, *A Carolina Rice Plantation of the Fifties* (New York, 1936). Also see Potter, 66, 80, 108.

10. *Charleston Courier,* Nov. 24, 1860.

11. Augustus D. Dickert, *History of Kershaw's Brigade* (Newberry, S.C., 1899), 12.

12. Olsberg, 116.

13. *Ibid.*, 168.

14. On the rise of insurgency in the individual slaveholding states, see Schultz, 200–230, and John McCardell, *The Idea of a Southern Nation* (New York, 1979), 277–335.

15. Schultz, 231–233.

16. *Ibid.*, 26–57, 134–149, 178ff.

17. Potter, 259.

18. *Ibid.*, 254.

19. A. W. Dimock, "Pledging Allegiance to the Confederate States of America," in K. Jones, 185.

20. *Ibid.*

21. *Ibid.*, 186.

22. Howard E. Danner, "Beaufort in the Civil War," June 30, 1960, 5, Beaufort County Historical Society.

23. Mrs. A. T. Smythe, *et al.*, *South Carolina Women in the Confederacy* (Columbia, S.C., 1903), 176.

24. *Ibid.*, 177.

25. *Ibid.*

26. *Civil War Naval Chronology 1861–1865,* Navy Department (Washington, D.C., 1971), vol. I, 23.

27. *Ibid.*, 29.

28. George P. Elliott, "Port Royal City," *DeBow's Review,* Sept. 1858, 410.

29. Donnell, 510.

30. J. A. Johnson, 80.

31. Pinckney, 4. The following battle description is taken primarily from accounts by Federal and Confederate Officers in *OR*, and from papers presented to the Beaufort County Historical Society, particularly Pinckney and Danner.

32. Brig. Gen. Thomas F. Drayton, C.S.A., to Capt. C. D. Walker, Adjutant General, Charleston, S.C., Nov. 24, 1861, in K. Jones, 231.

33. A. W. Dimock, "The Fleet Is Upon Us," 205.

34. Bern Anderson, *By Sea and by River: The Naval History of the Civil War* (New York, 1962), 57.

35. Laura M. Towne, quoted in the papers of Mrs. Robert F. Sams.

36. Richard DeTreville, "Sea Island Lands: St. Helena Parish and Its Citizens . . . a few chapters from a faithful unpublished History of the War of Secession," n.d., South Caroliniana Library.

37. Richard L. Johnson to Mrs. William Johnson, Nov. 11, 1861, Beaufort, S.C., copy in SCHS.

38. Lt. Thomas G. White to *Charleston Courier,* Dec. 2, 1861.

39. *Ibid.*

40. *Ibid.*

41. Nathaniel Berners Barnwell, 16.

42. White to *Charleston Courier.*

43. DeTreville, "Sea Island Lands," 1.

44. Charleston *Mercury,* Nov. 11, 1861.

45. Gen. Robert E. Lee, C.S.A., to Judah P. Benjamin, Nov. 9, 1861, in *OR,* Series 1, vol. VI, 312.

46. Stevens, 10.

47. From Sherman's "Official Report," reprinted in *War Letters of William T. Lusk* (New York, 1911), 98.

48. DeTreville, "Sea Island Lands," 1–2.

49. *OR,* Series 1, vol. VI, 44–75.

50. Gen. Robert E. Lee to Judge McGrath, "President of the State Convention about to meet in regard to preparations to defend the State, December 24, 1861," in Samuel Jones, *The Siege of Charleston* (New York, 1911), 72.

51. *Ibid.*

52. For a Confederate view of the siege, see Paul Hamilton Hayne, "The Defense of Fort Wagner," *Southern Bivouac,* March 1886, 599–608. For a Union view, see Luis F. Emilio, *History of the 54th Regiment Massachusetts Volunteer Infantry* (Boston, 1894), 67–127.

53. Gen. Robert E. Lee to President Jefferson Davis, C.S.A., in *OR,* Series 1, vol. XXXIII, 1097.

54. *Ibid.*

55. *Ibid.*

56. Dickert, 443.

57. Mark M. Boatner, III, *The Civil War Dictionary* (New York, 1959), 848.

58. Grady McWhiney and Perry D. Jamieson, *Attack and Die: Civil War Tactics and the Southern Heritage* (University, Ala., 1982), 134.

59. *Ibid.*, 62–68, 126–139.

60. For a vivid partisan account of the battle for Trevilian Station, see U. R. Brooks, *Butler and His Cavalry in the War of Secession* (Columbia, S.C., 1909), 236–270.

61. *OR,* Series 1, vol. XLVII, 197.

62. Lt. Gen. U. S. Grant, U.S.A., to E. M. Stanton, *OR,* Series I, vol. XLVIII, 405.

63. John Barrett, *Sherman's March Through the Carolinas* (Chapel Hill, N.C., 1956), 58–60; "Report of Gen. William T. Sherman," *OR,* Series I, vol. XLVII, 20.

64. "Confederate War Records of Daniel J. Chaplin," microfilm no. 33, 267, South Carolina Department of Archives and History.

65. Dickert, 536.

CHAPTER 12
1. Baker vented these sentiments in a letter to Dr. James Morrow, Oct. 27, 1860, South Caroliniana Library, Columbia, S.C.

2. R. L. Baker to James B. Campbell, Dec. 11, 1864, James Butler Campbell Papers, SCHS.

3. Baker to Campbell, July 25, 1864, in *ibid.*

4. *Ibid.*

5. James Butler Campbell Papers.

6. C. B. Farmer to Campbell, Nov. 19, 1864.

7. Bill filed by *Thomas B. Chaplin,* et al., v. *R. L. Baker, F. L. Roux,* et al., n.d.

8. R. L. Baker, letter to the court, n.d. (summer, 1864).

9. Baker to Campbell, July 25, 1864.

10. R. DeTreville to J. B. Bissell, n.d.

11. DeTreville to Bissell, Oct. 13, 1864.

12. *Ibid.*

13. Affidavit of Lawrence J. Witsell, Nov. 16, 1864.

14. Bissell to Campbell, Dec. 10, 1864.

15. Roux to Bissell, Oct. 8, 1864.

16. Roux to Campbell, Oct. 27, 1864.

17. C. B. Farmer to Campbell, Nov. 19, 1864.

18. Baker to Campbell, Dec. 11, 1864.

19. Roux to Campbell, Dec. 15, 1864.

CHAPTER 13

1. *OR,* Series 1, vol. VI, 5.

2. Stevens, 355.

3. J. A. Johnson, no. 22, 103.

4. The classic study of this endeavor is Willie Lee Rose, *Rehearsal for Reconstruction* (New York, 1964).

5. Allen, 37.

6. *Letters and Diary of Laura M. Towne,* ed. Rupert Sargent Holland (Cambridge, Mass., 1912), April 17, 1862, 8.

7. Edward L. Pierce, *Enfranchisement and Citizenship* (Boston, 1896), 121.

8. Lusk, 139.

9. DeTreville, "Sea Island Lands," 3.

10. Arthur Sumner to J. H. Clark, Jan. 23, 1863, Arthur Sumner Papers, Southern Historical Collection, Chapel Hill, N.C.

11. Towne, in Holland, xiv–xv.

12. Allen, 37.

13. *Ibid.,* 98; Towne, in Holland, 20.

14. Sumner to Clark.

15. Towne to "R," Oct. 23, 1864, in Rose, 364.

16. Pierce, 58.

17. *Ibid.,* 73

18. *Ibid.*

19. *Ibid.,* 122.

20. "Preliminary Report from the tax commissioners of South Carolina under the act of Congress June 7, 1862," Jan. 1, 1863, in RG 58.

21. Towne, in Holland, 21.

22. Lusk, 97.

23. *Free South,* Jan. 17, 1863.

24. DeTreville, "Sea Island Lands," 8.

25. *Free South,* Jan. 17, 1863.

26. Allen, 36.

27. *Ibid.,* 23.

28. William H. Brisbane to Joseph J. Lewis, Feb. 23, 1864, in RG 58, quoted in Rose, 294.

29. Allen, 198.

30. *Ibid.,* 172.

31. Edward S. Philbrick to William Channing Gannett, July 8, 1864, Gannett Papers, University of Rochester, Rochester, N.Y.

32. Towne Papers, May 25, 1864, Penn Community Center.

33. Henry Seabrook to Edward S. Philbrick, South Caroliniana Library, Columbia, S.C.; also quoted in *Letters from Port Royal,* ed. Elizabeth Ware Pearson (Boston, 1906), 316.

34. Pearson, *ibid.*; also quoted in Mason Crum, *Gullah: Negro Life in the Carolina Sea Islands* (Durham, N.C., 1940), 326–327.

35. Allen, 152.

36. "Preliminary Report from the tax commissioners of South Carolina. . . ."

37. *Ibid.*

38. Allen, 188.

39. *Ibid.,* 152.

40. *Ibid.,* 126.

41. *Ibid.,* 152.

42. U.S. Direct Tax Commission, Plat of the City of Port Royal, S.C., Oct. 20, 1864, RG 58.

43. *Ibid.*

44. J. A. Johnson, no. 22, 103.

45. DeTreville, "Sea Island Lands," 6.

46. Pinckney, 15.

47. DeTreville, "Sea Island Lands," 5.

48. *Ibid.,* 11.

49. Cases include: *E. J. Fishburne* v. *D. J. and T. B. Chaplin,* 1867, box 5-66; *Otis D. Prentiss* v. *T. B. Chaplin,* 1868, box 7-88; *Oliver H. Middleton* v. *T. B. Chaplin,* 1869, box 11-98; *William H. Cowl* v. *T. B. Chaplin,* 1871, box 15-33, Colleton County Court House, Walterboro, S.C.

50. Thomas B. Chaplin to Oliver H. Middleton, Dec. 10, 1866, in *Middleton* v. *Chaplin.*

51. *Ibid.*

52. Chaplin to Middleton, n.d. (Feb. 1867), in *ibid.*

53. Bill of Foreclosure, William H. Cowl against Thomas, Daniel, Ernest, and Virginia (since deceased) Chaplin, in *Cowl* v. *Chaplin.*

54. Daniel and Ernest Chaplin, answer to subpoena, Feb. 7, 1870, in *ibid.*

55. C. B. Farmer's answer to Cowl's second attempt to have the court serve a bill of foreclosure against the Chaplins, n.d., in *ibid.*

56. C. B. Farmer, appearance in court, n.d. (June 1871), in *ibid.*

57. For the Appeals Court rule on eligibility for homestead, see *Shelor* v. *Mason,* 2 SC 233, 1870.

CHAPTER 14

1. Hermine Munz Baumhofer, "Economic Changes in St. Helena's Parish, 1860–1870," *SCHM,* vol. 50, 1940, 1–13.

2. For a discussion of how freedmen in coastal Carolina named themselves, and of the significance of their names, see George C. Rogers, *The History of Georgetown County, South Carolina* (Columbia, S.C., 1970), 438–441.

3. Allen, 129.

4. "An Indenture made Jan. 2, 1865, between William Henry Brisbane, William E. Wording, and Dennis N. Cooley, U.S. Direct Tax Commissioners, and Marcus L. Penniman," *Book of Leases,* RG 58.

5. School Farm Letters, RG 58.

6. These items are in the School Farm Letters.

7. April 5, 1875, in *ibid.*

8. W. R. Cloutman to J. W. Douglass, April 20, 1875, in *ibid.*

9. *Opium Eating, an Autobiographical Sketch,* by "An Habituate" (Philadelphia, 1876), 83.

10. On the opium problem in the South at large, see David T. Courtwright, "The Hidden Epidemic: Opiate Addiction and Cocaine Use in the South, 1860–1920," *JSH,* vol. XCIX, Feb. 1983, 57–72.

11. *Beaufort Tribune and Port Royal Commercial,* March 22, 1877.

12. Ambrose Elliott Gonzales, "There Was Nothing, Save Flowers, Left to Give," in K. Jones, 311.

13. Towne Papers, Penn Community Center; an edited version of this item appears in Holland, 289.

14. Dr. William J. Jenkins, Application to Redeem Indian Hills Plantation, S.C. Direct Tax Applications to Redeem Real Estate Sold for Direct Tax, RG 58.

15. Dr. William J. Jenkins, Claims for Surplus Proceeds from the Sale of the Sandiford Place, S.C. Direct Tax Applications for Refund Surplus Proceeds of Sale of Real Estate Sold for Direct Tax, RG 58.

16. Affidavit of Dr. William J. Jenkins, in Application of Daniel Pope to Redeem the Daniel Pope Place, in S.C. Direct Tax Applications to Redeem Real Estate Sold for Direct Tax, RG 58.

17. S.C. Direct Tax Maps, vol. I, RG 217.

18. J. A. Johnson, letter to the Beaufort *Republican,* n.d., "Copied from clippings pasted into an old account book found in the Porter Danner house after its purchase by Mr. and Mrs. Howard E. Danner," Beaufort County Public Library.

19. School Farm Letters, 1886–1890.

20. *Ibid.*

21. Field Notebook of Joseph L. Townsend, surveyor, in RG 58.

22. D. F. Bradley to John Mason, May 21, 1889, S.C. Direct Tax Applications to Redeem Real Estate Sold for Direct Tax, RG 58.

23. D. F. Bradley to John Mason, June 15, 1889, in *ibid.*

24. E. A. Webster to John Mason, Feb. 22, 1860, in *ibid.*

25. *Palmetto Post,* Dec. 11, 1890.

26. *Ibid.,* Nov. 27, 1890.

THE JOURNAL OF
THOMAS B. CHAPLIN
(1822–1890)

Edited and Annotated with the
Assistance of Susan W. Walker

FOREWORD

Marc Bloch, the great French historian, once observed that "the migration of manuscripts is, in itself, an extremely interesting object of study," because it corresponds exactly to the "vicissitudes of life." Chaplin's journal illustrates the point. In December, 1928, Daniel Chaplin's youngest child, Fred, then fifty-one years old, sold his grandfather's diary to a Charleston pawnbroker for "liquor money." The pawnbroker immediately sold the volume to the South Carolina Historical Society for ten dollars. Four years had passed since Daniel died, and forty-three years since Thomas B. Chaplin appended his epilogue. Over the next half-century, a handful of genealogists and historians consulted Chaplin's journal. Willie Lee Rose used it extensively for details of antebellum life in *Rehearsal for Reconstruction*. Although the significance of the journal has long been appreciated by denizens of the archives, attempts to interest a publisher have been unsuccessful until now.

My aim in editing Chaplin's diary has been to keep faithful to his concerns and to preserve the character of the diarist, while making the book more readable. As a rule for what to leave in, I took a cue from Ulrich B. Phillips's *Life and Labor in the Old South:* "Let us begin by discussing the weather . . ." which is precisely what Chaplin had done almost every day. Still, I did delete many weather observations when conditions on a particular day were not unusual and did not interfere with the plantation routine. I also deleted some of Chaplin's references to health, social visits, teas, and billiards games. I left in the seasonal occurrence of agricultural tasks but omitted some day-to-day records of work. For example, each round of hoeing is reported, but not necessarily the daily progress made by the workers. I tried to retain the structure of drawn-out events such as sieges of illness and the annual preparation of the cotton crop for market, but I struck out repetitive detail. The result is some loss, then, of the dreary and obsessive side of life. Life seems a bit more eventful, and proceeds at a faster pace, in the edited journal.

In selecting entries to keep I tried to adhere to subjects which were significant to the diarist—a method of selection that assumes I understand him. I was helped by Chaplin's notes, the comments he added in the postwar years which call attention to passages like flags in an open field. In the interest of brevity and narrative unity, I deleted parenthetical remarks at the beginning and end of entries. Thus, the diarist may seem less digressive and more focused, less pained by tedium and more purposeful, than he actually was.

I did not chop sentences out of paragraphs or words out of sentences. Neither did I alter Chaplin's sequences or syntax. Most often I deleted whole entries, or whole paragraphs from entries. I did not indicate deletions with ellipsis points, as I felt they would slow down the reading and counteract the narrative thrust of the book. Ellipsis points that do appear were put there by Chaplin. Any diary is difficult enough to read because ongoing stories are dispersed across the entries, and it is up to the reader to pick out the parts and combine them.

I corrected or modernized Chaplin's spelling where a word may have caused confusion, but I left unchanged what I believed were slips of the pen. I regularized datelines and partially normalized punctuation, placing commas between words written in series, replacing dashes with commas or periods, and adding apostrophes, according to modern usage. I italicized the words Chaplin underlined for emphasis, the names of books and ships, and words in French and Latin. I used empty brackets to indicate illegible writing; other brackets supply a word or words left out by Chaplin in haste or error, words which are evident from context and where the insertion makes for smoother reading. Lines indicating blank spaces were put there by Chaplin. He meant to go back and fill them in later, but did not.

People who want to read the unedited journal may see the original at the Fireproof Building in Charleston. Also, the South Carolina Historical Society plans to make the complete diary available on microfilm in the near future.

The text contains two sets of notes—Chaplin's afterthoughts and the editors' clarifications. Chaplin's notes appear in the text wherever he inserted them, set off by asterisks as was his fashion, and occasionally initialed with a "C." Notes prepared by Susan Walker and myself appear at the bottom of the page. Their purpose is to maximize recognition and minimize confusion and strangeness. Every character who could be identified is noted. More is said about the white people than the black people because the whites left behind a more abundant record. Where genealogical information about a person is relevant to establishing the planters' social network, we have named spouses, parents, siblings, and sometimes aunts, uncles, cousins. Each person's relationship to Chaplin is spelled out. The first thing one gleans from the notes is that Chaplin lived surrounded by relatives. At least a hundred people mentioned in his journal were direct relations—not counting anyone more distant than second cousin.

Places, events, associations, and obscure allusions are also identified—the Croton Aqueduct, in New York State, for example, which deeply impressed the lowcountry planter, who worried perennially about his water supply. Agricultural terms are noted, and also the *meaning* to Chaplin of cotton prices and crop yields. In these instances, what the diarist has left unsaid is what most needs saying—how many weeks his workers can be fed, for example, from an acre's harvest of sweet potatoes.

About half the notes occur in the first third of the journal, when characters and terminology are introduced. The remaining notes identify new characters, explain changes in technological and material life, and follow the children of Chaplin's friends and neighbors—relatives all—as they mature and take their places in society.

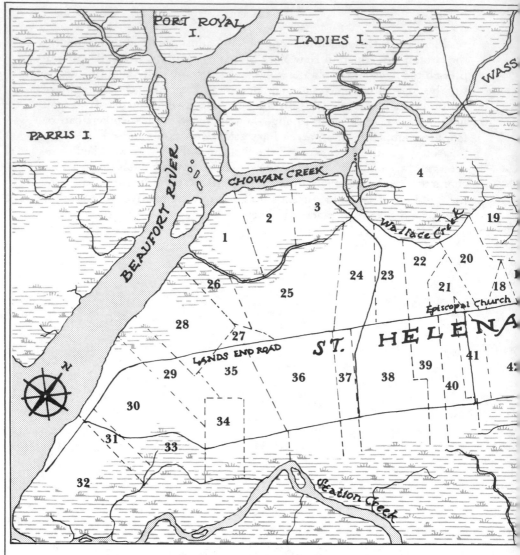

Plantations of St. Helena Island
(circa 1860)

Marsh ▢ Farmland and Woods

```
0      1/2      1              2
SCALE IN MILES
```

1. Littlewood Point—William A. Chisolm (250*) 2. Edward M. (Ned) Capers (266) 3. Gabriel Capers (267) 4. The Oaks—J.J.T. Pope (500) 5. Robert Fuller (500) 6. Polawanna—Dr. Lewis Reeves Sams (100) 7. Oakland—Dr. Lewis Reeves Sams (121) 8. Randall Croft (150) 9. Jenkins Neck (147) 10. Eddings Point—Joseph D. Eddings (604) 11. St. Helenaville Pine Lands—Joseph D. Eddings (90) 12. Village Farm—Capt. John Fripp (200) 13. Marion T. Chaplin (303) 14. Feliciana—Daniel Pope (448) 15. Indian Hills—Dr. William Jenkins (400) 16. Corner Farm—Capt. John Fripp (300) 17. The Parsonage—Dr. Lewis Reeves Sams (121) 18. The Fendin Place—W.O.P. Fripp (80) 19. The Wallace Place—Robert G. Norton (475) 20. The Perry Place—Joseph Perry (299) 21. Orange Grove—Edgar W. Fripp (225) 22. The

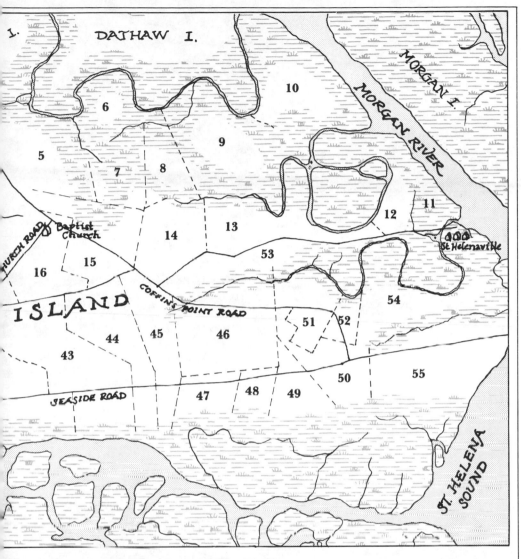

Pritchard Place—Oliver J. Pritchard (232) **23.** J.E.L. Fripp (221) **24.** W.O.P. Fripp (232) **25.** The Scott Place—Dr. William Jenkins (570) **26.** Isaac Fripp (300) **27.** Lonesome Hill— John E. Fripp (150) **28.** Bermuda—Edwin Chaplain (n.a.) **29.** Riverside—Daniel P. Jenkins (326) **30.** The Baker Place (Riverside)—Isabella Baker (328) **31.** Ben Chaplin (165) **32.** Lands End (434) **33.** Tombee—Thomas B. Chaplin (376) **34.** Curlew Hill—Paul Chaplin (n.a.) **35.** Paul Chaplin (608) **36.** Dr. William Jenkins (615) **37.** Jane Pritchard (160) **38.** The Sandiford Place—Dr. William Jenkins (600) **39.** Frank Pritchard (230) **40.** Henry McTureous (199) **41.** Ann Fripp (260) **42.** Seaside—Edgar W. Fripp (944) **43.** Frogmore—Thomas A. Coffin (1,060) **44.** Woodstock—Thomas G. White (610) **45.** Hope—Alvira Fripp (572) **46.** John Fripp's Big House—Capt. John Fripp (990) **47.** Mulberry Hill—Capt. John Fripp (500) **48.** Cherry Hill—Thomas A. Coffin (300) **49.** McTureous Lands—Thomas A. Coffin (531) **50.** Pine Grove—William Fripp, Sr. (750) **51.** Cedar Grove—Thomas B. Fripp (205) **52.** Hamilton Fripp (200) **53.** Thomas James Fripp (614) **54.** Fripp's Point— William Fripp, Sr. (750) **55.** Coffin's Point—Thomas A. Coffin (1,438)

*Acreage in parentheses.

Topographical features based on a map of Beaufort District by Robert Mills, 1825, and U.S. Coast Survey, "Sketch of Sea Coast of South Carolina and Georgia," 1863. Plantation placement based on U.S. Direct Tax Commission plats, township maps, and surveyors' notes, 1863–65, and drawings in the papers of Mrs. Robert F. Sams, n.d.

1845

Jan. 13th. We were very much astonished about 10 o'clock at night, by January[1] from H. Hill[2] making his appearance at the door. He brought letters to Capt. D. Jenkins[3] & myself, the purport of which was that the sheriff had taken 27 Negroes from the Point Place,[4] under a mortgage to Ladson & Bee[5]— It is my firm belief that R. L. Baker was at the head of this mean transaction and brought it about by making Ladson believe that he would not get his money unless he proceeded against the property immediately, or something to that effect. It is nothing but a spirit of revenge on the part of Baker.[6]

---

[1] A slave belonging to Chaplin's mother, Isabella Baker. He lived at the Point Place.
[2] Hickory Hill. A 1,200-acre, heavily wooded plantation owned by Chaplin's brother, Saxby. Located on the mainland, in St. Bartholomew's Parish, Colleton District, near Green Pond, upstream from Mrs. Baker's home plantation.
[3] Daniel T. Jenkins (b 1810), planter. Bachelor son of Col. John Jenkins and Sarah Chaplin. First cousin to Chaplin on his mother's side. Lived at Indian Hills Plantation near the center of St. Helena Island, and had a life interest in property at Lands End. Served as a trustee of Mrs. Baker's settled estate.
[4] One of two tracts—the other was Walnut Hill—that made up Fields Point, Isabella Baker's home plantation, occupying the point of a neck of land between the Combahee and Chehaw rivers, north of St. Helena Island, in St. Bartholomew's Parish.
[5] James H. Latzin and William C. Bee, partners in the firm of James H. Latzin & Company, cotton factors in Charleston. They held mortgages on properties owned by Isabella Baker, her husband, and her son Saxby.
[6] Robert Little Baker (1807–1867). Son of Joseph and Mary Baker, of St. Bartholomew's Parish. A bankrupt pharmacist from Charleston, Baker had married Chaplin's mother, Isabella, on June 14, 1843—his second marriage, her fourth. Three days later, Baker mortgaged her Fields Point Plantation and ninety slaves to Ladson and Bee. When it came time to pay the debt, Baker and Isabella quarreled over which properties to sell in order to raise the money. In a deed of appointment, replacing the old trustees of her estate with new ones, Mrs. Baker testified that her husband's interference with her wishes had caused Ladson and Bee to seize the mortgaged property and to sell several of the Negroes "at a great sacrifice."

Mrs. Baker's estate had been diminished by forty-six slaves since her marriage to Baker—thirty-one were sold to pay debts which Isabella had contracted while she was yet Mrs. Fields; nine she had deeded as a gift to her son Thomas, and six to her son Saxby. Thus, Baker's "spirit of revenge": to strike back at the Chaplins for scheming

Jan. 14th. I rode over to the Captain's to see him about the letter. Found him making a coffin for a little Negro that died last night from being beat by one of his women (Mary). He answered Mother's[7] letter by January, who returns tomorrow. The Major[8] & William[9] left for the main[10] this morning. I saw John Chaplin[11] and engaged him to attend to my crop this year. . . . Borrowed three cotton bags[12] from the Capt.

Jan. 15th. Killed beef for market,[13] which is the last. John L. Chaplin rode over in the morning. I gave him a list of 36 full hands[14] to plant for this year. January returned to the main today. Sent John[15] to Beaufort.[16] Rec'd a letter from J. W. Gray.[17] Tom Fripp[18] dined with me today. Rode over to the Riverside[19] to learn if the sheriff had been there also, as we heard. Rode with wife[20] over to Uncle Ben's[21] in the evening.

---

him out of fifteen Negroes, and to prevent them from getting any more of their mother's property, Baker maneuvered some of her choice possessions into the hands of his creditors.

[7] Isabella Baker (1785–1863). Daughter of John Cato Field and Elizabeth Perry. Previously married to Daniel Jenkins, her first cousin, once removed, on her father's side, and uncle of Capt. Daniel T. Jenkins; to Saxby Chaplin, Sr., her second cousin on her father's side, and father of Thomas B. and Saxby, Jr.; and to the Rev. John Fields, former rector at the Episcopal chapel on St. Helena Island. She owned five plantations and several hundred slaves.

[8] Daniel Perry Jenkins (1812–1891), planter. Son of Benjamin Jenkins and Elizabeth Perry (niece of the Elizabeth Perry who was Chaplin's maternal grandmother). Second cousin to Chaplin on his mother's side; first cousin to Capt. Daniel T. Jenkins. Lived with his mother on their Riverside Plantation, just above Mrs. Baker's Riverside Plantation, on Broad River. Bounded on the east by Tombee.

[9] Dr. William J. Jenkins (1818–1883), physician and planter. Brother of Maj. Daniel P. Jenkins; second cousin to Chaplin. Lived on a 600-acre plantation northeast of Tombee, on Seaside Road. Eventually owned five plantations on St. Helena. Dr. Jenkins had witnessed Isabella Baker's marriage contract.

[10] The mainland.

[11] John L. Chaplin, farmer and sometime overseer, did not own land. Second cousin to Chaplin on his father's side.

[12] Coarse sack material, English made, used to pack Sea Island cotton.

[13] A group of four, five, or six planters and overseers who took turns slaughtering stock and distributing the meat. This was Chaplin's last turn before the "market" was scheduled to end.

[14] Of the seventy slaves Chaplin owned, and the several he borrowed from his mother, thirty-six worked in the fields.

[15] Chaplin's slave, used as a messenger and drayman.

[16] Resort and trading town for Sea Island planters, on Port Royal Island, northwest of St. Helena. Population 800, in 1840.

[17] James W. Gray, master in equity for Charleston District.

[18] Thomas James Fripp (b. 1820), planter. Son of Col. Thomas James Fripp. First cousin to Chaplin, once removed, on his father's side. Lived in the northwest section of the Island, near St. Helenaville.

[19] Isabella Baker's plantation on Broad River, adjacent to Tombee. Since her latest marriage, also called the Baker Place.

[20] Mary Thomson McDowell (1823–1851). Daughter of Alexander and Sarah McDowell, of Charleston. She married Chaplin in 1839.

[21] Benjamin Chaplin (1776–1851), planter. Son of Thomas B. Chaplin and Eliza Fripp. Brother of Chaplin's father, Saxby, uncle of Capt. Daniel T. Jenkins, and an

Jan. 16th. Went with J. L. Chaplin, the constable,[22] to take Old Cuffy—found him at Cuthbert Barnwell's[23]—and brought him off and left him with Old Bentz, as he requested, until Saturday, when he is to be tried. The old fellow is very cunning—there is no getting a straight story out of him—he denies beating Old Sancho,[24] for which he is to be tried. Packed one bag of P.G. yellow cotton.[25]

Jan. 17th. Went to Beaufort with Sophy.[26] She called on Mrs. Kirkland.[27] Paid Bolger[28] and Mr. Tealy,[29] both bills I think very extravagant. Returned about 8 p.m. Two bags of P.G. cotton (yellow) packed.

Jan. 18th. Went to the clubhouse[30] to attend the trial of Old Cuffy, an old doctor and fortune teller. As I was the prosecutor I was in hopes that he would be sentenced to leave the parish. The magistrate however decided otherwise. His being found guilty he was sentenced to receive thirty-nine lashes, which he took without a murmur.

Jan. 19th. A very disagreeable, windy, drizzly day, quite cold, stayed indoors all day. This weather produces a great deal of sickness. I have 8 or 9 down with fever & chill in the last week. Charles, Amy, Betty & John are now sick with fever. Bought 3 gal. of brandy & 3 of whiskey on Friday 17th.

Jan. 20th. January laid up today. Killed the 5th hog for bacon this year. Ben[31] killed 4 ducks on the Island.[32]

Jan. 23rd. Sent to Beaufort yesterday for a piece of bagging and a barrel of Irish potatoes. Today I rode over the field with John L. Chaplin. I think

---

uncle by marriage to Dr. William and Major Daniel P. Jenkins. Lived next door to Tombee, on the southwest or Lands End side. He had no children.

[22] Also Chaplin's overseer.

[23] Cuthbert Barnwell (1797–1853), planter. Son of John Berners Barnwell and Jane H. Cuthbert.

[24] The owners of Old Cuffy and Old Bentz are unidentified. Old Sancho belonged to Chaplin. He was "a Negro doctor." See Feb. 20, 1846.

[25] Cotton stained by seeds crushed during ginning. It brought 6 to 8 cents a pound in 1845—one-fourth the price of middling-fine white cotton. A bag held 350 pounds.

[26] Sophia Creighton. Chaplin's sister-in-law, half-sister of his wife Mary. She lived at Tombee with the Chaplin family.

[27] Virginia L. Galluchat Kirkland (1814–1864). Wife of William C. Kirkland, Methodist missionary to Beaufort. See note, April 1, 1846.

[28] H. W. Bolger, cabinetmaker and furniture-store proprietor.

[29] John M. Tealy, carpenter.

[30] Meeting place of the St. Helena Island Agricultural Society.

[31] A favored slave who was allowed to use a gun. By statute, only one slave per plantation could have this privilege at any one time, but the rule was commonly ignored.

[32] Eddings Island, the westernmost of the "Hunting Islands," the outer or barrier islands between St. Helena and the ocean. Across Station Creek from Lands End. The place name "Eddings" has come to be spelled with two "d"s.

he understands the nature of my lands better than any man on the Island. He has given me several very good ideas of planting. My large sorrel mare broke out with the distemper today. I also saw a dog with the distemper and think it occasioned by the sudden changes in the weather, as it is nothing more than violent cold. I bought on Friday last, the 17th instant,[33] of George Law,[34] a bay mare called Fanny Douglass, four years old. I bought her expressly for my wife & hope she will like her as a saddle horse.

Jan. 24th. The Major and J. L. Chaplin went to Edings Island with me to take a hunt. Had a long and very exciting chase at an old buck, but don't succeed in killing him. He took to the marsh at Terrapin Creek. Sawney & Sam were getting out oars[35] on the Island today. Yesterday eve it clouded up and commenced raining very hard about dusk. The wind blew violently. Mrs. Wright[36] thought the house would blow down, but it has stood many heavier blasts.

Jan. 25th. Rose[37] was confined last night and brought forth a boy. I name him David.

Jan. 27th. Took a hunt on Edings Island. J. L. Chaplin went with me. We got two deer, a doe & a yearling. J.L.C. killed both, one with each barrel as they jumped together. Had a delightful day—returned after dark. Peter[38] sick, fever.

Jan. 28th. A very delightful day, like spring weather. Rode over to the Captain's in the morning. Finished ginning cotton. Planted Irish potatoes. Carpenters still working on the Island getting oars. Sent Isaac & Prince to the bridge for rafts[39] on Monday last. They have not yet returned though the weather has been so fair. Was advised by J. Chaplin to use spirits of turpentine up a horse's nose for distemper. It is to be done with a syringe. I have tried it on the sorrel mare & bay colt, they both appear to be better. Louisa & Hannah sick with fever. Dr. Jenkins presented his bill a day or two ago. I was very much surprised at the large amt., notwithstanding I have lost nine Negroes the last year.[40]

[33] On the seventeenth day of the present month.
[34] George Law (b. 1798), planter.
[35] Felling, hewing, and shaping hardwood timber into oars.
[36] Possibly Sarah Wright (b. 1818), wife of Charles Wright, of St. Bartholomew's Parish.
[37] A slave.
[38] A slave.
[39] Beams, spars, or rafters—long, thick timbers, shaped for use.
[40] A great loss of life and property, equal to about twelve percent of Tombee's black population.

Jan. 29th.   Packed the last bag of cotton. Prince & Isaac not yet arrived with the rafts. The rest of the men leveling ditches[41] & grubbing.[42] Tony getting out stakes.[43] Anthony Snr. sharpening.[44] Stephen getting out short stakes. Wind blowed very hard from the north in the morning. Calm towards evening. Mrs. C.[45] & myself rode over on horseback to Uncle Ben's.

Jan. 30th.   John Chaplin & Anthony,[46] with Stephen, commenced running out land.[47] Sam fixing cart. Tony with Sawney on the Island sawing. Farmer the painter[48] came over. Paid him $10 which is all I owe him. The Major & William[49] rode over in the morning, the former dined with me. I expected to give him a haunch of venison for dinner, but from the carelessness of the servants, the dogs got hold of it and devoured it all last night. Sent all of my cotton to Beaufort, 17 bales in all packed—B. Cream, 4—P.G., 10—stained of both kinds,[50] 3 bales. Admond, Paul, Titus & Anthony Jr. went with the flat. Commenced listing in marsh[51] today with the women. Men cleaning up ground. Old Cash came from the main on the 27th, returned on the 28th. I sent some sugarcane to Saxby.[52] I rec'd a letter from Mother by Castillo—answered thru January. The Negroes that were taken from the Point were sold on the 25th inst.[53] W. Jenkins thinks that Isaac Fripp[54] has killed a hog from him within the last day or two.[55]

Jan. 31st.   The flat did not get to Beaufort with the cotton until high water today. Got all the cotton on the wharf safe, though the flat was very much loaded to be safe.

[41] Cleaning and reaming drainage ditches.
[42] Uprooting shrubs and stumps with a heavy hoe.
[43] Cutting and shaping pointed sticks for use in laying out the tasks, or daily work loads, of the field hands.
[44] Sharpening hoe blades with a file.
[45] Mary Chaplin.
[46] Chaplin's foreman or slave driver, a slave himself.
[47] Setting out stakes to mark the tasks.
[48] A white artisan from Beaufort
[49] The Jenkins brothers, Daniel P. and Dr. William.
[50] A fine and a coarse variety of cotton, and the stained remainder of both. The proportion of stained to white cotton is unusually high—an indication of poor soil preparation or carelessness in handling the lint.
[51] Turning the marsh grass under the soil with hoes.
[52] Saxby Chaplin, Jr. (1825–1884), planter. Chaplin's younger brother. Lived at Hickory Hill Plantation, in St. Bartholomew's Parish.
[53] Prime field hands were selling for $550 apiece in Charleston, at this time. The value of slaves on the seaboard had been declining since the mid-'30s and in 1845 was near the bottom of the cycle. Prices would double over the next four years.
[54] Isaac K. Fripp (b. 1798), planter. Son of Archibald Fripp and Elizabeth Scott. First cousin to Chaplin, once removed, on his father's side. Lived on a 300-acre plantation north of Tombee, on Broad River.
[55] Fripp's Negroes are suspected, not Fripp himself.

Feb. 1st. Muster Day[56] in Beaufort—have to go again. We expect to shoot for the plow today,[57] with both artillery & rifles.

Feb. 3rd. Got some sycamore trees from C. G. Capers.[58] Set out some at home, about 20. Took up orange trees at Toomer's[59] & set them out at home in the yard. Planted 1 peach & 2 pear trees from Toomer's. Got oars stuff from the Island.

Feb. 4th. Clouded up last evening. Commenced raining in the night with a heavy blow. 8½ o'clock a.m. still raining. This is the first rain we have had since the 23rd of January—*12 days.* Put all hands shelling corn, as I thought the weather too bad for them to work out. Three Negroes sick—viz. Louisa, Phyllis, Moll, fever &c. Ben killed 2 English ducks on the Island yesterday.

Saw my old sow today with 7 pigs, about 5 days old. Carpenters repairing bridges. John & Amy are also sick today. The bay mare broke out with distemper today. I think smoking up the nostrils with tar, pine tops, feathers & powdered sulphur is better than anything that can be used. Put the tar in the bottom, sprinkle sulphur on it, set it on fire and pile on pine tops & feathers.

Feb. 5th. The wind blew very hard all last night and continues to blow this morning, more violent—if possible—and very cold, by far the coldest weather we have had this winter. Though it rained hard yesterday the sand is flying today in such a manner that it is hardly possible to go out of doors. Sent all the men to split rails[60] in Toomer's woods. The women working on the road near the old gate as the most protected spot from the wind. John, Amy, Phyllis & Moll are sick. Louisa out.[61] 9 o'clock a.m., the wind appears to rise. I am afraid it will do considerable damage, particularly to shipping. Trees & fences must suffer.

The wind lulled a little about 9 o'clock p.m. Blows in puffs up to this time, 7½ p.m., sometimes high, sometimes low. I do not recollect ever seeing such a continued blow, now 32 hours it has blown most violently, and likely to continue all night.

---

[56] Bimonthly meeting of the Beaufort Volunteer Artillery (B.V.A).
[57] Competitive target shooting—the winner gets a plow for the season. Plows were gaining favor on the Sea Islands after being shunned for 100 years.
[58] Charles Gabriel Capers (1775–1857), planter. Son of Charles Capers and Anne Thomson. Lived north of Tombee on a 500-acre plantation on Chowan Creek. He owned several other plantations, including one in Charleston District.
[59] A pine barren and a neglected orchard off Lands End Road.
[60] Making fence rails.
[61] Out of the sickhouse and back to work.

Feb. 6th. The wind fell last night sometime after dark, and today it is calm but very cold. I attended the meeting of the Agricultural Society today. Our new member J. D. Pope[62] found dinner.[63] Several resolutions were made, but only one of any importance, viz.—to convert the society into a horticultural as well as an agricultural. The motion lays over to the next meeting. If this resolution is not carried into effect, it is my intention to leave the Society. The Negroes belonging to the Est. of M.L.C.[64] were hired today. I bid them in very low—$138 for the five.[65] The Major was the crier. He did very well for the first attempt. Sent Ben to Beaufort, brought my new coat and vest. W. Fripp[66] left the Society today, because "it is said" he was not on good terms with myself.

Feb. 7th. Set out in front of the house 12 sycamore trees & 21 cuttings of the same. Also, 5 fig cuttings and a grape to every *coleus*.[67] Plowed up the yard (stable) and sowed oats. Carried Ernest[68] down with me. Stopped at "Cuz." I. Fripp's[69] on my way back & borrowed a blanket to cover Ernest with, as it was very cold.

Feb. 8th. All hands out today. J. L. Chaplin & T. J. Chaplin[70] went on the island with us. Killed two deer, but only got one, a large buck, just dropped his horns. Echo had pups (11) on the 5th inst. Drowned 6, kept 5 dogs.

Feb. 9th. Went to church.[71] Bay colt died about 3½ o'clock p.m. of distemper, or a complication of diseases. Intend starting for the main in the morning, *please God.*

Feb. 11th. Had a long talk with Mother concerning the disposal of her property. She came to the conclusion that she would deed it away to

---

[62] Joseph Daniel Pope (1820–1908), planter and lawyer. Son of Joseph James Pope and Sarah Jenkins. Member S.C. House of Representatives 1850–60, S.C. Senate 1863–65, and a delegate to the 1860 State Secession Convention.
[63] Members took turns "finding"—providing food and liquors at meetings.
[64] Maria Louisa Chaplin, one of Chaplin's two dead sisters. However, this was a slip. Chaplin should have written "E.I.C.," as the Negroes belonged to the estate of his other sister, Elizabeth Isabella Chaplin (1817–1840). See March 6, 1849.
[65] The normal cost of annual hire was ten percent of the Negro's market value.
[66] William "Good Billy" Fripp, Sr. (1788–1861), son of Capt. John Fripp IV and Martha Scott, brother of Capt. John Fripp. Husband of Sarah Harriet Reynolds, and father of William W., Alviro A., Clarence A., and J. Edings Fripp.
[67] A plant in the mint family set out for its showy foliage.
[68] Ernest A. Chaplin (1840–1875), Chaplin's oldest child.
[69] Chaplin and Fripp were first cousins, once removed.
[70] Thomas James Chaplin (1772–1855), planter. Second cousin to Thomas B. Chaplin, on his father's side.
[71] The Protestant Episcopal Church, also called Central Church, near the center of the Island. Originally a chapel of ease of the parish church in Beaufort.

Saxby & myself if possible.[72] If this can be done it will be a good thing, for Baker knowing he cannot get any part of it is trying to injure it as much as possible. Saxby had a little dancing party in the evening—or rather night for they danced until near 4 o'clock.

Feb. 13th. Intended to return home today, but was so unwell with a violent dysentery that I did not feel able to ride. Was quite sick all day & night. Saxby lost a prime fellow called Bristol.

Feb. 14th. Returned home from the main, found Peg, Lib, & [   ] sick. Peg has been sick ever since I left home.

At night made the following singular calculation, viz.—put a grain of corn on the first square of a chess board, and double it on every other, in this way—2 on the 2nd, 4 on the 3rd, 8 on the 4th, 16 on the 5th, 32 on the 6th, &c, &c. The calculations proved to be as follows—9 quintrillions, 220 quadrillions, 376 trillions, 793 billions, 429 millions, 935 thousands & 808. This was asked as a gift by the first inventor of chess of an emperor, who thought it quite an insignificant request, but it is not so. Peggy is still quite sick. Sent for Doctor Jenkins twice this day.

Feb. 17th. Rode over the fields with J.L.C. Commenced moving the poultry house & yard. Saw 2 geese & 1 turkey sitting, also a Muscovy duck. I am anxious to see what sort of ducks she will hatch out, as I have no drake of the same species in the yard. I have now six horses with the distemper, among them are Puss & Duchess. Isaac & Prince finished bringing shingle stuff[73] from the Isl. Old Judge splitting up.[74]

Feb. 18th. Peggy still sick (8 days). Anthony Snr. sick, Hannah pretending Do [ditto], January Do, Ellen sick. Sent Stephen & Ben to get some fish or oysters.

Feb. 19th. Called with the Captain on Wmn. S. Chaplin,[75] he looks very bad. I do not think he is long for this world. He speaks of going to the sea beach, when he is not able to sit up in bed.

Rec'd a letter from Thos. L. Webb, Esqr.,[76] containing very bad news, about lawsuits, judgments &c &c. Commenced levelling land for garden. Peggy still sick (9 days).

[72] One year later, Chaplin would swear in court that he did not try to influence his mother in making this decision.
[73] Cedar or oak cut into lengths for making shingles.
[74] Cleaving shingle wood lengthwise into usable pieces.
[75] William S. Chaplin (d. 1845), planter. Son of William Chaplin and Sarah Jenkins. First cousin to Chaplin on his father's side, and to Capt. Daniel T. Jenkins on his mother's side.
[76] Thomas Ladson Webb (b. 1810), attorney and cotton factor, partner in the firm of Ingraham & Webb. Son of Daniel C. Webb and Elizabeth Ann Ladson.

Feb. 20th. Ploughing up the spot for a garden. Commenced listing March corn land.[77] Put Fanny in the sulky. She does not appear accustomed to the draft,[78] as Dr. Warren[79] said. I rode over to Uncle Ben's in the evening, took tea with him. Walked with Dr. Jenkins & wife[80] over to their place. He slipped off the log, poor thing, & fell in the mud, soiled his stocking & shoe. What a pity. I made three very good shots with my rifle. If I do as well on Saturday, when shooting for the plow, I think I shall win it, but I am afraid I will not. The weather is very fine, though much sickness among the little Negroes.

Feb. 21st. Ploughing the new garden. Planted a few rows of green peas & lettuce seed. Tried old Hyder[81] in the plow—he performed very well. Tomorrow the *trial* comes off in our company, in shooting with the rifle for the plow presented to us by S. A. Benjamin.[82] I think my chance very slim. Judge sick today (fever). Finished shingling poultry house.

Feb. 22nd. This is the day for the trial of skill with rifles in the company. Went to Beaufort to attend muster. After falling in, we were marched up to Sams Point[83] (myself acting as 4th lieutenant) where the target was placed at 80 yards. Commenced firing at 12 o'clock m.[84] My number was 32 in rank of firing. My first shot was so bad that I despaired of winning the plow, several very fair shots being made previous. My second shot was much better, about 4 inches from the center, Capt. Barnwell[85] being then the best shot on the board. My third shot came round & was made, which decided all dispute, being within two inches of the center. The prize was mine, won by about one inch of Capt. Barnwell. Returned home about dusk &c.

Feb. 23rd. Attended service at the P.E. Church,[86] had the pleasure of hearing a Mr. Johnson, a very young man, the nephew of Mrs. McElheran[87] He was ordained last winter (1844). In my opinion, he is a very

---

[77] Breaking the top crust of the land and hoeing under the vegetation.
[78] Drawing or pulling a vehicle.
[79] Dr. John Warren, physician and planter, an old acquaintance of Isabella Baker. Lived on the Chehaw River, St. Bartholomew's Parish.
[80] Eliza Mary Chaplin (1825–1894). Daughter of Archibald Chaplin and Martha Fripp. First cousin to Chaplin on her father's side.
[81] A horse.
[82] Solomon A. Benjamin, Charleston clothier.
[83] On Beaufort's east side.
[84] Noon.
[85] Possibly Thomas Osborn Barnwell (b. 1812), planter. Son of Capt. Edward Barnwell and Elizabeth Osborn. West Point graduate and former army lieutenant.
[86] The Protestant Episcopal Church.
[87] Ann Eliza McElheran (b. 1809), Irish-born wife of Rev. David McElheran.

promising young minister, having a clear & distinct voice, good delivery, adhering to & explaining very minutely his text, viz.—Unto him that hath shall be given & unto him *that hath not* shall be taken away even that which he hath.[88] This is a portion of Scripture that I have never before heard explained, believing the text to be altogether contradictional, and am now not fully corrected, though more enlightened.

Feb. 24th.   Went [to] Beaufort, took Sophy & Ernest with me. Saw Dr. Croft.[89] He left in the steamboat for Charleston, on his way to Newberry.[90] Had him sworn by Johnson (Magistrate)[91] as a witness to the sealing and delivery of two deeds made by Mother in favor of Saxby & myself.[92] I sent my deed by W. B. Fickling,[93] to be recorded in Gillisonville.[94] Returned home about dusk. Peggy still laying up (14 days). Marcus & Belle sick (2 days). Frank still with the fever. Borrowed the Captain's cart. Borrowed Mr. Capers' boat. Sent seven hands in her to the main for Mother, expect them to return tomorrow, weather permitting.

Feb. 25th.   Very heavy fog in the morning, cleared off very warm about 9 o'clock. Rode over to the Major's for the purpose of waiting for Mother's arrival from the main. After waiting some time after supper I left for home, but just before I got to the yard a boy came galloping up on a horse

---

[88] Matthew 13:12. "For whosoever hath, to him shall be given, and he shall have abundance: but whosoever hath not, from him shall be taken away even that he hath."

[89] Either Theodore Gaillard Croft (1812–1870), planter and physician from Greenville District, or his brother Randall Croft (1818–1869) planter and physician, St. Helena Island. Randall Croft's wife, Charlotte M. Jenkins, daughter of William Jenkins, Sr., and Mary Chaplin Fripp, was a first cousin of Dr. W., Major D. P., and Capt. D. T. Jenkins. She was Chaplin's second cousin, once removed, on her father's side.

[90] Town and district in the northwest part of the state.

[91] David Johnson (1782–1855), Virginia-born lawyer. Member S.C. House of Representatives 1810–11, state solicitor 1811–15, associate judge of the Court of Common Pleas 1815–35, judge of the Court of Equity 1835–46, Governor of South Carolina 1846–48.

[92] Mrs. Baker exercised the power reserved to her by the second clause of her marriage settlement—contradicted by the first clause—to dispose of her property in any way she saw fit. To Thomas she deeded the Point Place—one-half of Fields Point—on the Combahee River; Dunham Plantation, at the headwaters of the Ashepoo; "a large number of Negroes" and half of all the cows, hogs, poultry, and horses belonging to the Point Place and Walnut Hill. To Saxby she deeded the lands of Walnut Hill, facing the Chehaw; Riverside Plantation, on St. Helena Island, bounded by Tombee and Broad River; a pine barren on Hilton Head Island "attached to and used with Riverside"; Negroes, cows, horses, poultry, etc. The deeds would be recorded in April and June.

[93] William B. Fickling, Charleston magistrate and lawyer.

[94] A pinelands settlement northwest of Beaufort. Site of the district courthouse and jail.

to say that the boat had arrived. So I had to return. Found Mother there, at the Riverside—we got home safe to supper.

Feb. 26th.   Went over to the Island to take a hunt. Had very little sport. Ben killed a very fine fat *doe*. Though he always gets a shot, this is the first deer he has ever killed. I had him well bedaubed with blood, for his luck.

Feb. 27th.   The Major sent to borrow my dogs. Himself and William Jenkins are going to take a hunt, but it is my opinion they will hunt without my dogs. The Major was too busy to go with my invitation yesterday but was perfectly at leisure to go with Dr. Jenkins today. They also invited me, particularly on *account of the dogs,* not that they care so much for my company, or to hunt with me, or they would try and make it suit them to go with me when I go. But on the contrary, I have noticed that they invariably go a day or two after I do, when they must know that I am too much fatigued to hunt again so soon, but the invitation is always attended with "If you can't come send your dogs." I am sorry, but my dogs are also tired.

Feb. 28th.   William Jenkins & myself went down to the village to play billiards. I beat him the rub.[95] The Major promised to go, but I suppose his *mama*[96] was not disposed to let him go.

March 1st.   This is the first day of *sweet spring.* But it looks more like winter than it did in February. Cloudy and cold. But this is generally a blustering month. I sent John to Beaufort yesterday. Among other things he brought a fine bunch of celery. I heard through him that a Negro woman was committed to jail for killing her husband by stabbing him. Did not hear who is her owner. Gave J. L. Chaplin a cowhide whip.

March 2nd.   Went to church. The Capt. spoke to me about some difficulty he expected to have with Mr. Jn. H. Webb.[97] No doubt it will be a serious affair, he requested me to act as his friend. This is rather unpleasant but I will do so.[98]

---

[95] A set of three or five games the last of which decides the winner when the previous games have been split.

[96] Elizabeth Perry Jenkins (b. 1780). Widow of Benjamin Jenkins. Her husband's brother Daniel was Isabella Baker's first husband. Isabella's mother, Elizabeth Perry, was her aunt and namesake. Chaplin calls her Cousin Betsy.

[97] John H. Webb (b. 1811), planter. Son of Daniel C. Webb and Elizabeth Ann Ladson. Brother of Thomas L. Webb, Chaplin's cotton factor.

[98] Chaplin has agreed to be Jenkins's second, or intermediary, should the quarrel with Webb come to a duel.

March 3rd.   Sent John to Beaufort in the buggy. Received a note from Treville,[99] stating that the Court of Equity had decided in favor of Mother's right & power to dispose of her property in any manner she pleases.[100] Planted sugarcane this day over at Toff's old house. Think it will do well, 2½ feet apart. Received a visit from Mr. Belcher,[101] found him very agreeable. He dined with us—we had a very fine Berkshire pig for dinner, the first I have ever killed. I let Fanny Douglass run a short distance against J. L. Chaplin's sorrel horse. She beat him without the least exertion. Expect to take Mrs. C. to the beach tomorrow if the weather permits. Peggy is still sick (21 days)—Louisa is sick today. Carpenters have not yet finished the new garden, palings[102] gave out.

March 4th.   Weather looks rather cloudy, but if it does not rain, we will start for the Island. Mrs. C. being very unwell, hope the trip will benefit her. Sent over for Uncle Ben's large boat to go to the Island in. Weather still unsettled—sunshine and clouds. However we are ready to start, I think we will go.

Started for the Island about 4 o'clock. Got down after dark, to W. L. Chaplin's[103] camp. Were very fortunate in finding it as it rained a little during the night.

March 5th.   Cleared off very pretty. Isaac came with the sorrel mare. Stephen brought the small boat. About 10 o'clock saw some porpoise running very near the shore. Went down to the edge of the water, saw a very large school of bass, drew the seine[104] immediately—caught 113 bass at the haul. Sent Stephen & Isaac in the small boat to Beaufort with 75 to sell. Went over to the old house up Moons Creek in the evening, camped there that night.

March 6th.   Went hunting. John killed a very large buck very near the camp. Put the horse in the boat & came home with last of the flood tide in

[99] Richard DeTreville (1801–1874), Beaufort equity lawyer and planter. Son of Robert La Boularderie DeTreville and Sarah Burton Ellis. Graduate of West Point and colonel in the state militia. Member S.C. House of Representatives 1830–32, and S.C. Senate 1835–54. Author of a bill in 1844 which forbade free Negroes to enter South Carolina. Lieutenant Governor 1854–56. A staunch advocate of states' rights and nullification, DeTreville was a delegate to the State Secession Convention in 1860.
[100] Knowing that his wife intended to deed away her entire estate to her sons, Baker had filed a bill to restrain her. The lower court decided in favor of Isabella.
[101] Charles D. Belcher (1822–1857), schoolteacher employed by C. G. Capers.
[102] Fence stakes or pickets.
[103] William L. Chaplin (1826–1851), planter. Son of Archibald Chaplin and Martha Fripp. First cousin to Chaplin on his father's side and brother-in-law to Dr. William J. Jenkins.
[104] A long fishnet with floats at the top and sinkers at the bottom, stretched across and pulled through a creek or the surf.

the evening. Had fair wind and made a quick passage, arrived about dark.

March 7th.   Stephen handed me $7.75—the proceeds of the fish. Sold very low, hardly worth the trouble of sending them. All hands listing potato land. Very dry to do so, but the season is so far advanced, we are obliged to list. Had a trial of speed between Duchess and Fanny Douglass. It was a very closely contested race, Duchess beating by about two lengths in the quarter.

March 8th.   I was very sick last night, with a violent pain in my chest & giddiness in the head. Sent for Dr. Jenkins. He bled me in the left arm, blood very bad, gave me great relief. Put on poultices & mustard plasters, & took castor oil, camphor & laudanum.[105] I feel much better this morning, but very weak and a little feverish. Col. R. DeTreville came here today to see mother on business. He took dinner & returned to Beaufort. The Capt. also rode over & dined. Sent John to Beaufort. This is the 4th time we have sent this week. I sent a haunch of venison to Mr. Capers. He sent me a few green peas, the first I have seen this spring. He also sent me some olive cuttings to set out. Treville says they will not grow.

March 11th.   Commenced laying out the garden. Planted some mangel-wurzel[106] & long blood beets.[107] D. P. Jenkins & his mother rode over in the evening, that is after they had dined, but before *we* had dinner. They left about dusk. John L. Chaplin went over to the Island by himself to hunt. He killed a large buck however, but could not get it home, not being able to bring it to the boat.

March 12th.   Commenced raining before day and rained off & on all day. During the intervals between showers I worked in the garden. Set out some onion sets, sowed green peas, carrots, parsnips, and some corn. J. Chaplin went in all the rain to fetch the deer he killed yesterday. It looked & eat very inferior, being so much in the water. The hands went out to make fence, but the rain drove them in. I put them to work on the road.

March 13th.   Ellen & Rose laying up. Peg still sick (32 days). All hands but two are making fence. A constant drizzle rain all day. Rained very

---

[105] A tincture of opium.
[106] A beetlike vegetable fed to livestock.
[107] The best table beet—according to Chaplin's guide, Francis S. Holmes, *The Southern Farmer and Market Gardener* (Charleston, S.C., 1842).

hard at night. Planted in the new garden, okra and squash. Set out 74 cabbage plants. John went to the village.

March 14th. Wind NW, likely to clear. John & Jim ploughing corn ground. 4 carts still at the mud.[108] Got a barrel of tar from Beaufort, also 1 lb. of tobacco & 100 cigars. The young sow had pigs last night. She had 7. One got mashed to death by the other hogs in the pen. Went out fishing with J. L. Chaplin, at Marsh Island. Tom Chaplin[109] took one drum.[110] I got the head & one side. Came home to a late dinner. Met the Captain returning from Beaufort on horseback. Old Adam planted some muskmelons & cucumbers. The melons are a peculiar sort, called the Smyrna melon, got of John Minott[111] on James Island. Got three hounds of Vidal's[112] man Noble, named Dido, Leade & Rock . . . on trial.

March 15th. Intended going down to Bay Point fishing, but the weather is rather cool & cloudy for water work. Will try my new dogs at a cat[113] today. Hannah sick with fever. Rose & Ellen went out, the former today, the latter yesterday. Called for the Major, & took a cat hunt. We did not succeed in finding one, had poor sport. This appears to be an unlucky day for me. When I returned home, I found the deputy sheriff[114] there, with a writ to serve on me, & what was worse he produced judgments, together with costs & interest, amounting to near $1500. I know not what to do. I have friends but none have money to help me. I fear my property will be sacrificed. It can be seized at any moment.

J. D. Pope has just informed me of another very heavy claim placed in his hands for collection. *Hard times, hard times.*

This was only the beginning. Lots more of the same sort & worse.

March 16th. Sunday. Went to church. Mr. Mc.[115] preached a very good sermon, he was more theatrical than usual.

March 17th. Went to Beaufort. Saw the ex-president of Texas, Mr. Lamar.[116] He is a very inferior looking man. No one would suppose from

[108] Carting mud from the salt marsh to the cotton fields.
[109] Thomas James Chaplin. See note, Feb. 8, 1845.
[110] A large food fish averaging three feet in length and thirty to forty pounds in weight, so called for the noise it makes, "resembling the tap of a drum."
[111] John B. F. Minott (b. 1804), planter, St. Andrew's Parish, Charleston District.
[112] James Vidal (b. 1815), planter.
[113] A bobcat—a blunt-tailed, yellow-gray cat, weighing twenty-five pounds on the average.
[114] William Mickler (b. 1800), blacksmith and deputy sheriff of Beaufort District.
[115] Rev. David McElheran (1793–1875), Irish-born minister of Scottish extraction. Became rector of the St. Helena Island Episcopal Church in 1835.
[116] Mirabeau Buonaparte Lamar (1798–1859). Born in Georgia. Fought in Texas's War of Independence from Mexico. Served as Secretary of War, Vice-President, then President (1838–41) of the Republic of Texas.

his look that he was ever the president of Texas. I succeeded in stopping the sheriff for a short time. Gave Treville a memorandum of property, to be deeded by I.C.B.[117]

March 18th.　　Called in the morning to see W. S. Chaplin. He is very low, I do not think he will survive many days. At W. S. Chaplin's I saw Aunt Martha Chaplin[118] and Cos. Martha Chisolm.[119] The former has not been over to see us. I do not regret it. Wm. Jenkins' wife[120] was delivered of a little girl on Thursday night, the 13th instant. I went on to Beaufort from Wm. Chaplin's. Attended the meeting of the *Independent Order of Odd Fellows.*[121] Was initiated & took the first & second degrees. This is altogether a charitable society, and I think the best by far that has ever been instituted. There is a *secret*—but it is only for the purpose of preventing imposition on the Order, and the benefits to be derived thereby. Capt. John Fripp[122] also took two degrees. He was initiated some time ago, say 1 meeting. I am so well pleased with this society that candidly I would not leave it for $500. I returned home about one o'clock at night.

March 19th.　　Quite windy this morning. A boat came over from the main yesterday, and brought a man by the name of DaCosta,[123] a sort of overseer for the fellow Baker. I believe he has instructions to *kick* me off the land whenever I was caught on it. What a farce! The being that has had his head turned by his supposed possession of considerable property, when he was a mean *pauper* & a bankrupt, to put on such airs of power and authority—It is ridiculous in the extreme. It is very likely however that his little authority that he is so unaccustomed to will be cut short in a few weeks.[124] I read a letter today from R. L. Baker to J. L. Chaplin, mostly concerning myself, as I appear to be an eyesore to that fellow, from some cause or other. It is very provoking to have one's name mentioned so often

[117] Isabella Chaplin Baker. Chaplin refers to an addition to the deed previously mentioned but not yet recorded. He is anxious to get his hands on this property, hoping perhaps to convert some of it to cash to save his own estate from his creditors.
[118] Martha Fripp Chaplin. Daughter of Paul Fripp and Elizabeth Jenkins. Wife of Chaplin's Uncle Archibald. She was Chaplin's first cousin, once removed, on her father's side. Her daughter, Eliza Mary, was married to Dr. William Jenkins.
[119] Martha Chisolm, wife of Samuel P. Chisolm. Maiden name—Martha Chaplin.
[120] Eliza Mary Jenkins.
[121] Benevolent organization that offered financial assistance to "distressed or disabled members," their widows and orphans. Established in South Carolina in 1841.
[122] John W. Fripp (1792–1865), planter. Son of John W. Fripp IV and Martha Scott. First cousin to Chaplin, once removed, on his father's side. One of the wealthiest men on St. Helena, Fripp lived at Big House Plantation, a 1,000-acre tract in the eastern part of the Island, one of four or five plantations he owned in 1845.
[123] Perhaps Joseph DaCosta, son of Isaac DaCosta, a neighbor of Ann Roux—mother of Mrs. Baker's trustee, Francis L. Roux. See note, Aug. 18, 1845. DaCosta has replaced J. L. Chaplin as overseer at Riverside.
[124] Once Mrs. Baker's deeds are recorded.

& appear to be of so much importance to so low & vile an insect as that thing that crawls about & calls himself R. L. Baker. J. L. Chaplin has nothing more to do with this being, and lucky he is to get clear of him, if he can only get his money for his services.

March 20th. Put coal tar on the bottom of *Pelican*[125] yesterday. Commenced painting her black with white streak today, for the first coat. Tommy working on the boats. Sam & Tony repairing trunks[126] over the creek. Several Negroes sick today, viz.—Betty, old complaint of the heart, January, Marcus (piles), Louisa, Peg, still in the house,[127] making 39 days.

March 22nd. Evans Chaplin[128] came to me today begging that I would give him some work to do, and give him victuals to pay for it, he did not want money. Said he had no place to stay. His Uncles Edwin[129] & Isaac[130] had turned him out of their houses, and he could get no work to do & no place to sleep & nothing to eat. I felt sorry for the poor fellow, though no doubt it is greatly his own fault that he is in this situation. I told him however that I would give him food & he could stay with me a while, and look for something to do. I put him to help paint my boat. He does it very well & appears very willing to do anything in his power to pay for his victuals & bed.

March 25th. This is Muster Day for our company on account of its being a general review in Coosawhatchie.[131] Mrs. C. & myself went to Beaufort in the carriage. The wind blew very fresh when we started but fell very much before we arrived at the ferry & we had quite a pleasant trip. A dinner was given by the officers of our company, in the arsenal shed. A very laughable occurrence took place. Just as we were all about to be seated, the table gave way "beneath the load of the feast" & down it all went on the paved yard, over on two men, that had a drop ahead, got caught under the table, and cut a very laughable caper. One man grabbed a ham, another a turkey, another a joint of roast beef &c &c. However, besides the breaking of several plates, dishes & glasses, we all

[125] Chaplin's sailboat.
[126] Large wooden casings for sluice gates which may be lifted and lowered to regulate the flow of water.
[127] The sickhouse.
[128] Evans Chaplin. Son of John Fripp Chaplin, Jr., and Ann Fripp. First cousin, once removed, to Thomas B. Chaplin on his father's side.
[129] Edwin Chaplin (b. 1798), planter. Son of John Fripp Chaplin, Sr., and Mary Fripp. First cousin to Thomas B. Chaplin on his father's side. Lived at Bermuda Plantation, north of Tombee, on Broad River.
[130] Isaac K. Fripp, husband of Evans's aunt, Charlotte Chaplin.
[131] Pinelands town and former seat of Beaufort District, about five miles south of Gillisonville, on the Coosawhatchie River, a tributary of Broad River.

got comfortably seated & enjoyed a very sumptuous dinner. Everything went off well & Captain Barnwell gave us a good drilling after dinner to settle both that & the wine. Only two men had to leave the ranks for not keeping their legs well under them.

March 26th.   Poor W. S. Chaplin died yesterday morning. Weather very fine. Finished painting the *Pelican.* W.O.P. Fripp & lady[132] called. Planted fodder corn in the garden on the 24th. Commenced planting cotton on Carter's Hill.[133]

March 27th.   Commenced banking potato land. Ploughing potato land. Finished planting 18 acres of cotton. Went to W. S. Chaplin's funeral—was late, having mistaken the word "ten" for "one" & went when it was all over.

March 30th.   Sunday. Got up about 9 o'clock, and felt very well, but while dressing was seized with a violent pain in the left side of my neck. The pain has continued all day, very much like stiff neck. Prevented me from going to church. Rested very bad at night, from the severe pain in my neck—could not move my head at all.

March 31st.   My neck still continues very painful. Have tried a host of things for it. J. Chaplin recommends the marrow out of a hog's jawbone. I have tried it and find it gives great relief.
   Bay mare took J.L.C.'s horse. Large sorrel has not yet refused.[134] Potato seed[135] have rotted very much, do not think I will have enough to plant. Rode out in the field in the evening where the hands were planting potatoes. The ground is in fine order for planting.

April 1st.   Planted potatoes. Did not have seed enough. Got two cart loads of Uncle Paul,[136] and one & a half loads of Capt. D. Jenkins.

[132] William Oliver Perry Fripp (b. 1820), planter, and his wife, Thomas Ann Taylor—called Ann (1826–1895). Fripp, the son of James Fripp and Ann Pope, was Chaplin's second cousin on his father's side. The Fripps lived on a 230-acre plantation north of Tombee, on Chowan Creek, next door to C. G. Capers.
[133] High ground on the northeast side of Tombee, bordering Uncle Paul Chaplin's land.
[134] Chaplin's bay mare and his large sorrel mare are being bred to John L. Chaplin's stallion.
[135] Small potatoes from the previous year's crop.
[136] Paul Hamilton Chaplin (1788–1866), planter. Son of Thomas B. Chaplin and Eliza Fripp; brother of Chaplin's father, Saxby. Owned two plantations between Tombee and Dr. Jenkins's Seaside Plantation. He was a bachelor.

April 2nd. Got Buckskin off Wm. Means[137] for the purpose of getting some colts.

April 3rd. Agricultural meeting. The Society was converted into a Horticultural & Agricultural Society. Had an election for officers—John Fripp[138]—pres., Edgar Fripp[139]—vice, W. W. Fripp[140]—treas., & Capt. Jenkins—sec.

April 5th. Fickling went to Beaufort. I went out fishing. J. L. Chaplin went with me. Took one drum & 25 blackfish. Got my anchor fastened in a rock and had to leave it. Old bay mare took the horse. Evans is still staying with me, but I must try & get him off. He is a bad boy, not worth charity.

April 6th. Sunday. Intended going to church. Dressed, brushed, examined critically my tout ensemble, being satisfied herewith was about to depart, when lo—my gloves were missing. A general hunt produced but *one* of the missing articles. What was to be done? To go with an ungloved hand was impossible. Besides that member presented a most inelegant appearance, having burnt it mahogany colored in my fishing excursions. But in the midst of my turning upside down of trunks and boxes there come up a sudden shower. Fortunate circumstance! I ordered my buggy back, ensconced myself in my elbow chair, and oh! Sin and Satan, spent the morning in reading the *Chevalier de Faublas.*[141]

April 7th. My wife begs me to write this sentence down. "A gentle and complying temper is amiable, but unless accompanied by discretion, will lead you into the most dangerous errors: to yield, where we *know* it is our duty to resist, is a weakness for which it is difficult to form an excuse: first be assured that your principles are just, and then let it be your glory to act in conformity to them." (My wife took the liberty to write the above. I always like to see persons practice what they preach.)

Went fishing, or rather went to look for the anchor I left in Broad River on Saturday last. Could not find the oar to which the rope was tied.

[137] William B. Means (1820–1897), planter.
[138] Possibly John F. Fripp, planter. Son of Paul Fripp and Amelia Reynolds; brother of William B. Fripp. First cousin, once removed, to Capt. John Fripp.
[139] Edgar Fripp (1806–1860), planter. Son of James and Mary Fripp. Chaplin's second cousin, once removed, on his father's side. Lived at 940-acre Seaside Plantation, northeast of Tombee, halfway across the Island along Seaside Road.
[140] William Washington Fripp (1825–1879), planter. Son of William "Good Billy" Fripp and Sarah Harriet Reynolds. Chaplin's second cousin on his father's side.
[141] *Les Amours du Chevalier de Faublas,* a bawdy novel by Louvet de Couvray, published in 1789. The hero enters society at sixteen and embarks on a series of love affairs ending in murder, madness, and suicide.

April 8th.   Commenced planting cotton with 8 hands. I went out fishing—lost the anchor I got from J.L.C. which I had lent him, and found the other at low water. Caught two drums as usual & returned home, having lost one anchor & found another.

April 10th.   Went out fishing. Wind blew very fresh—went to Bay Point,[142] caught nothing. Hoisted sail and went up to Bay Gall,[143] where I saw a good many boats. Dropped anchor. Fish commenced biting about the last of ebb tide. Caught 11 fish,[144] took 5 on my own line—making 7 I have taken myself & 21 in the boat this year. Had a fine sail home, arrived about dark. Planting cotton.

Fanny[145] refused the horse yesterday.

April 12th.   Fished at Marsh Island bank—took 4 fish. Went ashore about 3 o'clock & had a race between the *Pelican* & Capers' *Eliza*, 6 to 8 oars. The *Pelican* beat about 6 lengths. Ned[146] was very much mortified & disappointed. Evans Chaplin went to Edwin Chaplin's to be sent to Gillisonville.

April 17th.   Fished under Hilton Head shore.[147] Took 12 fish. J.W. 2,[148] Saxby 2, & I 4—the Negroes took the balance.

April 18th.   Took a hunt on Edings Island. J.L.C. killed a very large buck—found it very hot hunting.

April 19th.   Saturday. Mother left for the main with Saxby & J. Witsell. Sent Sawney, Ben, Sam and Paul in the *Pelican* to take them over to the main. They arrived about 10 o'clock at night, having stuck in the cut[149] a long time.

Went over to the Riverside after Mother left, to see Mr. DaCosta.

---

[142] A small summer retreat on the tip of Eddings Island, at the northeastern outlet—the St. Helena side—of Port Royal Sound. Established in 1817 when an epidemic in Beaufort killed 120 people—about one-quarter of the town's white population.

[143] An inlet on the Broad River side of Hilton Head Island, directly across Port Royal Harbor from Lands End.

[144] Drum fish.

[145] Fanny Douglass, the mare.

[146] Edward M. Capers (b. 1820). Son of C. G. Capers and Mary Reynolds. Chaplin's best friend and frequent companion. Living with his parents, Ned Capers did not have much to do.

[147] Atlantic shore of Hilton Head Island.

[148] John W. Witsell (1818–1892), planter, from St. Bartholomew's Parish. Son of Frederick C. Witsell and Catherine Hagood, and brother of Saxby's wife, Anne.

[149] Stranded in the creek at low tide.

Told him I would take the Negroes deeded to us by Mother.[150] He made no objection & has promised to deliver them to me whenever I demand them, notwithstanding Baker's orders. He appears to be a very gentlemanly behaved man, and does not intend to be made a tool of by Baker.

April 23rd. Went fishing—took 14 drum. While they were biting well a small boat came alongside with two of my boys in her, to call me ashore, that Mr. Mickler the present deputy sheriff wished to see me. More trouble—he has judgments against me for about $2500. I shall be obliged to sell Negroes. Lost my boat hook.

April 24th. Went to the Hunting Islands, to see what I could get off of the wreck of the English boat *Clio,* wrecked about 10 days ago at or near Bulls Point.[151] I got over 200 fathoms of rope,[152] 23 blocks, and some old iron &c, &c &c. The ship is not more than 100 yds. from the bluff. I went on board several times with the assistance of a long ladder. She stands about 25 feet above the beach—that is from the ground to her bulwarks. She has been well stripped of everything of any great value, except the hull itself and the iron in her, and about 20 tons of coal.

April 26th. Saturday. Stayed at home all day. Had violent toothache. Weather very hot & very dry. We have had no rain of any account since the 31st of March—26 days—and that was only a small shower, also a little shower on the sixth of April. It is a singular fact that I have never known it to rain at this end of the Island, that is the southwest end, that it does not rain, if ever so little, at the other or northeast end. And I have noticed that it has rained several times at the other end, & even as far down as the Episcopal Church & farther & we have not a drop here. Certainly there is a greater chance of making a crop there than here, for they get the rain, when we see the cloud, expect it, & are disappointed.

April 27th. Sunday, went to church. Was taken with a violent toothache, & returned home without hearing the service. There is to be a great baptizing at the Baptist meeting house today.[153]

Robert was taken very sick last night with an attack very like cholera. Man Tony was taken in the same way today. They were taken very sud-

---

[150] The deed in question was recorded on April 16. Actually, the Negroes were deeded to Saxby only.
[151] The western tip of Chaplin's Island at the entrance to Trenchards Inlet.
[152] Twelve hundred feet—six feet to a fathom.
[153] A baptizing of Negroes. At this time on St. Helena, only the Baptist Church baptized and catechized slaves.

denly with spasmatic pains in the stomach, with frequent operations[154] & excessive vomiting of green stuff like beet grass, and extreme debility in every part. Opium brings relief.

This is the day of my birthday, the 23rd year of my age——

April 30th.   Went hunting, killed nothing. Saw the ship[155] ashore. It was quite a curiosity to some of the men. She was sold to a Mr. King[156] in Savannah for 52½ dollars, so I do not expect to get anything more out of her. The men are now cutting her to pieces. Returned home about 8 o'clock. My tooth pained me very much. Sent for Dr. Jenkins. Had it extracted, it came out very easy.

May 2nd.   Stayed at home all day—had toothache. Find that the tooth is broken off in the gum.

May 3rd.   Went to Beaufort, parade day.[157] Got off from parade on account of my tooth. Returned after dark. Had a heavy shower of rain after I left the ferry. Was very much disappointed when I got as far as Wm. Chaplin's[158] to find there had not been a drop there. I do not think it rained farther this way than the marsh, if so far. This is the second rain they have had at the other end of the Island when we have had none for several weeks. Everything is suffering for want of rain. The little cotton that *is* up is dying. Potatoes and sugarcane also dying. The corn looks green in spots, but not growing. Water is getting scarce. My pump is almost dry—it sucks every evening. Nearly every pump & well in Beaufort has gone dry. Trouble gathers thicker & thicker around me. I will be compelled to send about ten prime Negroes to town[159] next Monday, to be sold. I do this rather than have them seized and sold in Beaufort by the sheriff—or rather sacrificed.

I never thought that I would be driven to this very unpleasant extremity. Nothing can be more mortifying and grieving to a man than to select out some of his Negroes to be sold. You know not to whom, or how they will be treated by their new owners. And Negroes that you find no fault with—to separate families, mothers & daughters, brothers & sisters—all to pay for your own extravagances. People will laugh at your distress, and say it serves you right, you lived beyond your means, though some of the same never refused to partake of that hospitality and generosity which

---

[154] Bowel movements.
[155] The shipwreck *Clio.*
[156] Probably William King (1804–1884), cotton factor and insurance agent.
[157] Day when the B.V.A. assembled for display, inspection, and procession.
[158] William S. Chaplin's plantation, on the road to the Ladies Island Ferry.
[159] Charleston.

caused me to live beyond my means. Those beings I shall find out and will then know how to treat them.

May 4th. Sunday—did not go to church—toothache all day. The Negroes pulled up the floor to one of the outhouses & killed 56 rats—fine Sunday's work. A few clouds flying about. Wind very fresh but no rain. Things look worse & worse. Rode over to J. L. Chaplin's to get him to take the Negroes up to Beaufort for me tomorrow.

Just as had finished writing the foregoing sentence, I perceived J. L. Chaplin, James Clark[160] coming down the road. After they had eaten dinner, they went to the Negro houses & took 10 Negroes, viz.—Prince, Sib, Moses, Louisa, Tom, Hannah, Paul, Titus, Marcus & Joe. Carried them over to the Riverside where Clark's boat was. Got them on board, but it was so rough the boat nearly swamped, so they had to come on shore & stop until the next day. I cannot express my feelings on seeing so many faithful Negroes going away from me forever, not for any fault of their own but for my extravagance. It is a dearly bought lesson, and I hope I will benefit by it. The Negroes did not appear at all inclined to get off,[161] but apparently quite willing and in good spirits, particularly Prince & Paul. I hope they will bring a good price in Charleston where I have sent them under the charge of Wm. B. Fickling, to be sold, and that I will not have to sell any more. Mickler the deputy levied on them as soon as they got in Beaufort, but Fickling jockied him and got them on board the steamboat quite safe.[162]

May 5th. Went to Beaufort. Could not go down to the boat to see the Negroes off, but am glad it is all over for it is the most unpleasant thing I have ever had to do, and truly hope it may never occur again. The Negroes at home are quite disconsolate, but this will soon blow over. They may see their children again in time. Returned home after dusk. DaCosta rode from the ferry with me.

NOTE TO 4th & 5th MAY.* *It was a trying thing then. But could I or anyone foreseen how things would be 19 years after, when every Negro was set free by "force of war" I & everyone else would have gladly put them all in their pockets.[163] Besides, I would not have felt bad about it, for in truth, the Negroes did not care as much about us as we did for them.*

[160] James S. Clark (b. 1811). The census of 1850 lists his occupation as "none."
[161] Off the boat.
[162] Some of the court judgments that forced this sale involve creditors in Beaufort. The deputy attempted to seize the property before it left the District. In Fickling, Chaplin has chosen an experienced and influential man to see the slaves safely to Charleston, where they will bring more through a broker's sale than at a sheriff's auction in Beaufort.
[163] Would have sold them then and there.

May 7th.   Heard the joyful sound of *rain* falling on the shed last night about 12 o'clock. Rained very hard until 5 o'clock this morning. A little more would not be too much, but God is the best judge.

May 8th.   Found my horse Tippo foundered[164] this morning. I think this is owing to a heavy fall of rain about 2 p.m. yesterday when he was very warm, just after I crossed Port Royal Ferry.[165] Saxby & myself went down to the Point today, to take possession. C. M. Myers[166] & E. M. Capers[167] accompanied us as witnesses. Called at Walnut Hill for Mr. Nix[168] the overseer, who rode down to the Point with us. When I told him that I had come to take possession of the property as my own in presence of C. M. Myers & E. M. Capers, this he forbid in presence of the same gentlemen. I then asked him if he acted as Mr. Baker's agent, and if Baker was responsible for what he did. He said he was Mr. Baker's agent, & Baker was responsible. I must see my lawyer before I proceed further.[169] We then returned to H[ickory] Hill.

May 9th.   My horse being too low to travail, had to remain all day on the main. Rode over to Myers' in the evening. Found the horse though quite stiff able to get along. Started about 8 o'clock from Saxby's.

May 10th.   Rode on until I got to J. R. Toomer's[170] place on Port Royal. Rode up to demand an apology for some scandalous talk he had taken the presumptuous liberty to make use of towards me. The fellow hesitated rather long for my patience to endure, so I merely gave him a genteel flogging with a small cane. Made him beg like a Negro, swearing that he would not prosecute or do anything else if I would let him go. I then left him and when I had driven about 50 yards, the coward took a flying shot at my back, but did no more harm than putting one shot in the horse &

---

[164] Lame; suffering from laminitis, an inflammation of the hoof.

[165] Ferry connecting Port Royal Island and the mainland.

[166] Charles M. Myers (b. 1797), planter. Husband of Sarah Jenkins, Chaplin's first cousin on her mother's side. She was the daughter of Col. John J. Jenkins (brother of Isabella Baker's first husband, Daniel) and Sarah Chaplin (sister of Isabella's second husband, Saxby). Myers's lands on the Combahee were bounded on the south by Fields Point.

[167] Ned Capers.

[168] One of several Nixes listed in the census as either overseers or farmers.

[169] Though the deed to Point Place has been recorded, Chaplin is not sure it will stand up in court. Hence his hesitation, lest he have to pay damages to Baker.

[170] John R. Toomer. Son of Col. John R. Toomer and Mary Elizabeth Baker—R. L. Baker's sister. Mrs. Toomer testified at her brother's equity hearing that she had overheard Isabella Fields say, on the eve of her marriage to him, that "she intended to make him comfortable." Toomer's "scandalous talk" may have to do with the Baker-Chaplin dispute.

shooting off the hat of my boy John.[171] I waited for him then, at Port Royal Ferry, but he did not come, so I came on home.

May 12th. Had a veal killed. Sent a bit to Captain Jenk., & Coz. Betsy.[172] Planted celery & sugarcane. Sent John to Beaufort, being very anxious to hear from Fickling. He intends returning from Charleston via Savannah.

John returned after I had gone to bed, brought a note from Fickling stating 7 Negroes were sold to a man near Georgetown[173] named Cowen. Marcus, Prince & Sib had not yet been sold.

May 13th. Saw my friend J. R. Toomer. He looks as though he had been pretty severely handled by someone—I wonder who it was? He came into Edmund Rhett's[174] office when I was in there. He appeared very much surprised to see me. He was with R. G. Barnwell,[175] Magistrate, and I suspected he intended to indict me for assault & battery, & sure enough it was so, but the affidavit was not properly drawn, so that he could not compel me to keep the peace—& he wished to do, the *infernal coward*. I demanded his securities also,[176] when lo! he was not to be found—

I stayed in Beaufort to the meeting of the Odd Fellows, was very much amused at the initiation of S. P. Reed, and Mr. D. R. Beaubian.[177]

May 14th. Clear & hot in the morning. Everything growing beautifully. Cotton nearly all up. Hauled potatoes.[178] Cloud rising in the south about 2 p.m. Clears off before sunset. Started 2 flats & the boat with 60 baskets of corn & blades,[179] with some furniture for the village.[180] Sent 9 hands including Ben & the carpenters.

[171] The younger of Chaplin's two slaves named John.

[172] Elizabeth Perry Jenkins—Cousin Betsy, the Major's mother—was Capt. Daniel T. Jenkins's aunt.

[173] Major port town of the rice kingdom, 110 miles northeast of St. Helena, 60 miles above Charleston.

[174] Edmund Rhett (1808–1863), lawyer and planter. Born in North Carolina. Son of James Smith and Mariana Gough, a descendant of Col. William Rhett. Brother of R. B. Rhett, South Carolina's leading secessionist. The children of James Smith adopted the Rhett name in 1837.

[175] Robert Gibbes Barnwell (1818–1899), son of William Wigg Barnwell and Sarah R. Gibbes. Became associate editor of *DeBow's Review* (New Orleans) in 1851, and U.S. consul to Amsterdam.

[176] Chaplin is threatening to sue Toomer for assaulting him with a rifle.

[177] Samuel P. Reed (b. 1812), physician and planter, and D. R. Beaubian (b. 1785), planter.

[178] Hoed dirt up against the potato vines to make a deeper bed, to encourage the growth of vines and protect the roots from scorching.

[179] The leaves of the corn plant, dried and used for fodder.

[180] St. Helenaville, a small pine-bluff settlement on the east side of the Island, overlooking St. Helena Sound. Chaplin owned a summer house at one end of the village and his mother rented a house at the other end, a half-mile away. Chaplin is about to send his family off for the long summer.

May 15th. Went very early in the morning to take a cat hunt with the Major, but instead of starting a wildcat we started 2 runaways belonging to Isaac Sandiford[181]—Charles & Peter. We got a number of fellows working in the adjacent fields & gave chase, but they were too cunning for us & gave us the slip, taking to the marsh after dropping their bag of provisions—cooking utensils &c &c. Returned and dined with the Major. Commenced thinning and hauling cotton[182] on Carters Hill. It looks very sick & puny for its age. Returned home about ¼ past 3 p.m. & found that our folks had not yet dined. Shame to say it, we rise *later,* dine *later* & go to bed earlier than anyone on St. Helena Island.

May 16th. As soon as I was up, heard that sheep had been killed in the pen last night. Went to investigate the matter, found the meat in old Sancho's house. Rode in the field after breakfast, had Sancho tried.[183] As soon as he found that he was found out he said that Mr. Sandiford's Charles (the fellow that we started yesterday) came and gave him the meat, but after several very doubtful tales I came to the conclusion that Sancho was leagued with the runaways. As he says that Charles was to return the same night & eat some of the meat with him & that he had retired into Toomer's woods for the day, rode over to the Major's, got the Capt. & himself to ride with me in search of the fellow. We traversed the woods & hedges in vain—saw nothing of the runaway, so returned home.

May 17th. Anthony did not catch Charles last night, but saw the other fellow that is out with Charles named Dick.[184] Did not catch him. But I am convinced that my man Sancho harbors the pair of them, as they have both been to see him. What shall be done with this old rascal?

Mother and myself rode down to the village. Went up to the house she has hired of W. B. Fripp.[185] She gave Nelly such directions as she wished, rode round to my house, looked around & returned home to dinner. Expected to find Dr. Jenkins down there to play a game of billiards with me, but he had gone down to Uncle Ben's to stay until Monday.

Finished thinning & hauling the first planting of cotton & commenced hauling March corn. The only Negroes now sick are Rose since yesterday, Tony—22 days, viz. since the 27th of April. Peggy has not gone out to work yet. In fact she does not *want* to do anything. She has now been laying up for 82 or more days.

[181] Isaac Sandiford, planter. Lived halfway between Dr. Jenkins and Edgar Fripp, on Seaside Road.
[182] Reducing the number of cotton plants per hill, and hoeing dirt up from the furrows against the stalks.
[183] Questioned.
[184] Chaplin had mistakenly called him Peter.
[185] William B. Fripp (1792–1853), planter. Son of Paul Fripp and Amelia Reynolds, Chaplin's first cousin, twice removed, on his father's side. He was married to Chaplin's first cousin Eliza Chaplin.

May 18th. Sunday. Went to church. Dined with Capt. D. Jenkins. Capt. C. M. Myers & the Major were there also. Returning home, stopped and got a veal of J. L. Chaplin.

In crossing the Sands Creek,[186] drove too much to the right, & got in the bog. My horse went under water three times, nothing to be seen but the saddle to the harness, my sulky wheels up to the hub in the mud. Puss managed however to drag me out after several very violent lunges & plunges. It would have been a very laughable sight had anybody witnessed it.

May 19th. Capt. Jenkins, Dr. Jenkins, Uncle Ben & myself commenced a veal market, to kill every Monday for a month. I killed this day. Started my boat & flat[187] with furniture & c to the village this morning. Will be glad when the trouble is over. Got ourselves & everything safe to the village, all to our little runaway scrape.[188] Uncle Paul's mule that I borrowed for the occasion took it into his head that he would not pass his master's road. So he, the cart & boy full drive up to his stable, throwing nearly everything out of the cart, among them a basket of crockery, and fortunately only two trifling pieces got broke.

My boat went on to the main to bring over some things for Mother. As they were returning, that rascal Baker lay wayed[189] them at the mouth of Chehaw River, armed with guns and pistols, ordered them to stop or he would shoot them. He then got on board the boat, and took it up to the Point landing.[190] Took Ben, Rinah & Daphne out, & all their things & locked them up. He intended also to vent his spite on Old Davey, but the old fellow was too cunning & got off into the woods. The others escaped out of the house when the scamp was at dinner, by bursting open the door. Simon & Ben came over to me that night in a small boat. My boat returned also in the evening. Rinah, Davey & Daphne were left in the woods. Just as Baker got on board of my boat, he saw Mr. Minott coming down the river. This frightened the fellow, as he would not have attempted anything of the kind if there had been a white man present.[191]

---

[186] A tributary of Station Creek which bisected Tombee and passed under Seaside Road.

[187] Flat-bottomed creek boat which draws very little water and can handle great weights.

[188] "All to" means except for. The "runaway scrape" refers to the incident with Uncle Paul's mule, not to Isaac Sandiford's runaway slaves.

[189] Waylaid.

[190] On the Combahee River.

[191] As usual, Negroes are the objects of contention. Baker does not accept his wife's deeds to her sons. He runs from Minott, a close friend of the Chaplins, because he feels unsure about his position. If the Appeals Court sustains the lower-court ruling, he could be held liable for damages.

May 22nd.   Sent the boat back to the main for the Negroes that got away from Baker yesterday.

Grouse was taken down very bad with the staggers.[192]

Grouse, poor Grouse.

May 23rd.   Boat returned before I got up in the morning. They found the Negroes at Perry's[193] & brought them over. They had no clothes but what they had on their backs. Sent the boat home. Ben & Violet went home in it, to work in my field the balance of the year.

Gained two hands

Col. Johnson[194] & William Fickling had a falling out the other day, about the trial of a Negro woman for assault & battery.

May 24th.   Killed a lamb to carry to the village.

June 4th.   Since the 24th of May my journal has been left at the plantation.[195] I have **not** been able to write any nonsense in it. E. Morrall[196] & the Capt. came home with me from church on the first, and dined. After supper the Dr. & Major came up. We all returned with them to the Dr.'s & took supper with him & spent Sunday very wickedly.

Had the Irish potatoes dug, 100 feet turned out 3 pks.[197] I intend showing them for the premium at the Society tomorrow.

Dr. Jenkins & Capt. I. Fripp have made up & played billiards on my table yesterday.

June 5th.   Meeting of the Agricultural Society. Capt. Paul Jenkins[198] furnishes dinner. Did not present my Irish potatoes, as the premium is only 25 cts. Weather very warm and dry—crops suffering for want of rain.

June 6th.   Had fodder corn planted in the stable yard, for the benefit of the milk cow & calf. Heard that man Bidcome,[199] down on the estate of

---

[192] Grouse was a horse. Staggers was the name given to various diseases which induced a dull, sleepy appearance and a staggering gait.

[193] William S. Perry (1797–1854), Combahee River planter. Son of Peter Perry and Ann Fripp, Chaplin's first cousin, once removed, on his mother's side. Uncle of Major D. P. and Dr. W. J. Jenkins.

[194] Benjamin Jenkins Johnson (1817–1861), planter and lawyer. Son of William Johnson and Elizabeth Whaley. A colonel in the B.V.A.

[195] Chaplin is staying at the village.

[196] Edward F. (Ned) Morrall, planter and attorney, St. Luke's Parish.

[197] Three pecks. A peck equals eight quarts, dry measure, or one-quarter bushel.

[198] Paul Fripp Jenkins (1826–1878), son of Col. Joseph E. Jenkins and Ann Jenkins Fripp. Chaplin's second cousin on his father's side. First cousin of Eliza Fripp Jenkins (Dr. William Jenkins's wife), and second cousin of J.E.L., W.O.P., and J.T.E. Fripp.

[199] A slave.

W. S. Chaplin, had caught runaway Dick belonging to Mr. Sandiford. He & Charles, his companion, were in the sheep pen, had two sheep tied. Charles escaped by knocking down one of the men.[200]

June 11th. Wednesday. Went down to the plantation to go to the Hunting Islands, on a fishing excursion for the amusement of Fickling, who has been a good friend to me, because he was a friend in need. Had very good weather, though very hot, did not have much sport. Our only amusements were bathing in the surf & digging turtle eggs, of which we got about 400—135 in one nest. The bathing was delightful, and Fickling enjoyed it very much.

June 17th. Tuesday. Capt. J. Fripp & Mr. J. J. Pope[201] went with me down to the plantation for the purpose of appraising all of my land & Negroes, as I wish to have them secured to my wife & children, and take out of the bank $10,000 of her legacy.[202]

The Negroes were valued at $14,605.[203] The land, both tracts, at $11,450.[204] Making the full amount of my property appraised—$26,055.

Took dinner & returned about dusk. Found Maj. Felder here ready with a dun for me, for lumber. He is the man, J. M. Felder,[205] of Orangeburg,[206] but a very cross, grasping, rough, ungentlemanly fellow. But he is rich & that pushes him along.

June 22nd. Sunday. Went to the Central Church. Very hot, very dry, no rain, crops going to the devil.

June 23rd. Had 6 hands all the evening cleaning up the hedge—on the creek—so as to get more air.

June 26th. Went to Beaufort in the afternoon with Bell[207] to stay with him until after parade on the 28th. Arrived in Beaufort about sunset. Mrs.

---

[200] Slaves from the estate of W. S. Chaplin, who confronted Sandiford's runaways.
[201] Joseph J. Pope (1793-1864), planter. Pope and Capt. Fripp were thirty years older than Chaplin.
[202] Mary Chaplin was left $15,000 in bank stock by her grandfather, John McDowell. Chaplin hopes to substitute land and Negroes for the stock, then convert the stock to cash.
[203] An average of $250 per slave, counting the very young and the very old, field slaves and house servants, full hands, quarter-hands, and slaves unable to work at all.
[204] Tombcc, worth $6,000, and an unidentified tract—possibly land recently deeded to Chaplin by his mother—worth about the same.
[205] John Myers Felder (1787-1852), planter, lawyer, and lumberman, of Orangeburg District. Son of Samuel Felder and Mary Myers. Member S.C. House of Representatives 1814-16, 1822-24, and State Senate 1816-20, 1840-51.
[206] Commercial and resort town in the pinelands, seventy-five miles north of St. Helena.
[207] Theodore Augustus Bell (1822-1882). Son of John Bell and Henrietta McKee. Lieutenant in the B.V.A.

Bell[208] was just dressing to go to a party at Col. Johnson's. Bell was quite unwell, had a slight fever so, as a good wife, she would not go, though she appeared to be somewhat disappointed. Spent a very hot night—no such breeze as we have at the village. Drank soda water &c by the woods, which was somewhat refreshing.

June 27th. Friday. The hottest day I think I have ever felt, almost perspired to death. Changed my linen about four times. Oats (100 bushels) came up in the steamboat.[209] My boat came up for them. Could not take but 23 bags—3 bushels each, leaving 10 bags. Sent word by Dr. Jenkins to Mrs. C. to send the boat up for the oats tomorrow. Mrs. Bell is to have a little party tonight.

A heavy cloud commenced rising in the north, about 3 o'clock—got heavy & heavier with peals of thunder & vivid flashes of lightning. The party was disposed of, after all the preparation. Just before dark in pops J. H. Webb with Julia Rhodes[210] on his arm. Soon after, say 6 o'clock, it commenced raining very hard. Slacked a little about 10, when in came Dr. Johnson,[211] H. McKee,[212] John McKee[213] & a Mr. Cunningham.[214] These were all that thought fit to attend a party this stormy night, but I think they made up for the rest in the *eating line.* I made myself sick eating ice cream.

June 28th. Saturday. The anniversary of our company—the plow & bugle to be shot for.

We paraded at 8 o'clock a.m. in citizen's dress. The rain last night made it more pleasant than it otherwise would have been, though it was very hot. We marched out to Sams Point & shot at the target. The shooting was only tolerable—25 in the target out of 75 shots fired. I knew my chance was lost at the first fire, so gave it up, having missed the whole target, owing to the blowing of my rifle burning me up with powder &c &c. Lieut. T. A. Bell won the plow, or, made the best shot. Lieut. Baker[215] the bugle, the second best shot. There was some misunderstanding in the matter. Baker understood, & so did some others, that the best shot had the

---

[208] Mary Chaplin Adams (1815–1890). Daughter of Benjamin Adams and Mary Rebecca Chaplin. First cousin to Thomas B. Chaplin on her mother's side.
[209] From Charleston.
[210] Julia Rhodes. Daughter of Thomas W. Rhodes and Elizabeth Jenkins. Niece of Capt. Daniel T. Jenkins.
[211] Either Joseph Fickling Johnson (b. 1813), or John Archibald Johnson (1819–1893), physicians and planters. Sons of William Johnson and Elizabeth Whaley. Brothers of Benjamin, Richard, and William H. Johnson, and Sarah Johnson Verdier.
[212] Henry McKee (1811–1875), planter and resident of Beaufort.
[213] John McKee, Henry's father.
[214] Either A. M. Cunningham (b. 1820), Irish-born planter, or H. L. Cunningham (b. 1812), planter, both of St. Helena Parish.
[215] John M. Baker (b. 1800), tax collector.

choice, so Bell claimed the plow & so did Baker.[216] It was put to the whole company & decided in favor of Bell. The company then broke until 4 o'clock p.m. I was however excused from drill on account of having a very painful *corn* on my toe. It is a great consolation to me to know that at least *I* have taken the shine off the plow that they would quarrel for.[217] A very heavy cloud making again this evening. I was afraid it would overtake me before I got home but escaped with only a few drops on me. It poured directly after I got in the house & rained the greater part of the night. I was sure that I would get a full share of this rain, as the heaviest cloud hung in that direction, but was disappointed—only a few drops fell on my parched fields.

June 29th.   Sunday. Went to the Central Church. A heavy cloud made up while in church, which cut Mr. M.'s[218] sermon short.

The boat got here just before day with the oats, left ten bags in Beaufort. Gave the first feed off them this morning. Heard of the death of Mrs. Cannon—Mrs. O. Fripp's sister, yesterday. Went to the village church in the afternoon. Rode up to Mother's after tea.

June 30th.   Dined with the Major at the plantation. Got 10 bushels of rough rice[219] of him. Returned home a little skeiweed.[220]
O fie fie!!!

July 1st.   Sent John to Beaufort. Rode up to Mother's in the morning. While there it rained very hard for two hours, the first time I have seen the water settle on the ground for a long time. Sent for W. J. Jenkins & D. P. Jenkins to witness the signature of three deeds executed by Mother in favor of Saxby & myself, D. Jenkins[221] & her creditors. These deeds cover all of her settled property.[222] *Now* what will R. L. Baker do? Go & keep accounts & paint coats of arms for jackasses, as he did before for a living.[223]

---

[216] One man thought the best single shot won; the other thought the best average of shots closest to the center of the target won.
[217] Chaplin had won the use of the plow at the last contest and has been using it.
[218] Mr. McElheran.
[219] Rice with the grain still in the husk.
[220] Either a word play on whis-key, or from "skewgee," meaning confused or uncertain.
[221] Daniel T. Jenkins was a first cousin to the two other Jenkinses.
[222] These deeds made a clean sweep of Isabella's estate. All her property, except for a number of Negroes selected out for sale and a family of slaves she kept for herself, now belong to Thomas and Saxby. The Bakers are left without any means of support.
[223] Baker painted portraits during the years he ran a pharmacy.

From sleeping with a fresh breeze blowing on me last night, I took a cold which gave me a little fever & sore throat this evening.

July 2nd.　　Felt very unwell all day—pains in all my bones & sore throat. Mother spent the day with us, she is also quite unwell. Had a little ice cream today—

DaCosta came down in the evening, after a couple of little runaways—Lundon & Morris.[224] Caught them at the village & took them home.

Felt very sick this evening. Sent for Dr. Jenkins. Wanted to give me jalap[225]—would not take it.

July 3rd.　　Went to the plantation. Left the two deeds[226] at the Captain's house, as he had gone to Beaufort by water. Dined with the Major. He paid me 10 bushels & 3 pecks of corn, being all that he owes me, & that for a long time.

July 4th.　　Friday. Anniversary of the Declaration of Independence of these United States. Felt too unwell to go to Beaufort, went to the muster house.[227] An oration was delivered by Mr. C. Belcher, Declaration of Independence read, or at least spoken by E. M. Capers—he had all by heart—prayer by Mr. McElheran. The oration was a plain, well-written speech, a very good repetition of the history of the Revolution, but not oratorically delivered. We dined about ½ past 2 p.m., drank 12 bottles of champagne, & returned to the village at about 5 o'clock all sober. Preparations were then made for fireworks, which came off about 8 o'clock p.m. I had the misfortune to get my right eye very much hurt from the bursting of one of the rockets. They went off very well. After which, the young ladies gave a picnic in Dr. Scott's[228] piazza. I did not eat any of this supper, but expect it was very good. I furnished 6 bottles of champagne—I know that went off very well.

Fool forgot about your 10 Negroes sold! Ah, Low! Low!

Date my weak eyesight from this same occurrence

July 5th.　　Saturday. My eye very sore. Tried bread & milk & slippery elm poultice. Something better towards evening. E. M. Capers came home

---

[224] From the Riverside.
[225] A purgative drug made from the tuberous root of a plant in the morning glory family.
[226] Two of the three deeds mentioned above.
[227] Meeting house of the St. Helena Mounted Riflemen.
[228] John A. P. Scott (1794–1874), physician and planter. Son of Joseph Jenkins Scott and Catherine Adams. Married to Chaplin's first cousin Sarah Ann Chaplin. The Scotts lived on a 750-acre plantation north of Tombee, on Lands End Road, bordering Dr. Jenkins's place. Jenkins eventually acquired it.

with me on the 4th, still here—**& *always here*** Dr. Jenkins, the Major, the Capt., B. Capers, F. Capers, E. Capers,[229] Ben & Tom were all in the billiards room today.
Regular rendezvous for all the village loafers

July 7th. Monday. E. Capers & myself went down to the plantation. Rode over the crop. He thinks mine as good as any he has seen on the Island, only, as with all the rest very backward, not blossoming as much as the rest. Dined with the Captain.
O this dining somewhere or other every day almost

July 10th. Peggy is at last confined. She had ***pretty*** good cause for laying up, being delivered of two fine boys. She has never had a male child before.
Elimus, one of the twins now alive, is 32 years old on the 10th of July this year of 1876

Started for the main this morning, the Major, Captain & E. Capers with me. Arrived on the main about 11½ o'clk. Met with no resistance from Mr. Nix. He would not give me up the keys, but I soon had the locks broken open & took what I wanted. When he found out I was determined he opened some of the doors.[230]

Brought, or rather sent over to the village, a quantity of furniture, 10 bushels of corn &c &c. Had a little rain there. Spent the night with E. Capers. Mosquitoes bit very bad, but it was quite cool.

July 11th. Got to the village in a hard rain about 3 o'clock. Ned did not come down to the Point in time so did not wait for him. Found Old Grace at the Point very sick with the dropsy. Employed Dr. Hazel for her. The boat returns to the Point this night. They have a very good crop over there.

July 12th. Saturday. Went home. Found a good mess of ripe figs on the tree. Three good showers of rain during the day. Planting slips as fast as I can.

July 14th. Monday. In the village all day. Played billiards & backgammon with E. Capers. The Major & his posse[231] stopped in the evening—he looked like a capon carrying chickens.

---

[229] Benjamin Capers (b. 1815), Francis T. Capers (b. 1828), and Ned Capers, three sons of C. G. Capers and Mary Reynolds.
[230] After this break-in, Chaplin was sued by Francis L. Roux for "pursuing a system of annoyance" against Mrs. Baker's estate, and obstructing him, Roux, from fulfilling his duties as trustee. See Aug. 15, 1845.
[231] Planters riding patrol—night watch—over the slaves.

July 16th.   Wednesday. Ned & myself went down to the plantation, dined, returned before dark. Went up to see Uncle Ben. Stopped at Dr. Jenkins', had a small dance there. Ned was the fiddler.

July 19th.   Sent John to Beaufort. Killed lamb for market. A few large drops of rain about ½ past 2 p.m., very hot. Rode with Sophy in the buggy up to Mother's,[232] found her very sick, though I heard she was much better in the morning. Had the carriage got. Made a bed of pillows in it & brought her to my house.

July 20th.   Sunday. Did not go to church, very hot. Mother some better. Ice appears to revive her very much. She eats it continually.

Peggy lost one of her twin boys on the 18th inst. I thought they would not live, they were so very small. Went up to the chapel in the evening.

July 21st.   Went to Beaufort. Dined with Bell. Returned before dark. Heard that S. A. Hurlbut[233] had stopped from Charleston very much in debt. I hope he has not got me into any difficulty as he had some business of importance to transact for me. Got Fickling to write Gray about him.[234]

July 22nd.   Remained in the village. Lent my buggy to D. P. Jenkins to take Mary Jenkins to Beaufort. Charles Belcher called after breakfast. Spent the day & night with me. We played 31 games of backgammon, he winning 16 & I 15 games—this, he said, he never knew to happen before to his knowledge. The weather was exceedingly hot today. The thermometer standing as high as 96 in the shade & 100 in the sun & wind—in the shade at 6½ o'clock & in the sun at 5¼ p.m.

July 23rd.   Went to the plantation. Took Belcher as far as Lawrence Fripp's[235] on, or out of, my way home. Carpenters still at the boat house.

---

[232] Mrs. Baker is now separated from her husband and living by herself in St. Helenaville. Major D. P. Jenkins testified that her relatives "had cast her off" when she married Baker, and welcomed her back in the fold only after she signed deeds in favor of her sons.

[233] Stephen Augustus Hurlbut (1815–1882). Son of Martin Luther Hurlbut and Lydia Bruce. U.S. district commissioner for South Carolina, in charge of registering bail and affidavits in civil cases. In the fall of 1845 Hurlbut left the job and fled the state because of financial troubles. He resettled in Springfield, Ill., where he became a friend of Abraham Lincoln, and a member of the Ill. House of Representatives. Lincoln sent Hurlbut on a special mission to Charleston in 1861 to sound out Hurlbut's former employer, James L. Petigru (see note, Feb. 25, 1846) about feelings in the state toward the Union. Hurlbut later won a commission as brigadier general in the U.S. Army, but charges of corruption led to his dismissal. After the Civil War he served in U.S. diplomatic missions to Colombia and Peru.

[234] Chaplin was trying to draw cash from his wife's legacy.

[235] James E. Lawrence Fripp (1817–1864), planter. Son of James Fripp and Ann Pope.

Sawney nearly cut two of his toes off, with the broadaxe. Gave the Negroes at the Riverside a small beef. Dined with the Capt.

July 24th. Killed beef for market. Rode down to Coffin's Point,[236] a part of the Island I have never been at in my life. On my way I met Capt. I. Fripp.[237] Rode up to his place with him for the first time I had ever been there. He is one of the most enterprising planters I know of. Has a great quantity of thrown-by machinery which he has tried & never succeeded with, such as gins &c &c &c.

Went to Coffin's to see Cockcroft[238] his overseer to buy some corn. Succeeded in getting 50 bushels at 75 cents.[239] He is a very obstinate fellow, appeared to be afraid I would not pay him in time for him to pay Coffin when he returned from the North. I am to give him an order on Mr. Gray for the amt. $37½,[240] payable the 1st of October next.

Alas, how little did I think then, that now, 32 years after, in 1876, I would be living on the same place, Coffin's—now Whitwell's,[241] almost as an overseer myself & a Yankee schoolteacher, & not worth shucks, much less 50 lbs. corn. Truly the vicissitudes of life are past the comprehension of mortal man. Coffin, Cockcroft and hundreds more are dead & a great blast of ruin & destruction passed over the country.

July 26th. Saturday. The steamboat came along about 7 o'clock. She came to opposite J. L. Chaplin's landing. The Capt., seeing several of J.L.C.'s family on the beach waving handkerchiefs &c, thought they wanted to get on board, but as soon as the yawl was lowered they scampered up the bluff. The Capt. was very much provoked, & hardly wanted to stop for me opposite D. Jenkins' landing. Bristol & Sancho put me on board in J.C.'s little boat. We arrived in Savannah about ½ past eleven o'clock a.m. I had never been there but once before, with the company on the 28th June and had no opportunity of seeing anything but a great crowd. I cannot say that I admired the place at all, it is one of the hottest & dirtiest places I ever saw in my life. Very few good looking stores. I got

---

Chaplin's second cousin on his father's side. Lived northwest of Tombee on Chowan Creek, next door to his brother, William Oliver Perry Fripp.

[236] A 1,400-acre plantation on the eastern end of the Island overlooking St. Helena Sound. One of several large tracts owned by Thomas Aston Coffin (1795–1863), who spent most of his time in Charleston. Coffin was the son of Ebenezer Coffin and Mary Matthews.

[237] Another Isaac Fripp, not Chaplin's "Cousin Isaac."

[238] Jonathan Cockroft (b. 1808), overseer.

[239] Per bushel.

[240] This money comes out of his wife's inheritance, for which Gray is keeping accounts.

[241] Samuel W. Whitwell (1816–1880), a northerner who acquired Coffin's Point during the Union occupation of St. Helena, in the 1860s.

so wet with perspiration that I was obliged to go into a clothing establishment & get a change dress even to a linen. We partook of fine ice punch & a very ordinary dinner at the Pulaski House.[242] Drank a good deal of iced champagne & left the Georgian city at 4 o'clock.

July 27th. Rode down home & over all the crop. Cotton looks very well, but backward. March corn tolerable—young, good & very bad in spots. Potatoes very bad. Peas miserable. 3¾ acres of slips planted, no rain to plant more. Had only a few drops last eve, though we had a fine rain at the village. Ground almost as dry as it was before. Cattle suffering for water.

These must have been happy days.

July 28th. Monday. Peas cannot sprout. Those that have come up are withered up. Commenced stripping blades[243] on Thursday the 24th inst. They are very much dried up but I think I will make more than last year. Mr. McElheran took tea with us. Walked up to Dr. Jenkins' in the evening. Heard today that the scarlet fever was in J. J. Pope's family & the whooping cough in Mr. James Fripp's[244]—hope we will escape.

July 29th. A very pleasant day, fine breezes. Stayed at home. Major borrowed my buggy to go to Beaufort. I walked a mile after supper by walking the length of my piazza 88 times, it being 60 feet long.

July 30th. Wife rode down to the plantation with me. The weather looked very fine when we started, but about 10 o'clock a cloud rose in the southwest & commenced raining about 12 m. Rained very hard for about an hour, but the ground was so dry it was not wet an inch deep. The sun shone out again for about ½ hour when we saw another cloud making up in the same direction. I rode over in the field, & while trying my potatoes it commenced to rain again. Took shelter with the Negroes in Adam Morcock's[245] house. It rained very hard for about ½ hour, with several very severe claps of thunder. When it slacked a little I concluded to take advantage of the interim & gallop home, but got a complete drenching, this being the first time I have been wet by rain this summer.

July 31st. Thursday. Planting slips with all hands. Hope we may have enough rain to finish, for it is now so late I will hardly get anything but

---

[242] Savannah's finest hotel.
[243] Pulling the leaves off the corn plants.
[244] James Fripp (1811–1880), planter. Son of Isaac Perry Fripp and Mary Pope. First cousin to Chaplin, once removed, on his father's side.
[245] Possibly William A. Morcock, of Beaufort.

seed potatoes.[246] Rode out with wife in the afternoon. Clouds rising in every direction—no rain. Rode up to the Major's after tea.

Mr. McElheran sent round a subscription paper for the purpose of raising money to have the well in the parsonage yard bricked—as he pretends—for the benefit of any person that may succeed him as minister on the Island. I have no doubt he expects to spend his lifetime here. **He did not & the shame of the people**[247]

Aug. 1st.   Friday. This stormy month comes in with not much prospects of rain or storms. Yet the sea may smooth in the morn and ere night be tossed by winds & waves. So it may be with this month. My opinion is, that as we have had no rain to set a crop of slips & peas up to this late season when it is (generally speaking) too late to ensure a crop, we will now be visited with tremendous storms of rain & wind, which will destroy or greatly injure the crops of cotton. But we trust to God—He alone can control the seasons, it may be all for the best.

Aug. 3rd.   Sunday. It commenced raining last night about 9 o'clock & rained steady all night. I never in my life heard such thunder as we had last night between 12 & 1 o'clock, such loud & rapid succession of claps of thunder & vivid flashes of lightning apparently nearer & nearer every time, it was really alarming. I thought the house or something in the yard would be struck every moment & still fear that some damage has been done in or near the village, for it seemed as if the whole artillery of heaven was opened on this spot.

Aug. 4th.   Got up 8 o'clock, found it still raining, wind blowing fresh from the east, & SSE. Very dark & dreary, looks more like continued rain than breaking. I fear it will greatly injure the cotton. The Captain is with me, very uneasy first **at** one window then another, hardly sits down for one minute at a time. This is the day I intended to be at Bay Point on a devilfish[248] excursion, but am very glad I am at home.

I was much astonished about 10 o'clock at seeing several gentlemen walking up from the other end of the village, but learnt that they only

[246] Because of adverse growing conditions, Chaplin expects his potatoes to be too small to eat and good only for use as seed the next year.
[247] See June 12, 1856.
[248] A species of ray; "a monster," wrote William Elliott, "measuring from sixteen to twenty feet across the back, full three feet in depth, having powerful yet flexible flaps or wings, with which he drives himself furiously through the water or vaults high into the air. . . . The chase of the devil fish [is] an established diversion of the planters of Port Royal Sound. They make Bay Point their place of rendezvous." (*Carolina Sports by Land and Water* [Charleston, S.C., 1846], 6.)

came to see what damage had been done to the bluff up here from the heavy rain last night. I took a walk up the village & was very surprised to see the manner the bluff in different places has been washed. At Mr. Hall's,[249] it washed within 20 feet of his house, the gully about 10 feet wide & 15 deep. At Dr. Sams',[250] about 15 feet from his fence is a gully. A small cave-in opposite John Pope's,[251] one opposite John Fripp's, & a tremendous chasm opposite D. P. Jenkins', about 30 feet wide, 20 deep, & about 8 feet from his steps. Another hard rain would wash away his steps. All the hands that could be started in the village were immediately pressed to fill up this large gully. Several persons have agreed to [provide] carts & horses with a boy & have it filled up at once, as it injures the looks of the village very much, that is, the front walk, for there is no siding pass on that part of the bluff. Everyone thought that my bluff would wash more than any other, but they were much mistaken. The bluff opposite my house did not wash at all, owing to the slant being towards the house & not to the bluff.

Aug. 5th. Tuesday. The wind has got to the NW & is quite cool—a thick coat very comfortable, & I do not think a small fire would be amiss. It would certainly be wholesome to dry the damp walls.

Went down home. The Capt. & myself rode his crop & mine. Found that the rain & wind had whipped the blossoms & forms off considerably.[252] Had to recover some of the slips.[253] The hands were scattered all about. Some letting off water out of the field, some supplying peas.[254] Sent Ben with the bay mare & cart to assist in filling up the breaks made in the bluff at the other end of the village. Though I doubt very much, if the same thing should happen up here, if they would lend their aid.

Aug. 7th. Went to the Agricultural meeting. The new member Geo. Law found his maiden dinner, & it was very good, & what is surprising, he found 6 bottles of liquor. There was no show of fruit as expected & agreed upon the last meeting. C. G. Capers brought a fine basket of grapes. W.O.P. Fripp, *one peach* & one little watermelon, & about ½ dozen potatoes, old & new crop.

[249] John W. Hall (b. 1810), planter.
[250] Either Berners Barnwell Sams (1787–1855), physician and planter, or his son, Melvin Melius Sams (1815–1900), also a physician and planter. The younger Sams was a second cousin to Chaplin on his mother's (Eliza Fripp's) side.
[251] John Jeremiah Theus Pope (1799–1864), planter. Lived at the Oaks Plantation, 500 acres on Chowan Creek, northeast of Tombee.
[252] The wind blew off both the cotton flowers and the young bolls behind them.
[253] Set out new cuttings.
[254] Replanting peas in places where they did not come up or were washed away.

Aug. 10th. Sunday. Fickling went to Beaufort to send the report of Gray's to the Chancellor Johnson.[255] Thinks that Johnson will sign the order for the transfer of stock &c. If so I will soon be clear of debt.

Aug. 13th. Went after devilfish. Struck a very large fellow, rope got entangled with my feet & nearly carried me overboard. I was so much strained with the effort of holding on to the [   ] of the boat that Dr. Jenkins thought I ought to be bled & it was done, which relieved me very much, but kept me very weak all the time I was down at the Point.

Aug. 18th. F. L. Roux,[256] Baker's accomplice, has served Mother, the Captain, Saxby & myself with what is called writs of prohibition, to prevent our taking possession of any of the deeded property.[257] I have put them in Treville's hands.

Aug. 19th. At home all day—
Commenced eating red potatoes, they yield very little, hardly worth digging. Do not get, on an average, more than 4 quarts to the task row,[258] and as they are sprouting, they will not grow but very little, if any more.

Bought sorrel horse, Slapbang, of J. L. Chaplin ($100)—well worth the money, being a well grown Island raised horse. Put him in the cart (for the first time) & he drew 7 bushels of potatoes 12 miles, with a heavy Negro man in the cart, besides other things, making a very heavy load for any horse.

Aug. 21st. Helen was delivered of a male child on Friday, 8th August, in the evening, name *Scipio.*
Would be 32 years old this month 1876

Aug. 22nd. Friday. Had a fine rain last night. Wife rode up the village, just returned in time to escape. Potatoes still turning out very bad, reds nearly gone. Will get corn from the main & give 2 allowances[259] more.

---

[255] David Johnson. See note, Feb. 24, 1845.
[256] Francis L. Roux, bookkeeper by trade. Son of Lewis Roux and Ann Buckle. The elder Roux may have been Baker's attorney at one time. Baker was released from a debt he had owed Lewis Roux upon Roux's death in 1842. Francis L. Roux was one of the two trustees—Capt. D. T. Jenkins was the other—of Isabella Baker's estate.
[257] These injunctions issued out of Roux's suit charging Chaplin and others with using "illegal and forcible means to entice the slaves so settled"—named in Mrs. Baker's marriage settlement—"to leave their work," thus threatening "to destroy the growing crop" and bring Roux "into great jeopardy."
[258] A yield of half a peck, or one-sixteenth bushel per standard length row of the daily task, or work load, of a field hand.
[259] Weekly or biweekly food rations.

Saw a schooner at Dr. Jenkins' landing. Suppose she has brought lumber for his dwelling house.

Aug. 25th.   Major & Capt. dined with me. Had a very rainy day, commenced to rain about 12 o'clock m. Cleared a little about dusk. Think it will rain again tomorrow, if the old sign does not fail, that is, it rained today when the sun was shining. Or the devil whipping his wife behind the door.

Aug. 26th.   Tuesday. Went home. Dined with the Capt. Learnt from him that his sister Emma[260] is determined to be married in the fall, to J. H. Webb,[261] contrary to the wishes of all her friends. I do not think it such a bad match.
& so it proved, they lived happily & if there was any fault it was on her side. Both dead now 1876
The Capt. takes it very much to heart.

    4 hands picking cotton, hoeing rice & breaking down corn. Sent 25 bushels corn home in the wagon. Brought load of blades & pumpkins back.

Aug. 31st.   Manny[262] got into a very bad screaming & fretting, & throwing dishes & glasses off the table (or trying to do so). I could not find out what he was crying for so came to the conclusion that he wanted a little switch pudding, when I straightaway gave him a little brush, but this did not stop him. When he expected as is generally the case that his mother would interfere & get him off—though she attempted to do so, I would not give way. Mrs. C. then took the foolish idea in her head that I had whipped the child *through spite to her.* This is not so, I own I was provoked at her interference, when I thought proper to correct one of the children. The only cause of my whipping the child after her interference was to show him that he would not escape always, through the interference of his mother, & by that means form an idea that I would not be allowed to whip him & therefore not obey me. I feel perfectly justifiable in what I did & will do it again, even if Mrs. C. gets *vexed,* & remains so six months or twelve.
& now 32 years after in 1876, the mother long dead, & the child a man with 3 children as spoiled as he was, I am of the very same opinion, & the mother lived to see her error. Mrs. C. & I had a sad experience of its effects on D[263]

---

[260] Emmeline Jenkins. Daughter of John Jenkins and Sarah Chaplin. First cousin to Chaplin on her mother's side. She was the widow of Thomas F. Fripp..
[261] Webb, who had quarreled with the Captain, is about to become his brother-in-law. He previously was seen in society with the Captain's niece, Julia Rhodes.
[262] Daniel Jenkins Chaplin (1843–1924). Chaplin's fourth child and second son.
[263] Daniel.

Sept. 2nd.   Went over to W. B. Fripp's pasture to shoot plover. Saw very few, did not get but two shots. Killed two birds & returned home by 11 o'clock.

Sept. 5th.   Sent the boat to the main for the 150 bushels of corn, as I do not think I will get paid for it & Nix said he would not give it to the Negroes.[264] Sent John to Beaufort in the buggy, to get groceries for Mother.

Sept. 6th.   Went to Beaufort to parade. Dined with J. D. Pope at Morcock's.[265] He acknowledged that he was really engaged to Kate Scott[266] to be married sometime before the 1st of January next. Boat came back from the main, left 18 bags of corn here, about 50 bushels, & carried 18 bags of corn home, about 70 bushels.

Sept. 8th.   Had the corn measured that came from the main—53½ bushels. Weather warm & dry, would like to have a little rain. The slips are all drying. Do not think I shall make seed for next year. Sent John to Beaufort.

Sept. 9th.   Let W.O.P. Fripp have ten bushels of corn. He is to get ten more & return it in new corn this winter. Old Judy came down in the cart today, so as to be here should Mrs. C. be taken sick, and Mrs. Cook not be here.[267]

Sept. 10th.   Lent the Major 7 bushels of corn for Cousin Ann Chaplin,[268] to be returned in new corn this winter.

Sept. 11th.   George Cuthbert[269] came to my house yesterday evening. Started this morning with me for the plantation. There we were joined by Capt. D. Jenkins & J. L. Chaplin and went down to Skulls Inlet.[270] We landed John Chaplin at the 1st bluff with the dogs, to hunt on towards the camping place. Found several persons at the inlet—Mickler, Graven-

---

[264] Baker's overseer Nix won't feed Chaplin's corn to the contested Negroes and risk giving credence to Chaplin's claim of ownership.

[265] Beaufort boarding house, operated by William A. and Susan Morcock.

[266] Catherine Scott (b. 1822). Daughter of Dr. John A. P. Scott and Sarah Ann Chaplin. Thomas B. Chaplin's first cousin, once removed, on her mother's side.

[267] Mary Chaplin is near her time to go into labor. Old Judy, a black midwife, has been summoned from Tombee to the Chaplin house in the village until Maria Cook, a white midwife, is available.

[268] Ann Fripp Jenkins Chaplin (b. 1818). Widow of William S. Chaplin. Daughter of Benjamin Jenkins and Elizabeth Perry; sister of Major D. P. and Dr. W. J. Jenkins. She is Chaplin's second cousin on her mother's side.

[269] George B. Cuthbert (b. 1805), planter, of Ladies Island, St. Helena Parish.

[270] A creek dividing Chaplin's Island from Fripp's Island (also called Prentis Island), in the chain of Hunting Islands.

stine, Slowman,[271] Haskell,[272] young Mickler[273] & Howard Bold.[274] They had caught a good many bass. We were not long at the camp before J.L.C. arrived with a very large buck. Very much troubled with mosquitoes at night, the wind having died away. Got little or no sleep.

Sept. 12th. At the inlet. Went fishing, caught a good many fine fish, no bass. J.L.C. went hunting, killed nothing. Set the shark line, hooked a very large one, carried off stake, line & hook. Heard that Dr. Guerard or Garret[275] lost 6 Negroes—drowned going to Beaufort with a load of blades. Nat Heyward[276] had a fellow that had run away from him, upset in a paddling boat & was out 2 days, & when found had all his toes eaten off by crabs & fish. He is the same fellow that let his master's horses run away in Beaufort the other day & got one of their legs broken.

Sept. 14th. Cuthbert[277] & myself went to the Central Church. Mr. McElheran preached from the text I gave him in an anonymous note last Sunday—And Jesus said unto them, I am sent only to the lost sheep of the house of Israel.[278] I paid great attention to the sermon but do not consider the passage very clearly explained, though I have a different understanding of it now from what I had. Yet it is not entirely cleared up in my mind that, as Christ himself says, I am *only* sent to the *lost sheep of the house of Israel*—that he could, or anyone else could, put a different or any other construction to the words than that *He* was sent to no other people, and more particularly to the *Dogs* as the Jews termed the Gentiles. And I am still left to think that if the Jews had accepted Christ as their Redeemer, the Gentiles never would have received the blessings of a Savior, for it was not until the Jews had rejected Him that He told His apostles to preach the Gospel to all the world. But this I have to say, that I will never be convinced that one passage of the Bible ought to be produced to satisfy any misunderstanding that a person may have of any other passage, and where one is a flat contradiction of the other, one or the other must be wrong—*& the Bible is said to be all truth.*

Sept. 15th. The report not true about the 6 Negroes being drowned in the late storm. Got an invitation to a picnic at Bluffton[279] on the 17th inst.

---

[271] James Slowman (b. 1795), planter.
[272] Isaac Haskell, a joiner, born in New York, and resident of Beaufort.
[273] Deputy Sheriff Mickler's son.
[274] Howard Bold (b. 1830), son of planter William Bold.
[275] Jacob D. Guerard (b. 1793), physician and planter.
[276] Nathaniel Heyward, Jr. (1816–1891), planter. Son of Nathaniel Heyward and Hettie Hutson Barnwell.
[277] Capt. George B. Cuthbert, C.S.A., was killed at Chancellorsville, May, 1863.
[278] Matthew 15:24.
[279] Settlement in St. Luke's Parish, southwest of St. Helena, on the road to Hilton Head.

Heard that Uncle Ben's Robert had stolen $30 from his master & sloped.[280]

Sept. 16th. George Cuthbert left my house last night to stay with Dr. Jenkins. W.O.P. Fripp rode down home with me, went over the crop, thinks it very good.
Note—*everyone that rides over another's crop always pronounces it very good— 1876*

Sept. 18th. Clear, cool & beautiful morning. My day for killing beef for market. Hope I will get a good one, as that fellow McTureous[281] had the impertinence to find fault with the last I killed, though it was better than his.

Sept. 19th. Went to Beaufort. Dined with Bell. Had a writ served on me.[282] Heard that Toomer intended to drop the state action[283] against me, and commenced a civil action on his part.

Sept. 20th. Heard that Edwin Chaplin's son Paul[284] shot his hand so bad yesterday at Bay Point that it had to be amputated just above the wrist joint. The operation was performed this morning by Dr. Guerard. James Fripp's little daughter not expected to live with the scarlet fever. Drove DaCosta's gray horse up from the plantation. He wishes to sell him. Will take seventy dollars for him, and I think he is worth it well.

Sept. 21st. Sunday. Had in yesterday 1989 lbs. of cotton.[285] Planted turnips on the 10th of this month. I planted seed from McMillan[286] some time ago, but they did not come up. Bought this time from Wm. Barnwell[287] & they came up in two days.

   J. Fripp's daughter Eugenia[288] at the point of death, with scarlet fever, some little better this evening. God grant I with my family may escape, for this would be a horrid time to have it in the family—considering the

---

[280] Ran away.
[281] One of the McTureous brothers—Henry, James, John W., or Edward M.—who owned lands at the eastern end of Seaside Road.
[282] See Nov. 1, 1845.
[283] Criminal charges.
[284] Paul Chaplin (b. 1832). Son of Edwin and Elizabeth Chaplin. First cousin to Thomas B. Chaplin on his father's side.
[285] Will reduce to about 500 pounds after ginning, or about a bale and a half.
[286] Capt. Thomas McMillan, planter.
[287] William Wigg Barnwell (1793–1856). Son of Edward Barnwell and Mary Hazzard Wigg. Father of R. G. and Nathaniel Barnwell.
[288] Eugenia Fripp. Daughter of James Fripp and Caroline Edings Sams. Second cousin to Chaplin on her father's side.

situation of Mrs. Chaplin, expecting to be confined every day, and we have so many little negroes in the yard.

Sept. 22nd.   Gave the marsh cutters 14 feet cords to cut for a day's work instead of 12 feet as they have been cutting.

Sept. 23rd.   Sun crosses the line, 12 hours long. Almost as cold as winter, fire very comfortable.

James Fripp's daughter, and Mrs. J. Fripp's[289] only daughter Eugenia died last night about 12 o'clock. Funeral took place this evening at 4 o'clock. Rev. W. Hall[290] officiated. I did not attend—or any of my family. She died of scarlet fever, only a few days' sickness.

Sept. 24th.   Mrs. C. felt so unwell in the evening, I sent off about 7 o'clock for Mrs. Cook. She got here about ½ past 11 at night.

Sept. 25th.   Mrs. C. not taken sick[291] last night as she expected. Mrs. Cook went back to Beaufort, but returned in the evening. Got my pistols from Bell for a few days.

Sept. 26th.   Sent the boat to the main for the rest of the corn. Went home. Did nothing but shoot pistols all day. Returned early.

Inst. after I got home, went upstairs. Mrs. C. complaining, had one or two pains. Knew the time had come. Stayed with her until about 8 o'clock. Sophy went upstairs, and soon after Mrs. Cook went up. I remained in the hall very quietly reading the newspaper, expecting to keep awake nearly all night, when about ten minutes of ten, I heard something like a young child cry. Could hardly believe it was over so soon, but Lo it was. A little *boy*[292] was born. ½ past ten saw him for the first time. Saw Mrs. Cook wash & dress him. He soon eat some butter & sugar. The largest child I ever saw when it was just born. Saw my dear wife, about ten minutes after ten. She does well. How much women suffer for men and how badly some & many of them are treated. I do not think that any male being after seeing how much his wife suffers for him, & can treat her ill after, can have any soul or heart, except so much as will keep life in them. I did not go to bed until after two o'clock though at any other time I

---

[289] Caroline Edings Sams (b. 1816). Daughter of Lewis Reeve Sams and Sarah Fripp. Second cousin to Chaplin on her mother's side.

[290] Wilson Hall (1819–1845). Son of William Hall and Ann Poyas. Studied for the Episcopal ministry but was converted to the Baptist faith. Hall died within three months of Eugenia Fripp.

[291] Did not go into labor.

[292] Eugene Thomas Chaplin (1845–1865), Chaplin's fifth child, and third son.

would have been sleepy. I did not feel so last night even when I went to bed. Left mother & child doing well.

*1876**Good God, the changes since then!!!! And that boy—fell, a victim to a cruel war, his bones molder in an unknown grave in North Carolina. He died from war, pestilence & famine, and cruelty while prisoner in the Yankee army,*[293] *in 1864. Who dreamed of the end when this page was written, 32 years ago. Now, poverty extreme, from affluence & wealth.***

Sept. 27th.   Everything going on very well, wife has a few after pains. Child sucked well this morning. Hope to God it will not have to suck a bottle & what is *ten times worse*, a Negro.

Weather getting much warmer. Mother came up to see her sixth grandchild—just half the number she has had herself.[294] She returned in the evening. Wife appears very well.

Sept. 30th.   Took the boat & went down to Fripps Inlet.[295] Got Uncle Ben's seine, caught very few fish. Heard there were a great many down there is the reason I went. Spent a very uncomfortable night—sand flies & mosquitoes very bad. Carried the tent sticks & forgot the tent. Slept under the sails. Caught but very few fish this night.

Oct. 1st.   Intended going home very early this morning, but the boat got aground & we could not get her off before flood tide. Did not get to the plantation until after sunset, at the village about 9 o'clock.

Oct. 2nd.   Rec'd a letter & answers to the bill filed by Roux against Mother, the Capt. & myself, to be approved by us, that is, as I understand it, we are to say whether we are willing to swear to them or not.[296] Treville sent his own servant over with the papers. I felt very unwell all day.

---

[293] A prisoner *of* the Yankees.

[294] Isabella Baker had one child by Daniel Jenkins and four children by Saxby Chaplin, Sr. In light of this, Chaplin's comment is mystifying.

[295] Bay and creek dividing Hunting Island from Fripp's Island, on the ocean side, in the chain of Hunting Islands.

[296] The answers, as sworn in Equity Court, were:

Mrs. Baker: ". . . when Baker proposed to her, she was disposed to believe, from his pecuniary condition, and the disparity in their ages, that her property was his main object, and would have rejected him, had he not repeatedly assured her that her right 'to do as she should be minded,' from time to time, and always, with every part of her property, after marriage, should be carefully reserved to her, and should always be acknowledged and held sacred by him. . . . She executed these deeds freely, without persuasion or advice on the part of her sons or anyone else. . . ."

Capt. Daniel T. Jenkins: ". . . has had notice of several deeds of appointment from Mrs. Baker to her sons, and being advised she had power under the settlement to execute them, is willing to recognize and give effect to them, and has made some exertions with that view, but owing to the difficulties interposed by his colleague Roux, the

Oct. 4th. Very cloudy this morning. Sent John to the ferry for Wm. Fickling, Magistrate, for the purpose of swearing Mother to her answer to Roux bill, which has to be returned to Treville this evening, as he leaves for Gillisonville tomorrow morning to have a bill of injunction signed against Baker & Roux.[297] He intends petitioning court to have a receiver appointed until the decision of court. Fickling returned in the evening— we played backgammon & billiards, I beat him three games at each.

Oct. 5th. Crickets hollow more tonight than I have ever heard them. *Note the sign.*

Oct. 6th. This day is one week since woman Daphne has been hired to Col. B. J. Johnson. Rode down to the plantation. Commenced breaking in corn. Hands from the Riverside helping us. Made a very poor day's work, broke only 219 baskets. Cotton opening now very well. Much sickness among the children & some grown on the place. John went to Beaufort in the wagon.
For Mother I suppose—'76

Oct. 7th. Rode down to the plantation. Very cloudy, some wind. Broke in 271 baskets of corn, broke in the best of it. Killed a small beef for the Negroes, very fat. Albert Pritchard[298] came to me for a letter of recommendation. Gave him one better than he deserved, but the fellow really appeared distressed. And I was sorry for him, and perhaps this letter may help him to get a good situation, and when he knows he is well off, he may act to remain so.
he did not—76
He is going he says to Charleston. May get in a store.[299]

Oct. 8th. Wednesday. E. & F. Capers came to my house or rather yard yesterday evening, had their horses put up, & went to the vill. Quite con-

---

other trustee, and Baker, and never himself having been in actual possession of the appointed property, he has been unsuccessful. . . ."

Thomas B. Chaplin: ". . . it is untrue that the reservation of power to his mother was inserted in the settlement by contrivance of herself and this defendant and his brother. He is prepared to prove that he was not within seventy miles of Charleston (where the deed was executed) either at the time of its execution or of the marriage, and did not see the settlement for several months after it was executed. . . . It is also untrue that he and his brother persuaded his mother to abandon Baker, &c. Equally untrue, by undue influence, they forced her to execute the deeds of appointment. . . ."
[297] DeTreville seeks to have Baker and Roux enjoined from going onto the disputed plantations or using the slaves and provisions on them. He also wants the court to remove Roux from his trust, leaving Capt. Daniel T. Jenkins as sole trustee.
[298] Albert Pritchard (b. 1815), listed in the 1850 census as a "hunter." The Pritchard family owned land on two sides of the Sandiford Place, on Seaside Road.
[299] He did become a storekeeper, but in Beaufort.

venient for them, but I will fix them. Finished breaking March corn. Made 917 baskets—equal to about 604 bushels. Commenced April or May corn. Do not expect to make half as much as I did March corn.

Oct. 9th.   Commenced my young corn, planted the middle & last of May. Turning out very badly. Had in 132 baskets when I left home. Killed another small beef for the Negroes. Minott[300] & the Capers went down to the Hunting Islands today. I believe Codding[301] went also. I pity them when the mosquitoes begin to sting. Called to see Uncle Tom.[302]

Oct. 10th.   Home again. Expect John Webb[303] from the main. Sent John to Beaufort in the wagon for things I expect from town. Finished breaking corn before dinner—made only 295 baskets in the whole.
late corn Picked peas in the afternoon. John Webb came about 4½ o'clock, landed at the wharf. Started from Grahamville[304] at 9 o'clock a.m. John got back from Beaufort, about 9 a.m. Brought the things I sent to Robb[305] for. **Note writing crooked**[306]

Oct. 11th.   Mr. Tom Reilly[307] & O. Fripp came over to the billiard room & played cards & billiards until dinner. Webb & myself took it out in wine & backgammon after dinner.
Note '76   Good old times, eh!
    One of the most gloomy days I have seen this season.
Note '76   The gloom of those days were sunshine to these.

Oct. 13th.   Very cold last night. Slept cold under one blanket. If the wind had not blown so hard, I am certain there would be frost. I have seen frost when it was not as cold as it was last night. Think if the wind falls we will have it tonight. Then goodbye to my cotton. Webb & myself dined with Dr. Jenkins, supped also. Fickling came over from Beaufort in the evening. Brought the good news that the chancellor had signed the order for the transfer of the stock.

Oct. 14th.   John Webb started home in my boat, with fair wind in evening. Gave him a Berkshire pig & a pair of East India geese.

---

[300] John Minott.
[301] Elisha Codding (b. 1799), C. G. Capers's overseer.
[302] Thomas J. Chaplin (1772–1855), planter. Son of Thomas B. Chaplin and Elizabeth Fripp. Young Thomas B. Chaplin's paternal uncle. Lived just east of Tombee, between his nephew and his brother Paul. He was a bachelor.
[303] John Webb (1800–1866), planter. This John Webb, a cousin of the St. Helena planter by the same name, lived in St. Luke's Parish.
[304] Resort town in St. Luke's Parish. Burned by Sherman in 1865.
[305] William L. Robb (b. 1820).
[306] Chaplin alludes to the effect of his drinking.
[307] Tom Reilly, cotton factor from Charleston.

Oct. 15th.   Fickling went back to Beaufort, I went also. Engaged Jos. D. Pope to assist Treville in the case with Baker.[308] Yesterday the writ of injunction was served on Baker & Roux, preventing them from going on any of the places as they have done to us. The boat returned from Webb's today. He sent me a very fine large boar. Do not know exactly what breed.

Oct. 18th.   Daniel & Maria[309] very restless all night (last). In the morning about 7 o'clock we were greatly alarmed by his being seized with a convulsion, after fretting very much for some time. Sent for Dr. Jenkins. He had four very severe [convulsions] during the day. Maria also quite sick with fever, occasioned I believe by worms. Manny much better in the evening, has not had a fit since dinner. Aunt Betsy[310] called, Mother is here also. Given up all idea of going away today, may go tomorrow, though very much against it, but the business is so very urgent. Hope to God they may be well enough whether I go or not.

Oct. 20th.   Both children much better, Maria up & dressed. And my having very urgent business in town I determined to go—everybody said the children were out of danger, and I could very well go—Started in the rain about 10 o'clock. Rained all day. Left Beaufort about 3 p.m., in a very heavy rain. Horrid night, constant rain.

Oct. 21st.   Arrived in town[311] about 1 o'clock p.m. Still raining. And O! my God how little did I think that at that time my poor dear Maria was no more. What suffering and distress at home—if I had known it at that time, what would have been my feelings, when I know I could not get back home until the next Friday. Met Fickling in town. The stock[312] had just been sold by the master, brought ten thousand five hundred & sixty dollars.

Oct. 22nd.   Called on Mr. Gray. Had a settlement with him in the evening.[313]

---

[308] Joseph D. Pope and Richard DeTreville formally became partners in 1853.
[309] Maria Louisa Chaplin (1841–1845). Chaplin's second child and eldest daughter.
[310] Elizabeth Hann Jenkins Chaplin (1785–1867). Wife of Chaplin's Uncle Ben. Daughter of John Jenkins and Mary Fripp, thus also Chaplin's first cousin, twice removed, on her father's side. Her brother Daniel was Isabella Baker's first husband. Another brother, Benjamin, was the husband of Elizabeth Perry, the mother of Daniel P. and William J. Jenkins, Chaplin's "Cousin Betsy." Aunt Betsy and Cousin Betsy were sisters-in-law.
[311] Charleston.
[312] From Mary Chaplin's inheritance.
[313] Gray represented Chaplin in the stock transaction.

Oct. 23rd. Drew the money out of the bank. Fickling & myself hired a hack & went shopping. We dined with Major Webb.[314]

Oct. 24th. Left the city at 9 a.m. and arrived in Beaufort about 3 o'clock p.m., there for me to receive the greatest shock it has ever been my lot to experience. My feelings of horror cannot be described, when on stepping from the boat on the wharf to meet Jos. D. Pope, who said he had something to say to me, and what was it? *That my child was dead.* My first thought that it was Manny, but no, the one that I thought the least ill of the two when I left home—*she* it was that had been taken away. She was taken ill shortly after I left on Monday, and on Tuesday at 10 o'clock she was dead. No one knows exactly what was the matter. I felt that the cold unrelenting hand of death was closed on her forever. Twas not till then that I felt my loss & the anguish & distress of my *poor poor* wife. She too in such wretched health. May God spare her & give her the strength to bear up in this our day of trouble & sorrow.

Oct. 25th. Saturday. Today was performed that *last mournful duty,* the burial of the dead. The service was performed by the Rev'd. D. McElheran at 11 o'clock a.m. at the Central Church where I deposited the remains of my daughter, whom it has pleased God in His wisdom to take from this world of sin, at her tender age.

Oct. 26th. Charming day. At home all day. Daniel much better. Wife still suffering much with her breast.

Oct. 27th. Took Ernest with me & rode down to the plantation. Returned to a late dinner. Cotton opening very fast. Could not see after much. Wife suffering most excruciating pain with her breast. It has risen very large and almost black. Daniel much better.

Oct. 29th. Saw J. R. Toomer. He has promised before witnesses that he would drop all proceedings against me, on condition that I would tell him who it was that told me he had spoken against me, which I agreed to do.

Our company[315] went into camp last Monday, or that is, a small part of it, to be encamped five days, but from the small number & some mismanagement they broke up in two days. There was also a procession of the Order of Odd Fellows on the 25th & as I heard, a fine address delivered by Jos. D. Pope. And all of this happened when I was burying my child. Sent Mary[316] home in the wagon. The carts came up in the evening to move us home tomorrow. Dr. Jenkins, Uncle Ben, Dr. Scott moved

[314] John Webb, of St. Luke's Parish. Later called Col. Webb.
[315] Beaufort Volunteer Artillery.
[316] The slave Mary.

today. Coz. Ann Chaplin, Jos. Pope & James Fripp moved yesterday. W.O.P. Fripp last week.

Oct. 30th. Flat did not come last night as I expected. Started off five carts & the wagon. Wife a great deal better. Stood the ride home remarkably well. Stayed at the village until after 3 o'clock & no flat came. Dined with Mother & came on down. Found all safe & sound. One cart left on the road, black colt would not draw. So here we are again. We have brought back as many as we carried, yet there is one missing. That one will never return, not to this home. She has gone to a home prepared for her in heaven. The flat did not start from here until this morning.

Oct. 31st. Cotton blowing very fast, the field perfectly white. Sent three carts & the wagon to the village for Mother & her things. The carriage went in the evening, the flat got here about dusk. Wm. Jenkins rode over in the evening. Heard that Coz. Ann Chaplin was engaged to be married to Wm. B. Fripp.[317] Had in this morning in cotton nine thousand eight hundred & seventy-two weight.[318]

Nov. 1st. Parade day of our company. Went to Beaufort. Glad to find after I got there that there was no parade, it was put off for another time. Paid O'Connor[319] his judgment against me. This is the last paper of the kind out against me, and now my property is safe, and secured to my family. Wm. Fripp Snr. spoke to me & agreed if I would pay half the cost to drop his suit against me, which agreed to. So the two cases against me for the next court are dropped, and well for me. Mother came down from the village. All of the things could not be brought in the carts & wagon.

Some rogue broke open the carriage house door yesterday but found nothing to gratify his thieving desire. Got a box of clothes from Edgerton & Richards.[320]

Note 1876 Said box of clothes cost more than enough to supply me with clothes at this time for two or three years.

Nov. 2nd. Found about seven hogs in my slips—destroyed about one task.[321]

---

[317] Ann Fripp Jenkins, widow of Chaplin's first cousin William S. Chaplin, and William B. Fripp, widower of Chaplin's first cousin Eliza Chaplin, were first cousins, once removed.

[318] About seven bales, after ginning and cleaning.

[319] Michael O'Connor (1795–1859), Irish-born Beaufort merchant.

[320] E. W. Edgerton and Frederick Richards, Charleston tailors. In 1851 they acquired exclusive right in Charleston to sell the new Patent Sewing Machine—an invention that spurred world demand for cotton—and secured the testimonial of Saxby Chaplin, among others, to use in advertising.

[321] One-quarter acre.

Nov. 3rd.   28 hands picked today, 933 lbs. of cotton. At this rate I will get in about 2 bales in 3 days.

Nov. 4th.   Put the two Johns, Ben & January at pulling hay.[322] Clear & cold all day. Think we will have frost tonight and a continuation of cold weather, as there were a number of robins seen this morning, the first seen in this neighborhood this season. Gave an allowance of corn this morning—16 b., 2 pks., 1 qt.[323]

Took Jack in the house as a waiter. The Major rode over in the evening. Finished shingling the boat house. My four sows have had a full service of the boar that J. Webb sent me. Daniel was quite sick again this morning, threw up a good quantity of bile. Gave him a little vitriol.[324]

Nov. 5th.   Muster Day on the Island, & an election for captain of the S.H.M.R. Company.[325] W. W. Fripp is the only candidate, and of course he will be elected.

Manny[326] was very restless last night, slept very little. The baby also very fretful. Dan threw up again this morning. Went out to the muster house, dined. I am one of the finders in January. W. W. Fripp was elected capt. of the company. The Capt. D. Jenkins stopped & took tea with me. Mr. C. G. Capers gave me today about two quarts of the California wheat seed, raised from a few heads I gave him about two years ago. I had lost all the seed I had.

Nov. 6th.   Yesterday I made the best picking of cotton I have made this season: 28 hands old & young, little & big, brought in 963 lbs.[327] Anthony Snr. & Stephen sick (fever). Took Ernest to ride on horseback. He rode Fanny Douglass, the first time he has ever rode so far by himself on a horse. We went all round the field.

Nov. 7th.   Friday. Yesterday was Thanksgiving Day, appointed by the church for this Island. There was service at the Episcopal Church. Send John to Beaufort. Sent for Dr. Jenkins to Daniel. He was restless last night & looked very bad this morning. The Dr. gave him calomel[328] & castor oil. The medicine operated & he seems much better this evening. Had

---

[322] Cutting hay with a sickle.

[323] Sixteen bushels, two pecks, one quart.

[324] Green vitriol, or copperas (iron sulfate), a caustic salt.

[325] St. Helena Mounted Riflemen, a volunteer cavalry outfit attached to the 12th Regiment, S.C. Infantry. See note, April 1, 1856.

[326] Daniel.

[327] Equal to about eight pounds of cleaned cotton apiece—or $2 worth of marketable cotton per hand, at 25 cents a pound.

[328] Mercurous chloride, a purgative.

twenty-eight hands picking peas. I offered a prize to the three best pickers, of pieces of bacon—different sizes. Peter took the first prize, Sylvia 2nd, & Robert 3rd. All hands picked in 3800 lbs. Pick again tomorrow if weather permits. Dr. Jenkins rode over again in evening to see Daniel. He is not much better.

Nov. 8th.   26 hands picking peas. Picked well in the morning. The idea of getting meat encourages them very much. Peter ahead 183 lbs. Sent John to the ferry with Black Hawk & the sulky. I have lent him to Fickling to go up to Gillisonville to court. Gave Daniel a dose of oil this morning. He appears to be something better.

Commenced raining pretty hard about 3 p.m. Ran the Negroes out of the field—did not quite finish the patch. Peter won the 1st prize, Robert 2nd, a tie between Helen & Isaac 3rd, & Amy 4th. **3657**[329]

Nov. 9th.   Sunday. Went to church in the morning. Heard that Capt. J. Fripp's child died yesterday (Mary).[330] Daniel quite sick again this evening.

Nov. 11th.   Gave the Negroes a part of the morning to get in their corn. Commenced digging slips about 10 a.m. Made a poor day's work. Got in 3 banks of leathercoats, pumpkin, Spanish & reds[331]—buried them in the garden. Dug about 6 or 7 tasks & did not see a single good sized eating potato. Dug in one or two tasks of roots.[332] Got about one bank. Gave the most of them out to the Negroes for allowance. I think I will make enough seed, but no eating potatoes of any consequence, perhaps not enough for house use.[333]

Nov. 12th.   Wednesday. Jno. Chaplin and Dnl. Jenkins went down with me to the Hunting Island. The Major, Uncle Ben & Wm. Jenkins went down also. The two latter returned the same evening. We had very good sport. I killed a deer not an hour after we landed, and broke the leg of another shortly after, which we ran in the surf and waited until it came out, when Wm., Major & self shot at it. I shot it down the last shot. The two

---

[329] Pounds of peas.
[330] Mary Fripp. Daughter of John W. Fripp and Elizabeth McKean. Chaplin's first cousin, twice removed, on her father's side.
[331] Four varieties of potato. Chaplin stored them in earthen banks, with from fifteen to thirty baskets—up to fifteen bushels—to the bank.
[332] Chaplin is harvesting potatoes he planted from both slips and seeds. The latter were also called root potatoes.
[333] Includes food for the Chaplin family and for the house and yard slaves who did not receive allowances but were fed from the provisions set aside for the house.

puppies were there—the deer not being shot dead, had a long fight with it, and they performed admirably. They never smelt a deer track before but took it naturally & ran like old dogs. Two deer killed before them this day. Ben killed a large boar, the dogs did not see it. Wife was quite sick with a pain in her side last night, but appeared much better this morning. Hands digging slips.

Nov. 13th. Went hunting very early. Started several deer, no one but Ben got a shot. He had a fair one, on the open beach, 19 yds., & missed. Dogs ran beautifully—no meat.[334] Weather very fine. Caught a few fish. Returned home in the evening, got home about 8½ p.m. The moon gave very little light, being almost a total eclipse.

Found wife quite sick. She had been very sick all day, but better. Some pain in her left side. Manny much better. Hands digging slips—finished the reds today, got only one bank of eating potatoes (reds). The Major's puppy got in the house before I went to bed & eat nearly all the haunch & loin to the largest deer. The potatoes are turning out very well, considering the time they were planted (middle of August) but the potatoes are small.

Nov. 14th. Friday. Wife a little better. Took Daniel to ride in the buggy. Commenced digging the yam slips, they turn out a good chance[335] of seed potatoes. While I was in the field, I was very much alarmed at seeing John coming down the road very fast. Said wife was very sick. Sent him right on for Dr. Jenkins. When I got home she was much better. She was taken by a violent pain in her stomach, which was greatly relieved by the application of flannel wet in very hot water. The Dr. came about 3 p.m., left medicines & went off. She is a good deal better this evening. I think she requires food and rest, which will do her more good than all the medicines in the world.

I have some slips uncovered which if it should rain would be ruined. Found that my rice which was put away in bulk in the corn house loft was a little molded. Must have been put up wet. Put Ben & John thrashing it out.

Nov. 15th. Saturday. Took all of the children down to Trenchards Beach on Edings Island. The day turned out much finer than I expected & we had quite a pleasant time. The trip & sea air appeared to benefit Daniel a good deal—he eat very hearty. The tide suited rather late, so thought it best to stop at Uncle Ben's & get the children home in his carriage, rather

---

[334] Chaplin withheld meat from the dogs to make them more eager to hunt.
[335] A large quantity.

than send them round in the boat after night. Wife better today. Still a little pain in her side.
Heard that Saxby's wife[336] was confined & has a son.[337]

Nov. 17th.   Monday. Still digging slips, turning out very well, all after the first day. Did twice as well as I had the least idea of. Three rows I dug today turned out 3 bushels of good eating potatoes & 2 bushels of seed & I have no doubt but many other parts of the patch would have yielded as much. From what I have heard & seen I think I am making a better crop of slips than any of my neighbors. Do not think I will finish before tomorrow morning, when if the weather permits I will pick in what peas are in the field, so that the horses can get it. The Major went to Charleston today pr. steamboat.[338] Sent by him for my Negro shoes & cloth.

    Received a letter from Col. Treville after I went to bed. He saw Baker & his two emissaries Nix & DaCosta very thick & thinks they or Baker is planning some way to run some of the Negroes out of the state. But I will keep a watch on him.

Nov. 18th.   Went to Beaufort. Saw Treville He advised me to go to the main & put the Negroes on their guard. Do not like to go at all—damn the place. Capt. Jno. Tealy returned with me, rode in my sulky that Fickling borrowed—he having just returned from Gillisonville the day before.

Nov. 20th.   Borrowed Dr. Jenkins' sulky. Started for the main. Went round by Capt. D. Jenkins. Drove Black Hawk & Priss. Got to White Hall Ferry about 10 a.m. Stopped a short time in Beaufort. Arrived at Hickory Hill about one hour before sunset. Found there—Myers,[339] E. Capers, F. Witsell[340] & Saxby. Stayed there that night, or rather went over with them to Myers', spent the night.

Nov. 21st.   E. Capers & myself went down to Minott's. Sax went to Walterboro.[341] Sax told me that his wife had a little girl[342] about 2 weeks, Friday. Spent the night at Minott's. Saw fellow Bristol, heard that Baker was

---

[336] Anne O'Hear Witsell (1827–1915). Daughter of Frederick C. Witsell and Catherine Hagood, of St. Bartholomew's Parish.
[337] See Nov. 21, 1845.
[338] By steamboat.
[339] Charles M. Myers.
[340] Frederick C. Witsell (1798–1850), planter. Saxby Chaplin's father-in-law.
[341] Summer resort and trading town for planters on the Combahee, Ashepoo, and Edisto rivers; inland seat of Colleton District, and site of the first nullification meeting, in 1828.
[342] Caroline Isabella Chaplin (1845–1935).

at the Point, pretending, as I think, to be an agent of Roux's, for I do not think that Roux has that power. I sent for Nix at the Point. He came over & I had a long talk with him. He acknowledged that Baker was on the Point Place & making use of the provisions, but could not get him to swear to the fact. However he said it before a witness which I think will answer.[343]

Note many years after— All of this was real foolery. None of that property ever benefited me or mine in the least. Mother died. Baker ditto, & the war swept off all the Negroes. The land lost also, & now owned I hear by Negroes. 1876

Nov. 22nd.   Sent John before day in the morning on one of Saxby's horses to take a letter to Col. Treville in Beaufort to know from him what course I should adopt. Ned had nothing much to eat, Minott not leaving the keys, so we went back to H[ickory] Hill. On the way had a glimpse of Baker—not man enough to distinguish. If I had known him, who it was—but Ned said it was his buggy. As soon as he spied someone, he jumped out of his buggy & got behind a pine tree with his gun. I had nothing but a pistol, therefore did not think proper to approach. Before I could get a gun however, he made off. We went on to H[ickory] Hill. John returned that night with a letter from Treville, which advised me to see Mr. Perry, his partner in Walterboro, and get out a writ against Baker.

Nov. 23rd.   Started for Walterboro in a cold drizzle rain. Could not see Perry—got C. B. Farmer,[344] a lawyer & magistrate, to draw up certain papers, left them for Perry. Stayed with Sax this night. Cleared off in the eve.

Nov. 24th.   Saxby & myself left Walterboro for H[ickory] Hill. Took Farmer with me for the purpose of swearing any men I could get as good witnesses. Very cold day, saw plenty of ice. Got to the Hill for dinner.

Nov. 25th.   Tuesday. Send down very early for Capers. He came up to dinner. We all rode over to Francis Nix's. This Nix attends to the business at the Dunham Place,[345] but lives at Barnett Elliott's.[346] We did not find

---

[343] Chaplin is collecting evidence for his case. Roux and Baker are under injunction to keep off the plantation.
[344] Charles Baring Farmer (1823–1885). Later became a commissioner in equity for Colleton District.
[345] Isabella Baker's 1,200-acre plantation at the headwaters of the Ashepoo River. She has deeded it to her son Thomas.
[346] Barnard Smith Elliott (1824–1850). Son of Barnard Elliott and Juliet Gibbes, of St. Bartholomew's Parish.

him at home, so we returned, having left a note for him requesting him to come to H[ickory] Hill the next morning.

Nov. 26th.   Nix came over very early. He said a good many things before witnesses, but I could not get him to swear. Took affidavits of E. Capers & F. Witsell of what both the Nixes said. I started home about 1 o'clock p.m., got across Beaufort Ferry about sunset, & at home about 7½ o'c. Commenced working the roads. Had out one-third of the hands only working at the Ferry Bridge. I had five hands there. They did not finish it.

Nov. 27th.   All hands commenced our division of roads. Met at Jno. L. Chaplin's seat. Worked down to Lands End, a thing they had not done for ten years.

     Mary[347] was confined whilst I was away, the night before I got back, child born dead—did not see it.

Nov. 28th.   I kept my hands back from the road today—for the work I did on the road last summer. Saw ice this morning, the first I expect that we have had here. Yesterday was very cold and windy, last night one of the coldest nights I ever felt. Send John to the village.

Nov. 29th.   All hands to working on the road, last day, first day I attended. Capt. D. Jenkins' overseer gave me 21 hands, all of my own & Uncle Ben's. Dined at the same line. Jos. & Tom Perry[348] found dinner. Commenced working again at 3 p.m. Could not finish the road as far as where we left off last year, by nearly a quarter of a mile. Knocked off at sunset, not to meet before next year. Tom Perry will be off the list by that time.

Nov. 30th.   Sunday, last day of this month. Very cloudy & cold. Mother & Sophy went to church. Daniel had the croup last night, coughed a great deal.

     Was a little astonished this morning at seeing a steamboat passing in Station Creek.[349] I have some distant idea of either seeing or hearing of one or two passing this way before. She just got by when she either got aground, or is waiting for the next high water.

     Gave out Negro cloth & shoes on the 27th inst. Cloth for field hands,

[347] The slave Mary.
[348] Joseph Perry (b. 1810), planter, and Thomas Perry (b. 1800), planter, sons of Joseph L. Perry.
[349] Tidal creek between St. Helena and Eddings Islands, parallel to the coastline. The Big House at Tombee faced Station creek.

men & women, price 45 cts. For children, & old Negroes, 38 cts.[350] Shoes 75 cts. pr. pair.

Dec. 1st. Monday. All hands assorting cotton.[351] 4 men on the Island for wood. My turn to kill veal for market, & the last did not have one fit to kill. My cattle are so very poor. I have never seen them in such bad order, and I expect to lose a good many before they get the field.[352] Had to send to try & get one from one of the three uncles.[353] Heard this morning that the steamboat that passed yesterday was sent for the purpose of examining & marking out the navigation through from Broad River to St. Helena Sound, for the purpose of one of the boats running from Savannah to Charleston passing through this way occasionally. I hope they will make a business of it. They will receive my support. About 11, two men from Anderson Dist.[354] (I do not know their names) came here this morning, to know if I wished any cattle spayed or horses altered, which appears to be their *profession,* and travel about for that purpose. I got them to alter my black horse Charley, which they did in short order. First put a twitch on him & did it while he was standing up without all the trouble of tying & throwing the horse. They said they could spay a milch cow, & she would continue to give milk as long as she lived without having another calf. They charged me only $2 for altering the horse & offered to insure his life for two more.

Gave out the first & only allowance of potatoes. Got a veal from Uncle Tom. It was in good order. Wind blew hard all night. Sent Ben after ducks—he got three.

Dec. 2nd. Got a new & very fine strong cart from Charleston with harness, sent me by Ingraham & Webb.[355] Got the signet ring sent me by Heyden & Gregg,[356] brought up from town by Fickling.

Dec. 4th. Saw a large steamboat pass in the creek early this morning, think it was the *Cincinnati* from Savannah. This is our Agricultural Society day. W. J. Jenkins finds dinner. Do not think many will attend such weather. Ordered the cattle turned into the field & minded out of the cotton. Went out to the Society house. Met only 4 members & two visitors.

---

[350] Six yards of cloth were allotted to every field hand, and five yards to every other slave, twice a year—at a cost, then, of about 7½ cents per yard.

[351] Separating white cotton from yellow or stained cotton, and picking out leaves and trash, preparatory to ginning.

[352] After the cotton was picked, the cows were turned into the fields to forage.

[353] Ben, Tom, and Paul—brothers of Saxby Chaplin, Sr.

[354] District in the northwest part of the state.

[355] George H. Ingraham (1804–1888) and Thomas Ladson Webb, cotton factors and plantation merchants, in Charleston.

[356] Sidney Hayden and William Gregg, Charleston jewelers and silversmiths. They also sold fire insurance.

Jenkins found an excellent dinner & no one to eat it. Returning, stopped at Uncle Ben's a few moments.

Dec. 5th.　Clear fine day. Rode patrol. Killed the first hog. Belcher called, dined & spent the night, played several games of backgammon. He intends leaving Mr. Capers if he cannot get more scholars so as to make it worth his while to stay. He leaves on Monday. Received an invitation to Catherine Scott's wedding. She is to be married next Thursday night, to J. D. Pope.

Dec. 8th.　All hands picking cotton. Phyllis has been in the house for a month, expecting to be confined every day, but came out today, as she is rather doubtful as to the time.

Dec. 9th.　Rode patrol at 10 a.m. I being leader, did not ride more than a hundred yards in the road & dismissed. Went on & got Tom Perry & his dogs & took a cat hunt. It rained so late this morning that we did not start one.

Dec. 10th.　Commenced yesterday to move my cow pen over the root patch[357] for next year. Sent 4 hands on the Island for wood. Carpenters ditto to bring off shingles. All the balance, assorting cotton. Tried to get a race between John L. Chaplin's little bay mare, though I ought not to run my mare as she is in foal, but he thinks his mare can beat mine. His mare would not keep the track. She bolted twice, the third time I let her start ahead, but she crossed over directly—I had ordered my boy not to leave his track—my mare almost touching the other & hand in hand. The next trial, my mare was 15 yds. ahead when the other mare bolted. J. Chaplin's mare is kept steady in the stable, & my mare most of the time in the pasture.

Dec. 11th.　Jos. D. Pope is to be married tonight, hope he may have good weather for the occasion. Went to the wedding at 7 o'clock. Commenced raining just before I got there. However there were a great many persons there, a host of Popes from St. Luke's.[358] There were four bridesmaids & 4 groomsmen. Everything went off very well—a very good supper, & very mean champagne. Dr. Scott retired soon after the ceremony was performed. He looks very badly. Pope had the whole of the Beaufort band[359] over, the music was poor enough. Returned home about 3½ o'clock in the rain.

---

[357] To fertilize his potato ground, Chaplin encloses his cattle on it.
[358] Joseph D. Pope's second cousins—Franklin P., Richard R., and William J.—from Hilton Head Island.
[359] Band of the Beaufort Volunteer Artillery.

Dec. 14th. Looks a little like clearing this morning. Rode over to Toomer's,[360] found my largest bacon hog dead. No one knows what was the matter with him.

Dec. 15th. Still raining. Wind got round NW about ten o'clock, think it may blow off about 12 m. Put all the men to shelling corn. Clears off about evening & blows violently. Blew down fences & trees, had to tie up some young trees in the yard.

Dec. 16th. Sent the boat & five hands to Beaufort. Commenced ginning with 7 hands, moting with 7, balance overhauling the yellow cotton to get what white there is in it.[361] Wind so high the boat could not go to Beaufort, hands returned, went to ginning, making 10 hands.

Dec. 17th. Wednesday. Clear & cold, very heavy white & black frost.[362] A little cloudy about midday, but clears. Sent the boat to Beaufort. Started 7 gins, but the day turning out so fine, put all hands picking cotton—a very good blow in the field. Gave Carter's Hill up to the cattle. They are dying so fast, 4 down this morning. Dr. Jenkins & Ed Morrall called. Lent all of the chairs to the Dr. for his party tonight, to which we are invited. Went to the party about 6 o'clock. Spent a very agreeable evening. It was quite a large party & an excellent supper, far better than the wedding. The bride & groom[363] were there.

Dec. 20th. Clear & bitter cold, the coldest weather we have had for 2 years. Freezing at 12 o'clock in the day, & the sun shining bright. Icicles hanging on the pump a foot long. All hands ginning. Phyllis was delivered of a girl child, name [   ].

Dec. 21st. Sunday. Very cold & windy last night. Clear & still this morning but too cold to do anything but sit by the fire, much less to go & sit for hours in a cold church. This is the coldest weather I ever felt on this island. Everything frozen—ice 3 inches thick. The creek in front of the house frozen across, which has not been the case since all the orange trees were destroyed, and I think they stand a slim chance this winter.[364] Their

---

[360] Toomer's woods.

[361] Seven slaves are working at individual gins, separating the cotton seed from the lint; seven are picking out the "motes" or stained bits and cracked seeds from the lint; the other hands are picking through the stained stuff to find scraps of the more valuable white cotton.

[362] A killing frost.

[363] Catherine Scott and Joseph D. Pope.

[364] Citrus groves had to be replanted after exceptionally cold winters. A climatic shift late in the century ended prospects for commercial citrus farming on the Sea Islands.

leaves now & also the cabbage & nearly everything else look as if boiling water has been poured on them.

Sent to borrow Uncle Ben's carriage to send Mother to the main tomorrow. Dr. Jenkins would not lend his. *Wife rules—*[365]

Dec. 22nd. Clear but not quite as cold as yesterday, however all the ponds are thickly frozen over & have not melted all day. All hands picking cotton. Mother started for the main. Drove my mares to the ferry. Tony went early with the carriage horses to go on from Beaufort.

Put a cow with a young calf up in the stable on the 20th to get milk night & morning.

Dec. 23rd. Heavy white frost. Clear in the morning, but soon clouds up which is generally the case after a heavy frost. Borrowed six oars of the Major to go down to the Island tomorrow. All the men getting wood on the Island. Killed a wether[366] in the morning. Sent pieces to Coz. Betsy Jenkins & to Uncles Paul & Tom.

Request my dear wife, as a Christmas favor to me, to continue my journal until I return from the Hunting Islands. To record some of her thoughts and observations, also any little occurrences that may take place during the absence of her husband, whether concerning the family or the plantation. If she does this, she will oblige her husband, & he will also do (or not do) what will oblige her while he is away.[367]

Dec. 25th. Thursday. Christmas Day. Dull. Dull. Dull. No rain but very thick & foggy, do not think we will be able to go down to the Island. Capt. & J. L. Chaplin came over in the morning to go—the latter *pretty well corned.*[368] Very sorry for it, but do not know what to do with him. If we go will have to take him down with us. Killed 2 beefs for the Negroes this morning. Looks a little like clearing—wind NW. Got a very early dinner & started for the Island. Got down & pitched our tent by dark. Cloudy all night, but we slept very comfortably. Not very cold.

Dec. 26th. Went out hunting very early. While the dogs were trailing, a large buck jumped up near to the stand I was at. Jumped out in the cove, & I got a chance to shoot. Hit him very badly with both barrels. J. Chaplin had a shot just after, but did not hit him. Got the dogs on, & after a beautiful chase of about an hour, caught him. My pups performed well.

[365] Eliza Jenkins felt a keen rivalry with her cousin Thomas B. Chaplin. She was a niece of Chaplin's Uncle Ben, and like Thomas she had ambitions toward the property of the childless old man. *"Wife rules"* is mildly insulting to Dr. Jenkins, Chaplin's lifelong competitor.

[366] A castrated ram.

[367] Mary did not write anything in her husband's journal at this time.

[368] Drunk.

They caught & fought him for a half hour before I came up with a knife to cut his throat. Wm. Jenkins & the Major came down about ten o'clock & joined us. After they came I shot a very large boar. Killed nothing more this day. I gave them a forequarter of the buck.

Wind blowing very hard from NW & very cold—but we had our tent in a snug corner, & a large fire.

Dec. 27th. Saturday. Very cold, thick ice. Wild ducks all left the ponds and took to the woods & rushes. Went hunting very early. Jumped two deer, large doe & yearling. I shot down the doe. We were all together. The Capt., J. Chaplin both fired at the yearling, but did not kill it. They think they both hit it, however we never got it. The doe was very large & very fat. We killed nothing more this day but a few ducks. Returned to the camp, took dinner, broke up & came home, got here about dark, after having spent a very pleasant Christmas & had much sport, neither of which we hardly expected when we started. Nor did anyone else—
Who were the "else"

Dec. 29th. Dined with the Capers. Called on the Rivers.[369] Spent a pleasant day. Saw one or two horse races. The Rivers are quite clever.
Whiskey drinkers, gone to nuts. 1876

Dec. 30th. Edward Capers, Robert Rivers & Mr. McElheran dined with me. All had a good deal to say, particularly Mr. McE.
All got tight on cider & whiskey

Dec. 31st. Frank Capers & C. Rivers came round to invite me to a party tomorrow night (New Year's), & to get John & Ben as fiddlers. I do not feel well, & do not intend to go, too much frolicking will not do. Drank too much liquor today. Wife emptied all the brandy out of the window. Which closes the old year, now for the New.

End of
The year of our Lord
1845

Note made 32 years after, & I suppose more brandy. When I think, an opinion is really worth something, & my opinion now, at this late day, when I am 54 years old, is candidly that that very throwing away my costly liquor out of the windows to prevent me from drinking it was wrong in the extreme, & did much more harm than good. It was continued, & even to this day, but it is wrong & useless waste & real foolery—I have no doubt that at least $500 worth in all has thus been destroyed for no earthly good.

[369] Robert (b. 1814) and Cornelius (b. 1824) Rivers, sons of George Chisolm Rivers and Elizabeth Reynolds.

1846

Jan. 1st.   Thursday, New Year's Day, A.D. 1846. Packed the first bale of cotton. Virginia,[1] Daniel & wife all sick—hope, according to the old saying, it won't be so all the year. Capers' party tonight. Send the boys but do not go myself. A little cloudy & windy in the evening & blows very hard all night. New Year's Day comes in with calm & sunshine & goes out with storm & rain. Is this to be the season of the year?

Jan. 3rd.   W. Jenkins, Danl. P. & Danl. Jenkins[2] called. When they left I took my wife, Ernest & Daniel out to ride in the carriage. The day looked so fine—but such a ride. Just as we were crossing a bridge on the causeway over the Sands, the plank being rotten, Black Hawk as he stepped on the second plank (& luckily for us the carriage wheels had not yet reached it), the plank broke. Hyder stepped on it almost at the same time. Their forefeet being over they both fell in backwards, breaking 3 planks, and the ditch being very deep, they could not touch and there they hung, with no part above the bridge but their forefeet, necks & heads. I jumped out as soon as I heard the crash & got my family out safe but very much frightened. John held the horses down with all his might by the reins, until I could loose the traces & pole straps, when we with great exertion pulled away the planks that were behind them, but there they hung on the sleepers,[3] & their forefeet on the plank in front for a half hour or more. When by pulling them backwards got their hind feet to touch, Hyder, as soon as his feet touched, he wheeled round & with surprising activity jumped over the sleeper as high as his neck, with very little injury. Think he is strained a good deal.

---

[1] Virginia Sophia Chaplin (1842–1867), Chaplin's third child.
[2] The Doctor, the Major, and the Captain.
[3] Longitudinal beams which support the crosswise planks.

Jan. 3rd.[4]   Saturday. Black Hawk being more bruised, having struggled more, being astride one of the sleepers could not get out until we prized away the outside sleeper & led him out. He is badly cut in 2 or 3 places, but they are both better off than I had the most distant idea they would be when I saw them hanging in the bridge. They drew us back home in the carriage and after being bathed in lye & well rubbed, are doing very well. Hawk a little stiff. Daniel was so frightened I thought he would have a fit.

Jan. 5th.   Heavy fog, cloudy. Took wife to ride.
Could I have been a very bad husband to forgive the brandy so soon? 1876
   Anthony Snr. very sick. Peter cut his foot very bad last night with an axe. All hands picking cotton, excepting sick & some on the Island for wood.

Jan. 6th.   3 carts hauling out cow pen manure. All hands planting oats. Sent John & Ben to the Island for game—returned with six ducks. Showery & sunshine all day, one very heavy shower, which I got caught in, being out in the field. Did not finish planting oats, have not land enough plowed. Driver Anthony very sick, sent for Dr. Jenkins to see him. He has a very bad leg from the effects of the sting of a stingray some years ago. Daniel was quite sick again this morning, taken in the same way—vomiting, before or at breakfast & ending in the most extreme debility & faintness.
   The carts are hauling manure on the Pine Sapling Field next to Uncle Ben's line. Mr. Tom Chaplin,[5] commissioner on roads, called today, to see after the bridge my horses fell in. He has directed me to summon out five hands from the Capt., Uncles Paul, Ben, & Tom, & one of my own to have it repaired, as he supposes in one day, & hew out stuff for it.

Jan. 8th.   Commenced getting out stuff for the bridge. The Capt. came over & assisted me, had five hands, got stuff in Uncle Ben's woods near the bridge. Delightful day, warm & clear. 3rd visit Dr.'s to Anthony. The commissioner rode down to see how we were getting on (quite consequential). All hands picking cotton except 3 on the Island for wood & Peter laying up with a very bad cut on his foot.

Jan. 9th.   Friday. Went to Beaufort to see Treville. The Capt. came over, breakfasted & went with me to Beaufort. Left the management of the

---

[4] Chaplin wrote and dated two entries on this day.
[5] Thomas Chaplin, Jr. (b. 1799), planter, of Ladies Island. Second cousin of Thomas B. Chaplin on his father's side.

bridge work to my fellow Sawney. A great many persons went across the ferry. Among them were Martha Fripp,[6] Julia Scott[7] & Mary Pope[8] on their way to Montpelier, Geo. to school.[9] Treville informed me that he had an order from the chancellor to put Baker in jail if he did not leave the Point & give up every part of the property he had in use. Baker has left the Point, but still has two of the Negroes in his possession, Aaron & August.[10]

Had a few hands picking cotton today, finishing out the field. There is still a good deal of cotton in the field, but this is the last day I shall pick this year, or season, for fear I shall be too late getting out what I have in. Some hands ginning. Quite cloudy this morning & I thought it would rain, but cleared off very prettily. John plowing & finishing planting the oats. Finished the bridge in very good style.

Jan. 10th. Took a cat hunt—started nothing. J. Perry, Major & Capt. were out with me. Started Tom with the ox cart at the manure, making 4 carts. All hands ginning, moting and assorting cotton. John still at the oats—not finished. Isaac acting as driver during Anthony's sickness. He does remarkably well.

Jan. 11th. Took Sophy to church in the buggy—weather quite cool, but clear & a bright sun. A meeting of the vestry was called today for the purpose of putting the following question to Mr. McElheran—viz., do you intend becoming a citizen of the United States & when?[11] I did not have the content of his letter in reply, but understand that it was not at all satisfactory to the vestry, & signified that the vestry had no right to question his politics. I do not know where this thing will end. Some of the vestry seem to be determined, that if he does not take the oath of allegiance, he must quit the Island, or the church at least. I think it a very uncalled for matter on the part of the vestry, and now that there is no likelihood of a war with England,[12] they had better let it drop. Mr. McE. has too much

---

[6] Martha S. Fripp (1825–1900). Daughter of Capt. John Fripp and Fripp's first wife, Caroline Chaplin. Chaplin's second cousin on her father's side.
[7] Julia Scott. Daughter of Dr. John Scott and Sarah Chaplin. Chaplin's first cousin, once removed, on her mother's side.
[8] Mary Pope. Daughter of J.J.T. Pope and Mary Townsend, of the Oaks Plantation.
[9] Montpelier Episcopal Female Institute, near Macon, Georgia. Under the direction of Rt. Rev. Stephen Elliott, Jr., the school offered a "full corps of competent Teachers for all branches of English Education, Music, Drawing, Painting, French, &c. . . ."
[10] Dispossessed by his wife's deeds to her sons, Baker has kept two of the contested slaves.
[11] Rev. McElheran was a native of Ireland.
[12] A compromise had recently ended the dispute between the United States and England over the northwest boundary of the Oregon Territory.

interest in this country to do anything against it. All the relations & property he is worth in the world are here, & he is a denizen of this state.

Jan. 12th. Monday. Went down to Trenchards, took Ernest with me. Stayed all night. Shot a few ducks, did not see any fish. Went out striking at night.[13]

Jan. 13th. Took a hunt, did not start anything but a cat.

Jan. 14th. Robert, Ben & Sancho sick since yesterday. Got along slow with ginning. Have only 4 bales packed today. Anthony still sick with his foot. Bought a hog from John weighing 136 lbs. gross, at $4 pr. 100, $5.44.
　　Planted a bed of green peas. Traded with J.E.L. Fripp yesterday—1 pr. of East India geese for 3 turkeys. Have now 54 geese all together.

Jan. 15th. Commenced to rain very hard just before day, wet gloomy day. Robert & Anthony still sick. All hands shelling corn, & finished assorting the last cotton picked, & overhauling the ginned cotton for the bag. Killed a hog, making the 4th I have killed for bacon this year. I have lost one & expect to kill 6 more. Think this weather will continue some time—it looks darker & darker. Lent my sulky to the Major to go on the main last Monday—he was to have returned today, but do not think he can, or will come. Had some rice thrashed. Cleared off & the stars shone out bright just after dark.
　　I have made a very short crop and it appears to me I never was so slow in getting it out. I will hardly finish this month. And most of my neighbors are nearly done listing their land for another crop. J. L. Chaplin still has a good chance of cotton to pick. He was picking last week 40 lbs. to the task. I did not think in the first of the season that his cotton would turn out much more than that in the whole. Wish he had done as well for me.

Jan. 16th. Had a pen made to put marsh in, in the middle of the Home Field. Put 5 good wagon loads of fowl house & hog pen manure on a bit of land back of the old garden to plant sugarcane next week. A few windy looking clouds around the horizon, wind S.W.

Jan. 17th. Planted sugarcane last year on the 3rd of March. Quite clear & pleasant. Went to Beaufort. Sophy went with me to see Mrs. Kirkland. Sent the boat up with Tony & four hands. Got 4 barrels of seed inst. potatoes, a barrel of molasses to sell to the Negroes for corn. Got also a box of

[13] Fishing for flounder or shark with pronged spears called gigs.

candles, can of lamp oil, & 10 lbs. of tea. Saw DaCosta, he is just from the main, and said that he heard that R. L. Baker was dead, that he died last Thursday in Charleston. I think the news is too good to be true. Saw the Major in Beaufort, he is just from the main. Heard nothing about Baker's death. DaCosta said that two men came up from town & told Nix to send & let C. B. Smith[14] know that his uncle was dead, & that the men went to Perry's, which last appears rather strange. Treville does not appear to believe the report. DaCosta leaves the Riverside tomorrow, not to return. Had the land plowed, to plant sugarcane. Packed the fifth bag of cotton. Got back home sometime before sunset. The wind blew very fresh from about 11 a.m., fell towards evening. Sun set in a cloud—said to be a sign that it will rain the next day, we will see. Boat did not get back until sometime after dark. Wife is trying to make hog's head cheese, but I think she will make a failure of it, not having a receipt[15] to go by. Out of the hog *I* cut up the other day, we got a jar of lard, & we did not get more than ½ a jar out of 3 hogs before. I know that we were cheated.

Jan. 18th. Saw H. Grayson's wife[16] at church, the first time I ever saw her. Think her quite pretty. Mr. McElheran has written another letter to the vestry, which they are satisfied with, so I suppose we will hear no more about it, as he has said he would stick to us in war or peace.

Jan. 19th. Monday. The Capt. came over to breakfast & we went in my buggy to Beaufort. He goes on to town in the boat today, to see Roux about the sale of the deeded Negroes.[17] Did not see anything of Baker's death announced in the papers. I think the report is false. Dined with Bell. Bell is selling his Negroes & intends to invest his money in merchandise.

Jan. 20th. Wind blew violently last night, & continues so this morning, with a little rain. If the wind falls we will perhaps have a heavy rain for the clouds are very thick & heavy. The Capt. must have had a rough time in the steamboat last night—he has never been in one before. Wind N.E., falls a little & rains harder about 10 a.m. Stopped the carts[18] & put the boys to ginning. If this weather continues any length of time it will greatly backen me in getting out the crop. The Captain will, or has had, a dread-

---

[14] Charles Blincoe Smith (1831–1897). Son of Thomas Smith and Mary Elizabeth Baker. R. L. Baker's nephew and a half-brother to John R. Toomer.
[15] Recipe.
[16] Caroline E. Brantley, wife of Henry S. Grayson.
[17] The slaves who had been singled out for sale by a deed of Isabella Baker. Most of them had not been sold by 1851.
[18] Stopped hauling manure.

ful time for his trip to town so far. I expect he wishes himself at home again. Received yesterday a whole budget of the *Southern Christian Advocate*,[19] a Methodist paper Mrs. C. subscribed to some five weeks ago. They have been laying in the office all this time, the P[ost] M[aster] not knowing who to deliver them to.

Jan. 21st.   Wednesday. Rained & blew very hard all last night. Part of the garden palings blew down. 12 gins running today. Killed 2 hogs. Dr. Jenkins & the Major called in the evening. The steamboat *Wm. Seabrook* passed through Station this morning. Ben went to haul wood with the new cart & broke, through carelessness, one of the shafts. Opened a barrel of molasses to sell to the negroes for corn, at 12½ cts. pr. pint allow., 75 cts. pr. bushel for corn. Anthony hobbled out today & cut up the meat. His leg & foot are still very much swelled & painful.

Jan. 22nd.   Put 2 hogs in the pen to fatten. Sent John & January to the Island for pine. Packed the 7th bale of cotton. I see the pasture horses are hankering about the stable, a sign the pasture is getting poor & scarce of grass. Tony went to the village for a set of curtains. No one has broken into any of the houses since he was there last—they find there is nothing to steal. John plowing ground to plant Irish potatoes. E. Capers came over from the main yesterday.

Jan. 23rd.   Friday. Put all hands leveling & trenching ground for Irish potatoes. Planted them, 3 barrels of seed, did not measure the ground. Planted sugarcane, all white cane, no ribbon, I do not like it. It is not as soft to eat, does not grow as large, & does not turn out as well. Planted on the 3rd of March last year, 1 month & 8 days later than this year. This may be planted too soon & may rot, but if it does, I have a plenty for seed & can plant again in February, which will be time enough for it to mature well.

E. Capers went home. Mrs. C. quite sick with a pain in her side. She took 2 blue pills[20] last night. Sent for Dr. Jenkins today. He bled her,[21] which gave some relief. Aunt Betsy walked over & paid us a visit this evening. Sent Tony to Beaufort to get some things I expect from town by the Captain. The steamboat passed from Beaufort about 4½ o'clock. She must have had a fine & quick trip. Weather very fine, though the wind got round east. Sent John to the Captain's for the things he brought for me

[19] A weekly publication friendly to southern institutions.
[20] Popular medication composed of powdered mercury and gum arabic, sometimes laced with opium.
[21] The practice of drawing blood—by means of an incision below the crotch of the elbow—was falling out of favor in the medical community.

from town. Got a few books from Hart,[22] among them a prayer book and a Bible, as a present for my wife from myself. Very prettily bound in green velvet & gold——

Baker is not dead & in better health than he has been for several years. Ordered the Negroes to shut up all their hogs or I would kill them.

Jan. 24th.   Sent the flat and four hands to Beaufort with 7 bales of cotton.[23] Put the four women that had no gin to follow listing in marsh back of the corn house. Put Ben plowing 3 tasks of ground that is completely matted with joint grass, to try & destroy it by turning it up from the alley onto the old bed, thereby exposing the roots and loosening it so as to rake out a great deal of it entirely. I hope I may succeed in destroying it, in this way, as it would save immense labor if it could be done with the assistance of the plow. My reason for plowing from the alley & throwing the roots up on the old bed, are these—where the alley now is, is where the bed will be for the coming crop, and I think the joint grass grows more from the roots that are covered up *under* the listing than from those that are turned or listed in from the old bed. For the roots from the old bed must be on the top of the listing, & consequently, easier hoed off than if they were in the bottom of both listing and banking, as the roots would not be so deep & strong. If this had been done before that very cold weather, I think, the roots being exposed would have been entirely killed.

Jan. 25th.   Sunday. Sophy, Virginia and myself went to church, took Ernest also. The Capt. & Major dined with me. C. Rivers & E. Capers riding in the former buggy ran against Capers' carriage returning from church. Rivers' horse kicked, broke off both shafts to the buggy & threw them both (the men) out into a deep pond of water.

Jan. 26th.   Phyllis came out to work. She has been in four weeks since confinement. 4 hands listing in marsh. Carting marsh from the stacks to the marsh pen. I rode over to the Captain's & went shooting doves with him. The Captain's man Sancho killed a large doe at Lands End on Saturday. J. L. Chaplin ran it off of Edings Island & it came ashore there, just at the old fort, & laid down in the grass, when the fellow went down and shot it. Packed the 8th bale of cotton today. Black Ben sick. Dnl. Jenkins gave John a ticket[24] to go & look for a master. I am not able to buy him. Hope he may find a master on the Island, or in the district.

[22] Samuel Hart, Sr. (1805–1896), Charleston bookseller to the plantation trade.
[23] The market was slow at this time, buyers for middling-fine Sea Island offering from 23 to 31 cents a pound.
[24] Written permission for a slave to be off the plantation. John formerly lived at Tombee, while belonging to the estate of Isabella Baker.

Jan. 27th. John did not find anyone that would or could buy him. I do not think he will find anyone that he would like to live with on the Island to buy him at private sale.

Rode over to the Captain's. The Major and myself dined with him— had for dinner a haunch of the deer Sancho killed at Lands End a few days ago. I shot several doves & robins in the Captain's field.

Jan. 29th. Five hands listing, 2 bales of cotton packed, making 9 in all. Carpenters on the Island getting out posts for Negro houses. W.O.P. Fripp returned the 10 bushels of corn yesterday that I lent him in the summer. Gave him a pair of East India geese. Do not intend to give away any more, as I have only 8 left & only 3 geese[25] among them.

Jan. 30th. Went down to Bay Point, took all the family. Would have had a very pleasant day had not the tide suited so late in the evening, which prevented us from starting until late. Had a great deal of trouble pushing the boat across the banks, most of which have formed lately. We did not get clear of the banks till after dark, and then to cap it all, it commenced raining very hard & we had nothing but one umbrella to keep it off. I had ordered the carriage to meet us at Lands End, but the tide was too low to go in the swash,[26] so we went up to the Negro houses on the bluff & bogged out.

Put Sancho in the field for the first time, Frank in his place with the cattle & Summer with the poultry.

Feb. 1st. Sunday. This month comes in with rain, but looks like clearing about 10 a.m. After I went to bed last night, John came in to let me know that Tippo was very sick. I dressed & went out—found that he had a colic. Bled him in the mouth & gave him a drench of mustard, turpentine, & warm lye. Covered him with blankets, had him well rubbed, & left him, he seems quite well this morning (rather weak).

I have to find dinner for the Society next Thursday, & I do not know what I can get. We can hardly find enough to eat at home. Have to trust to luck in getting venison & wild ducks, by way to filling up the table.

Feb. 2nd. Turned quite cold in the night, weather looks like snow. Sent six hands to get wood. 5 hands raking out the joint grass I had plowed up. Sent Ben on the Island to try and get some ducks for Society dinner. All the women overhauling some seed cotton. Three carts hauling out marsh. Sent Tony to Beaufort. Let Uncle Ben have a bushel of seed Irish pota-

---

[25] Females.
[26] A channel of water between the sandbanks and the shore.

toes. The sale of John is put off till next Monday. Killed a hog. Peter & Violet sick. Carpenters making a trunk to put in the lower part of the garden, & repairing some old ones in the field.

Feb. 3rd.   Went to the Island to take a hunt. E. Capers went with me. Col. Johnson, Dr. Jenkins, the Major & the Captain also went down. Started two deer, I had a shot, wounded a large doe very badly. It ran into the surf & drowned. Johnson killed a large hog. The other men dined & started back home after dark. E. Capers & myself stayed all night—I was so anxious to get venison for Society dinner.

Feb. 4th.   Went out hunting. Found the deer I shot yesterday, it came ashore in the night. It was very carefully hid in some grass, by the fellow Noble, who found it very early in the morning & was rascal enough not to let me know. Killed nothing else.

Feb. 5th.   Met the Society, found dinner, & an excellent one it was, five times as much as the men could eat, & I was afraid there would not be enough. There was a resolution passed to fine any member 50 cts. who found more than six dishes of meat for dinner, which is a very proper thing, it will prevent competition among members in finding dinner. Drove Duchess to the lodge in the sulky. She drew very well, but her shoulder got a little chafed, & I drove Steel back. The first time I ever drove her in single harness.

Feb. 6th.   Nix came over from the main in the boat to move the Negroes from the Riverside over to the main.[27] They are all to go but Morris, Judy & Amy. I had gone to sleep on the sofa, & dreamt that Saxby was dead, believing that what I had dreamt was all true, but it was only a dream.

Feb. 7th.   Took a dose of salts & pepper tea last night, feel much better today. The Major came over in the morning to know if Saxby was really dead. God knows how he could have heard what I dreamt last night so soon this morning. Someone of his Negroes must have been here & heard it. Very windy all day, the boat could not return to the main.

Feb. 8th.   Boat went to the main today, Sophy went to church. Quite warm & pleasant. Someone broke a potato bank last night. Made a search, found some potatoes in old Charles' house. Suspect young Charles & Tom, both staying in the saw house. They say they are innocent, I think

---

[27] Nix is removing Mrs. Baker's slaves from St. Helena Island.

them guilty. John went on Steel to the main to try & get Uncle Archy[28] to buy him. He is to be sold tomorrow, in Beaufort at public auction.

Feb. 9th. Monday. Sometimes the sun shines out bright—then again very dark—think we will have a storm shortly. Turned quite cold. Planted broad Windsor beans.

John is to be sold today in Beaufort at public sale. Killed 3 bacon hogs, making 10 killed this year, have one more to kill. The Capt. went to Beaufort in his boat—wind, I think, too high for him to get back. 9 hands listing marsh, 3 carts at stable compost on some low land.

John was bought by J.J.T. Pope for $300. Dr. Jenkins offered to buy him off Pope at 350

Note *in 1876 That offer of Jenkins was all sham, he had a fair chance of buying him if he wanted, & only offered because he knew Pope would not sell. He did all he could to keep Uncle Ben from lending me the money to buy him. All this came up after some years. Jenkins has always been my* friendly enemy.
but he would not sell. Pope bought him he says for a house servant or a driver, neither of which he is capable of being. John does not at all wish to belong to Pope. I have offered to hire him. He returned here at night, & is to go & ask Pope to hire him to me.

Finished packing the 12th & last bale of white cotton today. A little left to make a four yard bag.

Feb. 11th. Went to the main. Got over to Beaufort about 11 o'clock. Got a letter from Treville to take to Perry.[29] Left Beaufort about 12 m. The Major went as far as Gardeners Corners[30] in company. Arrived at H[ickory] Hill about 4 o'clock, found Saxby at dinner. I had dined with Dupong[31] at the Corner. Found Mother & all well. R. Witsell[32] was there. Col. Johnson paid me $28 on a/c of Daphne's hire. He is to give her up when this month is up.

Feb. 12th. Mother, Saxby & myself rode down to Perry's, dined with him. Met Minott there. Shot some robins, a great many there. Perry con-

[28] Archibald Chaplin (1783–1849), planter of Prince William's Parish, Beaufort District. Son of Thomas B. Chaplin and Elizabeth Fripp. Chaplin's paternal uncle and Dr. William J. Jenkins's father-in-law.
[29] Not DeTreville's partner in Walterboro, but William Perry, Sr., Chaplin's first cousin, once removed. Chaplin will ask Perry to receive the income from Isabella's estate until the court can decide on the Baker and Chaplin claims.
[30] Small settlement on the main, now called Gardens Corner.
[31] E.J.F. Dupong (b. 1812). Beaufort shopkeeper, born in Germany. The 1860 census identifies him as a brassfounder.
[32] Robert H. Witsell (1823–1862), physician, St. Bartholomew's Parish. Son of Frederick C. Witsell and Catherine Hagood. Saxby Chaplin's brother-in-law and Frederick and John Witsell's brother.

sented to act as receiver. Minott & Dr. Jenkins Sr.[33] are to be his securities.

Returned to H[ickory] Hill in the evening. Saxby is to send over shortly for the five Negroes he has over here. I will be glad to get rid of him, he is the most selfish man I ever saw.[34]

Note 1876* *My opinion then & it is unchanged now after 31 years more of knowledge of him. He has to work hard now to support in a plain way, his large family, but he is still very selfish. But surpassed by Dr. W. J. Jenkins in that* virtue.

Feb. 13th.   Started home—got to Beaufort before 11 a.m. Wind blew very hard, could not get my horse & sulky over the ferry, left them with Tealy. Dined with J. D. Pope. Came over the ferry & rode as far as Scott's road in his carriage, & from there in his sulky. Wind blew violently & rained before I got home. No one expected me, & did not know I was in the house until I got upstairs.

Feb. 14th.   Put the hands getting out yellow cotton. Saxby gave me a musical box when I was on the main, it is really a wonder.

the gift—not the box, that was not worth much

Wind so high could not get my horse & sulky from Beaufort. Rain held up, & all hands went out to work about 2 p.m. All the men ditching, & have been since Wednesday.

Feb. 15th.   Went to church—Mr. McElheran has not returned from town & we had Ben Chaplin[35] to read a sermon to us. He did very well, better than I expected. Sent Tony to the ferry for my horse & sulky. He came back & said that they could not be got across, the flat being lost & the ferryboat's bottom having been stove in last night or the night before.

Feb. 17th.   Very calm beautiful day. Had five carts hauling manure, finished all the compost.

Saxby sent January over with the boat for the five Negroes I promised to give up to him. I will send them—but Betty being sick I will keep her & Sam & he will have to send again for them. Commenced hauling sedge today.

---

[33] John William Jenkins, physician. Son of Richard Jenkins and Phoebe Waight. Chaplin's second cousin, once removed. First cousin to Major D. P. and Dr. W. J. Jenkins.

[34] Though united against Baker, Saxby and Thomas were rivals for their mother's property. "The five Negroes" lived at Riverside and had been deeded along with the land to Saxby. He was entitled to take them, but Thomas was miffed at how quickly he exercised his right.

[35] Possibly Benjamin S. Chaplin (b. 1795), planter. Son of Benjamin Chaplin, Jr., and Martha S. Reynolds. Chaplin's second cousin, once removed, on his father's side.

Feb. 18th. Cloudy. Sent January, Stephen & Charles Jr. over to Saxby. Daresay he will think I do even this for self interested motives.

Note 1876 During a long life, I do not now regret of any of the many acts of this kind I have done. I may have been often deceived, but if I was right only once I am content. He really never had any right to these Negroes, or any part of Father's[36] estate, & acknowledged it years after.

Rode over to Mrs. Pritchard's,[37] for the purpose of meeting J. J. Pope[38] by appointment, we being commissioned by the court, with three other persons, to appraise & divide the Est. of Tom Pritchard.[39] The other men have already been sworn & appraised the property in 1844, we had only to be sworn & to sign our names sanctioning the appraisement & division, which we rode over to J.E.L. Fripp & did. Mr. Pope, having drawn up a return beforehand, & I agreed to the same.

A man came here with a paper signed by a captain of a vessel, stating that he was deserving of charity, having been robbed by pirates in coming to this [country] from Switzerland with his family of everything he had in the world. And with the capt. & crew of the vessel sent adrift, by the pirates, with neither water or provisions, in which situation they remained for 2½ days, when they were picked up by another vessel & taken to Tenerife, one of the Canary Islands, where his family & parents now are, subsisting on charity, and he has come to this country to beg for enough cash to pay their passage to this country. He has already collected $170 & says it will take $250. I gave him $1 & he gave me the change to a ten dollar bill in specie.

Rained & the wind blew violently all night, every window fastening, almost, came loose, & I heard such a slamming & banging, as if the whole house were coming down———

Sent Sawney & Sam to the Island for some cedar trees. Set them out in front of the house, 8 of them.

These are now alive & large, are 31 years old   1876

Feb. 19th. Rained steady the whole day from daylight till dark, & looks like clearing. Nothing done out of doors today. Set it down as a completely lost day. We have so much rain now, that I am afraid we will have another very dry summer. We had unsettled weather this time last year, tho I had some hands cutting marsh. I would do the same now, but there is so much sedge[40] on the bay, have determined to try that. It is quicker

---

[36] Saxby Chaplin, Sr. (1780–1828), planter. Son of Thomas B. Chaplin, Sr., and Elizabeth Fripp.
[37] Ann E. Pritchard (b. 1802). Widow of Thomas Pritchard. Lived on the Seaside, midway between Dr. Jenkins's and Edgar Fripp's Seaside plantations.
[38] John Jeremiah Theus Pope. See note, Aug. 4, 1845.
[39] Thomas Pritchard, planter. Deceased husband of Ann.
[40] Marsh grass washed up by the tide.

work & I believe very nearly as good manure. The difference I can make up in quantity. I had another, & the last, hog put up to fatten yesterday, making 11 in all I had for bacon this year.

Feb. 20th. Dug up a parcel of live oak trees to set out. Sent three hands on the Island for pine. My potato banks were broken again last night. Searched all the houses but could not find the potatoes.
Oaks in yard now 31 years old 1876

Saw Free Billy,[41] he came over from the main to bring his sister Nancy to my old man Sancho, to see if he as a Negro doctor can do anything for her. She is deranged. I think he is an infernal fool for his pains. Their boat got away the night before last & has not yet been found. I have no doubt she has gone to sea, the wind being N.E. & an ebb tide. The boat belongs to Wm. Perry Snr. The woman has been sick for 2 years & will not speak to anyone.
Note 1876 *She got well, but not cured by old Sancho, and lived many years, died some 3 or 4 years back.*

Feb. 21st. Saturday. Got out 18 live & water oaks, had 5 hands at it all day. Sent Tony to Beaufort. Got a letter from Webb[42] saying that he had sent me 200 bushels of corn by the *District.*[43] Fed the horses today on sugarcane. They do not appear to like it atall, but will try & force them to eat it. Planted a task more of cane. Rose sick 3 days.

Feb. 22nd. Went to church, took Ernest with me. Heard that Edgar Fripp had presented the church with an organ.

Capt. D. Jenkins dined with me. Major called in the evening, lent him my sulky to go up to Gillisonville tomorrow, as a witness in our case. The Capt. & myself are also going, but not as witnesses. Had the balance of my cotton put on board the flat to go up to Beaufort early tomorrow for the steamboat to Charleston. I have made in all 12½ bales, but tightly packed. **$1750.00.** The flat will bring buck from Beaufort 200 bushels of corn, sent me by Ingraham & Webb. Send in the flat, 5 hands, Anthony Snr., Robert, Ben, Isaac, and Tony Jnr

Feb. 23rd. Monday. Started for Gillisonville, D. Jenkins went with me. Drove Hawk & Hyder. Got over to Beaufort about 11½ o'clock. My flat had got there, & had in a load, 61 bags of corn—2 bushels in a bag. Left 39 bags which they will return for tomorrow. We started from Beaufort about 12½ m., arrived at Gillisonville about 6½ o'clock p.m. Stopped at

---

[41] A free Negro, one of about fifty in the District.
[42] Thomas L. Webb, of Ingraham & Webb, cotton factors.
[43] The steamboat *Beaufort District.*

Mr. Firth's. There are 2 public houses in this place, one kept by Pat Ryan, but we preferred Firth's, as there was no barroom kept there & consequently a more quiet place. We met all the folks that went from our parts there—Treville, Fickling, Pope, Perry &c. My object in going up to court was to hear the case of Baker & Roux vs. myself & others.

Feb. 23rd. Monday. Treville informed me the evidence of Memminger & Jervey,[44] which was of the greatest importance, had not been received, & that it must be had at all hazards. We therefore set out in search of a man who was recommended to us by Firth, by the name of Finley. After a great deal of trouble we found him, & he agreed after long persuasion to go for thirty dollars. Start in an hour from that time, say 10 o'clock at night, & to return on Thursday at 11 o'clock a.m. He soon got his horse & though the night was very dark, bolted off at full speed through the pine trees. We returned to the house & went to bed a little better satisfied, for I thought at first that the case would be put off for the next court, which would have been too provoking. I would rather pay a man $100 to go to Charleston for the papers than have the case put off. I slept very well on a hard bed.

Feb. 24th. The Major got here about 10 o'clock. He will be examined this evening & will return home tomorrow morning. This is a dull place, nothing to do but to go to the courthouse & listen to what does not interest you in the least. There are a great many cases on the docks, ours is the 52nd & will barely be reached this court.

Feb. 25th. The man Finley got back today about 3 o'clock—but forgot to mention that the papers came yesterday by Mr. Petigru.[45]

Feb. 26th. Did nothing all day. Occasionally saw Baker, who is up here & stops at Ryan's. He is the meanest looking white man I ever saw. He

[44] Christopher Gustavus Memminger (1803–1888) and William Jervey, Charleston attorneys. Memminger drafted Isabella Baker's marriage settlement, and Jervey read the final version to Baker, hours before the wedding. The German-born Memminger served for twenty years in the S.C. House of Representatives. In 1860, Gov. William H. Gist sent him on a mission to Virginia, to seek a unified southern response to the sectional crisis. A signer of the Ordinance of Secession, he represented South Carolina in the provisional Confederate Congress, and was a Confederate Secretary of the Treasury. After the Civil War he campaigned hard for public schools.

[45] James L. Petigru (1789–1863), Charleston attorney employed by Baker. Like Memminger's, his practice was very lucrative. Praised universally for his honesty and quick mind, Petigru was always well received in court. Served as state Attorney General 1822–30, and in the S.C. House of Representatives 1830–32 and 1836–38. A devout unionist, he had tutored secessionists R. B. Rhett and Richard DeTreville, in Beaufort.

could not look me in the face. He has the boy Aaron with him & the horse John Bull.

Feb. 27th. Friday. Rained nearly all day, & very cold. Our case was called just before sunset, 2 bills were read & the court adjourned. Baker looks a little alarmed. His strong man Hunt[46] has not come to defend him. He will have to trust to Colcock & Hutson.[47]

Feb. 28th. Our case took up the whole day from 10 o'clock till dark. It was very interesting. Baker was completely used up, and looked like a sheep-stealing dog. Pope,[48] in his speech, called him a good for nothing bankrupt druggist from Broad Street,[49] and Baker looked as though he could eat him up. Hutson spoke first, followed by Pope, Colcock & Treville. The three latter made splendid speeches. Colcock did well but he had a bad case, the evidence was too much against his client. The case will no doubt be decided in our favor. The judge was heard to say that his mind was made up before Baker's side was heard, after hearing the bills & answers made, & the evidence given in. I suppose we will get the written decision in a few weeks. Treville has sent an order to Charleston to have Baker taken as soon as he gets there, for not returning the Negroes Aaron & August. Geoffrey & family were sold last Thursday in town. The two Nixes were at court, but not called in as evidences in the case.[50]

March 1st. Very heavy rain last night, continued till about 9 o'clock this morning, when it held up, & we started for home. Treville rode in company with us. Saw Baker about to start when we did. He had his doubled barrel gun alongside of him. We had no rain on us until we got to Gardeners Corner, when it commenced to pour, & continued until got home. Stopped a little while in Beaufort, the wind very high, was almost afraid to cross the ferry. We had to leave J. Pope's horse & sulky, for fear of hav-

[46] Benjamin F. Hunt (1792–1854), Charleston attorney, Massachusetts born. Served in the state legislature for twenty years and was chairman of the Judiciary Committee from 1849 until his death. Along with Petigru and Memminger, Hunt was a leader of the unionist party. "Many of the most difficult cases in Charleston and Georgetown passed through his hands," noted J. B. O'Neall, historian of the S.C. bar.
[47] William Ferguson Colcock (1804–1889) and William Ferguson Hutson (1815–1881), Charleston attorneys. Baker has spared no expense in choosing his legal counsel. Colcock served in the state legislature for eighteen years and the U.S. House of Representatives 1849–53. For the next twelve years he was collector of the port of Charleston. Hutson served in the state legislature for ten years and was a member of the 1860 Secession Convention.
[48] Joseph D. Pope.
[49] Business street in Charleston.
[50] Isabella's deeds to her sons were ultimately struck down. See note, Dec. 1, 1846. "Geoffrey & family" were among the slaves deeded for sale in June 1845.

ing too much in the flat, and as it was we came very near being sunk. The wind rose higher, blowing from the N. We were blown over on the Ladies Isle shore, & the only way we got along was by poling and we did so in good earnest. We were in great danger, not of our lives, but of losing our horses, two of mine & one of the Captain's. If they had got overboard they would have been lost, for we were near the shore, which was very boggy & they could not have swam off. The Capt. jumped overboard & with great exertion kept the flat off while we poled her along. She was then nearly half full of water. Pope & myself—or rather, I say, myself did not stay in the flat for fear [of] getting wet for we were completely soaked already, it raining hard all the time, & we had to put off our wet cloaks, & work the poles. After about two hours' passage we got on the landing—& safe. Though wet through we put on our wet cloaks, & all three got into the buggy & came on. Pope took the Captain's horse at Scott's road & went up. We got home safe, but I thought we would have found some of the bridges floated away. The whole road & everywhere else appeared to be one street of water. The highest part of the road was underwater & some places over knee deep. We got home about 9 o'clock. The house looked as if it was in a pond or in the creek, the garden completely afloat. Found all well. Capt. spent the night & I expect slept soundly after his fatigue, I know I did. Wind blew violently all night.

March 2nd. Monday. Anthony got all my corn from Beaufort last week—made two trips in the flat. I emptied it today—measured 2 bags, they did not hold out the 2 bushels by 5 quarts—equal to 18 b., 2 p., 6 qts. on the 200 bushels. 4 hands were on the Island last week getting rails. Have 51½ acres of cotton land listed and well manured. Have to list 44½ more.

96 acres in all

Commenced listing March corn land on Thursday the 26th Feb., did not finish. Listed potato land, finished today all to 1 task that the cow pen is now on. Commenced hauling out & scattering cotton seed on M. corn land, 1 pk. to the task row. Gave the 1st allowance of the bought corn today, it is very clean & good corn. Sent Tony to Beaufort. Got a letter from I. & W.,[51] cotton not yet sold. Killed the stall fed beef yesterday. J. L. Chaplin sent me yesterday a very large haunch of venison he killed last Saturday. I sent a part to Dr. Scott. His physician has told him to eat nothing but game. Had 14 pieces of the beef salted up.

March 3rd. Most of what I have written above ought to be dated the third & will so be read——

[51] Ingraham & Webb.

March 4th. Muster Day on the Islands. All hands listing M. corn land. Carpenters repairing trunks. Got 2 rafts of boards of Mr. Law[52] & had them brought home last week—1 raft of refuse & 1 of prime stuff—price 8 & 13 dollars pr. M.[53]

Sent the sulky to the ferry for Fickling. Rode on horseback to the muster house. Fickling did not get to the muster house until just as we were about starting home, so he lost his dinner. The Capt. & Major took tripe supper with me. Finished carting out cotton seed on corn land.[54] Commenced carting compost on ditto. All hands listing corn land. 3 sick.

March 5th. Commenced plowing corn land that is listed. Intend to plant after the plow without banking.[55] 3 hands have been making fence now going on 3 weeks.

A delightful breeze from S. which makes it quite pleasant. This is really spring weather, all the peach & plum trees are in full bloom. Jubah[56] went out today. 2 hands were sick—Phyllis & Belle.

March 6th. Finished manuring all the corn land on this side of the Sands & finished listing the same. All manured with cotton seed except the old slip patch, that with compost. Rode over to Toomer's. Saw 2 of my sows with 13 pigs. They have lost so many that I ordered Adam Morcock to attend to them, & put old May to making baskets, 2 a week. Mrs. C. rode over to Coz. Betsy's,[57] the 1st time she has been out on a visit this winter. Carpenters whitewashing.

March 7th. Sent Henry to Beaufort. Finished moving the pen over the root patch. Hauled the rails to make a pen over the other side by the mulberry tree to make compost for another crop. All hands cleaning out the ditch to drain the rice. Henry returned about dark, brought a letter from Tom Webb stating that 200 bushels of corn is now in Beaufort for me, Western corn.

✱✱*Note 1876   It was an awful drawback on a planter to buy corn. I got over it soon*

---

[52] George Law.
[53] Per thousand.
[54] Crushed cotton seed and the waste from ginning was used to fertilize corn land.
[55] To save work, Chaplin is eliminating one step in planting corn. Rather than plant in ridges thrown up with the hoe after plowing, he will have the corn planted in the ridges made by the plow. On higher land, the corn would be planted in the furrows.
[56] The name Jubah originates in one of several African languages: Yoruba (southern Nigeria) *juba,* "to acknowledge as superior"; Bambara (French West Africa) *juba,* "a hen which has young chickens"; Wolof (Senegal and Gambia) *juba,* "a tuft of hair on the head"; or from words in the Vai (Liberia) or Mende (Sierra Leone) languages. For these and other African name derivations, see Lorenzo Turner, *Africanisms in the Gullah Dialect* (Chicago, 1949).
[57] Also the home of Maj. Daniel P. Jenkins.

& had it to sell. & note how well I was manuring corn this season 1846, I bought very little after that & often sold corn & fodder. C∗∗

March 8th. Sunday. The atmosphere looks very smoky. Warm & pleasant—everything growing finely. Fickling, Sophy, Ernest & myself went to church. Saw & heard the new organ presented to the church by Edgar Fripp.
∗∗That organ was taken to Bay Point by the Yanks during the war, they ought to return or pay for it.∗∗

March 9th. Commenced banking corn land—will bank only the low ground around the ponds. Sent cotton seed to J.E.L. Fripp's to exchange with him for some of the Godly selection.[58] Carting stable manure on corn land the other side of the Sands, 5 loads to the task. Will plant 14 acres of March corn.
∗∗Note 1876 40 acres of an average 20—800 bu was not bad. I had to try, not that I made bad crops, but I fed higher & had more horses to feed than my neighbors generally. C∗∗
Tony fixing a place in the corn house to put the corn in. Jolly grubbing. Sancho, Samson & Adam making the cow pen. Sent the carpenters in the pine barren near the church to get our oars. Steady rain all day, all hands in the corn house shelling corn for seed. Had some slats nailed over the cracks in the corn house to prevent the rain from beating in on the corn—the weatherboards were put on smooth joint & they have swelled so much that the rain can come through. Dark & raining still. The carts returned from Fripp's, but did not bring the seed for fear of its getting wet. The flat has not got back. I hope they will wait until the rain holds up & not get the corn wet.

March 10th. A fine driving rain & dark clouds, most disagreeable weather. The hands went out to work very reluctantly. 4 carts hauling fowl house & hog pen manure on corn land.
Fickling & myself rode over to the Captain's & dined with him. The Major dined there also. After dinner we played cards & drank brandy & water till near sunset, when we started.
∗∗1876 did not drink whiskey in those days, brandy & rum & gin C∗∗
The Major took a seat in my lap, saying that he would drive my horses as far as his road & my boy should ride his horse. Off we went, the Major with the reins, I the whip, 3 cracks I gave & the horses were at full speed. I soon found that the Major could not hold them, & we were so very near to

[58] Seeds "selected" or bred by Edward Godley (b. 1820), planter of St. Peter's Parish, Beaufort District.

a very short turn in the road that it was too late for me to take the reins, so I hollowed out to the Major to drive over the beds around a large bush & thereby make a long turn, but no, he pulled them short to the right & over the buggy & us three went. Fickling first, I having the Major in my lap went last. As everything turned out it was one of the most laughable sights I ever beheld. Here lay the Major, holding his belly & hollowing Oh! Lord God—there Fickling, rising on his hands & feet with his_____stuck high in the air, asking for his watch (which had been thrown from his left vest to his right coat pocket) and hearing the Major groan so pitifully, crawled towards him & feeling his head, quietly asked him if his neck was broken. No, said the Major—but look at my nose. I think the Major more scared than hurt, his face as white as a sheet. I got off with a bruised leg & Fickling with a scratched nose. The horses broke the swingletrees[59] & got off with the pole, leaving the buggy unhurt, & what was more singular, it was righted up again after being turned over.

Note 1876* *I laugh even now & read this funny little scrap. How jolly we all used to be then, it seems but a few months ago it happened.*

The horses ran about a half mile with the pole, when they were found & brought back, none of the harness being broken, or the pole. Had two pieces of wood put in to answer as swingletrees & drove home. Horses did not appear to be atall frightened.

The flat returned this evening with the corn. Had it put up in the corn house, just as it is, bag & all. Gave out the first allowance of it, not as good as the other, it is a mixture of red, yellow & white, and very dirty.

If I had bought 400 bushels up to March I must have bought much more that year than usual.*

March 13th.   Dr. Jenkins, Fickling & myself went down to Trenchards & drew the seine. Caught a few mullets, got back before sunset. All hands planting corn.

March 14th.   Finished planting corn on this side the Sands. Fickling returned to Beaufort, but was very near not getting there for this reason. When they (he & Tony) got as far as Wm. Chaplin's road, the off fore wheel of the ill fated buggy ran off & threw the sitters out into the ditch, not hurting either of them fortunately. A fence rail ran through the top & tore it, the crossbar & pole broken, but no other damage done. They say the horses did not run very far with the buggy. Fickling got Perry's Jersey and drove old Hyder on to the ferry in it. Summer, the little boy that rode

---

[59] The crossbar to which the horses' traces are attached. Traces are chains which connect a draft animal's harness to a wagon or cart.

behind, was sent back on Hawk to inform me of the accident. I sent the wagon for the buggy.

March 15th. Sunday. Tony brought me information last night from Treville that I must go to Beaufort early this morning, which I did, & got there by 11 o'clock. Treville told me that Roux wished to have another writ of injunction served on me, on an attachment got out for contempt of court for my having in my possession some of the property now in dispute. I signed two affidavits & J. D. Pope went on Gillisonville with them to appear for me. I got back about dark.
What this was all for I never knew to this day 1876 C

March 17th. Heard that Uncle Ben when on his way to Beaufort yesterday met with a sad accident—*another upset.* His horse shied at something in the road, ran the gig in the ditch (which was half full of water), knocking him senseless & hurting him very much. Dr. Jenkins happened to [be] just ahead of him (which was most fortunate, for his head was under water & mud & he may have drowned), ran back & got him out & brought him back home. Sent Tony to Beaufort. He brought me a letter from Treville. The motion for the order was granted, but he has appealed. I do not know how this matter will end. Treville has sent up for the judge's decree, which I suppose will settle everything.[60]

March 18th. Wednesday. All hands banking corn land.[61] Carpenters pulling down the old tabby house,[62] got the top & one gable end & chimney down, I will get some very good lime brick from it. Rode over to see Uncle Ben, found him in a great deal of pain, cannot turn himself over in bed, and is likely to remain there for some time.

Sent a boy & got 19 crabs. If the day suits I try them myself tomorrow. Sent my buggy to Beaufort to be mended yesterday. Robert sick—

March 19th. John plowing potato root land. All hands banking & tracking corn land,[63] commenced planting the 14 acres. Went out drum fishing for the first time this year, took Ernest with me. Caught 2 drum—I one & Tony one—lost one. We had no prawn & caught no fish until I bought a

---

[60] See March 15, 1846. Though Chaplin believes he is legally in the right, Roux's maneuvering has shaken his confidence. Nine months will pass before the chancellor announces the court's decision in favor of Chaplin. See Dec. 1, 1846. On appeal, however, Baker and Roux will win.
[61] Throwing up a bed with hoes.
[62] An outbuilding that housed the old kitchen. Tabby is a cementlike substance made of sand, lime, crushed shells, and water.
[63] Laying out the rows, two and a half to five feet apart, depending on the "strength" of the land, then making the beds.

few from a Negro, though the prawn appear to be plenty. Ernest was delighted.[64] He never has been out with me before & never saw a drum caught. I fished at Bay Point & I understand that the Major, who fished at Middle Bank,[65] took 20 drum & bass. Ernest got a little seasick, but after he got onshore, was ready for another trip.

March 20th.   Finished planting March corn, ditto plowing potato land. Stopped one cart—3 carts putting sedge in the cow pen.

Kitty foaled just before day this morning. I had her in an enclosure but she got out somehow & made for the bayside where she foaled—a large, light bay horse colt, resembles, even now, the dame & sire. Got by Berkshire, he by Clock Sunday.

March 23rd.   Sent 6 hands on the Island to raft off the rails. Ben & John plowing cotton land, balance planting potatoes. Let Uncle Ben have 11 baskets of red seed potatoes. He, the Capt., the Major & W. Jenkins all planting today. My potato seed have rotted very little. I attribute it to their being covered so close & fresh dirt thrown on them whenever the bank cracked open, & after a rain. The leathercoats & pumpkin Spanish were completely rotted down to nothing. Sent Tony to Beaufort for some fruit trees, which I got R. Chisolm[66] to import from France for me. They cost me, landed in Beaufort, $26.29 &, if I can get them to grow, will be worth ten times that amt. Tony got back about 4 o'clock with the trees & a sack of salt, 1 box Cuba sixes,[67] & 1 box Spanish cigars. M. Petray & Sons, of Paris, is the firm Chisolm got the trees from.

March 24th.   In all the rain I went out & set out 43 trees in my new orchard of French trees. 2 in the yard called Maria Louise[68] (apple) makes 45. The ground got so wet had to stop for a good day. Some of the trees I had to put down in water, & many of them were sprouting. Dr. Jenkins sent in his a/c—could not pay it. Sent it back. Lent Capt. D. Jenkins 10 bushels of corn. Between the showers, planted 1½ acres of yam pototoes.

March 25th.   Finished planting potatoes, watermelons & muskmelons 7 days earlier than last year. Planted Smyrna muskmelon seed in the potato patch. Finished setting out the imported trees in the orchard—66 trees in

---

[64] Ernest is six years old at this time.
[65] A shoal in Broad River.
[66] Robert Chisolm (1807–1880), rice planter and horticulturist of St. Bartholomew's Parish. A proponent of olive culture on the seaboard, he exhibited olives, citrus fruit, and preserves at the 1850 S.C. Institute Fair.
[67] Six-inch cigars.
[68] Incidentally, the name of one of Chaplin's daughters and his deceased sister.

the orchard & 10 in the yard, 76 in all. I am afraid some of them will not take, as I had to set them out in the water that would spring in the holes, the ground was so very wet.

Rode over & took tea with Uncle Ben, he is much better. Saw J. H. Webb & his wife[69] there. Paid Dr. Jenkins his a/cs, by order on Treville for $500.

Note 1876*   *This gives the lie to some assertions I have heard that Dr. Jenkins made "that I never paid him my acct." He has scoundled me out of many a dollar for nothing

March 27th.   Friday. Borrowed Uncle Paul's boat, went out fishing. Uncle Paul sent his fellow Sambo with me. Fished on Middle Bank about an hour, did not get a bite, & the wind blew so hard we had to pull up anchor & run into Station Creek. Stopped at Station Island, made a fire, roasted oysters & stayed there till was low water. The wind fell a little & we went down to Bay Point—fished there until the tide was high enough to get up the creek, & came home, did not get a bite the whole day.

Hands banking ground & planting cotton. Lent the Capt. my sulky & the chestnut mare to go to Beaufort. Carpenters making oars[70] for the *Pelican.* Could get no stuff but sapling pines which are very poor, being full of sap at this season of the year, & very supple. March corn coming up very pretty.

March 28th.   Saturday. Went fishing, took 5 drum. Finished planting 20 acres of cotton.

March 29th.   Sunday. Fanny Douglass had a colt early this morning— bay, not a white spot, slight dark line down the back, very much like Kitty's only a very little darker & unfortunately a mare colt. It is as large as Kitty's, which is 9 days older.

Went to church. Capt. J. Fripp's horse broke both shafts of his gig & nearly killed his boy, all from the carelessness of the boy in taking the horse out of the gig.

March 30th.   Wind chopping around every point of the compass, finally got E. & N.E. & blew pretty fresh. 3 carts hauling rails from the raft to the line. 5 hands making fence on the line between J. L. Chaplin & myself, finished it about 2 o'clock. Put the same hands to cutting crotches to build the fence on between Est. B. Jenkins[71] & self. Balance of hands banking

[69] Emmeline Jenkins Webb. See note, Aug. 26, 1845.
[70] Oak and gum were preferred for oars.
[71] Cousin Betsy's Riverside plantation, known by the name of her late husband, Benjamin Jenkins.

ground & planting cotton. Sawney & Sam thrashing rice, thrashed 4¾ bushels.

March 31st.   Bay mare had a horse colt last night, dark bay on brown, both hind feet white.

April 1st.   Cold, windy, & rainy, thus is April ushered in. One of the dismal, gloomy days I ever spent. High wind from the east, & cold, with constant fine drizzle, drifting rain the whole day, and with all this to sit in the house all day with a dull Methodist minister[72] who seldom ever says a word except on religion, unless I happen to ask him a question. Would not look at anything stronger than cider, and not for the world sit in the room where a simple game of backgammon is being played. He came over expressly to take a drum fishing & I do hope the weather may clear off tonight so that we can do something.

Hands did some work today tho the weather was so bad. Making fence, banking ground &c &c. Finished carting out the rails. If this weather continues very long (and I fear it will not clear before the next change of the moon, which is on Friday next), I think I will get sick from staying in the house with these supercilious people. And I have been foolish enough to ask Kirkland & his colleague (a Mr. Franks) to come over & take a fishing bout with me when the fish are biting well. Mrs. Kirkland being my wife's old friend, I bear it all with as much patience as I am master of (& that is not much) & try to put on as solemn an air as possible.

April 2nd.   Just such a day as yesterday, cold drizzle rain, but not so much wind. Hardly went out of the house during the whole day. This weather has almost made Kirkland sick.

Puss had a bay mare colt about 11 o'clock today, exactly like Kitty's only one is a horse & the other a mare colt. Hard case that I cannot get a match.[73] Out of four colts from the same horse there are two pair that match in color, but one a horse & the other a mare.

April 3rd.   Mr. Kirkland & myself went out shooting. Killed a few birds, went out & caught a few crabs. Wind very high. Finished making fence

[72] William C. Kirkland (1814–1864), Methodist missionary to Beaufort and Pocotaligo. "He was an exceedingly amiable, sweet-spirited man. . . . In his tongue was the law of kindness, and in his heart a fountain of love. His preaching had the charm of simplicity and was directed with evident singleness of purpose to the conscience of the hearer." (Rev. Albert M. Shipp, *The History of Methodism in South Carolina* [Nashville, Tenn., 1884], 624–625.) Kirkland and his wife, Virginia, had two sons: William, Jr., who followed his father into the ministry, and James, who became chancellor of Vanderbilt University.

[73] A working pair.

yesterday, have about 4 cart loads of rails left. Hands banking cotton land. Yesterday was agricultural meeting day, forgot to go out.

April 4th. Kirkland & family went home. Finished banking cotton land on this side [of] the Sands. Put marsh sedge around the roots of my French trees. Rec'd. a list of names & Nos. from Chisolm—all in French, but will have it translated.

Major Felder came here dunning. Sent him off as he came—old rascal.

April 5th. Heard that Capt. J. Fripp's boy that got hurt last Sunday at the church from his horse running off has since died from the hurts he rec'd. Went out to church. Tom Fripp, Oliver Fripp, W. Jenkins, and D. P. Jenkins have all sold their cotton, which is from the same seed that I planted, at 32 cts. Webb is holding mine at 34, hope he may get it.

April 6th. All hands planting cotton, banking some salt land,[74] & digging ditches. Commenced plowing land to plant early peas. Numbered all of my new fruit trees. Sent Tony to Beaufort. Wife & myself rode over to Uncle Ben's on horseback in the evening, the first time she has rode on horseback for at least a year. Engaged Kudjo[75] to make my kitchen chimney.

April 7th. Went out fishing, very few boats out, fish bit very badly. Uncle Paul's Sambo[76] fished with me.

April 8th. Cloudy, wind S.E. Commenced listing in marsh sedge on the Bay Field yesterday. Went fishing. Finished the pillars under corn house, building the kitchen chimney.

April 9th. Rode over to the Captain's. He & Dr. Jenkins dined with me. Finished my kitchen chimney. Cost me $4 for the pillars & relaying the hearth to Sophy's room.

April 10th. Good Friday. Sent Tony to Beaufort. Finished planting fodder corn. All hands listing cotton ground. Capt. D. Jenkins came over & altered my sails & made them set a great deal better—my boat runs two points nearer in the wind.[77]

---

[74] Formerly salt marsh, now impounded.
[75] Slave belonging to Uncle Ben. *Kudjo* is a name in the Ewe language (Togo and Dahomey) given to a boy born on a Monday.
[76] See Nov. 27, 1853.
[77] Chaplin's old billowy sails have been cut and reshaped so that they can "sheet" flat, allowing him to sail two degrees on the compass closer to the wind.

April 15th. Beautiful day. Wind N.W., cooler. Went fishing. Finished banking cotton ground. Stopped the plows. Saw Dr. Jenkins in a new boat which he bought of C. G. Capers for $200.

April 16th. Planting cotton over the Sands, Godly selection seed. Supplying March corn. Never knew the birds so bad before, though the seed was well tarred, they will pull it, but can't eat it. Took nearly as much to replant as it did to plant. Went fishing.

April 20th. Monday. Went fishing. Listing corn land. Everyone of my fruit trees have taken.

April 21st. Finished listing corn land. Went fishing—biting very badly. Borrowed Capers' buggy to take to Bay Point tomorrow if I go. Cotton all up & pretty *regular,* all to some salt land near the house, & the first planted, which I think is owing to patting the dirt too hard on it with the hoe. Sugarcane coming up, but not at all regular.

April 22nd. Went with all the family to Bay Point. Stayed in Elliott's house.

April 29th. Moved all hands back home. The children look better, but the trip I do not think has done my wife any good. She complains still a great deal of the pain in her side. Heard that while we were away, that both Mrs. Tom & Jos. Perry[78] had died, one in childbed, the other very suddenly. Everything looks green, particularly the joint grass. Finished planting April corn. Cotton all up well, that planted last looks much the best. Potatoes coming up very well.

April 30th. Commenced hoeing potatoes, weather clear & hot, thunder in the evening but no rain.

May 2nd. Hoeing grass in cotton. Killed a veal.

May 4th. Went to Beaufort—paid my taxes, $50.19 cts. Sent Steel to Charleston as a present to T. L. Webb. Old bay mare refused the horse on the last day of April—Fanny ditto.

May 5th. Hoeing cotton. Killed a lamb & gave the Capt. half. Chestnut mare had a black horse colt. Sent Tony to the village with a cart to move Mother's furniture out of W. B. Fripp's house. He did not return at night.

---

[78] Fanny Kershaw Perry (1820–1846), wife of Joseph Perry.

May 6th. Went to the muster field to dine. A Mr. George Schley (Sly) & J. W. Pope[79] came home with me & spent the night. The former is a gentleman of Georgia, near Augusta, owns a large cotton manufactory, and is traveling about the country with samples of his Geo. plains, a woollen cloth which he wishes to introduce among the planters in this section for their Negro clothing, instead of their buying Northern goods. I hope he may succeed. It would relieve us a great deal from the heavy tariff on that article. His goods are thicker, stronger, as warm & *cheaper* than the Northern & I shall patronize him.

1876* *At a later day, we find we were mistaken. Not about that cry of "Tariff" how or when twas it. The cloth was better but higher, that was certain. But we ought to have supported Southern enterprise. I tried the cloth & found it to be as so presented. C*

May 7th. Thursday. Schley, Pope & myself went down to Trenchards to draw the seine, but got there too late. Schley has never been on the sea beach before & everything was novel to him. Was very much amused at him & he was perfectly delighted. Got a fine mess of fish from Grayson's[80] Negroes who were down there & made a hearty dinner.

May 8th. Clear in the morning, hoeing March corn. Clouds up about 1 p.m. Very heavy storm of rain & wind, did not last very long. J. Webb[81] & C. J. Colcock[82] came over to see me—were out in the river in all the storm but got here safe, all to a heavy ducking.

May 9th. Hauled potatoes. Reds look very fine, yams came up badly, & a good many died after commenced running.[83] Webb & Colcock insist on my going over with them[84]—concluded to go. Started in their boat, left orders for my boat to come over for me tomorrow morning. The wind was blowing very fresh from the S. but as Webb's boat was a good sea boat we thought we could get over very well, & started. Rowed down to Station

[79] John W. B. Pope (b. 1825), Charleston attorney. Son of Joseph J. Pope, Sr., and Sarah Jenkins. Brother of Joseph Daniel Pope.
[80] William J. Grayson, Jr. (b. 1820), physician and planter. Son of W. J. Grayson (1788–1863), lawyer and author of the polemical poem *The Hireling and the Slave*, a rejoinder to *Uncle Tom's Cabin*. William, Jr., lived on St. Helena until Jan. 1854.
[81] Maj. John Webb, of St. Luke's Parish.
[82] Charles Jones Colcock (1820–1891). Son of Thomas Hutson Colcock and Eliza Hay. Nephew of R. L. Baker's attorney William Ferguson Colcock. He was a director of the Bank of South Carolina and had an interest in a cotton factorage firm in Charleston. He also owned a plantation in St. Luke's Parish. Colcock and John Webb were brothers-in-law, having married Mary Caroline and Elizabeth Savage Heyward respectively, daughters of Thomas Heyward, Jr., and Ann Eliza Cuthbert, and granddaughters of Thomas Heyward, a signer of the Declaration of Independence. Colcock was a colonel in the 3rd S.C. Cavalry 1861–65.
[83] The plants died after they began shooting out vines.
[84] To the mainland.

Creek, & hoisted our sail, ran over to & across Parris Bank.[85] When we got on the other side Webb took the helm from me (who had been steering all the time before) & said he knew the way best & would steer the boat. We went along very well, sailing with a light south breeze, for the wind had fallen very much, when we saw a very black cloud in the N.W. apparently about four or five miles off. About a quarter past five we felt a few drops of rain, & the wind died away to a complete calm, when I proposed to Webb to take down the sails & row. He gave the order & the mainsail was made up, & the foresail brailed[86] up. During this time the rain came down in torrents, & the wind sprung up from the N.W., & before we could get down the foremast one of the most awful squalls struck us from the N.W., & in less than three minutes the boat was bottom up, & the wind fallen almost to a calm. We were in a horrid situation. We all got on the bottom of the boat, 4 Negroes & 3 white men. Everything floated out of the boat & we held on to one oar which we saved—was afterwards the only thing except one thwart[87] we had to paddle ashore with. The boat rolled over & over like a barrel though fortunately the water was smooth, for no sooner than the squall passed over it became almost a dead calm. We were about a mile from the shore & the wind driving us further off. The foresail was fastened to the boat by the halyard rope, which one of the Negroes by diving down succeeded in cutting off (Colcock had fortunately saved his knife by putting it in his glove), and we got rid of the sail. The boat would then lay bottom down for five or ten minutes at a time. During these times we would get rid of our clothes & boots, principally by cutting them off, & when the boat would roll over we would swim off until her bottom came up then get on it again. One poor fellow named Monday could not swim & though we got him on the boat twice the third time he went down, never to rise again, poor fellow, he was drowned without a struggle to save himself. This almost disheartened the rest of us, not knowing which of us would go next. We had not the most distant idea of being saved, for nothing but the mercy of God could save us, & the idea was beyond description that one after the other we would drop off & the one that could hold on longest would see the rest go, & what would be his feelings, no power to assist. But God had mercy on us. Though the boat had turned over some twenty times & we repeatedly managed to keep her on the bottom, her gunwales would be underwater & we could neither get the water out nor would she bear us inside, but all at once, when it was perfectly dark & we had nearly given up all hope, she righted up, leaving about 2 inches of the gunwale left out of water. We saw it was our only chance, & all with one feeling let go & supported ourselves in the water to

[85] A shoal in Broad River, just below Parris Island.
[86] Hauled in, by means of small ropes called brails.
[87] A rower's seat.

let her rise as high as possible, then held on with our hand & reaching over with other splashed out the water as well as we could, until we thought she would bear the weight of one person. One of the Negroes then got in, & with Webb's hat threw out water. (His hat & my cap were the only things we had to bail out with.) As she would lighten we would get in one at a time, until we all got in & felt safe. We then commenced to scull with oar & paddle with the thwart, but made poor headway against wind & tide. When we turned over it must have been ¼ of 6. I suppose we were in the water & on the boat 3 hours, & about 2 hours after we got in the boat before we got ashore. It happened in the middle of Broad River, between the mouth of Archers Creek & Rose Island. We went ashore on Rose Island & walked about a ½ mile to the cabin of two old Negroes belonging to Geo. Edwards.[88] We were very cold, having on no shoes & very little clothing, some with nothing but their shirts. Got by a fire & felt a little better—*we were on land.* We got two pieces of board from the old Negroes & hewed out something to answer for oars to try & get up to Webb's about 5 miles. Got a piece of tobacco from the old fellows & started. Though very much overcome we tried it. We three were to take it by turns to row, but Webb & Colcock were so weak I had to row nearly the whole way. They were all astonished to see that I could stand so much. We got safely up to Webb's about 2 o'clock. Colcock, when we were on the boat, said that one of us must try & swim ashore & get help so he took one of the masts & struck out, though we begged & instructed him not to try it, that he was too much exhausted & sharks would catch him. But he would not listen to us. He had not gone 100 yards when he found his strength failing him & turned back. When he got in ten yards of the boat, he gave out & called to us to help him, but we could not, & only encouraged him by words, telling him to hold on & not give up. We gave the mast a shove & Webb barely caught the end of it & pulled him to the boat, completely exhausted. I lost everything I had on board except my watch & pencil which were in my vest pocket. Lost my trunk with my best clothes, my gun & case, clock, saddle & bridle, shoes, coat I had on & shirt—gold sleeve buttons & studs.

May 10th. Sunday. Stayed at Webb's all day expecting my boat, which did not come. I was very uneasy, thinking that they might have picked up something or another that came out of the other boat & had either turned back to let the folks know at home or had gone in search of our bodies, supposing us to be drowned. A great many of Webb's friends came over during the day to congratulate him on his delivery from a watery grave. We all felt very sore from crawling over the keel of the boat.

[88] Either George Edwards (1776–1859) or his son George B. Edwards (1809–1860), planters. The Edwards plantation on Spring Island lay just west of Rose Island.

May 11th. I was rejoiced this morning to see my boat coming up the river—but what was my astonishment when she got near to see my wife & Dr. Jenkins in the stern. Early on Sunday morning on the beach between Lands End & the Est. of Benj. Jenkins, a parcel of things were picked up which were known to have gone in the boat with us, such as a demijohn with Webb's name on it, his liquor case, marooning box,[89] oars, rudder, mast, spouts[90] & my cigar case with my name on it. What were they to think but that the boat had turned over & we all drowned. The news soon spread, & boats were sent out in every direction in search of our bodies, for everyone was convinced that we had turned over on Parris Bank, or the things could not have got on this shore, that the boat had either sunk or gone to sea. The whole shore on Hilton Head, Parris Isl., Bay Point, St. Helena & even round to Trenchards & no sign of boat or bodies. We were given up by everyone. Persons told my dear wife to prepare for the worst, that all hope was lost, & she would never see me again alive. But she hoped on, & though persuaded by everyone to the contrary, she was determined to go over to Webb's & the last chance. She therefore got Dr. Jenkins to accompany her & very early this morning started off, & she was repaid for her trouble, for there we met again——
If I was worth the trouble—she *thought so anyhow.* C
She rested for a little while & we all started with light hearts for home. We arrived at Lands End about 1 o'clock. Everyone was astonished & rejoiced to see me, it was like being dead & again come to life. People crowded me on all sides. My poor mother was half crazy. She had given up entirely. I found Coz. & Aunt Betsy & Mr. McE. at home, it appeared like the house of death instead of life. After receiving their congratulations, Mr. Mc. proposed & we all knelt & returned thanks to God for his goodness.

May 12th. Clear—rode round to see my relations & friends—— Hoeing March corn, & hauling up what was planted in the list.

May 13th. My yam potatoes have come up so badly & so many have died after they came up that it looks horrid. I am afraid I will not get vines to plant slips. The reds are very pretty. My seed were sound, & I cannot tell what has rotted them after planting. Hoeing corn.

May 14th. Got a few red potato seed from the Major & supplied over a part of my yam patch.[91] Shall supply the rest with vines as soon as they are large enough. Hoeing and hauling corn. Rode over to the Capt.'s in-

---

[89] Box for carrying camping gear and food.
[90] Perhaps "spats," overshoes with cloth uppers.
[91] Replanted potatoes where the seeds had failed to sprout.

tending to take his boat & go down between Lands End & Bay Point, to try & find any things that may have come ashore, but the wind was rather high & we did not go out.

May 15th. Hauled up sugarcane—it has come up very badly. Filled up the vacancy with fodder corn. Hauling up March corn. Colcock's waistcoat was found at Lands End this morning. Manny sick with *colic*. Rode over to the Captain's, he not at home, gone to the Major's. Found the Capt.'s fellow Caesar very low. Sent a boy for Dr. Jenkins. No hopes of the fellow, has hernia.[92] Went to the Major's & told the Capt. what I had done, got a few more potato seed of the Major, to plant next Monday.

May 16th. Went down to Lands End, got a boat & rowed under the shore in search of things as far as Bay Point. Got nothing but a part of my gun case, it had broken to pieces, the gun of course lost. Killed a beef for the Negroes.

May 17th. Went to church. Heard a sermon touching very strongly on our late mishap. E. Chaplin[93] handed me a stick which he picked up near his father's which I knew to be Colcock's.

May 18th. Sent my watch to Charleston by Wm. B. Fripp to be cleaned.

May 20th. Cotton looks very sick in the jointer[94] & high spots—first planting looks much the worst, also badly broken. The cotton came up well, but died off.

May 21st. Still hauling & thinning cotton. Had all my rice thrashed & winnowed, turned out about 15 bushels rough, besides what I have been beating & thrashing all winter.

May 22nd. Went to Beaufort. Got up my Negro summer cloth, bought Schley's stripe. My watch was returned by Hayden & Gregg, not worth fixing.

May 24th. Sunday. Sent Anthony in the boat with 2 hands to Beaufort for my Negroes' summer cloth. He got back early & I gave out the cloth on the same day. Got striped homespun. Negroes are delighted with it.
    Went to church. Heard a most excellent sermon from the Rev'd. Mr.

[92] Strangulated hernia cutting blood circulation to the small intestine.
[93] Edwin W. Chaplin (b. 1827). Son of Edwin and Elizabeth Chaplin. First cousin, once removed, to Thomas B. Chaplin, on his father's side.
[94] Grass.

Young[95]—he is worth hearing. C. Rivers came to the Island, as I hear on a courting expedition.

May 27th.   Went down to Halls Bluff to fish for sheepshead,[96] caught two & two bass. Took Ernest with me. Peggy's child Grace was taken very sick last night. Sent for Jenkins. She has spasms, & I can find out no cause for them, save no doubt she has had a fall or hurt of some kind.

May 29th.   Jenkins called on Grace again—she had three fits in the morning. He gave her a great quantity of laudanum. She sleeps very little, almost constant spasms, complains of pains in her back, shoulder & side.

    The Capt. lost his fellow Caesar. Sawney made the coffin for him.

May 30th.   Grace died this morning about sunrise, had several convulsions last night. She was in her senses to the last.

    Sent the large sorrel mare to Isaac Fripp's horse on Tuesday. He gives me the colt for nothing.

May 31st.   Sunday.[97] "It is strange that creatures, who value themselves on account of a superior degree of reason to that of the brutes should take pleasure in sinking far below them. These such as *voluntarily* deprive themselves of the use of reason to continue ever after in that condition it would seem but a just punishment. Though this be not the consequence of one act of intoxication, it seldom fails to succeed a *course* of it. By a habit of drinking, the greatest genius is often reduced to a mere idiot. Drunkenness is not only in itself a most abominable vice, but it is an inducement to many others. There is hardly any crime so horrid that the drunkard will not perpetrate for the love of liquor. We have known *mothers* sell their children's clothes, the food that they should have eat, and afterwards even the infants themselves, in order to purchase the accursed draught.

    Intoxication is peculiarly hurtful to young persons It heats their blood, impairs their strength, and obstructs their growth; besides the *frequent use* of strong liquors in the early part of life destroys any benefit that might arise from them afterwards. Every act of intoxication puts nature to the expensing of a fever, in order to discharge the poisonous draught. When this is repeated almost every day, it is easy to foresee the consequences. That constitution must be *strong indeed* which is able to hold out under a daily fever: but fevers occasioned by drinking do not always go off in a day; they frequently end in an inflammation of the breast, liver, or

---

[95] Thomas J. Young (d. 1852) conducted services in Grahamville in the early '30s and served as rector of St. John's, Colleton, John's Island, until 1847, when he began assisting at St. Michael's Episcopal Church in Charleston.

[96] A prized foodfish that reaches thirty inches in length and fifteen pounds in weight.

[97] An excerpt from a temperance publication inserted by Mary Chaplin.

brain and produce fatal effects. Though the drunkard should not fall by an acute disease, he seldom escapes those of the chronic kind. Intoxicating liquors, when used to excess, weaken the bowels, and spoil the digestion: they destroy the power of the nerves, and occasion paralytic and convulsive disorders; they likewise heat and inflame the blood, destroy its balsamic quality, render it unfit for circulation and the nourishment of the body. Hence obstructions, atrophies, dropsies and diseases of the lungs. These are the common ways in which drunkards make their exit. Disorders of this kind when brought on by hard drinking, seldom admit of a cure. The habit of drinking frequently proceeds from misfortunes in life. The miserable fly to it for relief. It affords them indeed a temporary ease. But alas! This solace is short lived; and when it is over, the spirits sink as much below their usual tone as they had before been raised above it. Hence a *repetition* of the dose becomes necessary, and every fresh dose makes way for another, till the unhappy wretch becomes a slave to the bottle, and at length falls a sacrifice to what at first perhaps was taken only as a medicine. *No man is so dejected as the drunkard when his debauch is gone off.* Hence it is that those who have the greatest flow of spirits while the glass circulates freely, *are of all other* the most melancholy when sober, and often put an end to their own miserable existence in a fit of spleen or ill humor. It is of the utmost importance to check the *first* propensities to intoxication. After frequent indulgence in excess, the smallest self demise causes a faintness and depression of spirits which nothing can remove but the favorite dram or pretended cordial. Nay, more, the repetition of the last night's debauch is looked upon as the best remedy for the sickness of the ensuing day.

The effects of intoxication are often fatal. No kind of poison kills more certainly than an overdose of ardent spirits. Sometimes by destroying the nervous energy they put an end to life at once; but in general their effects are more slow, and in many respects similar to that of opium. A young man, for a spree, drank *ten glasses of strong brandy.* He soon after fell fast asleep and continued in that situation for several hours, till at length his uneasy *manner of breathing,* the coldness of his extremities, and other threatening symptoms, alarmed his friends and made them send for a physician. He arrived, found the young man sleeping, his countenance ghostly, and his skin covered with a cold clammy sweat. Almost the only signs of life remaining were a *deep laborious breathing,* and a convulsive motion of his bowels—

Oh friend; I go from thee　　　　Darkly to dwell
Where the worm feasteth free　　Givest thou no parting kiss:

　　　　Friend is it come to this
　　　　Oh Friend, farewell"

July 14th. Wednesday. Since the 30th day of June[98] I have not written a line in this journal, having moved to the village directly after & not having the journal with me. We have had a very wet spring, but since the first of this month quite dry, all the low grounds that were overflowed are drying up. Crops look however very promising so far. Corn in particular very fine. A good deal of sickness both with white and black. No deaths that I have heard of. I have four down now with fever. My family have escaped so far. I have suffered much with toothache. Had it extracted the other day by Dr. Jenkins, & he left me minus a piece of my jawbone, which gave me great pain, & is now very sore. The Capt. has been quite sick with fever—*now better.* I traded my sorrel horse not long since with E. McTureous for a bay falcon colt, 4 years old last spring, unbroken—do not think I made a good trade. A distemper, or epidemic, broke out among my horses about the 1st of August, which carried off six in a very short time. I have lost Puss & her colt, the large sorrel mare & her colt, Fanny's colt, the old bay mare. All died very suddenly. The Capt. has lost his sorrel colt & J. L. Chaplin lost two horses.

Aug. 13th. Saw caterpillars in my field on the 8th. Commenced to pick cotton with 2 hands on the 12th. Commenced eating potatoes on Tuesday the 28th of July. They average about a half bushel to the task row.

Aug. 19th. Capt. J. W. Fripp, D. P. Jenkins, the Doctor, E. F. Morrall, W. Morrall, W. W. Fripp & myself started about daylight for Coffin's Island to hunt. Got down about 6½ o'clock, drove the point, ran a large buck up to my stand, shot it with both barrels, wounded it very badly. It took the surf, came out in about 1½ hours. Had a very pretty chase at him on the beach with all the dogs (9). He could not get up the bluff, so took to the surf again. My dog Loud swam out side of him & drove him ashore, where W. W. Fripp shot him down, very fat, large horns in velvet.[99] Drove the next drive, jumped another, W. W. Fripp had a fair shot, did not kill it. Returned to the camp & soon had a fine dinner.

Aug. 20th. Thursday. Went to the plantation. Caterpillars have not spread much, they are now webbed up for a second brood.

Aug. 21st. Duchess had a horse colt, light bay, by Dr. Jenkins' sorrel horse Sheriff on Sunday the 16th of August.

---

[98] May.

[99] A buck's new horns begin growing around March 1 and are protected by a fibrous covering called velvet which he sheds in summer by rubbing the horns against a tree.

Aug. 22nd. Saw J. L. Chaplin & gave him my note for what I owe him. He has taken me in completely. I believed firmly that I agreed with him for $75 & he swears that it is for $175. There was no written agreement, & therefore he had me in his power, but I will know very well not to employ an overseer again without a written contract. Sawney drove a bull to death hauling posts from the pine barren, & for which I intend giving him a flogging.

Aug. 25th. Went down home. Found a little Negro very ill, Sylvia's child, Sarah. It died about 4 o'clock or 3½. A very hard rain passed on each side of the house, but no great deal at the house. All hands hauling peas. I have a very poor crop, the seed was worm-eaten.

Aug. 28th. Went to a party at Dr. Jenkins'.

Aug. 31st. Rode out with Dr. M. M. Sams[100] to shoot plover, got only one bird after a long & hot ride. Lost another colt yesterday, the last colt of my old cream mare given me by Uncle Paul. Do not know what was the matter, died in Uncle Ben's pasture, where it had been since last summer.

Sept. 2nd. Dined at the muster house with the company.

Sept. 3rd. Went down home. The caterpillars[101] have completely taken the field. There is but a very few leaves left, & in two days there will not be one. They are actually boring the hard pods. I never in my whole life saw such a sight, every leaf is completely covered, & they can be raked up by the quart, in the space of 3 feet on the ground. The turkeys eat themselves sick of them. In 3 days the color of the field has changed from a green to dark brown or red. You can drive for a mile with your gig wheels crushing millions all the time in the ruts. They are in each other's way & one half must starve to death. It is a general thing all over the Island, every crop is eaten or being eat up. I do not think there will be more than an average of a quarter of a bale per hand.[102] Finished eating my red roots. Yams are so

---

[100] Melvin Melius Sams (1815–1900), physician and planter. Son of Dr. Berners Barnwell Sams and Elizabeth Hann Fripp. Chaplin's second cousin on his mother's side.
[101] *Noctua xylina.* The moth deposits its eggs on the underside of the cotton leaves and the caterpillars emerge in two weeks. These voracious feeders begin eating the tender upper leaves and progress to the larger leaves before attacking the blossoms and young pods. First noticed in 1800, the cotton caterpillar thereafter was reponsible for severe crop damage on the Sea Islands. Dr. C. W. Capers noted in the *Southern Agriculturist* (May, 1828): "The rapidity with which these insects increase and the short time it takes to consume a large field of cotton is truly astonishing."
[102] A half-bale per hand was expected.

small I broke in some corn & will let them stand awhile. Slips look very poor. Considerable sickness. All hands picking cotton, average about 40 lbs.

Sept. 4th.   Went in the evening to a party at John Pope's.

Sept. 6th.   Cloudy & rainy, wind east, very fresh, think this weather will breed a storm. I am certain it will help caterpillars. Had Virginia Sophia, Daniel Jenkins & Eugene Thomas christened at the village church yesterday. No one present but the family & the Capt. D. Jenkins as godfather—except Aunt Betsy, Mrs. McElheran & Miss Young.[103]

Sept. 16th.   Thursday. Ben brought the beef, not remarkably good. At night John came with grits, did not know how much. Heard from one of the servants the corn was to last 12 days. Did not tho', only 7.

Sept. 25th.   Friday. The cart again today with 7½ bushels of corn for horses and one of cracked for cow. Tony gone to Beaufort, said for collars. Don't know what kind. Think if he had one of some kind for his own neck would not be amiss. Yesterday a bag of grits was sent Tom. I can't imagine how they continue to use so much.

Sept. 27th.   Sunday. Completely stormy today and cold enough for fire—they say caterpillars have entirely disappeared, I wish their ill effects had too.

Sept. 30th.   Wednesday. Anthony bought grits for the house, and the Negroes' allowance.

Oct. 6th.   Tuesday. Sent corn for horses.

Oct. 8th.   Thursday. Grits for the house, and cracked corn for the cow.

I went with Mrs. C. & Ernest as far up the country as Glenn Springs[104] for the former's health—was away about 5 weeks. Trip did Mrs. C. no good. Cost me about 400 dollars, which I wish I now had in my pocket.

[103] Maria Young (b. 1800). Teacher who boarded with the McElherans.
[104] Fashionable spa in Spartanburg District. The Governor moved his headquarters there every summer; lawyers, legislators, and judges followed, turning Glenn Springs into a summer capital. The spa had a reputation as a "market" for widows and widowers looking for mates.

After I returned I took the whole family down to Chaplin's Island. Sophy, Daniel & the baby having been quite sick during our absence in the up-country, I thought this trip would be of service to them (and so it was), & also prevent our taking the fever as we returned before frost. We were on the island two weeks. After our return from the island Daniel & Virginia were taken sick both with sore throat, the former I think salivated.[105] They are now both sick. So with all this trouble together with that of moving from the village this journal has hardly been thought of—Nov. 13th, 1846.

Nov. 12th.   Finished digging slips—made 27½ banks & 1 week's allowance, 11 banks' eating, 16 seed. Turned out tolerable in spots but very broken.

Nov. 13th.   All the women carrying out sedge on cotton land, 1 bundle to the row. Men moving the cow pen over to this side, also the hogs, 12 in number. Isaac's child Birch[106] was burned to death while I was on the island.

Nov. 14th.   Marked & altered 19 calves. Planted some peach & winter plum seed.

Nov. 16th.   Sent 4 hands to the Island to burn a lime kiln & get roller stuff.[107] 6 hands cutting rushes, all the women heaping up sedge.

Nov. 18th.   Sent 5 hands to the Island for wood. Ben ditto for wild ducks. 3 hands grubbing, all women listing in rushes[108] for cotton.

Nov. 24th.   Sent Anthony with four hands to Beaufort for a barrel of crockery from town.[109] I give the set six months to be broken, & the old ones half that time.

Started two carts putting sedge in the pen. All hands still carrying out the same. The damned catfish mouth Paul Barnes would not send the barrel because there was 60 cts. freight due on it.

---

[105] Produced an excessive amount of saliva—a symptom of "overheating" or a result of taking calomel or some other medicine containing mercury.
[106] Isaac and Amy's child.
[107] Lime obtained from burning oyster shells was used as a mortar, fertilizer, bleach, and disinfectant. It was commonly spread on the dirt floors of Negro cabins. "Roller stuff" refers to the oak limbs used as rollers in Sea Island cotton gins. These rollers had to be replaced frequently, sometimes daily, during the ginning season.
[108] Turning marsh grass under the ground.
[109] Charleston.

Nov. 27th.   Very heavy white frost this morning. Sent the boat to Beaufort for crockery. Amy[110] was delivered of a girl child.

Nov. 28th.   The boat returned after dark last night with the barrel of crockery, a dinner set & tea set—$56.25. The work of destruction has already commenced; the handle of one of the cups broken off this morning & by the mistress too.

Set out 4 grapevines & made a sort of trellis for them to run on should they live.

Nov. 29th.   Went to church. Returned & dined with Wm. Jenkins, the first time I ever took a meal in his new house. He has it nicely furnished.

Nov. 30th.   Monday, the last day of this last fall month. Commenced working on the Ferry Bridge. Met at the causeway at 8 o'clock, after long wrangling between several of the men over how the work should be done, everyone differing as usual, they commenced pulling down the bridge, & had not finished the middle pier when we knocked off at sunset. All is to be taken down & built anew, which I think will take them the balance of the week if not longer, for now the bridge is down the commissioners will be obliged to build it up again before they quit. Had only 5 hands on the road. Sent the balance of the men for wood, & the women to listing in marsh sedge.

Dec. 1st.   On the roads—finished pulling down the bridge & commenced to build up the middle pier, took everything down to the foundation. Commissioners wanted to keep us on the road after sunset. Came away about a ½ hour after sunset and let them return[111] us & be damned——

Received last night a letter from Col. Treville stating that the chancellor had given a decision in our favor in the case of Baker & c.[112]

Dec. 2nd.   E. Capers came home with me last night. Went down to the bridge—found that the pier head, or hog pen, as some call it, had floated off & from all appearances the work has been throwed back two days, the fault I attribute to there being too many directors on the work. I was one

---

[110] Isaac's wife.
[111] Report.
[112] Chaplin's triumph was short-lived. Baker appealed and the higher court would reverse the decision. Mrs. Baker's deeds to her sons would be declared invalid because they tended to defeat the chief object of her marriage settlement—to provide her husband with the means to support himself *and* her. Thomas and Saxby would be enjoined from interfering with Baker's management of their mother's estate for as long as Isabella and Baker both lived.

of the volunteers to stay on the bulkhead all night to prevent the work from floating off again. I got home however about 4 o'clock in the morning.

Dec. 3rd. Found the work all right this morning—did not get to the bridge before 12 m. Edgar Fripp & J. W. Pope had a few harsh words which I fear will lead to serious consequences.
did not, one afraid & other darsent (dares not)

Dec. 4th. Clear, went to the bridge again. We now think that the work will detain us until Wednesday. Oliver Fripp quarreled with E. Fripp today, whose turn will it be tomorrow. The Ladies Island hands have been working on the other bulkhead since Tuesday. They are doing the work in the right way & will get done before we will with fewer hands.

Dec. 5th. Saturday. Went on the road, things quiet today. More work done. Had all the hands, except 4 which I sent to Beaufort for Negro cloth & shoes, listing ground. Our commissioner allowed me one hand from yesterday for a crosscut saw I furnished on the road.

Dec. 6th. Let the horses rest today, did not go to church.

Dec. 7th. Found dinner on the road. Was fortunate in getting a haunch of venison of J. L. Chaplin for the dinner. The bridge & bulkhead nothing like done, now 7 days' work. We have had almost August weather in December for the work.

Dec. 8th. Excused from the road today—embraced the opportunity to rest. All the women & the men (not on the roads) listing ground.

Dec. 9th. Went again on the roads. Finished putting on the sleepers, & threw on the plank, but they were not regularly laid. Broke up after dark.

Dec. 10th. Excused from the road. Dined at the Agricultural Society. Went to Mary Jenkins' wedding. She married to George Chisolm.[113] Enjoyed myself very much, quite a stylish affair—broke up about 4 o'clock a.m.

Dec. 11th. Friday. At home all day recruiting from the last night's frolic.
and a big frolic it was, you bet

---

[113] George A. Chisolm (1825–1904), planter, of St. John's Parish, Charleston District. Robert Chisolm's first cousin, once removed, on his father's side.

Dec. 12th. Dined with F. Capers. Dr. Jenkins' horse ran away with the Capt. & Isaac Wilson,[114] smashed up Uncle Ben's gig.

Dec. 13th. Went to church, dined with the Captain.

Dec. 14th. Quite unwell, at home all day.
I was always unwell after these dinners

Dec. 15th. Bridge finished yesterday. Rec'd. an invitation to a party at Jos. D. Edings'[115] on Thursday next. Hephzibah Pope[116] is to be married to Wm. John Pope[117] tonight.
     Commenced ginning white cotton.

Dec. 16th. Ginning cotton. Lambeth[118] killed the last beef he got from me, making four in all—3 at $12 & 1 at $10 = $46. Hitched in a young yoke of steers to break for oxen. Sold a pair of turkeys to old Mrs. Lambeth[119] for $1.50. Cold drizzle rain all the latter part of the day. *Self very unwell.*

Dec. 17th. I continue to grow worse—most violent pain in my joints, shoulders, knees, ankles & hips, which proves to be inflammatory or flying rheumatism. Took to bed today.

Dec. 18th. Pains get even worse, nothing relieves me, tho I try everything imaginable.

Dec. 19th. In bed, no better.

Dec. 21st. Never suffered so much in all my life —worse. Can't get a Dr. to attend me.

Dec. 22nd. Still suffering great pain. Dr. Jenkins went hunting instead of coming to see me. Don't know anything of the weather.

Dec. 23rd. Wednesday. Sent my boat *yesterday* with seven hands & Anthony to Savannah to sell some poultry. Sent 15 pr. turkeys & 8 pr. of geese. I still very sick, no better.

[114] Probably Isaac K. Wilson, of St. John's Parish, Charleston District, then on St. Helena for the wedding of George Chisolm and Mary Jenkins.
[115] Joseph D. Edings (b. 1804), planter. Lived at 600-acre Eddings Point, in the northeast corner of the Island. Husband of Adelaide Fripp.
[116] Hephzibah J. Pope (1824–1849), of Hilton Head Island.
[117] William John Pope (1814–1852), of Hilton Head. See note, Aug. 7, 1851.
[118] John E. Lambeth (b. 1815), Beaufort butcher.
[119] Lambeth's mother, Mrs. C. A. Lambeth (b. 1790).

Dec. 24th. Several persons have called to see me since I have been sick. The Capt. left for the main today.

Dec. 25th. Christmas Day, which I spent in bed in the greatest pain. Boat got back from Savannah. Anthony says he sold the poultry for about $40, but could not produce more than about $24. He must have been drunk for he admits that three turkeys were stolen from him while he was sitting on the coop. He shall account.

Dec. 26th. Still sick, but a little better. Ventured downstairs because I could use my legs a little but paid for it. First time I have been able to stand up since Thursday.

Dec. 29th. Mother came over from the main to see me, hearing that I was sick.

Dec. 31st. Better, went downstairs. Had to go to bed directly after dinner from pain in my right hip.

Got 3 bags of cotton packed—
5 carts hauling manure—
All hands ginning—
End of the year 1846—

1847

Jan. 1st. Friday. Went outdoors & suffered for it by having to go back to bed, & there remain for a week——

I went over to the main with Mother on Friday the 15th, returned on the Wednesday after. The Major was married[1] on Thursday, the 14th inst. Brought over 4 hands from the main—Dick, Charlotte, Lucy and Lavinia. Sent over Ben, Violet & Nelly.

Jan. 25th. All the men ditching, women listing.

June 4th. Friday. I have neglected this journal for near five months, owing to sickness &c, but will carry it on after this . . . if possible.

Commenced moving to the village.

Fanny Douglass had a light sorrel mare colt, star on the forehead. Sent the flat to the Island with 3 cows & calves to E. Pritchard[2] in exchange for 1 cow & calf which he warrants in every way. Sent 3 carts to the village. All the family, except wife, baby & self went down. The crops this spring are very backward, at least a month. The season has been exceedingly wet, & the plants were attacked by the fly & root bug. Lost some cotton by the high tides in May, & by rain. Have at this time a very fine corn crop.

June 8th. Still moving. It appears we have more to move every year. Sent the flat loaded to the village, went the bridge way. Sent the cow down, also two carts, & will have another cart load tomorrow, including lime. Wife & self with baby went down in the evening. Do hope I will get

[1] He married Anne Jenkins, daughter of Benjamin Jenkins and Hannah Fripp, of Wadmalaw Island.
[2] Edward Pritchard (b. 1810), shopkeeper, later a lumber inspector in Charleston.

through with this trouble tomorrow. I have lost 17½ days' work in moving this year, besides stable boys & carpenter.

June 16th. Clear in the morning—commenced cutting oats. Rain came up in the evening, had to quit. Women hoeing cotton. Carpenter Prince working on the flats.

June 17th. Heavy wind from E. about 2 o'clock with very heavy rain. Finished cutting the ripest of my oats, & will no doubt lose them all, just my luck. Rained considerably all night.

June 18th. Wind E., very heavy weather. Expect this weather will continue some time, if so my oats are gone. Came down to the plantation. Hands banking ground & planting slips. Oats all laying down, wet & full of sand. Weather looks worse & worse.

June 21st. Came down home, found Jubah extremely ill, very much afraid she will die. Dr. Jenkins called to see her, said she has inflammation of the stomach. He dined with me & saw her at intervals during the day. She did not appear to be any better when we left. Planting slips with all hands.

June 25th. Came down, Jubah much better. All hands hoeing cotton.

June 28th. Anniversary of our company in Beaufort—forgot all about it, don't care a *damn*.

July 5th. Monday. The 71st anniversary of Independence celebrated today. Wind E. Very bad weather, rain all day. Went to the muster house, poor sport. Worse & worse every 4th on this Island, except in orations. The one today was delivered by Mr. Williams,[3] a graduate of West Point. The composition was excellent, but unfortunately his delivery was bad, & having an impediment in his speech which prevented him from speaking loud enough, he was not distinctly heard in the further part of the room. The dinner was excellent (but cold), toasts poor & few. In the evening we had a fine display of fireworks at the village. After which a picnic & a dance till two o'clock. So ended the celebration of American Independence on the anniversary of '47 of St. Helenaville.

July 6th. Came down home. All hands hauling cotton. Returned to village in the evening. Attended a party at Mr. McElheran's.

[3] Col. James H. Williams (1813–1892), of Newberry District.

July 9th. Came down. Sandiford[4] called, made a trade with him for a half Durham bull, will be 3 years old in December next. Gave him 2, two year old steers & an old cow & calf in trade.
How I used to be cheated & am still.

July 13th. Did nothing at the village all day yesterday. Came down in the morning. Planting slips in the oat patch on the other side, making in all now planted 11 acres & 1 task. Isaac Fripp called, & rode over the crop with me—he thinks it very good. E. Capers dined with me. Stopped at his father's on my way back to the village.

July 19th. I was very unwell the last part of last week with sore throat, & a slight fever once in a while. Thought I would have the mumps, but did not. Ned has been with me all the time.

July 26th. Broke Anthony & put Isaac in his place as driver. He took it very coolly. I have sent him to work out & pay me what he can.

——— ——— ——— ——— ——— ———

Oct. 12th. Since I last wrote in my journal, the hand of affliction hath been very heavy upon me. The Almighty has stricked forth his red right hand against me, the anger of Death hath cut off the fairest and loveliest of my flock. The soft eyes of my lovely little daughter Isabel[5] were closed in their last sleep on Sunday, the third day of October. Alas for the poor mother! The yet unopened bud plucked from its parent stem. Woe is me, my daughter. Isabel my daughter. It is the will of God! Where are my friends? In mine adversity they rejoiced and gathered themselves together; yea the very abject came together against me unawares.[6]

I am compelled to begin in the world again, not with forty, but *nine hands in the field.* And a large family to support & educate— Well, many have commenced with *much less* & made fortunes. I do not wish a fortune, but enough to live comfortably & honestly on & educate my children. I have seen enough of men to cause me to wish to have [   ] dealings with them. I know they do not care to deal with me *now, I am poor.* But, by God's help, I may be worth something one of these future days, when I know how I will be again sought after & counted. And I trust this great & sad lesson will be sufficient to teach me what & who they are, and to keep them at a proper distance.

[4] Either Isaac or James H. Sandiford.
[5] Isabella Caroline Chaplin (b. early 1847–d. Oct. 1847). Chaplin's sixth child, named after his mother.
[6] A paraphrase of Psalms 35:15.

I have been sold of land and Negroes, furniture, stock, possessions & everything I was worth in the world. I was fortunate enough to buy or have a little bought in for me[7] & on that little I *intend* to live. My village house was sold, & I am compelled to risk the summer with my family on the plantation. This alone creates in me great uneasiness, for if anyone should be taken very sick, I have not the means of removing them to any healthier spot, not even if it was on the same Island, for I would not intrude them on my *kind friends* of the [   ]. But, *God's Will Be Done.*

[7] Friends of the planter might buy his property in his stead—essentially, lending or giving him the money to save his goods. Or sympathizers might agree to bid low so that the dispossessed owner could buy back his property at a modest cost.

1848

April 7th. Friday. The weather is windy, cool and rainy today. This is the first rain we have had of any importance for ten weeks or more. Everything has been suffering for the want of moisture. I commenced planting cotton on the 4th.

April 8th. Finished banking potato land, and planted one task of the yellow yam potato. They are something new, & are considered by persons to be a great bearer. I manured the task with heavy coat of marsh under list, & 9 loads compost on the list.
(They turned out little or nothing, 1849).
    I was taken with the *mumps* on Wednesday the 29th of March—did not go very hard with me at first, but unfortunately on Saturday 1st. inst. I took a cold which drove the disease downwards into the testicles, when I suffered most excruciating pain for three days. I was relieved however on the 4th day by warm ointments &c. The swelling has gone down but left me with a most distressing ringing & buzzing in my head, & partial deafness & dizziness.
This deafness still continues—no worse or better—now 28 years 1876

April 20th. Can't get on with my journal somehow. I have had a hard bout of the mumps, but am a good deal better, only a very annoying ringing in my ears, partial deafness & giddiness in the head. Finished planting cotton yesterday (19th).
    Had a severe hailstorm last Saturday night. Some cotton up. Daniel has the mumps. Two Negroes sick. Mother came over from the main today. Commenced listing April corn land & plowing early pea land.

April 21st. Good Friday—went fishing.

April 27th. My birthday, though I may never see the end of it. Twenty-six years of age, Oh! How time has flown. But as yesterday I was united in marriage with *her.* It is but a day—still it is *nine years.* In *compassion,* I am content. I have suffered *nothing.* But I speak before my time, this is the *night before, I may not see the morrow. God's will be done.*

May 1st. Received a summons to meet the Board of Commissioners of Roads for this parish—one of which I was appointed by the legislature at its last session—at the meeting house on Ladies Island, for the purpose of laying out a public road from what is called the Old House Landing to Richard Reynolds'[1] Landing on Coosaw Creek in as direct a line as practicable, & *with* least injury as possible to the persons through whose land the road may run. We laid out the road, I believe, to the satisfaction of all parties except C. G. Capers, who appears to be very much put out, & I think reasonably so, he being the only one inconvenienced in the least in my opinion, & I voted against the road being put in that place. The proposition I made for the road to run in a direct line from the meeting house to the road opposite McKee's house, which would cut off at least a ½ a mile from where it now is to run, was lost I think by votes of the Ladies Island Commissioners, who thought it would be too much work for them, the road having to cross a swamp & had to be made by the public, when in fact it only benefited two persons. After laying out the road we all, or at least all from this Island, dined with Mr. Capers.

May 5th. Finished the 1st hoeing of potatoes. The weather is excessively dry. Everything suffering for rain. There is no use in planting anything for it won't or can't come up. Plowing my March corn—it is very broken, & what I have set out has died.

May 7th. Very warm today. Sophy & Ernest went to church. I pity my poor horses, plow hard all the week and pull that heavy carriage to church on Sunday. Edward Capers came here after supper & brought two drum & two whiting lines he made for me.

May 8th. Very hot, no sign of rain unless it was that I heard frog holler towards evening. Wife rode over to the Riverside with me on horseback. All the ponds & cow wells have dried up. One cow buggy is going into the swamp for water. *Hoeing cotton.*

May 9th. Sent the men to dig out the cow wells. This weather makes me think of the time I generally move to the village. This will not trouble me

---

[1] Richard M. Reynolds (1797–1861), planter, of Jericho Plantation, Ladies Island. His first wife was Margaret McKee (1808–1844); his second, Ann Eliza Oswald (1825–1859).

this year, & perhaps never again. *Edings*[2] *now owns my house*—I am sorry I ever built it. All my trouble & expense sacrificed *by the sheriff* for $820. The billiard table also gone, it once afforded me some gratification, but *never will again.* I spend this summer on the plantation, live or die. It is strange, I have not had a visitor for near a month *except Capers.* Property gone— *friends* decrease—better for me. They were the *friends of my property, not of me.* I have just heard that Robt. Brown & Son,[3] factors, have failed. He was a factor for a number of persons in this neighborhood & they have lost a good deal of money by him. Uncle Ben I learn has lost $250. He had better have taken his money & helped me in my trouble than *plead poverty* before he was ever [   ] & still have money in his factor's hands & to lose it too. I am sorry for him, it will near on to killing him.

He is dead long since, & knows not of trouble.

I never learned any wisdom from my misfortunes, just the same now as ever. But now, I am broken down in health, in spirit & in fortune. God's will &c 1876

May 9th. Tuesday. I am brought down through extravagance to a mere competency, from working 30 hands in the field to bare 8, all the rest little & big sold for debt, as would these, had it not been for *wife's legacy*[4]—*thank God.* Everything was sold, stock, horses, furniture & plantation carts & wagons, boats & flats. I have barely saved enough to carry on the place. My corn all sold, leaving me a bare ten bushels as my right by law, except what I was fortunate enough to buy in. My best horses have been *sacrificed*—fine colts that I had taken all the trouble to raise, & were then just old enough to use, were taken, sold for a trifle, & before it could be proven what they were fit for. All, all this for *extravagance* and *imprudence*—I hope I will *remember it.*

I have lived to see much harder times, war, pestilence & famine. I never [   ] at the horrid state I am now in. 1876

May 11th. Went down to Lands End to try the chance of a sheepshead at the Captain's ground, but met the Major who had been there & had not a bite, so I returned as I went. The Capt. dined with me—his visits are now rare. Commenced running two furrows in the cotton alley for the purpose of both killing what grass & weeds may appear there, but to enable the hands to do more hauling when they commence it. Looks very much like rain this evening. If it does not I shall not wonder, as it rains in every direction apparently & that is always the way, except just about

---

[2] Joseph D. Edings.
[3] Cotton factors in Charleston. Brown was born in Scotland.
[4] Mary Chaplin's grandfather, John McDowell, left her $15,000 in bank securities. See December 31, 1851.

here. *But God is just—he knows best—his will be done.* Took up Duchess's colt, Cowskin. The water is so scarce I fear he suffers.

May 12th. Overhauled my bacon, found it very much eaten by a black hairy worm. The eggs which produce these worms appear to have been deposited in the meat by a dark brown colored bug or fly, about the size of a firefly. These eggs first produce something in the shape & appearance of *skippers*[5] which eventually grow to these worms & eat into the meat until it resembles honeycomb. They appear to attack hams as a preference, not being often found in the fat of the meat, & as the gams[6] are generally coated with a strata of fat on the underside they do not often attack them. I have tried this method of preserving meat against these insects— viz., take a box lined with lead & almost airtight, put a thick layer of charcoal in the bottom, and alternately, a layer of meat & a layer of coal to the top, taking care to cover the top pretty thick with coal, & no other covering.[7] The weather is very cool today, hail somewhere. Killed a small beef in the afternoon.

May 13th. Very cool this morning, but clear. We slept under blankets last night & a fire would be comfortable. Finished hauling potatoes, & went on hoeing cotton. Make each hand haul & slack out a task of cotton for morning's work.[8]

May 14th. Wife went out to church—the first time for two or three years. I dined with Mr. Capers. Clouds up in the evening & looks like a change in the weather. Ed Capers came home with me & spent the night.

May 16th. Tuesday. H. McKee & Benj. Johnson[9] came today in two large flats for the cattle they bought at the sale. They left here about dusk for Coffin's Island, which they have bought, with 21 head. They intend putting the cattle on the Island & raising stock, make butter, sell beef &c &c. They are to return tomorrow for the balance—25 head.

May 17th. I took a ride with Uncle Ben in the morning all around the neighboring pastures in search of the cattle that are missing since the sale, but found only one, in the Major's pasture. There are at least 11 missing. Johnson & McKee returned for the remainder of their cattle today about

---

[5] Small, stout-bodied insects, resembling butterflies.
[6] The front thighs.
[7] Method recommended in Francis Holmes's *The Southern Farmer and Market Gardener.*
[8] The workers are hoeing dirt up to the cotton stalks and thinning out the weaker plants.
[9] McKee and Johnson were first cousins.

4 o'clock p.m. and left at 8 o'clock p.m. with 23 head, making in all 44 head, two less than they bought. They left me two cows, which would have made the 46, the No. they bought. But there are a number missing. They were satisfied however & told me I was *welcome* to all the rest *if I could find them.* Very kind, almost giving me what is my own. However I am not *particular.* I will endeavor to find all I can. I have now for stock—3 oxen, 2 3-year-old steers, 1 bull, 11 milch cows, 4 heifers & 9 calves, 0 yearlings, 0 steers and 0 heifers.

(*June 16th, all killed by rogues since the cattle were moved.*)

May 18th.   Finished plowing through the cotton, all but the five acres of Fraser's[10] seed, which I intend giving to my wife if it comes to anything worthwhile. Sent Anthony to Beaufort. I suspect that some of my hogs have been taken out of the pen—must see into it. A shower would be most agreeable to them, poor things. I put Jim & Frank at chopping through the corn planted with the plow. I find the earth so dry that I cannot throw the dirt well up with the plow.

May 20th.   Rained very hard last night, but did not last very long. Supplying over cotton this morning. Sent Isaac & Peter to Beaufort for my Negro cloth, & a plow & hoes. Clouds very heavy, & wet weather likely to continue. I did not get the cloth & other articles. They were shipped in the schooner *Science* which has not arrived.

May 22nd.   Finished supplying over all the cotton this morning. I think it will be all the supplying it will get, as it will be too late. But this rain will certainly bring it all up, else the next supplying will be with pea seed. All hands thinning & hauling up cotton, I taking it down to 2 stalks where it is healthy. My cotton at this time looks better I think than most that I see in the neighborhood & wants thinning in the low places very badly. The tap root having at last reached moist earth, the cotton grows very fast considering the dryness of the surface.

May 24th.   We had no rain last night as I expected, the wind blew very hard all night, which has nearly dried up what little we had yesterday. Sophy went to call on Mrs. Melvin Sams[11] in the morning. She has just returned from Columbia, where she was called to witness the death of her brother Thd. Black. She is sick & could not be seen today. My poor horses had a long drive for nobody's good, and certainly not for theirs.

All hands hauling & thinning cotton, it seems an endless job. My corn

[10] Seed developed by Frederick G. Fraser (b. 1794), planter, of St. Helena and St. Bartholomew's Parish.
[11] Eliza Black Sams.

suffers for want of dirt but I can't help it, will have the plows in it tomorrow. Planted some cauliflower and cabbage seed this day.

May 26th. Friday. Sent Isaac to Beaufort in the Major's boat for my Negro cloth &c. In the meantime they were landed from the schooner *Science,* on board of which they were shipped. She passed on to Savannah, & landed the things on her return trip, at Lands End. This is a fine way of doing business, the things were shipped on the 9th inst. I got up from town a double moldboard[12] plow to run in the alleys, throwing the dirt, for keeping the alleys clean, & make the hauling easy for the Negroes. Gave out Negro cloth in the evening. Gave out new hoes to Jim, Anthony, Moll, Peter.

May 29th. Finished plowing the old corn the 3rd time, & I think it will be the last. I will have it hauled up when it shoots the tassel & lay it by.[13] Started my double moldboard plow, in the Fraser seed cotton. It works remarkably well, & I think it an excellent article. I can have as much work done with it in one day as with two barshears,[14] & does the work better— that is, running in the alley, cutting out all the grass & throwing up the dirt on each side, of course not quite as high as a barshear would, as it runs in the center of the alley, & it can be used at any age of the cotton without injury to the roots that run off from the tap root, as the other plow would do. I am much pleased with it. My Fraser cotton looks very badly. It was planted late, & I attribute the cotton from the other seed looking so well to its being planted early.

June 1st. I borrowed Uncle Ben's boat & went down to Skull's Inlet to see if I could get anything from the wreck of a large brig, which went ashore on the beach about a week ago. Uncle Ben has been down twice, & got a quantity of odds & ends from the wreck, but I heard nothing of it before last night. I left here after sunset, & went down in quick time, across all the marsh in a direct line for the inlet. I never saw a higher tide, it was almost impossible to say which was creek & which was marsh. The Major's Jack & Sam went down with me. We found that the vessel had broken all to pieces, some parts on one island & some on another. We got nothing but some pieces of northern pine boards, copper & a few iron spikes. Saw two splendid masts of soft pine, would make fine boards, but could not manage them. I spent the night in a small camp on the beach.

---

[12] A curved iron plate attached to the plowshare which lifts, turns, and pulverizes the soil. The double moldboard throws the dirt up to *both* sides.
[13] Dirt will be thrown to the corn plants when the tassels, or male flowers, appear, behind which come the silk and the young ear. Then the corn will be left to mature.
[14] Plows with a single cutting edge.

Yesterday, I was out with E. Chaplin[15] on Parris Bank striking sharks—saw two but did not get a chance to strike either. The wind too high.

June 2nd. Out early this morning to find what I could—pieces of the wreck in every direction. E. Chaplin came down to the inlet about 10 o'clock a.m. Codding & B. Capers also. Pritchard was hard at work also. I returned in the evening with a good load. Left E. Chaplin down there—he will make the best of it. There is any quantity of wood & iron to be got for the trouble of cutting it out of hard oak, but no copper. The brig was a miserable old hulk, quite rotten. She is from Southport.[16] That is the name on her stern but I do not recollect her name. I have lost this day's work with four hands which I can very badly lose. I must make it up next week. I could get no fish on the Island, don't know the reason why.

June 4th. Sophy got a letter from her sister Sarah,[17] whom she has not heard from for four or five years. She is married to a Col. Burroughs, an Englishman & in the British army, so she says. She has a child 3 years old, & about having another (same authority). Hope that she may be happy & do well is the wish of one who knows nothing of her, nor cares to know anything.
⁎⁎28 years ago⁎⁎

June 5th. Each hand hauled a task in plowed corn (which I intend to give a good bed to & lay by) & then went into the potatoes. Had the ox cart hauling sedge on slip land, from 6 to 8 loads pr. task. I'm running the double moldboard through plowed corn to make it easier to bank. Frank with horse cart, hauling pea & yams from Riverside. Had ripe figs off the tree in the yard on the 3rd instant. Planted today, sugar, corn, & cabbage seed & cauliflowers.

June 9th. Ernest had a fever today. He was very foolishly allowed by his mother to go in the creek yesterday for crabs when I was away, & eat a quantity of plums which affected his bowels. This the beginning, & if another course is not pursued, will not be the ending. Planted some cucumbers today.

June 10th. Rode over to Uncle Ben's pasture to try & get home 3 yearlings I had there, but they are not to be found. The neighbors' Negroes have taken them for public property & killed them all. I strongly suspect

[15] Probably Edwin Chaplin. See note, May 17, 1846.
[16] Southport, N.C., at the mouth of Cape Fear River.
[17] Sarah Creighton Burroughs, Sophy's full sister.

the Major's Negroes. They are the greatest rogues in the neighborhood. I have had at least 20 head of cattle killed this last winter & spring.

June 13th. Stopped the plow & put Jim & Moll hoeing cotton. The grass is growing so rapidly that I can't keep it down. I fear I shall be badly stuck. Planted a few rutabaga turnips. Uncle Ben moved to the village yesterday—he must have got everything wet. However, I heard that the rain was not so heavy at the other end of the Island. The Major moved today.

June 14th. Cut oats—very inferior. Went to the Indian Hills & dined with the Captain. He has there a very good crop of cotton, corn & potatoes. Mother came over in the evening.

June 15th. Clear & very warm. Sheared my sheep, and marked 5 calves, altered 1.

June 16th. Very hot. Overhauled my meat—⅔rds spoiled. Black Hawk ran off with the cart & made a smash of it. He got himself so completely tied up that he could not move and squealed like a pig. He bruised himself very much but no bad cuts, all from the carelessness of Frank. I had just commenced hauling compost out on slip land, this will throw me back.

June 19th. Sent Isaac & Jim to Beaufort for some tar, which I intend to burn around the house this summer, hoping it may keep off fever.[18] The Negroes did not get back today, owing to the wind. Finished hoeing cotton, two hands howing April corn, 1st working. Saw cotton blossoms yesterday.

June 20th. Isaac got back this morning, said he was nearly swamped. The corn & cotton much blown down by wind last night. All hands hoeing April corn. Eugene has fever this evening.

June 21st. Commenced burning tar around the house at night. It will require a great deal—1 qt. does not burn 3 hours. Budded 13 buds of peaches & nectarines I got of J. Fripp today. Helen laying up, now 2 days. Jim had a tooth pulled today. Eugene has no fever today.

June 22nd. Finished hoeing April corn. Commenced giving the Fraser cotton the second hoeing & thinning down to a stand. Started two plows

[18] Malarial fever, caused by a parasite injected into the bloodstream by the bite of the *Anopheles* mosquito.

in the slip land again. Moll spreading sedge. Ordered Thos. Chaplin[19] today to summon two hands of Mrs. Reynolds[20] & repair the bridge near her house on Saturday next.

Prince & Jack commenced repairing my boat today—they did not do much today but will come early tomorrow.

June 24th. Let Dr. Jenkins have the use of my cow Huper, for the summer. He sent for her in the afternoon to take her to the village. I heard afterwards that his fellow Toby knocked off one of her horns in going down. She ran after him so tis said, & he struck her with a stick. I am sorry for it. I never get any good for my kindness, if you so call it.
Jenkins has been a secret enemy of mine for 30 odd years & is still, he keeps it up. W.J.J. now keeps a liquor shop in Beaufort—just opposite his boy [   ]
All kinds of work today. Some hands listing slip land where I can't plow handily, some banking, some spreading sedge (I have got through with the latter), one hand hoeing a spot in the potato patch where the vines do not grow, I can't tell why. They are up well enough but do not grow atall. They were manured with compost.

June 25th. Mother & Sophy went to church. Virginia has a fever today. Tony came over from the main yesterday. Got 5 gals. lamp oil & 2 gals. of vinegar by Hamilton's boat from Savannah today.

June 27th. Heard today that the cow I lent Dr. Jenkins is dead—got killed by a bull I hear.
He has forgotten that I ever loaned him a cow, 1876. He never paid for it
Carpenters painting my boat.

June 28th. I intended going to Beaufort to attend the anniversary parade of our company, but a heavy rain came up while I was at the Riverside & I did not go. The rain did not reach here, & not nearer than the line gate between here & the River. We had none all day. All hands hauling cotton. Tony & Simon went to Beaufort.

July 1st. Saturday. Clear & very hot. All hands planting slips, got in today 11 tasks[21] in all. The Capt. called in the morning. I called on J. H. Webb in the forenoon. He has the fever, has had it several days, brought on by exposure.

The carpenters finished my boat, charged me $8. She is now in pretty

[19] Thomas Chaplin, Jr., of Ladies Island.
[20] Mrs. Caroline Reynolds (1794–1853), planter.
[21] Two and three-quarter acres.

good order, but I did not have paint enough to give her a good coat. Had ripe watermelon today for the first.

July 4th. Independence Day. Hauling cotton. Intended going to Beaufort but had no way of going. Went to the muster house & dined with the St. Helena Company, from there to the village where they, by subscription, had a poor display of fireworks, and a picnic. At night we danced. I had a good supper. So passed the 4th July 1848. I stayed all night with Uncle Ben. The village looks as dull as ever, & has no charm for me. I hate the sight of it.

July 5th. Got my rifle from Mickler today. Cut my old seine & fitted it to my boat. All hands hauling cotton. P. W. Perry[22] & Tom Fripp had a quarrel at the muster house yesterday, did not fight. Perry sent for my pistols today. *All smoke.*

July 6th. Very hot. Finished plowing the cotton. Put both plows in the corn. Cut one of *Pelican*'s sails today to fit Jack. Shot a plover this morning with the rifle.

July 8th. Went over to the Point with Mother, was very much astonished when I got to the Riverside to find that wife had let Ernest go over also. She said that Mother begged so hard she could not refuse. We had it very hot indeed, & arrived at the Point about 3 o'clock. Saw a very heavy rain behind us from Hangman's Point,[23] & expected it to catch us, but we got ashore before it, & then it rained very little.

july 11th. Returned home, very clear & a most excessively hot day. Ernest & I both got much sunburnt. Found the hands hauling up April corn. They planted slips yesterday. All well.

July 13th. Commenced hauling the Fraser cotton. It has improved very much. Think this shall be the last working, unless I hand pick it. Killed beef for the market today, my kill second on the list. E. Chaplin has left the market, & J. L. Chaplin took his place.

July 15th. Planting slips—finished now 6 acres, will plant a few more for seed. Finished hauling the cotton. Dug in my Irish potatoes, they are very poor, have nearly all rotted in the ground. Very windy in the evenings, so

[22] Peter W. Perry (b. 1810), son of Peter Perry and Sarah Fripp. Chaplin's second cousin on his mother's side. He and Thomas J. Fripp, son of Col. Thomas Fripp, were first cousins.
[23] Point of land at the confluence of the Combahee and Chehaw rivers.

much so that we cannot light our tar lamps. It is very hot out of the wind. Sent to the village for a shoulder of lamb, not worth the trouble.

July 17th.   I rode as far as the lodge to meet a committee, of which I am one, the object of which is to give a dinner to the volunteers from this parish to Mexico.[24] It was decided to have the dinner in W. W. Fripp's barn on Tuesday the 25 inst. It is to be a sort of picnic. All hands supplying over some slips that did not take well. I had 50 water & 34 muskmelons picked & sent them to Savannah by Hamilton's sloop that sails tomorrow.

July 18th.   Uncle Paul's mule got into my pasture a day or two ago & last night broke into my field, letting in at the same time a drove of other horses. They eat & trampled my peas somewhat, & went on to Uncle Ben's & Paul's fields. I suppose the old man will try & get his mule up as soon as he gets into *his own field.* My colts are with the gang, & will be learned to jump also. I sent Jim & Isaac after them today. Hands listing up the orchard to plant some late slips & peas.

    A dull drizzle rain till near sunset, then set clear, and a rainbow—sign of clear day tomorrow.

July 19th.   Sign did not hold good this time, it rained nearly all night, and this morning broke gloomy enough as regards the weather. I spent the time reading a novel. The children making a great noise, & wife sleeping in the drawing room. The hands listed some in the orchard, & cleaned some cotton in the barn. The wind got round N.W. towards evening & I am in hopes it will clear. This weather may produce caterpillars. Jim did not get the colts yesterday but brought them today.

July 20th.   The Major came down to have a beef killed here for market, which he got of Prince, and which I let Prince have for some carpenter's work. He took breakfast with me. Aunt Betsy Chaplin called to see us.

July 21st.   Wife had a hot fever last night, better this morning. Put Jim plowing some ground to plant peas. Planted about an acre of peas in the orchard. Edward Capers called in the afternoon, he has been on another courting expedition, & got *kicked* as usual.

July 22nd.   Killed lamb for market this morning, another lamb in attempting to jump out of the pen got killed. I am head over heels in work.

[24] The war with Mexico began in January, 1846, when Texas was admitted to the Union, and ended in Feb. 1848. South Carolina sent 1,000 volunteers including, from St. Helena Parish, Richard DeTreville, William Adams, James Cantey, Robert Witsell, and Cornelius Rivers.

Blades to strip, peas to plant, slips to hoe, & my cotton getting very grassy. I shall brush over the hill part lightly, but am afraid to touch the low ground.

July 24th. Hamilton got back this morning. He sold my watermelons for 5 cts. apiece, muskmelon at 2 cts. I sent a few to Beaufort today, but got nothing atall for them except what Isaac took out of the stores. It is the last time I shall bother with it. Isaac Fripp called today & rode over my crop. He pronounced it very good, but advised me to hoe it again, & also to haul some of it. I will try it, though I am very much pushed for work— my blades are all drying up on the stalks, & slips want work.

July 25th. The reception dinner to the Mexican volunteers came off today in Washington Fripp's barn. It was a fine dinner & well attended, both by persons from the Island (and some of those who opposed it also), & from Beaufort. The Beaufort band was brought over which added greatly to the occasion.

Now for the worst part of the affair & what gives me much pain. I had drank too much punch & champagne like a fool, & as usual got boisterous & perhaps unsettling, while the toast & speeches were being given. This put my *friend* Dr. Jenkins (who has long been watching, cat like, to get an opportunity) up to saying something that he thought would expose me, & make my situation more conspicuous. I believe he proposed that *I be put out.* I was not *put out* however, & if Capt. D. Jenkins did not interfere (in a strange way to be friendly as he professes it to have been) he, the Dr., would have been *put out* of the window. I am truly sorry & mortified at the way I acted, but the Dr. *shall* be sorry too . . .

July 26th. Ben & Ed Capers called, they went on & dined with J. Webb. J. Webb called in the evening—all about yesterday's affair. I can think of nothing else.

July 27th. Stayed indoors all day, my mind very much worried. Sent for Ben Capers to take a letter to Dr. Jenkins.

July 29th. In the house all day. The hands are hoeing cotton, but I have not felt like going in the field since Monday. I hope they are not injuring the cotton, but I fear it very much, if they are not very careful.

July 31st. Commenced stripping blades. I don't know what can be the matter with my slips, a good many are dying after having run down to the alley. I think I put too little dirt in covering, & the hot sun has penetrated through to the vines.

Daniel had fever today.

Aug. 1st. Tuesday. July went out with a thunder squall & rain last night. A little cloudy this morning but pleasant. The rain has cooled the atmosphere. Stripping blades, finished the plowed corn and commenced the 11 acre March corn. Brought in what I stripped yesterday & packed it away. I think this & the old blades I have left will be sufficient for my own use. So I will have a parcel to sell next summer.

Daniel has fever again today, I fear it will be stubborn.

Aug. 2nd. Still at the blades. I shall have to stop tomorrow and haul my slips, see if that won't refresh them a little.

Daniel with fever again, also a slight chill. We do not know what to do. Wife thinks it is from worms. She is also very unwell.

8 o'clock p.m., Daniel's fever holds on still, since 10 this morning, & is as hot now as ever. We cannot get him into a sweat.

Aug. 3rd. All hands hauling up slips. If I do not have rain very soon to supply I shall lose the crop—it is almost too late now.

Sent Anthony to Beaufort. Got 4 bottles Dr. Townsend's Sarsaparilla[25] for wife, she is to commence it tomorrow, *it is a cure all,* but we will see.

Daniel had no fever today. We gave him quinine after a dose of oil, which I think has checked it.

Aug. 6th. No one goes to church these times, too hot. A shower came up about 12 o'clock m. but soon passed over, not even laying the dust even. The wind got round east directly after, & I am in hopes will bring it back, for we want it badly.

The east wind did bring it back, & we had a fine rain from 3 p.m. to near midnight.

Aug. 7th. Supplying over the slips with as many yellow yam vines as I can get. Peter & Jim came back today just after dinner. They say that Mother is quite sick. Tony came over in the evening and confirmed the news. He told me that old Capt. Wm. Murray is dead, died last week. I rode to Oliver Fripp's today. Expect I will go to the main tomorrow. I tried my potatoes today. They are not worth the digging, the bed is as dry as ashes in the center. I can't account for it, I banked it just after a rain.

Aug. 8th. Sophy and myself went to the main in Jack. What hands are left, planting slips. We got to the Point just at dark. Found Mother quite sick, but better than she had been.

---

[25] A widely advertised panacea for increasing "the secretions of the body," made from the dried roots of a tropical American *Smilax.*

Aug. 14th.   Commenced working the road. Sent on the Island (Edings) for boards & sleepers for the Sands Bridge. Sent 15 hands. The roll call 125 all together, a great many delinquent, which I shall return.

Aug. 17th.   Thursday. We have been hard at work on the causeway, but have not finished half, & what is done is not *well* done, for if we attempt to put it in complete order it would be a week's work with all hands. Joe Perry, Fraser[26] & myself have done all the work. Tom Chaplin Sr. & the Major have been on the road, but they come late from the village, & beg off early, so we get very little out of them. We have had dinner every day & rain two days very heavy. I had my tent pitched on the causeway which was some protection to us both from sun & rain. Joe Perry took 11 hands yesterday to get out stuff in Tom Perry's pine barren for the Club Bridge. He will be at it today also. We expect to get the stuff off the Island, also, today. Sent the flat & 8 hands for the purpose. I claim no hands for my boat & flat which the public have been using all week.[27] Yes, & ditto, horse!

Aug. 18th.   We finished the causeway & bridge today, & discharged all the hands except seven, which will be required to get out the stuff for the Club Bridge tomorrow. My hands have been all this week picking peas. Cotton is beginning to open pretty smart.

Aug. 19th.   I went out to see how J. Perry was getting on with the stuff in the pine barren. They will not finish today—discharged 3 out of the seven hands. Ordered 4 to return & finish the stuff on Monday, then we will keep two hands to put the boards on the bridge on Tuesday.

Aug. 21st.   We went to Beaufort to meet the Board of Commissioners about the Ladies Island Road again. I got there too late & was not sorry for it. Had a jury ticket served on me, and a tax execution for last year's taxes, which puts me in a bad fix. I must either pay or go to jail.

   Peg, Moll & Helen picking cotton. It is opening pretty thick in spots, particularly where it has rusted.[28] They picked about 40 lbs.

Aug. 24th.   Mother was taken with fever today. Picked in my pumpkins, made more than I expected. 3 hands picking cotton, they pick about 15 or

[26] Probably Frederick G. Fraser.

[27] Every planter had to contribute a certain number of slaves to the job, but the number could be reduced if he provided horses, wagons, tools, or building material. Chaplin could have sent some of his slaves home because he had allowed his other property to be used, but to set a civic example he did not.

[28] The leaves of the cotton plants have been blackened by a parasitic fungus.

20 lbs. each. I am inclined to the Fraser cotton. It is, I think, the best bearer, & holds on. Moll came out today, Amy sick, & Nelly ditto.

Aug. 26th.   Started to go up to Beaufort in my boat, to see Treville. When I got to the Riverside, heard that he had gone down the river fishing. I went down after him. Had an unsatisfactory conversation with him out on the river. He lent me a line & as it was strong ebb tide, I anchored & fished a little while. Caught about 12 blackfish & came on home to dinner. Hands hauling peas.

Aug. 27th.   Dr. Scott came down from the village in the morning to see Mother. I sent for him last evening, she seemed so sick. Heard from the Dr. that Capt. John Fripp had been thrown from his horse & his shoulder bone broken, and his son John[29] had fallen out of a two story window without much hurting himself. Also heard that W. B. Fripp's old fisherman Nero was drowned in Morgan's River[30] the other day.

Aug. 28th.   All hands picking cotton. I went out fishing. Had beautiful sport catching blackfish. Got also one sheepshead & a small cavally[31] in Broad River.

Aug. 29th.   Went to Beaufort in the boat. Saw Treville & had a talk with him about the tax writ I had served on me. He says I can't be made to pay the tax. The sheriff ought to have paid it, as *he* sold the property, and the property is not now liable.[32]

Sept. 1st.   Friday. All hands picking cotton—cotton opening pretty thick, all hands can't keep it down. Daniel has fever again today, Sam has fever also. Weighed off cotton—had in 516 lbs. clean.

[two pages missing]

Sept. 24th.   Sunday Wife is now on the mend, *thank God,* and with the Dr.'s advice, I am determined to take her to the village, as soon as she is able to be moved in a boat. I have got Uncle Ben's large boat for the purpose. W. B. Fripp has also very kindly offered me one of his houses at the village which I gladly accepted. The weather looks very cloudy & bad

[29] John B. Fripp (1834–1852). Son of Capt. John Fripp and Caroline Chaplin. Second cousin to Thomas B. Chaplin on his mother's side.
[30] Saltwater stream separating St. Helena Island from Coosaw and Morgan islands, emptying into St. Helena Sound.
[31] A narrow-bodied, fork-tailed game fish, related to the pompano.
[32] Chaplin's property sold at auction. See Oct. 12, 1847.

today, and the Dr. does not think wife can be moved before Tuesday, at any rate not before good weather. I have not time to think of the crop—all I know is that cotton is wasting in the field, & as white as a sheet all over. Daniel has had fever again for the last three days, & looks very badly. I give him *quinine.*

Sept. 25th. Wife appears a little better today. She sat up a little while, & tried to walk, but could not stand alone more than a baby. The boat was to have been brought here this evening, but I stopped it as wife declares she cannot be moved in it & will not. I will get Uncle Ben's carriage, & try & get her in that. The doctor was here today but will not return as he is obliged to go to town tomorrow night.

Sept. 26th. Wife seems a little better. She walked about the room a little with assistance. Dr. Scott sent his fellow Larry here today to help [   ] moving to the village. Uncle Paul lent me his [   ] cart & boy. I sent two cart loads of furniture down. Aunt Betsy called today. I did not see her, being in the field. Finished picking through my field yesterday and commenced again today. Cotton just as white as when I commenced it before. *I think,* tho I have not assorted & weighed off, that I ought to have in about seven bales.

Sept. 27th. Wife something stronger, but still has the pain in the stomach. I will move her to the village tomorrow if the weather will permit, which I think it will, it is quite clear & fine today. Uncles Paul & Ben both sent their carts here this morning to assist me, but I do not want them before tomorrow. This moving down to the village I *abhor* more than anything I know of, but it is the advice of everyone, & wife wishes it, so I suppose it *must* be done. I have no way of getting back & forth, except on horseback, therefore I shall stay the most of my time down here, go down about twice a week.

Tony came over from the main today, & brought a letter from Mother. She proposes for us to go over to the Point & stay with her. What an idea—jumping out of the frying pan into the fire. I would sooner think of carrying her to Halifax. I answered her letter & Tony went directly back.

Got a ram from Uncle Ben & put with my sheep today. My Negroes are not picking as much cotton as they ought with the blow they have. They only averaged me about 34 lbs today.

Aunt Betsy sent me, as a gift, this morning, 3 pr. of ducks. She sent a pair some time ago, making four pair in all, for which I am truly obliged.

Those times were very tight but I have seen worse & they do not get any better 1885

If I go to the village tomorrow I am not certain when I can come back; therefore do not know when I will scribble in this book again. The idea of staying down here by myself is not atall agreeable, but I am obliged to do it or stay at the village altogether & that I can't do. God grant that there will be no more sickness.

Sept. 28th. Thursday. Succeeded in getting wife down to the village. She lay on a bed fixed on Uncle Ben's carriage, & stood the ride much better than I expected, though she was very much exhausted. She was quite sick at night. Several persons called and were very kind. I dined with the Major (D.P.J.). Uncle Ben & Paul lent me their carts & Dr. Scott his 2 horse wagon & we got everything down very well, but the work will be to get back again. The thing I am glad of—I had to take out but *one* hand from the field.

Sept. 29th. Wife is much better this morning. I left her walking about the room. She is bothered with a bad cough which I too much fear will terminate in consumption. I returned home this morning with the carriage, to return on horseback sometime tomorrow.

Broke in not quite a task of corn, out of that made *entirely* with the plow, & got nearly a cart load. I think it will average about 15 bushels pr. acre. Bought from the Negroes, at 3 cts. apiece, about 250 pumpkins, & hauled them into the yard. They ought to last my horses till frost.

Dec. 11th. Many things have transpired since I last wrote in this journal—much and severe sickness in my family in the latter part of the summer or fall, which compelled me to get a house & move my sick family to the village at that late time of the year. But thank God they have all been spared to me thus far.

We have had a long spell of very warm weather lately, almost like summer, the grass is springing and fruit trees budding. I set out last week, or rather removed all my peach trees to the pear orchard, in hopes of ridding them of worms. I also set out about 30 sycamores on the avenue and stable lot. Finished picking cotton on Saturday or, rather, gave it up as the cattle had taken it & it is getting late. Had the hands making some of last year's cotton today.

Dec. 22nd. One of Mr. W. J. Grayson's fellows named Edward, being drunk, run one of his master's horses [   ] last night after dark. The horse being blind, the fellow run him plump against a pine tree about a hundred yards below the store & broke his neck, killing him as dead as a hammer. The boy was not hurt. I sent to Grayson to have him moved out of the road, & have a great mind to prosecute the Negro.

Dec. 24th.   Went to church & heard a very dull discourse from Mr. McElheran. He is getting worse & worse.

Dec. 25th.   Monday. Christmas Day. Mosquitoes were quite troublesome last night. The sun rose in a cloud this morning, but soon came out clear with very little fog but heavy dew, and bids fair to be a very fine day, but a warm one for the season of the year——

So far *Merry Christmas* is rather on the other extreme. But there is a party tonight at Pope's, I expect some amusement. Once upon a time, Christmas was to me a very jolly time, fun & frolic for a week, but times & disposition have both greatly changed.

Dec. 26th.   Sent Isaac to Beaufort—got some liquor from town.

Dec. 27th.   Last day of the holidays & I am glad, for then the Negroes will go to work & something for me to do.

Forgot to mention that I killed my 2nd hog on Monday, the weather being a *little* cool.

Dec. 28th.   All hands at work today, except Peter. I have ceased to mention him, he has been down so long. God knows what is the matter with him, I do not.

Dec. 31st.   Sunday, & the last day of this year of our Lord 1848—— I did not go to church, but like a bad boy I stayed at home, but was quite sick, throwing up, from too much liquor yesterday.

End of A.D.
1848

_1849_

Jan. 1st.   Monday—first day of a new year, A.D. 1849. I in bed sick all day, took a cold from cutting my hair, & took too much to drink, naught, naught, _very_ naught. All hands ginning—weather clear.

Jan. 2nd.   Worked in the garden nearly all day—planted onion sets, cabbages & Dutch turnips. The day & the weather lately has been very spring like, but no doubt as soon as the plants are up there will come a frost & kill them down——
    Peas are high enough to stick. Had a small mess of asparagus—very unusual for the season. All hands ginning.

Jan. 3rd.   Wednesday. Muster Day. How different the weather from yesterday—cold, windy and rainy—awful change—look out for cold sore noses & chapped lips. Found dinner at the muster house, Dr. Jenkins & Capt. W. W. Fripp found also—it was so cold at dinner we could hardly eat. The Est. of David Fripp's Negroes were hired. I hired three of them—Admond, Isaac & a woman named _forgot_,[1] do not recollect the price—they are to be delivered on the 20th inst. This I do not like, but hope I may do well with them.

Jan. 6th.   Saturday. Very bitter cold last night & today, though clear & fine sunshine. Rode over to J. W. Perry's to ask him to go my security for the hire of Est. D. Fripp's Negroes, he did not like to do it, so I did not press him, went to the store. Sent 4 hands to the Island in the flat for wood & pine. Rode over to Uncle Ben's in the evening, took supper—asked him to go my security for the hire of the Negroes—_he consented_. Wish I had asked him before. Clear & cold.
    Got some very good American tobacco at the store today & wife (good

[1] Molly. See Jan. 3, 1850.

at all things) made me some *very* good cigars out of it, as good as any American cigars I ever smoked. Had my sheep turned in the field, 12 in all.

Jan. 8th.   Monday. Rode over to Isaac Fripp's. Got from him the form of the note to be given for the hire of the Est. D. Fripp's Negroes. Went from there to Uncle Ben's, found him about to set down to dinner. Dined with him, he signed the note with me & I returned it to J. Fripp in the afternoon. Full moon tonight. Killed the hog I bought of Perry's Peter, making the 4th killed for bacon this year, one eaten up already, & 3 salted = 6 hams, 6 gams & 6 sides. Loaned Mrs. Pritchard ½ bushel of salt.

Jan. 9th.   Put Frank with horse cart hauling out sedge on *Williams* Hill. Took Isaac & went over to run out the cotton land for this year. Made 38½ acres on the Cowpen Hill, Williams Hill & Persimmon Field. Will plant root potatoes on each side of the road at the other end of the causeway. Packed the 4th bale of cotton—did not finish. 3 women overhauling for bag, 3 men assorting. Have about 2 allowances of potatoes left.

Jan. 11th.   Very cold this morning, the coldest weather we have had. Ice thicker than I have seen it for many a day. All hands assorting cotton. The infernal rabbits have attacked my peas, & eat them down pretty badly.

Jan. 12th.   Bitter cold last night & this morning—the orange trees look wilted. I fear they will be killed. I found another orange on the tree today, a very large one, but completely frosted. 3 gins going. Stopped Isaac to drive wife out visiting. She called on Aunt Betsy and on Mrs. Scott.[2] Says that Julia Pope[3] has a very pretty little girl child. Bought a hog from Scott's Cyrus—234 lbs. Sent the ox cart for it, & got it home.

Jan. 13th.   Saturday. Judge complains of pain in his knee, & cannot gin today. Only 3 gins going. Moll taken to her bed with fever. This sickness is bad for me in getting out my crop.

Jan. 15th.   Killed my 5th hog this morning & regret it as the weather has turned so warm. Rode over to see the Major—not at home—saw his little daughter, quite a pretty child.

Moll & Judge out today. Peter came to the barn to try & do something. He looks very pale & bad, but I am in hopes he is getting better.

---

[2] Sarah Ann Chaplin Scott (b. 1804). Daughter of William Chaplin and Sarah Jenkins. Wife of Dr. John A. P. Scott. Chaplin's first cousin on her father's side.
[3] Julia Scott Pope.

Early Dutch turnips just coming up. Cabbage seed have not made their appearance yet, fear the cold has injured them.

Jan. 19th.   Cloudy, cold & windy, occasionally a few drops of rain. Killed the 6th & largest hog. Made Isaac do it, Anthony being sick. I cut up the hog myself in the afternoon. Dr. Scott sent some powders for Peter.

Jan. 20th.   Peter seems worse since he has been taking the powders, had fever last night. This is the day I ought to get the Negroes I hired, but do not expect to see them till Monday.

Jan. 21st.   Sunday. Clear & beautiful day, not too warm or cold. Wife wished to go to church today, but Isaac had a colic & Jim had not a clean shirt, so she had to stay at home, not having a coachman. I & Daniel went. Heard that Dr. Jenkins' youngest child is very ill, not expected to live. Neither Aunt Betsy or any of the Jenkins family were out today in consequence, they were all over at the Dr.'s. How different when our poor little girl was dying.

Jan. 22nd.   The three Negroes that I hired came to me this morning about 9 o'clock, too late to take out a full day's work. Let the woman Molly have the day to fix her house, & sent her with the cart to bring her things. Let the men Isaac & Admond clean out their house & gave them 50 lbs. of cotton apiece to gin.

Heard this morning that Dr. Jenkins' youngest child died last night about 11 o'clock. All hands ginning again today.

Jan. 23rd.   Tuesday. Dr. Jenkins' child buried today at the E. Church. Rode to the store. Killed the 7th hog. Had five gins going today.

Jan. 25th.   5 gins going. Plowed up the ground for Irish potatoes. Got 2 new plows & 2 pr. of trace chains from town yesterday, 2 axes & 3 hoes. Also a barrel of very fine looking Irish potatoes for seed. Edward Capers dined with me and went home in the afternoon. Finished ginning all the cotton I had sorted, so will have to put all hands to sorting again tomorrow. This is a most tedious and bothersome way—I can't get ahead, will never have it so another year, but all the cotton must either be sorted in the field as it is picked, or before I commence to gin at all, then I will have none of this stopping every two or three days to sort cotton.

Jan. 26th.   Friday. Put Jim to plowing with the double moldboard, running it through the old alleys in the jointer spots, so as to expose the roots of the grass, & have them exposed to the cold, then to spread the manure in the trench & list on it—*an experiment.* Hope it will slack the joint grass.

Ox cart axletree broke down, put Isaac to making a new one. All hands sorting. Dined with Capers, the old man is better. Sent Anthony for oysters.

Jan 27th. Isaac did so little at the axletree yesterday I went at it myself today & finished it. Finished sorting the Godly cotton—will pack about 7 heavy bales of this cotton. Jim plowing, Frank & Summer carting. Dr. Scott came to see Peter, thinks his mind is worried by Negroes putting notions in his head that he is tricked &c. I will trick some of them if I hear any more of it.

Jan. 30th. Tuesday. Gave out the last allowance of potatoes, saved about a bank for the house. Stopped the plow & put Jim to the gin, 5 gins going today. Isaac not able to gin today, but he is out. Put him to bring downstairs the Fraser cotton. Finished the Godly, & gave out 3½ hands' work of the Fraser. There appears to be more cotton & less seed in the latter cotton, and it gins easier than the Godly.

Set out some strawberry plants, about 359. Intend to set out about 5 times that number, say 1800 plants.

Jan. 31st. Got a letter from P. H. Behn,[4] factor in Savannah. He has sold my one bale of cotton for 17 cts.[5] Paid Trenchards & Buckner[6] & Meeker. 2 gins going, balance hands assorting again. Set out another bed of strawberries. Rode to the store in the morning. One cart hauling out mud (cove mud).

Feb. 1st. Thursday. Agricultural Society Day. Capt. Jno. Fripp found dinner, & what is unusual, gave us dessert after. Mr. McElheran dined with us. Old Mr. Capers was out, he looks very badly. Dr. W. J. Grayson admitted a member. All hands assorting cotton.

Feb. 2nd. Carted manure in the garden for Irish potatoes. Planted 2 beds of strawberries. Ground quite dry. Lent the Major my flat to cut marsh for his mother. Wife complaining very much.
[   ] *poor wife was ill, sick, feeble, [   ] and miserable [   ]*
Says she is starved, can't get anything fit to eat. *Bacon & hominy* not good enough for *poor man's wife,* and I was not fortunate enough to raise turkeys

---

[4] P. H. Behn (b. 1820), cotton factor and merchant. Partner of John Foster.
[5] Per pound. A poor price, since common Sea Island was averaging 23 to 31 cents a pound.
[6] M. J. Buckner (b. 1821). Savannah boot and shoe merchant.

& rice last year, besides was obliged to sell *Negroes, land,* and *even furniture.* I might have done better had it not been for that.

Planted a bed of long orange carrots. My red sow came home today with 9 pigs, they must be about a week old, will hardly come in for next year's bacon.

Feb. 3rd.   Saturday. Cloudy in the morning & looked much like rain but clears off about midday, quite warm. Planted Irish potatoes, put a pinch of hog's hair *over* some of the sets, to try it, as recommended by Holmes. Routed the rats in the fowl house & repaired the nests. E. India goose commenced laying.

Feb. 5th.   Commenced to adopt the plan of soaking corn on the cob in saltwater for feeding horses.[7] I understand that it is a good plan, the horses eat cob & all, so require less corn.

Feb. 6th.   Clear & cold. I have to be eternally taking a cart off from the manure to haul wood, there is three times as much used as there is actual necessity for. Instead of the family sitting by one fire in the hall, both Sophy & wife sit in their bedrooms nearly all day, & of course have separate fires. One would suppose as they were raised in town, where all the wood they had was bought, they would be more saving . . . but to the contrary they seem to try how much trouble they can put me to in providing wood, and don't appear to care how much I am put back on that account with the crop. 5 gins going. Nearly everybody is listing ground.

Feb. 7th.   Packed 7th bale of cotton, half Godly & half Fraser. Dr. Scott called to see Peter, he acknowledges that he does not know what is the matter with him.

Had to sort cotton again today, only 2 gins running. I undertook to fix up my old dairy house for a smokehouse. Sent for Aimar[8] to do the brickwork—he came over & will go at it tomorrow. That is, I intend to have it bricked two feet underground to keep off rats, & have a brick tunnel made to convey the smoke through from the outside, so as not to have a fire inside the house.

Feb. 8th.   Thursday. Aimar came over early & commenced the brickwork, or foundation, under the old dairy, for a smokehouse. Got a little lime yesterday from Uncle Ben, it did not hold out to finish half of one side. Sent & borrowed 5 bushels from Mr. Capers. Isaac working with

---

[7] Recommended by Holmes.
[8] Augustus Aimar (b. 1824), Beaufort brickmason.

Aimar. Mother quite unwell today. Colds very prevalent, almost everyone has cold.

Feb. 9th.   4 gins going today. Judge sorting, Isaac with Aimar. Aimar working at the smokehouse. Uncle Paul sent his hands to work on Carter's Hill. Old Peter says he only wants to hire 26 acres—he told me he wanted about sixty acres. I hope he may take more than 26, however, that will bring me $78.

Feb. 10th.   Saturday. Wind high from east. Received yesterday by the flat that went to carry Myers's crop to Beaufort, my box of medicines from Savannah. Got a whole ounce phial of quinine.

Dined with Edward Capers. Heard that Uncle Ben had resigned the office of chairman of the vestry,[9] on account of certain things E. Capers had said, about his being too forgetful to be chairman &c. Ned is very impertinent & Uncle Ben should not notice him in the least.

Feb. 11th.   Sunday. Ben from the Point made his appearance just after supper, said that Baker had come over in the boat, he is at the Riverside & would not dare to bring himself here. I suppose he expects to take Mother back with him, but she is quite sick today, has fever & headache, & I know she cannot go & shall not.

Baker pretends he wants to see the Captain. I suppose he does & wants to get the Negroes over to the main from here & no doubt the Capt. will let him take them, though Mother does not wish them to go—he appears to be Baker's *trustee* now, & not Mother's; for he obliges Baker & not her. Baker sent some ducks & doves over here. I not atall admire this. Anything that Mother sends me or brings over herself I take willingly, but not what Baker himself sends, thinking of course to insinuate himself, &c. As Mother is in the house she can of course do as she pleases about it but were she not here, the birds &c should have been sent back, or thrown out. But he never would have been such a consummate jackass as to have sent them to me. The fellow will have a nice time of it tonight, in "his mansion house" on "his St. Helena plantation." (I wonder he don't call it his *homestead* as he did the Point.)

There is hardly a dry spot to be found in the house when it rains, & there is a pretty smart shower at this time (9 p.m.). I hope it may clear off, if only to get his cursed carcass off the Island. He will see the Capt. tomorrow if he likes & I suppose go on Tuesday.

Feb. 12th.   Monday. Cloudy, drizzly, windy and very disagreeable. Baker must feel very comfortable at the Riverside. All hands assorting cotton.

---

[9] Of the Episcopal Church.

Clears off about midday, cold. Heard that the Captain allows Baker to take over three of the men from the Riverside with him tomorrow—Robert, Ben & Tom. Old Charles was to go but he is sick. I suppose he will carry all of them another trip. As all the men are to go, the Capt. will hardly keep only the women. Baker is also to carry the blades, and I suppose corn, peas & all. The Capt. had better be Baker's trustee at once, for he certainly does not act like Mother's. It is a damned shame he had the law on his side, having resisted Baker in a suit he instituted to take the property out of his hands, & gained.[10] Besides, Mother, whose wishes he should consult, does not wish the Negroes to be sent to the main. And another thing, the Negroes risk their lives, or rather he risks them, in being moved from a comparatively healthy place to a sickly one, and to work in a rice field, after being accustomed to work in a cotton field. I think I ought to hold him responsible for their safety. He says he has too much trouble with the property. I know that he has very little, or none atall, I do everything I can to help him & he does not go on the place more than twice in a month. Sent Frank with the cart to the Indian Hills for some lime the Capt. promised me.

Feb. 13th. Tuesday. Frank returned from Indian Hills about dinner time, brought a note from W. B. Fripp saying I could have his house at the village for $80, to pay him $20 before I moved in & the balance at the end of the year. Hard times & tight bargains, but there is no alternative. I must take it. 4 gins going today, a little cotton left unsorted. Planted sugarcane, had the land cow penned for it. Planted beets yesterday.

Feb. 14th. Wednesday. Aimar came to work at the smokehouse, Sancho working with him. The cattle broke out of the pen last night & eat down nearly everything in the garden—onion, cabbage plants & turnips. 'Tis damned disheartening. Packed the 9th bale of cotton. 326 lbs.

Feb. 15th. Thursday. 5 gins. The Capt. came round & paid Mother some money—Daphne's wages. Aimar finished the brickwork to the smokehouse, tried it, & it does admirably, the cost, $9.00. I did not expect to pay more than five dollars. Let Aunt Betsy have some asparagus roots. I feel quite unwell today, very much like fever.

Feb. 16th. Was greatly surprised on looking out of the window this morning to see the ground almost covered with *snow*. It must have snowed

---

[10] Chaplin blames the Captain for having initiated the suits against Baker. Before litigation, Chaplin had enjoyed continual use of his mother's property, though title remained with her. Afterward, he had neither use nor title. Though Chaplin's side lost, the Captain had not suffered. Now he received his trustee's fees for expenses incurred in carrying out the wishes of Mr. Baker.

gradually all night, but the ground was not in a state for it to lie, & was only covered in spots. The tops of the houses were covered about 2 inches thick. Some snow fell after I got up, but stopped about 11 o'clock a.m. & about 2 p.m. there was hardly a flake to be seen. This is the first snow I have seen since I have lived on the Island. There was a snowstorm I recollect here when I was a boy. E. Capers came to see me yesterday evening & stayed all night.

Finished weatherboarding the smokehouse. Finished ginning all the white cotton, will have 10 packed bags, will not pack the last bale before Monday. The weather cleared off about 11 o'clock & no one would suppose there had been snow on the ground in the morning.

Feb. 17th. Saturday. Clear and cold. Run out, staked & burnt off the root patch, 4 acres. Isaac & Anthony with me. Put Sancho with Summer carting. 4 hands getting poles for the fence. Women cleaning cotton ginned yesterday.

Hear that Edw. Chaplin intends to sell all of his Negroes and go regularly into merchandising. One of his fellows came here today to ask me to buy him, fellow Cuff. That was out of the question for me to do, to sell one year & buy the next would be *fine* speculation on my part.

Feb. 19th. Monday. I received a summons while at breakfast, to go over to J. H. Sandiford's[11] at 10 o'clock a.m. this day and sit on a jury of inquest on the body of Roger, a Negro man belonging to Sandiford. Accordingly I went. About 12 m. there were 12 of us together (the number required to form a jury), viz.—Dr. Scott, foreman, J. J. Pope, J.E.L. Fripp, W.O.P. Fripp, Dr. M. M. Sams, Henry Fripp,[12] Dr. Jenkins, Jn. McTureous, Henry McTureous, P. W. Perry, W. Perry & myself. We were sworn by J. D. Pope, magistrate, and proceeded to examine the body. We found it in an outhouse used as a corn house, and meat house (for there were both in the house). Such a shocking sight never before met my eyes. There was the poor Negro, who all his life had been a complete cripple, being hardly able to walk & used his knees more than his feet, in the most shocking situation, but *stiff dead.* He was placed in this situation by his *master,* to punish him, as he says, *for impertinence.* And what [was] this punishment—this *poor cripple* was sent by his master (as Sandiford's evidence goes) on Saturday the 17th inst., before daylight (cold & bitter weather, as everyone knows, though Sandiford says, "It was *not very* cold"), in a paddling boat down the river to get oysters, and ordering him to return before

[11] James H. Sandiford (1795–1868), planter. His first and second wives were Perrys, and he was related through marriage to the McTureouses. Sandiford eventually moved to St. Mary's, Georgia.
[12] Henry Fripp (b. 1810).

high water, & cut a bundle of marsh. The poor fellow did not return before ebb tide, but he brought 7 baskets of oysters & a small bundle of marsh (more than the primest of my fellows would have done. Anthony never brought me more than 3 baskets of oysters & took the whole day). His master asked him why he did not return sooner & cut more marsh. He said that the wind was too high. His master said he would whip him for it, & set to work with a cowhide to do the same. The fellow hollered & when told to stop, said he would not, as long as he was being whipped, for which impertinence he received 30 cuts. He went to the kitchen and was talking to another Negro when Sandiford slipped up & overheard this confab, heard Roger, as he says, say, that if he had sound limbs, he would not take a flogging from any white man, but would shoot them down, and turn his back on them (another witness, the Negro that Roger was talking to, says that Roger did not say this, but "that he would turn his back on them if they shot him down," which I think is much the most probable of the two speeches). Sandiford then had him confined, or I should say, murdered, in the manner I will describe. Even if the fellow had made the speech that Sandiford said he did, and even worse, it by no means warranted the punishment he received. The fellow was a cripple, & could not escape from a slight confinement, besides, I don't think he was ever known to use a gun, or even know how to use one, so there was little apprehension of his putting his threat (if it can be called one) into execution. For these *crimes*, this man, this demon in human shape, this pretended Christian, member of the Baptist Church, had this poor cripple Negro placed in an open outhouse, the wind blowing through a hundred cracks, his clothes wet to the waist, without a single blanket & in freezing weather, with his back against a partition, shackles on his wrists, & chained to a bolt in the floor and a chain around *his neck*, the chain passing through the partition behind him, & fastened on the other side—in this position the poor wretch was left for the night, a position that none but the "most *bloodthirsty* tyrant" could have placed a human being. My heart chills at the idea, and my blood boils at the base tyranny— The wretch returned to his victim about daylight the next morning & found him, as anyone might expect, dead, *choked, strangled,* frozen to death, *murdered.* The verdict of the jury was, that Roger came to his death by choking by a chain put around his neck by his master—*having slipped from the position in which he was placed.* The verdict should have been that Roger came to his death by inhumane treatment to him by his master—by placing him, in very cold weather, in a cold house, with a chain about his neck & fastened to the wall, & otherways chained so that he could in no way assist himself should he slip from the position in which he was placed & must consequently choke to death without immediate assistance. Even should he escape being frozen to death, which we believe would have been the case from the fact of his clothes being wet & the severity of the weather, my *individual* verdict would be *deliberately* but *unpremeditatedly murdered* by his master James H. Sandiford.

Feb. 20th. Tuesday. 3 women chopping fennel.[13] Packed the 10th bale. Men splitting rails, ox cart hauling out rails & poles. Killed a calf, to get something to eat, & to save my breeding poultry, as wife is making havoc among them. I will not be able to send the flat to Beaufort as I intended. The tide suits very badly & the bale of cotton not ready.

Feb. 21st. Anthony did not put in all the cotton, only 343 lbs., leaving 54 lbs., that I cannot send down now. 4 women listing potato land, men making division fence. Uncle Paul won't help me. I don't see how he expects to plant my land, & have me to make all the fence. J. L. Chaplin will not make any on the other side, but it is nothing more than I expected *of him.* I swore, if his cattle come into my field this year, I will either shoot them or drive them to the store.

Feb. 22nd. Thursday. Sent 2 Isaacs, Judge & Admond to Beaufort in the flat with 9 bales of cotton. 2 women listing potato land. Molly chopping fennel, Anthony scattering cotton seed on corn land. Jim plowing corn land. Sancho hauling out rails. Flat got back after 10 o'clock p.m. Got my gun from Haskell that he had to stock, he has put on a very pretty stock, but the mountings are not fitted on neatly. The wood is Asiaberry,[14] a piece of one of the trees that grew in my yard. Set out by my father.

Feb. 24th. Had my bacon hung up in the smokehouse & made smoke to it. No. pieces—13 hams, 11 gams, 12 sides. I hope this quantity will last us the year. I killed 8 hogs, & there has been 3 hams, 5 gams, & 4 sides used already. Sent Anthony for oysters & put Amy scattering seed in his place. Will manure, at this time, about 5 acres & 3 tasks of corn with seed.[15]

Feb. 28th. Wednesday, last day of the month. February will go out & March usher in blustering, wind very high today from north & cloudy. Mother detained another day. The hogs bother my seed banks so much I made Isaac ditch around them & put up a sort of board fence. 5 hands

[13] Common fennel, said Holmes, "should be constantly cut down, to prevent seeding, which would cover the ground in a very troublesome degree." A preparation of fennel was used to relieve flatulence.
[14] The chinaberry tree. Its fruit was used as an animal wormer, and its wood for gun-stocks, furniture legs, etc. The appearance of chinaberry leaves in spring was a sign that it was time to plant cotton.
[15] Cotton seed waste.

listing in sedge on cotton land—day's work, 1 task & 5 beds. Moll sick. Molly chopping fennel. I will have them all at the cotton tomorrow.

Saw an invitation today to Mrs. Hephzibah Pope's funeral.[16] She died in childbed on Sunday night last, very sudden, the child alive. She has not been married long, this is the second child.

Sophy acknowledged this morning that she was wrong & spoke to me. I don't like dissensions, & let it pass over, but my "best plan is to have little to do with her in future."

** *Those family quarrels were very wrong indeed. So very different—for I married her & she is now my very good & loving wife 1876* **

March 2nd.   Mother went to the main. I went to Beaufort to see about hearing that this plantation is advertised to be sold for tax. Found it to be so, had to write Col. Treville for the money to pay up. Will then pay [   ] *protest* & demand redress from the sheriff, who ought to have paid the taxes, out of the proceeds of the sale of my property last year.

March 3rd.   Rode over Uncle Tom's. Borrowed $10 from him to pay for hogs I got of Perry's *Peter*, he is to be sold next week in Charleston, so had to pay him.

** *Never required me to pay back these loans.* **

March 5th.   Monday, cloudy & cold. Inauguration of Gen. Z. Taylor[17] as President of the United States this day.

Duchess had a horse colt last night. Head, neck & legs almost black & body bay. He is a colt from Capers' Shetland pony.

Put Jim at the plow again. Sent Frank to the wharf for some things came up in the steamboat for me. My hands are very much scattered today. 3 listing on Persimmon Hill, 1 on William Hill & 4 on Cowpen Hill. 2 in plowing, will finish today all that I can prepare for a first planting, that is, finish the first plowing. I will have to plant some land now, without manure, but will get some out for land to plant the last of this or first of next month.

March 6th.   Went to Beaufort to attend the Governor's Service of the St. Helena, Beaufort & Hilton Head beats,[18] and B.V.A. Company. The turnout was very small. Capt. Barnwell acted as col. & J. M. Baker[19] as adjutant. The battalion performed very well, and Barnwell highly com-

---

[16] William John Pope's wife. They had married on Dec. 15, 1846.

[17] Zachary Taylor (1784–1850), twelfth President of the United States. Fought in War of 1812, the Seminole War, and the Mexican War. Born in Virginia, Taylor was a slaveholder and owner of a Louisiana plantation. His daughter, Sarah Knox Taylor, married Jefferson Davis, future President of the Confederacy.

[18] Neighborhoods corresponding to state military subdivisions.

[19] The tax collector.

plimented by the Governor. The Governor, W. B. Seabrook,[20] was attended by two of his staff (Cols. J. Legare[21] & P. M. Hamilton[22]), by Major Gen. Schnierle,[23] & one of his staff (S. Chaplin). (I did not know that Saxby was one of his aides.[24]) The Adjutant & Inspector Gen'l Cantey[25] also accompanied the Governor. His Excellency made us a short speech, said he was pleased with our performance, but completely disgusted at meager turnout. Warned us of our danger, with regard our relations with the North, **humbug danger** and recommended our attention to military matters.

We have seen the end of which that was a beginning & a devil of an end of it. '76

We broke up about 2½ p.m. I dined with Bell. I received $100 dollars by mail from J. Webb, paid enough to Treville to settle my tax difficulty with Goltice[26] on Monday, amounting to about $43.

$57 left.

Went to call on Saxby in the evening. Got him to sign a release for me, as administrator on sister's[27] property, clearing me of all further liabilities, & my securities.

he had no right to any of that property.

Paid Haskell $5 on a/c of gun stock.

$5 too much

March 7th. Sent the release round to Uncle Ben to look at as he is one of my securities. All hands listing cotton land.

March 9th. Friday. Eclipse of the moon last night. Women listing cotton. 3 men digging out ditches in corn field. 20½ acres corn land plowed. 20 acres cotton land listed.

[20] Whitemarsh Benjamin Seabrook (1793–1855), son of Benjamin Whitemarsh Seabrook and Elizabeth Meggett. Member S.C. House of Representatives 1814–20, S.C. Senate 1826–34. Lieutenant Governor 1834–36, Governor 1848–50. A successful grower of Sea Island cotton on Edisto Island, and an authority on other coastal crops, Seabrook wrote extensively on political and agricultural subjects, and was a promoter of agricultural reform.
[21] James Legare (1805–1883), lieutenant colonel on Gov. Seabrook's staff. Charleston cotton factor and planter of St. Paul's Parish, Colleton District, and director of the Bank of South Carolina.
[22] Paul M. Hamilton (b. 1817), planter.
[23] John Schnierle (d. 1869), major general S.C. Militia. Member S.C. House of Representatives 1838–42, and mayor of Charleston 1845–47. The son of a German mechanic, Schnierle had studied law and devoted himself to his family's business.
[24] The aide's duties were to communicate the Governor's orders and to assist in preparing his military correspondence.
[25] James Cantey (1794–1860), adjutant general of the 5th Brigade, S.C. Militia. Fought against the Creek Indians and in the war against Mexico. Member S.C. House of Representatives 1838–40, and delegate to the 1852 Southern Rights Convention.
[26] The sheriff.
[27] Elizabeth Isabella Chaplin (1817–1840).

March 11th.   Sunday. Very smoky indeed, don't know where it can come from, unless from the burning of rice fields. Went to church. The Major, i.e., D. P. Jenkins, had his child christened. Learned that the cannon we heard yesterday were fired in Beaufort in honor & salute to ex-President J. K. Polk,[28] as he passed by in the steamboat from Charleston to Savannah.

March 12th.   Monday. Went to Beaufort. Dined with Treville. Had the release I got of Saxby recorded. Made my tax return, $14.80. 22 slaves, _____ acres land.

On my return found F. & E. Capers at my house, they stayed all night. 3 men tracking corn land to plant.

March 13th.   Ned & myself with two hands & 2 boys went out fishing. So foggy could not find the marks. Had one or two bites. Ned hooked one drum, but lost it. We caught nothing but a couple of toads, returned quite early. Had Ernest with us, he was awfully seasick, put him ashore on Bay Point.

March 16th.   Dr. Scott came here to see Peter. He heard I intended to send him to Whale Branch[29] to Frank Capers, as he has kindly offered to take him and try & cure him free of cost, but my strongest inducement to send him was that Dr. Scott recommended a change for him, that his mind was diseased. Told me to send him over to the main, but Peter expressing a willingness to go with Frank & an unwillingness to go to the main, I was glad of the chance to get him somewhere. Dr. Scott now thinks Peter's liver is diseased. Frank also says so, & says that he can cure him in two months. I hope he may. I will send him tomorrow.
He never returned but died soon after at Whale Branch.

March 19th.   The Captain came here to dun me for $120, justly due to him, but most unjust that *I* should have to pay.[30] I wish I was a thousand miles from here. All hands chopping in the listing and spreading manure on root patch. Jim plowing the same. I wanted to bank it up tomorrow, but the list is too dry, I must wait for a shower. Wish I had taken advan-

[28] James Knox Polk (1795–1849), eleventh President of the United States. Born in North Carolina, grew up in Tennessee. During Polk's term, 1845–49, Texas was admitted to the Union, California was ceded to the United States by Mexico, and the Oregon boundary was fixed at the 49th parallel. Polk was friendly to slavery and therefore popular in the South.
[29] Navigable creek connecting the Broad and Coosaw rivers, separating Port Royal Island from the main.
[30] Chaplin has hired several slaves from his mother's estate and now must pay her husband, Baker, through her trustee, Capt. Daniel T. Jenkins.

tage of the last but I was planting corn & did not wish to quit before I finished.

Sent Frank to Beaufort, did not get a letter from Webb with my a/c sales, though he wrote me on the 6th inst. that the cotton was sold.

March 24th. Saturday. Clear, calm, & beautiful day. Planting potatoes. Planted 3 tasks & 5 rows of yellow yams. Commenced common yams. Sent Isaac to Beaufort in the gig. Sent Anthony for oysters.

The day before yesterday I was served with a subpoena to appear at Walterboro Court next Monday week as a witness in a case of Levy, survivor of Benjamin & Levy,[31] vs. Baker, for articles Mother bought of them the summer she stayed at the village. I shot 6 rabbits today, had fine sport.

March 26th. Finished planting potatoes & planted some peas. I thought I would not have seed enough so sent off to Uncle Ben to beg, but I had *just enough,* not a dozen *pieces of cut potatoes left.* The weather is clouding up (4 p.m.) & getting much colder—fear for my potatoes.

March 30th. Friday. Finished listing cotton land, 35 acres. I'm plowing cotton land.

March 31st. Sent Anthony fishing—took nothing. All hands listing corn land for April corn. Jim got his foot badly cut somehow or other with the plow, it will lay him up some time.

April 1st. April, my favorite month, really comes in finely, & March went out with a shower. Did not go to church.

April 2nd. Monday. It turned quite cool last night, & is so this morning, but clear. Edward Capers came over last night & stayed with me till this morning. Sent Isaac to Beaufort. Planted water & muskmelons in potato patch. Each hand listed 1 task of corn land & then went & finished planting peas. Had to put Molly minding the potatoes and Sancho the corn. Put Frank to plowing.

April 4th. Commenced to bank cotton land—7 hands, bank one side. It does just as well after it is plowed, & anyone riding along would not notice but what both sides were banked up. Each hand banks 1 acre. I will get today 6¼ acres & ½ task banked, one hand being in some salt land which I will bank on both sides, & ditto 1½ tasks.

[31] R. Benjamin and B. Levy (b. 1790), Beaufort merchants.

Dr. Jenkins's Sam spayed my large black sow today. He spayed 3 shoats for me last week. They are all doing very well, but I am apprehensive of the old sow. She is very fat, and was a long time at the operation.

April 5th.   Thursday. Agricultural Society Day. Clear & very fine day—went out to the Society. This is the anniversary of the Society, & the day for the election of officers, which terminated in the election of Capt. Jno. Fripp, president, & re-election of Capt. D. Jenkins, W. W. Fripp & J. W. Pope, v. president, treasurer & secretary.

All hands banking—have today 13 acres, 1½ tasks. Will commence planting tomorrow, though tis said to be an unlucky day.

April 6th.   Friday. Dr. W. J. Grayson found dinner today at the lodge, he was elected a member the last meeting. He gave us an excellent dinner and got up in good style, considering he is a bachelor, we had a rarity—celery. Mr. McElheran dined with us. This is second time in succession, he must like the feeding.

Planted 7 acres of cotton in *William's Field, 1st planting.* Went out fishing, the river was very rough, we took 7 fish & a few blackfish. I gave the Negroes 4, the first they have had.

When I was returning home, just about the first bend in Station Creek, saw something white in the edge of the marsh, went up to it & found it was a dead *porpoise,* about 8 feet long. Apparently had not been dead very long, it was a very little tainted. We made a rope fast to it & towed it home. I will have it tried up,[32] & expect to get 4 or 5 gals. of oil out of it. This is the first one I have ever had a good view of. I saw, sailing out of Station, as we were coming in this evening, a beautiful white schooner, with red head or streak, with 4 men on board, two white & two black. One of the former looked very much like Col. F. Lance[33] of Charleston, quite an officer-like looking man. I don't know anything about the craft, where from or whither bound, one thing I know, is that she is a pealer at sailing.

The old sow that I had spayed, as I expected, died yesterday evening. The Negroes cleaned her & intend to eat the meat.

April 7th.   Saturday. Uncles Ben, Paul & Tom & the Major & myself joined and made up the fence from Uncle Ben's new ground to my division fence. My field is now fenced in, & I am very glad. Dr. Jenkins did not send a single hand, though the fence concerned him as much as any-

---

[32] Will render the fat.

[33] Francis Lance, commander of the 17th Regiment, S.C. Infantry; member of the S.C. House of Representatives 1856–58.

one else (just like him). Had 4 hands planting cotton, *13 acres planted.* Tried up the porpoise today, got about 5 gals. of good oil out of it. Tried it in the lamp, & it burned very finely indeed, no more smell about it than the best *sperm* oil. Anthony says it was not a fat one.

Heard a very melancholy occurrence today from Uncle Ben, viz., on the 5th inst. Taylor Danner[34] & his nephew, Joseph Danner[35], went out hunting wild turkeys. They took separate routes to the same tree, where they had roosted the turkeys the evening before. When they got near the tree, very early in the morning, they both saw a gobbler fly off the tree, and noticing the direction in which it lit, both crept towards it. The young man seeing something move in the bushes, as he thought, near the spot where the turkey should be, fired, and killed his uncle dead in his tracks, putting seven swan shot[36] in his body, two of which were mortal. The young man I hear is almost crazy. This should be a solemn warning to all hunters, *never* to *shoot* at anything without knowing what it is. Taylor Danner was a man that I believe was universally liked by all who knew him. I believe he was a man of family.

April 8th. Sunday. The Rev. Mr. Seabrook[37] preached at the Episcopal Church today, a very good sermon. He is from Bluffton, keeps a school there, the two young Capers go to him. A boat came from the main last night. 11 of my pear trees in bloom.

April 9th. Went out fishing, caught 3 drum. Some cattle got into my corn last night & eat it down pretty badly. If any come again they will not go out unless they are *carried.*

April 10th. 8 hands planting cotton on Cowpen Hill. Have 18¾ acres cotton planted. Ground very dry, want rain dreadfully. Anthony listing ground for tanyahs.[38] Rode to the store in the afternoon, bought some drum hooks & lead. Aimar has quit and Edwin Chaplin has a very nice store there in his place, and sells very cheap, "for St. Helena." Young Edwin stays there & keeps the store.

April 11th. Today is the tenth anniversary of my marriage. How many changes & vicissitudes *during those ten years.* Took Sophy & the children

---

[34] Possibly brother of Beaufort merchant William C. Danner, with whom Chaplin did business.
[35] Joseph Danner (b. 1830). Became an engineer in St. Helena Parish.
[36] Small pellets.
[37] Joseph B. Seabrook (1809–1877), Episcopal minister and schoolteacher from Edisto Island. Son of Joseph B. Seabrook and Martha Beckett. First cousin of Whitemarsh B. Seabrook. The Rev. Seabrook ministered mainly to blacks, eventually becoming pastor of a black church in Charleston.
[38] A root crop noted for its long storage life.

down to Bay Point, left them there to maroon for the day, & I went out fishing, took 9 drum. There were a good many boats out today, from all parts. Saw C. B. Farmer out with 3 young men, one was Andrew Murray, I believe, did not know the other two. There was a boat out from Edisto (Whaleys).[39] Don't think any did better than I did. Called ashore for the folks in the evening & got home about dusk.

Commenced banking ground for cotton, Persimmon Tree Field, 6 hands, took the two Isaacs with me in the boat. Make each hand list 3 rows in the Orchard in the mornings before they go out to work.

April 12th. Thursday. Went out fishing but caught *nothing.* The river was very rough, & the wind unpleasant. One of Uncle Paul's Negroes caught one drum in my boat.

8 hands banking today. The beds are so wide apart in the Persimmon Field that I have to have both sides banked, so only get 2½ tasks[40] pr. hand a day. Slow work but I don't care to plant it before we have some rain, the ground is too dry for any seed to vegetate. None of my potatoes have come up yet, and the peas, though planted just after a shower, have come up very badly.

April 13th. Friday. Wind fresh from the south. Went out fishing, caught 1 drum & a turtle, poor sport.

April 14th. Saturday. The sun set in a dark cloud so I think we may have rain soon. It is certainly very much wanted, the ground is as dry as ashes. Finished banking cotton land. Anthony went to Halls Bluff & caught three very fine school bass, better than going out in Broad River. I went in the boat & killed several very fine birds of the curlew tribe. Rode to the store in the evening, bought myself a coat & pair of pants of some black cloth called mohair.

April 16th. Monday. Clear but very cold, *heavy white frost & ice.* Everything looks wilted, I think all those that have their cotton up will have the pleasure of planting over. All hands planting cotton (Persimmon Field). Made Jim go & do some work in the garden. Hauled up the Irish potatoes for the 2nd & last time. They are about the size of a pigeon's egg. Went out in the boat & shot 19 May birds.[41] Planted cabbage seed for winter cabbage. Had a fine mess of green peas yesterday.

April 17th. E. Capers came here last night, spent the night. Sent Isaac to Beaufort. Finished planting cotton, 14 acres & ¾ the last planting, mak-

[39] The Whaleys were a prominent Edisto Island family.
[40] Five-eighths of an acre.
[41] Bobolinks.

ing in all 33½ acres, 13 in Williams Field, 5¾ Cowpen Hill, & 14¾ Persimmon Tree Field.

April 18th. Wednesday. I rode over with Ned & dined with him, he returned with me in the evening. When at Caperses' saw the large boat from the Point pass by, recognized Baker in the stern. Mother did not come over. By the by, heard that Baker & Dr. Jno. Warren of Chehaw[42] had a quarrel the other day at Ashepoo[43] & came to blows, in which Baker got knocked down two or three times & his eyes well banged up.

April 19th. This frost will finish what the last has left. Several persons are now planting over their entire crop. The corn & pumpkins and other tender plants look quite dried up. Finished listing April corn land. Adam cleaning up a patch for rice.

Ned & myself went out fishing, caught 2 fish. Saw Baker out in the river fishing, did not see him take anything. There were a good many boats out, but very few fish taken. We did about the best, several boats took none. Landed at Orange Grove[44] & rode home. Uncle Ben's & Uncle Paul's mules broke into my garden three times today. The last time I gave them a couple of loads of small shot to carry off.

April 20th. Friday. Clear & cool. White frost again this morning. This is uncommon, 3 white & 1 black frost in the middle of April. Ned & myself went out today, caught 3 in the boat, he one, & Uncle Paul's fellow two. I took *none,* but a fine parcel of blackfish. Mrs. McElheran & Aunt Betsy called on wife today. All hands banking corn land.

April 21st. Had to send all hands I could start in the evening to put out fire which was burning through the swamp, the other side of the fence we all made up the other day, & burning direct for the fence. Uncle Ben sent me word about it. He had been out & stopped the fire as far as his own fence was in danger.

April 22nd. Sunday. There is new moon today, & I am in hopes we will have some rain. Went to church. Noticed that the Captain had bought himself a very nice new buggy ($100). He can't be so very hard pushed for money, and I am glad, for it will not *greatly* inconvenience him if I don't pay him John's hire.

[42] Warren owned a plantation on the Chehaw River.
[43] At the crossing of the Ashepoo River and the stagecoach road to Charleston.
[44] Edgar W. Fripp's plantation, northeast of Tombee.

April 24th. Tuesday. Went fishing, took six. All hands cleaning up a patch to plant rice. Will plant corn tomorrow. Land rather dry but can't wait for rain. As good Billy Fripp[45] says, "It is flying in the face of Providence." Very few boats out fishing today, I expect the drum have been biting so badly, most persons have given up for the season.

April 25th. Wednesday. Came home from fishing a little after five, something out of humor, too annoyed by the Negroes, felt cross and made a little breeze with wife and the little ones. Caught six fish in the boat. Came home, went in the evening to draw the seine in Toomer's Creek, caught a few small fish, & some terrapins, got pretty well muddied & returned about sunset. Drawing the seine in those muddy creeks is dirty work, I don't like it. All hands planting April corn, tarred 1½ bushels to plant 10 acres. My corn will not hold out, I fear, to feed the Negroes till August. I plant about 30 acres this year. I must try to get a barrel of molasses, & some other articles & try and buy some corn from the Negroes.

April 26th. Finished planting April corn, & planted cotton corn. When going in the field who should I meet but Paul, a fellow I sold some years ago, now belongs to B. McBride.[46] He is a runaway, & has been out some months. He took good care to keep the fence between us when talking. He says he came to see me knowing that I would not take him, & wants me to buy him. That is next to an impossibility—

My red potatoes are coming up very well, the yams very poorly, and the crows are bothering them very much. The cold has mostly destroyed the blackberries, & they have little to eat. Cotton not coming up atall, the seed is perfectly sound in the ground. Old Charles came over to stay with me this morning to keep him altogether to attend cattle dairy &c. Uncle Ben's boat took 10 fish. Commenced supplying over March corn. Wife rode over to Aunt Betsy's in the evening.

April 27th. Friday. My birthday, 27 years old. It is a long time to have been in this world, considering the good I have done, which I fear amounts to precious little, but I hope & pray that my future years may be more usefully and better spent than the past.
Alas! Not so but decidedly worse, & bad to come 1885

Ernest & myself rode over to Uncle Tom's, & from there to Uncle Ben's & dined with the old folks. Dr. & Eliza Jenkins dined there also. Sent Anthony fishing in Uncle Ben's boat. They took 21 fish in the boat,

---

[45] William Fripp, Sr. See note, Feb. 6, 1845.
[46] Burwell McBride (b. 1787), rice planter of Prince William's Parish, Beaufort District.

Anthony caught 9 himself. The drum have just begun to bite. Finished supplying March corn, and commenced hauling up my potatoes.

April 29th. Sunday. Went to church. Julia & Catherine Pope[47] had each a child (daughter) christened today.

Sent some things to Peter. He has been very sick with an attack of colic, but is better. He is still with F. Capers. Don't think he will get well. Grouse has the staggers very bad again. He will make a die of it this time.

April 30th. Monday. Poor old Grouse died this morning—he had the staggers since Friday. I have had him a long time, & will miss him very much.

I am near neighbor now to the man I got Grouse from, J. Witsell[48] near Walterboro. How many changes.

Several of my pear trees appear to be dying. Had marsh sedge spread around their roots to keep the heat of the sun from them, which I suppose is the cause of their wilting.

May 2nd. Wednesday. Muster Day. I turned out in the Island company for the first time in my life, having quit the guards.[49] The tax collector came over to collect his taxes. There was also a man from Charleston, collecting agent for the *Mercury* newspaper.[50]

Finished hoeing March corn. Cotton not showing itelf above ground yet. The seed is perfectly sound & has not sprouted in the ground. My early peas that came up are nearly all killed. Young fruit are shriveling up on the trees, & the tree leaves are wilting for want of moisture. The ground is as dry as ashes for nearly 2 feet beneath the surface—nothing can vegetate.

May 3rd. Uncle Paul commenced the first hoeing of his cotton on Carter's Hill today. I intend to notice his management of it, & see if his field is kept in better order than my own.

It was

Had all my yellow cotton put into cotton bags to send to Grayson's tomorrow, he has agreed to gin it out for the seed.

May 7th. Monday. Some of my neighbors are planting over cotton again. Uncle Tom sent to me today for seed. I believe the seed is perfectly

---

[47] Catherine Scott Pope (b. 1826), wife of Joseph Daniel Pope.
[48] John Witsell.
[49] Chaplin has officially joined the St. Helena Mounted Riflemen, so he will no longer have to travel to Beaufort to meet his military obligations. See note, April 1, 1856.
[50] Charleston *Mercury*, the lowcountry's leading newspaper.

sound in the ground and only wants moisture to bring it up. I will wait for rain & see what comes up. Women hoeing cotton. Men trenching some more land for rice. Sent Anthony & Jim to Beaufort if the weather does not stop them. Had one or two smart showers between 12 & 2 o'clock, laid the dust for one or two inches. This is the best rain, as little as it is, that we have had here since I planted potatoes in March. There must, from the looks of the clouds, have been a good rain at the other end of the Isld. The clouds were only partial. There was a fine shower on Carter's Hill where Uncle Paul plants, & not a drop in my own field just adjoining. Looks clear towards night, but I am in hopes of more rain. Anthony got back from Beaufort about dusk.

May 9th.   Started in the afternoon to go to Whale Branch in the boat to fetch Peter. Before we got out of Station a tremendous storm of rain & wind came on us very suddenly & nearly swamped us in the creek. Turned back, got home after dark with a good soaking.
Lost my bearskin in the creek

May 10th.   Thursday. Quite clear & fine this morning. Started for Whale Branch, went by way of Beaufort, got there about dark, found Frank & Ned there.

May 12th.   Saturday. Peter said he could not get ready to come back yesterday, so I spent the day with the Caperses, & started early this morning. The hands have been hoeing cotton.

May 15th.   Tuesday. All hands hoeing cotton, the cotton is coming up very well. The last planting the best. I begin to feel the bad effects of my dunking. Had to put Moll to attend to Peter & O. Sam,[51] another hand out of the field.

May 18th.   Friday. The Negroes are hauling up potatoes. Had to put Sancho back to mind them. The crows are still pulling them where the vines are, some of them, down in the alley.
Nothing else for crows to eat

May 21st.   Monday. Went to Beaufort, in the boat, to attend a meeting of the Board of Road Commissioners, took Ernest with me. Brought home some boxes & barrels of groceries & dry goods sent up to me by Ingraham & Webb. Put the hands I did not carry to cleaning the yellow cotton. 1 hand finishing hoeing cotton 1st time through.

[51] Old Sam.

May 22nd. Finished the second plowing March corn. Had cotton seed thrown around the roots of some March corn that had no manure. All rest hands cleaning std. cotton.[52]

May 23rd. The tides have come so high lately that the saltwater has got into some of my crop, & destroyed about a task of corn & the same of cotton. Had to take all the men today & throw up a small bank around the places where it got in, to keep it out in the future. Women still at the cotton.

May 28th. Monday. Went to Beaufort to attend an extra meeting of the commissioners. The subject brought before the board was this: Two of the commissioners went to Ladies Isld. for the purpose of laying out the road granted by the legislature, and about which Capers & McKee[53] have had so much fuss. Capers had put up a fence & gate on the line where the road enters on his land, had the gate chained & locked, preventing the commissioners from going through with their duty. The meeting was called to decide what was to be done about it, and determined to indict Capers for the same, which I suppose will bring on a long lawsuit as Capers is fond of law.[54] Oliver Fripp also returned Mr. Capers for not returning one of his Negroes liable to road duty, and for taking four hands off the roads when he was working. This will make a split between those two.

May 30th. Wednesday. Put the women to thinning out cotton (William's Hill). Finished cleaning the std. cotton, all except what was taken out of the white cotton—Moll at that. Started the double plow in Persimmon Field. Commenced collecting sedge to make compost by putting a layer of sedge, then a layer of mud. I never saw mosquitoes so bad as they are tonight.

May 31st. Thursday. Women still thinning & men hauling cotton. I have but 6 hands in the field today, besides the plowman. Isaac sick, Moll minding Peter, Sancho in the potato patch.

This is the last day of May & I have not made any arrangement to move to the village yet. I must send my std. cotton to Savannah next week, hit or miss.[55]

---

[52] Stained, or yellow, cotton.
[53] Charles G. Capers and Henry McKee.
[54] Capers had sued McKee in 1840 after McKee dug a ditch across the road leading up to his house. See *C. G. Capers* v. *H. McKee,* 1 Strob. 164, 32 S.C.
[55] No white cotton was sold at this time of year. Yellow cotton was bringing 6 to 8 cents a pound.

June 2nd.　The cattle got across the creek & into the cotton field, but were found out before they did much damage. They eat a few hills of cotton. Had rails brought from the Riverside line fence & made up the water fence to keep them out hereafter. Packed the last of the cotton. Have 2½ bales of std. & a small packet of white. Killed a lamb, making the 3rd this spring.

June 4th.　Monday. Sent the boat & 4 hands to Beaufort to carry the cotton. 2 plows at the early peas. My March corn is tasseling, I must bank it up & lay it by.[56]

Aunt Betsy sent for Margaret, she went home today. Tis very strange, Aunt Betsy has so many Negroes about her that she says herself that they are in each other's way, & said that this girl could stay here even after she was done with Mary's[57] child, but for some cause she has taken her away before the child is big enough to take care of itself.

June 6th.　Wednesday. The crows are still so bad that I have to keep a hand in the patch all the time, equal to near 3 months' work of one hand lost, & I am very much pushed just now. The cotton *must* be slacked & hauled now. My April corn & potatoes want hoeing very much indeed & the March corn ought to be hauled up & laid up, now that it is shooting the tassel.

June 7th.　Thursday. Agricultural meeting day. Clear & the warmest day I have felt this year. Dined with the Society. No cotton blossoms could be shown. All hands hauling cotton. Thrashed out my peas, about 4 bushels. I begin to think about moving to the village. To have to go into that d—ned little stewpan is not agreeable, but "Necessitas non habat legas."[58] Sophy packed up some few things today.

June 8th.　Stopped both plows to give my poor horses some rest for their struggle next week. Fine shower about 5 o'clock p.m. Sunset clear Planted peas through a part of the March corn. Hoed out some of the rice. Sent Jim to the village to clean up the house. I rode through Uncle Paul's cotton on Carter's Hill today. I don't think it looks as well as some of mine, & better than none. Most of it has a yellow cast which is the case with some of mine in Persimmon Field, and I think the root bug has attacked it also.

(He made a better crop out of it.)

[56] It is time to give the corn its last hoeing and throw dirt up to the stalks, thus building a bed.
[57] The slave Mary.
[58] "Necessitas non habet legem": necessity has no law (Langland, *Piers Plowman*).

June 9th. Saturday. Clear & warm in the morning. About 12 m., a heavy cloud rose in the N.W. & about 1 p.m. a tremendous blast of wind & rain passed over, apparently only this end of the Island. I don't think the rain extended as far as the store. It was very violent but did not last more than ½ or ¾'s of an hour. I thought every tree in the yard would have been torn up by their roots. A great deal of my yard & garden fence was blown down, it is very rotten however. I never saw such a cloud of sand as blew over from the cotton fields on the other side of the creek, notwithstanding we had rain yesterday. It went in a body across the marsh to Edings Island so thick that you could not see the trees on the other side. I am sure that large seed could have been carried a long distance by this wind. Rode in the field after the storm was over, for it cleared off beautifully about 2 p.m. Some of fence was down, had it put up. The old corn is pretty well prostrated but not many stalks broken off. Did not go in the cotton. Supplied over about one acre of potatoes with slips, and put the Negroes to hoeing out some of the worst of the April corn, but the storm drove them in. Had to put all the men to fixing up fences. Made the women shell corn to carry to the village. Took down some bedsteads and made several little arrangements to make a move next week. I am very much pushed for work, & this taking off hands to move (for I have to send the flat) will throw me back still more, but there is no help for it.

I saw no hail in the storm today but I heard there was some hail. It came up very suddenly, caught all my young poultry out, & I believe drowned some of them.

Received a letter from P. H. Behn last night, acknowledging the receipt of my cotton, & enclosing an advance of $25.

June 10th. Sunday. Clear and the warmest I have felt this season. I wish I had a thermometer.[59] There was a heavy gust of wind last night, it blew very fresh nearly all night. I believe there was no rain. My garden fence was blown down again in one or two places, and the cattle were regaling themselves on my sugarane, okra, &c.

No one went to church today from this house.

June 11th. Commenced the miserable necessity of moving to the village. Sent the ox cart & two horse carts to Mary.[60] Sent the flat with furniture also. They will make a long trip of it if this wind holds so high & dead ahead. Only 4 hands in the field, hauling cotton. I have 22 tasks yet to haul.

---

[59] He gets one. See Aug. 25, 1856.
[60] The slave Mary.

June 12th. Uncle Paul sent me his cart today. Sent that & my cart loaded to the village. I went down with the carriage, took Sophy & 3 children. Left wife & Ernest for next trip. Got down about 11 a.m. The flat had not arrived as I suspected. I dined with Uncle Ben. Saw two young men there named Oswald.[61] The old man was bargaining with one of them for a tract of land on the Chaplin's Hunting Isld.[62]—he has bought it I believe. The old gentleman opened his heart & made me a present of his gig. It was quite a welcome present, I stand greatly in need of a vehicle at this time. Nearly everybody has moved in. I borrowed Dr. Scott's carriage, being very light, & left mine. Hyder seemed very weak coming home. This is hard work for the old fellows and they have no other fodder but marsh.

June 13th. Wednesday. We went down safely to the village in the evening. It was cloudy & pleasant. Wife stood the ride better than I expected, though she was very much fatigued. We got there before sunset. The flat got there last night & left for home this morning.

June 14th. Thursday. Came back from the village. Came along with Capt. Jno. Fripp & Dr. Scott, and went on with them to J. L. Chaplin's. Capt. John went there to look at a couple of Tacky horses[63] of Ben Chaplin's, which he bought—paid $150 cash & took them off with him. I came on home. The Negroes had got home & were in the field, but left the flat at Lands End. They said the wind blew so fresh they could not get her home, but I expect they had given out for they have had a long trip of it—3 days gone. I have all hands in the field again, but things look gloomy. The crops at the other end are too far better than at this. My cotton looks very bad, some of it dying. My potatoes are miserable, rain very much wanted. Finished hoeing potatoes & commenced hoeing April corn, that is in a bad fix, with weeds & drought &c——

I am down here by myself tonight, & sad & dull I feel.
I have felt sadder & duller since. 1876

June 15th. Friday. Dug in Irish potatoes. They are very poor, nearly all small. It will not answer to plant them on the same piece of land three years in succession, the ground gets too loose. Finished hoeing April corn all to 3 tasks, *1st working.* Got a few ripe tomatoes. Everything is backward and looks badly for want of rain, the ground is almost as dry now as it was in April. My young corn is all twisting up, & the old corn firing——

[61] John and Robert Oswald.
[62] Chaplin's Island (later Pritchard's) in the chain of Hunting Islands.
[63] Small, rangy horses that used to roam wild in the southern marshes.

June 17th. Sunday. Went from the village to the E. Church—no preaching. Went on to the Baptist & heard the last of a sermon. Returned to the village. Uncle Ben's Caroline very ill, not expected to live.
In 1876, she is alive still & living in Beaufort, a freed woman

June 18th. Monday. Paid Wm. B. Fripp $20 dollars on house rent. My yellow cotton sold for 5 & 6 cts. Returned from the village.

Hoeing cotton. Put Admond plowing a part of the old corn—breaking up the middle. Frank carting out manure on slip land. Wind very high all day. Killed a lamb, sent Benj'n Chaplin half in return for his quarter of veal. Sent a quarter to the village by the Major.

June 19th. Tide very high, flowing & injuring a quantity of my land. It got over the little banks I threw up some time ago to keep it out of my field. The tide has come much higher now, than then. Hoeing cotton, & it appears to do it more harm than good. The wind blows the cotton almost out of ground when the dirt is loosened around it, it is so very dry. A good deal of the cotton is dying. The infernal crows are eating my old corn as soon as the sign of an ear puts out. I never heard of their being so bad, they would pull the potatoes & plug every young watermelon if I did not put someone to mind them.

July 2nd. Peter died yesterday morning about 7 o'clock a.m., just lived to see July come in. They tell me he died quite easy. Said he was going to faint, & died off. He lived five months longer than I thought he would.

Very few of the slips I planted have taken. Cotton is improving, wants rain. Had a ripe watermelon on the 29th June.

July 4th. Wednesday—*Independence.* (Dined at the muster house.) Very cool & pleasant all day, the coolest 4th of July I recollect of. Went to a picnic in the evening, given in W. W. Fripp's new house.

July 6th. Friday. Came down. Planting slips, have 2 acres planted, & will have 2 tasks more planted today. Got 10 bushels of corn from Grayson. Had a ripe muskmelon & several water ditto. Returned Ben Capers' pony to him, he has sold him to his father.

July 16th. Some ice & other articles in Beaufort for me, & don't know how to get them to the village. The weather is too bad to send a boat or cart today, & there is no need of ice this cool weather. Mother sent the boat over from the Point on Saturday. All hands planting slips today, fine weather for that kind of work. I must try and get my cow down while the weather is cool.

July 28th.   Saturday. Commenced hoeing slips. I killed a beef that Uncle Tom gave me for market on Thursday last, & a lamb this morning.

Aug. 8th.   Went fishing with Grayson & Treville.

Aug. 22nd.   Wednesday. Clear & very hot. Two hands stripping blades off Negroes' corn, 3 hands picking peas, 1 hand minding field & turning down corn, 2 hands sick. One task of potatoes dug, for 9 days' allowance. Saw the first open pod of cotton in the field this day. Uncles Paul's & Ben's hogs troubling my corn field. Sent them word to send their cart for them the next time they got in.

Sept. 12th.   Wednesday. Have not been down for a week. Women picking cotton, it is opening here & there. Caterpillars at Dr. Scott's. The men cut some rushes this morning. I thought it too cool to put them in the marsh. Set them raking up sedge & floating it over on this side to be put in the pen. There is none on this side, the E. wind has driven it all across the creek.

     On the 9th inst. at 9 o'clock a.m. Mrs. C. delivered of a girl child.[64] Both doing well to date.

Sept. 17th.   I have been quite unwell lately, took a cold which gave me fever two nights, and inflamed my left eye very much, which made it very painful. I feel very much like fever today. Brought Daniel down with me today. I fear it is not right. Everything has the appearance of fever down here.

Oct. 4th.   Thursday. Clear & very warm. Went to Uncle Archy's funeral—he died at McPhersonville[65] of dysentery, on Tuesday the 2nd inst. at 5 o'clock p.m. He was buried in the family burying ground at Uncle Ben's. Had to put him outside the wall, no room inside.

Oct. 5th.   Had some rain down here, none at the village. Sent the boat to the ville with peas, blades & potatoes.

Oct. 6th.   Hands picking peas in corn field.

Oct. 8th.   Monday. Intended to commence breaking corn today but there is so much cotton open—put all hands at that until I slack it.

[64] Mary Frances Chaplin (1849–1851). Chaplin's seventh and last child.
[65] Summer residence for planters in the pinelands of Prince William's Parish, about twenty-five miles inland, featuring "a bowling alley for the young people and a billiard room for the men."

Oct. 23rd. Tuesday. Came down. Finished the April corn, it has turned out more and sounder corn than the March. I think I have made enough to last me if my slips do only tolerably & without waste.

Returned to village in the evening. The Savannah brass band gave a concert in W. W. Fripp's house at the village at night. It was very well attended. I went & took Ernest—he was delighted. I do not think however that it was anything extra, though new for the village. The band serenaded last night & this night also, & the music was decidedly better—sounded better than in the house. Those brass instruments do not sound good in a small room.

Oct. 24th. Wednesday. Came down in the afternoon, brought Ernest with me to stay all night. Broke in the cotton corn this morning. Got one cart load & each Negro a basket full, say about 35 baskets.

Oct. 25th. Thursday. Sent the boat to Beaufort for two barrels of *ice* Webb sent me unexpectedly on my part. Gave the Negroes a day to break in their corn. The cattle are troubling the field very much, don't know how to keep them out.

Last killing of the beef market today.

Oct. 26th. Put all hands picking peas for fear of rain. Though I have a good blow of cotton, I am inclined to save the provision crop *in preference.*

Nov. 8th. I should have moved from the village before this, but Mother has been with us, and very sick. She has got better and returned to the Point on Tuesday last, 6th inst. Everybody has moved from the village except Edings, Capt. Jno. Fripp & myself. I will get away as soon as possible, perhaps this week if the weather & wind will admit. Cotton is now blowing very fast, but I can't get my Negroes to pick as much as they ought, not being down here to weigh it myself. It is time to dig in slips, but I can't do so now. I think we shall have frost very soon, or when this wind falls, and gets more round north—it is now N.W. I have never stayed at the village as late as this before.

Nov. 9th. Sent the flat round to the village, also my ox cart and two horse carts. Uncle Paul & Dr. Jenkins are to send their carts down for me in the morning, when I expect to move. I have also borrowed Dr. Scott's & Uncle Ben's carriages.

Nov. 10th. Saturday. Very cold this morning, with heavy *white frost.* Pulled up stakes & made a general break for home. Five carts & the flat all loaded. I had no idea there were so many things in the house, nothing less could have moved me, everything was packed tight. The flat did not leave the village till late. We all got down here safe about 4 o'clock p.m. I suppose the flat will get here sometime tomorrow. Capt. O. Fripp also moved today, no one left now but Edings, except those that live there all the winter. This frost will make the cotton open, but will compel us to dig in our slips.

Nov. 13th. Tuesday. Dug the rows of roots today for a week's allowance for all hands & about three days' feed for horses, hogs, oxen & cow. Have about two weeks' allowance left. Got the last of my pea vines in today, a fine chance of them.
A good crop from a poor beginning*
Sent an order to D. P. Jenkins to summon out hands to work the roads on Monday next, the 19th instant.

Nov. 14th. Altered & marked 5 bull calves (2 ditto, left unaltered). Marked 7 heifers = 14. 6 ewes, 3 wethers—9.
Sent an order to Jos. W. Perry to summon out hands to work the roads on Monday next.
Prepared some arrowroot[66] given us by Capt. J. Fripp. Dr. Scott got about 1 quart, very pretty. The preparation is rather odious—but worth the trouble.

Nov. 16th. Friday. All hands picking cotton, the best blow I have had this year, & a good many hard pods left.

Nov. 19th. Monday. Commenced working the roads. Commenced digging slips.

Nov. 22nd. Thursday. Finished the road. Tom Perry as the substitute for Jos. W. Perry had charge of the Seaside Road, did very well as far as I saw (I did not go out the last two days). Edgar Fripp had charge of the Sands Bridge & bulkheads, had the bulkheads raised & packed in, it now looks much better. D. P. Jenkins had charge of the Church Road as far as the P.E. Church. We did not work the Club Bridge as I am in hopes that Edings will take that off my hands as Oliver Fripp has taken all the Pine Barren Road the other side the church from him. If he does not take it, I will have to work it.

Nov. 27th. Tuesday. This day I turn over a new leaf (as the saying is) with myself & everybody else about me white & black. With God's help, I will lead a different life myself. And by example, hope to induce others

---

[66] A tropical plant whose starchy root was dried, grated, soaked, and prepared as a beverage for invalids and babies. Recommended by Holmes for bowel complaints and dyspepsia.

around me to do the same. A reformation is actually necessary on the whole plantation & more *particularly* so in *myself,* and may God in His goodness give me strength & firmness enough to accomplish this good work, begun with such good intentions.

Alas! Alas! Man weak, unstable as water. It was not to be I suppose, as it was not.

Edward Capers dined with me.

That is break No. 1

Nov. 29th. Thursday. White frost again today. Clear & beautiful weather. All hands picking cotton. Finished the Persimmon Field, very little there to pick, do not think I will get but very little more out of that field. My other fields bid fair to hold on till January.

Nov. 30th. 4 hands to the Isld. for wood. Commenced William Field again to pick. Thrashed rice, got very little—2½ bushels. Birds eat near all. Lost one bacon hog, only 5 left, 1 put in pen today to fatten. Rode over to Dr. Scott's.

Break No. 2

From there I went to Caperses', dined there. Have not heard of any better crops of slips than mine. Capers made a good crop. Ned says six months' allowance (note: doubt it). Dug old oat patch. Got 16 banks (eating), 2 acres. Dug 16 acres field, got 11 banks (eating), 21 baskets each bank. I got 18/21 basket banks to 5 acres.[67]

Dec. 1st. Saturday. Sent Isaac & Jim to Beaufort, Anthony & Judge for oysters, balance assorting cotton.

Dec. 2nd. Anthony got back late last night with oysters. I was up, & feeling an inclination, took a very comfortable oyster supper about 11 o'clock, *solo & alone*——

Wish I had some now. Sept. 1885

Dec. 6th. Thursday. Attended the regular meeting of the Agricultural Society. Mr. Cockcroft showed there the largest turnip & potato I ever saw. The turnip, a rutabaga, weighed 12 lbs., and the potato, a brimstone red, weighed 9½ lbs. Set out onion sets.

Dec. 7th. I contemplated going down to seine one of the inlets to get some mullets, but *my wife* had so much to say about the matter, throwing out so many unnecessary *hints* and *insinuations,* that I gave up the trip, or

[67] Five acres yielded 189 bushels (18 × 21 ÷ 2), for an average acre yield of 37.8 bushels of eating potatoes.

rather *postponed* it *indefinitely*, at least until I can go quietly & *in peace*, and feel, or appear to be, more my own master, and regulate and control my own actions, and that too, without any unpleasant disputes about the matter.

This put off break No. 3

I sent 2 hands down for fish. Plowed up the Orchard. Intend sowing some buckwheat & Lucerne[68] in it if I can get the seed from Savannah.

Dec. 8th. Saturday. Sent Isaac to Beaufort. Adam fixing gins for use on Monday. Balance hands picking cotton. Will finish the fields today and commence over the Persimmon Hill again and get the most I can for the last picking in that field. The others I will hold on to as long as anything is to be got out of them. Two plows going in the Orchard. It is very rough plowing, but I must level it with the hoe & then plow it over before drilling it for the seed.[69] I am in hopes of getting it today. Went to see Uncle Ben in the afternoon—he was taken today with paralysis of the brain & tongue, & is completely speechless.

Never recovered

Dec. 9th. Sunday. Went over to see Uncle Ben in the morning—he was much the same.

Something queer in all this, someone interested

Went over & sat up with Uncle Ben all night.

Dec. 10th. Uncle Ben much better, spoke today.

roughly mumbled a word

A great many persons with him today. I will, if requisite, sit up again tomorrow night——

Commenced ginning 7 gins——3 hands picking——Rode Duchess's oldest colt for first time.

Dec. 16th. Sunday. Cloudy & heavy fog, has been damp all the week. Uncle Ben much better.

They only hoped so

Weather very bad for picking cotton.

Dec. 17th. Monday. Sent Frank to Beaufort with shoe measures to go to Charleston. Rode over to Caperses' to see him grind cane to make syrup. The operaton was quite simple. Ben Capers made the mill, which was very light & could be turned by a very small horse & grind or squeeze about 1000 cane per day. The juice was boiled in a very large pot (set in

[68] Commonly called alfalfa. A deep-rooted European herb in the pea family.
[69] Preparing a trench in the row to receive the hand-dropped seeds.

brick) till thick, then clarified with lime. I think he has made about 60 or 70 gallons of syrup, some of which I tasted & found delightful. I have some idea of having my cane ground & made into syrup; Ned Capers very kindly offered to do it for me himself if I would send it round to him with wood enough to boil it with.

Don't think I ever did so. 1885

Dec. 19th. Wednesday. Went to see Uncle Ben, found him much better & downstairs. J. H. Webb & his wife were there.

Did not last long

Grayson & E. Capers dined with me.

Dec. 20th. Put all hands out picking cotton, to get through the field before Christmas. A good many pods in the Point yet, shall pick it after the holidays. Packed first bale of cotton—340 lbs. Sent Frank to the village for my carriage.

Dec. 21st. Friday. Sun rose clear, but entered a cloud, which came on a heavy fog. All hands picking cotton, except two overhauling for [
]. Isaac & Sancho to Beaufort for Negro clothing &c &c. 1 bale of cotton packed—350 lbs.

Dec. 22nd. Saturday. All hands in the barn assorting, packed 2nd bale cotton, 350 lbs.

Dec. 24th. Sent to Beaufort—got Negro shoes & gave them out.

Dec. 25th. Tuesday. Christmas Day. Clear & cold. Isaac, Admond & Jim & Adam went to Savannah last night in the boat. Boat came over from the main with a raft of Negroes & some good things from Mother.

Borrowed Uncle Ben's buggy & drove my colts for the first time. They performed remarkably well, no tricks or disposition to kick or run, drove them over & called at Uncle Ben's to see him. He was worse, speechless. I don't think he can ever survive this attack of paralysis.

& did not

Dec. 26th. Wednesday. Went to Skull's Inlet with E. Capers, Frank, Gabriel[70] & Dr. Kirk.[71] Caught a good chance of fish. Killed one deer, & spent a very pleasant time.

Not so—it was rather the other way if I remember right

[70] Ned, Frank, and young Gabe—William Gabriel—Capers (1832–1882).
[71] John William Kirk (1803–1868), physician and planter of St. Luke's Parish.

Our two maids, Eliza & Nelly, took to themselves husbands this night. Their mistress gave them a grand supper (which they did not deserve). They were married by Mother's Robert, the former to Uncle Paul's June, & Nelly to Uncle Ben's man Taffy. Tis said they had great doings at the wedding, which I did not witness, being on the Island—in fact I did not wish to be here to see the tomfoolery that was going on about it, as if they were ladies of quality.

Christmas 1876, will be 27 years since those girls were married. They are both alive, & stranger, have the very same husbands. One has a married daughter I believe. They are now free, & live on my old place.

They had out, with wife's permission of course, very foolishly, my crockery, tables, chairs, candlesticks, & I suppose everything else they wanted.

& some of my good liquor made into a bowl of punch for the company

Dec. 27th.   Thursday. Very cold. I on the Island. Negroes got back from Savannah. Isaac too late to see his daughter[72] married.

Dec. 28th.   Commenced work again, 4 gins running. 3 hands picking cotton. I never picked cotton after Christmas before. Returned from the Island. I got nothing, but a bad cold.

Dec. 29th.   Saturday. Clear & cold, work same as yesterday.

All good resolutions were gone

Dec. 31st.   Monday. Last day of 1849. Ice for the first time this year, the old year goes out with a freeze—— Thus ends the year 1849. Can I look back and point out any actions of my own during the last twelve months, of which I feel proud? I fear not, may it not be so for the next twelve months to come, if it pleases God to spare my life so long a time.

Aug. 24th, 1876. It has pleased God to spare my life to this time, & I do not know that I can say more than I did above 27 years ago. Many changes & great ones have occurred. I am, in a manner, homeless, living at Coffin's Point, in a stranger's house, my old & other Negroes own most of my old place. Some Yankees own the house & I can't get it if I wished. What will be the end, I can't think & I sometimes hardly care now, 1876

Things got a little better, then about 1884 got decidedly worse. Wife & I prostrated with sickness & could not help ourselves. Daniel had us moved over to Walterboro, & now from Oct. 17th, we are living at Jim's[73] farm 2 miles from W.[74] & ought to be contented if we are not

---

[72] Eliza or Nelly.
[73] James Hagood Chaplin (1848–1930), son of Saxby Chaplin, Jr., and Anne O'Hear Witsell. Nephew of Thomas B. Chaplin.
[74] Walterboro.

1850

Jan. 1st. I have made a very short crop the past year—fear not over ½ bale per hand.

Jan. 3rd. Found dinner at the muster house.
What a tax these dinners were & for what use

Gave up the Est. D. Fripp's Negroes which I hired the past year. They were hired again today, to run from the 20th Jan. 1850 to 20th Jan. '51. I hired Admond at $53 and Isaac at $60. Rather a high price, but they wished me to hire them, and they will be of great service to me in many ways besides making a crop—for instance, I have only two men, and a quantity of fencing to do, & rail timber very scarce. If I wish to go anywhere in a boat, why, I have no oarsmen but two. I did not bid for Molly. She is old & of little use in the field & will not pay for herself. Frank Pritchard[1] hired her. She was very much disappointed and I was sorry for her, she is a good natured old woman. I had not the least trouble with her, she did what she was able to do.

Jan. 5th. Rode to see Uncle Ben. He was sitting up for a little while today, but still unable to speak, & has a very bad sore on one of his legs. Killed 20 robins, never saw them so numerous——

Jan. 7th. Carting out, with 2 carts, some cove mud on cotton land. 4th bale cotton packed. The robins have nearly all disappeared. Intend to go steadily on now with my manuring. Cart mud until I commence listing in marsh, then will go at the compost. I will try some mud this year on potatoes.

[1] Francis Pritchard (b. 1825), planter. Son of Thomas and Ann Pritchard. Husband of Sarah Sandiford, daughter of his neighbor James H. Sandiford.

Jan. 8th. Heard cannon firing throughout the day. Suppose they were in Savannah, celebrating the battle of New Orleans.[2] Hauling out cove mud on cotton land—— Plowed up patch for beets & mangel-wurzel. E. Capers called, dined & spent the night.
*He stuck *to us**

Jan. 9th. Edwin Chaplin called to collect his a/c, paid him by order on Uncle Paul Chaplin, $38.40.

I was engaged today staking out ground, and selecting such as I will plant this year in cotton. Made out in the Yard Field, Point, and Graveyard Hill, in all 29¾ acres, throwing out all the worse joint grass tasks.[3] I will have to take in 7¾ acres at the Pine Saplings and can get about 2½ in the garden. 3 gins going today, 2 hands assorting & Isaac making ox yoke, and bows.[4]

Jan. 14th. 2 gins running, 3 hands assorting cotton. E. Capers called & dined with me. He is going to the main tomorrow and I have some idea of going with him. Rode over to see Uncle Paul in the evening, asked him to go my security for the hire of Est. D. Fripp's Negroes—*but he would not.* It is mortifying to ask such a thing of anyone & to be refused.

Jan. 15th. Tuesday. Windy, cloudy, cold & very disagreeable. Went to Mr. Caperses' to go on the main with Ned. Weather too bad, did not go. Dined with them. Ned came home with me in the evening. I felt very much like an attack of rheumatism, bad pain in my chest, & shortness of breath. Had a hot fever at night.
This was the beginning of a shortness of breath that has troubled me ever since, more or less

Jan. 16th. Wednesday. Ned started home before breakfast, to go to the main. I was so sick all night that I told him I could not go with him, but felt so much better when I got up, and being anxious to embrace the opportunity of seeing Mother, that, notwithstanding my bad feelings, I went over to Caperses' to go. They did not go, & I am very glad, for I grew worse, and was very sick at night, with fever, violent pain in my chest, & rheumatism in nearly every joint. 5 hands picking cotton today.

---

[2] The last major battle of the War of 1812. A large British expeditionary force under Gen. Sir Edward Packenham was routed by an American army consisting of half-trained militia units under the command of Gen. Andrew Jackson, at a cost of 2,000 British and 71 American casualties. The battle occurred fifteen days after the signing of the Treaty of Ghent (Dec. 24, 1814), before news of the treaty could reach the city, and hence did not affect the outcome of the war.

[3] Several quarter-acre patches that produced more grass than cotton.

[4] Oxbows: U-shaped collars for oxen.

Jan. 17th.   Thursday. Pleasant day. I suffered very much with pains, particularly in my chest. Sent Frank to Beaufort to try and get something to relieve me. Got a vial of Flannagant's pain killer.[5]
Don't remember the medicine, Perry Davis's is the [   ] now.   '85
  Planted mangel-wurzel & turnip beets.

Jan. 18th.   Friday. Rubbed three times with the pain killer, think it has done me some good, feel some easier this evening, though I suffered a great deal last night and this morning. Finished ginning white & commenced the yellow cotton.

Jan. 19th.   4 gins at yellow cotton, one hand picking. I came to the unavoidable conclusion, to give up the hands I hired of the Est. of David Fripp. I am so unfortunate that no one will stand my security, & I am too proud to ask any & everybody. I have therefore given the Negroes a ticket to go to Isaac Fripp on Monday. I have no one to blame for it, but only set it down as a failure to comply to terms.
I suffered much mortification in those things, but where are they now, that were so particular & saving then—no better off today than I & some dead & gone, & their leavings belong to strangers. They saved, saved, for strangers

Jan. 21st.   Monday. Most dreadful day in every way. Rain, & sometimes very hard, from morning till night, & nearly all night, and *I* was in almost agony all day, though not *entirely* confined to bed. Sent Frank to Beaufort to get something to rub my rheumatic parts with. God knows how he will get there—such a day—he has not come back, 10 p.m.
  Finished ginning all the cotton, stained & all. Packed a pocket of white—250 lbs., making in white cotton, 5 packed bags & a pocket, in all 1900 lbs. clean cotton, or six bales & 100 lbs. Have not weighed the std. cotton, suppose I have about 200.
  Isaac Fripp would not accept of the security I offered him for the Est. D. Fripp's Negroes, so I came to the conclusion, & I think wisely, to give them up, and sent them to him today. I, in the first place, gave too much for them, I could hardly have cleared the hire, $113.

Jan. 22nd.   Tuesday. Clear as a bell this morning and a delightful day throughout. I rested tolerably well last night & feel much better this morning, though still painful. Walked out a short distance.
  Frank got back this morning. Jim went out & struck the first hoe

[5] Falligant's Rheumatic Liniment and Pain-Killer, advertised as "the best remedy ever discovered for Rheumatism, Pains in the Limbs, Joints and Swelling or Enlargements of the Bones."

towards listing in marsh, the only one. Judge getting stakes. The women all cleaning the yellow cotton. Isaac very sick, very much affected as myself, except the rheumatism.

Killed my largest & last bacon hog.

Jan. 23rd.   I was out on horseback a little while today, but all in a good deal of pain in my chest & shoulder, my feet so swollen & painful I could hardly walk about the house, & could not get on my boots or even my cloth slippers, had to put on an old pair carpet shoes. Isaac still sick but better. Had five hands out listing today, preparing what land I can plant in the garden. Wish I could well attend to this most particular work.

Jan. 25th.   Friday. 7 hands listing today. 5½ acres listed (marsh). Isaac is better today but not out. Planted carrots. Both carts hauling out marsh. Uncle Paul takes 30 acres of cotton land of me this year, plants the Bay Field, over the Sands. This will bring me in $90 at the lowest, but I candidly think that he ought to give me $3.50 per acre.

Jan. 26th.   Rode over to see Uncle Ben in the afternoon, he is in a very bad way. Isaac is still quite sick.

Marked my cotton—5 bales, 350 lbs., 1 pocket, 150 lbs., white = 6 bales & 66 lbs. 1 pocket, 170 lbs. stained, equal in whole crop to 6 bales, 236 lbs. Being at the rate of 217 lbs. to the hand, for 10 hands.

Jan. 27th.   Sunday. Received a letter from Mother today by Ned Capers. He returned from the main last night. Mother expects to come over very shortly. God, what we will find to give her to eat? We have killed the last hog & are out of everything fresh.

She always brought something

Jan. 28th   Monday. Sent Anthony with 3 hands to Beaufort in the flat with cotton. They got back quite early, before dark, round here to the landing. Sent 4 bags & 1 pocket of std. to Ingraham & Webb & 1 bale to P. H. Behn in Savannah——

Bought a bridle & bit from J. S. Fyler & Co.,[6] price $_____ . Mary went to Beaufort in the flat. 4 hands listing. Commenced a mullet or prawn net.

Jan. 29th.   E. Capers called, & dined with me. Carts at the compost again today. Isaac still quite sick. I do not feel as well today as I did yesterday. Put Adam tracking out March corn & potato root land. Will put some

---

[6] John S. Fyler (b. 1814), Beaufort merchant.

hands to listing corn land tomorrow. Gave out the last potato allowance this evening, two weeks' allowance more than last year, and save more potatoes for the house.

Feb. 2nd. Saturday. Ned & myself went to Beaufort, 5 oars. 5 hands listing.

Swore to, before J. D. Pope, magistrate, & signed my name to a paper drawn up by Treville in answer to a bill by Hastie & Nichols[7] of Greenville, petitioning to have more of Mother's trust Est. sold to pay them a debt. Brought home & sent to D. Jenkins another paper of the same kind, for him to swear to as his answer to same persons. Also one for Mother which I am to send over on the main to her.[8] For to send to the main is very inconvenient. I will have to take all the men off the place to send. **All this trouble on myself alone & not a bit of use for it**

Feb. 4th. Monday. Bitter cold, black frost. Wind very high. Don't think the boat can possibly get to the main. Every green thing in the garden looks completely stewed up with cold—green peas, that are in bloom, particularly so. What hands are left are listing corn land. Judy listed on Saturday, & was laid up today.

Feb. 5th. Tuesday. The Negroes that went in the boat came back *afoot,* about 11 a.m. They did not get further than D. P. Jenkins' creek and there the scamps stayed all day yesterday, & came home too late to do a day's work today. I put them to work however. Wind rose again at night & blew all night.

Feb. 8th. Sent Anthony and Judge to the main to carry a letter to Mother. They could not have finer weather. Moll sick yesterday & today. Isaac a little better. 5 hands listing potato land—will not have a day's work for all hands tomorrow. Finished the compost pen. It went over all the Home Field (cotton), and a few tasks of potato land. I will note down when the land is listed, how many acres the compost manured. I was busy today running out March corn land and potato patch, had only Jack with me. It is rather troublesome work. Killed a wether yesterday.

Feb. 9th. Saturday. Moll & Isaac still sick, this a great drawback to me. Sent Jim and Sancho to get wood, and put the women to getting manure

---

[7] William S. Hastie and James H. Nichols, *Charleston* saddlers and suppliers of "goods, wares and merchandise" to the plantation trade. In later years, Hastie and Nichols occupied different stores on the same street.
[8] The merchants are suing the Bakers *and* the Chaplins to recover three old debts: one contracted by Isabella while she was still Mrs. Fields; one contracted by Chaplin, with his mother standing security; and a third run up by Baker after his marriage.

out of the hog pen, cow house and stable, there is a very fine quantity of it. They did not finish getting all out. I must keep an account of how many cart loads I carry out. I calculate there are about two hundred loads.

Feb. 10th. Sunday. Mother came over from the main today, came all the way round by Harbor Island,[9] got here up to my landing about 4 o'clock p.m. I fear she has come too late for signing the paper. Anthony did not get to the main till Saturday morning. Mother left them at Hangman's Point on their way back today. I suppose they will be here some time tonight.

Feb. 11th. Anthony & Judge made their appearance this morning and went to work. Sent for J. D. Pope, magistrate, he swore Mother to the paper and sent it immediately off to Col. Treville, so this business is settled so far.[10]

Moll came out today. 7 hands listing cotton land, 3 tasks listed, manured with rushes at the Pine Saplings, and 3½ tasks mudded at the Graveyard.[11] Summer & Anthony getting the manure out of the stable, did not finish. Mother's boat returned to the main.

Feb. 12th. Yesterday I let J. L. Chaplin have a cow & calf so that he can get a little milk to put in his coffee. He & his family are staying at the Riverside, and are quite bad off. Ben Chaplin has turned them out of his house since last summer and, as I hear, does not help them out in any way, will not even let them have a little milk, though he has a large stock of cattle. I will lend him the cow for a while.
Bad off as I was, I helped that man then, & he actually wanted to claim the cow & calf as a gift

Feb. 15th. Judge out today, Moll still sick. Put a blister on her chest, did her much good. 6 hands listing compost.

Feb. 16th. Saturday. Sent Anthony, Summer & Sancho for oysters. 5 hands listing. Sent the cart to move Judy over from the Riverside. Whole amt. of land listed for cotton, 21¼ acres—viz., marsh, 9½ acres; no manure, 2 acres; mud, 5¼ acres; rushes, ¾ acres; cow pen compost, 3¾ acres = 21¼ acres——

E. Capers called and dined with me. He brought with him some sausages & spareribs, which, to us, was a godsend, as we were sorely put to it "to find" today's dinner, and from necessity had just put to death an old

---

[9] A marsh island just below the southeast tip of St. Helena Island, between St. Helena and Hunting islands.
[10] See Feb. 2, 1850.
[11] The Graveyard Field.

gander, which old Suky had pronounced as entirely too tough for human beings to masticate. So we will put the old fellow off for tomorrow's dinner, & have him well boiled.

Moll still sick. Saw Isaac walking out today. Anthony got back about midnight, got a fine parcel of oysters.

Found out later that Isaac was playing possum

Feb. 17th. Sunday. Mother & myself intended to go to church, but my old horses took it into their heads not to go, and when I did get them off, Hyder broke both of his traces, so we had to give it up. I went in the gig. Drove Mother over to Uncle Ben's & called for her on my return.

Feb. 18th. Isaac & Moll still sick. God knows when I will get all of my small force at work. So many mouths to feed & so few to work that it is *impossible* for me to get along. If there is not some arrangement made so as to have fewer Negroes about the yard and more in the field, I will not be able to make enough to *feed* them—to say nothing about clothing them, and yet, it appears that not one of those about the house & yard can be done without. I have now in the field, when they are all out, at any rate I plant for them,[12] the following: Including stable boy, Frank, for though I do not plant for him, he does the carting & plowing, Isaac 1, Peg 2. Jim 3, Sancho 4, Judge 5, Moll 6, Helen 7 and Amy, Mary and Summer equal to 2 hands, making in all that I plant for, 9 hands. Now, those about the yard, and those that eat & do nothing in the world for me: Mary, seamstress, 1; Judy, washer, 2; Suky, cook, 3; Charles, dairy, 4; Nelly, nurse, 5; Eliza, house, 6; Jack, ditto, 7; Sam, ditto, 8; Nelly, nurse, 9;[13] Anthony, garden, 10; May, hogs, 11; Old Nelly, nothing, 12; Judy, ditto, 13. Not counting the children & Old Sam, who can't do anything, but make 9 mouths more to feed. This shows out of 30 head to feed, only 9 work and make feed for them, then they expect clothes & shoes regularly. Another year will see us worse off than we are this——

Feb. 19th. Helen had an idea of laying up today but I saw that nothing much was the matter and made her go out to work. I am determined to look more closely into their complaints, and not allow anyone to shirk from their work and sham sickness.

Finished carting manure on potato land, 12 horse and 43 ox cart loads, some of it on corn land. 55 loads of manure out of stable—some left. Listed and manured nearly 1½ tasks of land for sugarcane.

[12] Field hands who receive their food in allowances.
[13] Chaplin has listed Nelly twice.

Feb. 22nd. Friday. Finished listing cotton ground, 28¾ acres. Commenced listing ground at the Saplings for corn, 1¾ acres listed. Anthony putting out long stakes to run out cotton field. Finished putting down short stakes for potato & March corn land yesterday.

Feb. 25th. Monday. Planted sugarcane, 1½ tasks. Moved cow pen onto a task of cotton land.

Feb. 26th. Tuesday. Finished listing corn land at Saplings, 4½ acres, 15 acres in all for March corn. Judge making hog pen.

March 2nd. Saturday. Sophy & I rode over to see Uncle Ben in the afternoon. The old man was much better, he could speak a few words. Women spreading manure on potato land, plowing ditto. Men getting poles. Sent Anthony to Beaufort. Cotton I sent to Savannah sold for 30 cents.

March 3rd. Went to church. Isaac got his hogs in the pen, one of mine that came up with his I put up. Am afraid I shall not get all of mine up this year.[14]

March 4th. Monday. Rode around my fencing with Uncle Paul. He sent his hands some time ago to make up my division fence, & I wanted to show him that they did little or nothing to it. He is to send them back again tomorrow to go over it. Had the women spreading compost on corn land at the Saplings today. I plant 4¼ acres March corn there this year on cotton land. 3 men cutting poles, will have enough cut today and go at the fence tomorrow. Summer & Frank carting out the poles.

March 5th. Women listing ground for early peas. Men at the fence. Dr. Grayson dined with me. E. M. Capers took two drum fish on the 4th inst. Had not the politeness to send us a steak.

March 6th. Wednesday. Muster Day. Ned came home with me & spent the night. A meeting was called at the muster house and resolutions passed to remove the muster house to a ½ acre lot of land to be given to the company by W.O.P. Fripp on his land between the two churches. It was agreed and I suppose this is the last of it.

March 10th. Sunday. Cloudy all day, no rain, did not go to church. Put Badger in the plow *yesterday*—he performed very well for first time.

---

[14] Hogs were given the run of the fields after harvesting, and usually were put in the woods to forage for up to ten months before being penned and fattened on corn. Chaplin fears he won't find all the hogs he has on the loose. Poor fences compel Chaplin to pen up his hogs longer than usual.

March 12th. Tuesday. Planted yellow yams, ½ acre, & ¼ acre of a sort of leathercoat potato, picked out of the yellow yam seed. Finished the gate, such as it is, made by Anthony & Judge.

Sent Jim & Sancho to Beaufort.

March 14th. Thursday. Planting potatoes. A smart shower came up about 12 m., which drove us in for an hour or two, but partially cleared, & I got over 5 tasks planted—brimstones, Mexicans and common yams. Planted beans in garden, & Lucerne a day or two ago——

March 15th. Finished planting potatoes, 3½ acres, 6 different sorts. Planted water & muskmelons through potato patch.

Note—My potato seed kept remarkably well this year. I did not get a bushel of decayed ones out of all I opened. Have about 3 banks left, besides what I fed out in the fall. Put the hands to ditching after they got through planting potatoes. A very heavy job to dig out the ditch from the pond or cow well by the Negro houses, out to the bay or creek.

March 17th. Sunday. Went to church. Heard great talk about a sea serpent 150 feet long, besides *several* whales seen lately in Broad River. Some say that George Elliott[15] and others went down from Beaufort with a cannon to shoot the monsters, & actually succeeded in giving one of them, I don't whether serpent or whale, a broadside or two, and sinking it. I fear we will get the character of telling "big snake stories" as well as some of our Northern friends. I also heard that Frank Capers was chased ashore by one of the monsters after shooting at it with a rifle, at Whale Branch.[16]

March 18th. All hands banking corn land. Exchanged a ½ bushel of corn with Dr. Scott for the same quality of early corn for seed. Got about a gallon of coal tar of Edwin Chaplin in return for some common tar I loaned him near two years ago.

March 21st. Would have planted corn today but the weather was too bad. Had all the corn tarred, ready for planting. Planted a task of guinea

[15] George Parsons Elliott (1807–1871), planter and leading antebellum promoter for the development of Port Royal Harbor. Son of William Elliott and Phoebe Waight. Brother of William Elliott, Jr., and Stephen Elliott, Sr. Member S.C. House of Representatives 1856–60.

[16] The sighting of the sea serpent was reported in the Charleston *Mercury* (March 18): "He is from 120 to 150 feet in length, and of proportionate bulk; has the head of a serpent, which he carries, when in motion, five or six feet out of the water; about ten feet from his head is a hump, resembling a huge hogshead, and as far as could be seen out of the water a succession of humps was observed." A few days later a party of men pursued the beast. "The object of their search . . . was resolved into four whales, in single file. . . ."

corn, mostly for fodder. I intend to plant more. Put some ashes on ground in the garden to be planted in corn.

March 23rd. Saturday. Finished planting March corn in the field near the potato patch. Planted 10 beds more of arrowroot, got the seed from Aunt Betsy.

March 25th. Major's Jack came here & did some work on my boat, paid him in corn & bacon.

March 26th. Tuesday. Most delightful day. All hands banking ground at the Point by the garden for cotton. Some persons have planted. Uncle Paul's hands are banking in Bay Field today. I rode over & dined with Capers. *Noticed* that many persons had not planted potatoes. I must trust Providence for mine, have been in the ground nearly a fortnight, found two rotten ones in grabbling[17] yesterday. They were yams of the last planting. The reds were sound, what I saw.

Got Mr Capers' coachman to trim Buckskin's hoofs, they were in very bad order. Someone stole some seed potatoes put up for hog feed, out of the gin house last night. *Suspect* Frank.

March 30th. Saturday. Disagreeable. Mother sent over two hands with some good things.

April 2nd. Tuesday. Planted cotton up to the Negro houses, 4 tasks deep from the yard, all round the Point & in the garden (the seed that Isaac selected in the garden). Rather wet to plant.

April 4th. Thursday. All hands banking cotton, Graveyard. Agricultural Day. I felt very unwell but went out, had a toothache nearly all day. Election of officers, the same were retained, with the exception of sec'try J. W. Pope, who having left the parish, Dr. Grayson was put in his place. Dr. Jenkins found a very excellent dinner. My find next, & cannot find as good.

We held a meeting, after the society adjourned, for the purpose of taking into consideration the proper time & place of holding a parish meeting for the purpose of expressing our feelings upon the death of John C. Calhoun,[18] senator from this state. There was some little jarring be-

---

[17] Digging or groping with the hands.

[18] John Caldwell Calhoun (1782–1850), theorist of the doctrines of states rights and nullification. Son of Patrick Calhoun and Martha Caldwell, of Abbeville District. Member S.C. House of Representatives 1808–10, U.S. House of Representatives 1811–17. Secretary of War 1817–25, under James Monroe; Vice-President under John

tween Dr. Scott & J.E.L. Fripp. The Dr. wished the meeting in Beaufort (at which place all agreed, with few exceptions, it should be held) called by our Representatives. Fripp wanted it called by the Intendant of Beaufort, which later was carried. The meeting is to be called for Monday, 12 m., 8th inst. The request was sent over by J. M. Baker. Esq., tax collector, who came over to receive tax returns. I made my return, amounted to $23. I enjoyed this meeting better than any I have ever attended. The dinner was good, & so were the liquors, and after dinner we were kept in a constant roar of laughter by a succession of stories by Dr. Croft, a guest, from Newberry.[19]

April 5th. I suffered agonies last night with my tooth. Did not sleep the whole night. A little better this morning, but my God how it did shoot in the evening. I got no ease till I put spirits [of] hartshorn in it, when it commenced to swell. Planted green peas in the garden. Hands banking.

April 6th. The baby was taken very suddenly ill this evening, taken with throwing up & tonight threatened with convulsions, don't know what can be the matter. We were just saying this morning how much she had grown and how well she looked.

April 7th. The baby very ill all last night, thought every moment she would have a fit. Finished banking cotton land yesterday evening.

April 8th. Monday. Anthony says he saw *white frost yesterday morn.* Baby sick all night, better this morning. Dr. Scott called about 12 m. & cut its gums. Planting cotton, the 3rd & last planting. Peg sick today. I suppose she thinks it is near the last, she may as well take a day. Finished planting cotton out & out.

April 9th. Fine day for fishing, but I do not hear that the drum are biting well. Uncle Tom's boat only took 5 yesterday & 4 today. Not worth taking hands off for, unless, as it is with him, I had nothing to do. I should have gone out today however, but had not lines enough and went over to

---

Q. Adams and Andrew Jackson 1825-32. Calhoun wrote the "South Carolina Exposition" for the S.C. legislature, declaring that a state was not bound by a Federal law it believed to be unconstitutional. He quarreled with Jackson over the tariff and over northern influence in the making of national policies. U.S. Senator from South Carolina 1833-43. Secretary of State under John Tyler 1844-45. Returned to the Senate in 1845 and served there until his death.
[19] Probably Theodore Gaillard Croft, brother of St. Helena Island physician and planter Randall Croft. Newberry was a prosperous upcountry town, on the road to Greenville, about 150 miles from St. Helena.

Caperses' and made a couple very fine & strong ones, out of the fine cotton that Ned Capers gave me last spring.

Planted 3 tasks of groundnuts[20] for wife. She promises to make the yard Negroes dig them in.

April 10th.   Baby still quite sick.

April 11th.   It appears that I am not to have a good day to go out, I went however today, and wished a dozen times I had stayed at home, though the weather looked at several times like breaking & turning out a fine day. It became overcast about 1 p.m. and rained very hard. I did not get very wet, thanks to my bear's skin, but had a very disagreeable time. We took two drum, and had two fine turtle given to me. Got home about 3½ p.m. The fish bit well on this morning's high water, about sunrise. James Fripp was out on the same drop I took (Parris Bank) & took 17 & lost several. He had a plenty of prawn, and very kindly gave me two or three dozen. There were a number of boats out, but none did well but him. Some even worse than I. This is my first day's fishing this year and an unfortunate one it was. I not only got wet, took but two fish, but Anthony lost my hook & tiller overboard, through awkwardness.

April 12th.   Friday. Very heavy rain last night. I consider myself fortunate in having my ditches all free, I see very little water settling in the field. My corn is all up very prettily. Potatoes up here & there very scattering; first & second planting of cotton coming up very well. All hands listing April corn land today. No fishing for me today, and I will not go out again till we have good weather.

April 13th.   Saturday. Clear, with high wind from N.W. I think we will have good weather for fishing next week, if not *I* stay at home. High wind is worse than rain for fishing. Have but 3 hands in the field today. Peg went out or I would have but two. Sent 3 to Beaufort & Helen & Jim sick. God knows when I will get through with my late corn land. At this rate, it will be May instead of April corn, and the ground is so low & wet I shall have to bank it. The day before yesterday was the eleventh anniversary of my marriage.

1868*   *now 28 years, wife long dead & only two poor children alas, all tho gone to heaven I hope. 1876, now only one left, poor Ernest is gone too. '76   It is most time for poor me to go & join the rest, if I was only prepared for it—I care not how soon now. Nothing left me [   ] but dear Sophy

[20] Peanuts.

Eleven long years and yet it appears as only yesterday. 7 children, 5 alive, only think.

Had to put Mary to minding the potatoes. I see the crows have found them out.

April 18th. Thursday. Very good day, but did not go out. I wanted all hands in the field today and I wished to be at home to start the plows in the corn land. All hands hoeing potatoes. They are all sprouting beautifully and would have been up much sooner if I had had them hoed to break the hard crust on the bed, which kept them down.

April 19th. Very pretty day. Went fishing, took 4 drum, I 3 on my own line, and Frank one, the first one he ever caught. Finished hoeing the potatoes. Hoed 5 tasks of early corn, & some cotton in garden.

April 20th. Saturday. Wind very high, but went out to Broad River. Had to come in early, it was so rough, but caught 6 fish, I 5 on my own line. This is the fifth time I have been out & have taken 9 drum, 8 in the last two days. Jack took the 6th today. A great many boats out. I hear that they bit well on Thursday, as high as 30 were taken.

April 21st. Went to church. Saw a good many red faces, the effects of drum fishing——

Engaged Wm. B. Fripp's house again for this summer, could do no better, and I suppose the family must go away from home. I am determined not to spend my summer there at all risks, I will go to Bay Point first.

April 25th. Thursday. Fine day. Planted April corn, later than last year, & not so well manured. Went fishing—poor sport. Saw a schooner anchored in the river, heard that Saxby and several others from the main were on board. Went aboard, found Saxby, Minott & wife, Farmer & wife, Bill Ford[21] & Andrew Fowler,[22] also a crowd of visitors from the Island. Of course not much more fishing was done.

Summer still sick, but reported better. . . .

April 27th. Saturday. Fine day. My birthday, 28 years old. Attended battalion review at the muster house, got the appointment of clerk of the company.

---

[21] William H. Ford, medical student. Later physician and vaccinator for the city of Charleston.
[22] Andrew D. Fowler, clerk. Later a customs collector in Charleston.

April 28th. Summer has no fever this morning, gave him quinine.

While at supper, Amy came in crying, said Summer was worse. When I got to the Negro house found him *perfectly dead.* Never was so surprised in my life. We were all under the impression that he was getting better, and was so reported to us by his mother and Old Judy, who were attending him, but since his death, they have just thought proper to tell me of several symptoms he showed that would have made it necessary to employ a doctor, and which I had no way of knowing except through the nurses. His last was rather strange. About sunset he vomited something as black as soot, and died in an hour after. I was not even informed that he had vomited, or something might have been done for him, even at that late hour. I certainly would have sent for a Dr., but he would have been too late. He was delirious a day or two ago, and though I was away from home, wife should have been informed of it, or myself when I returned at night, but these infernal stupids kept saying he was better till an hour before his death. I blame them very much, but it can't be undone now, but they ought to have a lesson for the future.

I wished to have a post morten examination, but could not get a physician to come. Summer will be a great loss to me. He was good steady boy, about 16 years old. He lost one of his eyes last summer, which seemed to affect him considerably. He always appeared in low spirits. Taken sick on Tuesday, died Sunday night.

April 29th. Monday. Clear & high wind, injuring the cotton, has killed nearly all in the garden. Planted it over today, also supplying over the whole field. Hoeing & hauling potatoes, most of them are now up very well. Corn & cotton both want working badly. Never saw grass grow so fast, but must clean my potatoes first. They were only hoed the other day.

April 30th. Anthony sick today. He is very much grieved at the death of his son.

May 1st. Wednesday. Went to muster. Paid taxes, by order on Ingraham & Webb. Anthony very sick, no doubt he will go next. All hands hoeing March corn, 5 tasks early corn hauled.

May 3rd. Finished hoeing March corn near the Negro houses—commenced hoeing corn at Saplings. Dr. Grayson & Ned Capers dined with me. Grayson is a whole souled fellow, got corned as a matter of course, fell out of his sulky at the gate. Started him off all right. If Ned don't blab the occurrence will go no further than this journal. Ned stayed all night.

Anthony very ill. Sent for Dr. Jenkins, gave him calomel. No better at night, up with him nearly all night. I like the old fellow but he never thought so because I cursed him sometimes. I will greatly regret his death, which I *hope* (I won't say pray) to God will not now take place. His mind is greatly worried on account of his son.

May 4th. Anthony, for his case is uppermost in my mind, is very much the same as yesterday. Dr. Jenkins called again this morning, thinks he has a paralysis of the tongue. Something like Uncle Ben, only the *brain* not so much affected. Finished hoeing corn at Saplings.

May 5th. Moved Anthony in his own house yesterday. He is worse this morning. Went to see him about 7 a.m., thought he was dying. Breathed his last with hardly a struggle about 10½ o'clock a.m., just a week all to a few hours, after his son's death. He is regretted by many, white & black. I miss him more than I would any other Negro that I own. Peace be to his soul.

May 6th. Monday. Warm, dry & windy, no sign of rain. Cotton dying all over the field. All hands commenced hoeing cotton, 1st hoeing. I fear it will only make it die worse, after loosening the dirt, unless the wind stops or we have rain. There has much died since I supplied it last week.

Got Uncle Ben's Paul to make a coffin for poor old Anthony. The body begins to smell very bad already, had it put in the coffin as soon as it came. Buried the body alongside of his son about 11 o'clock at night. Little did anyone suppose that in one short week at the same hour & day that Summer was laid in the ground that Anthony would rest alongside of him, cold in death, and no one can tell who, of all that were present, will be in the grave this time next week. I attended the funeral. There were a large number of Negroes from all directions present, I suppose over two hundred.

May 7th. Judy confined late at night (boy).
Born 7th of May 1850. Dennis 26 years old 7th May 1876.

May 9th. Thursday. Helen & Mary sick. Isaac supplying cotton. All hands transplanting corn, and setting up what has blown down.

Item—the cotton that I had hoed flat looks better & cleaner today than what was ridged down. The grass in the latter is green after the rain, in the former it was shaken up & is *dead.* Finished thinning & transplanting all my March corn. If the transplanted corn takes, I will then consider that I have a good stand. Hoed guinea corn—

May 10th. Went out to fish for whiting, but when we got on the drop, told Jack to throw out anchor, when the rotten old rope broke, & away went the anchor to the bottom, and we made our way back home. Mary came out today, or rather was *whipped out*. Started Frank plowing the March corn near the potato patch.

May 11th. Saturday. Helen reported to be speechless this morning. I went to see her. Am inclined to believe there was some pretense about her not being able to speak. She recovered her speech & senses remarkably quick and was able to get in & out of bed herself, after I had been to the trouble to sending for a doctor. Sent first for Dr. Jenkins, but circumstances of a domestic nature prevented him from attending. He sent a prescription after a second note, which wife wrote contrary to my desire. Sent for Dr. Scott, he came immediately. I showed him Dr. J.'s prescription—he recommended it highly, said he would have done the same. *Item*—I doubt it. Went on with Dr. J.'s prescription. The woman got better. Heard that J. J. Pope Jr. was married a few days ago to a Miss Mikell[23] of Edisto.

May 16th. Thursday. Hoeing cotton & potatoes. Finished plowing corn at Negro houses. Dr. Scott sent a mare to my horse on 15th yesterday. She took & is to return next Friday week. W. W. Fripp sent his mare, but sent her back, as the horse had a mare that day. He is to send back next week.

Capt. W. W. Fripp sent me an order as clerk. I did not think the office would be so troublesome or I would not have had it. The order is to summon all defaulters from militia & patrol duty to go to Gillisonville to court martial. It will take about 16 summonses.

May 21st. Jim & Judge both lying up today. Made them come out but no use, they will have their time out. Jim I think was really sick with diarrhea. Isaac I think is beginning to skulk, if he has not been doing so for some time. I made him take his hoe today, thinning & hauling cotton.

Went round to serve a summons on the defaulters, *note*, I must look into this. I doubt if it is the duty of clerk—served all but J. W. Perry. Dined with Mr. Capers. They were all distressed, Mrs. Capers[24] being quite ill. Ned went over in the boat for his sister, Mrs. Minott,[25] while I was there. I made a trade with the old man for his buggy, a very strong, serviceable & convenient article, with seats for four, & will carry all *my* family as well as a carriage. The old man *rather* stuck me, the hiding being much motheaten, no pole or harness, or wrench to take off the wheels. I

---

[23] Emily H. Mikell. Daughter of Isaac Jenkins Mikell and Emily C. Price.
[24] Mary Reynolds Capers. Wife of C. G. Capers. Mother of Ned, Frank, Gabriel, Jr., Ben, and Tom Capers and Ann Capers Minott.
[25] Ann E. Capers Minott (b. 1825). Wife of John Minott.

gave him my colt Badger, & am to give him $40 in one year or when my next crop is sold.

✱✱ *The buggy worth about 40 dollars & no more. It was serviceable*✱✱

Item—Gabriel Capers has been expelled from the Citadel Academy[26] for disobedience of orders.

Item—Mr. Capers is very much afraid that he had 60 bales of cotton burned in the late fire in Charleston.[27] The cotton was in the hands of Smith & Coffin. They lost all the cotton in their hands, so Capers's must be gone, & his money too, if the cotton was not insured.

May 23rd.   Some black rascally rogue killed a sheep yesterday evening in my pasture. It was done in broad daylight, just before Charles went over to pen the cows. The blood was not dry when he found it. I saw someone just about the time the thing must have been done, from the upstairs window, standing near the cow pen. No doubt it was the very rascal, I would give $5 to know who was the sheep stealer.

Wife took a notion to visit today, so we went over to see Mrs. D. P. Jenkins[28] & her little baby. Took our baby[29] with us. She was dreadfully afraid to ride in the buggy, but soon got fond of it. Mrs. Jenkins could hardly believe she was the little thing she called "a scrap of a baby" last fall. Old Hyder pulls the buggy easily, and wife is very much pleased with it.

May 24th.   All hands banking up March corn, finished all to 3 tasks. Still plowing pea land. It is late for early peas but I can't help it, I must plant with this rain. Gave the Negroes a small beef, they are working pretty hard at this time. Judge came out & thinned some cotton today. Dr. Scott sent his mare back to the horse—she refused. I think she is in foal. This brings me nothing, as I owe him money. He sent another mare but she was not in season.

May 25th.   Saturday. Drove wife, with the baby & Virginia over to see Cousin Sarah Scott. Wife has got to be such an intolerable coward, & so nervous, that I dislike to drive her anywhere. She blames me & quarrels & finds fault with everything for the most trifling thing. She says she places no confidence in my driving or management or judgment—after eleven

[26] Military academy in Charleston, founded as an arsenal after Denmark Vesey's abortive uprising in 1822. Its rigorous curriculum and strict standards of discipline resulted in a low rate of completion for the "pay cadets."

[27] The fire of May 17 was set by "an incendiary" in a cotton shed and spread quickly to surrounding wharves and office buildings, destroying more than 5,200 bales of upland cotton and some 435 bales of Sea Island cotton—the total valued at $325,000.

[28] Anne Jenkins Jenkins.

[29] Mary Frances Chaplin, called Missy.

years' experience with her & only two accidents, *neither* of which was any fault of mine. *Now,* she must find someone else to drive her, with whom she will feel more safe, and in whom she can place *confidence.* I can drive well enough for the safety of *my own neck.*
(*1876*) *How foolish this all looks now—only nervousness*

May 28th. Tuesday. Hands planting rice[30] through April corn for morning's work, did not finish. Hoed & hauled some joint grass tasks of cotton in the yard field. Sent Isaac to Beaufort in gig. Judy came out—child 3 weeks old tonight.

Commenced that hateful of all things to me, moving to the village, by sending that black lady Mary with her cart load of things. It always takes a cart to move her Ladyship. I expect to get the family down on Thursday.

May 29th. The Captain sent me two carts from the Indian Hills, & two from the Seaside, with Uncle Paul's cart. I loaded them all & sent them down. They are to return for another load tomorrow when I expect to get the family down. I will try to get wife to stay down with me for a few days. I must observe that Uncle Paul (good old man) lent me his cart for two days when Uncle Tom, having nothing for his horse to do, would not lend me his cart atall.
some good reason for it

May 30th. Loaded and sent off 6 carts, to the village. Sent Sophy and all the children except Ernest. He & his mother are to wait till I go down. Went down to the village myself and had everything fixed as well as I could *considering* that Sophy has not spoken to me for more than two weeks. I have made up my mind not to speak to her *again,* unless she makes the first advances.
All this was so childish
The children were very anxious to come back with me from the village, particularly Virginia. I have moved this year with less trouble than I ever did. I said, *it* was because wife did not go down with the rest but she won't hear of it. Had today 2 carts from the Indian Hills, 3 from Uncle Ben's (Seaside) with the assistance of my oxen, and one cart from Uncle Paul (good old man).

May 31st. Friday. All hands hauling cotton, I never saw grass grow so fast, and this rain will help it. Rained very hard last night with much thunder & lightning. Very warm this morning. The house is so still it

---

[30] A dry-culture, high-ground variety of rice grown for home consumption is being sown in the furrows or alleys between the corn rows.

makes one feel lonesome. Ernest is very dull—he must miss the other children very much.

June 6th. Thursday. Found Society dinner, had much trouble, would have had more, but Mother sent Simon over to help me, also turkeys & hams. Hands at home ridging down April corn.

June 8th. My crop looks very well, corn & potatoes particularly. Finished hoeing young corn & commenced hoeing cotton, that in the garden is very grassy & weedy but good. I expected to find a blossom there today but did not, some forms are very large. Rice is up well, birds pulling it. I showed the largest stalk of cotton at the Society on Thursday. Fine weather for killing grass, and I have made up my mind, if my field gets grass so soon after this working as it did after the last, to flog *every Negro in the field.*

June 10th. Monday. All hands hoeing cotton, listing in the Orchard for slips for morning's work. Helen sick again. She & Moll were both sick last week. She has two bad jointer tasks, is I think one cause.

June 12th. Wednesday. All hands hoeing cotton—hoed through the 1st planting. Hauled up & laid by all the early corn (for last task) except that at the Saplings. That I laid by some time since it got but two workings & a plowing, but it will get no more. The two tasks in the garden & 5 tasks at potato patch have had two hoeings & two haulings. It is now silking & looks finely. I will lay by my March corn next week. Will haul up the first planting of cotton tomorrow. Found one or two good sized red potatoes in the patch today. Got 9½ bushels of corn from Wm. J. Grayson yesterday.

June 14th. Friday. Saw a cotton *bud*—will open tomorrow. Had okra & cucumbers to eat on the 12th. Helen has been sick all this week. *Obstruction.* Wife was quite sick yesterday at the village, cholera morbus.[31]

June 17th. Monday. Mother returned to the main today, Sophy went with her. She (Sophy) runs a great risk, but she is so dying to get away *somewhere* that I am glad she has gone. They wanted to take Eugene with them, but I would not hear of such a thing. Brought Ernest down with me. He will have to go to school tomorrow, to Miss Augusta Chaplin,[32] his

[31] Acute gastroenteritis. Symptoms include vomiting, diarrhea, and general prostration.
[32] Augusta S. Chaplin (1825–1852). Daughter of Benjamin S. Chaplin and Laura Butler. Chaplin's third cousin on her father's side.

first "entrae." I shall send Daniel also. Eugene says he wants to go, but he is rather *juvenile.* Virginia will go to Mrs. Mc. next Monday.

June 19th. Wednesday. Sent Ernest & Daniel to school to Miss Augusta Chaplin. They were a little diffident at first but soon got quite delighted. This is the first time I have ever sent any of my children to school. I will have to stir myself to keep them at it & pay for them. I rode out with Dr. M. M. Sams to his plantation. He has a very fair crop.

June 24th. Monday. Very hot & excessively dry. Hands hoeing peas for morning's work. Hauling cotton today, 2½ tasks each. Helen sick again, since Friday. Mary[33] confined about bedtime, girl child. She made a great fuss about it.
Amy died at 2 or 3 years old.*

June 29th. Had a watermelon today, not perfectly ripe. Cut mustard & flax yesterday. Owing to the drought the seed has not filled out well & is small, but the mustard is strong. Isaac finished regulating cotton today.

July 1st. Monday. Dr. Scott lost his little baby Oliver[34] on Friday night. Sent Isaac & Frank to Beaufort. Peg sick. All hands hauling April corn.

July 3rd. Wednesday. Heavy rain last night between here & the village. Wm. S. Chaplin's Est., Edgar Fripp & Grayson all planting slips, & not a drop down here. Helen, Peg & Amy sick yesterday—two came out today. Peg still laying up.
    Mother came over.

July 4th. Thursday. Anniversary [of] Independence. Dinner at muster house. Oration by Dr. Wm. J. Grayson, well written, badly delivered. Splendid speech from Col. Treville.
secession I suppose, & what did it all end in 1876
Toasts, champagne &c &c. Picnic at night in the village.

July 9th. Tuesday. Killed veal for market. Negroes making great complaints, don't want to work. Made up my mind to whip all round. Had to dig out cow well.

July 17th. Wednesday. Amy sick, bled her. Peg & Mary hoeing cotton. 3 listing pea ground, rest stripping blades.

[33] Young Mary, not the Mary they depend on for moving.
[34] Oliver Scott. Son of John A. P. Scott and Sarah Ann Chaplin. First cousin, once removed, to Thomas B. Chaplin on his mother's side.

July 19th. Friday. Everybody is busy getting up a dinner to be given on the 24th inst. to R. B. Rhett.[35] A good many persons are invited, and upon the whole it is to be a fine & grand affair for St. Helena. The partitions in Grayson's house to be knocked down for the table, & a stand erected outdoors for the speakers.

July 22nd. Monday. Very heavy rain with much thunder and lightning last night, which appears to have been pretty general all over the Island. Planting slips today, the first I have planted & I doubt if my neighbors are any better off. It is so late I expect to get little else than seed potatoes. The drought has been almost unprecedented, & I fear provisions will be very scarce another year. Roots are very backward, corn nearly all lost, & too late for a crop of peas or slips. There was a heavy wind last night with the rain, which prostrated the corn very much, also the cotton. Though this rain will benefit everything else, I think it will make the cotton cast off much of its fruit.

Great preparations making at the village to give Barnwell Rhett a grand reception. Mother's boat came over from the main last night, brought me about 500 clapboards to make yard fence. They are not enough for the village yard, & think of bringing them down here.

July 24th. Wednesday. A great day in the annals of St. Helenaville, a grand dinner given to the Hon. R. B. Rhett. Everything having been arranged in good and tasteful style, which did much credit to the committee of arrangements, by way of erecting a stand for the invited guests of distinction, neatly entwined with evergreens & covered with a canopy. And after testing our patience for about an hour the guest arrived, was conducted to the stand & introduced to the audience, among were the fair of the ville, by Capt. Jn. Fripp. Mr. Rhett then addressed us in a very able & spirited manner for nearly an hour. After the speech, refreshments were offered & freely partaken of by some. Then came dinner, done up in excellent style. After dinner & on the appearance of champagne, there were excellent speeches made by Col. B. J. Johnson, Edmund Rhett, & J. Pope, Jr.[36]

I offered a few remarks in my own way & style

I intend a further account of this day's affair in another place.

---

[35] Robert Barnwell Rhett (1800–1876), attorney and planter with extensive holdings in St. Helena and St. Bartholomew's parishes. Son of James Smith and Marianna Gough. Brother of St. Helena legislator Edmund Rhett. An avid secessionist, Rhett was state Attorney General 1832–36, member U.S. House of Representatives 1836–49, and U.S. Senate, succeeding John C. Calhoun in 1851. He resigned the next year after the 1852 Southern Rights Convention affirmed South Carolina's right to secede from the Union, but took no direct action.

[36] Joseph D. Pope, son of J. J. Pope.

July 27th.   Saturday. Blank.
**I getting over the champagne of yesterday, many others doing the same. Grayson put
out home to hide his headache**

July 29th.   Sent to Beaufort for 40 bushels of corn come up from town
for me.

Aug. 2nd.   Friday. I have a few tasks of ground banked for slips, but if it
does not rain by Monday, I will put it in peas.

Aug. 5th.   Monday. Very heavy tornado at the village and pretty general
gale on Saturday. A good many trees blown down & some struck by lightning. Wind from about N.E. Not much rain at the village—or down here,
but very heavy about the middle of the Island. Corn blades are shredded
as with hail, though there was none that I know of. Planted a task of slips
this morning, then, as the ground was rather dry, put the hands to stripping blades, what is to be had of them, which will be trifling. Picked my
pocket full of cotton today. It is opening here & there all over the field.
    Our little baby is quite sick—teething & bowel affection in conse-
quence . . . has been under the Dr. for several days, and is no better.

Aug. 6th.   Baby much the same. Dr. Scott thinks she has a tumor on her
neck. It is very painful & stiff.

Aug. 7th.   Wednesday. All hands stripping blades, except Peg & Mary
hoeing burr grass in cotton.

Aug. 14th.   Commenced cutting marsh, 3 hands. Cotton opening so fast I
expect I will have to put more hands picking. Will have 3 hands at it tomorrow. Finished all the blades, cotton field corn & all except the April
corn. Isaac turning down corn.
    Commenced on my red potatoes for allowance yesterday. They turn
out very badly in the place they commenced—took about 15 beds for half
week's allowance. I expect it is the worst spot in the patch.

Aug. 19th.   Monday. E. Capers came down with me, rode over the crop.
& took drink after as a matter of course, if we had any to drink   1876

Aug. 21st.   Wednesday. Gabriel Capers came down with me to shoot
plover, found none in my pasture—did not go in the field. 5 hands picking
cotton, men hauling peas.

Aug. 24th. Saturday. Tremendous storm of wind and rain from S.W. Did much damage, more than all the drought did. Nearly if not quite destroyed the peas & blew out a quantity of cotton for me as I had a good blow.

Aug. 31st. Saturday. All hands hard at the cotton. 3 picking off the ground. Cotton opening very fast. Will get through the field on Monday I think. Peg came out & sorted some cotton. I do not expect to get anything out of her till after her confinement, which will not be before the last of Sept. or first Oct.

Heard that Catherine Pope had a girl baby a day or two ago. **J. D. Pope**[37]**

Ernest came down with me. There is no fruit to eat, & he seems quite *dull.* Negroes picking as high as 60 lbs. cotton, but ought with the blow they have, pick 80 & assort it. Peas have improved since the storm, but have not and never will entirely recover, at least my own will not. **Damn other people's**

Weighed off the first cotton—1758 lbs.—which is all I have assorted. Rain came up about 2 p.m., did not last long. Made the women assort cotton & the men haul a task of slips each. Cleared off prettily & I put the women out picking again.

Sept. 2nd. All hands picking cotton (Tabby Point). They will not finish the field tomorrow and the cotton is very white behind them.[38]

Sept. 16th. Sunday. Eliza was confined of a child, female— **Martha**

Sept. 25th. Peg confined, girl. This is the third birth among my Negroes this summer and all females:

   Mary confined 25 June, female, name, Amy; **died**
   Eliza confined 16th Sept., female, name, Martha; **Alive**
   Peg confined 25th Sept., ditto, Emmeline. **alive, grown woman**

Sept. 27th. Canadian stallion sent on by T. A. Coffin for the Agricultural Society arrived last Saturday, dark bay, not a handsome horse by any means—price, $156 in N.Y.

All hands picking cotton. Have in over five bales.

---

[37] Catherine Scott Pope's husband.
[38] Cotton is opening very fast. The part of the field already picked is white again though the pickers have not finished the first round of picking.

Oct. 16th.   I have been sick at the village ever since last Wednesday with something like, if not quite, the broken bone fever.[39] I am better today, but should not have ventured out, but was so anxious to get down & see after things that I could not resist.

Not like this time

Find that the hands have picked through the heavy blow of cotton, but there is still cotton to pick. I will pick some of the whitest spots today, and if they get through well, will try and get in some of my corn this week. I have broken in all the corn, 4½ acres at Saplings. Got 33 baskets besides what I have been eating off of for two months. It has not done well. My fellow Sancho took himself off on Monday last, on account of Isaac's attempting to flog him for beating his (Isaac's) daughter Mary. Sancho came in today. *Note:* Isaac has never been able to find it in his *tender heart* to find a *whip* to make my Negroes do their work, but as soon as one of his family was molested he could directly *feel* it his *duty to inflict punishment*. I shall be lenient with Sancho on this account, but the girl shan't escape.

(evening) Did nothing to the culprits today, as I shall have to return tomorrow. A few drops of rain.

Oct. 17th.   Thursday. Clear & remarkably warm, like a midsummer's day. Came down late, left wife quite unwell.

Commenced regularly to break in corn, took the 10 acres April corn first—as I expected, turns very badly indeed. I cannot exactly say how much as I am breaking it in the shuck. Got 7 wagon loads broken in this way, out of about 6 acres. All the corn I got was on low spots. I will finish the April corn tomorrow, early, and commence on the March corn, about 9¼ acres, which I expect to turn out well. My peas are bearing badly, upon whole I shall be miserably short of provisions. I have but about ½ acre roots left, worse & worse. I stay down here tonight, well enough all day but at night, *miserable.*

Oct. 20th.   Found Mrs. C. quite sick. Ernest & Eugene had fever (slight).

Oct. 22nd.   Commenced breaking the March corn near the Negro houses— it turns out very well. Returned to the village in the evening.

Oct. 23rd.   Wednesday. Came down & brought Mrs. C. & Ernest with me to stay till I finish breaking corn. Am in hopes the little change will benefit wife. Hope Ernest will not get fever, it is a risk for him. Corn turning

---

[39] Breakbone fever, or dengue, a tropical disease causing fever and severe pains in the joints. Uncommon in South Carolina.

well.[40] If my whole crop was as good—I should make an abundance of provisions, slips or no slips.

Oct. 24th. Must confess that I wish wife back at the village, for more reasons than one. She is dissatisfied with everything & everybody, myself *in particular,* and so intolerably cross—but poor soul, she is *ailing,* & I must only hold my peace, & so *prevent* her finding fault with what *I say,* if she does with what *I do.* I must bear with what I have brought on myself, by doing that which has given her power over me, to *upbraid* me *justly,* and she knows how to take advantage of this power. But "those who live [in] glass houses should not throw stones."
Alas, alas, I am sorry more than once for what were trifles then. Poor wife, poor me, 26 years after, & I can only say I am sorry, but I did nothing in bad blood

Oct. 25th. Friday. *Finished* breaking in corn about dinner time. Though my April corn failed, the March corn has nearly made up for it. I got out of 8¾ acres 192 bushels, about 24 bushels average pr. acre. Gave the Negroes the balance of the day to get in their own crop. Tomorrow, they will pick peas. The cotton ought to be got in, but I must try and save what few peas I have made, not more than two days' picking.

Oct. 28th. Went to Beaufort to meet the Board of Road Commissioners. This is the last meeting of this board, as their term of service expires at the meeting of the legislature next month. We had very little business before us. Passed a resolution to assess the inhabitants of St. Helena Island ten per cent on their general tax this year, payable in May '51.

Oct. 29th. Killed veal for market. Sent Isaac to making up the garden fence. All hands picking cotton. Uncle Ben moved home. Stood the ride very well.

Oct. 31st. Sent mother's boat round to the plantation with as many things as we could do without. This is a great help to me in moving—save at least 5 cart loads & I do not calculate on much help this year. Dr. Jenkins moved today. O. Fripp is gone, Dr. M. M. Sams goes tomorrow, no one left but Capt. Fripp, W. B. Fripp & myself. I will get part of my folks down tomorrow. Sent Mary & her cart load down yesterday. Played the farewell game of billiards with Capt. Fripp in the evening & beat him 60.

Nov. 1st. Sent my cart down with one load. Brought wife, Ernest, Virginia, & Daniel down in the buggy. Pretty good load for one old horse; however, we all got down safe about 12 o'clock, which is one great load off

---

[40] South Carolina grew more corn in 1850 than in any census year until 1900.

my mind. I shall not go down till the morning for those left behind, but will send the ox and horse cart tonight.

Nov. 2nd. Saturday. Went down to the village very early this morning, found Uncle Ben's carriage already there, also 3 carts from the Indian Hills, one from Uncle Paul, with two of my own, I managed to get all & everything safely down by dinner time. From the quantity of things I had already sent home, I had no idea that there was enough left to fill six carts, but so it was, & a tight jam to fit all in then, could not have done with any less.

So here we all are once more, safe & sound. All hands picking cotton, except Moll & Eliza digging groundnuts & Isaac fixing up garden fence. Weather in the evening looks like a change.

Nov. 4th. Monday. Put all hands picking in the last of my peas. I have barely made seed. I will now pull up the vines for fodder.

Nov. 5th. Jim & Frank pulling up pea vines. All hands picking cotton, good blow, & wasting, will have everything I can start at it tomorrow. . . . Oliver Fripp called on me to make some arrangements about getting lumber for the public bridges, & working the Ferry Bridge. We agreed to send 25 hands from each division, making 75 in all, & work next Monday, 11th inst. O.F. will work his division of the road at the same time. I would like to do so also, but it does not exactly suit me. In the first place, people generally are digging in their slips & in the second, I will not get through my blow of cotton by that time. I can see no benefit a person derives from being commissioner, if it is not his privilege of working the roads whenever it is most convenient for himself to do so, that is, when he can best spare his own hands from home. I will have to get 2000 feet 2-inch plank for the bridges in this division, and have authorized O. Fripp to get them for me in Beaufort at the same time that he gets stuff for the Ferry Bridge, which will take over 5000 feet, besides sleepers & bulkhead bridges.

Query. Can there be anything more unpleasant to a man of family than that his wife should be a victim to the following demoralizing and injurious habit? Habits which entirely destroy all social and domestic enjoyments & comforts and prevents all chances of prosperity. The wife says it rather makes her appearance (this is, when she makes it atall for the day).

Sometime between 11 a.m. & 1 p.m. remains out of her chamber one or two hours more or less, *sometimes* takes her place at the dinner table, but always takes her breakfast in bed. After dinner, retires for an hour or two to *indulge* either in [   ] or what is worse, to half fill her mouth with snuff, and lie in bed, when, if per chance a little of the saliva escapes down her throat, a fit of vomiting is invariably the consequence, then farewell to the small quantity of nourishment her sedentary habit allowed her to take at dinner. She leaves her chamber *generally* just about dusk, when she walks out, to take a [   ] walking about the yard—frequently remaining out of [   ] after dark. Sometimes remains down to tea, but should she retire before, & her tea is sent to her, [   ] the servant not unfrequently finds her unable to speak, and why? Her mouth is *full of snuff;* should she remain to tea, she retires immediately after, not to bed, to sleep, oh! no, but to put *snuff in her mouth,* take a *novel* & lie on her back till twelve or one o'clock at night, unless, per chance, she enacts the vomiting scene over again, & thereby loses her *tea.* At a late hour she goes to bed finally in a very ill humor with her "good man," & everybody else for she is perhaps sleepy by this time, there to remain till the late hours previously mentioned, the next day, to live the same routine of life over & over again, each succeeding day, not to mention one or two *other* items. I envy not that man's conjugal blessings.

Beautiful description wants only* truth *to make it quite charming.

Alas, it was too true, but it is past & gone & forgotten, & if she is in heaven, I hope she has forgiven.

O God, what a woman was lost. What a mind—sunk in despair & grief & disappointment

Nov. 6th.   Went to muster. There is to be a colonel's review in Beaufort on the 28th instant, our St. Helena company *not* compelled to go by law, but unanimously agreed to go, at the request of the Colonel John Webb. There was an attempt to get up an independent mounted volunteer company on the Island, but signally failed, as everything of the kind does, and will always do on this Island.[41]

Nov. 7th.   Thursday. Got a buck sheep from W. J. Grayson yesterday, almost too late to get his breed this year. Marked and altered of fall lambs this morning, 3 wethers & one black ewe which I will kill. I wish to get rid of all the black breed.

Good mutton under black wool though

All hands picking cotton today, good blow but cotton very much stained.

Nov. 8th.   Marked & altered 3 bull calves. Marked 1 heifer & marked 2 young bull calves, 1 bull (saved for breed), making 7 in all. Sent Isaac to

---

[41] Because of the difficulty of traveling to Beaufort, the St. Helena Mounted Riflemen were exempted from battalion and regimental duties provided they would meet on their own muster ground on review day. The St. Helena Company did indeed succeed as a viable local unit. It was dissolved, after the fall of Port Royal and the defeat at Port Royal Ferry, by order of Gen. Robert E. Lee, in Jan. 1862.

get out a well frame. I will be obliged to dig a new well or fix up the old one, one will be as much trouble as the other.

Nov. 9th. Saturday. Busy all day making a well frame, finished it, & a very good one it is for the first attempt to make one, either myself or Isaac. I must try and get it in next week if I can. Uncle Tom sent me a fine piece of beef today. He killed a beef for Edwin Chaplin & kept a quarter for himself. I wish he would kill one for me also. I have not a beef to kill this winter. Nearly all the neighbors have dug in their slips, and got a *very few* fit to eat. I will let mine stand a little longer, if it does not get too cool. They are growing fast now, and there has been no frost to hurt them, besides I have a good blow of cotton. It is time I should have my arrowroot prepared, but there is no water on the place fit to do it with. I never since I have been on the Island knew it to be so dry, not a pond with a drop of water in it, and everything suffering, even to the poultry.

Nov. 10th. Sunday. Dined with Capers, did not see the old man. Mrs. Capers looks remarkably well, better than I ever recollect to have seen her, her summer's trip has much benefited her. Ben Capers is making a boat to send to the fair in Charleston,[42] & then to the world's fair in London.[43] She is beautifully got up & he deserves a premium for her. **Fudge, old bogie work none '76**

Nov. 11th. Monday. All hands picking cotton. Commenced working the Ferry Bridge. Oliver Fripp has charged I did not go out. Isaac getting out crutch & pole & cutting of boards for well.

Nov. 12th. Rode down to see how the folks were getting on with the Ferry Bridge. They had all the boards & unsound sleepers taken off, and the bulkhead nearly fixed, but the new sleepers had not got to the ground today. The carpenters were fixing the railing, ready to put up when wanted, and a very substantial one it will be. We intend having the work as it ought to be this time, the first work our Board of Commissioners have done to it. Oliver Fripp finished working his division of road today, all to a very little to do tomorrow, and discharged his hands all to a very few. He has agreed to take some of the road off of my division, say from the Baptist Church Bridge to Wm. Chaplin's road, or the 8 mile post, a part of the road which of very little consequence, nothing to do to it but cutting a few bushes.

[42] The second annual "Fair of the South Carolina Institute for the promotion of Art, Mechanical Ingenuity, etc." opened on November 18. Exhibits included specimens of cotton, rice, sugar, tobacco, wheat, flour, rosin, and turpentine. A "monument to J. C. Calhoun in sugar" graced the fair-grounds. C. B. Capers sent to the fair "a cypress canoe, [and] specimens of live oak and bay."
[43] The "Great Exhibition of the Industry of All Nations," at London's Crystal Palace.

Nov. 13th. Commenced digging a well, between the corn house & the poultry house, on a little knoll or hill. The ground was as dry as ashes for 5 or six feet down, then found some moisture, and at about 9 feet a little water commenced to spring in a bed of iron ore. I fear the water will be enjoined by it—will, however, get it as deep as possible, & into a bed of white sand (all this by 2 o'clock p.m. when we knocked off for dinner).

3 p.m., went at the well again. Water does *not* spring fast, have not yet struck a regular spring. Found lumps of the iron rock much larger than this morning, and very difficult to get out, which makes the work go on slowly, and I am very much afraid I will have to give it up entirely & dig somewhere else but I am still in hopes that this is but a thin strata of ore & that good water will be found below it. The well is not much inclined to cave. I will not be able to do much at it tomorrow, having to go to the bridge to see how they get on there. I will rig something however, to bucket out the water, and make Isaac & Jim work out as many of the lumps of rock as possible.

Sent all the women to make a finish of the groundnuts, which they did and not much at that. I don't think that wife will get, in all—after they are sorted &c—more than 15 bushels, a miserable turnout for 3 tasks, not worth the trouble planting and digging. However, this is the last of them, and I will now have all hands at the cotton.

Nov. 15th. At the well again. Got through the strata of iron rock & struck a good spring in light colored sand beneath it. Dug until the water flowed in faster than the Negroes could throw it out, when I put in the frame & got it nearly half boarded up by 1½ o'clock p.m. I am in hopes of having good water. It drinks very well as it is unsettled.

3 p.m., planked & filled up the well nearly to the top. Threw out all the water & left it to spring and settle for use, for the old well is now completely given out, & we are very near *entirely* out of water to use for any purpose whatever, and what there is, is muddy.

Nov. 16th. Saturday. Sent Isaac to Beaufort for a box of medicines &c from Turner.[44] Sent Frank to the village wharf for some articles come up in the *Etiwan* for me from Charleston.

Received a letter by Pope's John[45] from Mother—came by way of Beaufort, where she has sent some things for me & left them with Daphne. Frank got back about 4 o'clock, bringing a very heavy load, more, I was convinced, than I had any reason to expect, but there proved to be a

---

[44] T. M. Turner & Company, druggists in Savannah.
[45] John used to belong to Mrs. Baker. He was purchased at auction by Pope on Feb. 9, 1846.

hhd[46] of crockery for J.J.T. Pope, that the fool of a Dutchman[47] at the wharf had sent as my own. J.J.T.P. must send first. Isaac got back about dusk, brought the box from Savannah, but heard nothing of the things sent to Daphne by Mother. He could not have brought them, for the bridge is not done, & he had to walk from the bridge to the ferry. Joe Perry wrote me a note, that the bridge would not be finished before Monday or Tuesday next, & requesting me to be there on Monday & to find dinner. Will see about it.

Nov. 19th.　　Aunt Betsy sent over eleven hands to help me dig slips—what a godsend, went ahead now rapidly.

Nov. 20th.　　Wednesday. Weather continues good. Finished digging slips. Aunt B.'s hand came over again today. Potatoes did not do as bad as I expected. Made 15 banks, 3 of eating, 12 of seed. Made enough eating for the house use, but not to give an allowance. Seed aplenty & to spare if they do not rot. Ox, Captain, died, don't know from what.

Nov. 21st.　　Thursday. Put Isaac & Jim at the garden fence. Forgot to state in proper place that I put Buckskin in the gig on Monday last. He drew finely & quite gentle. My horse cart is broken, my ox dead, and God knows how I shall get along.
I did however, very well, long after

Nov. 22nd.　　Friday. Fence finished. Turned out my hogs—3 sows, 6 pigs, 3 shoats & 2 barar.
ows[48]

Nov. 23rd.　　Saturday. Cut & banked some small sugarcane for seed. Will let the rest stand till next week as Ned Capers promised to come over and make arrangements to grind it for me.
which he never did

Nov. 26th.　　Tuesday. Very little cotton to pick. Cattle constantly coming in, will have to shoot
& did kill

---

[46] Hogshead: a cask containing sixty-three U.S. gallons, liquid measure.
[47] Fenn Peck (1807–1873), Connecticut-born sea captain. Besides transporting cargo, Peck carried the mail between Charleston and Savannah, making stops at Beaufort, Bluffton, and Hilton Head.
[48] "Barar," in the entry, is a mistake for "barrows"—castrated hogs. Chaplin was trying to correct the spelling in his note.

Nov. 27th. Wednesday. Can't wait on Ned Capers any longer.
of course not
Had my cane all cut & buried. Took all hands all day—commenced feeding horses on it, they eat it very well.

Nov. 29th. It's an old saying that all signs fail in dry weather, but I'm believing that if we don't have a heavy rain soon, there will be a rise in the price of beef next year.
Don't recollect how it turned out, '76
Sent 3 hands to the Island for wood. Sent Isaac to get out roller stuff, a job that I have neglected entirely too long. Set the women picking out what little cotton is open, when I think I may as well let my stock have it, tho there are a great many pods yet to open. I know that the *old folks* will turn their large stock in *their* fields & I will not be able to keep them out of mine.
The rich old folks don't remember the poor young ones

Nov. 30th. Rode over to see Uncle Ben, drove Buckskin in the gig. Found the old man much the same, very emaciated. D. Jenkins & Dr. W.J. Jenkins came in while I was there. We walked over to see the Dr.'s cotton gin, just erected. He is not much pleased with it, gets but 150 lbs. clean cotton ginned per day. I don't think he has it a proper fix, or it would gin what the inventor says, 4 or 500 lbs. Lunched with the Dr. on some of his delicacies, being just from town, where he usually lays in a supply of nick-nacks.
Item—Noticed that the Capt. had treated himself to a splendid gold hunting watch & chain, cost, $110.
Item—W.J.J. in the tip of the fashion.
He was coming out then
Sent old Judge for oysters. All hands assorting cotton. Isaac still at the rollers stuff. Planted some rye in the Orchard where I had slips planted.

Dec. 2nd. Monday. Gave to Benjamin Chaplin the youngest[49] an order to summon out hands from Lands End to Edgar Fripp's to work the roads on Monday the 9th inst. Also appointed the Major, D. P. Jenkins, overseer of all. Sent 3 hands to the Island for wood.
That wood was always a great tax & is still, '76
Not now, '85
Balance of hands assorting cotton. Judy grating up arrowroot. I will not make as much as I expected, the weather has been so dry. I have to

---

[49] Benjamin Chaplin (b. 1831). Son of Benjamin S. Chaplin and Laura Butler. Chaplin's third cousin on his father's side. Miss Augusta Chaplin's brother.

keep Isaac almost all the time bobbing about, till I can hardly see what he does.
"*Bobbing all round,*" in fact, now in 1885, I get plenty of wood by hard work, but plenty.

Dec. 3rd. Tuesday. Sent the flat again for wood. I want to lay up a supply so as not to be troubled when I do commence ginning. Sent the women out to pick, but they get so little cotton that I will wait on it a while, & either gin or sort. Wm. Jenkins sent one of his mares to Buckskin today. I will not charge him anything.
Why not—he charges me for everything
Judy grating up arrowroot today, and did not finish, tis a troublesome job.
& not of much profit

Dec. 4th. Put Judge to keep the cattle out of the field. Rode over in the evening to see Uncle Tom, & to try and get a steer from him for an ox, but he had none to spare. I must try Ben the Roarer.[50]
Think I got one from Isaac Fripp with luck

Dec. 5th. Thursday. Attended Agricultural Society meeting.
came very often
Not much business before the Society.
& what there was, is of no account & never is
C. E. Capers fed. One thing came up before the Society, that I will make note of, viz., the Society last year got Mr. Coffin to buy for them at the North a Canadian stallion. Mr. Coffin (who was present today), spoke to two different persons requesting them to *look out* for a horse of that description for him. As it turned out, both persons bought horses for Mr. Coffin, one of them, he sent on to the Society, as mentioned before, the other is now in Charleston.
The horse we have received was, at a meeting of the Society, put up for keeping, to the *lowest bidder* for 12 months under certain conditions & limitations as regards serving mares &c &c. Dr. Grayson underbid Mr. Cockcroft, by $10, agreeing to keep the horse 12 months for $110, all proceeds from the horse to go to the Society, & the Society responsible to him for the keeping, $110. The matter I think clear enough, but, at this meeting, I think actions rather uncourteous in two respects were taken regarding this horse. In the first place, Mr. Coffin *offered* the Society a choice between the two stallions, the one rejected by *them,* to remain as *his* property, & be sold by him at his own risk, and the one retained by the Society

---

[50] Possibly Chaplin's Uncle Ben.

he would keep on the following terms. He, Mr. Coffin, would keep the horse, at the risk of the Society. Whatever he made by serving mares would go to pay for his keeping, subject to the limitations of the Society, say $5 for members & $10 for non-members. If the horse made $200, it went towards his keeping. If he made *not one cent,* the keeping would be at Mr. Coffin's expense solely & wholly. This proposition, though a good one, had to give way to one from Edgar Fripp, who proposed to keep the horse at his *own expense,* to use & manage him at his discretion. Each *member* to pay $5 for a colt, this money to go to the *Society's funds.* The horse to stand for mares from *non-members,* at a price discretionary with the keeper & said fund to go toward paying for his keeping.

Item—My opinion is, Edgar *Fripp is an ass.* He shows *for rich* with Tom Coffin & is determined that Tom shan't out do him in philanthropy, ∗∗*generosity*∗∗ but as the saying is, this time, "he has burnt his shirt." But he *stickles so little to do "small things"* that I have no doubt that when he gets Kitty and all *his* other mares in foal from the horse (free cost) which is his right in the bargain, he will tell the Society to find some other keeper, he will be tired of it. *We will see.*
∗∗*& we did, he never got the horse. I believe Capt. Jno. Fripp bought him of the Society. I don't know who got the money in hand*∗∗

Dec. 9th. Monday. Commenced working the roads. I had to go to Beaufort to meet the Board of Commissioners, got there too late. The Board met, & appointed Capt. J. Fripp & Mr. Jos. Hazel[51] commissioners on their part to lay out the notorious Capers & McKee Road on Ladies Island.

Dec. 10th. Working the roads. Got through with the Sands causeway bridges, & brushed over the road on the *Seaside,* as far as Dr. Scott's road which runs through to the store, this road I intend to put in complete order. Daniel P. Jenkins & Edwin Chaplin found dinner, dined at the line between Drs. Scott & Jenkins.

Dec. 11th. Wednesday. Very few hands on the road. Besides those taken off for work on the Ferry Bridge there are more *reported sick* than I have had since I have been comm.

Dec. 13th. Friday. Sent the boat to Beaufort, Negro cloth, shoes, &c, and a bale of goods for family. A very large bill, but payday must come. The boat got back after dark.

---

[51] Joseph Hazel (1798–1885), highly successful grower of Sea Island cotton. Father of Dr. W. Gowan Hazel and Thomas Hazel.

Dec. 14th.   Saturday. Gave out Negro cloth & shoes. Both good.

Dec. 16th.   Monday. Let Old Judy go to Beaufort to see Daphne, she being sick. Wife sent 2 bushels of groundnuts to sell by her which with 11 bushels sent to town on Friday, & 1 bushel kept at home, makes 14 bushels to the *great crop,* of ¾ acre, nearly ⅔rds poppers.

Dec. 19th.   Thursday. Had Isaac putting in some sashes, but he did it so miserably that I sent him off & went at it myself, though I dislike the work, the smell of the putty makes me sick.

Dec. 20th.   Friday. I was busy fixing the back room step all day—3 gins going. All the women picking cotton in the garden, as it looks much like rain I wish to pick what is open, it is the only piece I have saved from the cattle. The cattle all gathered around the well today, there is no water for the poor things on this side. I ordered a cow well dug tomorrow. Isaac has lost a great deal of time fixing the garden fence, and yet the hogs are continually breaking in, first one place then another. I made up my mind not to raise any more, unless tis one sow for a roaster now and then. Eat or sell all the rest, or what I would prefer, give them to someone to raise on shares. One thing is sure, I will not be bothered raising till I can make a better fence, it is decidedly better to buy bacon. A hog raised as I have to raise them, 7 months in the pen, eats his head off 3 times over.

Dec. 21st.   Saturday. Had the women picking cotton, men digging cow well. Packed the first bale of cotton, 340 lbs.

Dec. 23rd.   Monday. Sent 3 hands to Island for wood. Women assorting & moting.
Moating *is the proper way to spell it. No—it is not. Mote—moting
Killed a hog for bacon.

Dec. 24th.   Sent Frank to Beaufort for a little box that wife expects from town with nicknacks for the children. He got back after dark with the box, containing a few toys, candy &c for Xmas gifts for the children.
     Flat with wood got back about 12 m.

Dec. 25th.   Wednesday—*Christmas. Merry Christmas,* yes, merry to all the world but me. Here I sit moping at home all day, no pleasure, & *I care for none but* to see the *children* enjoy themselves, which they appear to do every other day as well. I will try and amuse them by setting off a few little fireworks Webb sent up tonight.
& *what better amusement could I have had*
One *of those children, Dan'l & the only one alive now, has 4 children of his own, they call me Grandpa, I can't afford them fireworks*

I only wish the Negroes were at work. I had nothing to give them but a few turnips, but they are satisfied, **pretend to be** and I suppose will enjoy *themselves,* though *I don't.*

Dec. 26th. Old Sam died just before day this morning. Poor old man, he is gone at last. Twas a relief for him to die. It is now nearly three years since he was taken down to his bed, perfectly helpless, horribly afflicted with paralysis, convulsions, and perfectly blind. Twas a blessing to take him.

There was an instance out of many—an old man had to be fed, clothed & a woman did nothing else than attend to him for 3 years before he died & he wanted for nothing. How did his wife, who attended him then, & died herself, since made free, why she died of smallpox, in the most wretched manner, not even her children would go near her and she regrettably [   ] before she died, but then, she was free!

Dec. 27th. Friday. The last day of the holidays, and I rejoice at it. Cloudy & not very cold, but disagreeable. Commenced raining a little about 1 p.m. Has the appearance of a spell of dismal weather. Capers will have a bad night for his party. I rode over to Uncle Ben's in the morning, and not expecting to see any but the family, was rather shabbily dressed, when there, George Chisolm and his wife[52] came in, then the three Jenkins girls,[53] Miss Chisolm[54] & Dick Jenkins[55] from Wadmalaw. They all looked quite fine, compared to me, but what do I care. They all dined with Dr. Jenkins I believe, from there they go to *the party, if* this weather does not prevent, for it is now raining pretty hard (4 p.m.). *If* it were a fine moonlight night, I don't know, but I would go myself. I have had nothing like amusement this Christmas, & I feel that I am always welcome at Caperses'.

I must have had the blues at this time, & felt disgusted with the world generally.

Dec. 28th. Sent Frank to Beaufort. Sent Jim and Sancho to the Island for wood. Started to pack second bale of cotton, did not finish it. Had only 300 lbs. Ginned, will finish it on Tuesday. 4 hands assorting. Planted in the garden today a bed of green peas & two rows of radishes.

---

[52] Mary Jenkins.
[53] See note, Jan. 30, 1852.
[54] One of George Chisolm's sisters, either Sarah Caroline or Ella Louise.
[55] Richard E. Jenkins, planter. Son of Richard Jenkins and Martha LaRoche, of Wadmalaw Island. Second cousin to Chaplin on his father's side. Brother of Rev. P.G.T. Jenkins and Benjamin Jenkins (husband of Adelaide Chaplin). Second cousin, once removed, to Maj. D. P. and Dr. W. J. Jenkins. He and the Jenkins girls were third cousins.

Dec. 31st.   Tuesday. Dismal, rainy day, & very cold. The old year, 1850, goes out with a frown. Last year went out with a freeze but no rain. It is cold enough for ice today, but too wet, all appearances of a spell of miserable bad weather. I hope it may be better tomorrow, as I have to find muster dinner——

All hands assorting cotton, except Isaac, finishing the bag commenced on Saturday. Too wet to gin. I feel very unwell today with a troublesome & very disagreeable pain through my right breast & shoulder, must be either pleurisy or the liver, both bad enough, God knows.

End of the year of Our Lord, Eighteen hundred and fifty, and I am no better off spiritually or temporally.

1851

Jan. 1st. Wednesday. Found dinner & attended muster at muster house. 4 gins going today.

Jan. 4th. Edwin Chaplin came dunning—paid him $431¼, by order on Uncle Paul.

Jan. 7th. Tuesday. Fixed braces under the old kitchen piazza, which was about falling down. Rode over to see Mr. Capers about getting an ox from him. Succeeding in getting what I call a very fine one, better than my own old ox—price $20, paid by order on Uncle Paul.

Jan. 8th. Tom Capers[1] came here for some asparagus roots for Mrs. Minott & his father, and some seeds for the latter. He dined with me. Packed the 3rd bale of cotton. Did not weigh the cotton, but think it is the heaviest bale packed yet. Must be 375 or more—

Jan. 10th. Old Charles got back from a visit to his wife last night, he has been gone twelve days. Johnson, that bought Phoebe at *the sale*, has gone to Texas, has not taken Phoebe with him, but sold her to a man, as Charles says, named Bob Fitch, who wishes to sell her, & asks $150—wish I could buy her.

Jan. 13th. Monday. Election held today for sheriff, candidates are Youmans, Heap & Stone.[2] Went out and voted for Youmans. When I left

---

[1] Thomas L. Capers (1834–1853). Son of C. G. Capers and Mary Reynolds.
[2] William Youmans (b. 1805), merchant, planter, and clerk of court, of St. Luke's Parish. Joseph H. Heap (b. 1806), planter, of Prince William's Parish. Benjamin R. Stone (b. 1800), planter and mechanic, of St. Peter's Parish. The three candidates represented three of the four parishes of Beaufort District. Youmans won the election with 534 votes to Heap's 322 and Stone's 29.

there were 17 votes taken—Youmans had 15 of them, Heap 2. Oliver Fripp had dinner brought out & Grayson & myself dined with the managers.

Jan. 14th. Packed 4th bale of cotton, 318 lbs. Sent Judge for oysters, 2 gins only running. Gave Isaac & Amy tickets to join the Baptist Church. Commenced with ox cart hauling out mud.

Jan. 15th. Wednesday. Set out onions & planted a bed of peas yesterday. Packed the 5th bale cotton, 320 lbs. Did not quite finish it, will do so in the morning.

Very cloudy in the evening. Sophy & 2 of the children went over & dined with Aunt Betsy Chaplin—a rare occurrence for any of my household.

Judge & Peg both laying up, Judge with a tumor on his hip, which I fear I will have to get cut out; Peg, with a rising breast. Singular thing that her breast should rise. I would as soon think of a bag made of dried skin, which it very much resembles, suppurating, & coming to a head. **Poor soul, she did not long survive her freedom. She was not a bad woman at heart & very attached to my family.***

Jan. 16th. Killed the second & last bacon hog. Rather warm to save it, but I suppose it will be saved as the other was by eating it all before the salt has time to penetrate.

The water in my new well continues so very offensive, in smell & taste, that I have to get all the water we drink from Uncle Ben's. This we have been doing for some time. It is very troublesome, & I will have to dig another well as soon as I can possibly spare the time. I think of trying on the hill near the old tabby. Wife & Sophy (wiseacres) both think that the best water is to be found there. Their reason I cannot comprehend, but when I get a chance I will try the spot. I had a well in the old garden once, near the spot, but it soon went dry.

Planted a row of poppy seed along the garden fence side of the path. The infernal hogs have destroyed nearly all my rye which was growing very prettily. I have to keep the sows in the pen. I have offered them for sale.

Jan. 17th. Some rogues broke my potato banks last night, took out about two bushels, also stole some turnips, & went out the back of the garden. Isaac tracked them, as he says, as far as the Major's. He saw here & there where they had dropped turnip tops. I went over & searched the Major's Negro houses, but discovered nothing. It is useless to go out looking for anything lost in that way. If I lose anything more I will make my Negroes accountable for it. Judge came out today, but Peg still in her house. Wife made an attempt to lance her breast, but failed of course. Only two gins going today. I got on slowly, Isaac has lost almost the whole day following tracks, to no purpose.

Jan. 18th. Saturday. I had my cotton that is packed turned out of the house into the yard, thinking to improve the weight, by the action of the dews and perhaps a little rain, but I fear this is too much rain for it. I must take it now however, hope it will not be injured, I would have served myself a fine trick.

Jan. 20th. Monday. 4 gins going and I intend to try & keep that many going till I get through. My cart is nearly all the time bringing wood, & one hand cutting it. I will get no manure out at this rate. Had the women assorting cotton today, there is one or two bales yet unsorted. Set out another bed of onions, making 4 in all, but I put them much further apart than heretofore, nearly twice the distance.

A certain event, *failed.*
I wonder what that was, I have forgotten 25 years after

Jan. 21st. Isaac Fripp's Negroes broke my potato banks last night. I thought they were the Major's Negroes the last time, but now the proof falls on Isaac K. Fripp, no knowing who the thieves are——

Jan. 22nd. Wednesday. Joined hands with Benjamin Chaplin & sent my flat to Beaufort with his crop of cotton & five bales of mine. I hear that there is a chance of selling for 32 cents in town, & this would be a good opportunity of getting what I have packed to Beaufort & only send one hand. The weather looks so bad in the evening that I am sorry I sent.

Jan. 23rd. I am now very sorry I sent by the flat to Beaufort. In trying to gain time I am likely to lose, if the fellow Jim I sent should get sick from being out in this weather.

Two of Mother's Negroes came over from the main via Beaufort today. They have had a bad day, rain nearly all day. They saw nothing of Jim & the flat in Beaufort (strange). I have heard nothing of him since he left.

Jan. 24th. Friday. Fellows got back with the flat. Brought a can (10 gals.) oil, vinegar and 1 gallon for wife from T. M. Turner & Co.
Do not name it
Packed 6th bale cotton on Thursday—320 lbs.

Jan. 26th.   Sunday. Went to church. E. Capers set the tunes to the surprise of everyone.

"Rock of Ages"   expect he did wish to be hid in the cleft rock.

Jan. 27th.   Monday. 4 gins going. Had to flog Jim & Sancho about their bad ginning. Peg still laying up with her breast.

Rode to meet Uncle Paul at Carter's Hill, he is to plant down to the cart path this year. Don't know how many acres yet. He has just begun to list over there. I am extremely backward in getting out my crop, consequently will be late planting.

Jan. 28th.   I feel quite wretched today, nothing but trouble, trouble, trouble, enough to break the spirit of any man. I feel very much like *giving way altogether.* God knows what the end will be, ruin & destruction, every side, no stay or stop, *on, on, on,* to the end of life, which cannot last long. Better or worse *must come.*

And O God, what have I not experienced since then. Those were even halcyon days to [   ] since —1876.

Rode over to see Uncle Ben in the afternoon. He is much the same, perfectly helpless. Mr. McElheran was there. The old gentleman was quite affected when Mr. Mc. took leave of him. His mind is quite weak. Eliza & William Jenkins & Uncle Paul came over while I was there. No one pretends to speak to Uncle Ben. He either does not understand anyone or it is because he cannot answer a question.

Jan. 29th.   Wednesday. Axle to ox cart wore off. Sent Isaac to get out a new one. Put Frank to gin in his place. This is another drawback to me, both in ginning and getting out manure. Oh! How I wish I had a carpenter. I must try & hire one for a few days to fix my boat before painting, at any rate.

Jan. 30th.   Thursday Very busy all day making an axletree for the ox cart, did not quite finish it. I intend putting irons on the bottom, which will make it last much longer & run easier. I put one in last year without irons, & it is worn off already. 4 gins going. Think I have another bale ginned. If I get the axle done in time, I will have it packed tomorrow.

Peg still laying up. She never knows when to come out when once she gets in the house.

Jan. 31st.   Finished the ox cart axletree before dinner, and a very good one it is, for my make. I can do some things as well as other people. Commenced packing the 7th bale of cotton—320 lbs. Did not finish it. Think I will get two more, have nearly another half bag ginned now. Came near having a very serious occurrence today. Mr. Frank,[3] the careless rascal, had a fire in the stable this morning, & in leaving just kicked some loose trash over it, thinking to smother it, but it caught the sill & bottom weatherboarding & if I had not fortunately discovered it, it would soon have been in a blaze, & the high wind would soon have ended it.

Feb. 1st. Saturday. Ice again this morning. I do not think it thawed all day. This is decidedly the coldest spell we have had this year, or this winter.

No ginning today. Sent Jim & Sancho to the Island for wood, Isaac & Frank to Beaufort. Made Judge finish the bag commenced yesterday. He made a bad job of it, & did not get all the cotton in by 24 lbs., which will make the bag fall 4 lbs. short of the 300. Besides I shall have to put a patch over the mouth of it. Some of the women overhauling for bag, & some moting. I think I have nearly another bag ginned, will pack it on Monday.

There appears to be some disease among my geese. One died yesterday & one today, do not know what the cause is.

Peg still laying up. This is her 17th day—15 working days. She *must* go to work on Monday. Isaac did not get back from Beaufort till 10 o'clock p.m. Brought a new black frock coat made for me by Morgan[4] in Beaufort, price of making, $8.

Feb. 2nd. Sunday. Went to church. Heard today of the death of Miss McTureous,[5] eldest daughter of James McTureous (deceased). She is to be buried tomorrow at the Baptist Church. She was baptized either last Sunday or the Sunday before.
Did this cause her death? "So it is said"!-!-!

Feb. 3rd. Monday. Sent Ernest & Daniel to school to Miss Augusta Chaplin, over at the Bluff.[6] They are to go over every morning in the buggy & return at two o'clock. Sophy went over with them this morning. Killed a yearling beef which Aunt Betsy gave me. Sent her a quarter. She only took off the loin, & sent the leg back.

Feb. 3rd. Monday. Packed the 8th bale cotton, 320 lbs.

Feb. 5th. Wednesday. Clear and pleasant, not too cold or too warm.
So it must suit. . . .
Finished preparing land to plant beets and carrots. Planted 13 rows

---

[3] The slave Frank.
[4] Charles Morgan (b. 1813), tailor, born in England.
[5] Elizabeth McTureous (1834–1857).
[6] St. Helenaville.

(short) of carrots, the long orange kind, & 1 row of early Horn. The Captain of a vessel came up here to see if he could get some cotton. I would not send what I have, would rather keep it till I get it all out. The vessel belonged to Capt. Vincent of Charleston, named the *William & John*. **The same vessel came to the Point since the war, about *1871, 2 or 3*.**

Feb. 6th.   Thursday. Agricultural Society day. Attended. D. Patterson[7] joined Society. Passed a resolution to sell the stud horse on next muster day.

Feb. 8th.   Packed 9th bale of cotton, 308 lbs. Jim snagged his foot very badly, laying up in consequence. This a great drawback. I may get one more bale of cotton.

Feb. 10th.   Monday. Election today & tomorrow for delegates to Southern Convention.[8] Edmund Rhett, Capt. John Fripp & I believe R. G. Barnwell[9] are candidates, only two to be elected however. I will not go out to vote till tomorrow.

Feb. 12th.   Sent Jack to cart manure, but his having to drive the children to & from school so much interferes with it that I will have to put someone else at it. Old Judge I expect.

Feb. 14th.   Friday. Finished all the Godly cotton except the yellow. Judge commenced packing the 10th bale of cotton. Will not finish it today as the cotton ginned today is to go in it, & make a pretty heavy bale, gave out a little more than the usual measure for the bag. I have from the seed Ned Capers gave me (Ashburton I believe), 480 lbs., which I will commence ginning tomorrow, it will make a little pocket, worth something. I think I might as well get out my yellow cotton at once, depends on the weather.

Feb. 15th.   Saturday. Commenced ginning the Ashburton cotton. Finished the 10th & last bag of Godly—350 lbs.
     Note. I have made on 26 acres of Godly 3242 lbs. of clean white cotton, equal to ten 300 wgt. bags & 242 lbs. over, and average 124½ lbs. per

---

[7] Davis B. Patterson (b. 1808), planter.
[8] A state convention for the purpose of choosing representatives to a southern congress which was to discuss secession and other strategies to counter declining southern influence in national Federal policies.
[9] Robert *W.* Barnwell (1801–1882). Son of Robert Gibbes Barnwell, Sr., and Elizabeth Wigg. Member S.C. House of Representatives 1826–28, U.S. House of Representatives 1829–33; U.S. Senate 1850–52. President of S.C. College 1835–41. Member of the Secession Convention and the Provisional Congress of the Confederate States. Confederate Senator from South Carolina 1861–65.

acre. 11,329 lbs. of seed cotton, equal to 435¾ lbs. per acre, average weight, not calculating the yellow cotton atall, that I will add anon.

Jim ginned some today. *Planted some more sugarcane.* Set out a parcel of black & yellow fig sprouts.

Feb. 16th. Went to church—heard that Capt. John Fripp & Edmund Rhett were elected delegates to the convention. Barnwell got thirty odd votes. He is however elected as a delegate from Charleston, & stands 5th on the list.[10]

Feb. 18th. Tuesday. Finished ginning and packing all my cotton except the stained, in all ten bales & a pocket of fine from the garden. Got it all in the flat to send to Beaufort tomorrow. I will send 3 bales & the pocket to Savannah & two bales to town. If I can get money will go to Savannah myself.

Feb. 19th. Wednesday. Clear. Sent the cotton to Beaufort, & started to go to Savannah myself. Dined in Beaufort with Bell. Steamer did not get in till dark, got off late, suppose 9 p.m. Got to Savannah about 4 a.m. next morning, went to American Hotel.

Feb. 20th. Thursday. Called on Behn & Foster, delivered cotton. Drew $50. Changed lodging from American to Pulaski House, better accommodations.

Feb. 21st. Friday. Did little or nothing all day. Cotton not selling, could not get 28 cents for mine. Went to circus at night. Not much account, same thing over & over.

Feb. 22nd. Saturday. Intended to start home this evening, but cotton not sold, & Behn advised me to wait (wish to God I had not done so).

March 1st. Saturday. Started from Savannah, 9 o'clock at night. Weather bad, & has been so for nearly a week. Been in Savannah all this time, doing worse than nothing, & cotton not sold. Can't help what is past. Landed in Beaufort about 4 a.m., could get in nowhere, so had to wake up Daphne & stay there till morning. Found Frank there. Sent him home as soon as it was light for the buggy. Went across the ferry about 10 a.m. Sunday morning.

[10] Fripp, Rhett, and Barnwell all attended the state convention on April 26, 1852. Rhett and Barnwell supported immediate secession by South Carolina even if no other states would follow. Fripp voted with the minority (136–19) against the principle that a state has the right to secede.

March 2nd.   Sunday. Rode home in a hard rain, found all well, but self.

March 4th.   Tuesday. Got out of bed for the first time since I came. Great deal of sickness on the place. Isaac very sick, & I expect they have all had their turn since I have been away.

March 5th.   Wednesday. Went to muster, so could not get in the field. There has been a report here since I have been absent, that I had left Savannah on the Saturday that I intended & had gone on to town. Made everybody very uneasy, & particularly wife, who actually wrote on to Webb to know if I were there. All a lie of some of Mrs. Ann Fripp's[11] Negroes that went to Savannah to sell turkeys, & who I never saw. Negroes make more mischief than any other class of beings in the world, they can't tell a straight story. I have turned up alive anyhow, if not sound & well.

March 7th.   Friday. Wind high, but could keep out of the field no longer, so footed it all over. Find that the Negroes have done better than I expected. They have 10 acres of cotton ground listed, 3½ acres (all) potato ground, 4 acres (old root patch) corn land, and are listing in cotton seed at the Cassena Line Gate, for corn today—only 6 hands, including little Mary. Sancho carting & Judge grubbing. The hogs have played the devil with my potato banks. Shot one of the sows last night.

March 8th.   Saturday. Did not go in the field. Must get a saddle. Listing in cotton seed. Isaac no better. Trimmed up all the trees in the Orchard.

March 14th.   Sent flat & 4 hands to Beaufort for corn &c &c, don't suppose they will get back before tomorrow morning. Hands listing 2¼ acres for March corn at Jenkins' corner, to make the complement of 18 acres, in this way—4 acres, old root patch, 11¾ acres at Cassena Line Gate, & 2¼ acres at Jenkins' line.

     I never knew colds & coughs so prevalent. I have a dreadful one, and all the family old & young are troubled with colds & coughs. Virginia and Missy[12] very bad indeed. The Negroes also are all more or less affected. (Eat the first drum fish, sent us by Ben Chaplin.)

March 15th.   Saturday. Negroes got back from Beaufort before day. Had a pretty good load, 100 bushels of corn, very good and clean corn, but the measure does not hold good by my measure, loses about 4 quarts or more

[11] Ann Jenkins Chaplin Fripp, widow of W. S. Chaplin and wife of William B. Fripp. See note, Sept. 10, 1845.

[12] Mary Frances.

on every bag of 2 bushels. 2 barrels molasses, & 6 sacks salt to sell to the Negroes for corn, 1 barrel Irish potatoes from Savannah, besides several small boxes. Webb sent me a saddle, a much better one than I expected. Did not receive a letter, so do not know the price of any of the articles.

Received a letter from Behn, in Savannah, he has sold my cotton for little or nothing, 23 cents for Godly, & only 30 cents for the fine cotton. I can't pay my debts in Savannah, & don't know what to do. Would to God I had never gone there at all. Turner will give no more credit till he is paid so I don't know what wife will do.
She did do

March 16th.   Sunday. Aunt Betsy sent us a piece of drum fish today. J. L. Chaplin took five yesterday. Sent all to town, where he gets $2 apiece for them. Did not go to church.

March 17th.‡   Dear husband, I opened your book to put a little extract in it and read your last items, one when you comment about Turner not giving credit on *my account*. Don't give yourself uneasiness for *me*. I have always endeavored to spare you any trouble I could, in this case I only reap the punishment due to my own weakness, believe me *you* are one of the best husbands. I can only hope you will not long be troubled with a wife so frail, weak and suffering. God help you my husband. You have but one fault that may work your ruin—for the sake of *our* children check it. Think not of the poor frail wife. I will pray for you here and if it be possible, hereafter——
Was it possible, if so I know she did pray for me

March 18th.   Tuesday. Busy all day fixing up the yard fence. Finished banking up the old root patch & each hand listed a ½ task of cotton land. I see that my dear wife has again, very contrary to my wishes, written some of her ideas in this foolish journal. But Oh! My dear wife, you may write till doomsday and never *then* can you express what I feel, I am not given to *manly words* . . . but I feel more than words can express. Try not by word or action to hide from me what *you feel*. The very *attempt* but makes your situation the more apparent. I *know* what you *feel* & *suffer* & the inability to relieve is death *to me*. Try not to hide it, it but makes things worse. To *know* that *you want* what you once valued not is more than I can bear, but I will bear it or die in the attempt.
Pretty oh!

March 19th.   Sent Frank fishing with Jno. Chaplin. Killed a veal, to get something *to eat*. We are dreadfully bad off in the eating line. What bothers me & worries me is that when there is a small fowl or any dish, not very

‡ Mary Chaplin wrote this entry.

plentiful, prepared for a meal, that neither wife or Sophy will take any of it. Seeing, I suppose, that the children & myself could eat it all, they deprive themselves, for fear *we* should not get enough. Now I am determined to prevent this, and if it is the last *cow, sheep* or *hog* that I have on the place, it shall be converted into provision, so there shall be no stinting.

Judge & Jim getting fence stuff, Sancho hauling it out. All the other hands listing in mud for cotton.

March 21st. Friday. Morris[13] came over to take charge of my little force today. He says he will do his best.

Planted 6¼ acres of early corn. Planted 1 bushel of seed. Jim & Judge tracking—4 feet in old root patch, & 4½ all the other corn land. Sancho & Frank hauling mud.

March 22nd. Planted 4 acres of corn in old root patch, & planted 1 task of brimstone potatoes. I would plant my full crop of potatoes, but the ground rather dry to bank. I must plant next week.

March 23rd. If this was any other but the Lord's day, we might bank up potato land, but maybe it is all for the best. Tis time potatoes were planted, but this is Sunday, and we must not write of affairs so worldly, and yet, ten to one, we do *worse* if such a word as *worse* can be discovered in an English vocabulary.

March 24th. Monday. Morris very attentive. Over here very early this morning. Got the key & had the corn tarred to plant before I got up. Planting today in the piece next to the line gate, 7¾ acres, 1 bushel & 4 quarts given out to plant it, this is more than the usual *quantity,* but I wish it planted thick to allow for the depredations of the birds.

Note. Morris is very punctual, and far exceeds my expectation. A new broom sweeps clean, we will see how long the broom will last.

March 25th. **Note—it did not last very long.**

March 30th. Sunday. I have been sick for some time, & am now very unwell. I know very little of how things have gone on.

Uncle Archy's son William,[14] I hear, died on the main at his mother's last Wednesday, and was buried alongside his father at the church here on Friday last. I was sick in bed & could not attend.

My cotton sold in Charleston for 27 cents—discouraging.

[13] A trusted slave from Isabella Baker's Fields Point plantation.
[14] William L. Chaplin (1823-1851). Son of Archibald Chaplin and Martha Fripp.

March 31st. Monday. All hands banking potato land. Finished manuring Cowpen Hill & William Field, & commenced carting it over to the Persimmon Tree. Set out beets, the long blood were very broken—in fact very few came up, when the turnip beet came up beautifully, & I thinned out nearly enough of them to supply all the bloods. I have proven that beets will not vegetate well in very low land, but require a light but medium soil.

April 1st. The month of all others, the month, the 27th of which I first saw the light, nearly twenty-eight **nine** years since, ushers in with one of her delightful, balmy sunshine days. It has been warm all the day & we sat with open windows till late in the evening. Finished banking potato land today, with one hand's work in cotton land. Morris very attentive. Looked over my cotton land today, & find I have but 17 acres listed. However I shall cut potatoes to plant tomorrow to plant next day.

The last of my molasses was sold today.[15] I have not measured the corn taken in. The salt sells badly, perhaps it will do better when drum fish get to be plentiful.[16]

April 4th. *Item*—In looking over my account sales of the last year's crop, I find that I have made with 3¼ hands off of 28 acres of ground 3480 lbs., or 11 three hundred bales & 180 lbs. over of clean white cotton, the net proceeds of which is $856.11. If I had sent it all to town to I. & Webb the proceeds would have been $877. My cotton held much better weight in Charleston than Savannah, and brought 4 cents more per pound. *Would to God I could have sent it all there. Would to God I had not gone to Savannah,* but what is done cannot be helped, I must try & do better hereafter. **I hope I did**

April 6th. Capt. Daniel Jenkins has been appointed commissioner of roads in this division in my place. I have very strong suspicions that some of my *friends* have been *officiously* busying themselves to get me out of the office—*they,* if such be the case, did not dream that they were doing me a favor instead of an injury. I suspect D. Jenkins & the Dr., for I understood from the former today that he had told our representative, Ben Johnson,[17] that he did not know that I would serve another term if appointed, & recommended Dr. Jenkins, but he got stuck in himself. I suppose he is satisfied however, & thinks it quite an honor. I wrote a letter to Johnson while he was in Columbia & mentioned that both Oliver Fripp & myself were

---

[15] Chaplin bartered molasses to his slaves for corn.
[16] Drum fish were preserved by salting. Chaplin has been distilling salt from salt water but cannot find buyers for the product.
[17] See note, May 23, 1845.

willing to serve, yet both Oliver & Edings[18] are reappointed & I thrown out. This looks suspicious; Edings refuses to serve & W. W. Fripp is put in his place. I am rather glad, than otherwise, that I am not put in again, but, as I know that I have tried to do my best to keep the roads in order, and suit the convenience of the people as far as possible in the times of working, I shall endeavor to find out if anyone has been displeased with my conduct in office and wished a change.

John L. Chaplin sent us a roe & bit of drum fish today, the third piece we have had this year.

April 7th.   Monday. An election held today for ordinary[19]—R. G. Norton[20] & E. F. Morrall[21] candidates. Ned is determined to have an office. I fear he will get beat again, the polls only open for one day & not many persons will go out. I went out & gave him a vote. This is the 4th election held this fall.

All hands listing cotton land—nearly everybody's cotton is up. My corn is coming up very well. Had to put Mary to minding potato patch.

April 9th.   Wednesday. Uncle Paul paid my land rent today by order on Robert Brown & Co.[22] I will have to go to Beaufort on Friday & have it cashed. We never were so hard up for something to eat.

April 10th.   Planted 2¾ acres cotton in garden, with the seed that Isaac selected from the Godly. Wife rode over with me to see Uncle Ben & Aunt Betsy. It *should* have been a pleasant visit, as she goes out so very seldom, but the wind was so very high & right in our faces going, & then my good wife got herself in such a bad humor that she scolded me all the time going & returning. 5 hands banking for cotton on Cowpen Hill.

April 11th.   Friday. Twelfth anniversary of our marriage. Went to Beaufort, got the order cashed that Uncle Paul gave me, got a few articles from town, sugar, bacon, tea &c. Sent the boat up for the things. All hands banking for cotton.

April 12th.   Finished hauling out compost. Put off my boat, she does not leak a drop.

[18] James Thomas Edings Fripp (1822–1863), planter. Son of James Fripp and Ann Pope. Brother to Lawrence (J.E.L.) and Oliver (W.O.P.) Fripp. Chaplin's second cousin on his father's side.
[19] Judge of probate.
[20] The incumbent, Robert G. Norton, planter. Lived on Lands End Road, St. Helena Island.
[21] Edward (Ned) Morrall, planter.
[22] Cotton factors, in Charleston.

April 19th. Saturday. Finished planting cotton, and commenced supplying over early corn.

April 22nd. Tuesday. Turned suddenly cool last night & quite cool this morning with high N.E. wind. Fell about 9 o'clock and I went out fishing. Caught one drum & a bass. I caught the drum, 2nd this year, Charles the bass, the first in the shape of a large fish, he says, since he was a young man.

Governor's review today in Beaufort. I did not feel like going. Hands listing ground for early peas. That infernal old May has let the hogs break in the garden & root up all the arrowroot. I did not know they would eat it, but they chew it up just as they do sugarcane.

April 23rd. Went fishing, took 3, drum as usual, making the 3rd, Jim took 2. Gave one to the Negroes, first they have had. Hands listing pea land, about 3½ acres listed. Heard they had great doings in Beaufort yesterday, a dinner &c &c &c. I am not atall sorry I did not go, in fact, I expected something of the kind is one reason why I did *not* go. Saw in the river today Minott & Farmer. They were in the *Pelican,* the old boat I *once* owned. She looked quite snug, new set sails, centerboard &c.

May 1st. Thursday. Hands hoeing corn at Jenkins line. Started Frank plowing corn yesterday, got very little out of him, he takes so much time to carry the children back & forth to school. Set out some tomato plants. Hoed through my potatoes, first time. Reds up prettily, the rest not so well.

May 2nd. Hoed the 9 tasks corn at Jenkins line, & 3 hands hoeing 1 task each of cotton on Cowpen Hill, 1st hoeing.

Had to put Helen to mind the peas, the birds are so bad after them. Jim sick & Eliza washing in the place of Judy, who has a falling of the womb, & her mistress says she must not stand up much, and put her to sewing.

The Old Judy lived for many years after, passed through the horrid Civil War with all its suffering & loss, and returned to Beaufort with Bill Jenkins[23] family & Uncle Paul & died there about 1870 or 71. I don't think she ever saw her old home after she left it 1860*

May 3rd. Saturday. All hands hoeing cotton. Jim still in his house, but he is not very sick. I caught him plaiting a palmetto hat, setting up in bed.

[23] Dr. William J. Jenkins.

May 7th. Wednesday. Poor old Uncle Ben died sometime today, in the evening I believe.
34 years to 1885

May 10th. Saturday. No invitation has been sent here, so I sent over to know at what hour the funeral would be, as I *accidentally heard* he would be buried today, and I am determined to go tho I am not fit to go. Took Ernest & Virginia over. Sophy would have gone, but as no invitation is sent, she would not. I don't care, I know *whose* doings it is. The funeral took place about 11 a.m., good many persons attended. He is buried at the church. It was better for him, he is out of the great misery he must have suffered now more than 16 months. Poor Aunt Betsy, I am sorry for her, but she has been expecting it a long time, and she is satisfied he has gone to heaven, where the two good souls will soon be again united. Would to God I was even half as well prepared, I would almost be satisfied to go at once. But there is a vast difference.

May 12th. I expect we will stay on the plantation this summer, as I cannot get a house at the village and Tom B. Fripp,[24] who now owns the house we had the last two or three summers, will not let me have it without the cash ($50) by the 1st of June. I believe it is only a pretext not to let me have it, for I hear that the Caperses want it, also, & they are all great friends. However, for myself, I prefer staying here, and if we are prudent will, no doubt, escape fever.

May 15th. Thursday. Hauling corn in potato patch, 1st hauling—very dry but I cannot wait any longer. I hear that Dr. Jenkins & Aunt Betsy moved to the village today. J. F. Townsend & wife[25] are over at Aunt Betsy's, they leave today.

I know that I am a fool, but sometimes I think I am *a very great fool.* For instance, in the management of the children, particularly Ernest—some-

[24] Thomas B. Fripp (1829–1862), planter. Son of William B. Fripp and Eliza Chaplin First cousin, once removed, to Thomas B. Chaplin, on his mother's side. Brother of John E. and William P. Fripp. Lived at Cedar Grove plantation, in the eastern part of the Island.
[25] John Ferrars Townsend (1799–1881), of Edisto Island. Son of Daniel Townsend and Hephzibah Jenkins. Studied law and devoted himself to politics and agriculture. Renowned for his successful cotton crops, his seed selection techniques and his experiments in fighting the cotton caterpillar. Member S.C. House of Representatives and S.C. Senate for sixteen years. Delegate to the State Secession Convention in 1860. His wife, Mary Caroline Jenkins (1813–1889), daughter of Richard Jenkins and Phoebe Waight, was Chaplin's third cousin, once removed, on her mother's side. She was a first cousin to Dr. W. J. Jenkins, Maj. D. P. Jenkins, Capt. D. T. Jenkins, Charlotte Jenkins Croft, and Emmeline Jenkins Webb, and a niece of Aunt Betsy Jenkins Chaplin.

times wife will say, "Good man, if *you* don't do something with that child he will go to destruction, or commit murder." Then she will tell Ernest, "If you do so & so again I will positively send you to your father to be punished, or I'll tell your father." Ernest repeats the fault, or act. Well, *perhaps* I *am* told, *but* I must first promise not to punish him, & this is done over & over. Sometimes, but rarely, I catch Ernest in the very act of committing a fault, or have every reason to believe that he has. I punish him, directly I am asked what it is for, and very often (I won't say always), after some wrangling, I am told (perhaps in the presence of the child) that I punished him unjustly. I say to myself, well, if this is to be the way (for it always vexes me to be spoken to in this way before the children), that I am not fit to judge whether or no a child deserves punishment, you can manage them yourself in future, I will say nothing, you be both mother & father, mistress & master. The next thing I hear, with much fuss & to do, "Good man, you must *positively* do something with Ernest, he is so impertinent to me you would not believe." I say, "Why don't you punish him?" "I am not able, you must do it; now when he is impertinent again, I will send him to you to be punished." "Very well," I say, *"just* send him with a note to that effect," but he is never sent, & if I am told, why, I must *let him off this time,* but the next time he won't get off so well, I can tell him. Then again, "Good man, the little Negroes are ruining the children, I couldn't tell you half the badness they learn them. That little demon Jack must be sent out of the house, he *shan't* stay another day." Jack is sent out. Next thing, Jack is mounted behind Ernest on a horse & sent off together to get plums, or Ernest is put under Sam's protection, & sent one or two miles to get mulberries, on foot. They have one or two creeks to cross, which are nearly dry at low water, & no danger of *them,* but it happens to be high spring tide & these little creeks become deep & unfordable even for a horse, and I had forbidden Ernest to go. I speak about this, and the risk they run & the long distance they would have to walk round these creeks, and for what good? I am told that I deprive Ernest of every *privilege, don't want* to see him do anything that every little boy of his age is allowed to do, and *only* let him enjoy himself when I am out of my *senses* (with liquor). *I am done.*
[penciled note of 1876, six lines illegible]

May 18th.   Sunday. Did not go to church. Old Judge lost his wife today. She belonged to Mrs. C. Reynolds, & was very valuable to her.

May 19th.   Monday. Finished hoeing through my cotton 1st time. Sent Charles to try & get whiting, but he caught none. Got Negro cloth from town on Saturday. Gave it out today. Cost 9 cents per yard.
Good or bad crop the clothes must always be got

May 20th. Aunt Betsy sent me today (the good soul) 5 pieces of bacon & a large kettle of lard.
(*I have no doubt, even then, she had to hide the deed from Dr. Jenkins*[26])

May 21st. Sent Jack to Beaufort in the boat that takes up Miss Augusta Chaplin. I hear she is to be married to Jos. Perry, & goes up to purchase "fixings in Beaufort."

May 22nd. Helen sick, they say to be confined. I am very much pushed for work. My cotton should be hauled, my corn hoed & hauled, & potatoes must be worked. The cotton in the garden wants thinning & hauling very badly. Finished plowing my early peas today. They are up badly, but Uncle Paul says his are worse.

May 27th. Tuesday. Duchess had a mare colt, very small & think a bay color.

May 28th. Wednesday. Helen is confined of a girl child, name Tenah.

May 29th. Everything looks discouraging—cotton is actually dying by the task, some places not a hill alive on a row. Cause of a very high wind & ground so dry last Saturday, 24th inst., I shall be obliged to supply a good deal over, the first rain, God knows when that will be. Finished hauling all my March corn, that is getting yellow & twisting up. Commenced with Frank, cutting rye. Everything looks withered & dying in the garden, Irish potatoes nearly all dead.

May 31st. Saturday. May would not go out without a shower. Looked cloudy this morning, & about 8½ o'clock sent down a *very delightful* shower, in fact a hard rain, & just such a one as soaks the earth. It will require a good deal of it to thoroughly wet the ground. I have not been out to see what the hands are doing. Saw some hauling cotton. I will now be able to set out plants in the garden.
    I must supply over my cotton where it has died on Monday. The rain in the morning of this day lasted till 10½ o'clock, pretty steady all the time, when the sun came out scorching hot for a short time, when the wind commenced blowing fresh from east, with heavy clouds, occasionally fine driving scuds of rain, quite cool and disagreeable, up to night——

---

[26] Aunt Betsy's husband, Uncle Ben Chaplin, has just died, leaving considerable property to his niece Eliza Mary and her husband, Dr. William Jenkins. Chaplin received nothing from Uncle Ben's estate. See June 14, 1851.

My Negroes were hauling cotton today when their own sense should tell them they ought to be supplying. Uncle Paul's hands were supplying Carter's Hill.

With all the rain today, in some places I kicked up dry sand with my foot & the ground does not seem to wet down more than 1½ or 2 inches.

June 2nd. Monday. All hands planting over cotton, this is unfortunate, but cannot be helped, the cotton is literally *killed* in places and must be planted over. Finished the whole field, & made Judy & Charles plant over the garden cotton.

Frank & Jack cutting rye, about half done, don't think it will yield much. Aunt Betsy was down home today from the village. She has been sick, the boy said. She sent over presents of caps, collars, lace &c to wife & Sophy. She is a good soul.

June 3rd. Commenced shearing my sheep. Sent Frank to Beaufort.

Miss Augusta S. Chaplin was married in the evening to Jos. W. Perry—the children & myself were invited to the wedding, & we went. Quite a plain affair, just a little tea, cake & cordial. I think the match quite a suitable one. The party was made up of the McTure., Pritchards, Perry, Fendin[27] &c. J. H. Webb was there.

June 4th. Wednesday. I have more beets & carrots than I know what to do with, no cow up to feed them to & my horses won't touch them. *Finished rye.*

June 8th. Understand that C. Ben Capers was married in Charleston on Thursday night last, 5th inst., to a Miss Yates,[28] & brought his wife up in the s[team]boat yesterday, to Beaufort. So the old bachelor is spliced at last, & I believe all parties are satisfied with the match. Old Mr. Capers was on the Island on Thursday, & is here now. He was sick & did not go down to the wedding. The rest of the family went down.

June 10th. Veal market commenced. Lamb market commenced last Saturday. Finished hauling cotton, all to 1 task. Thrashed at 1½ pecks of rye & had it ground to flour, turned out about ½ bushel of flour, besides the bran. Made some bread of it, very dark, but eat very well. Requires to be re-sifted, through a finer cloth than I could get today.

---

[27] James W. Fendin (b. 1814), planter. Lived on Lands End Road, across from Edgar Fripp's Seaside Plantation.
[28] Eugenia Yates.

June 13th. Friday. Hauled up & laid by corn in old root patch. J. H. Webb & myself with my three boys went down to Trenchards to get terrapins—found only two & a few eggs, got back late.

When we got home, were very agreeably surprised to find old Moveum[29] at the landing & Mother in the house. She came round by the village & got here before high water. Gave Old Morris permission to go to the main to see his wife.

June 14th. Saturday. Hauling up early corn, will have to leave it unfinished on Monday & hoe out the Cowpen Hill cotton before I go at it again, although it is now in tassel & ought to be laid by at once, but the cotton is suffering. I have not seen a blossom yet. There are several on Carter's Hill *I hear.* Put Jack carting mud in cow pen.

Heard that Wm. J. Jenkins, Paul Chaplin & Daniel Jenkins are left executors to Uncle Ben's will. Wm. Jenkins is the only one qualified or that will qualify before next year. His children & the Captain get nearly all the property.

W.J.J. got it all. *Uncle Paul's Negro Aaron* [   ] *great good it did them.*

Mother's hands went to Beaufort in my boat. Sent Isaac with them to see if Webb has thought proper to send the things I wrote to him for on [   ]. He had better do so.

June 15th. Sunday. Went to church. Saw Mrs. C. B. Capers. She is neither ugly or pretty.

June 17th. Rained steady but not very hard during the whole day, don't think there was 15 minutes that there was not rain falling, a regular soaking rain. Got no work done out of doors, had some rye thrashed, about 1¾ bushels. Mother is quite unwell today.

June 18th. Supplied the whole root patch over with slips, it was very much broken. The seed did not come up in the brackish land atall, & is perfectly sound now & appears just to be taking root. However I supplied over with vines, as I think the chance is best to make anything from them. Opened some drains, to let the water off potatoes. Jim cutting bushes in slip patch. Isaac tracking same. I wish I had my slip land listed. I will not put it off so late again. This is a fine time to plant, if I was only ready.

June 19th. Thursday. Helen came out today, 3 weeks after confinement. Made her haul cotton in the garden. Eliza thinning on Cowpen Hill. Jim cutting bushes.

---

[29] A nickname for Old Morris or Old Mary who helped with the annual move from the plantation to the village.

June 20th. I discovered today that the cursed crows have plugged every watermelon in my patch from the size of my fist to the largest, some larger than my head. They are the most destructive devils in the world. Hogs are hardly worse and they are of some use, but God only knows what crows were made for.

Moll sick today, hope she will be out tomorrow.

June 21st. Saturday. Killed a lamb & sent it down to the village. I thought I had lost my new net, given me by J. H. Webb not long ago. Suspected some of Mother's Negroes of stealing it, but heard today that it was left at Bull's Point when I went down there, & J. W. Perry found it, & it is now at his house quite safe, thank God.

June 22nd. Sunday. Nelly taken sick, & confined last night before midnight, had a boy child, name Willis.

July 11th. Friday. Heavy storm of rain & wind after midnight last night—still raining this morning. Turned out the hands to plant slips, I must not lose this chance of rain. I think I can very nearly finish what land I have listed tomorrow. Planted a little over 5 tasks of slips.

July 14th. Monday. Full moon & very high tide, with pleasant S.E. breeze in the evening. How infinitely more pleasant & comfortable down here than the close, swelling situation we occupied at the village the two past summers. Peggy came out. Virginia's birthday—9 years old I believe. Hands hoeing cotton. Eliza & Moll laying up. Ernest complaining tonight, fear he is getting fever. He does enough to give it him.

July 15th. Killed veal for market. Went to the lodge & gave it out, & a very fine one it was. All hands hoeing cotton, Cowpen Hill. Eliza sick, or rather, laying by today. Sam taken with fever. Second allowance of the last corn from town.

July 16th. Mother's boat came over yesterday & she went home today. Sophy wanted to go with her but as I would not consent to let Eugene go with them she would not go. I think it is well she did not, for she would be almost sure to have the fever.

All hands out today, hoeing cotton. Grayson sent to me today for the corn borrowed from him, but I have not got it to return to him.

July 17th. Thursday. Uncle Paul killed beef for market today, 2nd killing & both times I got the back piece. The book is made out wrong. Mr.

Reynolds kills next time. If I get an inferior piece again I shall return it to the killer.

July 20th.　　Sunday. Went to church on horseback. Dined with Capers, had quite a feast of fruit, some very fine peaches & pears.

July 21st.　　Monday. Frank sick, bowel complaint. Sent Jack to Beaufort.

July 26th.　　Saturday. Isaac taken with bowel complaint on 26th inst.

July 30th.　　Wednesday. Wife, poor soul, had fever last night, & is quite sick today. She is exceedingly imprudent, which is the cause. I can't induce her to take the least medicine.

July 31st.　　Got up early and killed a beef for market, in fine order, & tho I thought it rather small, I think it quite as large as any that has been killed this year except Uncle Tom's, & *larger* than some.

Had the hands in the garden till ten o'clock, preparing land for turnips. Turned out & commenced stripping blades.

Had Webb's gun, so I went out & killed two plover. They were small & not fat. Saw a good many, but the first I have killed—having no gun of my own.

Aug. 2nd.　　Saturday. Set out *208* drumhead & flat Dutch cabbage plants. *Manured* with soft salt mud under a light list, & compost & fowl house manure on the list, then banked pretty heavy. The plants are rather old & tough, & some of them very large in the stalk, but I am pretty sure the grubs will not attack them. Some of the plants are fine. I think this is early to set out for winter heads, but the plants are so old & the weather very favorable for the work, I would not delay longer. I will keep a few of the smallest for a later season.

My guinea squashes are bearing very well, the first I ever had to bear, or even to come up—*only those* that were left in the seed bed have borne, the transplanted ones have not grown. I worked & manured them today, which may stand them, but will be late. Hands hauling slips & cotton.

Aug. 6th.　　Wednesday. Got in all my oldest blades. All hands picking shiny peas, got in 24 sheets. Pulled the last of the beets out of the garden & gave them to the Negroes.

Aug. 7th.　　Thursday. Agricultural Society day, a good many persons out. I had the finest water & muskmelons & vegetables out, among the latter, a fine guinea squash, the first I ever raised. Dr. Scott found a very excellent dinner. Several strangers were there, Dick Pope, W. John Pope,[30] & Yates,[31] Ben Capers' brother-in-law.

Sent 3 hands & fixed up the fence between Benj. Chaplin Jnr. & myself.

Aug. 8th. All hands picking peas except Isaac. Had him with me making a new axletree to my horse cart, finished it, & a very good one it is. Only wants skeins[32] or irons to it.

Uncle Ben's Paul repaired my little boat & I brought her home today. It is done very well indeed, & will now be of the greatest service to me. Mosquitoes very bad for the past three or four nights.

Aug. 9th. Saturday. Finished picking peas this morning, first picking, got 60 sheets in all. I expect to get nearly as many more off of 4 acres. Supplied my late peas, they are not as much broken as some I see about. Sent 2 hands to strip Morris's corn at the river. Had 4 tasks of slips hoed. My last planting of slips look very mean, a good many vines are dead.

There was a picnic at the village last night. Oh! Ye Gods.

Aug. 10th. Sunday. Clear & hot . . . went to church.

Heard that J.T.E. Fripp & his wife[33] have made up matters & come together again. She wrote for him & he went over to her, took out on the sound in a boat, met the steamboat, boarded her, & cleared out for Savannah, a regular runaway match. They are to spend the rest of the summer in the upper part of Georgia. I think they have done what is right & what should have been done long ago.

Aug. 11th. Hoeing slips, 3 hands cutting marsh. Isaac getting wood for a kiln.

Aug. 12th. Tuesday. Stripping blades off Negroes' corn. Commenced eating potatoes, turn out very badly indeed. I am much disappointed in the land I planted, I was sure it would produce fine potatoes.

---

[30] Richard R. Pope (b. 1817) and William John Pope (d. 1852), planters. St. Luke's Parish. Sons of William Pope, Sr. William John's mother was Sarah Green Tucker, his father's first wife. Richard's mother was Sarah Norton, the senior Pope's second wife.
[31] Eugenia Yates's brother.
[32] Metal covering protecting the axle shaft.
[33] Elizabeth Amelia Fripp (1826–1867). Daughter of Charles E. Fripp and Mary Minott. Chaplin's second cousin, once removed, on her father's side. She and her husband were second cousins, once removed. Private James Thomas Edings Fripp, C.S.A., was killed in a skirmish on the Combahee in 1862.

Aug. 13th.　Wednesday. Clear & very oppressive weather. Mosquitoes intolerable night & day.

Mother came over, got here to dinner. She brought my gun, nicely fixed. Hands stripping blades.

Aug. 14th.　Put one hand picking cotton in the garden. Mother's Negroes went up to Beaufort in my boat. Women hauling slips.

Missy very ill indeed. Poor little thing, she suffers.

Aug. 15th.　Friday. I went out to try & get a plover for wife, left Missy, we all thought, better. While in the pasture, Sam was sent to tell me "she had fits." God only knows how I felt when I saw her. My heart sunk within me, I felt choked, I felt that death had seized upon her poor little body. Oh! But not on her soul. *That* as pure as if already an angel. God will take her to him, for her good, and I hope for a chastising to us all. She suffered much. Oh! Too much, but God relieved her, her spirit fled about 3 o'clock p.m., fled, yes, fled to everlasting peace, rest, enduring rest forever.

Sent 3 hands to Beaufort to get a coffin for the remains of my angel. Oh! For the *poor mother*, how she suffers, tis agony to behold. More even, than the death throes of the child—the mother, the woman, the strong minded woman, to see the little one she has so suffered to bring into the world, go out of it, taken from her in a few short months, & in such agony. Oh, who knows what that innocent suffered, would to God I could have borne some, if only a little—but who, which could bear the hereafter best, there is no comparison, only as there is between the condemned sinner & the heavenly angel.

Aug. 16th.　Saturday. Aunt Betsy's horse was taken sick after she got down to her place yesterday, & she sent to get Hyder to carry her back to the village. She did not come over.

The Negroes got back from Beaufort about 3 p.m. today. Busher[34] made the coffin. Sent Jack to the village to request Mr. McElheran to perform the service at 9 o'clock tomorrow morning, at the Episcopal Church. No one else invited except Uncle Paul.

Aug. 17th.　Sunday. I went to perform the last melancholy duty to my poor little *Missy.* Got to the church before nine o'clock, & had the grave dug close alongside of *the two that went before*—three daughters almost in one grave. May God spare the rest to us and may they prove a comfort,

[34] Edward B. Busher (b. 1815), joiner.

now & hereafter, to their poor heart stricken mother, & a consolation for those she has lost.

✱1868. Two more gone since & the mother too left, and they are of no manner of use or consolation to anyone, or even themselves.✱

The service was performed in the church, no one present but Uncle Paul, the minister & myself. We were enough. About ¼ to two, we laid the remains of the precious one in the cold, cold grave. Peace, eternal peace & joy is hers. She was of God, and he has recalled his own, to dwell with him in heaven. I did not stay to attend church but came directly home. So ends the distressing duty of consigning one's own flesh & blood to the grave.

Aug. 18th. Monday. Commenced making lime kiln 12 feet across. Planted more turnips, those I planted have very few come up. I will supply them over. Negroes hoeing burr grass in cotton. 3 hands cutting marsh.

Aug. 20th. Wednesday. Went shooting plover. Rode as far as Webb's, promised to go fishing with him on Friday. Women picking peas, 24 sheets in.

Aug. 22nd. Friday. Fine day. Went out as per engagement. Had pleasant day & tolerable sport. Took a good many blackfish & one large sheephead & a shark.

Aug. 23rd. Sunday. One of the most dreadful hurricanes I ever *saw*. Did much damage to my young corn & all the cotton. Blew down my boat house. It lasted all day, with some rain. A regular equinox.[35]

Aug. 25th. Tuesday. All the women picking cotton in *the field,* do not get any great deal, 10 or 15 lbs. each——
    Men still cutting marsh. Isaac burning lime kiln.

Aug. 26th, 27th, 29th, 30th. Picking cotton & cutting marsh except one day, the men had to go & fix up marsh dam, which the high tide broke. Tony went to the main in my boat on 26th. Left the boat he came over in at Riverside.
    It was most fortunate that my only boat was not under the house when it fell. She was taken out when I went fishing & never put back, & all the damage was one broken oar.

[35] As severe as the storms which occur around the fall and spring equinoxes.

Sept. 1st. Monday. 39 cords & one large rick[36] of marsh cut. Hands still cutting. 5 tasks of potatoes dug down, patch going very fast. Turn miserably & get no better.

All women picking cotton, one hand picking in the garden. Isaac pulling the fallen boat house to pieces to save the stuff. Most of it is very good, & I shall use to repair my Negro houses which need it greatly. The shingles are good.

Sept. 3rd. Muster Day, but I never thought of it till it was too late to go. I was calculating on going tomorrow, confounding the Society day with Muster Day, Wednesday & Thursday.

Sept. 4th. Broke in the balance of the early corn *on the road,* which I commenced the other day. In all, 2¼ acres, got 65 baskets of sound corn.[37] After finishing this, went and cut pea vines, cut about 6 tasks. I fear it will rain tonight and spoil what I have cut.

2nd killing round in beef market commenced.

Sept. 8th. Monday. All women picking cotton. They don't get more than an average of 20 lbs. Hauling in pea vines with 2 carts, will not finish today, & hardly tomorrow. Mother's boat, or rather, her Negroes in my boat got here yesterday. Brought a sort of job carpenter over (Peter) to help me fix up my piazza. Brought also a barrel of ice, which is very acceptable.

Sept. 9th. My turn to kill veal for market, 2nd round. Rain drove the Negroes from picking cotton in the morning. Went out & raked sedge in afternoon. I went out blackfishing. J. H. Webb & John & Wright Rhodes[38] went with me. Caught a fine parcel of blackfish, one sheephead, & a shark about 9 feet long.

Sept. 10th. Wednesday. Nearly finished framing Negro house for Isaac. Still hauling in pea vines, will hardly finish tomorrow. Mother's Negroes went back to the main. Peter stayed, to help me with my carpenter's work.

---

[36] Stack.

[37] Equal to 32½ bushels, for a per-acre yield of 14½ bushels.

[38] John Jenkins Rhodes (b. 1829) and Richard Wright Rhodes (b. 1834). Sons of Thomas W. Rhodes and Elizabeth Jenkins. Brothers of Julia, Emma, and Frances Rhodes. The Rhodes children were first cousins to Chaplin, once removed, on their mother's side. John H. Webb was their uncle through marriage to the Captain's sister Emmeline.

Sept. 11th. All women picking cotton, average about 36 lbs. per hand. Sent Isaac & Jim to get out roller stuff in Mother's pine barren at the church.

Sept. 12th. Friday. Sent Jack to Beaufort for elixir of opium. Sancho & Frank hauling pea vines. They are now almost too dry, but I will haul them in, if only for manure. Picked the last of my pumpkins—did not make a good crop, got only about 250 all together.

Sept. 18th. Thursday. Frank & Jim both sick. I worked on the Negro house nearly all day.

Sept. 20th. Saturday. Negroes not picking as much cotton as they should. There is a tolerable blow in the field.

Frank came to work today. Isaac with fever, laying up. Much sickness on the Island, principally fever.

Sept. 21st. Sunday. Isaac had not the fever in the morning, but his precious wife went off to church instead of coming to me for quinine for him as she was directed, & consequently the fever came on again in the evening. Jim took quinine all day, & has no fever tonight.

Sept. 22nd. I rode over to Lawrence Fripp's according to a message received from him yesterday, requesting me to meet him. He was not there, did not come from Beaufort. (Catch me going to meet him again.) I rode over & saw Oliver, however, & had a pleasant chat with him. Jim out to work today, Isaac still with the fever. It went off about 10 a.m. & I commenced with the quinine. Gave him 4 doses through the day (large ones). He had no fever at night.

Negroes picked a little better today. I must try and break in some of my corn (at last) this week.

Sept. 24th. Wednesday. Isaac came out & did some work on his house today.

Oct. 5th. Sunday. Mother, Sophy, Virginia & Ernest all went to church. Ernest rode there & back on horseback for the first time.

Oct. 7th. Broke the early corn today. It is short & shells off very much, but turns out better than I expected. Got 100 baskets off of 4 acres, only 7 baskets less than the 4 acres of flint corn off of old root patch.

Oct. 8th. Wednesday. Have 8½ acres of corn to break besides the cotton field corn. Finished 7⅗ March corn but could not get it all housed, had to leave about 3 cart loads in the field till tomorrow. Broke it in, in the shuck,[39] so I could not measure it, but am satisfied it turned out well & was the best corn I had.

Oct. 9th.   Thursday. Finished everything in corn out & out this morning & gave the Negroes the rest of the day to break in their corn. They, generally, are making a good crop, the best I have known them to make for a long time. They had good land & low, which suited the season. Some of them have excellent corn, better than any of mine. I like to see this & will always encourage it. I think I have made enough to last me if my potatoes do well.

I got very little out of the cotton field, only one cart load & that very mean. Should have done better if I had planted flint instead of gourd seed corn.[40] I heard Uncle Paul say that he never made a better crop of corn than he has this year, but once in his life.

My cowpeas have put out poorly, & if there is not rain soon, I will make very few & they will not be full.

Oct. 10th.   Friday. I worked all day on Isaac's house. All the women picking cotton. Sent the men to the Island[41] for wood. Mother's boat came over for her. She goes tomorrow herself.

Oct. 11th.   Mother went to the main. Aunt Betsy, hearing that wife was sick, came to see her. Got here just after Mother left. I drove Mother over to Caperses' & she started from there.

Sent the flat & 3 hands again to the Island for wood. They have not brought off all they had cut. I am very anxious to have my cellar filled with wood & pine for winter, which will save me the trouble & bother of taking off hands when I commence ginning to go to the Island, or the carts when I am getting out manure.

Oct. 12th.   Sunday. Wife very sick. She has been sick a long time but is worse than ever now. I fear it will be long ere she gets better, if she ever does at all. I want very much to go to Beaufort tomorrow & try & get some medicine for her if she is not too sick for me to leave her.

Oct. 13th.   Went to Beaufort, the first time I have been there for many months, almost a year. It was quite a busy day there. In the first place

---

[39] Corn picked and stored with the shucks still on.
[40] Flint corn is small and hard-grained. Gourd corn is softer and sweeter and the grains are larger, but it does not like the salty environment.
[41] Most likely Eddings Island.

there was an election for members of a Southern Congress[42] (that will never meet). Then, it was Muster Day for the Artillery Company, and the anniversary meeting of the Southern Rights Association,[43] & which I became a member today. After parade the company had dinner under the oak trees in the suburbs of the town, to which I was invited. The dinner was a good one with champagne & other liquors & wines, over which there were five fiery secession addresses delivered by Messrs. De Treville, E. Rhett, Trescot,[44] J. D. Pope, & G. P. Elliott, which were all loudly cheered.[45]

Oct. 15th. Wednesday. Hands picking cotton, cotton very much stained. Jim cutting wood, Frank sick. Worked on Isaac's house all day, got one side shingled up. Wife still very sick but better than yesterday.

Oct. 17th. Friday. Sun rose clear but clouded up soon after. Sent Isaac & Jim to Beaufort for some things I expect up from town. They did not get back, the weather not permitting.

I was engaged all day putting in glasses in the windows, which were sadly in want of them, but they are broken out almost as fast as I put them in. I have put in the last 6 months an entire box of 10 × 12 glass,[46] except what panes were broken in the box.

Mr. C. G. Capers called on me today, wants me to sign a paper, after having signed Lawrence Fripp's petition for the ferry. It is this. When Lawrence Fripp asked me to sign his paper, I had heard nothing of this idea of petitioning the legislature to so alter the charter of the White Hall Ferry so as to *oblige* whoever received the grant of said ferry to substitute a team & steamboat for a flat, & horse labor for manual labor. But still if this cannot now be done, I recommend L. Fripp for ferryman, and if it

[42] Although the other slave states did not answer South Carolina's call for a southern congress, secessionists and cooperationists—opponents of separate state action—decided to go through with the election of delegates to test public opinion. The secessionists lost in five of the state's six congressional districts, winning only in Chaplin's district, which embraced Beaufort, Colleton, Barnwell, and Orangeburg districts.

[43] A secessionist organization with local units around the state. Though not an important force after 1852, it had helped to coalesce anti-Union feeling, and it set the tone of the decade-long secession debate.

[44] William Henry Trescot (1822–1898), planter, lawyer, orator, "the father of diplomatic history in the United States." Owned plantations in Prince William's and St. Bartholomew's parishes. He was Assistant U.S. Secretary of State in 1860, member S.C. House of Representatives 1862–68. Trescot held various diplomatic posts after the Civil War. He was married to Eliza Cuthbert, first cousin of Mary and Elizabeth Heyward, the wives of Col. John Webb and C. J. Colcock, respectively.

[45] DeTreville, Pope, and Edmund Rhett's brother R. B. were delegates to the 1860 State Secession Convention.

[46] The windows in the house contained nine lights over nine.

can be done, I recommend him still, provided he keeps the said team on steamboat.

Oct. 18th.　Saturday. Isaac got back from Beaufort about 11 a.m., brought articles sent for—2 dozen ports, ½ dozen pints wine, 2 galls brandy, 1 qt. laudanum.

Oct. 25th.　Stock troubling field very much, principally Uncle Tom's, but they have only been in Uncle Paul's cotton, not in mine.

Oct. 26th.　Sunday. Let all the hogs out of the pen, & I suppose they will be in my slips very soon—will know of the damage (if any) tomorrow. Wind fell & cleared off in the evening, quite cool, wind rose again at dark & blew part of the night or I suppose we should have frost, tis plenty cold enough.

Oct. 27th.　Monday. Hands picking cotton, but will pick peas tomorrow.
　　Wife so very sick I could not go out, in fact, she has been so for more than a fortnight, but I think her worse today. Mother came over today.

Oct. 28th.　Wife no better today. She eats nothing at all. Tis agony to witness her suffering.

Oct. 29th.　Finished picking peas in the morning. Turned miserably bad, only got 22 sheets in all, 5½ acres. Hands went after the cotton again. Uncle Paul digging slips. Hear that they are turning out a bushel to the bed.
　　I do not think wife is any better today. She is so weak—takes no nourishment and talks inadheredly[47] at times, poor soul.

Oct. 30th.　Thursday. Rained this morning & continued cloudy all day. Hands could not pick cotton, had them assorting. Had the men in the garden preparing a piece of ground for the purpose of setting out some strawberries when we have rain enough for the purpose. Also had them clearing round & manuring my fruit trees.
　　Sent Isaac to Beaufort.
　　I think wife a *shade better* today, *thank God*. The sun shines out just as I am writing, 5½ o'clock, so tomorrow may be clear.
　　I feel quite drowsy & feverish this evening, having set up with wife the greater part of last night, & exposed myself somewhat this morning. Have a sore throat & feel feverish. God grant I may not have fever at this time.

[47] Incoherently.

Oct. 31st. All hands picking cotton. Killed a yearling steer, as much to get the feet to make jelly for wife as to get something to eat. Rather warm to keep it fresh any length of time, but am in hopes it will turn cooler.

Nov. 1st. Saturday. Wife very sick all day. She cannot last much longer. At night—Oh! What a night, she appeared to be *sinking* fast. I laid down to sleep about 12 midnight, but Rinah soon called me, said wife called me. I went up, & found her worse, I think dying. Daylight came (2nd) & still she was not revived. Dying, irrevocably dying.

Nov. 2nd. Sunday. The saddest day of my life. My poor, poor wife breathed her last, and was relieved of all her sufferings (many & great they were) about 12 o'clock today. Scarcely with a struggle, her pure soul departed, to realms of peace & love & joy, above, where will be no more sorrow & care, and where her troubled soul will be at rest. My poor children, *you* have lost that which never, no, never can be replaced, a *mother's love*, a *mother's care.* Your dear aunt has promised to do all in her power to prevent your want of the latter, but alas! How can she replace the former. May God bless her for all she *has* & *will* do for *you,* my poor orphans.

My heart is desolate, there is a coldness there that can never be warmed, a blank that never can be filled. May God give me strength to perform properly & faithfully that fatherly part, which I so solemnly owe to you, & which is my sacred duty. And to Sophy—Oh! What a debt of gratitude & love I owe to her, pray for me my sister, as I shall pray, that I may truly & faithfully perform the trust bequeathed to me by *one you* loved & who loved you so well.

Nov. 2nd. Sunday. Rained hard part of the day. Sent Jim & 3 hands to Beaufort for coffin. Sent to E. B. Busher for it. Wind very high.

> The relatives, Friends and Acquaintan-
> ces of Mr. and Mrs. Thos. B. Chaplin are
> invited to attend the *Funeral* of the *Latter,*
> at the Episcopal Church on *Tuesday,* the
> fourth (4th) instant, at 12 Oclock M.
>
> The Rev[d] D. McElheran is *particularly*
> requested to attend.
>
> St. Helena Isl[d]
> Nov. 3[d], 1851‡

Nov. 3rd. Jim got back sometime after night. I went over myself *for what he brought* & landed at the Riverside.

‡ Funeral invitation was inserted in the journal on a separate leaf.

Sent Jack to the village with invitation to funeral, and Mother's Ben on the same errand to those persons on their plantations.

Funeral to take place at the P.E. Church at 12 m. tomorrow.

Nov. 4th.   Mother & the children went with me to the funeral, Aunt Betsy kindly lending her carriage.

Attendance very numerous. The last solemn rites were performed at the appointed time, and *the dear loved one* rests by the side of her three departed *babies,* & her soul now communes with theirs in heaven. God's will be done.

Nov. 5th.   Wednesday. Clear, but all dim to me. I see nothing, & yet I see too much, every object that meets my eye, every voice I hear, but tears the bleeding heart afresh.

Cousin Sarah Scott & Miss Young called, I suppose to offer consolation. How vain, how futile the effort, tis useless & too late, we need it not—Mother came down, but Sophy did not see them, quite right.

Nov. 6th.   Thursday. Clear & cold, high wind and very cold at night. Aunt Betsy called. No one but Mother saw her. I *could not,* neither did Sophy wish to do so.

Nov. 7th.   Friday. Very cold. Heavy frost. High wind all day. I fear my slips will be injured but I can't help it now. I cannot dig this week, all hands are picking cotton, except men cutting poles for potato pen.

Nov. 9th.   Through the carelessness of Jack, Black Hawk got his right eye knocked out. He says Buckskin kicked him in it. The ball is completely broken.

Nov. 10th.   Monday. Mother returned to the main. I, very reluctantly, let Ernest go with her. I am sorry to see that Ernest is so anxious & willing to go from us, but he is too young as yet to know better & only looks to the indulgence he gets from his grandmother.

Commenced digging slips. I shall make a short crop of them. They are tolerably thick but not large, some spots are very good. Ben Chaplin's & the Major's horses have destroyed a good many for me. They are bad neighbors, and if I possibly can find means, I will fence them both off.

Nov. 11th.   Tuesday. Finished the common yams. Made 2 banks of eating & 4 of seed. Commenced the yellow yams, the first task I started turned *remarkably* well and very large indeed. I got a large bank of eating & a few baskets of seed from eleven rows.

Nov. 12th. Dug potatoes in the morning but the rain drove us in about 12 m. Got about 2 cart loads dug, the last one of eating potatoes & some seed got wet, & would not bury them, will wait for weather to dry them first. Spread the seed in the gin house, the eating I had put in the potato yard & covered with stalks. I fear this weather will continue for some time, & prevent my digging potatoes.

Nov. 13th. Set out some strawberry plants in the Orchard. Clear in the evening, but the sun set in a cloud.

Nov. 14th. Friday. Made a desperate push & got in all my slips, did not get them all covered till after dark. Used the plow to side down[48] or would not have finished. Made more than I had had any expectation of, about 2 months' allowance, I think, & a plenty of seed. My reds did very well, wherever there was a root, they were thick, but they were very broken.

Nov. 15th. Saturday. Sent Isaac, Jim & Frank to Beaufort, got groceries—flour, sugar, coffee, &c, also box of dry goods, caps for boys, shoes, & clothes from I. & W., Charleston. Bill large, $115.[49] These things *must* be had & more to come yet.

Picked in my oranges, got about 15 dozen. A great many have been eaten by the family, & stolen by the Negroes.

Nov. 24th. Monday. Commenced working on the roads, Capt. Daniel Jenkins commissioner. Women assorting cotton, finished what is picked.

Nov. 27th. Little Edwin Chaplin came here & worried me a great deal. He wants to get my little black horse. I told him he could not get him, but he is such a little ass, & *knave.* He has begged his father for an old out of date note he has of mine, & is fool enough to think I would let him have the horse for the note. He is such a contemptible little puppy I can't write any more about him.

Commenced plowing up the yard & plant rye.

Nov. 28th. Friday. I & Daniel rode over & dined with Ned Capers. He was at home quite alone, the family being all in town.

Ben Chaplin has fixed up an old pair of shafts in a botched up sort of fashion for my gig, and sent it home today. They are almost stiff enough for cart shafts.

---

[48] Knock down the sides of the potato hills with the plow. A risky procedure because the plow blade could bruise the potatoes.
[49] By 1851 prices equal to the receipts from one large bale of cotton.

Nov. 30th.   Lanced Isaac's thumb, he suffers greatly, and it looks very bad, much swollen.

((one month has passed . . . 4 Sundays))

This month goes out angrily and blustering.

Dec. 1st.   Monday. Had 3 gins at the yellow cotton today. I want to get it out of the way. The women were cleaning last year's motes,[50] there is a good deal of good cotton in them, which, though it cannot be cleaned for market, will answer to make a good mattress. I must see that so much good cotton is not pulled out with the motes this year.

Isaac's thumb is still very bad, the whole arm is much swollen.

Dec. 2nd.   Finished cleaning out the motes of last year, there are two good sheets full that would be good cotton if it had not been picked out with so much mashed seed in it. I *consider* that at least 20 lbs. or $6 worth of cotton was pulled out of my last year's crop by the utter carelessness of the moters, pulling out too much cotton with a cracked seed or mashed leaf. This would at the same rate amount to a considerable sum to a large planter.

Dec. 3rd.   Wednesday. Moved cow pen. Rode down to the Indian Hills with Wm. Jenkins behind his *new* horses and in his *new* buggy, quite a turnout. Returned to dinner. Hands picking cotton.

Dec. 5th.   Friday. Had a notion to go down for fish but did not. Edgar Fripp, Capt. D. Jenkins & Benjamin Chaplin Jr. & myself agreed to form a beef market, to begin on Wednesday next, each get a quarter, & kill once a fortnight. I to kill first.

Dec. 10th.   Wednesday. I killed first beef for market, in fine order. The Captain did not send for his piece. As I understand, he is one of a large party to go to the Hunting Island today. I suppose this *great occasion* has driven something else out of his head.

Finished ginning all the yellow cotton. Hands picking.

Dec. 11th.   Thursday. Clear & quite warm, beautiful day. Sophy rode on Buckskin with me in the field, and around by the Riverside (a circumstance worthy of note). She did not like his gaits much, not knowing how to manage him. He rode rough and consequently made her rather *sore,* but she has not rode for a long time, and if she will only keep it up & with a little padding I think she will get tough enough to stand a ride without

---

[50] Stained bits of cotton picked out after ginning.

being sore, and soon learn the horse to go as easy as he does with me. All hands picking cotton, last & light scraping.

Much sickness among the Negroes. I had 4 down on Tuesday, including Isaac with his hand, & he, I fear, will do nothing this winter. Today there are none but him from work. His hand still looks very bad, it runs but is still much swelled.

(*Dec. 2nd.* In the following record of births, deaths, & marriages in my own immediate family & in those connected with it in any way—and some, or *one* at least, if far from being palatable to me, to suffer the appearance of, in *this* book, much less so in the holy family Bible, commencing with myself—I do not *intend* to *be* or to state anything but what may be relied on by *future generations* as *strictly correct,* for it is for this purpose that *it* is recorded, that they may be informed how their ancestors went and came.)

[forty-one lines crossed out]

Dec. 17th. Wednesday. Cloudy and as I expected, found it sleeting pretty smartly at daylight. *Very, very* cold. Sleeted till about 9½ a.m., when there fell a mixture of sleet & snow. This continued till about 12 m., when it stopped sleeting, but continued to snow, though not very hard. Having a pretty good foundation of sleet, which made a good show on the ground, the snow was laying very well at 2 p.m. Started 5 gins this morning, but the day is so cold that I let the hands off at 12 m. to go & get wood to keep themselves warm.

At dark still sleeting & snowing.

Dec. 18th. Thursday. Sleeted & snowed a good deal last night to judge by the quantity on the ground, it being pretty well covered. Today is clear & bright, but very cold, the snow is melting where the sun can get at it but everything freezes in the shade. I think this is decidedly the coldest weather I have felt since I have been living on the Island & last night the *coldest* we have had this winter. How changeable this climate is, no doubt now that in a few days, it will be warm enough to sit in the house without a fire.

5 gins running today.

Freezing all day—the sun shone bright & clear, as the snow would melt on the roof t'would run down & form icicles from the eaves of the houses.

Dec. 20th. Saturday. Clear & pleasant today, some snow still on the ground here & there in spots. 3 gins going today. Jim packing 1st bale cotton. Mother sent over today. She was too unwell to come herself as she intended. Sent us a treat in the way of wild ducks & a wild goose. She will be over next week.

Dec. 21st.   Sunday night. Spent the greater part of the night of this, the very day seven weeks after the lamentable occurrence recorded above, in the melancholy occupation of reading & rereading some of the correspondence of *our early love . . .*
These letters were lost, left in a desk at house.
Oh! What *pangs* & *heartaches* did I not experience while reading & recalling to memory those incidents and passages of happy, happy days, long past, *never,* oh! *never* to be recalled, those treasured & ever to be remembered expressions of *earnest,* constant and *affectionate, doting* love. Oh! Those blessed *loved epistles,* how I *now* treasure them, would to God I had read them once every week, had learnt them by heart, the dear hand that penned them *might not* now be cold in death, & I *had* been a kinder, better husband, & *now* a better man. On the other hand, when I read over some of my own old letters *to her, to her,* who so sacredly treasured up the worthless trash, what feelings of shame, for their *misspelled, ridiculous,* nonsensical, *unworthy* nature, to be addressed too, to *one* so *infinitely superior* in intellect, so divine, so heavenly. What feelings of *utter remorse* & *unselfforgiving* for the wonted neglect, to avail myself of those *years* of happiness & the thousands of opportunities to treasure up, and shield from all harm & sorrow that precious gem it was my (great) good fortune to possess . . . Oh! Fool, fool that I was to be so blind not to have valued above all *earthly*—"ay" all—*every* other gift, *that heart so pure & so good,* ever *affectionate, loving & trusting,* so *wholly my own,* but tis *gone,* lost to me forever & ever, & I am desolate—yes—utterly desolate & alone, for who, who *can ever be to me what she was? None, no not one living being.*
1868, How much truth in the above time has shown, very nearly all I held dear has actually passed away from me. With property has gone fortune, children, the dearest of my flock, one sacrificed to his country,*[51] *another to her love or perceived love for a worthless object,*[52] *two left & such, not only worthless to themselves & to me but one a disgrace to his name*[53]
That one has redeemed himself by taking us under his care & support. 1884*
and the other forgets his father for himself,*[54] *who, I surely believe would see me suffer & is without one sympathizing feeling or assisting hand be raised to help me. Nothing but a return of fortune would call him to my side. This is as true as the above. 17 years ago.*

[51] Eugene.
[52] Virginia.
[53] Daniel.
[54] Ernest.

✱✱1876, 8 years more have passed & I am back on old St. Helena once again, but tis so, yes, not at the old home. I live at Coffin's Point, tried & proven by experience, 1868, a stranger's land & in a stranger's house. Still I am not desponding altogether, I manage to live, only dear Sophy & I, we are almost the only ones of the old inhabitants that have got a foothold here again.✱✱

✱✱But we left it again in 1884, Daniel having persuaded us to move over to the main near Walterboro. We had been very sick & the change was a benefit & here I suppose we will lay our bones.✱✱

The thought has often (lately) fixed itself upon my wondering imagination, *how could such a being* as *she was, love so dotingly, disinterestedly* love such as *I* am, tis past my comprehension, yet I know twas so, yes, positively, & without the least foundation of a doubt. And *she* is *gone, gone*— Oh! The golden opportunity that I have let escape me of rendering *her happy*, yes, happy, not *only here*, but hereafter. What do I not deserve, what will I not have to answer for to my maker. But *tis past*, and she is no more. Rest on sweet one. My *heart*, that was *all your own* when living, is now with you & you alone, in death, even in the *cold, cold grave*. There is no room, no place for it in this wretched body of mine. "Tis earthly, but not of earth."[55] *Farewell farewell*, Oh! *Remorse, Remorse*. I am *thy slave, now & forever*. Years may pass & scenes may change; all I hold dear on earth may pass away. Oceans may roll between *her* sacred resting place & I, yet *thou, thou* wilt always pursue, always retain thy unrelenting grasp upon my wretched spirit, *always & forever*.

Dec. 23rd.   Went to Beaufort. Got sales of 1 bale std. cotton sold by Tom Reilly—10¼ cents.

Got back to late dinner. Got Sophy's & Virginia's bonnets.

Dec. 24th.   Wednesday. Mother & Ernest came over today. Both well. I think she is pretty well tired of Ernest. I knew she could not manage him, but he did as he pleased. He looks well. Ben Chaplin killed beef for market . . . 2nd killing.

Dec. 25th.   Thursday. Christmas Day, clear, and devilish dull.
✱✱This must have been a very dull Christmas. Why so?✱✱

Dec. 29th.   Monday. All hands at work except Nelly—ris.[56] breast. Packed 2nd bale white cotton.

---

[55] I Corinthians 15:47–48. "The first man is of earth, earthy: the second man is the Lord from heaven. As is the earthy, such are they also that are earthy: and as is the heavenly, such are they also that are heavenly."
[56] Risen.

Dec. 31st. Wednesday. Fog in the morning, but the sun soon shone out bright, but almost directly clouded up and a light rain commenced to fall. But being anxious to get to Beaufort, on account of a message I received from Col. De Treville last week, stating that he wished particularly to see me on some important business connected with myself & the children, I started in the buggy, taking Ernest with me but much regretted doing so afterwards. It rained on us all the way to the ferry, one or two hard showers, & one very hard after we got to the ferry. The boat did not get over till after 2 p.m. We got to Beaufort just in time for dinner, which we took with Bell. Weather continuing bad & not being able to see Treville till late, I concluded to stay all night with Bell. Sent word to the boy on this side the ferry to take the horse back to Mr. Hazel's at Eustises,[57] & return for me in the morning. Saw Treville at night, 7 o'clock, & settled my business with him, *somewhat* to my satisfaction, but not altogether so. The matter we spoke of was this; soon after the death of my dear wife, I wrote a letter to Mr. J. W. Gray.[58]

Important

(who is, or was, trustee by appointment of court, to the legacy left my wife by her grandfather Jno. McDowell[59]), requesting him (Gray) to inform me in what light *I* now stood in regard to *this* property, which was substituted for the legacy of bank stock.[60] In answer, he said that he considers the property at the death of their mother wholly the children's[61] & sent me a clause of McDowell's will to that effect, and advised me to petition the Court of Equity to appoint me guardian of it, & I would then remain in possession of it as heretofore. I placed the letter in Treville's hands for his advice. He says the court will require me to give security or two securities to the amount of double the property, say $30,000. This it is almost impossible for me to do, not to say anything of the unpleasantness of asking anyone to become my security.

He, however, advised me to do this —not to make *any application*, but just to let everything stand as it is, at least for the time, that he thought I ran no great risk in doing so; that no one could make me accountable but the children when they became of age, & *then* I would have a *set off* (which I will mention further on); that when Gray made his next report, to the court, of legacies in his trust, *if* he would be *only* content to say that the

[57] Patience Wise Blackett Eustis (1786–1860), planter. Widow of Gen. Abraham Eustis. She owned part of the big Pine Barren tract on Port Royal Island. Joseph Hazel handled her business.
[58] Master in equity for the Charleston District. See note, Jan. 15, 1845.
[59] John McDowell, Mary Chaplin's paternal grandfather.
[60] See note, Oct. 13, 1845.
[61] McDowell had instructed that in case of Mary's death, the stock "be divided share and share alike, principal and interest, between her children. . . ." (Charleston County, *Will Book F,* 1818–26, 261.)

person for whom he held the property in trust had died, *leaving children,* to *whom* the property now devolved, and there was therefore no longer any necessity for his trusteeship, the court would *very* probably take no further notice of the matter, and the property might remain as it is forever. And he *thought* that Gray *would* be satisfied with only saying this in his report. *But,* if he (Gray) should feel it his duty to move or recommend the court to appoint some person (giving due security) *guardian* or *receiver* of *the property,* the court would do so, and it would then be necessary for me to make the application, if I could find security, and in the meantime I could look out for security. And if I could not find security for myself, he would advise me to get some friend or relation that *could* give security to apply for the appointment, and such person to appoint me agent for the property, to make return to *him* annually, so that *he,* as the proper person, could make his return to the master in equity *annually.* This would be *rather mortifying,* but if I can do *no better,* I must be glad to do even this, if even I can do this, for Treville says that the court would appoint *any*one giving security and it may be an *entire* stranger, one who would (and many they are) take the trust of an estate for such a long time (till the children are of age) just for the commissions & other benefits they may derive from the property. Of course, such a person could not be guardian of the *children*—they could not be taken away from *me,* only the property, and to pay me for the support of the children *only* what the *court allowed.* And to end the matter in the end, *the whole concern* would go to the devil, or into the pockets of such a person as would make the application, for such ends as mentioned above. O my God, tis too bad, tis too bad, enough to drive me mad, the very thought, it cannot, *shall* not be while there is breath in this body of mine——

And thus ends the *eventful,* the never to be forgotten year of eighteen hundred & fifty one. . . . Yes, go, grim & gloomy as is thy departing visage, thou leavest behind *hearts* more gloomy still, *perhaps* to linger out in sad despair, another Anno Domini.

End of A.D. 1851

***1876** *The property did remain without interference by anyone, entirely in my hands until the war, which did scatter it most woefully. In 1875, I redeemed about 100 acres of the place in my own power, & still hold it but can't realize anything from it atall.*[62] **

[62] This was land that Chaplin had substituted for his wife's bank stock. See note, June 17, 1845.

1852

Jan. 1st. Thursday. The first day of another year, and a dark, cloudy & cold one it is, but no rain.

We returned from Beaufort *in time* for a good New Year's dinner, prepared at home for us by *good Aunt Sophy,* which was very relishable after *herring & mackerel* at Bell's.

I must not forget to state that I was greeted with a "Happy New Year & God give you many more" by my very particular cousin friend, *good* Billy Fripp,[1] my God, Happy New Year to *me.*

The Beaufort Ferry passes today into other & I hope, better, hands than those of Jno. Tealy. Wm. A. Morcock has the contract from the last session of the legislature, over J.E.L. Fripp who also applied. Fripp had the largest number of signatures from the Islands, which I believe has generally governed the discussion of the legislature. But I understand the fact that Bythewood,[2] who owns the land on this side, at or adjoining the ferry landing, signed Morcock's petition influenced, very much, the committee in making their report. I do not think this was *right.*

Jan. 2nd. Friday. Put Judge to do some work in the garden, I intend to take him for a gardener altogether. He is ruptured, and not fit for other work. Mother's boat came over at night. She goes back with the boat. When she is on the main, she always writes as though she were *dying* to get away, but this time, she seems *dying to get back.* Her Negroes brought over 4 wild ducks, which makes 18 I have had this winter from the main, better, far, than we ever get over here.

Jan. 3rd. The appearance of the weather today has been very singular, alternate bright sunshine & heavy, dark clouds, no rain & a deep red sunset. This appearance is auspicious in my mind.

[1] William Fripp, Sr.
[2] B. R. Bythewood (b. 1800), planter. Owned Whitehall Plantation on Ladies Island, and a tract of land on St. Helena.

Aunt Betsy moved to the village today, don't know & can't conjecture her object in doing so, unless it is to save Dr. Jenkins the expense of boarding his children with Mrs. McElheran.

I rode as far today as Edgar Fripp's, to take a measure of his corn house, which I did in presence of Mr. Harvey,[3] his overseer. Fripp wishes to contend for the premium offered by the Agricultural Society for corn and had to have his corn measured by witnesses, members of the Society.

Packed the 3rd bale cotton today, 325 lbs. All hands out, but Isaac. God knows when he will be.

Jan. 6th.   Tuesday. Clear & windy & cold so Mother did not go home. Put some of her Negroes ginning.

Jan. 7th.   Wednesday. Clear & cold. Mother still put off going—— Found dinner at the muster house, went out, but did not stay to dinner, for reasons of which I am & ought to be ashamed.

Jan. 8th.   Thursday. Clear. Mother went home today. Peg & Frank still laying up.

Jan. 12th.   My hogs came up & I took the opportunity of putting one in the pen. Mother left Robert over here with me, I will try & make him useful in some way.

Jan. 13th.   Tuesday. Somewhat surprised to find it snowing quite fast this morning and the ground pretty white, and continued to snow till about 2 o'clock p.m. and at times harder than I ever saw it snow *here,* but it was very light and dry & did not lay. Sun came out bright about 4 p.m. & by dark the snow was pretty well melted where the sun got at it. Weather very cold, some think even colder than the last cold spell & snow we had. I never knew it to snow twice in the same winter since I have lived here. This, so far, has been a severe winter & not half over yet.

Negroes did nothing today but shell their allowance, and the men cut some wood.

Received a letter last night from Mr. Seabrook saying that [he] would take Ernest in his school.[4] I will take him as soon as I can.

This the singular looks of heavens predicated. The winters are even colder now in '75, 6 & 7 than then, but no snow. We are getting northern seasons as we get older.

---

[3] James T. Harvey (b. 1825).
[4] Rev. Joseph B. Seabrook's "Classical and Mathematical School" at Bluffton.

Jan. 19th. Monday. Sent Robert to Beaufort, by land, to get shoes for Ernest as he did not get them on Saturday. Hardly think he will get across the ferry, the wind is so high. All hands ginning & moting. Robert got back about 10 a.m. He had a severe time, very high wind & very cold all day.

Jan. 20th. Tuesday. A singular light appeared (for the second time this winter & once in the fall) last night in the northern horizon. It was of a rose color, not very bright, it must be what is called aurora borealis or northern light, an appearance of very rare occurrence in this latitude. This has altogether been a very uncommon winter.

    Gave out the last of the cotton to gin today. 4 hands' work. There will be near 500 lbs. of cotton to pack, don't think I will get it all in one bag.

Jan. 21st. Had the men tracking the old root patch for March corn, and the women spreading cotton seed on corn land. Agreed with Dr. Scott to send a hand in the place of his fellow Billy. I want him to go with me to Bluffton tomorrow if the weather suits.

Jan. 24th. Saturday. Started with Ernest for Bluffton on Thursday, weather very cold, but calm & clear. Got as far as Dr. F. P. Pope's[5] on Hilton Head where we stayed all night, and went on to Bluffton yesterday morning, as early as we could get breakfast. Got to Bluffton at 11½ o'clock. Saw Mr. Seabrook & made all necessary arrangements with him as soon as could. Did not stay more than a ½ or ¾'s of an hour, as the tide was far spent & I wanted to get home last night. Ernest was dull all day, but did not cry, except when I told him goodbye & kissed him, when he shed a few tears, after a hard struggle to repress them. Poor fellow, he will find it a little hard at first but it is all for his good, and I think he will be very contented & happy after a little while. I believe Mr. Seabrook to be an excellent man and will take every care of his comfort as well as his studies. Ernest is rather young to be sent away from home;[6] but I feel satisfied he is in good hands, & that neither of us will ever regret his going there. I expect much from him & hope I will not be disappointed.

   I was, most sadly, sadly, poor fellow. He is I hope in a better world now, 1876
   I was mistaken, Seabrook was & is a poor shoat. Ernest learned very little, he stayed there about a year. Seabrook is now teaching & preaching in Charleston. 1876

[5] Franklin P. Pope (b. 1812), planter and physician, St. Luke's Parish. Son of William Pope and Sarah Norton. Brother of Richard R. Pope and half-brother of William John Pope.
[6] Ernest is twelve years old.

Jan. 25th. Sunday. Cloudy all day. At home all day, quite out of sorts, dull & desponding.

I have seen years of hell since, '76

I can't help my thoughts wandering constantly to Ernest. It seems to me he is now cast upon the waters of life, for weal or woe, to sink or swim.

Jan. 26th. Monday. Sent 4 hands with the flat to Beaufort with cotton. Six bales, weighing 1975 lbs.[7]

300, average 329, very short crop indeed, the shortest I ever made

Hands with the flat did not return at night. Don't know what keeps them.

Jan. 27th. Tuesday. Flat got back at dark. They did not get to Beaufort till last night, owing to the Negroes' oversleeping themselves night before last & losing the tide, for which they shall be punished. Fortunately the steamboat got to Beaufort late & they were just in time to put the cotton on board. Very few hands listing today, the tough ground has scared them. 2 laying up, Eliza yesterday & today, & Mary today, & both *pretend* to the same thing—viz., falling of the *"body."*[8]

Rode over to see the old gentlemen, Uncles T. & P. today, the first time since last summer. Uncle P. has sold his cotton for 29 cents.

Heard that several blackfish, a species of whale, have been found dead at Bay Point & other places by Edwin Chaplin, J. H. Webb & others, out of which a good quantity of oil was extracted. I can't imagine the cause of their death, unless 'tis cold weather & shallow water.

Heard that on Monday night, 19th inst., J. E. Lawrence Fripp, on his way from Beaufort in his boat, got capsized, he & four Negroes, who were all very fortunately saved by Mr. Capers' Negroes, who heard their cries for help & went to them, they being near Mr. Capers's plantation. 2 of the Negroes had swam ashore, but the other two & Lawrence were with the boat (which was bottom up) & very nearly exhausted when picked up.

I got from Charleston, landed at the village wharf on Sunday the 25th, 1 barrel of Irish potatoes, keg of butter, keg nails & 3 plow points.

Jan. 28th. Wednesday. Fine day. Heaviest white frost this morning I have seen for a long time. There was also ice. All hands out today. Put Elsie in the field, & took Eliza about the house till she gets a little stronger.

Rode over to see Uncle Paul. Received from him an order on his factors, R. Brown & Co., for the balance due me for land rent the past year,

---

[7] See Feb. 10, 1852.

[8] Prolapsus: the protrusion of the uterus through the vagina, the result of weakened pelvic support tissue.

amounting to $57. I had already drawn $42. He will not require any of my land this year, having a plenty now of his own, since Uncle Ben has left to him & Uncle Tom during their lives his Carter's Hill tract. I do not in the least regret that Uncle Ben did not leave me anything, and I do not regret that he left Uncle Paul land, but I *do* wish or, I would rather, that he had left him three times the value to the land *than the land,* for it deprives me of the *very convenient* little opportunities of drawing a little money from Uncle Paul, on the strength of leasing him land, which has been of great convenience to me.

That land now belongs to Jenkins, confiscated during the war[9]

Jan. 29th.   Thursday. Mother's boat came over. She has sent for Robert, nothing more than I expected. I am very sorry to have to give him up. He was of great use to me, & would make an excellent house servant, but it can't be helped, he must go. Mother sent me some wild ducks (all I have had this year came from the main), some rice, a peck of oats, &c, also a large trunk for Ernest. Come too late, may be able to get it to him after a while.

Robert was sent back & became my head man but he was no house servant. Remained driver till the war, & became quite distinguished by the Yankees conferring on him the title of D.D.[10] He died very lately. 1876

Robert proved an old rascal. I left everything in his hands & he never saved a single thing for me & has always kept out of my way since peace. He might have saved something if ever so little

Jan. 30th.   Friday. Had 3 hands listing potato land. Have not finished the corn land however. Have over 2 acres to list in old root patch yet, besides 8 or 10 by the pond.

Very unexpected visit from the three Misses Jenkins—Caroline, Amanda & Isabella.[11] Hear that Mrs. Emma Webb has dropsy, & that Dr.

---

[9] Dr. Jenkins redeemed the land in 1876.

[10] Doctor of Divinity. Robert was a leader in the black community during and after slavery.

[11] Caroline (1830–1882), Amanda (b. 1832), and Isabella (1833–1883) Jenkins, daughters of Benjamin Jenkins and Mary Chaplin. Chaplin's second cousins, once removed, on their mother's side, and third cousins on their father's. Emma Jenkins Webb was their first cousin, once removed; the Major and the Doctor were their uncles; Randall Croft was married to their first cousin Charlotte. "Mrs. Caroline Chaplin, wife of John F. Chaplin, and daughter of Mr. Benjamin Jenkins . . . was one of those lovely young ladies who grew up on the Island of St. Helena, and ripened into womanhood a few years before the war. Possessed of an independent fortune each, these young lives were bright with hopeful promise. They were nieces of our old friend, Dr. William J. Jenkins, and in days before the war, like him, their affluent circumstances gave them the means of dispensing much hospitality, added to their refinement and culture, their attractions engaging the attention of a large circle of friends. . . ." (*Palmetto Post,* Beaufort, S.C., Oct. 26, 1882.)

R. Croft was accidentally shot in his arm by his own gun while riding down to Edwin Chaplin's in his buggy yesterday, & that the Major's horse threw him last evening, but did not hurt him a great deal.

Mother's boat returned today. Robert with them. Sent my boat with 3 hands to Beaufort with 2 bales of cotton.

Helen sick. Have expected it a long time.

Feb. 2nd. Monday. Finished listing potato land, all to 2 tasks. Sent Mary to Beaufort in the gig to carry money to pay Fyler & Danner[12] their bill for 1851, amounting to $31.31 cents.

I had Morris & Isaac running out the field, or rather trying to do it. It is the most jumbled up concern I ever saw. Can't get it straight no how we could fix it. Told *them* to go on putting stakes as near to their places as they could, & gave up running the ground for a while. All our work today was useless, but I will try it again soon.

Feb. 7th. Saturday. Clear & too warm for what I have done—killed a hog, the last one I have.

Forgot to mention that someone broke my potato bank last Tuesday night. Don't know, *of course,* who it is. Wish I did. I have established a sort of night guard now, & if the banks are again broken I will make my own Negroes responsible. It is *rather* an uncommon instance of *instinct,* that an entire *stranger* should pass all the seed holes and break the only eating potato hole I have. Very suspicious, very.

Feb. 8th. Sunday. Made an attempt to go to church on horseback. Started but several events transpired against me. The wind was right in my eyes, soon filled them with dust. My horse seemed lame, in fact *is* lame. The saddle girth broke just as I passed Dr. Jenkinses', & I turned back, sat myself down & read *David Copperfield* the rest of the day.[13]

The fact is, I did not leave home in a very pleasant humor. Things don't seem to swim *smoothly.* Sophy—something wrong there, my fault no doubt; but she is *cold* & distant, short to me, *does* everything as usual, but, as though it were her *duty,* not a *pleasure.* I don't love this. She owes *me* no duty, and I can't expect her to have *pleasurable* feelings in doing anything for *me,* tho I would like to *think so.* But I *owe her* a duty, and will *try* to perform it. Please God. She made a pudding today, for the *children.* Maybe she thinks I am vexed. I aint much so *with her.* I was a little put out by a little scrap of paper I came across a day or so ago, but I would not have

---

[12] John S. Fyler and William C. Danner (1825–1885), merchants.
[13] *David Copperfield,* by Charles Dickens, was published serially in the late '40s and first appeared in a complete edition in 1850.

shown that I was, for quiet sake. But I suppose it *was* to be so, & it will *always be so, at times.*

Old Charles made me very mad this morning, but I got over that in time for church. Mother sent a trunk with some things from the main. Sancho brought it from the meeting house.

Feb. 9th. Monday. I was all day engaged in running out ground, and am happy to be able to say that I have succeeded much better than the previous attempts, but have not got through yet. I will go on. To my joy & astonishment Jim came to work today & has no measles atall. But we are almost sure to have them here, for they are so near, only next door (Uncle Paul's). All hands at work today except Eliza. Someone must "lay up" always.

Feb. 10th. Tuesday. All hands out today, *uncommon.* Running out land again. Succeeded beyond my expectations, will perhaps finish running the cotton land tomorrow. I have a little more than half the cotton land listed. I will fall short of manure. The marsh will give out tomorrow. I may, or ought to cut marsh or rushes for the field next the Sands.

Sent Jack to Beaufort today. My cotton is sold, for 29 cents, net proceeds $540.16. God knows if it will pay Webb. I don't think so. I have not received a/c current.

Two letters came today from Bluffton, one to Sophy & one to me from Ernest. I don't think *he* wrote them, at least I hope not. I don't complain of the *writing,* I would be rejoiced to think he could write atall so soon, but the spelling is bad. He got someone of his mates to write for him. He seems dissatisfied, and complains much in his letter to his aunt, wants cake & *money* sent him. I must keep my eyes open. I *myself* am an instance of what money can do for a boy at school. He says he does not get enough to eat. This can hardly be so, he means, I suppose, not enough of cake. I have one his grandmother sent, & will try & get it to him. I must keep my eyes on that same grandmother. This is the first letter I ever received from my child, my first born, my first son, first son's first letter. But I should not say all this till I know that *he* wrote it. I think he did not. Will see.

Feb. 11th. The chimney to my room took fire last night just as I was about going to bed. The Negroes in the yard gave the alarm. Looked out, & the yard was in a complete blaze of sparks, some falling on the roof, but the wind was so high that it blew them off. Had this not been the case, the house must surely have caught, & everything being so very dry, together with the miserably constructed roof (almost impossible to get onto it & not without the greatest risk), nothing in the world could have saved it.

We were all much alarmed. I know I was very uneasy & apprehensive. Such an event as our house being burned is shocking to think of.

Have 28½ acres of cotton land marked & run out. I don't think I will plant any more than that. There is so much joint grass to contend with & I am obliged to plant so very largely of provisions. If I plant, as I contemplate, 25 acres of corn, 4½ root potatoes, 28½ of cotton, 4½ of early peas, 7 of slips & 5 of late peas, in all will make 74½ acres, which, with 10 hands will be about 7 4½/10 acres per hand.

Feb. 14th.   Saturday. Sent Edgar Fripp a load of cotton seed in exchange for a load of his. I am to send another load or 2 for it. Think he might have been neighborly enough to swap even with me.

2 hands cutting rushes. Frank hauling it out on land. Will have to cut again on Monday, not having enough yet. Sent Isaac to Dr. Jenkins to let him look at his finger. I fear he will lose a joint of it. A strolling organ player from Corsica came here about sunset, & asked to stay all night. I let him stay & he gave us some tolerable good music. His instrument played ten tunes.

Feb. 15th.   Sunday. Took all the children to church, but there was no service. I hear that Mrs. McElheran is very sick. Sent the organ man off this morning. A great many Negroes in the neighborhood sick with the measles. We have been very fortunate to escape so far, but I expect to hear of it being on the place every day.

Feb. 17th.   Made a contract with Morcock, ferryman, to cross the ferry till 1st Jan. 1853 for $15.

I am much more forward in my field work than last year. I had just finished ginning the 18th Feb. last year & now I am nearly done listing all my ground. I hope to finish all, except for slips and early peas, next week.

Feb. 19th.   Thursday. Put 3 men getting rails to repair fencing, and started the plow in corn land.

Mother sent Robert over from the main with some wild ducks. He is not to stay however, & she *hints* that Elsie may be sent for. If she is sent for, I shall give Mother to understand that, as it appears she has no *authority* to send or leave Negroes over here, from the main, I shall hereafter decline her doing so.[14]

---

[14] Since the court restored R. L. Baker's control of his wife's estate, authority to manage her slaves rests with him.

Feb. 21st.   Saturday. Sent Jack to Beaufort for a dress of Sophy's made there. Finished listing corn ground, 23 acres. I may list about 3 acres more to plant some early corn. 3 hands splitting rails. Isaac & Thomas hauling sedge to pen.

Feb. 24th.   Partly bargained with Uncle Paul today to sell him Buckskin for $150. I am to have him gelded when the weather gets a little milder, & then he is to take him.

Gave the first allowance out of the corn broken in, in the shuck. Saw Dr. Scott & wife today in the road. He informed me that Mr. Seabrook was really to break up his school in April & remove to Charleston. Sorry for it.

Feb. 25th.   Finished listing early pea land.

Smoked bacon in a barrel, do not like the plan, will not adopt it in future. 1st planting Irish potatoes coming up.

Feb. 26th.   Thursday. All the women throwing out rails, except Moll. She listing a little more pea land to make 5 acres in all for early peas. She will finish tomorrow. Someone, I think, has killed one of my shoats. Finished carting out rails for the new fence across the Riverside Field. This is only a commencement of what I *have* to do.

Feb. 27th.   Planted rye in the yard yesterday & today, also some poppy seed.

Feb. 28th.   Saturday. Judge & Charles repairing fence. Had to quit the cross fence till I get some more rails carted there. Wants about 250 more rails to finish it. I have enough split in the Riverside woods but wish to get them where they will be handier to the fence. I want those in the Riverside woods for the Jenkins line fence.

Received a/c sales of the cotton I sent to Savannah, sold at 23 cents = 6 cents less than I got in Charleston,[15] loss on the lot, $28.98 cents. Very bad, this is the last cotton I will send to Savannah. Received also my a/c current from I. & Webb. I owe them now $385.20 cents. Cotton sent to Savannah netted $105.10. If I had sent it to Charleston I would have got $137. My whole crop netted just $645.16. We must live on very little this year.

[15] The 29 cents per pound Chaplin received for his cotton in Charleston was in the upper range for common Sea Island, indicating he had a clean crop.

March 3rd. Wednesday. Muster Day. Mr. A. A. Fripp[16] was elected first lieutenant of the company.

He died 3 or 4 years ago, quite bad off & quite gray   1876

Baker was to come over & receive tax returns today, but did not.

Women banking corn land & men making fence. I see that my neighbors are banking potato land. I will wait for a while. There will be more rain.

March 4th. Thursday. Men making fence, women banking corn & potato land. Got a cart load of sugarcane seed from Capt. Jno. Fripp. W. W. Fripp sent a mare to Buckskin.

**All of Buckskin's colts turned out well. The colt from this was long in use & a fine horse. **

March 6th. Saturday. All the women banking potato land. 3 hands at the fence got on very slowly.

Fencing was always a tax on this Island. Now, they make none but tie up the few cattle they have. 1876

March 8th. Monday. Planted flax, mustard, saffron, & 1st bed of beans. Transplanted sage.

Jim very sick with measles. Helen sick, hope not the same.

March 10th. 2 hands cutting potatoes to plant. They have rotted considerably. Commenced plowing cotton land. Finished carting rails. Isaac went at the fence. Women banking corn land.

Employed myself today making a gate for the Sands causeway.

March 11th. Thursday. Commenced planting potatoes, planted a little over 7 tasks of common yams, all the seed I have. My seed will surely fall short & I know not where to get more.

Finished the gate I was making, all to putting up. Put all the rails I had on the Orange Grove fence yesterday. Sent 2 hands today to help the Major finish the rest of it (the fence), about 4 tasks. He sends also two hands.

March 15th. Monday. Jim & Helen both came out today. Put them to shelling corn to plant as the ground is too wet for Jim, who is just out from measles.

---

[16] Alviro A. Fripp (1830–1871), planter. Son of William "Good Billy" Fripp, Sr., and Sarah Reynolds. Chaplin's first cousin, twice removed, on his father's side. Eventually but briefly, he owned a 570-acre plantation on the Seaside, east of Tombee.

Washington Fripp sent his mare back to the horse today—did not refuse.

March 16th.　Tuesday. Rain from about 8 a.m. and continued with
hardly any intermission all day. Spent a very gloomy day. Don't know
what I would have done to keep off a fit of blue devils, had it not been for
a novel & cigars.

Commenced planting corn, but rain drove in the hands. Had all the
corn shucked out. It may last me till July. Thrashed out what peas I had
left & put away what I wanted for seed.

Sophy & I sat up (wonderful to tell) till one o'clock, as the Irishman
said, "tomorrow morning," chatting about God knows what. She is a
good soul, God bless her. She is, or shall be, my guardian angel. *Could* she
be anything else? Oh! Me.

**She has been both & a most excellent wife to me & mother to my children. Every-
body has faults, hers are few, & circumstances, trouble, disappointments of many
kinds have somewhat soured her temper, & I should be more patient with her, but I
am also a sufferer & can't always govern my temper, but, without boasting, I think I
do, or try to do so, more than she does　1876**

March 17th.　Item. What shall it be? There is an item, yes, & it shall be
here recorded, but *not now*. I am not likely to forget it. I will only observe
that Sophy & myself are getting into a very bad habit of sitting up very
late at night, even to trespass on the "small hours"——

March 19th.　*Wonderful,* found it *snowing* quite fast this morning. The
ground is too wet for it to lay, & it melts as fast as it falls. This is certainly
an event, or it *happens* to *commemorate* an *event* the most strange, which is to
compose the above *Item.*

I suppose, or rather, calculate, that my planted potatoes are all lost,
the ground is so wet & it is quite cold today. God knows where I will get
any more seed.

It did more good than harm

Cleared off prettily after m. but cold all night. Got very little work out
of the Negroes, they banked a little corn ground.

March 22nd.　Monday. All hands planted corn. Amy & Frank sick since
Saturday, hope they have not the dreaded measles.

**Thought more of measles then than small pox since they have all had the latter
during the war.**

Finished planting corn—24¾ acres. I will plant no corn in April as
formerly. Put all hands to ditching in the evening, except 2, they are sup-

plying over the early corn. What is up looks yellow from the recent cold, and the birds have pulled it very badly.

Item—I hardly see any use in tarring seed corn, the birds pull it off & destroy it after it comes up, if they don't eat it, & they might as well eat it after they pull it. The tar only prevents them from eating it—not from pulling it.

March 23rd. Frank broke out with measles. I think Sancho has them also.

2 hands hoeing out joint grass, all the rest ditching. Finished all the ditching that I think wanting in cotton and corn land. Will have a good deal in the land I intend putting slips in.

Set Charles to whitewashing in the house.

Mother came over, got up here to the landing just at supper time. She had a rough passage & came round by the sound. She brought Robert over, he is now to stay with me, *I hope* always.

And he did, till the war, and lived and died on the place. I made him driver. He did very well, but was not faithful to his trust when the war broke out, never saved me a single thing & got all he could for himself. 1876

March 26th. The secret is out. Sophy, dearest Sophy will be mine. Mother has been told of our love & she is agreeable. God bless everybody, & us in particular.

(April 4th   Coldness, 1st want of confidence)
Sept. 5th, 1876. Coldness, the 40,000th want of control of temper.

March 30th. Tuesday. I had just gone to sleep last night, when I was aroused by old Suky knocking at the door & bawling out that "Marse Ernest come" & sure enough he had come, most unexpectedly, for his vacation was not to begin till next week, but Seabrook had changed his mind. Ernest came in the steamboat from Bluffton yesterday, & landed in Beaufort, where he fortunately found Pope's John who was afoot, but he got him as far as the Indian Hills somehow, walked part of the way. The Captain loaned them his buggy and a mare, & they got down here about 11 o'clock last night. Ernest looks remarkably well & fat. He is still very diffident, & says William Scott[17] wrote the letters for him, he cannot write yet, & is still not pleased with Bluffton.

3 hands planting cotton. Planted 5 acres, 14 in all. Sent Robert to Beaufort for Ernest's trunk.

[17] William Scott (1840–1867). Son of Dr. John A. P. Scott and Sarah Ann Chaplin. Chaplin's first cousin, once removed, and Ernest's second cousin. He was Ernest's age.

April 1st.   Thursday. Agricultural anniversary meeting. D. Jenkins' find——

Finished banking cotton land except 2½ tasks. Got some seed arrow-root of Capt. J. Fripp. Isaac hauling sedge to manure 1½ acres more land for cotton.

Paid my taxes—$22.63.

April 3rd.   Saturday. I went to Beaufort. Things did not come from town that I expected. Dined with Bell.

Finished planting corn through cotton fields & listed 2 acres of land, manured with sedge for cotton. Birds very bad at the corn that is coming up. Have Thomas & Mary, old Isaac there with the gun also. I cannot see the use in tarring the corn seed.

Bought a fine straw hat ($1.50) & a coarse one [   ] for myself today, & one apiece for the boys (50 each).

April 5th.   Monday. Sent the boat & 4 hands to Beaufort for Haskell, & the work he is doing for me.

Fence around graveyard at church

Wind fresh all day, with rain, prevented them from coming down. Gar den, thinned & set out beets & turnips, planted celery, pepper. Supplied mustard, set out a few tomato plants.

April 6th.   Tuesday. Clear, wind high. Haskell did not get down till about 12 m. today. Got the stuff all to the church with 2 carts. Rode to the church with Haskell in the evening. He came back, stayed with me. Planted the 9 tasks of cotton.

April 9th.   Friday. Gave the Negroes the day, being Good Friday.

April 10th.   Saturday. All hands ditching. Sent the boat to Beaufort for things I expect from town—did not get them. They are to be sent the [next] trip of the boat, so I. & Webb writes me. This is the 2nd time I have sent & been disappointed.

April 12th.   Monday. Planted 5¼ acres early peas.

Rode over to Uncle Paul's. He is just from town, & has bought himself a new buggy, & wonderful to tell, given *me* the old sulky.

April 13th.   Went to church. Did nothing but a little priming to the pal-ing. Haskell must finish it before I will do any more— Saw Edgar Fripp at the church. He has W. T. White[18], stonecutter from Charleston, up here,

---

[18] William T. White owned a marble and stone yard.

putting up a family vault for him in the churchyard for himself & wife. **Said vault was a fine affair & did not have to wait very long for its occupants, Edgar & wife.[19] The Yankees broke it open during the war hoping for treasure. It is now somewhat out of order. 1876**

All women hoeing corn, men ditching.

April 14th. Wednesday. Cloudy this morning (good weather cannot last). I went out fishing, first time in my boat this year. Did not get a single bite & saw very few fish taken, although there were a great number of boats out. I got a good soaking coming home, for a very heavy rain came up. So this ends my first day's fishing. Perhaps a bad beginning may make a good ending.

April 15th. All hands hoeing corn. Sent Robert to the village & got the sulky Uncle Paul gave me.

Heard that the fish bit very well at Bay Point yesterday. Some boats took from 12 to 15.

April 16th. Went fishing—took 3, lost 2. I caught 2 & lost 2 myself. A good many boats out, very few fish taken.

April 17th. Saturday. Went to Beaufort in the boat. Took Ernest. Started very early & got back about 3 p.m. Got all the things I sent to Charleston for, also 100 lbs. of leaf tobacco that I did *not* send for. Edward Chaplain got a passage up with me, he got drunk & I would not bring him back, or rather, he could or would not come back.

April 19th. Monday. 3 hands hoeing cotton, 1 hand hoeing corn, & balance hoeing potatoes.

Subscribed to the *Southern Literary Gazette*[20] when I went to Beaufort last. 2 hands sick with bowel complaints.
Alas—those "things from town"

April 27th. Tuesday. My 30th birthday. No more fishing, no drum biting.

April 28th. Mrs. Augusta Perry, wife of Jos. W. Perry died yesterday.[21]

---

[19] Eliza Fripp (1810–1860). Daughter of Isaac Perry Fripp and Mary Pope. Edgar and Eliza both died in 1860.

[20] The *Southern Literary Gazette* styled itself "a large and elegant family Journal." Published weekly until its demise—shortly after Chaplin took out a subscription—this magazine of literature and opinion boasted "a larger amount of original matter than any other paper in the country." It cost $2 a year.

[21] Formerly Augusta Chaplin, third cousin to Thomas B. Chaplin and his children's teacher.

Childbed I hear. I attended her funeral at the Baptist Church at 4 p.m. today. Poor Joe, I feel very sorry for him, only married last June, this the first child. She was a most excellent woman, & a *real* Christian. This is the second wife Perry has lost in the same manner & his brother Tom's wife died in the same way.

April 30th.   Friday. Very warm & clear. Went to Beaufort & took Ernest for the purpose of sending him on in the steamboat to Bluffton, but he found out that Dr. Scott's sons were not going till next Friday, and took on in such a manner & begged so hard for me to let him stay, that I consented, & brought him back home; this will put me to much trouble, I know, but I knew no one going on to Bluffton who I could put Ernest under the care of, & Ernest is so intimate with Bill Scott that I thought he would get along better, & not mind going so much. He promises not to make any fuss next Friday.

May 3rd.   I see no chance of our getting a house at the village for this summer. I saw Dr. Scott yesterday, whose house I expected to get and although Farmer has declined taking it, *I* cannot get it, as the Dr. has concluded to keep it for the benefit of his *servants* who, he says, are accustomed to staying at the village, & he is *afraid they* will get the fever on the plantation. This is real *St. Helena friendship.* I predict that Long Tom Chaplin[22] will stay in the house this summer, from what I have heard, and from what I know of Dr. Scott's deceitfulness. Let it go——
His servants, that were, have learned to stay on the plantation & the Dr. any place he could get. Poor fellow, long dead both he & wife, good people they were   1876

May 4th.   Tuesday. Cloudy this morning with high wind from east. Put all hands (except 2) transplanting & thinning corn. Finished all the corn & I think I will now have a good stand. 2 hands supplying cotton. Gave out my last allowance of corn. This is too bad, I never had such a thing to happen to me before. I sent to town for 100 bushels last week.

May 5th.   Wednesday. Cotton looks dreadful bad this morning. I fear it will not all recover, & I have just finished supplying this morning. I suppose I will have to go all over it again, if I have seed. My early peas are *very* broken. Raked up about a quart in the loft, & sent Moll & Mary to supply them as far as they will go.
    Muster Day—

---

[22] Possibly Thomas Chaplin, Jr., of Ladies Island.

May 7th. Friday. Took Ernest to Beaufort & sent him on to Bluffton. He went off very well this time. Saw Col. Jno. Webb on board the steamer on his way to Bluffton & put Ernest under his care. Steamboat came so late I lost the tide & stayed all night at Morcock's. I expected some corn up from town, but it did not come.

May 10th. Monday. Eliza Jenkins called, pretty much a business visit. She wanted me to give Wm. Jenkins a clearance for $50, as *my share* of [the] rest & residue of Uncle Ben's estate. I told her *I* had no share in Uncle Ben's estate, he had left me nothing in his will, & I had no legal claim; that, if Dr. Jenkins would draw up a release, I sign it & let the money go to its proper source, to Uncle Ben's widow. I am bad off enough, but damned if I begrudge others.

May 13th. Dr. Jenkins called & offered me the $50. I took it, gave him a release, folded it up in a sheet of paper, & directing it to Aunt Betsy Chaplin, requested him to deliver it. Now, if Aunt Betsy thinks proper to make me a present of it, I am not too proud to accept, but I am, to take it in the way it *has* come.

Hands hauling potatoes.

May 14th. Borrowed Uncle Paul's flat & sent up to Beaufort for the corn. They got back at 12 midnight & no corn. What in the devil has got into Webb? This is too bad. My Negroes on half allowance and not a quart of corn in the corn house for horses. I never was in such a fix before. Had to borrow a bushel of Jno. H. Webb[23] to feed the horses on.

May 15th. Saturday. Tried to borrow 10 bushels of corn from Uncle Paul. He *would not oblige me* with more than 5, as I could not return it in any other than gourd seed corn, & he did not feed his Negroes on anything but flint. Selfishness is meanness if not a vice. I offered him more corn than I receive on every bushel—it would not do. "Charity covereth a multitude of sins. Tho a man giveth his own body to be burned, if he hath not charity, it availeth nothing."[24] But I forget, charity is not often found on this island of St. Helena.

Loaned J. H. Webb old Hyder to send to the village for Dr. Jenkins, to his wife. She is quite sick. Hyder has a sore back—no matter, the man's wife is sick.

---

[23] John H. Webb and Thomas L. Webb, Chaplin's cotton factor, were brothers.
[24] I Peter 4:8. "And above all things have fervent charity among yourselves: for charity shall cover the multitude of sins." I Corinthians 13:3. "And though I bestow all my goods to feed the poor, and though I giveth my body to be burned, and have not charity, it profiteth me nothing."

May 17th. Monday. Sent Robert to Beaufort. All hands hoeing cotton. Aunt Betsy called today. Virginia is to stay with Aunt Betsy this summer, by invitation given the other day.

May 18th. Tuesday. Too wet to hoe today—put all hands thinning the cotton hoed the past 2 days. Sophy & I rode over to Jno. Webb's.[25] His wife is a little better but not out of danger. She has dysentery.

The Captain has a good stand of cotton, but very grassy.

May 19th. All hands hoeing 1½ tasks apiece of cotton, & ½ task early corn. Cotton has improved very much since the blow, much of it that I thought dead is now putting out young leaves almost from the roots.

May 20th. Thursday. Some hands thinning & hauling, some hoeing, cotton. Robert & Charles cleaning up & whitewashing my room. I want to get it in good order, painted &c &c &c, not only to make it comfortable for the summer, but in anticipation of a *certain event, to take place in the fall.*

May 21st. Started the flat for Beaufort about 12 m. Wind rather high, but they may get up, & I hope to God I will not be a third time disappointed in getting the corn from town.

Sent 8 dozen bottles to Beaufort to sell.

May 23rd. The flat got back about breakfast time, & thank God, brought 50 bags of corn. I measured 2 bags, they lack about 2 quarts of containing 2 bushels, the quantity they are sent for. Emptied it all out, & gave out 2 weeks' allowance, after dinner. I hope the corn will last me, in fact, *it must*—— The bags I return.

Judy confined about 10 a.m., girl, named Daphne.

May 24th. Monday. I & Sophy rode down to the village & carried Virginia. Spent a pleasant day enough, the folks that were there were very clever. We visited McElhcran, & Bill Jenkins, dined with Aunt Betsy— first rate dinner, ham & turkey. J. H. Webb is there, his wife, tis thought, is a little better. I played several games of billiards, the table in shocking order.

May 25th. Returned the 5 bushels of corn I got of Uncle Paul. Finished painting my chamber, all to the sashes.

May 26th. Sent Robert with Buckskin to Ben Capers to be altered but he came back as he went. Old Capers has a lame mare that he picked up

[25] At Lands End.

cheap in town, and I suppose he has an idea that he can palm her off on me, & possess Buckskin, but it won't go. He told Robert to carry the horse home & tell me to come & see him, for a trade. Ben told Robert to bring the horse back again early tomorrow & he would alter him. I will send him.

May 27th. All hands hoeing & slacking cotton at the Tabby. Sent Buckskin to Ben Capers early this morning. He altered him, & the horse was back here by 8 o'clock a.m. He appeared to be in great pain after he got home, laid down very often & the strain to get up again made him bleed very much. The bleeding slacked towards evening & he seemed much easier. Sent the buggy to the village for Webb's two boys,[26] who are to stay with me till his wife gets better or worse. They got here about 6 p.m., just after a shower.
One other little act of kindness on my part & such as I seldom receive myself

May 29th. I rode down to Lands End with the boys (Webb's & mine). While they were getting some vegetables out of Webb's garden I borrowed a rod & line & went down to Station to try the sheephead. I hardly hoped to catch any, or more than one, but I had luck & sport far, far beyond my anticipations, for I caught 11, *eleven* fine sheephead & lost several bites—& left them biting. But I had to quit, as the tide was rising & I had two creeks to walk across. I left 2 fish with old Captain Wood of the lightship, 2 with Sancho for use of line, brought 7 home, out of which, I sent 2 to Uncle Tom.

May 31st. Monday. The last day of the spring month. Dismal & rainy, rained all last night, and still raining this morning and continued the whole day, without intermission. Hardly put my 2 feet out of doors all day. Negroes did nothing. Raining hard & wind rising at 9 p.m. with not the least appearance of breaking. This is the longest spell of rain we have had for a very long time. Very high tide & a quantity of marsh sedge coming up. This is unfavorable weather for Buckskin. I am obliged to keep him in the stable, and he has swollen very much & is quite stiff behind and drawn up.

June 1st. Tuesday. There is a good deal of water laying about, but not as much in the field as I expected, and only around the ponds. Tides come very high & much sedge floating about but the wind won't let it come up where I want it. Supplied root potato patch & hauled peas today. I had to send two hands to let the water off the corn around the Negro house pond & the big pond.

[26] Thomas P. (b. 1838) and Philip G. (b. 1840) Webb.

June 2nd. Wednesday. Beautiful morning, clear as a bell & pleasantly cool, more like real spring than any weather we had during spring. Finished hauling up peas. Banked up early corn and laid it by. Commenced hoeing 15 acre field of corn, it is very grassy indeed. Went down to Webb's sheephead ground, caught 6, would have caught more but broke my hook & had to quit.

June 3rd. Thursday. Agricultural Society day. Dr. Jenkins found an excellent dinner. He brought out a basket of champagne which is to be paid for out of Edgar Fripp's premium money for corn. It was all drank and very few, if any, went home perfectly sober.

All hands hoeing corn. Buckskin doing well.

June 6th. Sunday. We all went to church except Webb's boys, poor fellows, they have no clothes fit to go in. Saw Virginia at church, she looks very well.

June 8th. Veal market commenced. I killed first, tolerable good meat, and sent to the lodge. I fear I shall not be able to keep in the beef market this summer, having no beeves, & don't know how or where to procure them. Hands hauling corn, I think they will finish the 15 acre field tomorrow. Corn looks very fine, don't think I ever had a prettier crop (taking the whole) of corn, since I have been planting. Saw some stalks as high as I can reach with my umbrella & shooting five & seven silks.[27]

June 10th. Thursday. Sent Robert to Beaufort & my buggy pole to Henry Fripp to be mended, if he can do it. I got it broken while riding out yesterday evening.

4 hands listing slip ground, Isaac tracking ditto, 2 hands hoeing corn & 2 hands cotton. Mary hauling some high tasks of potatoes.

Took a swarm of bees today, making 8 in all.

N.B. They left in the evening, *damn them.*

June 13th. Sunday. Went to church. Heard that two Negroes are to be tried for their life tomorrow in Beaufort for murder, all belong to Lewis Sams[28] I believe.

June 14th. Judy came out of her confinement (3 weeks). Hands hauled a task of potatoes & hoed a task each of cotton.

---

[27] The corn is blossoming.
[28] Either Lewis Reeve Sams (1810–1888), physician and planter, and Chaplin's second cousin, or his father, Lewis Reeve Sams, Sr. (1784–1856), planter.

July 1st. Some villains have been killing my sheep—3 last night & 2 when I was away. Charles says the two were killed by dogs. I don't believe so now. I must make some effort to find out about it, & if possible to stop it. Sent for J. L. Chaplin to meet me at the pen as I heard that his dog was seen where the sheep were killed. He came, found his dog there & shot him, but we could find no traces of the meat or the rogues.

July 2nd. Friday. Clear in the morning, heavy rain about dinner time. J. H. Webb came down & after we rode over his crop he dined with me. I lent him my sulky & horse to go back to the village. He came down with Dr. Jenkins & it is strange, or rather, *mean* in him not to let him have some way to get back, & I so much worse off for horses than he.

Men & 2 women ditching. Finished hauling through cotton, & commenced again to hoe. 2 hands regulating cotton. Webb thinks I have a pretty good crop but it is very broken. My early peas are bearing finely.

July 4th. Sunday. Independence Day. Celebrated I suppose, tomorrow. Poor will be the celebration on this Island, not even an oration can be got up nowadays. We will have a dinner as usual tomorrow. Cloudy this morning. Heavy rain about daylight. Brightened up a little, & I & the boys went to church. The church in mourning for the death of Bishop Gadsden.[29] Virginia came home with me. I fear tis running a risk, but as there is holiday tomorrow, Aunt Betsy told her to come and stay till Tuesday when I will take her back. This must positively be the last time she spends a night down here this summer.

July 5th. Monday. Went to muster. T. B. Fripp's first turnout as captain of the company. He treated to a basket of champagne, which of course made everybody quite lively. There was an election for 2nd lieutenant & ensign, which created a little excitement. E. W. Chaplin[30] elected 2nd lieutnt. & E. B. Reynolds[31] ensign.

All hands planting slips—2 acres, 6¼ in all.

July 7th. Wednesday. Clear & hot, and very, very hot for *me,* for I had a scorching fever from 10 o'clock a.m. till midnight, when it went off. Took

[29] Christopher Edwards Gadsden (1785–1852), Episcopal bishop of the Diocese of South Carolina from 1840 until his death. During his tenure he consecrated twenty-two new churches, including the new building of the St. Helena Protestant Episcopal Church in Beaufort. A classmate of John C. Calhoun at Yale, Gadsden officiated at Calhoun's funeral in Charleston, in 1850.

[30] Edwin W. Chaplin was Thomas B. Chaplin's first cousin, once removed, and first cousin to Thomas B. Fripp, captain of the St. Helena Mounted Riflemen.

[31] Edward B. Reynolds (b. 1829). Son of Richard M. Reynolds of Ladies Island. Listed as "artist" in the 1860 census.

a dose of hippo[32] about 12 m., which brought a little bile. Took salts at night, operated well before morning. I have not been so sick for many years before. I think the fever proceeded from cold I have taken, & my fool's trip to the main laid the foundation.

All hands hoeing cotton. 4th hoeing.

July 10th. Saturday. Heavy rain this morning. Sent Robert & Jim to the main with the things that came from town for Mother, also with a hint to her that she had better come over, for I was quite sick (from Sophy). Dr. Jenkins & T. B. Fripp came to see me. The Dr. gave me a large dose of quinine, which made me as deaf as a teaspoon. I have no fever today, the first time it has been off since I was first taken. Hope to God it may keep off, being no agreeable companion. Dr. Jenkins, T. B. Fripp, Alviro & Papa, Good Billy,[33] & the 3 Misses Jenkins, &c &c &c, leave on a Northern tour of pleasure, *criticism,* & *discovery,* on Monday, 12th inst. Ye Gods! I want them to bring *me* a small piece of the North Pole, a specimen of the Croton Waterworks[34] (not to speak of Fair Mount[35]), and just the *tip end* of the Bunker Hill Monument,[36] a *dish* from Saratoga,[37] & a piece of the *National Conventions,*[38] if any to be had for the asking——

---

[32] Ipecacuanha, or ipecac: an emetic drug from the dried roots of a tropical plant in the madder family.

[33] "Papa" *is* "Good Billy."

[34] An article on New York City's Croton Aqueduct appeared in the Charleston *Mercury* in Jan. 1851. The aqueduct carried water from upstate to Manhattan through 200 miles of pipes. The *Mercury*'s correspondent was astonished by the "enormous waste of water by the population," which was a source of complaint by the aqueduct's managers.

[35] Fairmount Water Works, in Fairmount Park, Philadelphia, was visited in 1842 by Charles Dickens, who found the elevated reservoirs "no less ornamental than useful, tastefully laid out in a public garden, and kept in the neatest order."

[36] Boston's monument to the Battle of Bunker Hill, the first major battle of the American Revolution, was beset by financial problems and controversy through its completion in 1843. South Carolina architect Robert Mills protested that his design had been used—slightly altered—without acknowledgment.

[37] Saratoga Springs, in New York's Adirondack Mountains, attracted not only invalids but "the gay and fashionable." Southern planters flocked there in summer. William J. Grayson painted a gloomy picture of his stay at the spa: "We went through a month of Saratoga as summer idlers commonly do; inhaled the dust of the streets, drank the Congress water; rushed with the crowd to dinner and supper; occupied a room ten foot square; slept on a hard mattress of straw or corn shucks; and paid for all these enjoyments the long bill that Northern watering places inflict on Southern simpletons." (*The Autobiography of William J. Grayson,* ed. Samuel Gaillard Stoney, *South Carolina Historical Magazine,* vol. 49, 1948, 218.)

[38] Only weeks before the St. Helena travelers departed, the two major national political parties held their presidential nominating conventions in Baltimore, a popular stop on the tourist train North. After reaching a hopeless deadlock, the Democratic party nominated a compromise candidate, Franklin Pierce, of New Hampshire, on a platform which included a denunciation of "Abolitionists and all others" who tried "to induce Congress to interfere with the question of slavery." The Whig party convention was equally tumultuous. On the fifty-third ballot, General Winfield Scott was

All hands hauling cotton today, 4th hauling comm[enced]. I would rather Morris had put them to listing pea land, but I can't see after it.

July 11th. Sunday. Rain again this morning. I had no fever all day—but was very sick last night, & all day with diarrhea, or dysentery. Had many operations, almost all *blood* & blood matter. It makes me very uneasy. I dread this even more than fever. Operations not so frequent in the evening.

July 13th. Tuesday. Mosquitoes very bad. I feel much better this morning, no fever, and bowels in much better order. Hope I may continue to improve.

All hands hoeing cotton. . . .
well if I had gone then, 1885

July 14th. Virginia's birthday—she is 10 years old. How time flies. Sent Isaac to Beaufort for some ice &c &c.

Some hands stripping blades off early corn, balance hoeing cotton. I have not another allowance of corn. If my early corn is not fit to eat by next week, I don't know what I shall do.

July 16th. The hands picked 9 baskets of peas this morning. I will have to give them out as part allowance next week, and feed the horses on them altogether. Only wish they had ripened three weeks ago. I am sorry I have not got my peas ground ready to plant with this rain, it is high time they were in the ground. I always plant too late. All hands listing pea ground, 5½ acres listed today in all. Started the plow through the listed ground. Heavy growth of wild peas on the land.

July 17th. Saturday. Sent Robert & Frank to Beaufort last evening for some groceries I expect from town. They got back about 10 a.m., got all the things, but a bag of coffee that was lost.

Killed lamb for market, 2nd killing for me on 2nd round.

Picked 8 baskets of peas this morning, 17 baskets in all.

July 19th. Monday. 3 hands planting cowpeas, 3 sick, the rest banking peas ground, Jack plowing.

Sent Robert to Beaufort with Ben Chaplin to try & find my bag of coffee. Heard that Edwin Chaplin had brought it from Beaufort for me. Sent there after it—got the bag of coffee.

---

nominated for President. Pierce won the general election, defeating Scott and Free-Soil candidate John Hale in all but four states. The bleak campaign, however, was in sharp contrast to the noisy conventions.

Drove Buckskin in Uncle Paul's buggy. He drew finely, a little lame yet. I will send him over tomorrow, when the old gentleman can hand me over $150, the price he is to pay me for him & a very good one it is.

July 20th. All hands banking ground & planting peas. Gave out half allowance of peas, & half of corn, almost the last of the bought corn.

July 27th. Tuesday. Bought 7 bushels of corn at the store, 75 cents per bushel. My early corn not yet dry enough to break in. All hands hauling slips. Finished all to 2½ tasks. Brought in blades in the evening.

July 30th. Friday. Went to Beaufort in the buggy. Stayed till the steamboat came. Saw Mr. Seabrook on board on his way to Bluffton from a trip to town. Sent a pair of shoes by him to Ernest.

Dr. Jenkins & party returned from their Northern tour. They have been absent just 18 days, & been as far as Albany. Traveled so fast that they saw nothing, fatigued themselves almost to death, and returned quite sick of their trip, no wonder.

They complained of not getting rice to eat, & could not stand that*

They had no way of getting to the village, no one expecting them of course, so I offered them the use of my buggy, which they accepted, and as I had no other way of getting home, I had to go along with them. I took Eliza & Caroline Jenkins with me on the seat, & W. Jenkins & John Fripp[39] rode behind. Mr. McElheran took Amanda & Isabella in his gig. He stood up behind & drove them. Such a cavalcade—but we *got on* very well, & to the village about tea time. The folks were all taken by surprise and I surely did not expect when I left home of getting there before I returned. I took a cup of coffee with Aunt Betsy, and eat supper with W. Jenkins. John Fripp loaned me Tom Fripp's horse & buggy, and I left about 9 o'clock. Got home after 11 o'clock. They all seemed very anxious for me to stay all night, & I felt quite sick & tired enough to do so, for I left home sick in the morning, but I knew Sophy and Mother would be uneasy, so I determined to come. Left my old horses and buggy with William, to come down in the morning. I did not know that John Fripp went with the party, but he could not let his sweetheart[40] go without him. Tom Fripp did not come back with them, but went on to Niagara, & showed sense in doing so. He & Alviro Fripp are together & will no doubt enjoy themselves. I think it a pity that people should have it in their power to go traveling and seeing the world who cannot appreciate or enjoy the means in their hands.

[39] John Edwin Fripp (1831–1906). Son of William B. Fripp and Eliza Chaplin. Brother of Thomas B. and William P. Fripp. First cousin, once removed, to Thomas B. Chaplin, on his mother's side.
[40] Isabella Jenkins. She married John Fripp in 1853.

July 31st. My buggy got home this morning, horses looked quite used up. All hands stripping blades, pond field.

Aug. 1st. Sunday. Had fever all last night & all day today.

Aug. 2nd. Monday. Fever cooled this morning but came on hot again at night. I sent for Wm. Jenkins yesterday, but he could not come as his wife was quite sick. He wrote me quite a friendly note, & sent 6 blue pills which I took.

Aug. 4th. All hands hoeing slips & brought in the blades stripped yesterday. I feel much better today. Came downstairs & even took a ride in the field. There is, I hear, much sickness in the neighborhood. Dr. Jenkins told yesterday that he had 20 Negroes down with fever.

Aug. 5th. Thursday. Benj. Chaplin killed beef for market today, we being on shares this year. I got him to kill the first beef but as there is only 6 in the market, I will draw off, pay Ben Chaplin for half his beef & not go round again.

I attend meeting of Agricultural Society. Mr. Capers found dinner in my place & I am to take his turn——

I found an open pod of cotton & carried out.

Aug. 8th. Sunday. Did not go to church. Much sickness among the Negroes. Mary's child Amy, the youngest, died in convulsions this evening. She was only sick a few days. Peg's youngest child had fits yesterday, but got over them.

Heard that caterpillars were seen in Uncle Paul's cotton field.

Aug. 14th. Sent Robert to Beaufort to buy some medicine. I have used all I have. Never heard of so much sickness all over the Island.

Finished turning down corn. Six tasks of peas still to work.

Aug. 15th. Sunday. Went to church. Got there too late to go in.

Aug. 16th. Monday. All hands out today—thank God, and all picking peas. This is the last of them, & only a little over a half a crop. The last picking are quite black from so much rain.

Aunt Betsy came down to her place today, & sent Virginia over to spend the day with us. She looks very well & we think has grown tall, the dear child. She seems so delighted to be at home. I took her over to return with Aunt Betsy in the evening.

Broke in ½ an acre of early corn, 17 baskets. Making now in all, broken off of 1½ acres, 40 baskets, or about 20 bushels. Picked in 130 pumpkins.

Aug. 18th.   Wednesday. Clear & hot. Robbed my beehives, 8 of them. They turned out pretty well & very fine honey.

Aug. 22nd.   Sunday. Cloudy. I foolishly went to church. Had rain on me nearly all the way there & back. Very few persons were out. Coz. Ann Fripp & the Jenkins young ladies,[41] they were just leaving in a hard rain as I drove up. Mr. McE. told me he had read *prayers,* but no preaching.

    Sent Jack to village to ask Dr. Jenkins to come down & see Mother. She is worse.

    The day is fixed—3rd of September.[42]

Aug. 24th.   Tuesday. Gave out the first allowance of potatoes (reds). They are only tolerable. Took nearly a task for ½ week's allowance. They will not improve, nearly *all* are large to eat. So must be satisfied.

    Marion Chaplin[43] killed a most mean veal for market today. I won't stand this. I give the best I have & some members of the market try to kill the meanest they have.

Aug. 26th.   Thursday. Aunts Betsy & Martha came down to see Mother today. She seems quite sick. Virginia came with them and little Sissy Jenkins.[44] The two girls stayed to dinner. Sophy & I drove them over in the evening. We then drove over to the Riverside, to see if we could do anything for J. L. Chaplin & family, having heard that they were all sick. Found them all looking badly, but Tom the only one in bed. The old man looks horrible. Promised to send them some medicines & comforts, from our own slender store, and a servant to help them till they get better. I am truly sorry for Mrs. Chaplin.

Aug. 28th.   Saturday. Was quite sick all last night, not much better this morning. No fever till ? p.m. Came on hot, took blue pill. Operated well during the night.

Aug. 29th.   Sunday. Laid abed & took quinine all day.

---

[41] Cousin Ann Fripp was Caroline, Amanda, and Isabella Jenkins's aunt.

[42] Chaplin and Sophy would be married on the *second* of September.

[43] Marion Thomas Chaplin (1825–1865), planter. Son of John F. Chaplin and Ann Rebecca Fripp. Husband of Sarah Fripp. Chaplin's first cousin, once removed, on his father's side. Lived in the northeast corner of St. Helena Island, above the village.

[44] Daughter of Dr. William Jenkins and Eliza Chaplin. She and Virginia were second cousins.

Aug. 30th. Monday. No fever this morning, came downstairs very weak.

Storm—I neglected to state that the wind commenced blowing violently on Friday about midday, from south. Continued till Saturday morning, with driving rain Friday night. I hope this is the [last] storm of the season for it has done little damage & a trifle in comparison with the storm about the same time last year. I have not heard of or seen any caterpillars in my field as yet.

The last week's allowance of potatoes took something over a task. All the women picking cotton today. I weighed one sheet, 20 lbs. Cotton opening prettily. There is and has been much sickness. I have only one sick today out of the field. Sophy sick in bed all day.

Aug. 31st. Tuesday. Clear & pleasant mornings. I have no fever today, feel much stronger & better, & hope I am clear now, please God. Sophy is also better today & downstairs. Mother is also about, thank God for all. Potatoes do not turn out as well today as they did the last allowance day. Don't know the reason.

Daniel & Eugene both taken with fever today, and both at the very same time began to complain. I have been looking for it for some time.

Sept. 1st. Daniel has no fever today, Eugene has, went off in the evening. All the women picking cotton, average about 33 lbs.

Sept. 2nd. Thursday. Neither of the boys had any fever this morning, but Eugene's came on about 10 a.m. quite hot.

This is doubly unfortunate, as Sophy & myself had arranged to meet Mr. McElheran at the church today, & be married. And, altho the matter was partially, or rather in a fair way of being postponed, we nevertheless made up our minds, late this morning, that our plans had better be carried into effect today, for reasons I shall hereafter state. Consequently I wrote and sent a note to Mr. McElheran to meet us at the church at 4½ p.m. Sophy wrote one also to Aunt Betsy requesting her to be there & to bring Virginia. I sent to ask Uncle Paul. These are all we expect (I am writing at 12 m., the *results* will be stated after). The only thing I truly regret is that my dear Mother is not able from recent illness to be present. She could not stand the ride to the church. I should feel much more happiness could she see me married to the *only woman I know* that *I believe* can contribute to my future happiness and the welfare of my children, for who can feel that love for & interest in *them* as *Sophy,* the *loved* & *loving* sister of their *dear mother.*

Now for our reasons, or rather *my* reasons for thus seemingly hurrying the matter. We are, or have been, all sick. The children are now sick. It is necessary that we should help & attend each other, the children in Sophy's room, & my wish to be near or have free access to them at all &

anytime, which cannot be done with propriety under present circumstances; we were *engaged*, & have been so for some time, & would be married at some time. Why defer it? I can see no reason, or at least no *pressing* one, living in the same house, in constant communication, and in love, engaged—tis better we were man & wife, & I trust God we will be before five o'clock this evening.

8 o'clock p.m. Tis all over. We went to the church a little before 5 o'clock. Met Mr. McE., Aunt Betsy & Virginia & Uncle Paul. I requested Uncle Paul to act the part of a friend in the ceremony of giving away, which he did, and with much grace. The ceremony was very soon over & we were pronounced man & wife.

Received the congratulations of all & hurried off home, for we left Eugene with a hot fever on him. Poor Virginia. She cried bitterly to return with us, but that of course was not to be thought of for a moment. We took Daniel with us, but poor fellow he had fever before he got home. Sophy & I thought *surely* that our engagement was a profound secret. We had told it to no one in the world except Mother, but *there* was the source through which it got out. *She* told it to Saxby, though I begged her to tell *no one*, & he least of all would *I* tell. Saxby told it to Minott, & I suppose everyone else he knew. Minott gazetted the village with the news; I will know hereafter how to keep my own confidence.

I never have & never will* *1877

The Negroes today averaged about 37½ lbs. cotton.

Sept. 3rd.　　Friday. Supplied over turnips. Sent Robert & 2 hands to Beaufort.

Sept. 4th.　　Saturday. Robert got back this morning, brought a barrel of ice & bale of cloth for sheets from town. Weighed off cotton. Have in, 1005 lbs. assorted.

Sophy has been quite sick all day, hot fever. She had fever yesterday, but not so sick as she has been today. Gave her today, 30 grs. of blue pill. Neither of the boys have not had any fever today. God grant they may have no more. This is fine beginning of our honeymoon.

Sept. 5th.　　Sophy is quite sick all last night, much better this morning. The boys are quite lively, but I shall ply the quinine again today. Mother has treated herself to another dose of "Lobelia Inflata"[45] today. She takes too much medicine, when she requires stimulants. If she don't mind, she will get so "Inflatulated" she will go up like a balloon one of these odd days.

---

[45] An emetic herb in an alcoholic solution.

Sept. 8th. Wednesday. Rain. Rain. Very heavy last night & this morning, held up about 12 m. No cotton picked this week. Broke in 2 tasks of early corn for the house use, 22 baskets.[46] Have 2 tasks left for seed.

Sept. 9th. Thursday. When will this rain stop? It is ruining the cotton. The seeds are actually sprouting in the [   ] & much cotton beat down in the dirt, [   ] What is open in the pod is mostly rotten [   ] I have the hands picking today, but [   ] they pick looks very bad.

I have not been able to find any caterpillars myself, yet. Don't think, if they had taken the field, that they would have done more or as much damage as the rain has. This is the 7th day it has rained. The fine show of top fruit I had has nearly all cast off, and many small pods rotted. Slips & peas look fine, but this wet weather, I think, will make the peas rust.

Mother's boat came over from the main today. They have also had much rain over there.

Sept. 11th. Saturday. I was in hopes that this day would be clear, but, as fate has so decreed, rain last night, some sunshine & several showers today, just sunshine enough to induce me to have my cotton put out. Then before you are aware, a shower comes up & soaks it all again. Raining at bedtime, and less appearances of clearing than last night. However, let us be thankful for [   ] ravages of storm & rain has been of the [   ] devastating character in the upper [   ]
All this as nothing to war & famine

Sept. 12th. Sunday. This is the tenth day we have had rain, but the wind about 4 p.m. got round to N.W. & it looks clear on that horizon. Besides the weather has turned considerably cooler, so I am in hopes & am of the opinion that we will have a clear day tomorrow.

Burned the lampers[47] out of Tom Jones' mouth today. Hyder very lame, can hardly walk.

Sept. 13th. Monday. Clear & delightfully cool this morning. Gave out the 4th week's allowance and have dry down 5½ tasks, all hands picking cotton.

Sept. 18th. Saturday. I felt very badly last Tuesday, & all day Wednesday—on Wednesday was taken with fever again, fourth time. Up the next morning, but down again with chill & then fever about 10 a.m. Just kept

---

[46] Twenty-two baskets per half acre, or twenty-two bushels to the acre.
[47] Lampas: a swollen palate in a horse, caused by congestion.

up long enough to cross the creek & shoot a beef for market, & had to kill one of my match steers. Would rather have given, if able, $20 than to have done so, but could not help it. Fever held on till early this morning, when I took large doses of quinine, & kept it off all day.

Aunt Betsy came here & brought Virginia. Sophy & I rode over to leave her with Aunt B. in the afternoon. I was hardly able to stand it, but the ride did her good. Daniel taken with fever today, 2nd time for him. Poor little fellow, he looks very badly.

Last kill of lamb market today. O. P. Fripp killed for me.

Sept. 20th.   Monday. Clear & pleasant. Mosquitoes very bad again. Heard Uncle Paul was sick, went to see him. Found him better. Daniel had fever nearly all day. Some Negroes picked as high as 50 pounds.

Sept. 21st.   Tuesday. Daniel still with fever, gave him 12 grs. blue pill today. Mother has fever again, I feel much better.

Negroes did not pick well today.

Sept. 22nd.   I rode down to the village, dined with Aunt Betsy. Played several games of billiards.

Virginia was not well, & has not been to school this week. The child looks very badly. She had a little fever last night, and sore throat today. I wish it was so that she could stay with us, she ought never to be from home. Daniel better today. Gave him oil to carry off the blue pill. It operated finely, & he had no fever & should have taken quinine all day, but my not being at home, he did not get it.

Sept. 24th.   I went to Henry Fripp's shop to try and get my sulky springs fixed, but he made them worse than ever, for I can't use them atall. I will have to send them back to him.

Simon went to Beaufort for ice, but got none. Don't know why Webb does not send it every Friday.

Sept. 29th.   Wednesday. Beautiful day. All hands picking, except Isaac, he at an endless job, making up garden fence of old railings. Amy I took out to attend Sophy, but as she is better & downstairs today, I think I will send her back. Charles does little or nothing as usual. Hands picked well, for my Negroes, over 50.

I have in now assorted 3028 lbs., and I judge, about 2000 not assorted.[48]

---

[48] Once ginned and packed, this quantity will reduce to three bales.

Sept. 30th.   Thursday. 12 hands picking cotton today.

Borrowed Dr. Jenkins' large tent in anticipation of going to the Island next week with the family, but it would suit me badly to go now. I ought to break in corn next week, or the peas will come on me when I can't pick them. I don't think I can ever pick them all, they are bearing so well.

Oct. 1st.   Friday. Negroes picked badly (yesterday), only averaged 33⅓ lbs. They picked at the Sands, where the cotton very short, the worst of the crop. But I think a little cowhide will make them do better.
All talk about cowhide with me.

Had all hands this morning while the dew is wet, picking what late shiny peas are ripe. I have only 3 tasks. Negroes picked well today, they averaged 47 lbs., the highest, Peg, picked 57 lbs. 13 hands brought me in 610 lbs. I consider this very good.

Mother sick again today. I think she and I both eat too many boiled mullets.

Oct. 2nd.   Saturday. Mother's large boat came over for us all to go to the Island next week. This is a trip I make with the greatest reluctance. I will not, if I can help it, take a single hand out of the field for this unnecessary jaunt. I will have all the trouble & worry of getting things ready, and it is so long since I have been on a maneuver, I hardly know what to do, or what to prepare. I think we will all be sick of it before it is over, perhaps sick bodily as well as mentally.

A boy named Isaac, belonging to Mother, came in the boat. He has run away from his employers in town. Don't know what Mother intends doing with him, think she had better send him back again, but how she is to do so is the question.

Sent Robert to Beaufort.

Negroes picked today better than yesterday. Peggy got as high as 60 lbs., and the average, 49⁸⁄₁₃ lbs. Gave Mother's Negroes 2½ bushels of potatoes to last them till we come from the Island. They say the potato crop at the Point is very poor, & will not last 2 weeks longer.

Oct. 4th.   Everything astir to go down to Skull's Inlet. So my journal must rest till we return.

Gave out 7th allowance potatoes and 2nd of yams. My reds lasted 5 weeks. The yams, so far, do better than the reds did.

Oct. 7th.   Thursday. We returned from the Island today, all of us worse off than when we went down. In the first place, Sophy had fever before we got out of sight of home. She got better, and tho unwell on the Island, she returned without fever. We camped on Chaplin's Island side of Skull's Inlet, a very good place, quite open to the sea, & at low water a splendid beach, some places more than a mile in width. We got fish enough to eat, none to bring home, except one cavally. Our tent was very comfortable, but the mosquitoes and gnats were intolerable. Our nets were no protection. There was no sleeping at night. Mother stood all very well, and of course, was made the most comfortably off, but she got into one of her tantrums, and made things unpleasant. I was taken with fever on Wednesday, and was determined to leave on the next day. And so we did. I was sick all night & Thursday morning, till late. We did not get off before about 11 a.m. Had a warm but quick trip, got home early in the evening. I went directly to bed, & know nothing more.

Oct. 9th.   Saturday. To our great astonishment, Mother got ready and went home to the main today. She appeared to be angry with everyone for what, God knows. She told none of the family goodbye. I did not see her, being in bed with a hot fever on me at the time she went. I hardly thought *she* would leave *me thus*—perhaps never to meet again, but so it is. Sophy got up to see her off & give her breakfast, & did everything she could to make her comfortable, but she hardly noticed her, actually treated her with contempt, not deigning to say goodbye. This manner of *marked* insolence that Mother has treated *both* my *wives* in succession is beyond endurance, it *ought,* it *must* and *shall be resented.*
How foolish this appears now so many years after '76
The wind blew fresh nearly all day, on the rise all the time, and at night there was a violent storm of wind and rain. The windows were blown loose, glasses smashed and rain beating in, and though I was quite sick, had to get up and fasten windows as well as their broken bolts would admit. And finally we had to leave our room and make a bed on the floor in the children's room. There was no servant in the house except a stupid little girl. The storm came from south & S.W. It lulled just before day, but there was no sleeping all night.

I thought often of Mother, and wondered if she escaped it. I hope to God she did, for no boat could have stood it. I never knew the wind to blow so fiercely—the house rocked like a cradle.

Oct. 10th.   Sunday. This morning the sun is out bright as ever, but everything shows the effect of the wind. Cotton all wiped out, trees almost bare of leaves, the old mill house blown down, and my cotton house careened over about 6 inches. Some of my field fence blown flat. I had that fixed up immediately. In all, not as much damage as I expected there would be.

Oct. 12th.   Tuesday. The storm has blasted the peas so much that I put all hands to picking—got 29 sheets. I was very sick all day, in bed, fever.

Oct. 13th. Thank God I was able to get up today & take a little walk—very weak.

All hands at the peas, 33 sheets today. Sent Judge for oysters which I relished exceedingly, but they made Soph. sick.

Oct. 14th. I feel much better & stronger, thank God, but my dear wife is quite sick. It is first one, then the other. She—in fact—we both look very badly. I never saw myself look so badly in my life, neither have I seen her look so thin & pale.

∗∗*1868   Pity we had not both died then and there.* ∗∗

Negroes picked 36 sheets peas today.

Oct. 15th. Friday. Quite cool this morning, clear and one of the most delightful days I ever felt or saw.

I saw caterpillars in the cotton today for the first time, but the Negroes saw several days ago. They can do no harm unless they eat the pods—there is nothing else left for them to eat. I made a finish of my peas today, I have picked all. There is not a second picking, but I shall save as many of the vines as I possibly can. I have made in all, 131 heavy sheets, weighing on average something near 75 lbs.

Oct. 16th. Saturday. 3 hands picking cotton, all the rest cutting pea vines. Killed a yearling bull for the Negroes. Altered & marked 3 others the same size.

Oct. 19th. Gave out 9th allowance potatoes. Got in all the pea vines that I had cut, & these I think are more than I can possibly use this winter, independent of the fine crop of blades I made. I am in expectation of being able to sell 4 or 5 thousand weight of blades next summer. All hands picking cotton, and a little better than yesterday. There is a very good blow in the field, and the hands should pick more.

Oct. 21st. Drove Tom Jones in the buggy with Duchess. He drew *remarkably* fine. I never drove or handled a horse for the first trial that pleased me so much. He is one of the *gayest* movers I ever saw, and withal, very gentle, no disposition to kick about him, but *very* full of life.

Commenced digging potatoes *expressly* for horse & oxen feed—

Oct. 24th. Sunday. Clear & pleasant. We all went to church. Tom Jones & Duchess in the buggy. Jones is a tip top horse, I like him more than ever. He bids fair to be a horse of first rate bottom[49] & much life.

∗∗*proved just so* ∗∗

---

[49] Great endurance.

Heard that Mother has been very sick since she went to the main. Nothing more than I expected. She did not write, but I heard through Tom Fripp who has been to the main. She would not let me know of her sickness for fear I should go over.

Oct. 25th. Monday. Gave out 10th allowance of root potatoes. Commenced breaking corn, had every Negro I could muster at it, in all about 16 hands.

I was getting up again in the world

Don't exactly know how much ground I broke over, something about 6 acres, got in about 14 horse cart loads. Corn very sound & good quality, considering all the rain & wind we have had.

Oct. 30th. Saturday. Rainy all the morning. Had the Negroes whipping out cotton. Weighed off 2659 lbs., unassorted—

Aunt Betsy brought Virginia down today. She returned in the evening. Had rain on them.

Oct. 31st. Sunday. Clear & warm. Daniel & I went to church. I came home sick & had fever all night & all the next day.

Flora had a calf, some few days ago.

Nov. 2nd. Tuesday. All hands but 4 picking cotton, 2 making garden fence, 1 carting sedge, and Amy cooking. Suky very sick.

This day is one of sad mourning to me, being the 1st anniversary of the most melancholy event of my past life.

Alas—how many have I passed   Oct. 3rd 1868

Nov. 7th. Old Nelly died last night, complete old age.

Nov. 8th. Monday. Clear & very cool this morning. I went to the village to take Virginia, returned to 3 o'clock dinner. Saw Ned Capers at the village, we played a couple of games [of] billiards. He confided to me that he was actually engaged to be married to Caroline Scott.[50] This is somewhat astonishing.

& it was all fudge & conceit on the part of Ned. He is not married to anyone yet, & Caroline married Ben Bailey[51] of Wadmalaw Island. 1876

**1877. Ned, like myself, has no home. He is with his brother Frank, staying at my old place on this Island, keeping a little shop & has a col'd living with him, the only wife he ever had or will have. He looks quite old & broken, perfectly white. **

Had hands digging groundnuts today. Got about 4 baskets.

[50] Caroline Scott (b. 1837). Daughter of Dr. John A. P. Scott and Sarah Ann Chaplin. Sister of Catherine Scott and Julia Scott Pope. First cousin, once removed, to Thomas B. Chaplin on her mother's side. Ned was seventeen years her elder.

[51] Benjamin Bailey (b. 1830). Son of Benjamin Bailey and Mary W. Townsend.

Nov. 10th. Wednesday. I was sick in bed all day, 11th attack fever.

Nov. 11th. Thursday. Rain all day, very high tides. Hands in barn cleaning cotton.

I feel much better but have to keep the house this weather. God only knows what I would do but for my dear, attentive & affectionate Sophy. May God bless & protect her always.

Oh my God why could she not continue so.

Nov. 13th. Saturday. Very high tides. Water got into places I never saw it in before. Mother sent me 3 bacon hogs. All the women digging groundnuts. More trouble than profit, considerably. I don't think I shall ever plant any more, only to get a few to eat.

Same opinion in 1885

Nov. 17th. Wednesday. Cloudy, warm, and damp all day, several light showers. I commenced digging slips, bad weather for the work. I will not cover them up however till they get a good sun on them, and if this weather lasts I will feed them away.

Some brimstones dug today turned out well, about 2 bushels per row, & very large. Dug today a little over 2 tasks of ground. I see that my cattle are beginning to trouble the field already.

Killed one of the hogs for pork.

Nov. 18th. No sunshine to dry the slips dug yesterday. I fear I will lose them. Negroes assorting cotton & groundnuts.

Mother's boat got over to the wharf after dark with 2 more hogs.

Nov. 19th. Friday. Cold this morning, but no frost. Heavy black clouds around the horizon. It seems I am destined to lose my slips. Digging slips with all hands, not turning out as well as on Wednesday, but pretty good. Dug about 1 acre—making 1¾ acres in all dug. 6 banks eating, 3 of seed, 20 to 25 baskets in the former and from 15 to 20 in the latter.

Nov. 20th. Saturday. Heavy frost this morning, but I have heard of no ice. 12 hands digging today. Have in 9 banks of eating potatoes up today, have over 5 acres to dig yet.

The Rev'd Jos. Wallace[52] was buried today. He died on Thursday, of fever I believe.

I went as far as Uncle Paul's slip patch. I do not think his potatoes are

---

[52] Joseph Wallace (d. 1852), Presbyterian missionary and planter. Lived on a 475-acre plantation north of Tombee, on Wallace Creek, a tributary of Chowan Creek.

turning as well as mine. I heard he was making a great crop & I think he is making a good one, but not more than I am to the hand. He does not plant large.

Nov. 24th. Wednesday. Hard at the slips still. They are turning out very finely, I don't think I ever made a better crop, or one as good. I will hardly get through digging this week. There will be nearly 3 acres left after today, and I have in now 18 banks eating & 12 banks seed. I put in from 15 to 20 large baskets in the seed banks, & I think the eating potatoes will average 28 baskets per bank.

Nov. 27th. Elsie went out of the field sick this morning, with griping of the bowels, as she said, but in about an hour after she was delivered of a boy child. She has stuck out boldly to the last that she was not in a family way, and may say so now, with some truth.

Nov. 28th. Sunday. Heavy white & black frost this morning, the first ice I have seen. Eugene & I went to church. Brought Virginia home with me, to stay till Tuesday or Wednesday. I wish her to meet Ernest tomorrow. I have to go, or send to Beaufort for him.

I hear that cotton is selling well in town. Edgar Fripp sold the same cotton that I plant for 53 cents. Hope it won't fall before I get my crop down. Factors in town think it will rise to 60 cents. God grant it may.

Dr. Jenkins has bought another fine horse, $230 blood bay. How long will *he* last?

Nov. 29th. Monday. Went to Beaufort to meet Ernest & brought him home. He looks rather thin, but much improved in manners & harmony.

Dug in all my root potatoes today, gave out the last allowance the 14th & put the balance by for horses & hogs. The former seem to be quite tired of them.

Dec. 2nd. Thursday. I had chills & fever in the morning, but wore off, so that, though feeling very bad, I went to the Agricultural Society. There was much business before the Society. Edgar Fripp & A. Cockcroft were competitors for the premium on corn. Fripp got it ($25) by something less than 2 bushels over Cockcroft, having made twenty eight bushels per acre, average crop. The premium for slip potatoes was applied for by Mr. Cockcroft, but as everyone that had an idea of applying had not finished digging, it was agreed to let it lay over till the next meeting, in February. Dr. Scott & Edgar Fripp will also be competitors, and I think I will try my chance also, and with strong hopes of success.

Dec. 3rd. Finished digging slips. Made in all of slips, 28 banks of eating potatoes, averaging 28 baskets per bank, and 17 banks seed, averaging 15 baskets, making 45 banks in all, and, if they do not rot, at least 6 months' allowance. But, I will feed out to horses, hogs, &c, which will make it much less. I have made about 105 large baskets of eating potatoes per acre at the lowest calculation. Gave Jn. L. Chaplin a cart load, about 15 baskets.

Cut my sugarcane & put it all up for seed, make so little. Dug arrowroot, did well & buried it, till I can grate it.

Turned out my hogs.

Dec. 4th. I was indoors all day, suffering greatly with piles, a dreadful complaint. I have been troubled for a long time with the bleeding piles, but never had anything so painful before. It must have turned to the blind & internal piles. I am uneasy about it. All hands picking cotton, except those at the fence round the potato banks, which was finished today.

All of Uncle Paul's & Uncle Tom's cattle were in my field today, though they know I have not given up my field. I sent them a message about it, but Uncle Paul thinks it of very little consequence. It is however the first & last message they will receive about it. I will resort to other means.

never did tho'. The old fellows were of too much use to me to do anything with their cattle. I got a beef now & then

Dec. 9th. Thursday. The women turned out & finished the cursed groundnuts. After all the trouble & time, I may say, lost—we have only made about 14 bushels of good ones. I am done with the article as a crop to sell.

Dec. 12th. Two of the boys & myself went to church. Hear that cotton is selling remarkably well in town. Godly from 42 to 44, Fripp's seed, 54 to 56, better than I ever knew the same quality to sell since I have been planting.[53]

Dec. 13th. Monday. Commenced ginning with 4 gins.

Dec. 14th. Tuesday. Clear & cold. Killed 3rd hog from the main.

Dec. 20th. Monday. I have been sick since the 13th, one day with chill & fever, and the rest of the time with a severe attack of piles. I never had them to lay me up before. Oh! They are awful. I got no ease from anything, till on Saturday. I got on Saturday a couple of boxes of Dr.

[53] "Good demand at firm prices" characterized the market, reported the Charleston *Mercury*.

Upham's Pile Electuary[54] from town, which has done me so much good that I am able to come downstairs today, but still suffering.

While I was sick the two hogs that were in the fowl house in the yard, broke out. One was caught, but the largest has not been taken, tho all the ginners were at him two or three days. I don't expect ever to hear of him again. I am not able to go after him, not being able to sit, let alone riding on a horse——

Dec. 22nd. Wednesday. Mother came over with a plenty of nice things as usual. Sophy had fever last night.

Packed first bale of cotton, 333 lbs. I am improving—better appetite.

Dec. 23rd. Thursday. Packed 2nd bale, 330 lbs. All hands assorting cotton.

The medicine I am taking is very powerful in its operation on the bowels, but it does me much good & I will persevere.

It made a complete cure of me, no return of the piles, now 25 years. I have had fistula[55] since, which is worse if possible. Had to use the knife. 1877

Dec. 24th. Friday. Sent 4 hands & boat to Beaufort with 2 bales of cotton. I want to get a share of the good prices.

I rode a little way on horseback, but made me sore——

All hands assorting cotton. I have heard nothing of the hog yet.

Dec. 25th. Saturday. Christmas. Not merry by any means, but happy enough.

I, Daniel & Ernest went to church. Not many persons out. Heard of the death of Wm. Jn. Pope. He was buried near his wife[56] at the Baptist Church. Death quite unexpected.

The family all dined together, quite cozy. I rode over to see Uncle Tom, & as far as Wm. Jenkins' in the evening.

Dec. 26th. Sunday. Mother, Virgina, E. & myself went to church. Quite a large congregation. Heard that cotton has fallen from 3 to 5 cents.[57]

---

[54] "An internal pile remedy . . . for the cure of Piles, Inflammation of the Liver and Spleen, Inflammation, Soreness, and Ulceration of the Stomach, Bowels, Kidneys and Bladder; Inflammatory and mercurial Rheumatism, Impurity of Blood, weakness and Inflammation of the Spine, and for the Relief of married Ladies." (Long-running advertisement in the Charleston *Mercury*.)

[55] A deep-seated inflammation.

[56] Hephzibah Pope, who died Feb. 25, 1849. Chaplin last remarked seeing William John Pope at an Agricultural Society dinner on Aug. 7, 1851.

[57] Prices for finer varieties were holding up, but prices for common Sea Island were "exceedingly depressed and continually dropping." (Charleston *Mercury*, Dec. 24, 1852.)

Dec. 27th. Monday. 4th allowance. Clear & quite warm. Heard one or two mosquitoes at night. Went out & shot birds enough for a pie.

Dec. 28th. Tuesday. This is the last day of the Negroes' Christmas holidays, & I am really glad of it. I hope now we will have some good weather for ginning.

Dec. 29th. Wednesday. *All* hands went to work today, 4 gins going. Let Charles go to see his wife last Friday. He has not got back yet.

Dec. 31st. Friday. Last day of the year 1852. Only 3 gins running today, as I had to sort some cotton.

Sophy & myself called on the Dr. & Eliza Jenkins. They were not at home, had gone down to the village.

End of the year of our

Lord, 1852.

I think from the looks of the writing above, that I must have been quite jolly those last days* ***

1853

Jan. 2nd.   Sunday. Clear & beautiful day. Everyone of us went to church, and everyone seemed to embrace the fine day, for I never saw so large a congregation in the church. There are several strangers on the Island, most of them come to the approaching wedding, I suppose. I saw today at church, the teacher that Capt. J. Fripp & Co. have employed, the Rev'd. Mr. Perdue, he is called, a very decent looking man.

I got a letter from Ingraham & Webb by Clarence Fripp[1] today. He has sold my 2 bales cotton for 42 cents, much less than I expected. I calculated on 48 at least. This is my luck. They wrote me, that if I had sent a lot of 5 or 6 bales, they could have got 45 cents. Very poor get off, I wish I was well clear of them.

Jan. 3rd.   Packed the 3rd bale of cotton—332 lbs.

Gave out 5th allowance of slip potatoes.

Let Charles go up to see his wife the day before Christmas, & he has not yet returned. Uncle Paul's Sambo, with whom he went, has returned without him——

Jan. 4th.   I went to the wedding of John Fripp and Isabella Jenkins. Married at the church, at 4 p.m. There was quite a large crowd, more than at Frank Pope's wedding. Everything went off in style—there were seven bridesmaids & 7 groomsmen.

Jan. 6th.   Thursday. Clear, not so cold as yesterday. Packed 4th bale of cotton, 337 lbs.

Went, Sophy & myself, to the bridal party at Coz. Ann's Seaside house. Quite a grand affair, & well attended. Enjoyed ourselves much at

[1] Clarence Augustus Fripp (1831–1876), physician. Son of William "Good Billy" Fripp and Sarah Reynolds. Brother of William Washington, Alviro A., and J. Edings Fripp. Chaplin's second cousin on his father's side.

the party, but had a very disagreeable & provoking time getting home. Old Hyder balked, the night very dark, & we were a long time getting off, but finally got home safe, about 4 a.m. At the party, we were invited to another to be given by Coz. Ann at the same place next Thursday.

Jan. 12th. This has been, so far, a very mild winter. Peach trees have been in bloom all winter, and black frost only twice as yet. Mother, Sophy, & myself went to the wedding of Caroline Fripp[2] & William Chisolm,[3] married at the church at 4 p.m. We got there a little late. A good many persons attended, but I don't think as many as were at Isabel Jenkins' wedding.

Jan. 13th. Thursday. Cloudy & some rain after dark, just as Sophy & myself were about starting for Coz. Ann Fripp's party. We went however, did not get wet. Cleared off before time to return. We had it pleasant enough while there, but the devil to get back. The cursed old brute, Hyder, behaved worse than he did at the last party. I think we must have been two hours trying to get him off. Did not get home much before day. There were not as many persons as there were at the bridal party but everybody seemed to enjoy themselves quite as much. This is, or ought to be, the last party I should attempt to drive Hyder to, particularly if Sophy goes.

Jan. 17th. Monday. Very cold, black & white frost in abundance. 7th allowance. Mother thought it too cold for water work, & so do I. Sent her boat & hands to the Island for a load of wood.

I borrowed Aunt Martha's carriage & Sophy took Virginia to the village to school to Mrs. McElheran. She commences boarding with her from today. She ought to have gone two weeks ago. I am satisfied she will do better than when she stayed with her Aunt Betsy—tis better for her to board where she schools. Sophy started late & got back about dusk.

Jan. 18th. Tuesday. White frost. Mother went home today. She had some head wind I think.

Jan. 19th. Wednesday. Very cold. Black frost, pretty thick at that, & white ditto, like snow. Everything quiet once more. Nobody here now but Soph., the two junior boys & self.

---

[2] Caroline Fripp (b. 1824). Daughter of Capt. John Fripp and Caroline Chaplin. Second cousin to Chaplin on her father's side.
[3] William Adolphus Chisolm (b. 1828), planter. Son of Samuel P. Chisolm and Martha Chaplin. Brother of George A. Chisolm. Lived at Littlewood Point, west of Tombee on Broad River, which Caroline's father gave to William and Caroline for a wedding present.

All hands assorting cotton. Should have mentioned, in its place, that I packed 6th bale on 15th.

Jan. 20th. I took a regular tramp & killed a few birds. 4 gins going. Packed 7th bale. Forgot to note, I killed my last & largest hog on Monday 17th, the old fellow I thought I had lost, he ran off so long.

Robert came out, he has been sick nearly a week.

Jan. 21st. Negroes got done their tasks (ginning) very early. They do not think the "Fripp's cotton" gins harder than the "Godly" tho 'twas so represented.

Jan. 22nd. Heard that Eliza Jenkins, the Dr.'s wife, was confined last night. Did not learn the sex of the child. Aunt Betsy came from the village & brought Virginia yesterday evening. I don't wish her to come home so often. It is not for her good to do so, and not convenient for me to send her back.

Jan. 24th. Monday. Packed 8th bale of cotton. 8th allowance slips. Have a most infernal cold in my head. Two Negroes sick, something like *pleurisy.*

Jan. 25th. I had six bales of cotton put on board of Capt. Murray's[4] steamboat *Experiment,* the first cotton I ever sent, except by way of Beaufort. I went aboard myself at Wm. Jenkins' & came on as far as the mouth of my creek, met my flat & took the cotton aboard. All hands assorting cotton——

Jan. 26th. Sent a lot of cowhides over to Lands End, to go aboard of Murray's steamer. He is to sell them for me in town.

I attended the estate of Joseph Wallace's sale today. Nothing but perishable property sold, and nearly everything bought in for the widow, at trifling prices. I went to try and buy a cart but there were none there worth having, & they were to be bought in, so I left before the sale was over. There were a great many persons attended, several from Beaufort. Several Tacky horses sold very high, for twice their value, at least.

5 gins going again today.

Jan. 27th. Thursday. Clear & very cold, the coldest weather we have had, that is, the ice is much thicker than any we have had. I wish I had a nice little ice house, I would collect some of the thickest, & put it up——

Two of my chaps, Sam & Thomas, were out audacious enough to break open my stable door last night, as cold as it was, and take out Duch-

[4] John Murray (b. 1800), ship captain.

ess on which they both mounted & rode down to Lands End on an errand for that old vixen, Old Judy. I will tickle them for it.

Jan. 28th.   Sent Robert to Beaufort in gig.
Contracted with Morcock for the ferry, for $15 for the year.

Jan. 29th.   Killed my old blind ox, Old Swiedan. He was in better order than I thought he was. I salted up 21 pieces, saved eight good pieces fresh, & gave each Negro a good piece.
All hands assorting cotton today. Finished assorting nearly all, think I will make out two more bales.

Jan. 31st.   Monday. 3 gins going. Isaac getting out ox cart pole. Rec'd from Mother yesterday $10.50, for the 10 bu. groundnuts she took with her to sell for us. Bring $1 pr. bushel. 9th allowance slips. My ewes have 12 lambs, at this date. Two have died, I suppose the very cold weather the cause.

Feb. 2nd.   Sophy & I rode over to Dr. Jenkins', she to call on Eliza, who has a baby girl.

Feb. 3rd.   Agricultural day. Edgar Fripp found some champagne, & Tom Jones beat his horse in a quarter, best 2 in 3. Close race. Ned Capers lost 2 baskets of champagne to Alviro Fripp.

Feb. 4th.   I put a young steer in the yoke with old Swan last Monday, & today put them to the cart. They did very well.
Finished all the yellow cotton except 90 lbs. I expect to have about one bale of it.

Feb. 5th.   Saturday. Cloudy and quite warm. A smart drizzle came up about midday. Finished all the cotton, but cannot pack the yellow today. Packed the 10th and last bale of white.
Unfortunately lost my young ox. The two got fastened somehow, under the old shed last night, and the young one found dead in the yoke this morning. Choked I think, & also very much bruised. Had him cleaned for the Negroes. I am now in a bad fix. God knows how I will get out my manure with only one horse cart.
Sent 3 women today to pile up sedge for root potato patch. I have only 307 lbs. of yellow cotton. Gave out 10th allowance of slips today.

Feb. 7th.   Monday. The Captain D. Jenkins was good enough to loan me an ox, a very large one, which I went over & got today & put him to work with my old Swan. He is taller than my ox, in fact, one of the tallest I ever saw, but I hope, and think, they will work together very well after a while. Packed a bale of yellow cotton, the 11th bale in all, 10 of white.

Edward Capers dined with me. *Wonder.*

Feb. 8th.   Ernest's birthday—he is now thirteen years old. It is distressing to think he is so very backward. I don't think he is capable of even writing a letter home. If he does not improve more this session at Seabrook, I shall be induced to take him away, and try some other school——

Sent 2 hands to get rails, they got poles. *To be flogged.*

Feb. 9th.   Murray's steamboat passed, and left groceries &c &c, he brought from town for me. He sold my cowhides for 8¼ cts. pr. lb. I have not had a regular settlement with him, but received $5 in cash, & paid him freight, $4.12½, making in all, $9.12½ for the hides that he has accounted for. I got from town, barrel of Irish potatoes for seed, and onion sets, & other garden seeds, ½ barrel flour, do. br. sugar, 25 lbs. crushed ditto, 50 lbs. coffee, 1000 cigars, 5 lbs. tobacco, 2 gals. brandy, 2 gals wine. Hoes (12), & axes (2), 10 gals. burning fluid. I have concluded that much more gas[5] is used than oil, & something dearer in the end, but it gives a better light, & is much cleaner than oil.

Feb. 10th.   Put 2 bales of cotton on board of Murray's boat to go to town, the last of my white cotton. I will keep the bale of yellow later. Have not heard from the last lot sent down——

Finished listing in what little marsh I have, manured 6⅛th acres. I never was so backward in my life in manuring, the land is not ready to be listed. I am having some marsh sedge listed in, & if I can find the compost will have some of it put on the list.[6]

Feb. 12th.   Saturday. Clear & pleasant. Hard at work repairing cart. 4 hands listing potato land. 2 hands listing cotton ground. Jim & Peg sick. Put up 3 hams in whitewashed bags. Planted Irish potatoes, and set out onion sets. Green peas just coming up.

Feb. 14th.   Monday. Finished the horse cart that I have been working at since Friday, and did it very well indeed, *considering.* I only hope there will be no more breakdowns directly.

2 hands listing potato land, & the balance heading out sedge for cot-

[5] Liquefied coal gas.
[6] Some marsh grass which had washed up with the tide is being turned under the soil; some will be mixed with compost and laid *on* the ground.

ton. 2 tasks pr. hand. Peg sick, damn her. She is always sick when I am most pushed for work. Gave out 11th allowance of slip potatoes.

Feb. 16th.   Wednesday. Set fire to the broom grass at Toomer's line. The fire crossed over, the wind being very high, & burned some of the Major's Orange Grove fence.

Feb. 26th.   Saturday. Clear. I am very backward in field work. Got my accounts from cotton—bad sales.[7] My crop brought, net, $1374.37.

Feb. 28th.   Monday. Blustering and somewhat cloudy, & likelihood to rain all day. All the women listing corn ground, had some corn land listed Saturday, which was manured with sedge. Carting out seed today for corn land, 1 cart load pr. acre.

There is an election held today for representative to Congress. I do not go out, only one candidate, "Colcock,"[8] and I am busy.

Gave out 1st allowance of corn to full hands, will give the potatoes to little Negroes & old ones. I want to try and save what I have left of potatoes, & if they keep, sell them later.

Sent Robert to Beaufort for a new cart I wrote to town for. He brought it late at night, the wind being so high, he could not cross the ferry. It cost $25, and I think it a strong, well built and light cart. I got also harness with it.

March 1st.   Tuesday. March comes in a little boisterous. Clear however & pleasant. Listing corn ground. Somehow I can't get the men at field work. I have much fencing to do yet, all my division fence to repair. I suppose Uncle Paul won't help me. He plants some of my land this year, & I see he is just cutting marsh to manure it. I have Isaac & Robert today running out and straightening my corn field. There is hardly an old task stake to be seen.

I have the new cart at work today, making 3 carts. I hope now to make some better progress in getting out manure. If I had had this cart a month ago I would have been done listing.

March 2nd.   Wednesday. Muster Day. Baker[9] came over and received tax returns. Made my return, also returned 13 Negroes of the trust estate, by request of Danl. Jenkins (trustee).

There was a subscription got up for a new muster house—sadly

[7] Not bad at all—39 cents a pound.
[8] William Ferguson Colcock, one of R. L. Baker's attorneys. See note, Feb. 27, 1846.
[9] John M. Baker, tax collector. Chaplin has thirteen slaves on loan from his mother's estate, on whom he must pay an annual property tax.

wanted. Subscriptions were freely made, & some money paid down. I think, now after the third attempt, that the house will be built. There were about $170 made up yesterday.

March 6th. Sunday. Went to church. Sent Virginia back to the village with Mrs. McElheran. Sophy went for her on Friday.
Got my crop money from town, by Oliver Fripp, $408.50.[10]

March 7th. Monday. Went to Beaufort, paid several debts there, to Barnwell & others. Bought a new bridle & martingale,[11] set of waiters,[12] handle basket, &c.

March 9th. Ned Capers left the Island on Monday, to take charge of his father's plantation near Charleston. The Captain went to town on Monday. Jno. H. Webb got back from town last Sunday—he bought a cart & horse.

March 10th. Paid Dr. Jenkins $15.50, medical bill. I hardly expected he would present one, but am glad I was able to meet it. Only $2.50 was for myself, or rather, for his tieing up Isaac's finger. The balance of $13 was for his attendance on Mother last summer. Baker ought to pay it. Dr. Jenkins never hears that I have money, but what he can find an a/c to send me. He charged very high for his visits to Mother, $6.50 each—*however, it is paid.*
That man has always been a sort of secret enemy of mine* *1876*

March 12th. Saturday. Foggy & cloudy all the morning. Cleared off prettily about 2 p.m. All hands, 11½, banking potato land. Ought to have 12 tasks banked today, but Jim quit with permission to see his wife who he heard was dying.
***1876 She is alive & fat as a hog now.**
Just heard of her death (Charlotte) Sept. 1885
She got better, I heard from Uncle Paul in the evening.
Items. Capt. Jenkins sent me my watch today, which he carried to town with him to have repaired. He sent it by Robert, who went to the village to carry & fetch Virginia's clothes. Cost of repair, $3.50. Paid & received a receipt, for $49.62½, to Mrs. McElheran for Virginia's tuition for past 3 quarters, including stationery, books &c &c.
Item. J. H. Webb got a horse from town today. Cost (original) $130 & add. one week's stable in town, & the passage.

---

[10] Net return, after Ingraham & Webb have deducted what Chaplin owes them.
[11] Straps that run from a horse's head to its girth to prevent the animal from rearing.
[12] Small serving trays.

March 13th.   Sunday. All of us went to church. Mr. McElheran gave one of the most nauseating sermons I have ever had the misfortune to hear. A lady in church observed that "the people wanted a change," & that "he would do no good if he preached here for thirty years." I will qualify the assertion, and give him his *lifetime* be it for one thousand years.

I hear that cotton is going up in prices.[13]

March 16th.   Planted early corn, 1 acre. Women banking corn land, men making fence (division). Sent Robert to Beaufort.

March 19th.   Saturday. Planted some more corn today, making about 7 acres in all. Men splitting rails, they make slow work. Put Moll to attend to the poultry, hope she will do well. She complains so much in the field that I concluded to take her out, and make Judy do full day's work 3 days in the week.

March 20th.   We all went to church, heard a very good sermon from Mr. Perdue. His delivery is not good, but he sticks to his text. Got a drum fish from J. L. Chaplin, $2 price, 1st I *eat*.

March 22nd.   Tuesday. Had most of my cowpeas thrashed, and shelled some corn. Cut a few potatoes in the evening. Let Mother's driver Bristol have 10 baskets of seed potatoes—yellow yams, brimstones & Spanish. He is to send me other seed in exchange.
Never got them

March 23rd.   Mother's boat returned. Got a hog from the R. side, she brought over for me. The men at the fencing again today. 6 women planting potatoes. Planted 1 task & 6 beds of yellow yams, & 1 task & 15 beds of Spanish. I have now planted 2¼ acres, as follows—reds, 1½ acres; yellow yams, 1 task, 6 beds; Spanish, 1 task & 16 beds = 2¼ acres.

March 25th.   Good Friday and a fine day it is. Sophy, the children & wonderful to tell, *I* went to church. Miss Young *complimented me,* by saying I was the *best young man* on the Island. If a man goes to church regularly he is called a "good man."

March 26th.   Saturday. Sent up to Beaufort & got my Negro cloth (from town), also family dry goods for the summer. Everything quite reasonable. Bill am'ted in all to a little over *$180.*
more than I make in a year now   '77

[13] "Medium fine" Sea Island was bringing 43 to 53 cents and rising.

March 30th. Wednesday. Men making fence in Toomer's woods. I think this will be the last time I will have to make that fence, as Capt. D. Jenkins now owns the land, & he will no doubt run his wire fence on that line, & we will join and make the fence on the line between us down to Cedar Hammock.

April 1st. Friday. Weather now & for some time has been fine & pleasant. Finished the Toomer fence, which is all *my* fencing. All hands planting corn. Finished all but 2¾ acres at Grove's fence. Commenced plowing cotton ground.

April 2nd. Saturday. Sent Robert out fishing. He caught one.
Finished planting corn, 26½ acres in all.

April 4th. Monday. March seems to have fallen into April. Clear, but wind S.W., very high again today. Heavy cloud in the north & N.W. about noon. Wind got round to N.W. & brought the dark clouds over. Commenced raining hard about 3½ p.m. & sun shone out for a moment at 4¾. Slight shower, then sun set clear. Wind high.
9 a.m., sent Robert in the buggy to Beaufort to meet Ernest, expecting him today. This is a very bad time for him, but I hope, if his holidays have begun, that he may come safe. He got home, at last, about 8 p.m., cold & hungry, but well, thank God, and did not get wet. He looks quite thin.
I got a new saddle from town today. Cost, covered with Buverteen, & heavy stirrup irons, $24.75.
think I rode that saddle through the war & it galled every horse I put it on
J. H. Webb's cost $36. I would not swap.

April 5th. All hands spreading compost for cotton today. They do not, when they spread & list, whisk it fine enough & I thought this is a good plan to have it well spread.

April 7th. Anniversary of the Agricultural Society. I went to the meeting. Officers elected —Jno. Fripp, president, Capt. D Jenkins, vice pres., Alviro Fripp, treas. & T. B. Chaplin, secretary. I was not much inclined to take office, but did so, with the intention & wish of seeing the proceedings of the Society more particularly recorded and preserved.
All gone to rats now, house & all　'79
Wonder what became of the Society property. There was considerable money besides silver forks & spoons in Treas.'s hands. W. G. Capers treas.

April 9th. Saturday. Clear & warm. Put on the coat & a cold was the consequence. All hands banking *cotton land.* Very late, but hope to come out in the end. I would rather plant late, and have my land in *good* order, than to plant early & have my land badly prepared.

There is none, however, that I call *well* prepared.

April 12th. 1st planting cotton, 7½ acres.

April 14th. All hands banking cotton land. Finished all but that I took up at Orange Grove line. Finished plowing, only 11 tasks left, & my horses are so often in the buggy I won't plow any more.

April 16th. I plant this year 6 acres of cotton with seed I got of Grayson. He calls it the Edings selection from the Owens seed, which he recommends as a great bearer & fine cotton.

April 17th. Sunday. All of us went to church. I & Ernest rode horseback, the rest in the "caravan."

April 18th. Quite cool this morning and last night, almost like winter. Had to put on thick clothes. Went to Beaufort & paid my taxes, Ernest went with me.

Finished planting cotton out & out, 36 acres.

April 21st. Went out fishing. Took 6 in the boat. I took 3 myself. All hands hoeing corn. Birds pulled it badly.

April 22nd. All hands supplying corn. Went out fishing. Took 6, lost 5. I took 2. Fish bit better than yesterday. Some boats took as high as 13. Saw Minott out fishing.

April 23rd. Saturday. Clear & very warm. Put on full suit summer clothes. Sent to the village yesterday for Virginia. She has a week's holiday.

Did not go out fishing—feel rather sore and tired. Sent out one hand in Uncle Tom's boat. 3 hands making hog pen & moving cow pen. Women supplying corn, it is very broken. Jim caught one fish in Uncle Tom's boat. I hear that they took 10 in the boat. Killed a lamb today— very small & poor, but we want a change from fish.

April 25th. Monday. Went fishing. Took the three boys[14] with me. They were all very seasick, Eugene the worst of all. He did not hold up his head

[14] Ernest, Daniel, and Eugene.

the whole time. Perhaps it may do them good. We took 7 fish, took 3 on my line, Jack 2, Frank 2, lost some 5 or 6. A quantity of sedge came up on the bay near the Negro houses & house landing. I put all the hands piling it up. At it all day, and did not finish. This is lucky, as it is so near the cow pen.

April 27th.   Wednesday. My 31st birthday. Went fishing, took only one—I caught that. Saw or heard of very few fish being taken. All hands hoeing cotton. No cotton up however, but field getting grassy.

April 28th.   Went fishing. I caught all that was taken in the boat, 1 drum & 1 bass, besides a few blackfish—I think the fishing season is well over. Very few are now taken. I landed at Lands End.

April 29th.   Friday. Stayed at home & painted my sulky. Paris has fixed it very well. Isaac making ox cart axle. Jim & Frank filling up stable. My young mare Moonlight had a colt on the 26 or 27th instant. All hands hoeing cotton.

April 30th.   Saturday. Hazy and warm. Hoeing & hauling potatoes & hauling corn. Very dry, cotton can't come up. Last day of April & I don't doubt I will have to plant the most of my crop over, for I fear the seed has laid in the ground so long it must be injured. Isaac finished cart axle. Finished filling up stable with dirt & lime.

May 6th.   Friday. Carried Ernest to Beaufort to go on to Bluffton. The steamboat did not come from town. She was detained, for the accommodation of the delegates to the Episcopal Convention now in session in Charleston,[15] to bring them up on its adjournment. Steamboat not to come along till tomorrow 10 a.m. Left Ernest with T. A. Bell, he kindly promising to see him on board. I paid several bills &c in Beaufort, being enabled to do so by the very kind generosity of Uncle Tom, who sent for me & gave me this morning $150. God bless the old man. This is more than any relation I have had ever done for me.

May 7th.   Sent Jack to Beaufort to see if Ernest was safe aboard. He said he was, and in good spirits. Several boys for the same school were on board.

[15] The Sixty-fourth South Carolina Episcopal Convention, at which Rt. Rev. Thomas F. Davis was elected bishop of the Diocese of South Carolina to succeed Bishop Gadsden. See July 8, 1855.

May 15th. Sunday. A very slight sprinkle during the morning, did not prevent us from going to church. Virginia came home with us, very much against my wish, but as we all go to the village tomorrow I suffered it.

May 16th. Whitmonday.[16] We all went to the village. Took Daniel to Mr. Perdue (whom & lady I very much admire) **don't think** & left him there to board & school. The tuition is the same "pr. quarter" as Mrs. McE.'s, tho board less. But we have not determined upon exact amt. Daniel seemed a little crestfallen at parting, but stifled it as he generally does his feelings.

Had not an unpleasant day, with the exception of Sophy's having a toothache all day, and Mr. McE., the old quack, put, or gave her to put into it, something that made her sick all the evening. Saw the Capt. at Aunt Betsy's. He has had & is now laboring under a severe attack of rheumatism in his right shoulder & arm. What if he had it from head to heels as I had?

All hands were thinning corn today. I have let it stand in hopes of rain to transplant when I thinned, but it is getting too large & must be thinned.

May 17th. Tuesday. Still no rain, no rain. I don't care to go in the field again till it does. Went to see E. W. Chaplin, who I hear is much hurt by a fall from his horse. They had taken him up to Beaufort.

May 18th. Rode over Uncle Paul's Carter Hill cotton. It is quite as bad as my own.

May 19th. Thursday. Very warm & dry, dry, dry. I never saw such a dry spring. We will soon have to dig cow wells. Carting out some chinqua-pin[17] posts, and throwing them in saltwater. Sent 2 hands to cut poles to make sheephead ground.[18]

May 20th. Friday. This is strange weather, & stranger climate. Today is cool enough to sit by a fire, & a thick coat. East wind, & high. All hands hoeing & hauling cotton land, for there are few plants to hoe.
made a sheephead ground

May 21st. Saturday. Clear & pleasant. Sophy & I took Eugene and went down to Bull's Point on a little maroon.[19] Had a very agreeable time.

---

[16] The Monday following Whitsunday, the seventh Sunday after Easter, which commemorates the descent of the Holy Spirit on the day of Pentecost.
[17] The dwarf chestnut, a fine-grained, durable wood.
[18] Wood frame sunk in the salt water to promote the growth of barnacles and oysters, on which sheepshead feed.
[19] A hunting, fishing, or camping party.

Found & brought home several good boards. There must have been a lumber vessel wrecked off the coast, as a great many boards have been picked up. Uncle Paul got near 200, Pritchard[20] as many, & Joe Perry got some. I wish I could have got them all.

May 26th.   Thursday. Traded with Benj. Chaplin Jnr. my largest young mare & colt for his sorrel horse, Silver Heels, & got a veal to boot.

May 28th.   Boat got back from Beaufort. Brought set of sulky harness, molasses & salt for Negroes, white sugar and 1 M cigars for self.

May 30th.   Horse Silver draws very well with Tom Jones. Do not match in size & color, but very well in gait. I don't think I made a bad trade. The horse works well, and can be used at once. The mare with a young colt would be useless for some time at least, and my old horses want help.

May 31st.   Tuesday. Heavy thundercloud in the evening. Commenced to rain after dark & we had quite a fine rain at night. This is a godsend. I hope now to get my cotton up, and not have to dig cow wells out. Killed a veal & sent Mr. McElheran & Mr. Perdue each a leg. May was determined not to pass without giving a sprinkle to parched vegetation.

June 1st.   I put the hands to supplying root patch with slips, & supplying early peas, & planting cowpeas through some of my corn. My potatoes are very broken. Worse crop I ever had so far, no knowing what they may do yet.

     I rode to the lodge today to meet the rest of the committee, appointed to have the house put in order for the reception of J. D. Pope, who is to deliver an address before the Society tomorrow. We scoured the floor, arranged benches &c. No one met me but Oliver Fripp.

June 2nd.   Agricultural Society day, and quite a gala day we had. Jos. D. Pope delivered an address on agriculture, before the Society, by special invite. The address was a very good & eloquent one, and quite a number of ladies graced the occasion with their presence, besides several gentlemen, not members. Edgar Fripp gave us a good dinner, a basket of champagne was drank, & after much jollity we broke up. A. Cockcroft resigned as member of the Society.
because he lost the premium for corn

---

[20] Edward Pritchard. See note, June 4, 1847.

June 4th. Saturday. Went up to Beaufort in the boat, took Daniel with me. Sent to town for ice,[21] as I heard there would be none in Beaufort till July. Got a 10 gal. can of gas from town.

June 7th. I went down to Webb's sheephead ground & took 11 sheephead. Sent Jack to the village with 5, to Capt. Jno. Fripp, Dr. Scott, & Mr. Perdue.

June 9th. Went to the village. Played billiards, dined with Dr. Jenkins. Uncle Paul is so much put out with Buckskin, that I offered him Silver Heels to use while I took his horse & tried to do something for him.

June 11th. Drove Buck & Tom Jones in the buggy, they drew finely. Went over & took Uncle P. to ride. He was astonished to see his good for nothing horse draw so finely. Buckskin not atall lame, hoof & frog[22] wanted trimming. Don't think this has been done since he had him.

June 12th. Sunday. Dry & hot, none of us went to church. Drove Sophy with Buck & Tom in the buggy. She likes them, and wishes Uncle P. would let me have him back again. I would not offer to trade "Silver" for him, but if *he* offers, it is a trade. Anything to please him. They (Tom & Buck) draw much better than "Silver" & Tom. Pope's John drove them today, and says he does not care to sit behind better horses.

June 13th. Monday. Still dry & hot. The young cotton is dying. A famine this year I expect. Corn all dried.

June 14th. Tuesday. Still no rain.

June 15th. Wednesday. " " " Everything going to the devil.

June 17th. All hands hauling where cotton ought to be. Sent to Beaufort. Got ice, soda &c from town.
Going in for luxuries again

June 18th. Some of my Negroes have served me rather a shabby trick today. I gave Robert permit to go to the main in the evening, to return tomorrow night, and six others, Jim, Sancho, Frank, Elsie, Helen & Nelly,

---

[21] Ice was cut in winter from frozen lakes in New York State, stored until summer, then shipped to southern port towns. Planters would buy the ice from their cotton factors or other merchants, who sold it by the barrel or on contract—so many barrels of ice per season at a prearranged price.
[22] The horny pad in a horse's sole.

took themselves off also, & without permission. I blame Robert for their going. He "knew of it," & the thing has been planned for more than a fortnight, & he told me nothing of it, which a driver, he should have done. They all shall be punished, but I have not decided how.

June 20th. Monday. The *runaway* Negroes got back from the main last night. I saw Robert this morning, he looks quite sheepish. Gave all but him a good flogging. He seems to be well punished in seeing this done & doing it with his own hands.
Unjust—he alone should have been punished

June 23rd. Thursday. I was sick in bed with fever all day. This is dreadful. What will become of us? I must try & get old Mayer's[23] house on Pine Island[24] & move there. This would be bad, everything would be neglected at home, but we must try & find a healthier place.

June 27th. Monday. I got some cotton seed from Mr. Harvey, Edgar Fripp's overseer, on Saturday, but I think the ground too dry to plant them, & I will only plant to try & fill out the field—not that I expect to get anything of consequence from it. I do not think I have *now*, more than ⅓rd of my crop—cotton, corn, potatoes & early peas—that I can calculate on making anything off of. All hands are hauling & thinning cotton today. Two carts hauling compost for slips. Have a very bad boil coming under my arm, just in the armpit.

June 28th. Went to Beaufort. The crops on the Beaufort road look better than they do hereabouts. Saw my old company, the "Beaufort Artillery," parade, being their anniversary.

July 4th. Monday. Independence. My boil is very painful, but I rode out to the muster house. Got not much good by it.

July 5th. Killed my first veal for market, one I got from Benj. Chaplin Jnr. Mother came over from the main. Heavy cloud in the evening but no rain, much disappointed.

July 6th. Wednesday. Clear in the morning, but clouded up, & a splendid rain commenced falling about 5 p.m., and continued pretty constant till dark. This is decidedly the best rain we have had for 10 weeks. All hands hauling cotton at Grove line.

[23] John G. Mayer (b. 1790), planter.
[24] Island at the entrance to Village Creek, across from St. Helenaville.

July 7th. Thursday. Thunder & some appearances of rain, but had none. Ground wet about 2½ inches deep. Put all hands to banking slip land. Would not plant, wait for next shower. Sent Jack to Beaufort.

Sophy is trying the Galvanic Belt,[25] now 7 days.

July 9th. Uncle Paul sent me word that my horses troubled his field. They went through the Major's good for nothing fence. I sent today and had it made up, won't do it again. Neither he or the Major sent to help fix the fence.

July 11th. Heavy cloud again in the evening & near all night, with much lightning & thunder but only about *three* big drops of rain. The whole heavens were overcast & I was almost sure of a rain, *but no,* disappointed again. Finished listing peas land, 8 acres. Hoed some potatoes, where supplied with slips.

I never knew roots supplied with slips to do anything much, 25 years

Had a severe chill, & hot fever nearly all day. Have also a very dry & distressing cough. Look very badly, worse than any time last summer. God knows what will be the end of all this. I feel wretched & uneasy.

July 12th. Tuesday. Very fine rain, lasted from dinner time, 3 p.m., till dark. I think there has been heavy rains all round from west to east, round northward.

Mr. McElheran came down & dined with us. Rather a rare occurrence *these times.*

July 13th. I was sick in bed with chill and fever all day. Chill came on violently, early in the morning, and scorching fever followed. Took an emetic, & threw up a quantity of bile. Feel better in the evening, but very weak——

Mother's boat came from the main yesterday & brought me about 2 bushels of peas for seed. Very glad of them. I shall now be able to plant about 16 acres to try & help out the bad provision crop. I must also try to get in as many slips as I possibly can.

[25] Advertised as "the most valuable medical discovery of the age," Dr. Christie's galvanic belt, bracelets, necklace, when activated by "the magnetic fluid" as directed, were alleged to relieve "asthma and respiratory illness . . . gout, spinal injuries, rheumatism . . . and all nervous diseases." "The great peculiarity and excellence of Dr. Christie's Galvanic Curatives"—and undoubtedly a source of their appeal—"[is that] they arrest and cure disease by *outward application,* in place of the usual mode of drugging and physicking the patient, till exhausted Nature sinks under the affliction." The belt cost $3.

July 14th. Sophy rode down to the village & got Mr. McElheran to go with her over to Pine Isld. to take a look at Mr. Mayer's house, which we have some idea of getting for the rest of the season. He asks $50. Rather high, but we may save much sickness, at least, the rest of the family. I am fixed already. Had no fever today. Sophy returned about sunset, likes the house and situation very well, but I am not sure that we will go there. Many things may prevent.

Just as the buggy was coming up to the yard gate, the blind dropped off one of the horses. He was not much frightened, but the folks were, black & white. They all jumped out. No accident happened fortunately.

July 18th. Monday. Had another smart rain again today. All hands & the cook planting slips.

July 19th. I rode down to the village & spent the day pleasantly enough. Dined with Dr. Jenkins. I think I shall give up the idea of taking old Mayer's house, the situation is too unhandy.

July 20th. All hands listing peas ground over on the Riverside land or track. I want to plant 6 or 8 acres more. Finished planting slips, 8 acres. I don't know that I shall plant any more. Think I had better plant peas.

July 22nd. Finished banking peas ground & planted a few. Sent 3 hands to Beaufort in boat for ice &c. Sent Jack to village to carry children's clothes & bring lamb in the morning. Wrote a letter to Mr. Perdue, requesting him not to let Daniel be so much down the village, & out late at night, as I heard he was.

July 24th. Sunday. Went to the Baptist Church. Saw six darkies baptized & heard a miserably poor discourse from Mr. Mellichamp.[26]

July 26th. Tuesday. Stripped some blades, brought in what stripped yesterday. Hoed cotton, very grassy.

July 27th. Mother's boat came over. Walked over the Captain's crop—it is very good, best, all in all, I have seen. All hands hoeing cotton, cotton casting off very much.

July 28th. Mother could not go to the main. Hands hoeing slips & cotton (not her hands).

[26] Stiles Mellichamp (d. 1872), assistant rector at St. Helena's Episcopal Church, in Beaufort, 1851–53.

July 29th. Mother started for home very early. She sent me word from the Riverside that there was a large sill at the mouth of Station Creek. I went out & brought it home, a fine sill, 40 feet long.

(*Put it under piazza*)

Hands hauling slips & hoeing cotton. Sent 2 hands to Beaufort for ice.

the ice a perfect godsend

Aug. 3rd. Wednesday. Sophy, Eugene went out fishing with me. Had a smart rain on us—caught one sheephead. Found Ned Capers at home when we got back. He brought me two Shanghai chickens, both molls unfortunately.

Fine bantams they would make[27]

Aug. 5th. Friday. Ned, Gabriel & I went out to Broad River to get fish & sea air. Got a fine chance of whiting, no sharks or blackfish as Ned objected to go over to the middle rocks.

Aug. 7th. Sunday. I went down to the village. Attended morning service there, dined with Aunt Betsy. As a heavy cloud was rising I did not stay to evening service, but started back a little after 5 o'clock. There were very few persons attended church.

Joe & Tom Perry are both very sick with dysentery. Dr. Jenkins lost a woman with the complaint yesterday. It seems quite prevalent. Both my little folks are well at the village.

Aug. 8th. Monday. Killed 1st plover.

Virginia came down with Aunt Betsy, who sent her over here to dine with us. She returned in the afternoon.

Finished stripping all my own blades. Do not think I have made as much as I did last year. I have the Negroes' corn yet to strip, which I am in hopes will give me enough to last me for I do not expect to make many pea vines.

Aug. 9th. Tuesday. Very sultry day. Rain wanted again for slips, peas, cattle. All hands hauling cotton, last hauling for all except some very young cotton here & there, which must be worked again. Commenced cutting marsh, 4 hands. Cord for day's work—length 10 feet, height 5 ft., width 5 ft. This is not enough, but will try it for a while.

---

[27] Chaplin was noting that Capers had given him "molls" or hens when he wished to have "bantams" or roosters, possibly to keep for fighting; or he may have been commenting that the chickens thought to be hens turned out in fact to be roosters.

Aug 10th. Finished working cotton, all to some very young that will require another working in spots here & there.
Repetitions common
    Mother sent a boat over to the village for Virginia to go over & ac-
company her to Walterboro. I heard that the boat was small & only
"three (hands)" or *boys* sent to row, & no female servant to take care of
her. I will not let her go.
Right too

Aug. 12th. Friday. High winds (S.E.), heavy clouds about, but no rain.
Joe W. Perry died last night about 12 o'clock. Buried today at 5½ p.m.
    Had to put all hands digging cow well. The wells & ponds are drier
than ever. The late rains have had little effect on them. Mother sent back
today. Sent larger boat & Virginia went.
Worse trip but one she ever made

Aug. 13th. Saturday. Sent to Beaufort for ice. Women hauling peas. 3
men cutting marsh. 15 cords cut.

Aug. 20th. Saturday. Picked a little cotton yesterday and the day before
with one hand. Sent to Beaufort—but got no ice. Got ½ barrel flour from
town, & 2 hams. D. P. Jenkins dined with me—he brought Daniel with
him.

Aug. 27th. Finished all the Negro blades, and hoed some young cotton
here & there. Got barrel ice from Beaufort. 54 cords marsh cut. Frank sick.

Aug. 29th. Monday. Gave out the second week's allowance of roots.
Supplied over some broken places in the slip patch. They may make some
seed.
    Rode down to Lands End in the evening. Saw Melvin M. Sams,
camping there, wanted me to go to Edings Island with him tomorrow to
take a hunt. I declined. John H. Webb goes to Bluffton tomorrow. Sent
him a box to take for Ernest, & 15 watermelons, part of them for himself,
the balance for Ernest. Webb has no melons.

Aug. 30th. I killed two plover today, as fat as I ever saw. Killed my second veal for market, fat—

Sept. 3rd. Saturday. I seldom ever saw such heavy rain as fell about daylight & just after, it appeared one sheet of water descending. Somewhat
seceded about 9 a.m., but continued gusty & showery all day. Sent 3
hands to Beaufort, *that is,* if they can get there.

Sept. 5th. Monday. Gave out 3rd allowance of roots, reds, do not turn any better, have nearly finished them. Hands did not get back from Beaufort till last night. Steamboat did not come till yesterday. All women picking cotton.

Mary had a boy child before 12 o'clock last night.

Jno. C. 1868 15 years old

Sept. 6th. Went down to the village for the purpose of meeting Virginia, & perhaps Mother also, as I expected them to come over yesterday from Walterboro. But they had not—neither did they come today. I waited till after sunset. I expect the late rains have swelled the swamps near Walterboro & made them impassable.

Sept. 7th. Went to muster, the captain being absent, the 1st lieut. did not parade the company, the day being very hot. 5 persons were appointed by the com'ss. officer to select a spot to put up the new muster house. Edgar Fripp having given the company a spot of ground on the opposite side of the bridge from the old house, which is more shaded and higher ground, we pitched on a spot there, on the bank of the creek. Several members agreed to send hands tomorrow and clean off the ground.

Sept. 8th. Sent 2 hands & went myself to have the ground cleared for the m. house. J. H. Webb, A. A. Fripp & myself were the only whites present, & 12 or 13 blacks. Found the work more than we expected, will take 2 days. A.A.F. agreed to send more hands (tomorrow). We had lunch &c & stayed all day.

Sept. 9th. Sent to Beaufort for ice (Isaac & Charles).

Sept. 10th to 13th. Constant rain & shine, every day very little done. I had no indoor work. The showers followed each other so fast, I could only rake sedge & carry some to the pen. Frequent cases of fever.

Sept. 16th. Bad time for the crops. Little cotton to pick & no weather to pick it in. I hear of caterpillars on the Island, but have seen none. Their appearance in my crop would ruin it completely.

Sent in the evening to Beaufort for ice & Robert to the village to bring the children down early tomorrow to spend the day.

Sept. 17th. Saturday. Heavy rain before day, and another shower after sunrise. The children came however, nothing would stop them. They were so anxious to get home that they say they hardly slept last night. They got a smart shower on them, but did not get much wet. I am dreadfully uneasy. Heavy rain with little or no intermission prevented their return.

They must stay, being rainy. One night may not make them sick. They were both overjoyed that it should rain & they would stay. Innocent things, they know not the disadvantages, both so much rain for their interest in the crop, but for their health. Their not having any *fear* of *fever* I think is in their favor.

Sept. 19th.   Gave out 5th allowance roots. They turn out so badly that all hands dug till 12 o'clock in getting them. Picked some cotton in the evening, & sent the men to getting lime kiln wood. Heavy rain towards the N.W. which drove the Negroes in, but the rain did not reach here and I am glad of it. We have had quite enough at present.

Sept. 20th.   Tuesday. Clear & pleasant this morning, and I was in hopes of a clear spell, but a very heavy rain came up suddenly about 1 p.m., then cleared, and then another just as heavy came on about 4½ p.m. This is altogether bad work for planters. The open cotton will rot badly, for we can't get it in, or dry what is in. It is now near the equinox, & I doubt if we have any settled weather till it is past.

Sept. 22nd.   Thursday. Clear all day, & quite cool. Had a fire in the morning. Cotton opening & rotting.

Sept. 23rd.   We all rode down to the village today. I called to see W. B. Fripp. He has been & is now quite ill with dysentery. The doctors think there is little hopes of his recovery. His sons[28], who are gone traveling, are expected back today. Sent Robert to Beaufort for ice, & other articles from town. Got 2 ovens, a tin roaster, steel grist mill &c.

Sept. 25th.   Sunday. Went to see Tom Capers, who I hear has returned from a trip to the North, where he went for his health, and returned in much worse health. I found him looking *extremely* bad, very thin, almost a shadow, a confirmed case of consumption.

Sept. 26th.   Eugene's birthday, he is 8 years old. I gave him a sheephead for his birthday dinner, as I went to J. H. Webb's ground today with Dan'l Jenkins & caught 3 sheepheads. None others were taken. The wind was too high for sport.

Sept. 27th.   I went to Beaufort, dined with Bell, got home about dusk. Nothing new in Beaufort. The *two stores,* Danner's & Fyler's, are full of new goods, but as usual, very high——

[28] Thomas B. and John E. Fripp. Pvt. Thomas B. Fripp, C.S.A. was killed at Pocotaligo, Oct. 22, 1862.

Sept. 28th. Fished for sheephead at my ground, but did not catch anything but toadfish. Weighed off 1431 lbs. cotton, the first I have weighed off. This is all I have in, except a little of that from the seed Grayson gave me.

I have never known the mosquitoes so bad in all my life. There is no peace for them even in daytime.

I set fire to the lime kiln today, burnt very well.

Oct. 1st. Saturday. Took off two hands to send to Beaufort. I will however finish breaking corn today. Turning out some better, but none good, all ½ shuck.

Note—The Major's (D. P. Jenkins') hogs have been troubling my field all the summer. I have sent him & his driver several messages about them, all to no purpose. Yesterday the whole drove came in my corn. I had one shot, & another wounded. They are now very much scattered & several of Jenkins' Negroes are looking them up today. There were some 15 head up at my corn house last night & this morning.

We received today, a little after 3 p.m., invitation to the funeral of Wm. B. Fripp. He died last night. His two sons who have been traveling this summer have returned in time to see him alive. This is the 4th death of white male adults this summer.

Oct. 3rd. Monday. Gave out 7th & last allowance of root potatoes. Received an invitation to the funeral of Thos. L. Capers, today, to take place tomorrow at 11 a.m. This was some*what* unexpected. When I last saw Tom Capers, I was strongly impressed with the *idea* that the poor fellow could not long survive, but I had not the belief that his end was *so near,* but he is now *no more.* His *venerable* father and two of his brothers, Gabe & Frank, were at the funeral of W. B. Fripp yesterday. Little did they suppose at the time, *that today,* their duty would be to call around their family hearth *the friends* of their beloved son, & brother. The ways of Providence are not to be scrutinized. God *gives,* God *takes away,* who shall dispute——

Oct. 4th. Went to Tom. L. Capers' funeral. There were a good many persons attended, notwithstanding the weather. The family are very much distressed. Ned was not there.

Mother's boat came over with some things for my Society dinner.

The centre sleeper to Capers' bridge fell in while some of the funeral party were crossing. No damage done. We all had to take out & lead over.

Oct. 5th. Everyone in the yard busy preparing for my Agricultural dinner tomorrow. I went to Webb's sheephead ground in the evening, fished till after sunset, but did not get but three small sheepheads and 4 young drum, which will make one dish and a very acceptable one too.

Oct. 6th. Thursday—Agricultural meeting. I found dinner, which was pronounced very good. Dr. M. M. Sams & A. A. Fripp came home with me after dinner and, by a previous arrangement, we went down after dark to Trenchards where we met Wm. Elliott Jnr.[29] & Wm. Barnwell Jnr.[30] comfortably encamped.

Oct. 7th. Friday. At daylight we were in the woods, & at 8½ o'clock had a large doe at the camp. Sams killed it. We started 4 altogether, but none others were seen. Returned to camp at 12 m., had dinner on cavally, bass steaks, & venison. Took a pleasant sail in Elliott's boat after dinner, & seeing some appearance of bad weather, we concluded to start back that evening, altho we had intended to stay & hunt the next day. We got up home at 9 p.m., took lunch & to bed. I found Eugene in my bed, he having sore throat.

Oct. 9th. Had my haunch of venison for dinner. Did not taste well, "twas badly clotted with blood." Feel rather sore from brier scratches.

Oct. 13th. Deputy Sheriff Thompson[31] came here & served me with a writ. Sent of Fyler, Danner & Co., & be damned to them. I would not see Thompson. He left the paper, & went. I have no idea of *again* entertaining sheriffs.
How coolly I took such things then

Oct. 14th. 93 sheets cowpeas in—
this could pay Fyler

Oct. 15th. Have much trouble with stock of all kinds. E. M. Capers dined with me, he looks well.
I guess, new wig
Picking peas today, will not get through the first picking of the patch, but must get at the cotton on Monday. Have in up to this day, 133 sheets peas (cow).
equal to 99 bu.

Oct. 16th. Sunday. Daniel came home yesterday & stayed all night, returned with us to church. We heard a sermon by Rev'd. Gervais Jenkins,[32]

---

[29] William Elliott, Jr. Son of William Elliott and Phoebe Waight. Brother of George P. Elliott and Stephen Elliott, Sr. See note, July 6, 1856.
[30] Possibly William F. Barnwell (b. 1840). Son of William Hazzard Wigg Barnwell and Catherine Osborn Barnwell, daughter of Capt. Edward Barnwell and sister of Thomas Osborn Barnwell.
[31] Possibly David L. Thompson, born in Scotland. Listed in the 1850 census as a "farmer" and in 1860 as a "planter."
[32] Paul Gervais Trapier Jenkins. Son of Richard Jenkins and Martha LaRoche, of Wadmalaw Island. Brother of Richard E. and Benjamin Jenkins.

not a very good one, but far better than I ever expected he would ever be able to preach. He was thought to be **_religious_** crazy once.

Oct. 17th.   Sent Jack in the cart to Beaufort for my barrel of ice. The weather is so cool it is hardly needed, but as I have to pay for it I might as well send for it. I did not want to take off hands to send the boat, besides I have taken out very little of my contract for the ferry this year. Jack got back after dark.

Oct. 21st.   Friday. All hands picking peas, 19 sheets, 152 in all.[33] Killed a shoat for pork, quite small. Hear that the Major's (D.P.J.'s) driver killed one or two of Uncle Tom's cows yesterday.

Oct. 22nd.   Joined hands with J. H. Webb & went to Beaufort in his boat. Head wind going & returning. Brought home groceries, dry goods, &c that came up from town for me. Got home about 8½ o'clock p.m. Negroes picking peas, 19 sheets.

Oct. 26th.   All hands picking cotton, and I must keep them at it, as long as the weather permits & there is any to pick. I have not finished the peas, but can't take more time at them. Have in 200 sheets, and I suppose I could get 60 or 70 more if I could pick them now.

Oct. 27th.   All hands picking peas. They ought to be at the cotton—got 29 sheets. I went down to the village, dined with Aunt Betsy. Brought Virginia & Daniel home.

Oct. 31st.   Monday. No ice came for me by last boat, so I suppose Webb has stopped it for the season. It is not wanted this cold weather. All hands picking cotton. They do not get much. Don't know why the pods do not open. Tides come very high—new moon tomorrow.

Nov. 4th.   A great deal of water has fallen, and much bottom cotton fruit is under water. All hands picking except a few men getting rails for potato pen.

Nov. 5th.   Saturday. I went to Beaufort in Webb's boat. Got my Negro cloth & shoes from town. Shoes $1 pr. pair. Cloth for grown Negroes, 43, for children, 35 cts. pr. yd. Everything high except cotton.[34]

---

[33] For the day's work, the hands picked 1,425 pounds of peas, or 14 bushels. To date, Chaplin has harvested 11,400 pounds or 204 bushels.
[34] The market "is in a dormant state . . . the principal cause being the high price expected by holders and not countenanced by the trade" (Charleston _Mercury_, Oct. 28, 1853). Prices for common Sea Island ranged between 40 and 50 cents a pound, 6 cents lower than a year ago.

Nat Heyward & J. L. Barnwell[35] came down from Beaufort with me, on their way to Bay Point where Heyward has hands at work moving his house, which has again washed in, the 2nd time in 12 months. As the weather looked unsettled & dark when we got to Lands End, & Heyward's boat not meeting him there, as he expected, both he & Barnwell rode over with me & spent the night. Quite a surprise. Sophy *got quite vexed on the strength of it.*

Nov. 6th. Heyward & Barnwell left after breakfast, and met their boat at Lands End. Eugene & I went to church. Gave the Negroes their shoes in the evening, and will give them each a flogging tomorrow for not picking more cotton yesterday.

Nov. 17th. Thursday. My neighbors are all digging slips, but getting all seed, very small. Some made one & some two banks of eating to the crop. I think my potatoes are still growing & if the weather continues warm, they might as well be in the ground, for slips dug & put in bank in warm weather are very apt *to rot.* There is very little cotton to pick at this time, & a good chance to dig, but the weather is better to pick what little cotton there is than to dig. So I will hold on.
Helen confined. Girl, name Kate.

Nov. 19th. Neighbors' stock destroying my slips so much that I shall be compelled to dig. Will commence on Monday.

Nov. 20th. Sunday. Clear & quite warm. We all went to church. Heard that Daniel was sick.

Nov. 21st. Sophy & Eugene went to the village to see after Daniel, & if necessary, bring him home. So I am alone for part of a day at least. Commenced digging slips. The acre near Ben Chaplin's line has little or nothing left—has been dug for me. Some leathercoats doing tolerably, considering. Very few large potatoes. Got today, 28 heaped baskets of eating potatoes, closely assorted, & _____ baskets seed. Ben Chaplin came round to summon out hands to work the roads next Monday. I returned 3 hands.

Nov. 24th. Finished digging red slips & commenced my yellow yams, which turn out well, but small. I have made 2 allowances of reds, & 2 of leathercoats.
I sent 2 hands with John H. Webb's in his boat, to Bluffton for Ernest.

---

[35] James Ladson Barnwell (1834–1924). Son of William Wigg Barnwell and Sarah Gibbes. Brother of Thomas G. and Robert G. Barnwell.

Webb was to have gone himself but is not well. He sends Sancho (Captain) in charge of the boat.

Nov. 25th. The wind lulled in the evening, & the weather turned very cold. Finished all the slips except the common yams. Have about 2 or 2½ acres of them to dig, will not finish tomorrow. Saw a good many robins in the evening. I think this is sure sign of cold weather. Have in now 294 baskets slips, 6 weeks' allowance, besides seed, 10 banks.

Nov. 26th. Saturday. Rode over to Webb's last evening late, thinking that Ernest might come over Broad River in the evening, but the boat did not appear in sight at dark. Went over at 11 a.m. this morning. The boat was just in sight. They all got ashore at 12¼ p.m. quite safe. Ernest says they started at 7 a.m. yesterday, but the wind was so high they stopped at an overseer's house on Scull's Creek & stayed all night. I am glad he is now (1 p.m.) at home safe, and looks quite well, but very little grown.

Nov. 27th. Eugene & Daniel went to church with me, the rest did not go. Virginia looks badly, has a sore mouth & a bad cough, the latter I think no trifling matter. I will not send her back to school for the balance of Mrs. McElheran's session.

I hear that Uncle Paul's man Sambo is in the Savannah jail. He went off to Savannah when his master went to town last week, & got taken up. Uncle Paul says he will sell him. I think it the best thing he can do with him.

Nov. 28th. Monday. The sale of perishable property takes place at the Estate of J. W. Perry's today.

Dec. 1st. Agricultural Society day. Dr. M. M. Sams, a new member, finds dinner. The President was absent, and the Vice President took the chair.[36] There was nothing done, but eating & drinking, & a great dog fight. Some men came near making up a horse race, & some trying to swap horses. I succeeded in making up a winter beef market of four, viz., Edgar Fripp, Dr. Jenkins, C. G. Capers & myself, to kill once a fortnight, each one take a quarter.

Dec. 2nd. Friday. Ben Chaplin's cattle are eating my cotton. Went out and shot two. Told him about it, he does not seem to care if I shoot them all, for he knows the most of them will die this winter.

[36] Capt. John Fripp, president, and Capt. Daniel T. Jenkins, vice-president.

Dec. 3rd.   Concluded not to kill any more of Ben Chaplin's cows. I might be made to pay for them, & they are not worth 1 dollar pr. head. Put a prime hand to mind them off, for, as I have a great many unopen pods, & the weather favorable, I may get more cotton.

Dec. 6th.   I was *sick* all day. Mr. & Mrs. Perdue spent the day. He was in my room with me all the morning. He cheered me a good deal. He says that the company of gentlemen who employ him say, that *after January*, he may take all *my* boys but, *only* the board money will go to him, the tuition money, at 12½ dollars pr. quarter, must go into the regular fund to pay his salary. This *I* think is very ungenerous, but Perdue says he will take my boys, no others, notwithstanding, & I have determined to send them all three in January.

Dec. 7th.   Wednesday. I am not much better but got up. Killed the first beef for our winter market.

Dec. 8th.   John L. Chaplin's daughter Caroline marries tonight, Capers Lowry[37] of Walterboro.
***1868, 15 years. He died of yellow fever in Charleston about 1870 or 69, very bad off* **
***Jno. Chaplin has now two boys grown   1877* **
***one I hear committed suicide by jumping down a well somewhere in Florida. He has lost his wife also some time ago 1888* **

Dec. 11th.   Sunday. Clear & cold, *heavy frost*. I & the children went to church. Old Mrs. Caroline Reynolds was buried today. She died on Thursday night. She was sick nearly all last summer with the prevailing dysentery & never entirely recovered from it.

Dec. 12th.   Monday. Clear & cold, white frost & ice, the first ice I have seen formed this winter. Started 2 gins, 4 hands picking. Very little cotton open. This frost will burst the grown pods.

    Ernest went to Beaufort with J. H. Webb, in his boat, to have a jacket made. He did not get back till late at night.

Dec. 14th.   Wednesday. Clear & very pleasant. I believe John Webb goes with his family to the Hunting Islds. so we may expect bad weather soon.

---

[37] Capers Lowry (1829–1870). Son of Isham Lowry and Mary Ann Brown. Listed in the 1860 census as an overseer in St. Bartholomew's Parish.

Dec. 15th. Killed 2 bacon hogs, for the first. Packed the 1st bale cotton, do not know the weight, part being packed in the fall. Rec. invites to Caroline Jenkins' wedding.

Dec. 16th. Friday. Very unexpectedly saw Sawney[38] today. He has come down on a raft to Beaufort. He belongs to the Est. of Felder,[39] but once belonged to me. He was very glad to see me, as I was to see him. He has got to be quite an upcountry Negro & says he would like to belong to me again. Would to God he did. He was a favorite Negro with me.

One of my best & largest bacon hogs is missing today, hope it is not lost.

Dec. 20th. Mother sent her boat over, and begs us all to go over & spend Christmas with her. She is not well, & can't come over here. I think we will go on Friday.

Dec. 22nd. Thursday. All hands picking cotton. Killed the 3rd hog for bacon.

We—Sophy, Virginia & myself—will no doubt go to the wedding[40] to-night, &, if the weather will allow, to the main tomorrow, so this journal will lay by till our return (4 p.m.).

Dec. 23rd. Friday. Went to the wedding, fine affair of course, fine supper, bride handsome, fine fun—
at Dr. Jenkins' house
Started for the main this morning, the wind was fresh but fair, went by Beaufort. Clouded up, wind rose, heavy rain & squall of wind took us in Coosa.[41] Broke the spirit to sail, scared Sophy, children seasick, but we got to the Point safe just after dark. Very cold.

Dec. 24th. Saxby & family came down today. He has five children, all well. I never expected that we all would ever meet again in the old house, and a house full we all are, 9 children & 5 adults. They all promised to come & pay us a visit in April. God knows how we will manage.

Dec. 25th. Sunday. Christmas Day. The ground is covered with snow this morning but not thick, trees covered icicles. Clear but bitter cold.

[38] Sawney was a carpenter. See July 23, 1845. Chaplin had been forced to sell him in 1847.
[39] John M. Felder. See note, June 17, 1845.
[40] The wedding of Caroline Jenkins and John Fripp Chaplin. Dr. Jenkins was her uncle.
[41] Coosaw River.

Saxby & I rode up to Farmer's. Took him up & went on to Minott's. We all returned & dined with Mother. She had a very fine dinner, too much in fact.

as she always did in those days

(I hear that the snow or sleet & cold weather extended to the Island.)

Poor Mrs. Minott is now living at my old place in a room, in my old cotton house, & is very bad off indeed, quite thin   1877

I hear she died in a hospital in Charleston after her husband some years ago very bad off   1885

Dec. 26th.   Sax & I rode out again, had some good sport shooting partridges. Sax is a good shot, & has a good pointer, also a fine broke water dog. We dined at the Point, and are to dine with Minott tomorrow. Farmer asked us to dine with him today & meet Mr. & Mrs. Minott, but for some reason or other Sax would not. I thought it strange, as Farmer expected us, & they seem intimate.

Dec. 27th.   Tuesday. Rode up in the morning to dine with Minott. Saxby's family came also, my folks did not. Farmer & family were of the company. They seem to be quite a musical set over there. They all play on some instrument. Sax & his wife play several tunes together on the piano & violin. Minott, Farmer, & Sax play together on the fiddle. After dinner, or late in the evening, I went with Sax & family to Hickory Hill. They are to have a dinner party tomorrow. Farmer will not join (he is right).

Dec. 28th.   We went after ducks today, had good sport. I killed the most. After late dinner, I took a cold ride to the Point, in Saxby's carriage, left Jack to start home with my horses tomorrow. (I forgot to say I had them sent round on Saturday.)

I have now not even a house much less a carriage   '77

Saxby drives a wagon for a living   70–77

my poor brother died in 1884 & I am now living in the same house he died in near Walterboro   1885

Dec. 30th   Friday. Weather too bad to go out in a boat, put off our trip.

Dec. 31st.   Saturday. Weather worse than yesterday. Rain & wind & cold.

1854

Jan. 3rd.   Everything looks snug. I find a good blow of cotton. All hands picking & have picked while I was away, about 200 lbs. They brought in about 10 lbs. apiece today. Gave out last allowance of slips.

Jan. 5th.   Took out the first hogs killed, & boiled over the pickle, & poured over again, 3 weeks since killed.
Have no hogs to kill now   1885

Jan. 6th.   Went to Beaufort. Took the three boys to get them each a pr. of boots. Got back before sunset.
    I heard today that Aunt Betsy has offered her village house to rent, offered it to Randolph Sams,[1] who declined it. This is rather unkind to me. One would suppose she would have offered it to me, knowing as *she does*, how much I would like to get a house at the village on account of saving the children's board. Dr. Jenkins, & no one else, is at the bottom of this, he can't bear to see me or mine get along, or be advantaged in any way.
He was run off
    Helen's last child died today, regularly murdered.[2] The little thing was bruised & hurt in several places. The mother deserves a good whipping, & I think she will get it yet.
    Packed 3rd bale of cotton, 369 lbs.

Jan. 8th.   Having heard that Aunt Betsy would hire out her house, I wrote her on the subject, & stated above. Tonight I received a message

[1] Robert Randolph Sams (1827–1910), planter and dentist, St. Helena Parish. Son of Berners Barnwell Sams and Elizabeth Fripp. Brother of Berners Bainbridge and Melvin Melius Sams. Chaplin's second cousin, on his mother's side. Randolph and Aunt Betsy were first cousins, once removed.
[2] Helen's girl Kate was born on Nov. 17, 1853—her third baby since 1845. See July 21, 1855, and the next-to-last entry in the journal, dated simply Oct. 1860.

from Mr. McElheran, through Uncle Paul, that I could have the house. Much more than I expected.

Jan. 9th.   We all went to the village. Left all the children, the 3 boys with Perdue, & Virginia with Mrs. McElheran. *Now* they are *all* at school. Virginia will commence music lessons on the piano this quarter. I do not feel inclined to move to the village till next May. I will try & get Mother to come over to take the children with her till we can move.

Packed the 4th bale of cotton. 344 lbs.

Jan. 11th.   Aunt Betsy called to tell us goodbye this evening. She moves to Beaufort this week. I hear that Dr. Jenkins moved in 3 flats to Beaufort yesterday & went with his family today. Aunt Betsy spends this night with Coz. Emma Webb[3] and returns to the village tomorrow.

Jan. 12th.   Thursday. Quite a thunderstorm last night, vivid flashes of lightning & severe claps of thunder (equal to a summer storm). Very heavy rain & wind, from S. or S.W. Cloudy & some rain this morning but looks like clearing, about 10 a.m.

I suppose that the occasion of the wealthy Dr.'s moving to & taking up his abode in the great city of Beaufort, was thus celebrated by the great artillery of heaven, an occurrence worthy of note.

Jan. 13th.   Finished packing the 5th bale cotton this morning, 404 lbs. Will send them off to Beaufort tonight. Borrowed Uncle Paul's flat for the purpose.

Heard today of the death of Coz. William Perry. He died very suddenly after eating dinner yesterday. An invitation was sent over to the Island to T. J. Fripp to be sent round.

15 years   12th Jan. '69
23 years this 1877, only think

Jan. 14th.   Sent 5 bales of cotton to Beaufort to go to town. Sent Thomas in gig to village with children's clothes. They are all well & satisfied. Mother's boat came over yesterday. Received a present from Saxby, in the shape of a large country built, oak arm rocking chair, cowhide seat. Very cool & comfortable.

Robert & Isaac got the 2 oak chairs I had, & never offered [   ]

Jan. 15th.   Sunday. Clear & pleasant. Sophy & I went to church. Saw Daniel & Virginia, the other two could not come. Eugene has a bad boil,

---

[3] Emma Jenkins Webb. Aunt Betsy's niece and the Captain's sister. Wife of John H. Webb.

and they are all very well satisfied. Capt. John Fripp informed me that he intended to withdraw from the company of three that employed Mr. Perdue. I am sorry for this. I would rather one of the others withdraw & let me in with Jno. Fripp as one of the party, & continue the school. I received today a notice that I have been appointed, with others, to appraise & divide the Estate of David Fripp between his children, David & Mary Fripp,[4] to take place on Thursday at Hall's[5] Store.
don't recollect anything about it   1885

Jan. 16th.   Attended an auction sale of perishable property of W. J. Grayson.[6] A great many things were sold, some very cheap. I made I think, two very good bargains, viz., a very good set of graniteware crockery, dinner set &c, for $11, and 6 painted chairs (wood) for $4.80 = $15.80. Coffin, T. A., had previously bought many of the things, furniture &c with the tract of land.

Commenced moving cow pen over slip land. I am having the balance of my white cotton whipped with switches, as is done with yellow cotton, but not as much whipped. This by way of experiment. I think it makes the cotton look better, at least it serves to show the specks better, to be picked out.

Jan. 17th.   Went to Grayson's, paid for & got all my things home safe. Sophy is quite pleased with my bargains. We needed some crockery, particularly if Saxby & fam. come over in April. Packed 6 bale cotton. Heard last week that Saxby lost his large machine house by fire.[7] Did not learn his loss otherwise, i.e. in cotton in the house, tis supposed it must be considerable——

Jan. 19th.   Thursday. Drizzly, & very disagreeable. Wind E. Finished ginning the last of the "Fripp" cotton, only one hand's work for today. I do not think it will fill another bag. Commenced assorting the Grayson cotton. I think I will get a bale of that.

I could not meet W.O.P. Fripp today, as I agreed to last Sunday, for the purpose of dividing some property between David & Mary Fripp.[8] The weather & my health does not permit exposure.

---

[4] David and Mary Fripp, children of the late David S. Fripp, son of Archibald Fripp and Elizabeth Scott. Young David and Mary were second cousins to Chaplin on their father's side.
[5] John O. Hall (b. 1817), Beaufort merchant.
[6] Grayson had moved off the Island.
[7] Saxby operated steam-driven cotton gins.
[8] Oliver Fripp, like Chaplin, was second cousin to David Fripp's children.

Jan. 20th.   Sophy went to the village for the children.

Finished the Fripp's cotton, *2513 lbs. by my weights.*

All hands commenced assorting the "Grayson" cotton.

Commenced hauling out marsh.

Finished assorting the Grayson cotton, 1281 lbs., allowing 10 lbs. on the hundred, about 357¼ lbs. pr. acre, and very broken it was.

Sophy got back with the children, all safe, about 4 p.m.

Jan. 21st.   Packed the 7th bale. Put in all the Fripp's cotton I had left, 310 lbs., but the bag holds more. Will fill it up with Grayson's frost cotton. Whipped out the yellow cotton (seed). Think I will get a 300 weight bag of it.

2 hands listed a couple of tasks. Manured with marsh. Sent 2 hands to Beaufort in boat from Webb's, had not returned at dark. Suppose the weather has kept them.

Jan. 22nd.   Sunday. Old Judy very sick, think she will make a die of it.

Jan. 24th.   Grayson's seed cotton gives 25 lbs., sheet included, from 100 lbs., sheet included, of seed cotton. I will not plant any more of it unless I get 5 cts. more for it than for the Fripp seed.

Jan. 26th.   Commenced planting oats in slip patch, with two women & Jack with the plow. 2 men ginning & 2 women following, & finish the last of the white cotton. Total 2845 lbs., *my weight.* Isaac, Frank & the 2 carts hauling out the stuff I had got out for poultry house in the fall. 2 hands chopping fennel.

Jan. 28th.   Saturday. I & Robert ran out some cotton land. All women chopping fennel in corn field. 3 hands ditching. Sent Jack to village. Planted Irish potatoes yesterday & today.

Jan. 29th.   Sophy & I went to church. Virginia was the only one of the children out from the village. Heard that Wm. Chisolm had moved to the village from Johns Island, & what is bad, brought the whooping cough with his servants.

Jan. 30th.   Monday. Various work going on. 2 hands ditching, 1 hand tracking root patch. Women chopping fennel. Finished carting out marsh & commenced at the cowpeas again. Sent Jack to Beaufort, to carry the plow I return to Webb & Ingraham.

Old Judy died about 3 p.m. She has been sick for some time, & so completely helpless it is better for her to be in the grave.

Feb. 7th. 1854.   Robert came in this morning to tell me that he found the smokehouse door *open*. Said when he left home he left 8 pieces of bacon; finds but five (5) and 1 of chine.[9] They say their *master* gave some of the little Negroes meat. Don't know how much. Jack was left to lock the door, can't say if he did, for it was open in the morning.

Feb. 11th.   Vaccinated the 3 boys, Jack, William, & Scipio, who were done by Dr. Croft on the 4th instant, which took. The following Negroes, Mary's two children, Sarah & John C., Judy's 2, Trim & Daphne, Peg's Isaac & Emmeline, Elsie's John, Sam, Pat, Martha, Thomas, Jonah—12. The rest could not be got at.

The Negroes did not get back today that I sent up to Beaufort yesterday. Can't imagine the cause. The wind was fresh from east, all day, but I do not think too high for them. I did not finish listing corn land on account of their absence. Have about 3½ tasks left. Will make in all 26½ acres. Commenced carting compost on corn land.

Feb. 12th.   Sophy & I went church. Saw Virginia & Eugene. Got a letter from T. L. Webb saying he had sent a can of gas for me by the *Etiwan* to village.

Feb. 13th.   Sent to the village for the can of gas, but did not get it. How provoking. No one has seen it. Finished listing all my corn land except 1 task, which is manured with mud, as an experiment. Want it to dry before spreading. 3 hands ditching corn land.

Feb. 14th.   Sent again to see if anything can be heard of my can of gas. Sent Robert this time, as I sent Thomas yesterday. I thought he may have gone wrong, but no better luck. Suppose it is lost. Mother sent over this morning, sent me some yellow cotton to put with my own when I pack it.

Heard from Webb last week, which I forgot to note, that my 5 bales of cotton are sold for 38¢, less than I expected, but from the state of affairs in Europe &c persons think I have done well.[10]

Feb. 18th.   Finished all my compost, stable and all. Have 9½ acres cotton land listed, manured *with marsh*. Will stop splitting rails after today, & commence making fence on Monday.

Killed the 7th & last hog yesterday, put it in pickle today. Had one of the first hams cured for dinner today, to try it, & found it most excellent &

[9] The backbone.
[10] War between Russia and Turkey had increased European anxiety over foodstuffs and depressed the demand for cotton. The Czar would die in March, encouraging hopes for peace and stimulating the cotton market.

juicy. If I can only keep them through the summer, I never wish to eat better cured bacon.

Wish I had a few of them now. Have nothing & none to get but mean [   ] bacon '77

Feb. 19th.   Got my can of gas, 10 gallons.
Where was it I don't say

Feb. 20th.   Commenced making fence line between my own & Riverside tracks. Posts that have been swelled in saltwater, & rails nailed on them with 12 d nails, rather slow, but easier than the old way.[11] 6 hands still listing in marsh. Got a box of medicine from town.

Feb. 21st.   Getting on slowly with the fence. I have nailed on every rail myself so far. Women still listing in marsh, & Amy still in the Negro house sick. Planted beets.

Feb. 22nd.   Wednesday. Washington's Birthday. 3 hands still at the fence, not more than half done. Women at the marsh, think I will finish in two more days. 14½ acres now listed in, of marsh. Amy still laying up, now 12 days. I'll take it out of her when she does come out. Finished plowing all the corn land, manured with cotton seed, & commenced plowing cotton land. Planted carrots.

Sent to Mr. Perdue on Sunday last, by Ernest, an order on Ingraham & Webb for $107.66. The amt. of Daniel's board & tuition up to Dec'r. 1853.

Feb. 24th.   Friday. Beautiful weather, warm spring day. Finished my post & rail nailed fence as far as the corner Station tree between the Riverside, Curlew Hill & my track. I will not go further till I know where Uncle Paul intends running his fence. I am in hopes he will make a fence on the line, between us, extending down to Station Marsh. Sent the fellows to work on my division fence till I hear from Uncle Paul. Sent Jack to the village. Amy came out & chopped some fennel today.

Mother moved over to the village yesterday, & at once took all the children to stay with her, so their board terminates this day. I don't know that Mrs. McElheran will deduct anything for Virginia as she boards by the quarter, but Perdue will deduct for the boys, for they board by the month, which I think is the most correct.

---

[11] Formerly the posts were notched and the rails were slipped into the notches like pegs.

Feb. 25th. The marsh I had cut last summer manures just 19 acres, 1 task & 7 beds. I shall have to cut about 3 days' work more as I cannot get mud enough for all the land I have left.

Feb. 26th. Sunday. Sophy & I went down to the village on a visit, to Mother & the children.

Feb. 27th. Monday. Clear & fine, at the village all day. The hands at home securing the sedge that has come ashore.

Feb. 28th. Tuesday. We got home about 11 a.m. Robert has made good work with the sedge. I will have more than enough to manure all the cotton land not already manured. The 3 men still at the division fence.

March 1st. Wednesday. Muster Day. Acted as orderly sergeant for the first time, having been appointed to the office.

March 2nd. Melvin Sams came down with his dogs & we took a cat hunt. The dogs, after a short chase, caught a very large cat. No one shot at it. D. P. Jenkins, Paul Chaplin, J. H. Webb & D. Jenkins joined in the hunt. The two latter & Melvin dined with me, & Sophy gave an excellent dinner.

March 3rd. All hands listing cotton land. Finished listing all the sedge that came up, 6¼ acres & 14 beds manured with it. Have, up to date, 31¾ acres cotton land listed, & all well manured. Uncle Paul concluded today, to run his fence down to the line between us, and as soon as we can, will make the entire line fence between us.

March 4th. Saturday. Sent flat with Robert & 3 hands to Beaufort for 100 bu. of corn. Did not get back today. Counted up all the land taken up for cotton, & make it out just 38 acres. Robert makes it much more. Don't think I made the mistake. Sent Jack to the village with children's clothes &c.

March 5th. Sunday. Went to church, and heard Mr. McE. wade through one of the dryest, [most] nonsensical & longest sermons that any poor devil ever sat under, & Communion Sunday withal. He can never confine himself to his one text. I should advise him to take some dozen, & he may be able to touch on some of them during his preaching.

My flat has not come today. I don't know what to think of it. I hear that the corn was in Beaufort, & got put in the flat at 9 o'clock last night.

(Note) Flat got back in the creek, but too late to get up to the landing, left in corn in her all night.

March 6th. Unloaded the flat, & measured two bags, which, as is always the case, did not hold out by 3 or 4 qts. Women opening mud to dry before spreading. 3 men finishing the piece of fencing between Uncle Paul & I. Will not get through today. Carts hauling posts & rails. Gave out the first allowance of the bought corn. Commenced spreading the compost over potato land. Finished opening the mud.

March 8th. Women listing in mud. 4 men splitting rails to finish fencing. This is very bad for me. Uncle Paul's rails gave out, & he does not seem disposed to help me out. Plowing the corn land manured with compost.

March 10th. Friday. Finished listing cotton land, and my fencing out & out——
Went to the village after dinner to stay till Monday (perhaps) for the purpose of having some corn put up that I expect from town pr. steamer *Etiwan.* Frank plowing corn land.

March 11th. Found the steamboat at the wharf this morning, got my corn, 30 bushels, & had it put away. Returned the bags to town that came with corn last week.

March 13th. Banked potato land. 1 hand tracking to plant corn. Isaac Fripp called to *beg* potato seed. Promised to let him have some if could spare them. Moll planted some cotton in her patch, near the yard.

March 16th. Commenced planting corn. Planted about 12 acres. I out fishing, joined hands with Webb. 11 drum taken, I only caught one, the only one I got on my side.

March 17th. Sent a side of fish to the village to Mother. All hands banking corn land.

April 2nd. Sunday. Clear, cold north wind. Went to church. Large congregation & good sermon. This weather knocks up all drum fishing for a while.

April 3rd. April has really taken the place of March *as regards to season.* Sent 2 hands to Beaufort but don't think they got there this morning, wind too high. All hands that are out, planting cotton, the 1st planting coming up—to be killed I suppose.

Gave out 4th allowance of bought corn.

April 5th. Planted arrowroot. Finished planting cotton, out & out, 42¼ acres & 7 beds. *Heard* that Uncle Paul got through yesterday, & Uncle Tom today.

April 7th. Friday. Gave the Negroes the day to plant for themselves. Sent Robert to the village to put the corn I have there in bags, to be brought round in Mother's boat.

April 8th. Sent 3 bales of cotton to Beaufort in Uncle Paul's flat. Joined hands with the Captain, he sends his cotton also.

April 9th. Sunday. E. M. Capers came to fish this week with me. He gave me 8 Shanghai eggs, which I set under a hen immediately.

April 10th, 11th & 12th & 13th. We fished in Webb's boat with various success, highest No. taken, 11.

April 20th. Thursday. Clear & moderate. Caroline Scott married today—Benjamin Bailey of Wadmalaw. We were invited to be at the church, but none of us went.

April 22nd. Saturday. Went out & took 2 drum, the 3 boys went with me. Let Robert go to see his wife.

April 24th. Finished 1st hoeing of corn, & commenced hoeing potatoes.

Planted over some cotton, injured by frost.

Saxby sent Scipio over for some papers connected with Mother's property.[12] I had none of any importance to send him.

April 26th. Wednesday. Took all the family down to Bay Point, where they spent the day. I went fishing, took 4 drum. Codding caught 45.

---

[12] Mary O'Connor, widow of Beaufort merchant Michael O'Connor, had sued R. L. Baker for a debt he had run up while he and Isabella were living apart. A clause in Mrs. Baker's marriage settlement stipulated that in case of separation, Isabella, not her husband, was to receive the income from her estate for "her own separate use." Saxby was preparing to jump in and sue the trustee, Francis L. Roux, on the grounds that the reversion of payment to Mrs. Baker had terminated Baker's interest in her property, which now ought to be delivered up to him, Saxby, and to Thomas, too. Mrs. Baker's deeds to him and his brother, claimed Saxby, had "become active and of immediate operation." The court would disagree with this interpretation of events, and Baker's "life estate" would be left "unaffected."

April 27th.　Went fishing, took 10 drum. My birthday. Got home to dinner, 32 years old.

April 28th.　Went fishing. My last day—took 7.

May 1st.　Monday. I have Irish potatoes & squashes & peas fit to eat. Cotton very grassy. Corn look very fine. I, unfortunately, have to buy more corn & in debt to I. & Webb, near $400 at that.

May 3rd.　Went to muster. Danl. Jenkins treated to a basket of champagne as his farewell treat to the company. He is over 45 years old & is now on the list of alarm men.[13] Two other men were taken off the roll yesterday & put on the alarm roll, James Fendin and D. B. Patterson. Baker, tax collector, was over, & gave an order for my taxes, $42.42, including the Negroes I have from Mother, & the Riverside land.

There were several men corned today, & some little quarreling, in consequence.

May 5th.　Friday. All hands hoeing cotton. Commenced moving to the village by sending down Mary & family to clean up the house.

May 7th.　Got Uncle Paul's flat to move to the village as soon as I can. I am waiting now for Mother's boat to come over, & clear weather.

May 8th.　Monday. Sent the children down to the village to school. Mother's boat came over, & we will all go tomorrow. Sent off a flat load of movables to the village.

May 9th.　All hands hauling cotton. Sophy, Mother & Eugene went round the village in Mother's boat, and, though I sent so many things in the flat, they had a good load & I had to send a cart besides, & make some of my Negroes walk. I saw things put to rights & [　　] down in sulky. So now begins the long & weary summer at the village.

May 13th.　Saturday. Flat got back with 49 bags of corn in the evening, late. Did not go to the village. Clear, hoed potatoes.

May 18th.　Thursday. Clear & fine, had very heavy blow at vill. yesterday, & heavy rain last night, not so much down here. Much grass in corn

[13] When a white man turned forty-five he was removed from the list of active militiamen and placed on the reserve list, called the alarm roll.

& some of the cotton. All hands hoeing. Peg miscarried yesterday, child born dead. Don't know the cause.

June 1st. Wednesday. Finished hauling corn, and commenced hoeing cotton. Traded with J.J.T. Pope my mare Duchess & colt, for his dark brown mare Mettle (I now call "Ida") & $20 to boot. Don't think I have made a very good trade, but, "Ida" is young, 6 years, & ready for present use. Duchess old, & of very little use but for breed.

Sept. 7th. Commenced blowing from the east, and got to be a very heavy storm, or hurricane of wind & rain, lasted without intermission till Saturday, 12 m., when the wind fell a little, but still continued blowing pretty hard, and a heavy storm of wind & rain again at night with much thunder & lightning. I never saw such a storm in my life.[14] Neither has the oldest inhabitant. Crops are all ruined. Trees blown down & uprooted, fences all down. Friday there was the highest tide I ever saw. The water was 2 feet deep in my yard & extended almost to the stable. Much of the cotton, corn & potatoes were under water. My grass cut, marsh carried off. All the large bridges on the Island gone.

Sept. 8th. Friday. Tremendous gale, or hurricane. Trees & limbs flying in every direction, fences all down.

[14] Driven by ninety-mile-per-hour winds, the ocean inundated plantations along the entire length of the Sea Island cotton and rice regions. The storm center passed inland between Jacksonville, Fla., and Savannah.

1855

Jan. 8th. 1855. Virginia commenced this year's board with Mrs. McElheran.

Jan. 15th. Daniel went to board & school at the same place.

Jan. 23rd. Ernest went to board with Mr. Morcock in Beaufort, & commenced school at the "College"[1] on the 24th.

Jan. 25th. Eliza confined. Boy, named Prince.

Feb. 3rd. Sowed English peas, lettuce, spinach, radishes. Packed 11th & last bag of white cotton (very light). Finished cutting cotton stalks to plant the Home Field over again this year.

Feb. 8th. Planted sugarcane.

Feb. 9th. Sent to Beaufort & to the village for the children. Commenced listing root potato patch.
   Planted cucumbers & guinea squash in turnip cups.[2]
Failure

Feb. 12th. Monday. Children returned to school. I went to village & to Mrs. James Fripp's[3] Estate sale. Did not stay to see many things sold, & I could buy nothing. Capt. J. Fripp bought the village house for the low price of $425.

---

[1] "Dedicated to Virtue, Liberty, and Science," Beaufort College was established in 1804 as a combination primary school, secondary school, and college; in later decades it functioned strictly as an academy, or secondary school.
[2] Hollowed-out turnips used for germinating seeds before setting them out in the garden. Recommended by Holmes.
[3] Mary Pope (1796–1854). Widow of James Fripp, and mother of W.O.P., J.E.L., and J.T.E. Fripp.

March 19th, 20th & 21st. Planted potatoes. Seed rotted very badly, barely had enough.
Covered with pine trash, bad plan

March 30th. Ernest's 1st quarter in Beaufort ends. Sent for him. Daniel's 1st [quarter] at Mrs. McElheran's ends. Went to the village & brought him home. Paid Dr. L. R. Sams $100 for 3 boys' tuition at Perdue's. Paid Mrs. McElheran $500 for Virginia on a/c.

March 31st. March goes out weeping dreadfully, steady & driving rain all day. Had the hands ginning cotton. March goes out very much as it did last year, rain & very heavy blow, colder this year.

April 1st. Sunday. April comes in clear & very pleasant, the only day like spring we have had. What a contrast to the storm of yesterday, but the rain is of much service.

April 2nd. Monday. Full moon. Commenced banking cotton land, altho I have not finished listing, but will take advantage of the late rain to bank up what I have listed. Put the men at the ditches. Election for Ordinary today. Cast my vote for Morrall.

April 21st. Saturday. Turned cool & cloudy during last night, wind very high. Cloudy & continues to blow from N. & E. all day. Lulled in the evening. Potatoes blew out of ground & had to cover them up. Supplied over corn.

I was called early in the morning to see old Uncle Tom Chaplin, & saw the poor old man breathe his last about 10 a.m. He has been almost bedridden for five months, suffering very much. He is now better off. God rest his soul. Few knew the goodness of his heart. He was a few months over eighty-three years of age, & perhaps the oldest inhabitant of this island.
30 years since he died, 1885, would be in April 113 yrs.
Having repeatedly expressed a wish to be buried in the family burying ground, near his house, his afflicted brother feels it his duty to have it done, though the tabby enclosure is quite full, & no room for another coffin, his remains will be interred close to the wall, & a small tabby or brick wall enclose the grave, & join to the old wall.
(Which was accordingly done)

April 22nd. Heard that D. P. Jenkins' kitchen was struck by lightning, & his cook very seriously injured, her life uncertain, a dog nearby killed dead. Rode over after the rain and assisted in putting the body of poor old Uncle Tom in his last house, the coffin. Returned to dinner, & attended the funeral at 5½ o'clock. My *best friend* is now beneath the sod. God rest his good soul. The funeral was numerously attended.

April 24th.   Tuesday. Fished, took 2.

April 25th.   Ditto. E. Capers with me, took 2.

April 26th.   do.   do.   "   "   "   5.

April 30th.   Sent Ernest & Daniel to school in Beaufort, they board at Morcock's. Ned Capers went up with them in the boat, I did not feel well enough.

May 3rd.   Virginia & Eugene went to school to Mrs. McElheran at the village.

May 9th.   First hoeing. The men ditching, a work that I am doing a great deal of, & hope the work is not thrown away. I lost most of my slips for the want these ditches last year. My corn is suffering for want of work, and so is my cotton, but I will take worse first, & turn all hands in the corn tomorrow. Nelly confined, boy child, name Dick, 17th inst.[4]

May 10th.   Capt. D. Jenkins called to see me, extraordinary.

May 15th.   All hands hoeing cotton, & started the plow through it. Sophy & self went out fishing, took 4 sheephead. She caught one, the first fish she ever caught in her life——

May 16th.   Wife & self went to Skull's Inlet. Had a very pleasant time. Got more fish than we and the Negroes could eat, sheephead, bass, mullets &c.

May 17th.   Thursday. We got back about 12 m. today, and met bad news at home. Nelly's child died just before we got ashore. Amy says with lockjaw. I don't know the cause. It was well, or rather not sick, when we left yesterday. I am unfortunate. This is the fourth Negro child I have lost

[4] May 17. This item was added to the entry after Dick's birth.

since last fall. There is something wrong, & I will find it out yet, the one that is to blame had better be in hell.

∗1868, no loss if all had died then & there∗

May 21st. Monday. All hands hauling & transplanting corn, 3 hands quite sick with bowel complaint, which seems quite prevalent, particularly in blackberry time. Sent all the children back to school, and we are by ourselves again.

May 26th. Saturday. Sent the sulky to the village with children's clothes, and Sophy begged for Eugene to come home. I don't like it, but consented. Hoeing cotton.

June 1st. Friday. Sophy begged again to let Eugene come. Consented for the last time this summer.

June 2nd. Heavy storm of rain & wind last night. Rain beat in & house leaked much.

Was greatly astonished to be called up this morning with the message from Robert that Sam had broken open the corn house last night, & that he was then tied in the corn house. Got up quick, found that the door had been wrenched open, tearing off the lock, about 1½ bushels loose corn gone, also all the meat I had bought for the Negroes except 4 small pieces. Robert says he knew that Sam was off the place last night. Had been to him, R., to borrow a bag to carry corn to the store. Sam being house servant, took no allowance, could have no corn. Further that he saw a track from & to the Negro houses, which he says is Sam's track. Sam accounted for the corn to my satisfaction. Robert says he found the corn house open after the rain, or before day. Clear & moon bright, the reason of his being up at that time, he had a dream or vision which made him uneasy. He also felt uneasy yesterday. Says he "always does when anything bad is about to happen." He gets up & goes to the stable & then to the corn house which he finds open & finds [   ] track in the "moonlight" but [   ] Frank about the track [   ] R.'s opinion (Frank would [   ] the place all last night [   ] guard last. Robert did not tell him, though Robert knew that F. was going—as well he did that Sam was.)

Up to Saturday 9th, heard nothing of thief or meat. Never expect to. Consequence. Will buy no more meat for the Negroes. This was fine fat rump pork, good enough for anyone to eat, & if they can't keep others or themselves from stealing it, they will get none atall. Here is a whole barrel of meat, the very best stolen by perhaps *one* or *two* Negroes, depriving the others of getting any atall, but, such is their character & nature. It was not, in my opinion, taken by any living off the place.

June 4th.   Sent Eugene back. Rolled down some grassy cotton.[5] Nothing more of the stolen meat or the thief. Believe Sam to be innocent of the theft, *rather* suspect Robert & Frank themselves. **Looks very snaky.**

June 5th.   Heard that the hailstorm on the 27th May did terrible havoc with the crops of corn, cotton & potatoes. Many persons have to plant nearly their entire crop of cotton over, at the Indian Hills all but 15 acres. The greatest sufferers I have heard of are, Aunt Betsy, Capt. J. Fripp, Edgar Fripp, Coffin, Edings, Capers, Sarah Perry & John Pope. Hailstones, they say, as large as **birds'** eggs.

June 15th.   Mother came over from the main, brought the boys with her from Beaufort. Very wrong at this time of the year. Sent boat to Beaufort for corn & ice. Thinned out all my cotton to one stalk, grows fast.

June 16th.   Saturday. High wind & cool last night. Boat got back from Beaufort with 25 bu. or rather 12 bags of corn, no ice. Damn Webb, no letters or papers.

June 20th.   Wednesday. Finished the second hoeing of cotton. Commenced banking up corn to lay by. It is rather old to work, much of it in tassel & silk, but can't leave it as it stands, hoed down & plowed. Finished the last plowing in it today.

June 22nd.   Sent cart to Beaufort, & got first barrel of ice from town.

June 29th.   Finished ginning yellow cotton, & cleaned it. Rode to Coffin's to see Ned Capers about fixing my flat. Sent boat to Beaufort for ice & sent bale of seed cotton[6] to go to town. 2nd barrel ice.

June 30th.   Hoed cotton, too grassy to haul.

July 2nd.   Monday. Sent Frank to Beaufort to carry a jug that was sent through mistake. Ernest & Daniel, very unexpectedly to me, came back with him. They brought a note from Morcock, stating that he could not board them any longer. I don't know where to get board for them & fear

---

[5] Chopped out the grass and heaped it in the furrows.
[6] Yellow cotton.

they will have to stay here which will not only be dangerous, but much valuable time lost from school.

July 3rd. Sent the sulky to the village with Virginia's clothes and to make matters worse, Sophy must be so foolish as to send for Eugene, unknown to me—too bad. Daniel went in the sulky.

July 4th. Heard that J. T. Harvey caught a Negro, runaway from Mrs. Wallace,[7] stealing watermelons out of Edgar Fripp's garden, & flogged & ducked him in such a manner that the fellow died. Harvey was arrested & lodged in Beaufort jail. His family are there with him. I am truly sorry for them. Don't think Harvey had any intention to kill the fellow—pity some more runaway rascals could not be killed. Harvey has applied for bail. I don't know the opinion of the public on the case.

July 7th. Saturday. Sent cart to Beaufort for ice. Got none, damned provoking & so hot. Ernest went also, in sulky, to see after & bring his & D.'s clothes. Did not half attend to his business. Thought more of his dress & buying for his grandmother, cake of course, than anything else. Rained hard in the evening.

July 8th. Sunday. Very hot. Went to church, heard a most excellent sermon from Bishop Davis,[8] who is on an official visit to this church.

July 10th. Tuesday. *Note.* Forgot to state in proper place, that on Friday night, 6th inst., 2 sheep were stolen out of my pen. Followed the tracks the next morning to a swamp, the other side of Dr. Scott's, but saw nothing of meat or rogues. I am sure they are two of Isaac Fripp's Negroes, runaways & the same fellows, by the tracks, that broke into my corn house a while back.

Went as one of the appraisers of the Est. of Uncle Tom. Daniel Jenkins & J. H. Webb were the other two appointed. It was a mere matter of form, as Uncle Paul gets everything. Sent Frank to Beaufort with a letter to Mrs. Bell to try & get her to take Ernest & Daniel to board. She says her house is full already.

More robbery. Discovered that my little rascal William, who I had

---

[7] Widow of the late Rev. Joseph Wallace. Harvey was the overseer for Mrs. Wallace's neighbor, Edgar Fripp.

[8] Thomas F. Davis (1804–1871), Episcopal bishop of the Diocese of South Carolina from 1853 until his death. Before taking holy orders, Davis was a successful lawyer in North Carolina. Under his lead, the diocese founded a theological seminary in Camden, S.C., where he had been rector of Grace Church. Antislavery agitation in the northern churches motivated southern Episcopalians to train candidates for the ministry at home.

minding the crows off the watermelons, has been the worse crow himself, & does the thing quite systematically. He turns over a melon, cuts a hole on the underside large enough to admit his hand, eats out the inside, where he finds a ripe one, then turns the melon back again, not breaking it off the vine. There it lays, looking as sound as ever, no one would suppose it hollow. In picking some today, we found no less than 23 or 25 in this fix. *Cunning,* very.

July 11th. Uncle Paul made me a present of three old pictures, or engravings, battle scenes that used to belong to my father, and hung in this house when I was a child. After many years, they have got back to their old places again.

July 12th. Thursday. Finished planting slips, 7 acres. Beef market commenced. Uncle Paul killed.[9]

July 14th. Saturday. Sent to Beaufort, got a barrel of ice—3rd barrel this year & very acceptable this hot weather. Daniel went to the village to spend the day with Virginia & Eugene. This is Virginia's birthday. She is 13 years old, & not in good health by any means.

July 16th. Monday. All hands hauling cotton. Mother's boat came over & brought me a veal.

July 17th. Rode down to the village to see the children. Played 11 games of billiards, beat 5 of them. Dined with W. P. Fripp,[10] clever fellow.

July 18th. Wednesday. Very hot. Finished hauling cotton, some of it for the last I think. Had to side haul the tallest. Commenced 1st hoeing of slips. They look very fine. Capt. D. Jenkins called & rode over my crop with me. He thinks it all very good & clean. He thinks my early corn good for 20 bushels pr. acre. I finished stripping blades off it today. Put Frank to hauling sedge in cow pen. I have neglected my compost very much. The young mare, "Moonlight," had a horse colt, about two days ago. Finished hoeing slips & hauled up some

July 19th. Thursday. Very hot, thunder in the morning. All hands listing pea ground, rather late, & ground very dry.

[9] It was Uncle Paul's turn to butcher and distribute beef.
[10] William Paul Fripp (b. 1834), planter. Son of William B. Fripp and Eliza Chaplin. Brother of John E. and Thomas B. Fripp. Chaplin's first cousin, once removed, on his mother's side. Second cousin of Capt. John Fripp, whose daughter Martha he married.

Undertook to boil some watermelon water down to syrup, an experiment. Have heard it was very fine. Will know the result tomorrow.

July 20th. Friday. Sent to Beaufort for ice, got 1 barrel. Letter in the office for me with proceeds of stained cotton. P.M.[11] would not send it without a note. Will send again tomorrow. Listing pea land.

July 21st. Saturday. Got my a/c sales for stained cotton. 3341 lbs., at 13 cents. Rec'd $40——
Daniel went to the village. Drove too hard & gave Buckskin the thumps.[12]
Just like him still—1868
Cannot get board for the boys in Beaufort. Will be obliged to keep them at home and try & teach them something myself. Finished listing pea land, & hauling slips. Helen confined with a girl child on Thursday night, the 19th inst., name Kate.

July 26th. Thursday. Mother's boat came over for her. Brought me two heifers & two bulls, yearlings, for breed & oxen. Pompey brought over a small poplar boat which I bought of him for $10. Finished banking pea land.

July 30th. Commenced picking early peas—7 hands, 14 sheets, 3 tasks. 2 hands at marsh again. Have not cut since first day. John E. Fripp & W. A. Chisolm came to ride over my crop. As I was upstairs & could not come directly down with a sore foot, they rode off, without seeing the crop, except the worst part along the road.

Aug. 1st. Finished 1st picking of early peas. Got 42 sheets.

Aug. 4th. Saturday. Sent to the village for the children. We are to go to the bay on Monday, weather permitting. Got Aunt Betsy's large boat for the purpose.
Finished an ox cart I have been working at for several days. A great quantity of sedge came up on my shore.

Aug. 5th. Sunday. Clear & not very hot out of the sun. All the children are here, & there is one constant noise. We will go to the Island tomorrow.

[11] Postmaster.
[12] A thumping or beating in a horse's chest; involuntary contractions of the diaphragm, like hiccups.

Aug. 9th. Thursday. Excessively hot. Had a storm of wind & rain last evening. All hands planting cowpeas. Planted 6 acres & 1½ tasks. Seed gave out. Negroes wasted it. I was too unwell all day to see after it.

Sophy sick all day, fever quite hot, & weather ditto, though there was a breeze.

Aug. 10th. Friday. Very hot. Stripping blades in cotton field. Sent to Beaufort for ice. Boat got back after midnight, brought ice & also some groceries &c, 6 doz. ale. Sophy quite sick all day, very anxious for the ice. Got some for her as soon as it came, did her much good. This is the 7th barrel, got 125 lbs. this time.

Aug. 13th. Monday. Commenced eating red potatoes. Turn about ½ bushel per row, good many small ones. Had to dig water for cattle. Sent Virginia & Eugene back to school. Sophy better today. Put 2 hands to picking cotton. They brought in one piled basket each.

Aug. 14th. I wish to make a fence between Ben Chaplin & myself. My cattle would no doubt have had water enough, but for his drove of cattle & horses. He will not dig, & depends on my wells. I have also to dig a well for house & plantation water.

Aug. 16th. Thursday. Hot & dry. Clouds about, but no rain. Commenced digging a well in the yard, between old kitchen & stable.

Aug. 17th. Friday. 4 hands at the well & frame. Came to water at about 7 feet. Caves so bad I can't go much deeper. Finished stripping blades out & out, Negroes' corn & all, & have made a fine crop. Sent to Beaufort by land for ice. *No* barrel.

Aug. 18th. Finished my well today. Water, I think, will be good but at present it tastes too much of the pine from the frame. 3 hands picking cotton yesterday & today.

Aug. 20th. Monday. Stopped with the potatoes & gave another week's allowance of corn. I think the potatoes may improve a little in size. 6 hands picking cotton, 2 hands cutting fence posts, 2 hands getting boards for cotton arbor[13] off the old house at the Riverside. Carting out rails for fence (B.C. line).[14] Rain drove in the cotton pickers, and I made them

[13] An elevated frame for bleaching the seed cotton in the sun, in hopes of making it whiter.
[14] The boundary with Ben Chaplin.

plant slips in the land listed & banked near the yard. It is very late for them, but with a pushing season they may make some seed.

Aug. 21st.   Carted boards from Riverside, & finished the cotton arbor. Too wet to pick cotton, so made the women clean the weeds out of the yard. 2 hands cleaned up the path for the B.C. line fence. Finished turning down standing corn & commenced turning cotton corn.

Aug. 23rd.   Thursday. Jim making a gate to be put where the Ben Chaplin line fence joins the Public Road. 7 hands picking cotton. Did not weigh, but guess they averaged 25 lbs. Sent 4 hands to Beaufort in boat at dusk, in the evening, for some things I expect from town. I heard the steamboat leaves town at 11 p.m. tonight. She ought to be in Beaufort by daylight.

Aug. 24th.   My boat has not come back at dark. I can't imagine what keeps them. Some hands picked as high as 30 lbs. of cotton today, 7 hands averaged about 27.

Aug. 25th.   Saturday. Boat got back from Beaufort about 10 o'clock last night, brought the pump I wrote for, a wooden one, the best I think after all. Cost about $13. Got the 8th barrel of ice, the 2nd of 125 lbs. weight. 630 lbs. cotton in. Finished putting down posts for line fence (B.C.). Commenced nailing on rails, but got out of nails. They were too small, got for 12 d, but not more than 10 d. Sent for 20 d's[15]—Jim & myself making gate.

Aug. 28th.   Commenced putting down my pump & making the platform. Pump rather long (15 feet), will do better for the well. I still intend digging at the old tabby.
Never dug it though
    4 hands ditching at the fence today, 3 tasks to 4 hands.

Aug. 29th.   J. H. Webb & myself rode over the Riverside old house to find out the situation of a white girl, Susan Chaplain,[16] who I heard was staying there, in a very destitute state, being turned off by her relatives, and cheated of the little all she had. We found her bad off, no provisions, bed or furniture. We will help her what we can until she is otherwise provided for.

[15] Twenty-penny nails.
[16] Chaplin's spelling of her name indicates he does not claim her as a relative.

Sept. 5th.   Wednesday. Went to muster, gave up my book as clerk of the company.

Sept. 7th.   Friday. Got 10th barrel of ice, 4th 125 lbs.

Sept. 11th.   Tuesday. Very dry & hot, averaging over 50 lbs. cotton pr. hand. I believe that Ben Chaplin has been turning his stock into my pasture again. If I catch the thief it will not be well for him.

Sept. 12th.   Very unexpectedly Mother came over today. We did not expect her till the 19th when she was to come & bring a beef for my market on the 20th, but she came today, & brought the beef too, which, poor thing, just lived to get ashore when in the Negroes' attempting to get it out of the boat, it gave up the ghost, had its throat cut, & will be a godsend to my Negroes, for I can do nothing else with it.

Sept. 13th.   Thursday. Clear & dry & hot. Everything is suffering. Nothing but dews keep plants alive.

Sept. 14th.   Friday. Clear, & the hottest *morning* yet, 11th barrel ice, 5th 125 lbs.

Sept. 15th.   Broke in my early corn, 2½ acres. Got 110 baskets, which ought to be equal to 55 bushels, or 22 bu. pr. acre, better than I expected.

Sept. 20th.   I killed beef for market, & a very fine & large one it was, the best I have seen. J. H. Webb called to see me. I have been up all day & no fever. Hope it may keep off altogether.

Sept. 21st.   Friday. Clear & hot. I feel so so today. Sent boat to Beaufort last night for ice, and other things. Got *12th barrel ice, 6th of 125 lbs.* Also, 1 barrel or 500 pts ale, ½ barrel flour, 2 boxes soap, & 50 lbs. coffee.

Sept. 22nd.   The mosquitoes are & have been for some time, though so dry, *most numerous* & savage.

Sept. 24th.   Monday. Clear & cool this morning, the cool weather is a great relief. Much sedge has been carried by the E. wind to the other side & handier for my compost pen. On account of so much dry weather, I have made but little compost. It does not rot down so fast in dry weather, tho there has been much sedge thrown in the pen.

Sept. 25th. Cotton falling out of the pods very much, & having to take it off the ground puts me back in picking very much. Some hands picked over 50 lbs. today.

Sept. 26th. Rode to the Indian Hills & dined with Capt. D.J. He is breaking in corn, & making a very fine crop of it. Plants about 55 acres & will make about 1200 bushels.

Sept. 28th. Commenced raining after daylight, and we had fine showers up to 12 m., looked like clearing about 1½ p.m. All hands assorting cotton. Frank started for Beaufort for ice before the rain this morning. Set out all the cauliflower plants I had, only 18, also a lot of Milan cabbage plants, & some red top turnips, from some seed that Old Charles had planted very thick in mistake for cabbage seed. Got 12th barrel ice, 6th 125 lbs.

Sept. 29th. Some rascally Negroes stole last night out of the poultry yard every duck I had except 6 Muscovys & 1 mongrel. God knows who they were, I don't expect ever to find them. Robert says it was Frank's yard night.

Oct. 1st. Monday. Getting in very little cotton, and a great deal of stained cotton in it. I suppose about one third of it is yellow, & nobs.

Rode to Edwin Chaplin's[17] to see him about two of his fellows who are strongly suspected of stealing my ducks, & I am almost sure, from what I have heard, that his fellows Orchard & John are the rogues. Edwin Chaplin promised to try and make them confess, by punishing them. I very much doubt if he gives himself any trouble about the matter, but if I catch those fellows, God help them.

Oct. 3rd. Rode over to D.P. Jenkins'. He breaking in corn, crop not turning out well, very small ears, and much rotten. J. H. Webb (I hear) makes about 25, or 7 bu. pr. acre of corn planted through cotton, i.e., 4 rows cotton & 1 of corn.

Oct. 5th. Went to Wm. P. Fripp's plantation by engagement & dined with him in company with Dr. Gibbs, F. & G. Capers, & A. A. Fripp. Went from there to the village & stayed with Alviro Fripp all night, attended a cotillion party given by what they call a "cotillion club," which club is composed of three young men of the ville, Dr. Jenkins, A. A. Fripp

[17] At Bermuda Plantation, west of Tombee on Broad River.

& W. P. Fripp. Everything went off pleasantly, &c. Got 13th barrel ice, 7th 125 lbs.

Oct. 7th.   Sunday. Clear & cool, did not go to church. Rode to Mr. Capers' in the evening to see him about my lost ducks, as Edwin Chaplin had sent me word that ducks were seen at his man Noble's house, by one of his (E.C.'s) men. Got no satisfaction, expected none. Sent Frank to Beaufort with a note to Walker Bold,[18] as I heard that fellow Noble had engaged ducks to him. Frank did not return today.

Oct. 8th.   Frank came home in the evening, no answer from Bold. He, out of Beaufort, his brother knew nothing of the affair (Charles).[19] Wanted to break corn today but rather too much cotton to leave in the field till I finish breaking.

Oct. 10th.   Wednesday. I was quite sick last night with pain in my right side, put on two mustard plasters & took laudanum before I got any relief atall. Quite unwell today & remained in bed.

Oct. 12th.   Friday. Quite cold last night & today. Heard there was frost last Monday morning. Did not see any. Fires kept up all day, cold & fresh north wind, think there must be frost this morning, if not, nothing but the high wind prevented, it is plenty cold enough for it. I am something better today, but far from well. (14th barrel ice, 8th 125 lbs.)

Oct. 13th.   Saturday. Not as cold as yesterday, but quite *airish.* Have the cotton so much slacked that I commenced breaking in my cotton corn. Some of it does very well. Got 97 baskets, but did not finish by 17 tasks.

Oct. 15th.   Finished breaking my cotton corn, entire yield, 108 baskets, equal to 54 bushels of corn.
more or less
Some white, or flower corn, selected from out of my flint corn, 2¾ acres, gave 116 baskets, or 58 bushels. 1 acre common flint (no manure), 20 bushels, or 40 baskets. Broke in, in all today, besides a few tasks of cotton corn, 193 baskets. Mother's boat came for her tonight, I believe she goes tomorrow.

Oct. 16th.   Mother returned to the main. Her boat brought over yesterday a bale of cotton which I am to send to town & have sold for her.

---

[18] Joseph Walker Bold (1832–1893), physician and planter. Son of William Bold; brother of Howard and Charles Bold and Jane Bold McKee, Henry McKee's wife.
[19] Charles Bold (b. 1825), physician. See note, above.

Oct. 17th. Wednesday. My corn turns out well today. Finished the Home Field & commenced the Ward corn,[20] 10 acres of it. 10 acres of my own selection, of which I planted the same number of acres as of the Ward to see the difference of yield each, having the same work, the Ward having the advantage (if any) in land, & equally manured, my corn turns about 19 bu., 3 pks. & 4 qts. pr acre (average). Some white corn that I selected from my corn, turned 19 bu. per acre (average). My early corn averaged 22 bu. Some acres of my *common flint,* not included in the acres of the same sort, mentioned above, turned 20 bu.

Oct. 19th. Friday. Sent to Beaufort for ice, 15th barrel. Finished breaking in corn. Made in all, cotton & early corn, 1173 baskets, allowing 2 baskets to the bushel, equal to 586½ bushels. By measuring the *bins,* the calculation gives me more corn, 624½ bushels. With a fair prospect of slips, I must have an abundance of provisions for the coming year, thank God. By basket measurement, as I had to mix the corn before I got through breaking to measure the bins, my cotton corn gave me 54 bushels; white corn selected from my corn, 3¾ acres, 58 bushels, 12½ acres my clear flint, 248½ bu.; 10 acres Ward corn, 168½ bushels. My flint corn beat the Ward corn 3 bu. pr. acre, trial of 10 acres, 26¼ acres in all planted. 2¾ of early corn gave me 60½ bu.

Oct. 20th. Hands digging groundnuts. Marked & altered 7 bull calves. Marked 5 heifers. Ernest went to the village to carry Eugene.

Oct. 22nd. Monday. Finished the groundnuts. They turned out well, but I don't expect to get many when the Negroes have got through with them. They generally pick out the best part and call them poppers. Only planted 1 task this year, & that gives too much trouble. All hands near 2 days, and one hand will be 3 or 4 longer in picking & drying them.

Oct. 26th. Friday. Very cold in the morning, heavy white frost. Uncle Paul told me he saw ice. Women picking cotton. Sent the boat to Beaufort with Mother's bale of cotton. Cotton not selling.[21] Got 16th barrel of ice, & the 10th of 125 lbs. & the last, for I have ordered it stopped. Got also from town, 2 cart collars & do. saddle, 5 gals. treacle & 3 of whiskey. Mother sent her boat over with a bacon hog & 6 ducks, good soul.

---

[20] Named for Nathaniel Ward, a planter noted for his high yields of corn and potatoes, and for his system of crop rotation.
[21] The Crimean War had driven up food prices in Europe and drained money away from the cotton market. In addition, the weather had been favorable to picking, and a large crop was anticipated, further depressing prices.

Oct. 28th.   Sunday. Delightful day. No service at the Episcopal Church. I went to the Baptist meeting, quarterly meeting, a great crowd of blacks were there. Some 30 were baptized. Rev'd Wm. Richards gave a very good & long discourse. He held forth under the trees, the old meeting house having been pulled down & removed to the village. The Baptists are about to build a large brick building on the old site, the bricks are already on the spot. I expect Wm. Fripp Snr.[22] is the chief mover & supporter.

Oct. 29th.   Could not commence digging slips today as I expected. Too much cotton open, put all hands at it, will get through the thickest of it today. Grated up arrowroot. Made very little, never saw it turn out so badly—got but one basket of seed & one of large roots out of nearly ½ task.

Oct. 30th.   Tuesday. Commenced digging slips. Turn out most splendidly. The piece of ground near the pond at the Negro houses turned out potatoes as fine as I ever saw. I did not measure them closely, but am sure I got no less than 50 baskets & 15 of seed to a little over one ¼ acre. Near the road they are equally as thick, but not so many large ones.

Nov. 6th.   Wednesday. Showery, but dug. No rain till night, had not the yesterday's potatoes covered. Finished digging today, made a very fine crop. 44 (I think) large banks of fine potatoes, but this weather will rot them badly I fear. Have not entirely covered any of them with dirt, and some banks only with vines. Dug a few rows of roots in the evening. Have about two tasks more to dig.

Nov. 10th.   Saturday. Dug in the balance of my root potatoes. Got 33 baskets large & a cart load of small ones. Picked in my peas, all that are ripe, & will give up the rest to the stock. Got about 12 sheets. Turned out my hogs, a plenty of food for them.

Nov. 13th.   Tuesday. Heavy fog, which blew off cloudy. Sent Virginia back to school. She has been at home all last week on account of the weather, losing too much time. Hands picking cotton, getting very little. Some pods left.

Nov. 14th.   Wednesday. Clear & quite warm, like spring. Uncle Paul finished digging slips today. He has only made 4 banks of eating, & had only 9 of seed besides what he gets today. Very poor turnout for 30 hands.

---

[22] "Good Billy" Fripp.

Nov. 15th. Thursday. Clear & quite warm. Had windows, or air holes, fixed to my potato banks.

[sixteen lines cut off page]

Nov. 17th. 3 hands (men) throwing up some small dams on the other side the Sands to keep the tide off land I will plant next year. Jim getting out trunks for dams, 3 of them. Women assorting cotton. Frank carting mud.

Nov. 20th. All hands assorting. Never saw so much stained cotton in the same bulk of white before. Fully ⅙th is yellow. Got ½ bushel early corn seed from W. A. Chisolm. He got the seed from Philadelphia last spring, called the Pennsylvania flint. Uncle Paul went to town yesterday, by the *Seabrook.*

Nov. 22nd. Hauled home 3 trunks I had got out for dams. Set Jim to making axle tree for cart. I have to convert my ox cart into a horse cart as my old ox Lion has pretty well given out & I can't find a match for the other ox. Commenced hauling out the manure I made in the hog pen by throwing in sedge last summer for cotton.

Nov. 23rd. Sent to Beaufort for Negro cloth & blankets I expect from town. Rode out to where Oliver Fripp's division are working the roads. Dined with them at the Indian Hills house. Marion Chaplin found dinner.

Nov. 24th. Hands that went to Beaufort got back this morning. Gave out cloth & blankets in the evening—no shoes this year.

Nov. 25th. Sunday. Went to church. Large congregation, over 70 persons. Poor sermon.

Nov. 26th. Monday. Commenced moving cow pen over potato land for next year. There is much broom grass on the land & I want to have it trampled in. Gave out 1st allowance of slips.

Nov. 27th. I worked hard today making a new cart body.

Nov. 30th. Friday. Sent Frank to Beaufort for liquors expected from town for my agricultural dinner. One box sent up I did not get; have to send again on Monday.

Dec. 1st.   Did not finish cart body. Worked on it, *in the piazza.*

Dec. 3rd.   Monday. Commenced ginning the Scadings cotton (Sophy's crop), with 4 gins. I have it whipped a little, after it is ginned, with switches. Will do all my cotton in the same manner. I know that if the factors & buyers knew of it, they would say the cotton is too much handled, but not knowing it, that the cotton is beautifully prepared. I have tried it before with success.

Dec. 4th.   Ernest & myself with Wm. Jenkins, John Jenkins[23] & the Major went from William's Landing & took a hunt on Edings Island. Had poor sport. Started no deer, the dogs were young & unbroken. I killed a fine wild English duck. We returned & dined with Wm. J. This was Ernest's first deer hunt, & a very poor one.

All hands assorting, & cleaning the cotton ginned yesterday. Makes 2 days' cleaning, one day's ginning, & not finished yet. It is so full of dry leaves. It is the fine cotton & I want it put up first rate. Could not gin today on account of having a carpenter here fixing some of the gins, & putting up a new one.

Dec. 5th.   Wednesday. Mother sent Simon over to help with my dinner. We are all busy preparing for it. Finished the cart body, & have only now to make the shafts. I do not think that anybody else has as much trouble to find a public dinner as we do.

Dec. 6th.   Thursday. Found Society dinner. I left home about 10 o'clock, after seeing underway, & dinner nearly done. They were started off in good time, but the black mare in the small cart got frightened somehow, ran off & kicked off the front of the cart, fortunately spilling only some sauce. Old Hyder in the other cart took everything on in safety to the lodge, & we had a very good dinner & a plenty, all in good time. Very few were out & little done as usual.

Dec. 7th.   Friday. Mother's Negroes went home. I gave them some potatoes &c &c.

Ernest went down to the village & brought Virginia in the sulky. Her holidays begin today.

[eighteen lines cut out]

[23] John Jenkins, planter. Son of Col. John Jenkins and Sarah Chaplin. Brother of Capt. Daniel T. Jenkins and Emmeline Jenkins Webb. First cousin of Maj. D. P. Jenkins and Dr. W. J. Jenkins, on his father's side, and first cousin to Chaplin on his mother's side.

Dec. 10th. Monday. Clear & very cold. White & black frost.

Dec. 12th. Wednesday. Packed the "Seadings" cotton (Sophy's), only 264½ lbs. Good many pods in the field but can't wait till they open, if they ever do, tho I will not head up.[24]

Dec. 16th. Sunday. Somewhat cloudy, but went to church. Good many people out and some strangers, that is, women that have married off the Island, came on with their men to spend Christmas. Jolly folks.

Agreed with the Captain to mark my fine cotton in his mark (E), & send it up in his flat tomorrow, to go to town & be sold with his bag of the same already in town. He, & Reilly, the factor, think that the cotton will bring more by increasing the quantity. I do too.

Dec. 17th. Had the bag of cotton headed up to go by the Captain's flat, but his Negroes started off after the rain last night, so it was left. I however sent it off to Beaufort in a cart. Packed the 1st bale Fripp's seed, on Saturday 15th. Gave out 4th allowance slip potatoes today. I can pack another bag tomorrow, but the cotton is not quite clean enough. It gins badly this damp weather. I can't get a full day's work. Rain fell lightly several times today. Killed the only bacon hog I had, & *that* Mother sent me.

Dec. 21st. Webb returned from Beaufort, brought for me, viz., 6 gals. gas, ½ box raisins, 5 lbs. crush sugar, ½ doz. wine & 1 gal. brandy. Stopped the gins, to have back cotton cleaned up.

Dec. 22nd. Ernest & I went over on the Island to shoot ducks. Continued to rain all day, with some high wind, & we got nothing but a good soaking, *no ducks.*

Packed the 3rd bale cotton, 320 lbs.

Dec. 23rd. Sunday. Gabe Capers & Wm. P. Fripp dined with me on wild turkey. Gabe Capers heard, after dinner, that his father's house in Beaufort was burned down last night, together with 16 others. He went immediately home, is to go to town tomorrow. The house, I believe, is insured.[25] Wm. Fripp spent the night with me. He is a good fellow. I like him much, & hope he may always prosper.

---

[24] To "head up" the cotton is to prepare it for market.
[25] The Charleston *Mercury* reported that ten or twelve buildings and homes were damaged in the Beaufort fire, including property of C. G. Capers, Capt. John Fripp, Mrs. Maria Cook, and Alexander Cockcroft.

Dec. 24th.   Wm. P. Fripp left about 1½ p.m. for Dr. Jenkins' where he dines today. He rode over some of my land today, & has an idea of leasing some from me if he does not succeed in *buying*.

Gave out corn allowance for Xmas.

Dec. 25th.   Tuesday. Christmas Day. Nothing doing or to be done. Weather cloudy & very heavy fog. Two of the boys went to church, more for the ride than anything else. Killed a small beef for the Negroes. I could but badly spare it. Rode over to Webb's in the evening—the Capt. was there. Very heavy rain at night, house leaked very badly.

Dec. 27th.   Thursday. Concluded to give the Negroes another day, making 3. Ernest & I went down to Trenchards, to shoot ducks &c. Took 5 hands in boat. We will stay all night. Cold & wind fresh, but we got down very well, & early. Pitched the tent, & made everything snug, then went to the pond, not a duck to be seen. Sent out after fish, did not get the first teals. Went to bed early & slept very comfortably indeed.

Dec. 28th.   Sent the hands across the river casting—they did not get the first fish. Went to the duck pond before sunrise. Killed 3 ducks. Commenced raining after sunrise, & continued all day. Broke up camp & started home in the rain, arrived about 12 m., well drenched with rain. Very little to repay us for it. All the hands that were at home went to work. Had 3 gins running.

Dec. 31st.   Monday. Last day of A.D. 1855, and a very dismal rainy day it is. Looked like clearing last night, but today it has been raining harder & steadier than ever, the day one constant pour, & cold at that. Nearly out of wood & pine & no getting any. Very little work got out of the Negroes. They barely finished Saturday's task today, & badly done. All hands assorting today. Have still two or three days' work at assorting if the rain holds on, & then, God knows what the hands will do. Can't gin this weather, As the moon quarters this morning & the weather does not break, I fear it will hold on for some length of time.

So Ends the Year of our Lord
    1855
And now for A.D. 1856.

1856

Jan. 1st. Tuesday. This day eleven years ago I commenced this journal, and kept it up, with a few blanks, ever since. If it is not of much account in itself, it has occasionally afforded me some satisfaction in referring to it. **& *it does now at this late day afford me some pastime 1869, 1877 & still 1885***

I have heard it said that the first twelve days of the year would be a simile of the twelve months of the year, with regard to the weather &c &c. We will try it. This the first day, *is,* rain in the early morning, very cloudy all day, but no rain after 10 a.m., damp & cold, but not very cold. Gave 6th allowance slips. Hands assorting Grayson cotton, not finished. Sent to the Island for pine. Jack went to the pond, got only two small ducks.

Jan. 2nd. I went to muster. Found dinner with 3 others, Wm. Jenkins, Wm. Chisolm & George Fripp.[1] There was a good dinner though neither of us found much. I had again to shoulder the musket, having resigned my clerkship. I still hold the noncommissioned office of orderly sergeant, & today commenced my 3rd year.

Gabriel Capers made me a present of a fine plantation whip.

Jan. 3rd. The boys commenced their studies again today. I fear I shall have to tie myself down to teach them another year, I see no chance of my raising money to send them to school. In this state, it seems that all rules & regulations of schools are opposed to the diffusion of learning among those not rich. Board & tuition are exorbitantly high, and board, in this neighborhood, hard to be obtained. I shall make application to get board

---

[1] George W. Fripp (1832–1862), planter. Son of Isaac K. Fripp and Charlotte Chaplin. First cousin, once removed, to Thomas B. Chaplin, on his mother's side. Private George Fripp, C.S.A., was killed at Okatee, S.C., in Aug. 1862.

with Mr. Wells[2] in Beaufort for my two oldest boys, but do not hope to succeed.

Jan. 4th. I went over to Col. John Webb's place in St. Luke's, with John E. and W. P. Fripp—*they,* to look at his land &c with a view to purchase; *I,* only on a *visit.* I furnished two, out of 7 hands, & we went in D. P. Jenkins' boat. Started from the Riverside at 25 min. after 11 a.m., went by way Archers Creek, passage a little rough at times. Arrived safely & cold at Webb's about 3½ p.m., who received us warmly, as also did his wife. This is the first visit between us since Webb, Colcock & self got the famous ducking in Broad River.[3] We had a late dinner, spent a pleasant evening. Though very cold, we all took a look round the beautifully laid out yard, & very well regulated buildings. The young men were highly pleased with all they saw, so far. Had some music after tea, by Webb's three pretty little girls, the oldest a little over Virginia's age. They have 6 children, 3 girls & 3 boys.

Alas where are they all now! Webb died some years ago, his children who are alive are married.

He, Webb, left 6 children. He died in 1866 or 7, in Charleston where he was in business. His daughter Annie[4] has married twice, O'Hear & Howard. Next daughter[5] married Horry——

Jan. 5th. Saturday. Commenced raining last night and continued off & on all day. I kept indoors chatting with Mrs. Webb[6] & a friend of theirs, a Dr. Ellis,[7] who is a very excellent fellow. The young men & Webb rode over the plantation, were pleased, & bought, don't know the terms, but that John Fripp made the purchase for himself, alone. They did intend to buy together. The price I think is $15,000, besides some mules &c extra.

Jan. 6th. Sunday. Clear & bright, but bitter cold, & still, we started home. Arrived at D. P. Jenkins' about dinner time. I soon got home, and found all the folks well, & Mother & Saxby's little daughter Lou[8] with them. She came over on Friday, the day I left.

Jan. 9th. Sancho sick, therefore one gin stopped. Judge sick, says he had a fit & fell in the fire, hand burnt. Applied soot & lard. Amy still very bad off with dropsy.

[2] Thomas J. Wells, former classics teacher at Joseph Seabrook's school in Bluffton.
[3] See May 9, 1846.
[4] Anne Webb (b. 1840).
[5] Martha Webb (b. 1842).
[6] Elizabeth Savage Heyward Webb (b. 1822).
[7] Edmund Eugene Ellis (1818–1883), physician and planter.
[8] Maria Louisa Chaplin (1847–1931). She became the wife of Chaplin's son Daniel, her first cousin.

Jan. 10th. Thursday. Clear as a bell, but bitter cold, the coldest day of the year, so far. Packed the 5th bale crop cotton. 302 lbs. Got a/c sales of my wife's bag of Seadings cotton sent to Reilly, only 45 cts.[9] Net proceeds $109. She will only get $50, as we have got some things from Reilly, amounting to the balance, & very high at that. He has not sold Mother's cotton. I shall not send down any more directly.

Sancho still sick, has, I think, pleurisy, bad thing.

Jan. 12th. Saturday. A most tremendous fall of rain last night, the heaviest we have had for a long time. It lasted till a late hour this morning. My old house leaked worse than ever, every room flooded. The wind got south this morning & drove up a fog, but no rain, & a little brighter & warmer at 11 a.m. No ginning today. Hands cleaning & assorting.

Jan. 13th. A cursed mink did some damage in my poultry house last night. Killed 4 ducks & 2 hens. This is third offense, but we put an end to him this morning, a very large fellow.

Jan. 14th. Monday. Cloudy and cold. Packed 6th bale cotton—300 lbs. crop.

8th allowance slips today.

The winters have been colder & colder ever since 1856 now 1885

Jan. 15th. Sent Virginia back to school. She should have gone two weeks ago, but we have really not had a fit day, besides Mother & Saxby's little daughter being here. I did not hurry her. I wish I had some other school to send her to. 6 gins today.

Jan. 17th. Went to Edgar Fripp's and made a trade with him (wonderful). Gave him old ox Lu and $250 for a pair of young steers, not horned, very likely & strong made. Think I have made an excellent trade. The single ox was of no use to me, & I could not get a match to him. Edgar fussed a good deal, but he really wanted my ox, thus the trade. I went on & dined with W. P. Fripp.

Jan. 18th. Went as far as Dr. Scott's Seaside place, where Edgar Fripp & myself agreed to meet with our oxen. We soon made the exchange. I don't think he is displeased with his bargain. Sent Robert in cart for things I expect from town, did not get anything. My letters must have miscarried. Ernest went also, for some things for his grandmother (mostly for himself I expect). Packed 7th bale cotton, 307 lbs.

[9] Fine cottons were bringing 50 cents a pound and better.

Jan. 21st.   Monday. Horrible, this morning. Very high northwest wind, & heavy black clouds, no rain, too cold. Mother's large boat came over for her, in spite of the weather. They must have been out of their senses. Came by way of the sound, too. There were two *better* days last week, when Tony was *here,* but he would not go, as he said the weather was too cold. Such ruined Negroes I never heard of.

Packed 8th bag cotton, 300. Gave 9th allowance slips.

Jan. 22nd.   Tuesday. Very bitter cold last night & all today, coldest weather for years. Thickest ice I ever saw here. Commenced to gin the Grayson seed cotton, 100 lbs. seed gins 25 lbs. ginned cotton.

Jan. 23rd.   All the ponds are frozen quite thick, and the ice did not melt all day. Oil, milk &c frozen. Mother has not gone, too cold for her to go in a boat. Some of her Negroes went for oysters. Sun set red & cold.

Jan. 24th.   Thursday. Clear & delightful, but still very cold. Mother left for home via Beaufort, so we are solo. Finished ginning the Grayson cotton, will not have 300 lbs. of it, have not weighed off.

Put Jim to making cart shaft to my *bought* cart.

Amy's case of dropsy must soon terminate in death. Poor thing, she is in an awful condition & suffers very much, large blisters are constantly forming on her legs, & bursting, I have done all I can for her. No doctor could save her if there was one *to be had.*

Jan. 25th.   The ground is so porous or *puffy* from the constant freeze, that a fall of rain would make it very miry & sloppy. Sent a cart & boy for things I expect from town—hoes, spades &c. Got them. No. 4 hoes. Ernest went also. Rec'd a letter from factor Reilly enclosing the balance due on Sophy's bag of cotton, i.e., $18. She also got a set of curtains & a nice little bonnet for Virginia, a knife apiece for the boys also

Jan. 29th.   Amy very bad off, don't think she can last much longer. She has lived, now, longer than I expected. One eye, today, is completely closed by the swelling & she is almost speechless. Does not complain of any great pain. Upper part of the body more swelled than the extremities. No one went out to church.

Feb. 1st.   Friday. Packed 10th bale, 308 lbs., Grayson seed.

Feb. 2nd.   Saturday. Never saw such weather, constant cold, the severest & most constant. The oldest men never experienced the like.

Feb. 4th.   Monday. Still very cold, ice never melts. Finished ginning white & commenced yellow cotton. Have some white & clean.

Feb. 5th.   Tuesday. Colder, if possible, than ever. The Sands so frozen over that the boys cannot cart over it. The whole bay is a sheet of frozen saltwater, a beautiful sight, as the sun is out. Nothing to do but to keep warm.

Feb. 6th.   Dined with W. P. Fripp. He takes 30 or 40 acres of land from me, on Carter's Hill, $3 per acre. Packed the 11th & last bale white cotton, Fripp's seed. 269 lbs. Hands ginning & cleaning yellow.

Feb. 7th.   Thursday. Put the hands out to chop bushes & clean around fences today, but it is another of the very bad days. Rain hard nearly all day. Hands had to come in & do some cleaning in the barn. This is too bad, first day out, & driven in, & I so *very* backward, more so than I ever was, as I have *so many* bushes to cut in the Bay Field, and burn a *mass* of broom grass. God help me.

Agricultural meeting, no meeting atall. I rode out in the rain about 1 p.m. Edgar Fripp had to find dinner. I found him at the lodge alone and quite disconsolate at not to have a crowd to eat his fine dinner. He was determined, however, to have a part of it, at least, put on table for the pair of us, but just as we were about to sit too, Gabe & Frank Capers came up, so we had a mock meeting, called the roll, marked absentees, and set down to his very excellent dinner. Not more than a fourth was served up, & that was enough for 20 men. We discussed agriculture, politics, & *wine* till 5 p.m. when the *Society* adjourned. Raining all the time, but not very cold. The rain melted all ice, the first time it has completely melted for many days.

Feb. 8th.   Friday. A nasty disagreeable drizzle all day. Kept the hands out all day, did not finish the fence or rather fire path. Uncle Paul won't make his, Old Noodle.[10]

Feb. 9th.   All hands at the fence path & cutting bushes, lots of the latter. Sent to the village for Virginia yesterday. It was misty & a shower of rain on them, but they (Ernest & her) got home safe & dry about 4 p.m. I rode over to Uncle Paul's. He still refuses to hoe & clean round his fence. If it burns I can't help it.
He was obstinate sometimes, but a good trusty old man. Survived the war & died in Beaufort in 1870 I think.*

---

[10] A simpleton or silly person, used affectionately.

Feb. 10th.　Sunday. Went to church. Saw the two Crofts[11] from Greenville.
they are both dead since the war

Feb. 12th.　Some of my pipe smoking Negroes were so very foolish as to carry fire over in the thick broom grass where they were cutting bushes, and let it get away. Of course, it soon spread, and was a matter of impossibility to stop it. There was no other way but to let it go, and it did, with perfect fury, and was soon over. The stubble did not burn close as I would wish it, the grass and ground being so wet, and I had no idea of burning it for some days yet. The hill part burnt pretty well.

Feb. 13th.　Wednesday. Commenced listing potato land with 3 hands. *Where* the cow pen has been moved over, I have 6 loads of stable manure *under the list.*

Feb. 14th.　4 hands listing for potatoes. Cutting bushes. Sent flat off about dark, with 3 hands & Robert to carry 11 bales cotton to Beaufort to go to town, 8 bales for Ingraham & Webb, and 3 bales to Tom Reilly. Grayson cotton to latter.[12]
　　Gave Robert a ticket to go & see his wife. He is to return on Monday next. Amy is not dead, but she had better be, being in an awful state, sore from head to foot, from the bursting of blisters. She is also speechless, & can eat nothing but liquids.

Feb. 16th.　Saturday. Amy died about 2½ o'clock p.m. today. She has lingered long, & it is really a relief to her, & others, for her to die.
　　The flat got back from Beaufort about 10 a.m. These two days are lost for field work. Listed in four tasks of marsh for cotton, in all, 6½ acres.

Feb. 17th.　Sunday. Rec'd $10 from Reilly pr. letter yesterday. Had coffin made & Amy buried. Coffin $4.

Feb. 25th, 26th, 27th, 28th, 29th.　Listing corn ground.

March 4th.　Tuesday. Exchanged 2 cart loads of cotton seed with Edgar Fripp. His is a selection from the Fripp's seed, which will plant. He swapped even, for a wonder.

March 6th.　Thursday. Finished listing corn land, 24 acres, all manured with cotton seed. Had very heavy work at it. 2 women spreading manure

[11] Theodore Gaillard Croft and his wife, Elizabeth Webb D'Oyley.
[12] The "common" cotton goes to Ingraham & Webb, and the finer grade to Reilly.

(sedge & mud) on cotton land. Started Frank plowing corn land, very tough & full of roots & stumps.

March 7th.   Commenced ditching corn land & plowed potato land. Started Robert & Charles running out land, commencing at the Public Road. 4 women spreading manure.

Mother sent over. Ernest does not care to come home.

W. P. Fripp called, but would not stay to dinner.

March 8th.   Rode to the store and gave Salinas[13] an order for $50. He is a cheat &c.

March 11th.   Tuesday. 2 hands banking corn land. 6 ditching. Robert makes poor work running out land, I had to put a little straight today. Stopped one cart, the other hauling sedge.

Mr. McElheran called today, great event, the first time he has been here for about 5 years. Dr. Jenkins, Dr. R. Croft, John Webb, Frank Pritchard & Uncle Paul called up for me to ride patrol. I had forgotten it, went out, & got well sprinkled.

March 12th.   Dug out 2 ditches through potato patch. Hear much complaint among the neighbors about their potato seed rotting. Several are planting. Wm. Jenkins finished today, & D.P.J. is now planting, but says he has not seed enough. I cannot & will not let any of mine go till I have planted, and that will not be for some days to come. Rode down to Webb's, to meet several men for partridge shooting, Dr. Croft with two fine dogs, Gabe Capers with 1, Dr. Jenkins, the Major, A. A. Fripp. Some of them took a cat hunt early in the morning but started nothing, had no good cat dog. The *varmints* are plentiful. We got only 4 partridges & 1 snipe, poor sport. Dined with Dr. Jenkins in company with the above party except Webb & the Major. W. P. & C. A. Fripp also dined with us. Dr. Croft's family are also at Dr. J.'s on a visit. Croft has two very interesting daughters[14] who gave us some tolerable music on the piano.

March 13th.   Thursday. Put all hands cleaning yellow cotton.

Note. Webb & Ingraham sold my crop about *3 weeks ago for 31 cts., damned bad & provoking.*[15]

---

[13] See April 20, 1858.
[14] Mary Sarah (1837–1922) and Charlotte Matilda (1842–1922), daughters of Randall Croft and Charlotte Jenkins. Chaplin's second cousins, once removed, on their mother's side.
[15] Common Sea Island was bringing an average of 35 cents.

March 14th. Finished banking potato land, all but ½ acre, 1 task of which I may not plant in potatoes. I had to go at running out the ground myself, Robert made such bungling. If I had done it at first, the whole would now be done.

Sent boat & 4 hands to Beaufort, went late, not back at dark.

Deputy sheriff called & served a writ on me, sent of Wood[16] in Savannah.

March 15th. Saturday. Decidedly the most beautiful day we have had this year. Boat did not get back from Beaufort till 2 p.m. today. Brought the following which came from town—1 pr. cart wheels, very good, but very high price ($25), ½ barrel br. sugar, 3 doz. ale, 3 gals. whiskey. Ought to have brought 5 gals. gas, but steamer did not put it out in Beaufort, hope to get it on Monday. Rec'd letter from Reilly stating that my 3 bales of cotton were sold for 35 c. & Mother's 1 bag for 28 cts. She will be provoked when she hears it, it ought to have brought more. All hands but 1 banking corn land.

March 19th. Wednesday. Robert sick yesterday & today. Jim & Frank making new hog pens, have now the sows separate from the other hogs. 5 hands ditching, 5 banking for corn.

W. P. Fripp rode up & took luncheon with us.

Hear from Webb that Emma Rhodes[17] is positively engaged to be married to that infernal squirt John R. Toomer. The fellow has lately graduated at medicine, so has his half brother C. Blincoe Smith.[18] Who is there that cannot get a diploma from the S. C. Medical College after this?

(Toomer jilted Emma R.)

Served her right for being such a fool

March 21st. Good Friday. Sent Robert to Beaufort. Finished staking out all the land east of the Cassena Line Road. Jim doing some job work about poultry house. Planted pumpkins & cucumbers in the garden for hogs, expect them to come off in time to plant the turnips on the same ground in September. Will not finish plowing or ditching corn land tomorrow as expected. Received from Reilly the proceeds of my 3 bales

---

[16] Ezekiel F. Wood (b. 1812), New York–born boot and shoe merchant.

[17] Emmeline Rhodes (b. 1831). Daughter of Thomas W. Rhodes and Elizabeth Jenkins. Chaplin's first cousin, once removed, on her mother's side. The Captain's niece, and Webb's niece by marriage. Her family was unhappy with the match.

[18] Toomer and Smith were sons of R. L. Baker's sister Mary Elizabeth, whose first husband was Thomas Smith; her second, Col. J. R. Toomer, Sr.

cotton, & Mother's 1 bale. Net amt. of my bales, a/c 35 cts., $312.50, Mother's ditto, $82.56. Rec'd in cash $243, Mother's part to come out.

March 22nd. Exchanged 5 pecks of corn with Tom Hazel[19] yesterday, to be planted 2 feet apart, 1 stalk to the hill, each stalk brings from 5 to 8 ears.

Mother sent over from the main, all well, I sent her by Bristol $30——

March 24th. Monday. Clear and pleasant, few clouds at sunrise. Finished running out all my land in the Bay Field, but have not got the short stakes put down. Finished ditching corn field. Have been a long time at it, but have the land now in good order. Moved the cow pen from the potato patch on the other side, and put it back of the corn house, to manure some land there for pumpkins & cucumbers for hogs. One of my young sows had pigs last night (6).

March 25th. Commenced planting potatoes. Planted common reds, brimstones, yellow yams & leathercoats, 2 acres & 2 beds in all, just half my patch. Finished driving down short stakes in Bay Field.

W. P. Fripp called, & lunched with me. He wants all the potato seed I can let him have. I hear that Uncle Paul has not enough by 5 tasks.

March 28th. Friday. Clear, sharp N.W. wind and very cold. White frost & ice this morning. Irish potatoes & tomatoes plants, also young peach & plum blossoms, well scorched. Let Uncle Paul have 1 bank of seed potatoes. I hear that this will finish his patch, all to ½ task. Went to Beaufort, the first time for something like 18 months. Paid several small a/c, & returned by 4 o'clock.

2 hands tracking & balance banking corn ground. Hope the cold will not injure the planted potatoes.

March 29th. Finished banking corn land, 25½ acres. Selected Ward corn for seed. I believe in selecting.

April 1st day. Rode to the muster house and cast my vote for Tyson for Col. of 12th Regiment.[20]

[19] Thomas Hazel (b. 1826), planter. Son of Joseph and Ann Hazel. Brother of Dr. W. Gowan Hazel.
[20] Reuben H. Tyson, planter, of St. Peter's Parish, Beaufort District, was elected colonel of the 12th Regiment—one of six infantry regiments constituting the 3rd Brigade, 2nd Division, S.C. Militia. The St. Helena Mounted Riflemen were attached to the 12th, as were the B.V.A. and the Beaufort Beat Company, until 1858, when the three St. Helena Parish units were consolidated into an independent battalion.

April 2nd.　Wednesday. Cloudy. Rained severe showers after 10 a.m., one very hard, which caught & gave me a soaking. Hands planted corn morning & evening.

April 3rd.　I am quite sick from my wetting yesterday, violent pains in my side & chest, very hoarse. Think I also have a touch of the liver complaint, but hope not. Could not attend Ag. Society. Finished planting corn.

April 5th.　D. P. Jenkins called to see me. W. P. Fripp also. I feel a little better, took salts. W. P. Fripp has had from me 3 cart loads of seed potatoes, got the last today.

April 7th.　W. P. Fripp is a strange man, though I think him a good & honorable one. To my surprise he sent me today 7 bushels of corn in *return* for the potato seed I *gave* him. I was somewhat hurt and mortified, for I did not expect it, and have repeatedly refused any return. I have put up the corn till his return from town, then will see him about it.
I was rather too generous.

April 8th.　Very late spring, everything backward.
W. C. Danner called a dunning. No money for him here.

April 9th.　Heard that J. H. Webb has fished every day this week & no drums. Counted up my cotton land today, & find that I have not enough by 1½ acres without planting some very low land. I was so sure there was even more than enough, or I might have taken some of the high land I have in corn, for cotton. The price of cotton has gone up some 6 cents in town. Too late, for me at least. Planted ½ task of groundnuts in garden. Commenced compost pen, for slips I expect. Very little sedge on the bay, this side, to put into it.

April 10th.　Sophy, the boys & I paid a visit to old Coz. Betsy Jenkins, the Major & wife, the first visit we have made together for many a day. May it be the forerunner of better things. The Major, *good man,* took communion in the Episcopal Church last Sunday. Sophy & the boys rode to Edwin Chaplin's store in the evening, & found him not, *gone fishing.* I had to stay at home, thank God, as I had a carpenter here, fixing my pump.

April 11th.　Friday. Cloudy, windy & cool again. Spring weather cannot last. I have planted, in corn, Hazel seed, 5 acres, Ward, 11, my flint, 9½ = 25½.
Sent to the village for Virginia. She got home about 4 p.m., but the

school has not broken up for holiday. Don't know whether to keep her or not.

Today is the 17th anniversary of my first marriage, Friday (the 11th came then on Wednesday), 17 years ago, a long and eventful period. **Alas! Alas! There have been "periods" & events since that have far surpassed anything previous to this date, war & famine & want & loss of property & children— everything but the one dearest of all—my wife—God grant she may be not taken yet from me 1877**

I will make out 40 acres for cotton, by taking some land intended for slips.
"It is but a slip from the sublime to the ridiculous"

April 13th. Went to church, but there was no service, Mr. Mc. having gone to Florida for his health. He must be very bad off for money, dun me so hard & can travel for his health.

Saw old Mrs. Daniel C. Webb[21] at church with Mrs. Capers. It is many years since I last saw her. She looks older, but very well. Did not remember me atall, had to tell her who I was.
I never saw her afterwards, been dead a long time now. 1877

April 14th. Monday. Not done listing yet. Started the plow in cotton field. Frank broke up the *small* plow & had to take the large. (Dr. Scott sent his large grey mare to Tom Jones. She took him.)

April 15th. Corn sprouting out. Planted rice through the lowest places in corn field, that is, I commenced this morning, & will plant a little every morning till finished. Planted wild orange seed about the yard for the purpose of making hedges & walks. J. H. Webb sent me a side of drum, the first I have seen this season. Quite a relish.

April 17th. Thursday. W. P. Fripp spent the day with us. Finished listing cotton land, never was so backward before.
I have often said this, but got on somehow.
Robert says there are 40½ acres listed for cotton. I can only make out 40 even. Commenced to bank cotton ground, got about 2¾ acres of salt or brackish, & very rough ground banked.

April 19th. Saturday. Planted 3¼ acres salt ground cotton, Fripp's seed, and 2 acres Seadings, on left of cart road. Stretched net yarn over potato patch, but it does not keep off the crows.
I have succeeded with it since

---

[21] Elizabeth Ann Ladson Webb, mother of John H. Webb, Chaplin's neighbor, and Thomas Ladson Webb, Chaplin's factor. Her husband, the late Daniel H. Webb, had been a leading cotton factor in Charleston.

April 20th.　Sunday. Went to church. Saw Saxby, Minott & Nichols from the main. They are staying with Capers. Saxby is to come here to stay a few days, tomorrow. I dined with Capers.

April 21st.　Monday. Clear, but rather high wind for fishing, though there were many boats out. Saxby came down from Capers', with Minott & Nichols.[22] The wind got so high that Minott could not get back with his boat, so they all three came and spent the night with me, all jovial fellows & we had a pleasant & fine time of it.

All tight I suppose

Mother came over from the main today, with Ernest, & two of Saxby's little daughters, Carrie & Lou.[23] They had a rough time at the mouth of Station Creek, but got here safe. Mother complaining much of cold & toothache. No fish caught.

April 23rd.　I took Saxby round on a visit to some of the neighbors, to Uncle Paul's & Coz. Betsy Jenkins'. Sax had a great desire to see what he has been told was the belle of St. Helena, Amanda Jenkins. He did not find her as handsome as he was led to believe she was. *Acknowledged* however that she was very agreeable & sociable.

About 1 p.m. according to my invitation, in or through respect for those that were in company with Saxby, several gentlemen arrived to dine with me, viz., Minott, Nichols, Frank & Gabe Capers. I managed with very little liquors & wine, & a plenty of substantials, to make them all appear & [at] least to feel very happy, and all things passed off well. Mother was quite sick today which created some drawback to our hilarity. I like Nichols very much. He is a *very* well educated man. He gave me pressing invites to come over to the main & see him, & to Walterboro. I have not paid due attention to my field this week. Hands have finished banking on the left of cart path, & commenced on the other side. Saxby left with the rest to go to Capers' tonight. The three are to start tomorrow & stop a night at Morgan Hammocks[24] one night before they proceed to the main. I say they will have bad weather.

April 24th.　Thursday. Somewhat cloudy in the morning, but cleared off fine & warm, calm, & the best weather for fishing we have had this week, if not season. I went out in the creek with the three boys & caught a fine mess of whiting &c. All hands planted 6¾ acres of Seadings cotton, have 12 acres in all planted, 8¾ of Seadings.

---

[22] Joshua Nichols, rice planter of St. Bartholomew's Parish.

[23] Caroline Isabella Chaplin (1845–1935) and Maria Louisa Chaplin. Daughters of Saxby Chaplin, Jr., and Anne O'Hear Witsell.

[24] Northeast of St. Helena Island, near the mouth of Morgan River.

Cousin Ann B. Fripp paid us a visit today. Saxby, Minott & Nichols have a fine day for their trip.

April 27th. My birthday, 34 years old, or thereabouts.

April 28th. Mother with Saxby's chicks started for home.

April 30th. Wednesday. Dry weather continues. Went fishing. Caught 2. Captain's boat, my hands.

May 1st. When will we have rain again? My cotton, what I *have* planted, is not up, but those persons that have cotton up say it is dying off. Perhaps my being so late will not do harm. I am tired of one & two fish for the trouble & loss of time. The children went today, and the old number 2.

May 2nd. Friday. Same old cry, hot & dry. Planted some cotton the first of the week, but banking again today.

May 4th. Sunday. Boys went to church, I did not.

May 7th. Muster Day. Wm. P. Fripp, D. Jenkins, & J. H. Webb found a very fine dinner.

The tax collector came over & I paid my taxes, $50, by order on I. & W. I was notified of my appointment as Commissioner of Roads for this division, to serve out the unexpired term of Jn. E. Fripp.[25]

May 8th. All hands planting cotton & made a finish out & out, 40 acres, according to Rob. D. P. Jenkins & family called on us in the afternoon.

May 10th. Saturday. Dry as ever. Went fishing with Webb. Caught no drum. They must have taken their departure from these waters. Webb thinks he hooked one but did not see it. Got a fine lot of small fish. So the drum fish season ends.

Gave the Negroes the day for themselves.

Sent to Beaufort, got no mail, postmaster negligent.

May 12th. Monday. Clear & pleasant, a few clouds made up about noon, & evening, hope they may thicken. All hands hoeing corn, 1st time. Sent Virginia back to Mrs. McElheran. She was much opposed to going, as she has been under the impression that she would go to Walterboro, but this was out of the question and was put into her head by her grandmother.

[25] Fripp left the Parish after buying Col. John Webb's plantation in St. Luke's.

May 13th. Killed a yearling, partly for the Negroes.

May 15th. Sent boat to Beaufort with 1 bag of stained and a packet of white cotton, near 500 lbs. in all. The boat to return tomorrow & bring some goods I expect from town—*if they are sent by I. & W.*

May 16th. Friday. Clear & warm and as far from rain as ever. Boat got back from Beaufort, brought the things I sent to town for, viz.: family summer clothing, 2 sacks of salt, 6 hams, ½ barrel of meat for the Negroes. Hope it will not be stolen, as that was last year, when my corn house was broken.

May 17th. Finished first hoeing of corn, and hoed a little cotton that happens to be up, in the salt ground. Took the boys down to Bulls Point. Spent a pleasant day enough. Got no fish or terrapins, but Ernest shot nearly one hundred birds, May birds &c, some of them extremely fat. We got back at sunset. Sophy was at home all day alone.

May 19th. So clear at 2 p.m. I despair of rain. Not one 50th part of my cotton is up, & God only knows when it will ever come up. Seed sound & dry. Sent 3 hands to split rails in Dr. Jenkins' pine barren. He kindly offered me the timber. All the rest of hands hauling corn and hoeing a little cotton today.

May 20th. Tuesday. A pretty smart shower about daylight, but it was what is called a *partial* shower, for though it rained *smartly* at the house & yard, in fact, all this side of the Sands, there was scarcely enough to lay the dust in the field. There was very little at Uncle Paul's, & little or no signs of rain at Bill Jenkins'. Cleared off before noon, no more rain. Started 2 carts to hauling rails, good long way to cart them. Got only 4 turns apiece, must have 6 tomorrow. Elsie sick, so there are only 5 hands in the field. Had them thinning & hauling some cotton that is up in low spots.

May 21st. Wednesday. Cloudy, wind north, and east. Smart shower here at the house, about 11 a.m. but very little fell over in the field. Wind very high & clouds of sand flying about. I think the young cotton on high ground will be injured. Heavy rains passed each side of this place towards Bay Point, & to the back of this Island. Hands hoeing cotton.

May 22nd. Blew a perfect gale from north all day. There was no going out of doors for the clouds of sand from distant fields, Uncle Paul's in particular. Had to stop the carts from hauling rails. Made one or two attempts to rain, but wind too high, only a few driving drops came over.

Cotton that is up must be very much injured. Hands hoeing cotton, don't see how they stood the dust. Only 7 in the field.

May 23rd. Friday. The wind blew nearly all last night & there was a light shower sometime during the night. Commenced raining about 10 a.m. today & there were several heavy showers during the day, & still raining & cloudy at dark. This rain is a godsend & will bring up all sound seed that is in the ground. But I fear my cotton seed has been too much backed with the hot sun & dry ground to sprout readily. Will wait on it a few days. The wind yesterday has injured & killed much cotton. Planted crowder peas through 16 acres of corn. Will finish the rest with the shiny pea. Did not split rails today, there ought to be 1200 now split.

May 24th. Planted shiny peas through some corn, & hauled corn. Nearly everybody on the Seaside planting over cotton regularly. Uncle Paul & Dr. Jenkins have but few hills alive in high land, and seed very scarce. My cotton, after all, is best off, for very little had come up & the seed still good in the ground.

May 26th. Went to Beaufort to attend a meeting of the Board of Road Commissioners, of which body I have lately been appointed to fill out the unexpired term of John E. Fripp, late commissioner for this division, removed from the Island. Some important business before the board, but all, I think, decided. One of the actions of the board was on a memorial of Thos A. Coffin, laid on the table of a former board, asking to have or be allowed to alter a short portion of public road running through his land. Referred to St. Helena commissioners, but authorized under conditions. The board also decided that the road on Port Royal Island known as "Broad River Road" was not a public highway and that that known as the Battery Road was.

Dined with J. D. Pope & returned early.

Giving potatoes 2nd hauling, and hauling corn. Isaac went to do some work in the field, fear of a doctor, for I have asked Dr. C. A. Fripp[26] to come & examine him tomorrow.

May 27th. Dr. Fripp came down to see Isaac, cupped him but got but very little blood.[27] During the operation Daniel fell down in what I called a hysterical fit. He soon got over it.

[26] Clarence A. Fripp. See note, Jan. 2, 1853.
[27] Heated cups were applied over an incision in the patient's skin. The vacuum created by the cooling glass drew blood.

June 5th. William P. Fripp marries (tonight) Martha, daughter of Capt. John Fripp. A good match I think. Bill is a good fellow & I hope he does well. They are to have a grand wedding. We were invited, but can't well go. Daughter will I hope.

June 6th. All hands going regularly through first hoeing cotton. Seems to improve the cotton. I have taken a good crop of bees this season. I had but 5 hives & now have 17, a great turnout. One swarm taken today; 3 that had been taken went off, not counted. Quite a fine little shower in the afternoon, did not last long. More in the field than at the house. Not enough to supply the root patch with slips.

June 7th. Commenced a lamb market. I killed first, today. Uncle Paul, Harvey & Trowell are the others.

June 9th. Finished 1st hoeing of cotton, *regularly through.* I have now a very tolerable stand.

June 11th. Commenced 1st hauling cotton, putting the old cotton at 2 stalks to hill, the young slacked to 3-4 & over, according to age. Corn is tasseling here & there, very low. Fear the crop generally will be short. The Capt., Webb & some others complain of not having vines even to supply their roots.

June 12th. Thursday. Agricultural Society day—not the regular day, the meeting was postponed on account of the marriage of the president's, Capt. J. Fripp's, daughter taking place the 1st Thursday. Dr. C. A. Fripp found dinner. T. G. White[28] was elected a member. I heard at the Society some very startling reports about Mr. McElheran. Whether true or false, they are calculated to injure his character as a minister very much, if not to entirely ruin it, as well as to injure Mrs. Mc.E.'s school. One report originated with *little* Caroline Chisolm,[29] a very imprudent & forward girl. She says that Mr. Mc. offered her great indignities & rudeness, of a very indecent & indelicate nature, while she was in his study, where she had gone for a book. She has, I hear, contradicted herself several times, & I think the matter altogether false as far as she is concerned. But I have determined to remove Virginia from the scene of *such* scandal, and will go & fetch her tomorrow. Uncle Paul very generously & kindly gave me $300 to pay Mrs. McE. what I owe her.

---

[28] Thomas Grimke White (b. 1825), planter. Lived on 610-acre Woodstock Plantation, between Lands End and Seaside roads.
[29] Possibly the daughter of William S. Chisolm and Mary Missroon.

This to do *about Mr. Mc. was all a most abominable scandal, he left the Isld in consequence. Now dead 1877*

June 13th. Went to the village. Requested Mr. McE. to give me a statement of all his claim against me up to date, & he did make out an enormous one—over $600. They wanted to appear very much surprised that I should take Virginia away, & Mrs. Mc. was quite angry, but I spoke to them calmly & determinedly. They at length said I was perfectly right.

June 16th. Monday. Finished the 1st hauling up of cotton, had it slacked, not thin enough. Looks very well. Some spots rather yellow.

Virginia has been quite unwell since she came home. She has, I think, been too much excited of late.

June 17th. Tuesday. Clear & sultry. Commenced hoeing, hauling up & laying by corn. It does not look very good. Some tasks I will have to hoe, but most of it can & will be hauled as it is.[30] Jim laying up with a splinter or shell in his toe.

June 20th. Friday. Very hot. Heavy cloud passed round. Ernest went to Beaufort. Sent boat up also, got gas, vinegar & 1st barrel of ice from town. *The* Captain called. We rode over to Uncle Paul's, but the old man was not at home. Cotton growing very fast, wish I had thinned it all down to 2 stalks.

June 22nd. Sunday. Very hot. Went to church. Found more people out than I expected after all the talk about Mr. McElheran. I hear that the Bishop[31] is to be over here on Tuesday, & Mr. McE. is to be brought up before him on very serious charges. The Bishop is to preach on Wednesday, Central Church.

June 24th. Tuesday. Too hot for Negroes to work in corn all day. Ordered that they should do part of their task in the corn, & finish in preparing slip land.

June 25th. Wednesday. Went to church, the Bishop preached a very fine sermon. Mr. McElheran read the service, at the close of which, the poor old man[32] made a short farewell address to the congregation. It was a very

---

[30] Where the soil around the cotton is overgrown with grass, the vegetation will have to be chopped out before the earth can be drawn up to the cotton stalks.
[31] Rt. Rev. Thomas F. Davis. See note, July 8, 1855. Bishop Davis consecrated a new chapel in St. Helenaville in 1859.
[32] McElheran was sixty-three years old.

melancholy scene. He has taken his leave of the people with whom he has been connected as pastor for nearly twenty-five years, forever, and I am sorry to say, under circumstances not the most favorable to his character. I am truly sorry for him, and can say no more.

I don't think so now.

Every person present was more or less affected. Many tears were shed & much sympathy displayed towards his family. He leaves for Charleston on Monday next, to return for his family in a week or two. Such is the way of the world.[33]

The very persons that were most against the old man were the very ones to make the greatest fuss when he left—the deceit of the world—but they have suffered more than he has

He left on Monday with all his family & effects.

& the Isld has gone down lower & lower ever since & now is no more than a Negro settlement

June 26th. Nelly was confined last night, child born dead. My luck with little niggers.

June 27th. Friday. Clear, hot & dry, almost as dry as a few weeks ago. Everything looks wilted. Finished hauling up & layed by my corn, that on the high ground looks bad enough, and without rain in a day or two, I consider it lost. Put all hands thinning & *partly* regulating cotton. Sent Frank to Beaufort for ice.

Tom James Fripp offered me some time ago to trade his buggy for my black mare. I sent her down to him today to look at. He has kept her, & it is a trade, I can't say a good one on my part. The mare is of great use to me, & I want a buggy, for I have nothing for wife or daughter to ride in. The buggy is not old, & a very nice one, & will at all events keep me from borrowing.

Got 2nd barrel ice. A tremendous storm of rain, wind, thunder & lightning came up about 6 p.m. Before the rain commenced, there was a dense cloud of sand came over the Seaside places, equal to the sand clouds of the desert. I think it must have hurt the cotton. The wind was very high, and drove the rain in every direction. The wind blew from N. & N.E. Thunder & lightning were very severe. The rain stopped before it was quite dark.

---

[33] Rev. David McElheran moved to Mt. Pleasant, S.C., across the Cooper River from Charleston. The official church history records his death in July, 1875, at age eighty-two. "He had been living in Mt. Pleasant since his resignation from St. Helena's . . . in 1856, and instantly assisted gratuitously in Christ Church Parish for all these years." (Rt. Rev. Albert Sidney Thomas, *History of the Protestant Episcopal Church in South Carolina 1820–1957* [Columbia, S.C., 1957], 369.)

June 28th. My corn was so much blown down by the storm last evening that I had to put hands to work righting it up today. Some stalks are broken entirely off. The cotton, particularly that which was thinned down, leans very much, & the buds much washed by the rain, but do not think it is much injured. I hear there was some hail, saw none.

3 hands listing slip land, very tough work. More rain fell than I expected to see, had to let off water from corn & cotton.

Sent & got the buggy which I traded the black mare with Tom Fripp for. It is in very good order, and I don't think it a bad trade on my part. Sophy & the children seem to be much pleased. Uncle Paul's people are planting slips today.

June 29th. Sunday. As there is no one to preach & no preaching, we all stay at home.

July 1st. Black sow had six black pigs last night. 6 hands listing slip land, 3¾ acres listed.

Rode to the store. Saw there Dr. Scott, Ben Bailey, Tom Jim Fripp & Joe D. Pope. Joe is out on an electioneering tour. He has an opponent in Jn. A. Johnson[34] for the legislature, and I expect he will have a light run if he is not beaten. Johnson is said to be popular in Beaufort & no doubt is, but I go for Pope.

July 3rd. Young spotted sow had 7 pigs last night.

July 6th. Sunday. Mr. S. Elliott[35] preached at the P. E. Church today, but none of us went out, not hearing of it till late.

July 7th. A duck taken out of poultry yard last night, Jim's guard. Intended to flog him but let him off for the present as it is supposed the thief was a wildcat, a track being seen in the vicinity.

July 10th. Thursday. Showers the last three evenings, sultry mornings. Banked up & planted slips wherever I could. Hoed cotton occasionally. Cotton begins to look very bad, many yellow leaves appearing.

Beef market commenced. I made out the book. Uncle Paul, 1st kill.

---

[34] John Archibald Johnson. See note, June 27, 1845.
[35] Stephen Elliott, Sr. (1804–1867). Son of William Elliott and Phoebe Waight. Brother of George P. Elliott and William Elliott, Jr. First cousin of Bishop Stephen Elliott, of Georgia, and General Stephen Elliott, commander of Confederate forces at Fort Sumter. Regarded as "one of the most experienced African missionaries," Rev. Elliott built "a large Church, seating 600, at his own expense, for the Negroes, and administered it himself." (Thomas, 358–59.)

Heard that the old gentleman was sick, went over to see him. Met Capt. D. J. going there also. The Capt. sits up with him tonight. The old man has fever, and requires someone to be with him. 4th barrel ice.

July 13th.   Sunday. Heard that Rev'd. Wm. Barnwell[36] would preach today, but as there is no certainty about it, did not go out.

Note. Got no ice on the 4th, though it was down on the freight list of the boat. Sent again on the 6th, got none, but got a barrel on the 11th, being 3rd barrel & one lost.

July 14th.   Lost a hen out of the yard last night. Sure it was a cat that took it. This saves Jim a flogging. However, to my great surprise, the fellow took himself off before I got in the field today. He went to work as usual this morning, pretended to go to the well to get water, & did not return. I could not believe he had run away, & sent hands to hunt for him, without success. He no doubt heard of the loss of the hen last night, & expected a flogging, though it was not his guard, but Frank's. It is a very foolish trick in him, not only do I lose his work, but I fear he will be a ruined Negro forever. I went & took all his clothes from his wife's house, in the evening. I don't think she knew anything of his intention, and the act was on the impulse of the moment with him.

This is V. S. Chaplin's[37] birthday. She is now 14 years old.

July 15th.   3 hands listing more land for slips. The women hoeing cotton—cotton looks miserably, much yellow leaf, bottom fruit lost irretrievably.

Nothing heard of Jim. 2nd day.

Mother came up the creek this morning before we were up. She started last evening, & rowed all night, wise plan, the days are so hot. Mother looks very well. Sophy was quite sick last night & this morning, better today.

July 16th.   Nothing of Jim. 3rd day.

July 17th.   I have only 7 (out of 12 hands) in the field. Too bad. Nothing of Jim, 4th day. I will keep a regular account of the rascal's time & make him pay dearly for it whenever I get hold of him.

Hoeing cotton.

---

[36] William Hazzard Wigg Barnwell (1806–1863). Son of Robert Gibbes Barnwell and Elizabeth Hayne Wigg. Brother of Robert W. Barnwell and Mary Gibbes Barnwell, wife of Bishop Stephen Elliott, of Georgia. The Rev. Barnwell assisted at the Parish church in Beaufort and outlying chapels.

[37] Virginia Sophia Chaplin.

July 18th. Got 4th barrel of ice from town, via Beaufort. All hands haul-ing cotton. Upon the whole I think the general crop is in a very unpromis-ing condition. The slips may, & I hope they will, do well. I have not finished planting, banked up one acre today, perhaps that will be all I can plant, making, I think, 6¼ acres in all.

Nothing of Jim—5 days—won't he catch it?

Bay mare *took* Tom Jones, *3rd time yesterday.*

July 19th. Saturday. Let Robert go to see his wife, don't like it atall. All hands hauled 1 task each, & balance of day's work hoeing.

Nothing of Jim, *6th day.*

July 20th. 7th day, nothing of Jim.

July 21st. Monday. Planted one acre of slips, I expect they will be the last. I have, I think, 6¼ or 6½ acres planted in all. Heavy rain last on Sat-urday night & ground quite wet enough.

8th day & nothing heard of Jim yet. Damn him—

July 22nd. Rode to the store. Heard that J. G. Barnwell[38] went down yesterday to Tybee Lighthouse[39] to fight a duel with J. D. Pope. They are to fight with rifles, 40 yds. Bill Fripp[40] told me about this affair on Satur-day. He said they were to fight that day, as Pope had gone down the day before with his friends. I understand that Barnwell had given Pope the lie, & Pope challenged. I don't *know* the particulars, so do not attempt to write them.

9th day, no Jim yet.

July 23rd. All hands hauling cotton.

10th day, no Jim.

July 24th. 8 hands listed & lightly banked 2 acres of land for peas—rather late to plant them, but I could do no better.

11th day of Jim's new *career,* &c.

July 25th. Friday. Gave F. M. Pritchard an order to summon out 6 hands & fix the bridges on the Seaside Road.

W. P. Fripp, A. M. McTureous & myself have been appointed manag-

---

[38] John Gibbes Barnwell (b. 1816), planter and lawyer. Son of John G. Barnwell and Sarah Bull.

[39] On Tybee Island, at the mouth of the Savannah River, just across the Georgia state line, a popular spot for lowcountry gentlemen to settle their "debts of honor."

[40] William P. Fripp.

ers of an election to be held on Monday and Tuesday next, for representative to Congress, to fill the vacancy occasioned by the resignation of Hon. L. M. Keitt.[41] *He will be returned sure.* I wrote the notices today & Bill Fripp put them up.

Walked over W.P.F.'s crop at the cottage. It is as bad if not worse than my own.

12 days Jim has been out. I will have to catch him.

Planted 3 acres of cowpeas. I am very late, but I notice several persons are just preparing the ground, & some have not commenced to do that yet. If I had seed I would plant more.

July 26th.   13 days for Jim.

July 27th.   Sunday. Clear & warm, fine breeze after 10 a.m. No preaching. The Capt. & Webb spent the morning with me, mint juleps &c &c.

Jim made his appearance about dark, his *hide* may keep cool for a while.

July 28th.   Monday. Went to the church & held the 1st day's election. Took only 4 votes. Bill P. Fripp found a lunch, I to do the same tomorrow.

Gave Jim a very moderate punishment, say about 60 paddles, put on his bare hide, with my own hands.

All hands hauling cotton. Had put round some very yellow looking cotton, on high ground, about a tablespoon full of salt to the hill.[42] Did so with about *6 tasks.*

July 29th.   Tuesday. Closed the election for congressman. W. P. Fripp carries the box to Beaufort tomorrow.

Aug. 9th.   The grass caterpillar has taken my peas in the corn, had to pick them in, ripe or not.

Dined & played billiards with Wm. Jenkins. He has his table up in a very nice house. Five guests dined with him today. He can get any quantity of these with the amusements & refreshments he can offer. He & family, I hear, take a flight to Greenville on Monday, on a visit to Croft.[43]

Let D. P. Jenkins have 12 bushels of corn.

[41] Lawrence Massillon Keitt (1824–1864), lawyer, from Orangeburg District. Son of George Keitt and Mary Wannamaker. Member S.C. House of Representatives 1848–52, U.S. House of Representatives 1852–60, and delegate to the 1860 Secession Convention. With C. G. Memminger, he helped frame the provisional and permanent constitutions of the Confederacy. Col. Keitt was killed at Cold Harbor, Va., in June, 1864, while leading a charge of the 20th S.C. Volunteers.
[42] Recommended in Holmes's *Southern Farmer and Market Gardener.*
[43] Theodore Croft.

Aug. 10th. Sunday. No preaching. Understand that there will be on the first Sunday of every month. Very hot & dry.

Aug. 14th. Water getting scarce. Had to dig out my well, very dry. If it continues, will soon have to dig cow wells.

Aug. 15th. Had land that I have had the pen on for the last 8 nights listed up for turnips, but the ground is dry to such a depth that after turning up, it is too dry on the bed to plant. Finished hoeing slips. Picked some peas & turned down some corn. Got 8th barrel ice. Peck says he paid the ice keeper for the barrel I ought to have got last week.

Aug. 18th. Monday. Planted rutabaga turnips, hauled up peas, & stripped some Negro corn of blades.

Webb & the Captain returned from the main, where they went to look at a plantation Tom Rhodes[44] had bargained for, for Webb. He will take it, price $3000, 3 yrs.' credit.

Aug. 21st. Thursday. Rode to the Indian Hills with the Captain, looked over the crop, which is very good. Dined with him & returned early. Finished stripping my cotton corn, good blades.

Aug. 22nd. Got 9th barrel ice from town, via Beaufort, also 1000 cigars, from I. & Webb.

Eliza confined about 8 p.m. Girl, name Amy.

Aug. 23rd. Water very scarce. Can't get any through the pump, had to rip off a board & bucket it up.

Hear that the Captain was taken with fever this morning. Went to see him.

Aug. 25th. Went to Beaufort, near four months since I was there last. Dined with Pope. Heard very little about the election. I managed to spend $10, got home about dusk. Bought a thermometer, $1.25, whip, $2.25, umbrella, ditto.

Aug. 26th. Had to put 4 hands digging a well, water is very scarce. All the women drying blades which I found were spoiling in the house. Saw some cotton caterpillars yesterday. Hear they are at several places on the Isld.

---

[44] Thomas Wright Rhodes (b. 1796), planter. Husband of Elizabeth Phoebe Jenkins, Chaplin's first cousin on her mother's side. Father of John, Wright, Julia, and Emma Rhodes. Webb and Capt. Daniel T. Jenkins were Rhodes's brothers-in-law.

Aug. 29th.   Friday. Cloudy, high wind & several light showers. No doubt the storm is brewing. 10th barrel of ice. Picked what peas I could find in corn field, they are black & moldy.

Aug. 31st.   Sunday. It blew from S.E. last night fresh, one heavy shower, cloudy all day, & some rain. The storm is on us in earnest. Commenced blowing *hard* about 4 p.m. from S.E., the same quarter the storm of '54 came from. By 9 o'clock p.m. it seemed to have got to its height, and rained at intervals, *like ten devils,* but the wind only then began to blow smarter, & I thought at times it was harder than during the gale of 1854, and so it continued all night, rain & wind & wind & rain. There was very little rest for us. The house rocked like a cradle & leaked. So August goes out like a raining hell.

Sept. 1st.   Monday. Wind fell some before daylight, and I expecting to see this morning a perfect wreck of houses & trees & fences, but I was agreeably disappointed. I did not see a single tree down & only a small part of my yard & garden fence. Much of my field line fence is down & though the tide came very high, I don't think any water went in the field. I would not look at the cotton, Robert says it is whipped and beat down tremendously. Many larger pods knocked off. Commenced eating root potatoes. Dug near ½ acre for allowance, the part of the [field] near the woods, & where I hardly expected anything. Hands did nothing after digging their allowance but make up fences and throw up a little sedge.

Sept. 2nd.   A quantity of sedge came up in the storm & I had some put in the pen & some piled. Two hands picked each a small basket of cotton. My cotton, being young, is much injured.

     Daniel Pope[45] came here today to visit Ernest & dined. He is a clever young fellow.

Sept. 3rd.   Wednesday. Went to muster, great affair, this St. H.M.R.C.

     No cotton picked. Hauled up young slips & stripped the last of Negro corn. Gave F. M. Pritchard an order to summon out part of the hands to work the roads next Monday.

Sept. 5th.   Sent to Beaufort, got ½ barrel sugar, box of soap, & 3 gals. whiskey.

     All women picking cotton, got very little.

     Got 11th barrel of ice.

---

[45] Daniel T. Pope (b. 1840). Son of J.J.T. Pope and Mary Townsend, of the Oaks Plantation. He was Ernest's age.

Sept. 6th. Saturday. Dug potato allowance, turned out better than last week, did not finish the 3rd task. Uncle Paul dug 10 tasks last week & did not then get allowance.

Sept. 7th. Sunday. Clear & pleasant. Thermometer stood 82 at 1 p.m. Heard there would be preaching today. Went to church, but there was no one there.

Sept. 8th. Monday. Commenced working the roads. I found dinner. There are few hands, & we get along slowly.

Sept. 9th. 25 hands picking cotton. The Captain & Webb found dinner, on the road. Burnt a lime kiln. Thermometer 84 at 11 a.m.

Sept. 10th. Wednesday. Still at the road. The men are generally attentive, but will take the whole week, anyhow. Oliver Pritchard[46] & Edward Reynolds fed us very well. Joe D. Pope & Lawrence Fripp dined with us.

Pope gave me the correspondence in connection with his affair with J. G. Barnwell. He wishes the Captain to see it.

Sept. 13th. Saturday. Finished the roads today, all that can be done to them now. They *were* in such miserable order that I think we have done well.

Got 12th barrel ice yesterday.

Sept. 23rd. Commenced breaking corn. I believe Uncle Paul and John Webb have both commenced today. Commenced on the corn I got of Hazel. The ears are small & long, cob very small, grain also. Clear flint, several ears to the stalk. Can't say that I like, but it appears to have turned out very well today. I measured 148 large baskets, but it was not all I broke today off of 4½ acres. Only 5 acres planted. An unfortunate, or rather I should say, *fortunate* affair happened to Ernest today. He was out shooting, by himself & some distance, half mile or more, from the house, when, *directly* after discharging both barrels of his gun, in attempting, or in the act of reloading, with the mouth of the powder flask at the muzzle of the gun, the powder running down the barrel, it discharged, in consequence no doubt of the gun being very dirty, & some damp powder remaining, being on fire, coming in contact with the dry powder as it descended & thence to the flask above. The flask was blown to atoms, the nozzle of the gun shattered, & Ernest considerably hurt, his right arm

---

[46] Oliver Pritchard (b. 1836), planter. Son of Thomas and Ann Pritchard. Half-brother of Frank Pritchard. Lived northeast of Tombee on Lands End Road.

badly bruised, cut & burnt, his clothes set on fire & he of course much frightened. He however must have shown great presence of mind, from his own account, for there was no one near. He tore off his burning cravat, put out the fire on his coat, picked up his cap (which was blown to some distance) & the gun, and made for home as fast as he could. I met him crossing the Sands, as I was going in the field. I noticed his face was very smutty, but did not know or dream that anything had happened to him until he, in a very cool manner, told me. I directly gave him my horse & returned to the house with him. Sophy was a little frightened at first, but we set to work directly and examined his wounds, two on the right arm & one on a finger, a burn on his left hand. They were all very painful, but none dangerous, only flesh wounds. We dressed them, & after a while he seemed comfortable. It was surely a providential & narrow escape, and we all should, and do, sincerely thank God for his mercy.

Eugene gave us a fright last night, or just before day. He was a little feverish yesterday, and woke up in the night in one of his old screaming fits, which are very distressing, & I think dangerous. It is hard to quiet him, but we did so after a while. I gave him some blue pills, & today a dose of oil, which operated well. He was feverish all day but some better in the evening. And I truly hope he will not have another attack tonight, or hereafter.

Sept. 24th. The thermometer last evening at 9 o'clock was at 66. What a sudden change! And at 7 this morning it stands at 54. Feels very frosty, clear, calm & delightful. Thermometer at 12 m. 63, 2½ p.m. 66 & at 7 p.m. 64.

Got from 5 acres Hazel corn, or Milne corn as some call it, 180 baskets = about 15 bu. pr. acre. 6¼ acres of the Ward corn broke today only gave the same number of baskets, i.e., 180. Have in today 360 baskets in all.

Sept. 26th. Friday. Clear & pleasant, very dry, and mosquitoes horrible bad again. Finished breaking corn, all to the cotton corn. Have made 639 baskets of assorted corn & 72 baskets of nubbins. Making 426 baskets less than last year, & planted only ¾ acre less land. I finished breaking on the the 19th October last year, 23 days later than now. I will have sufficient of provisions if my slip crop does well, I have still 50 or 60 bu. old corn left, & will make some peas. 13th barrel of ice.

Sept. 28th. Sunday. Went to church. Mr. Stephen Elliott preached, the first time I heard preaching since Mr. McE. left us.

Sept. 29th. Monday. Gave the 6th & last allowance of red potatoes. Gave the Negroes the day to break in their own corn.

Sept. 30th. Thermometer 68 at 6½ p.m. All women picking cotton. Got more than any day yet, & only a little over a basket full apiece.

Oct. 2nd. Attended meeting of Agricultural Society. Capt. Dan'l Jenkins has quit the Society.[47]

Oct. 3rd. Sent boat to Beaufort. Got gas, vinegar, keg nails, &c, & *14th barrel of ice.*

Went fishing with Webb & the Captain for bass. Caught no bass but had very pretty sport catching whiting & trout. Picked about 20 lbs. to hand of cotton.

Oct. 8th. Wednesday. Cool & high east wind, cloudy in the evening. Hope it will soon rain, can hardly get water to drink. 118 cords marsh cut. Will not cut but one day more, I think. Broke in cotton corn, very false, got but 15 baskets sound & 9 of nubbins.

Oct. 11th. Saturday. Water to drink & use for other purposes I never saw so scarce in my life. Had to dig another small well for the Negroes. My horses have to be sent to the cow wells for water, which is not fit for them to drink. I suppose, soon, we will have more rain than we want for getting in what little cotton we have. I don't think I have in now, *more* than one bale, if that.

John H. Webb dined with us, he came over to show Ernest how to put together the bateau he with Jim have been knocking at for the past fortnight. It now looks as though something of a boat may be made of it.

Oct. 12th. Sunday. There was, as usual, no preaching, so we all went a chinquapinning[48]——

Oct. 13th. Monday. Gave 8th allowance root potatoes.

Election commences today, for Congress, legislature, & tax collector. I, as one of the managers, went out on the regular hour. At the closing of the box today, there were only two votes polled for Johnson, 37 mistaken.

Oct. 14th. Tuesday. Attended the polls, closed with 82 votes for representation, about 9 for Johnson.

On account of the indignation felt by several—in fact all the voters on

[47] Jenkins had been secretary and vice-president of the Agricultural Society. He also had recently been retired from military duty.
[48] Picking the edible nuts of the chinquapin tree.

the Island, for the votes of Henry Verdier,[49] Dick Pope & old Mr. J. D. Pope,[50] put in the box yesterday, the two former voting on the [   ] of lots given them by Dr. Scott, at the village, several persons, among them Capt. J. Fripp, W. Fripp Snr., W. P. Fripp, Wm. J. Jenkins, & M. T. Chaplin,[51] who had said that they would not vote atall, came & voted for Johnson. I think myself that these votes were *legal,* but they ought not, & I am very sorry that they ever were put in our box. It will greatly injure J. D. Pope. He will most likely be elected this time, but his chances here-after will be more than doubtful. Several that had already voted for him regretted it, under the circumstances. There was considerable excitement at the polls today.

Pope was elected* all pretense *senator next time*[52]

Oct. 16th.   Thursday. One of the most disagreeable days I ever saw. Rain almost all last night, & almost incessantly today. I however went to Beau-fort to carry the box of votes. Rained on me all the time. Got there about 11 o'clock a.m. Votes counted in the council room at 12 m., only 3 manag-ers present. I read off the votes & Dr. Gowan Hazel[53] & Henry Verdier kept count. Considerable excitement in Beaufort. Many bets made & lost, principally by Johnson men.

Vote stood, Beaufort Poll, 19 majority for Johnson.

”   ”   St. Helena Poll, 24 majority for Pope. 24 − 19 = 5, total majority for Pope.

I got back after dark, did not get wet. Dined with Pope.

Oct. 18th.   Saturday. Mother sent her large boat over to the village yes-terday for us to go to the main. We cannot go *that* way, but start from here by my own conveyance this morning. I keep one of her hands to go in the boat with me & send one of mine to go in her boat. I believe I have or-dered & directed everything right before leaving home for ten or twelve days. My orders to Robert are all written down in my memorandum book. If I live to return I will see if they are all executed.

This journal will now be *blanked* till my return.

Thermometer at 54, & very clear & calm.

[49] Henry Verdier (1817–1864), planter. Son of John M. Verdier and Caroline McKee. Killed in Virginia in 1864.
[50] Chaplin probably means Joseph James Pope, Joseph Daniel Pope's father, who was a Beaufort resident at the time.
[51] Marion T. Chaplin died of typhoid in a Union Army prison hospital in Greensboro, N.C. in 1865.
[52] Pope was elected to the *Confederate* Senate, in 1863. (He also supervised the printing of Confederate currency.) This note, written after the Civil War, pokes fun at Pope, belittles the office of Confederate Senator, and implies that secession had been a grand but ruinous game.
[53] W. Gowan Hazel (1829–1893). Son of Joseph and Ann Hazel. Brother of Thomas Hazel. Dr. Hazel drowned in the hurricane of 1893.

Nov. 1st. Saturday. Clear & pleasant. Heavy white frost, both on the main & here, the first we have had. Left the Point at 10 o'clock this morning, and after a pleasant passage arrived safely at home between 6 & 7 p.m. Found everything going on well & all hands well. A very good blow of cotton in the field, & the peas have been picked through once, & the first time, during my absence, just one fortnight this day, a week longer than I expected.

Nov. 2nd. We arrived at the Point the day we left here after a pleasant passage, to a late dinner, say 4 p.m. Found Mother quite well, Ernest had got there about one hour before us. Horses quite fresh. Plantation generally & house & outbuildings particularly, in a very dilapidated condition. No care at all taken of them. Sent my boat back on Monday.

Paul Fripp[54] spent the day with us. Very clever little man.

Changed my mind when in after years I knew him better, as I did

Nothing to do here, no dogs to hunt. Minott not here, left the same day we arrived.

Went to Walterboro on Tuesday 21st, found Saxby at H. Hill, dined with him there, & he went on with us (Ernest & self) in the evening. Got there about dusk, found Virginia & Saxby's family all well. Stayed with him all Wednesday. Did nothing & saw none but the family. Saxby has a very pretty residence. Left for the Point on Thursday with daughter. Saxby came down as far as his place with us. Got to the Point to late dinner, found all well.

I was t–l on the trip home[55]

Friday & Saturday. Nothing to do but read & look at vessels passing & repassing. Felt quite sick all day Sunday.

Sophy, Virginia & self called on Mrs. Charles Fripp[56] & sons on Monday. Drank tea & spent a pleasant evening enough. She had called on Sophy while I was in Walterboro. Sophy was highly pleased with Mrs. Fripp.

Tuesday, Wednesday & Thursday. Nothing to do. Saw nothing of the Fripps, the young men had gone fishing. Plenty of wild ducks in the marshes, but had no way of getting at them. Paul Fripp sent me two wild ducks. He killed six of them yesterday, & some fine whiting. Minott came home on Thursday. We did intend to start on Friday, but Minott sent to ask me to hunt with him, so we went. Drove up to his house to breakfast. Hunted—started two deer, did not get a sight of either, no one got a shot.

---

[54] Paul Hamilton Fripp (1828–1871), planter. Son of Charles E. Fripp and Mary Minott, of St. Bartholomew's Parish. Chaplin's second cousin, once removed, on his father's side.

[55] An ironic reference to "teetotal"—abstinence from intoxicating drinks.

[56] Mary Minott Fripp (1795–1860).

Gussie Myers[57] hunted with us, quite a fine young man. We all dined with Minott. Cousin Eugenia Perry[58] dined at the Point with Mother. We got down before dark, started home on Saturday, and thank God, here we are again. Ernest however did not come with us, he wished to stay & I allowed him to do so. Jack came round with the buggy & got here a little after dark. All the way from the Point in one day is a long drive, but my little horses stood it bravely. They are good.

One of them, "Buckskin," lasted a year after the war began & died on the main. I rode him through our campaign in the cavalry.

Nov. 4th.   Killed veal for market, the last. Had to keep 2 pieces besides my own. Would not have joined had [I] known that there were only 6 in the market.

Weighed off cotton. Have in the very small quantity of 2196 lbs. Fripp's seed & 417 of Seadings = 2613.

Nov. 10th.   Monday. Gave out 12th allowance of roots. Dig almost every day for hogs. Got no ice last Friday. Had 16 barrels in all, equal to 2000 lbs., or 125 to the barrel.

Nov. 13th.   Thursday. Went down to Fripp's Inlet on Tuesday, in search of fun, fish & ducks, got a few of the last two & none of the former. Had good weather. Had the boys with me. Returned this day about 11 a.m. feeling somewhat seedy. Weighed off 428 lbs. cotton.

Nov. 14th.   Sent boat to Beaufort for Negro cloth & shoes. Cloth appears tolerable, 30 cts. for grown & 25 for little Negroes. Got no bill of shoes & groceries. Dry goods bill $175.25. Very big & nothing to pay with.

Nov. 18th.   Tuesday. Frost this morning, & Thos. said he saw ice, but he is such a liar. However, I think it was quite cool enough. Killed a small shoat for pork, very small & not fat, but must have something to put into hungry mouths. Have a fine blow of Fripp's cotton, picking about 50 lbs. pr. hand.

Nov. 19th.   Everybody I can start, picking cotton. I am late getting in my slips. All my neighbors are either done or digging.[59]

Nov. 22nd.   Yoked the two young steers I got from Edgar Fripp last winter. They cut up some fine shines. This is the first young yoke I ever fas-

---

[57] Charles Augustus Myers (b. 1834). Son of Charles M. Myers and Sarah Jenkins.
[58] Eugenia Field Myers Perry. Widow of Isabella Baker's first cousin, William Perry, Sr. Aunt to Major D. P. and Dr. W. J. Jenkins.
[59] Harvesting potatoes.

tened together under my own eye. Hope they will turn out well for they are a fine looking pair. The white one is rather stubborn now.

Nov. 23rd. Sunday. Virginia & I went to the Baptist Church. Heard a Mr. Duncan[60] preach, a very rampant sermon, & the first in the new Baptist Church.

Nov. 25th. Finished the brimstone & common red slips. Made 1 bank leathercoat seed, 2 of brimstone, with some of leathercoat seed mixed with them, 2 of common red seed. Very few eating potatoes so far.

Nov. 29th. Saturday. Finished digging slips, about 12 allowances. Dug in about two weeks of feed of root potatoes, & have more than one week's allowance left in the field.

Nov. 30th. Horses worked so hard during the week, did not go to church. No preaching at the P.E. but there is at the Baptist Church.

Dec. 2nd. Ernest got here after we all went to bed. Landed at the Major's, got a horse & came over. He had a long passage from the main & rough. Mother will, perhaps, come by Christmas. She writes that she is not well.

Coz. Betsy Jenkins gave me 100 oranges & a few lemons, also 50 oranges for Mother, & 5 lemons.

Dec. 3rd. Mother's boat returned. Sent "her oranges" to her.

Dec. 4th. Thursday. Agricultural meeting. Nothing done of any consequence (as usual) except eating a good dinner, furnished today by W. G. Capers.

Dec. 5th. Cut the few sugarcane I had & put it up for seed. Sent Frank to Beaufort, got a keg of butter, and some Christmas presents for the children. Daniel's birthday, 13 years old.

Dec. 8th. Monday. Clear, heavy white frost & ice. The thermometer 40 at 8 a.m. & 44 at 5½ p.m.

Gave out 17th allowance of root potatoes. All hands still picking cotton, tolerable blow.

---

[60] Either William Duncan (b. 1815), Baptist minister and planter of St. Helena Parish, or Hansford D. Duncan (b. 1785), Baptist minister of Barnwell District and second husband of Lavinia Chaplin, Thomas B. Chaplin's second cousin, once removed.

Dec. 9th.   Ice again, picking cotton. Played billiards & dined with Dr. Jenkins.

Dec. 11th.   Thursday. Picked some cotton. Played billiards with Dr. Jenkins. Beat me 4 games, making 6 games he is ahead so far.

Dec. 22nd.   Monday. Mother's boat came over for us all to go the main & spend Christmas with her. The children started today in the boat. Calm but cold. We, S. & myself, deciding to go by land. Wind blew high at night, made us very uneasy on account of the children.

Dec. 23rd.   Tuesday. Very cold & wind high. Salt as well as fresh water frozen. However, hoping to get across the ferry, we started, buggy, two horses & Thomas[61] on mare. Got to the ferry, could not cross, and not having "a dollar to pay for an old gray hoss" & half frozen, returned home, glad to get there, soon made ourselves comfortable, but very uneasy.

Dec. 24th.   Wednesday. Very cold, but calm. Started again, the same outfit as yesterday. Got across the ferry & drove down to the Point by 7 p.m. Found all well & safe, but the boat stuck in the cut on Monday night & the children were very uncomfortable.

[61] A young slave.

1857

Jan. 6th.   Tuesday. After passing a somewhat pleasant time on the main, we arrived safe at home yesterday evening about sunset. Found all well & right except Old Charles whom I find very sick, pleurisy. Ernest came round in the buggy today. Horses all right.

Jan. 9th.   Virginia & I rode to the village to see about the new school-mistress, Mr. & Mrs. Wm. Johnson,[1] very plain people. Like them. Agreed with them, after some persuasion, to take Daniel & Eugene to board & school. Aunt Betsy kindly offered to take Virginia to stay with her[2]—very good thing for me. Johnson's terms rather more severe than Mrs. Mc's. No alternative, must submit, but for a while. Have to pay all in advance. Can't send the children immediately, as I have *not* the cash.
He proved a humbug, entirely.

Jan. 10th.   The Captain & Webb dined with me on wild turkey. Webb is on the eve of moving to the place he has bought in Prince William's Parish.

Jan. 13th.   Tuesday. Started my young oxen to work. They were very wild. Had to put Frank & Jack both with them.

Jan. 17th.   Saturday. Oxen get along very well with Frank alone. Put Jack to the gin. Packed the 3rd bag of Fripp seed cotton. Sent boat to Beaufort with two bales of *Seadings,* 585 lbs. Heard that the Major got 55

---

[1] William H. Johnson (1811–1892). Son of William Johnson and Elizabeth Whaley. His wife, Flora Lee Love, is said to have been a cousin of Robert E. Lee. Johnson succeeded Rev. David McElheran as minister of the Episcopal Church on St. Helena Island.
[2] Since Uncle Ben's death in 1851, Aunt Betsy has been splitting her time between St. Helenaville and Beaufort.

cts. for his Owens seed. Think I ought to get 10 cts. more for Seadings cotton is selling pretty well.[3]

Wind rose after dark & blew a gale.

Jan. 18th.   Sunday. One of the coldest & most disagreeable days I ever experienced. Rain, last night, & this morning very hard, then snow & sleet the balance of the day.

I lived on the Isld 12 years from 1872 to 1884. During that time had very cold winters but no snow

Jan. 19th.   Monday. Last night was excessively cold. The thermometer is down to 20 in the house at 8 a.m. this morning. Everything is frozen up— eggs, milk, vinegar (pepper), & ink, all frozen hard. Every piece of crockery that water was left in overnight is cracked. One cow died in the pen on Saturday night. Would not have them penned last night.

Jan. 20th.   Took Virginia to the village, & left her there with Aunt Betsy to go to school. She will have another week holiday next week, for Mr. & Mrs. Johnson goes to town on Monday next. Thus, nearly or quite, one month of the 1st quarter is completely lost. I will not take the boys down till Johnson returns.

Jan. 23rd.   Friday. Cloudy all day & very cold. Thermometer at 26 in the morning, 30 midday. This has been the longest spell of cold weather I ever knew here.

How many of those "longest spells" & "most disagreeable days"

Jan. 27th.   Tuesday. 3 carts hauling out manure. Finished compost on potato land, 8 loads per task.

Jan. 29th.   Finished ginning white cotton, only 1443 lbs. Fripp seed & 580 lbs. Seadings = total, 2023 lbs. in all to 40 acres, $50^{23}/_{40}$ lbs. pr. acre.[4]

Killed 2 hogs, making 9 this year, very small.

Jan. 31st.   Webb has sold my two bags Seadings cotton,[5] 53 cts., 7 less than I expected, and weight fell 10 lbs. short. Robert to blame, he

---

[3] Middling-fine cottons were bringing upward of 55 cents a pound. Finer grades were selling at between 60 and 70 cents.

[4] At this rate, it took six acres of cotton to produce one bale—a miserable yield, down a third from Chaplin's crop of 1845, and half the average yield on Sea Island plantations.

[5] The previous year Chaplin had sent his fine Seadings cotton to Tom Reilly. Neither factor, Webb nor Reilly, was giving him satisfaction.

weighed the cotton when I was on the main. Webb complains of the cotton being badly prepared, too much handled. I did not whip it this year, is the reason.

Feb. 2nd. Monday. Carried Daniel & Eugene down to the village to school, to Mr. Johnson. The 3 children commence their ⅔rds of a quarter today, for which ⅔rds I paid Johnson $90, which I consider a most unconscionably high price. Only the two boys board with him.

Feb. 5th. Thursday. Cloudy. Agricultural Society day. Society broke up in quite a row, originating from some remarks of Mr. Edgar Fripp, about some one or more members trading with Negroes. Some very hard words passed among members, and I do not think the Society will meet again, and if it does, it will be with greatly reduced numbers.
In about 3 years after they were all scattered

Feb. 7th. Saturday. Commenced listing in marsh, 2 tasks & 5 beds pr. hand. Hauled out some mud.

Feb. 11th. Wednesday. Windy, cold & disagreeable. Finished carrying out & spreading marsh. Manured with it 23 acres.

Feb. 12th. Hands listing in marsh. Put Tenah in the field as ½ hand this year.

Feb. 14th. Had all hands chopping bushes & weeds & pulling up stalks, laying them in the alleys &c in corn field. I thought of burning the corn stalks, but have concluded to list them in, they surely must have *some* fertilizing power, if ever so little. My young oxen are so much used up that I stopped them today for rest, and shall run two horse carts next week.

Feb. 15th. Went to church, saw the children, all well & satisfied. Dan'l says he has got ahead of Benny Scott[6] in all his lessons.

Feb. 16th. Sent flat to Beaufort with 5 bales cotton. Finished cutting stalks & weeds in corn field. Commenced hauling sedge on root patch.

Feb. 17th. Gave out 2nd allowance of corn. I fed on potatoes (roots & slips) just 5 months & 1 week.

[6] Benjamin Scott (b. 1842). Son of Dr. John A. P. Scott and Sarah Ann Chaplin. Brother of Julia, Catherine, Caroline, and William Scott. Chaplin's first cousin, once removed, on his mother's side. Daniel Chaplin was one year younger than his second cousin Benny.

I took advantage of this damp weather to list up some potato land, had 6 tasks listed. Manured with 6 loads of sedge & 8 loads compost all under the list. I will plant half my crop in this way & the other half, 6 loads of sedge under the list & 8 loads of compost on top.

Feb. 18th. Commenced listing in cotton seed for corn. Finished little better than half the potato land, 9 tasks.

Feb. 21st. Saturday. Smoky or hazy all day. Jim got back from Beaufort but did not bring all the things, he will have to go back on Monday. Got 5 bu. seed oats.

I went to the Island hunting with Dr. Jenkins & party consisting of the two Drs. Croft, Capt. J. Fripp, Edgar Fripp, Dr. C. A. Fripp, & Col. Ed. Croft,[7] and also ladies, Mrs. T. G. Croft,[8] Misses Mary Croft[9] & Amanda Jenkins, Eliza Jenkins & children—quite a crowd. Dr. T. Croft killed the only deer, a doe. Spent a pleasant day. Got home after night. Aunts Betsy & Martha called here while I was away. Their visits are few & far between, in no other way are they like angels' visits. I am invited to join another hunt on Wm. Fripp's Island[10] next Tuesday but, as I, it seems, cannot go on any such excursions without being met with ill feeling at home in consequence, I shall not gratify myself.
You shall never complain of this again

Feb. 24th. Played billiards with Wm. Jenkins. Took a sail in the Captain's new $1000 boat. She is a splendid boat.

Got 1¼ acres of oats planted. (Heard drum fish biting.)

Feb. 25th. Went out drum fishing with the Captain in his fine boat, did not get a single bite.
He was in a hurry to put a drum fish in her
This is Ash Wednesday.

Feb. 26th. Listing in mud for cotton. Hereafter I will have as much mud thrown up in the summer as I can. It is so much easier to spread than the green mud. I shall have to turn in & cut some marsh for I am out of manure, & the compost will not be more than enough for corn. I manure this

---

[7] Edward Croft (1836–1892). Son of Theodore G. Croft and Elizabeth Webb D'Oyley, and nephew of St. Helena planter and physician Randall Croft.
[8] Elizabeth Webb D'Oyley Croft.
[9] Mary Sarah Croft (1837–1922). Daughter of Randall Croft and Charlotte Jenkins. Chaplin's third cousin on her mother's side. Amanda Jenkins's second cousin, and William and Eliza Jenkins's first cousin, once removed.
[10] Fripp's Island, between Chaplin's Island and Hunting Island in the chain of Hunting Islands.

year very heavy, for I made a good quantity of compost, & cut more marsh last summer than I have done for many years. Went out fishing for a little while with the Captain in the morning, but did not feel a bite.

Feb. 27th.   Went to Chaplin's Island hunting with Wm. Jenkins & a large party, ladies & men. Had very fine sport. Killed two deer. I had a hand in killing one of them as it came out of the surf. Put 3 hands cutting marsh. Listed cotton land. Heard that several drum fish were taken in Broad River yesterday.

March 1st.   Sunday. Sophy went to church with me, the first time she has been there for about two years. Communion Sunday.

March 7th.   Saturday. Finished banking potato land.
    Started off for the main in sulky. Don't know what I go for— Tomfoolery.

March 16th.   Monday. Got back from my trip, fool trip to the main. Had not much pleasure over there, but some very bad weather, which kept me longer than I intended. Saw Mother & Saxby. Spent one night with the former, balance of time with Saxby. Saw most of the Witsells. Sophy got uneasy and sent Ernest over in the Captain's buggy.
    Sam has been pilfering in the house, and was caught. Sophy sent him in the field. I will give him *ginger,* & bring him back.

March 27th.   Sunday. Started about 10 a.m. for Gillisonville as juryman at court. Horses in very bad order.
    Dined at Catherwood's[11] in Beaufort. Went on to John H. Webb's. Found the Captain there, stayed all night.

March 30th.   Monday. Started very early, had to get up to court by 10 a.m., 25 miles. Got up just in time. Very hard & dusty road, had time to wash off before I went into the courthouse, was immediately put on the grand jury. Had very bad accommodations at the hotel. Took cold, plenty to eat & very good.

March 31st.   Tuesday. On the jury all day.

April 2nd.   Thursday. Rain, came down. Stopped at Webb's, came on to Beaufort. Horses used up. Could not cross the ferry. Stayed all night with Catherwood.

[11] Samuel P. Catherwood (b. 1825), Irish-born druggist.

April 3rd. Friday. Could not get the horses over this morning—high wind. John Chaplin came over in the boat to meet his wife on this side, and as he kindly offered me a ride home in Miss Amanda's carriage, which came down to bring his wife, I came over with him. Had a very pleasant ride & got home about 2 p.m. All at dinner & very glad to see me & I to get home. Jack with the buggy did not get home till 4 p.m. Thunder & lightning last night, severe. Found all my folks well.

April 4th. Saturday. Find all my horses bad off with distemper. Find that Robert has 23 acres of cotton land banked, so I started all hands to planting cotton.

April 5th. Sunday. Weather good, no one out to church. Ernest went to the main in his bateau with 2 hands.

April 11th. Saturday. Clear & delightful this morning.
   This day, eighteen years ago I was first married. To look back upon the past & remember how, through all these long years, I have experienced love, happiness, pleasure, pain, misfortune, trouble, *anguish* and _____. God *alone* can read the heart and it is for the good and quiet of all.
   Planting cotton today with 9 hands.
20 more *long & very eventful years have gone by, & where am I, Coffin's Point, St. Helena, a poor broken down man without home or friends or fortune, but* alive.

April 12th. Easter Sunday. Cloudy all day. Went to church. Noticed that my friend W. P. Fripp communes in the church. Hear that he did so for the first time last Sunday. All is well that ends well.

April 16th. Went out fishing with the Captain. Took *no* drum, but got a fine lot of fine whiting, which I think superior eating to the drum fish.
   Hands preparing land to plant (4 acres) of cotton on the other side the creek. No manure—

April 17th. Friday. The finest day we have had this month. Finished planting 4 acres of cotton on the other side the creek, making a clean finish of the whole 46¼ acres. Commenced to list land for early peas.
   Went fishing again, took a fine chance of whiting but did not even hear a drum fish bite. Took Daniel & Eugene out with me.

April 19th. Heard last evening that Eliza Jenkins was very ill, *miscarriage* I hear, 9 children in 16 years.

I see that my first planting of cotton is coming up prettily, but looks rather yellow from cold winds.

April 20th. Went out fishing in the Captain's skiff with my two boys, took 41 whiting. Only two other boats I saw out.

April 21st. Tuesday. Clear, calm morning, but, as usual, the wind rose about 11½ o'clock & blew quite a gale from south or S.W. Fished a short time in the Captain's bateau, took about 30 whiting & *think* there were two *drum bites* lost carrying the hook. The wind got so high I had some difficulty in getting ashore. The Captain went up to Beaufort, I think he will have a hard time getting back, if he can *atall.*

April 24th. Friday. Gave the Negroes the day—fished. I took 1[12] today (*not* yesterday).

April 27th. **35th birthday**
Went to Beaufort to meet the Board of Commissioners of Roads. A new board was formed today, and myself elected chairman. J. M. Baker reelected clerk & treasurer.

I went fishing with the Captain today, 3 fish taken, my boy one. Hear that fish are biting well up the river.

May 1st. The Savannah Guards[13] are to visit the Beaufort Artillery today. They will not be favored with good weather for the frolic. The Artillery gives them a dinner &c &c. I was to go over, but the weather took too bad.

May 3rd. Sunday. I & the boys went to church. I was in great hopes that they would all go back to school tomorrow, but Mr. Johnson gave notice today that he would attend the church convention this week in Camden,[14] so I suppose there will be no school.

May 5th. Had to put 4 hands to gin out std. cotton. I have to do this to get some money to get necessaries for house & children.

May 6th. Went to muster. Gave order on I. & W. for taxes.

May 9th. Saturday. Sent bag cotton to the village wharf, to go to Reilly.

---

[12] Drum fish.
[13] The Savannah Volunteer Guards Battalion, organized in 1802, the oldest infantry corps in Georgia.
[14] Inland commercial center and resort town about 140 miles northeast of St. Helena.

May 14th.   Finished 1st hoeing of corn & commenced hoeing cotton. Ground dry, very bad stand.

May 16th.   Saturday. Clear & pleasant. Hoeing cotton. Got from town, 5 gals. whiskey, & 5 gals. gas.

May 17th.   Sunday. Went out to church but the parson did not come. Rained while I was at the church, and set in for, apparently, a steady rain at 5 p.m. with *some* thunder & lightning.

May 19th.   Finished transplanting corn. Supplied crowder peas with shiny. Thinned broom corn. Planted 6 rows of Peabody corn, the seed given me by Capt. J. Fripp. He gave $5 a peck for it.

May 21st.   Thursday. Very cool, fires comfortable night & morning. All thick clothing put on.

Commenced hauling my corn for 1st. Cotton damned *grassy,* let it stand. Grass *will grow,* cotton *won't.* Trust to luck.

May 28th.   All the corn that I sent out in salt land quite dead, let it go, no use.

May 29th.   Friday. Sent 3 hands & flat to Beaufort for 60 bushels of corn I sent for, hardly think it will be enough. Bad thing to have to buy provisions. And corn & potatoes both backward & broken this year.

May 31st.   Sunday. High wind last night, and pretty fresh today. Flat got back, however at 1 p.m. Brought very fine corn, the best I ever bought in town, but a high price—$1.03 & bags 18¢ apiece, freight &c &c, puts the cost to me here, $1.18 45/60 pr. bushels, not including loss of work of hands.

I did not go to church today. Daniel seems quite sick. I did not wish them to come home, but &c—

June 2nd.   Tuesday. Finished hoeing cotton & commenced to haul. Sent the boys back to school. Thomas came back & said that Dan'l had the fever before he got to the village. We will go down tomorrow.

June 3rd.   Hauled up early peas & laid by.

Sophy & I went to the village to see Daniel. He was not in bed but quite unwell all day, has a very sore throat. Left him easier in the evening. Dined with Aunt Betsy. Got home at sunset.

June 4th. Thursday. Attended Agricultural meeting. Had an election for officers. Captn. J. Fripp was reelected president, W. G. Capers, treas. & T. G. White, secty. I declined a reelection. Finished plowing corn.

June 6th. Saturday. Started double mold plow through the cotton.

June 8th. All hands hauling corn. Cotton wants thinning and hauling, but must wait till I finish corn.

Gave 2nd allowance of bought corn.

June 10th. Wednesday. Played billiards with W. Jenkins & beat him.

June 17th. *Moonlight* took the horse freely today, so not in foal. A dark cloud arose about 4 p.m., and there was a light rain about 7½ p.m., did not last long and barely laid the dust, tho I expected a fine heavy rain. Hauling cotton 2nd.

June 18th. Thursday. This is the day, according to some "know alls" that the famous comet is to demolish the earth.[15] Don't care if it does. Crops won't be wanted & creditors will be perfectly satisfied.

June 20th. Saturday. Isaac Fripp called & spent the morning. Mother & Ernest arrived about sunset. Almost unexpected, for we have been looking for them so long that we ceased to *do so.*

June 22nd. Giving the corn the last hoeing. Cut a part of the oats, balance not ripe enough.

June 24th. Wednesday. Had a beautiful & most refreshing rain today, from 9 to 11 a.m. It does great good & I lose no work, for it held up in time for hands to finish their day's work. Last hauling corn.

June 25th. Several persons planting slips. I am having slip land listed, 1¼ acres today in all. Some hands hauling corn.

July 2nd. A good show of bloom in cotton. I saw the first about the 29th June.

Gussie Myers was married today in Beaufort to Fanny Rhodes.[16]
20 years ago 1877, both living at last acct

[15] Possibly Donati's Comet, "The Great Comet of 1858," which was to appear in the sky a year later than expected.
[16] Frances Rhodes (b. 1836). Daughter of Thomas W. Rhodes and Elizabeth Jenkins. Sister of Emma, Julia, John, and Wright Rhodes, and niece of Capt. Daniel T. Jenkins. Fanny and Gussie were first cousins.

Much fuss going on about a picnic to come off at that hole of dissipation, St. Helenaville. Ernest will go & Sophy must send something for the boys to find. My horses will suffer.

July 4th. Saturday. Independence Day. Had a very fine dinner at the muster house, 2 baskets champagne, & speeches from Col. Johnson[17] (not political) & T. G. White. Short ones from Isaac Fripp & Chisolm.

July 5th. Sunday. Clear & warm. Went to church. Large congregation, tolerable sermon &c.

July 7th. No slips planted yet. I will have to plant all the peas I can, & have very little seed to do so.
The coons are breaking down my corn, near the swamp.

July 8th. The Captain dined with us. Wife had a pudding made of starch, & extras which was considered very fine by all hands.
Listed pea land with all hands (not those that eat the pudding).

July 9th. Planted slips for the first & late at that, no rain through the day. Think they will die.
They did not, for up to date, have had much rain.

July 17th. Friday. 7th barrel of ice. Commenced to plant cowpeas. Very heavy rain in the afternoon, much heavier in the field than at the house. Have had to open ditches and let off water. My ditches do not draw well. Cotton grows very fast. Corn looks well.

July 19th. Sunday. Mother's boat from the main got here about daylight. Brought from Beaufort for me 40 bushels of corn, cost $1.10, making 100 bushels this year.

July 20th. Gave out 1st allowance of 2nd lot of bought corn. Very heavy wind at dark. Storm. All hands hoeing cotton.

July 30th. Sent boat to Beaufort in the evening. Carry back 5 bags of corn I got by mistake, marked S.H. Also to sell some tomatoes & watermelons. I have not many melons, but an abundance of tomatoes this year.

July 31st. Boat got back from Beaufort after dark, did not expect them on account of wind.

[17] Lt. Col. Benjamin J. Johnson was killed at First Bull Run, Manassas, Va., on July 21, 1861.

Hauled up slips, 1st time. 9th barrel ice. Tried root potatoes, hardly a potato to be found. I don't think half the patch would give me (now) one allowance. Common reds the best of the 5 kinds I have planted. *Vines,* very fine.

I cannot give more than 3 or 4 more corn allowances.

✱✱*I want to state here that when the war broke out, W. G. Capers was Treasurer of the Agricultural Society of this Island and he had all of the property & money of the Society on his hands, 1 doz. or 2 doz. each of silver forks & spoons among them & for which he never accounted to any of the living members. Now 1877, there are alive that I can remember, myself, T.B.C., W.O.P. Fripp, C. A. Fripp, W. G. Capers, W. J. Jenkins, no other that I remember   Tom White✱✱*

Aug. 3rd.   Monday. Flat too wet for Jack to work on. Hands hoeing late peas, they look very pretty.

Wind on Saturday & yesterday, which was very high at times, blew down & broke off much cotton and corn, & some fencing.

Aug. 4th.   Went out with Sophy & Ernest, fishing, poor sport. Had a light sprinkle of rain on us, very little rain also, at the house, but there was a *very heavy,* tremendous rain over in the field, and all the N.E. part of the Island, the heaviest we have had this year. Slip patch flooded, some corn fields also, one bridge carried away on the Seaside Road. Had to summon out 15 hands to have the same repaired. Trowell in charge.

Aug. 5th.   Picked peas & made turnip pen.

Went to see after bridge. Requires 10 planks to fill up the wash. Sent them by Dr. Jenkins' cart.

Aug. 6th.   Thursday. Went on to Agricultural meeting. Nothing much done, some foolish wrangling & a horse race. T. G. White, elected secretary the last meeting, has resigned & left the Society altogether. Edings Fripp[18] came home with me, took tea & returned to the village.

✱✱*Fickle fellow Tom W. He is now practicing law in Beaufort. Gave up medicine & took law & politics.✱✱*

Aug. 12th.   Commenced to strip blades with women.

✱✱*W. G. Capers was treasurer of the Society when the war broke out & he had all the valuables of the Society in his hands, silver spoons & forks & money, & never accounted for any of it.✱✱*

[18] Joseph Edings Fripp (d. 1862). Youngest son of William Fripp, Sr., and Sarah Reynolds. Brother of William W., Clarence A., and Alviro A. Fripp. Chaplin's second cousin, on his father's side.

Aug. 14th.   Stripping blades. Cotton getting the *yellow* leaf very badly. The Captain's crop has fallen off in consequence. 11th barrel ice.
Wish I had one now   '77

Aug. 16th.   Nelly confined about 5 p.m. today, girl child name_____.

Aug. 17th.   Monday. Clear & very warm. At the blades again, rather a long job.
     C. A. Fripp was taken ill over at Dr. Jenkins'. The latter borrowed my buggy to take him to the village.
     Commenced taking honey, got myself stung.
(not the first stinging I have had)

Aug. 18th.   Have some sick Negroes, & with those attending on them that I get on slowly with the blades. I am little over half done. Weather very favorable indeed.

Aug. 19th.   Put up 3 quarts of tomatoes in self sealing cans to keep for winter.
They kept very well indeed.
     Got nearly all of today's blades wet.

Aug. 20th.   Planted rutabaga turnips—fear the seed not good. Sent some vegetables down to Bay Point yesterday to try the market. Did not sell any.

Aug. 21st.   Friday. Cloudy, N. wind, quite cool, bad weather for cotton, & just the thing for caterpillars——
     Cut marsh & picked peas yesterday & today.
     Clear in the afternoon, 12th ice.

Aug. 24th.   Monday. Went fishing with the Capt., Webb & Adams,[19] got a fine lot of small fish & had a pleasant sail.
     Finished stripping standing corn & commenced cotton corn blades.
     Gave out the last allowance of corn, will begin with potatoes next Monday, good, bad or indifferent. Capt. commenced today. Believe that 1 task did *not* give him much more than ½ week's allowance.

---

[19] William Adams (1804-1884). Son of Benjamin Adams and Mary Rebecca Chaplin. Brother of T. A. Bell's wife, Mary Chaplin Adams. First cousin to Thomas B. Chaplin on his mother's side.

Aug. 25th. Finished stripping blades but did not get them all cured & housed.

I dined with the Major. Saw W. P. Fripp.

Aug. 26th. Mother sent boat over, all well. Got in all my blades, & a very fine crop I have made. I may, & *may* not strip the Negroes' corn.

Nelly's child died last night or this morning, 10 days. I am sure it had a hurt, mashed or had a fall. Miserable wretches, they won't tell of it, but the lash will bring it out. This is the 3rd child Nelly has lost in as many years.

Aug. 27th. Thursday. Killed my first beef for market, & the last kill of the first round. It is a very good beef.

Sent 2 hands in the evening in boat to Beaufort with a veal to sell. Engaged at $8. It is well worth it.
I must have been hard up!!

Aug. 29th. Saturday. The boys got home to breakfast as I expected. I brought Virginia home about 11 a.m. They spent a happy day. The Captain dined with us, & the children all went back in the evening. Gave out 1st allowance roots, 1 task 5 beds.

Sept. 2nd. Wednesday. Did not go to muster.

There is to be another of those damned parties at the village on Friday night, given by Edings Fripp. We are invited but none will go but Ernest.

Sept. 4th. Friday. The weather has been threatening all this week, wind from E. & N., sometimes pretty fresh. 14th barrel ice, 1 barrel tar. Ernest went down to the party with buggy & Jack, in his glory no doubt.
poor fellow, gone gone

Sept. 7th. Sent Ernest to Beaufort. Heard that Reilly has sold my bag of yellow cotton for 16 cts. Sent an order for the money. He has been a long time selling it, ever since May.

Have 68 stacks marsh cut.

Sept. 9th. Wednesday. Had the women finishing the early peas, picked the last. I did not make as much as I ought, badly worked, but with their help I will not have to break in corn for allowance as *one* of my neighbors have to do.

The Captain (very unexpectedly) bought today a pair of small horses from Alviro Fripp, $300. We met Alviro at Uncle Paul's, trying to sell to him.

Sept. 10th.   84 cords of marsh cut. 6 hands picking, got as high as 20 lbs. to 1 hand. Did some thrashing & will get more tomorrow.

Sept. 11th.   Sent Frank to Beaufort. He did not get back.

Heard that Virginia has been so imprudent & foolish as to be riding out on horseback with that damned little ass Edings Fripp.[20] There are already reports about his attentions to her among the scandalmongers of the village. I feel mortified & angry. It *shall* be put a stop to, & at once. If this is what I pay $15 pr. quarter for, she might as well come home, & she shall do so if I hear any more of it.

I fear she did worse than E.F. in the end.[21]

Sept. 12th.   94 cords of marsh, cotton opening slowly. Frank did not get back till 9 p.m. Brought the ice, 15th barrel.

Sept. 13th.   Sunday. All of us went to church, I believe the first time this summer. Did not see any of the children, they were not out.

Sept. 14th.   Monday. Election for Ordinary of the district. Went to the church to hold the election as one of the managers. Heard sometime after that Fickling[22] is elected.

Sept. 18th.   Friday. Sent boat to Beaufort, 16th ice.

Went down to the village, Soph., Ernest & I go to a party given by Amanda Jenkins. S. & I went mostly to see after Virginia. Very nice party, good supper &c &c &c. Stayed with Aunt Betsy. Minott & wife came there but could not be taken in.

Sept. 19th.   Saturday. Dined with W. Jenkins. Came home in the evening, very tired. Confound these parties, I go to no more.

Sept. 20th.   Heard the Captain was sick, went to see him. Been sick since Thursday, fever.

Sept. 21st.   Monday. 4th root allowance.

Went over to the Captain's, he still has fever. Stayed with him all day

---

[20] Joseph Edings Fripp.

[21] Virginia married John Wilson Glover (1846–1882), son of John C. and Jane C. Glover, of St. Bartholomew's Parish, in April 1867. She died in childbed in Oct. of the same year. In 1870, Glover married Camilla F. Jenkins, daughter of Daniel Field Jenkins, brother of John Jenkins, first cousin to the Captain, the Major, and the Doctor, and third cousin to Chaplin on her father's side. Glover and his second wife named a daughter after Virginia. In 1874, Glover was struck and killed by lightning.

[22] William Fickling, of Ladies Island. Husband of Sarah Johnson, sister of William Johnson, Sr.

Fever cooled in the evening & I brought him home with me. Saw Uncle Paul over there in the morning.

Sept. 22nd. Tuesday. Captain still in bed, but no fever today. Uncle Paul came to see him. All hands picking cotton. Pick tolerably.

Sept. 23rd. Wednesday. The Major called to see the Captain. He has no fever. Soaking quinine.

Sept. 24th. Uncle Paul called. The Captain up today. Came downstairs, & we rode over to his place in the buggy.

For a wonder Uncle P. stayed to supper with us, the first time he ever took a meal in my house. All owing to the Captain's being here however. Ernest complaining. Hope he will not have fever.

Sept. 25th. Sent to Beaufort, 17th ice.

Captain & I rode over to Uncle Paul's in the morning. Met Aunt Betsy coming down here to see him, Virginia with her. She spent the day. The Captain keeps his ponies over here to ride about with.

Ernest down with hot fever, poor fellow. It is not long since he was boasting he never had fever.

Sept. 26th. Saturday. Ernest still with fever. Gave him 20 grs. of blue pill. Operated well but fever does not go off. Quite sick.

Sept. 27th. Ernest's fever still holds on. He alarmed us by being very delirious for a short time. Sent off to the village for Dr. C. A. Fripp.[23] He got here about 1 or 2 o'clock. Considers Ernest very sick, put on blister & gave calomel. He went back to the village after dinner to get more blistering ointment, as he feared what I had would not draw. He got back late, after 10 o'clock. Ernest still very sick, the Dr. thinks remittant fever with a touch of pneumonia. Up nearly all night. I, feeling quite unwell myself. Had to lay down. Sophy up all night.

Sept. 28th. Monday. Ernest a very little better in the morning. Dr. left medicines & directions & left himself about 8½ a.m. The Captain went home, did not return. Uncle Paul called in the evening. Sophy & I up nearly all night. E. quite sick.

Sept. 29th. Tuesday. The Captain & Dr. both came this morning. Ernest *very* sick. Fever does not leave him a moment, & very hot. Vomits very

[23] Clarence Fripp became a surgeon in the Confederate Army. After the Civil War, he moved back to St. Helena and practiced medicine among the freedmen.

often, can keep nothing down. Capt. went home to dinner, but returned again at dark, hearing that E. was worse, which he is. Dr. C.A.F., Sophy & I up all night. Captn. went to bed feeling badly. Ernest extremely ill all night, had to give him laudanum & brandy to keep life in him. A little stronger pulse towards morning. Sophy almost despairs.

Sept. 30th.   Wednesday. Ernest a very little better this morning, but the fever never leaves. The Dr. went home, Captain ditto. Com. breaking corn. High wind last night & turned suddenly quite cold. Had a fire made this morning. E. continues the same all day. Moved him in one of the front (east) rooms, more comfortable. Sophy & I up all night by turns.

Oct. 1st.   Thursday. Agricultural meeting, of course I can't go. Dr. came about 10 a.m., found Ernest considerably better, but still the fever holds on. Giving him quinine in large doses. Dr. returned before dinner, goes to the Society. Ernest very restless, has sick stomach, but we got some rest. I kept up till after 1 o'clock, but Sophy is so worn out I persuaded her to go to bed. Ernest took some paregoric & slept the last part of the night & so did I.

Oct. 2nd.   Friday. Ernest very much better, & may now be considered out of danger. The Dr. came but did not stay long, only directed the quinine to be continued. E. almost if not quite clear of fever for the first time. Took some more substantial nourishment.

18th barrel of ice.

Erskine Chaplin called today & took up his brother Paul's[24] note to me for $80.

Oct. 3rd.   Saturday. Ernest still without fever, & says he feels better. Dr. C.A.F. paid another visit.

Broke in my cotton corn, the best crop I ever made through cotton, 11 cart loads. Measurement, 100 bushels.

Simon came from the main. Mother heard that Ernest was sick, but not that he was ill.

Oct. 4th.   Sunday. Ernest much better, & came downstairs for the first time, in the afternoon.

Oct. 5th.   Monday. Clear & cool all day. 6th root allowance. Dr. C. A. Fripp called to see Ernest, & discharged his patient. E. was downstairs

[24] Erskine (b. 1837) and Paul Chaplin. Sons of Edwin and Elizabeth Chaplin. Brothers of Edwin and Elvira Chaplin. First cousins once removed to Thomas B. Chaplin on their father's side.

nearly all day. C.A.F. gives a party tomorrow night, but did not give us an invite. Dr. Jenkins gives one on next Friday night, & sent us an invitation today.

Commenced breaking corn. Used the flat to bring corn from the Sands crossing. By this means, got in about 20 cart loads of very fine corn. I am gathering so far a fine crop of provisions & fodder. I broke about 6 acres of ground today, but some of it was very broken salt ground. I think the whole, as it is, yielded an average of very near 30 bushels pr. acre.

Oct. 6th. Got in 18 cart loads of corn today, & some in baskets. Turned out better than yesterday. Broke only about 4½ acres, very sound corn, hardly any rotten or nubbins, one of the very best crops I ever made. Used the flat again today, it facilitates matters very much. The Captain was here today for a little while, he is not atall well. Ernest continues to improve & has a very good appetite.

Oct. 7th. Breaking corn, about 254 baskets out of 5 acres. Broke some of the flint corn, my selection. I have now, about 11 acres to break, & hope to get done by Friday night. Weather permitting.

C. A. Fripp was to give his party at the village last night. I suppose it came off & was a *St. Helenaville allumination affair.*[25]

Oct. 8th. Thursday. Cloudy & rain off & on all day, very heavy at dark, & looks like a set in affair. Wind high from the N. & E. Did not get but 8 or 9 cart loads of corn broken in, it still turns out well. Every task gives a cart load of 16 baskets, equal to 32 bushels pr. acre.[26]

Oct. 9th. Friday. Rain all day. Could not break corn. Thrashed out oats, sorted cotton & got some sedge floated from the other side the creek & put in the cow pen.

Oct. 12th. Monday. Finished breaking in corn, made the best crop I ever made. 32 bushels to the acre average or _____ bushels, besides 100 bu. cotton corn. Gave the Negroes the evening. Tried my slips, got 7¼ bu. yellow yams.

Oct. 13th. Tuesday. Gave the Negroes the day to get in their own crop. I believe they have done very well.

Gave out 1 task & 6 beds yesterday of roots for allowance.

[25] Chaplin is mocking social life in the village, especially the practice of holding parties for the alleged purpose of enlightenment.
[26] An excellent yield ($4 \times 16 \div 2 = 32$), twice the production of earlier years.

Oct. 17th.   Saturday. The children all came home, and all look badly & have violent colds. I don't wonder, from so much frolicking at that damned eternal village. I will keep them at home for a few days and run the risk, for I do not think they can be worse off, particularly the boys.

I, sick in bed all day, liver attack. No one thinks this serious, but they will see to their sorrow. The Captain came to see me.

Oct. 18th.   I was quite sick today. The Captain very kindly came & stayed all day with me. We spoke of going to the inlet the last of the week for a day or two, & taking all of my folks in his boat.

Oct. 24th.   Saturday. The wind rather high & ahead but we got off at 10 o'clock on Thursday and got to Skull's Inlet, after a hard row about 2½ p.m. Pitched our tents and made snug, for the weather looked threatening. Got one small sheeps head & a few other small fish for supper. We had a little rain on us at night. Friday the weather was cloudy & clear off & on. Caught several sheephead, and other fish, much as we could eat, white & black. Got very few mullets & small. Rain at night & tent leaked a little. Started home at 11 this morning, got here at 1 p.m., fair wind & the best day we have had.

I killed last market beef on Thursday, gave it out before we left.

Oct. 25th.   Sunday. The fruits of the trip—we all have very bad colds, & one constant cough throughout the house. I quite sick at night. Two Negroes sick.

Oct. 30th.   Friday. I have been quite sick, downstairs today, very weak. Much sickness among the Negroes this week. Sometimes 7 or 8 down— only 2 today.

Oct. 31st.   Rode out & dined with the Captain. Sent to Beaufort, got no ice. Suppose it is stopped, hope it is, I have just ordered it so, in a letter today. Have had 21 barrels this summer.

Hear that Dr. Jenkins & the Major have moved home, I don't know when, so they think there is no danger.

I have only weighed off 3 bales of cotton, & have in, I suppose, not more than 5 bales.

Nov. 1st.   Sunday. Ernest went out, but no preaching, as he heard that Mr. Johnson's sons ran off and broke his sulky.

Nov. 5th.   Rode to Capers'—the old man is quite sick. Saw Minott, Gabe, Frank & C. A. Fripp.

Assorted cotton, have to pick.
Sent 3 hands to the Island for clapboard.

Nov. 13th.   Friday. Virginia came home, fell out with Johnson. Let that go for some capers of the boys.

Nov. 16th.   Monday. Sophy & I rode down to the village to see Johnson about the children's difficulty. Everything was explained & we felt satisfied.

We had a heavy rain on us when returning. Ernest went with us & took a boat Mother had sent over for him, & went to the main. He no doubt got wet. We brought the boys home. They got soaked.

Nov. 20th.   Friday. Heavy clouds made up last night to the N.W. There were sleet & rain this morning, & all day. Ice formed, destroying everything in the shape of vegetation, and I fear that our chance for any more cotton not yet open is more than slim.

Nov. 23rd.   Monday. Commenced digging slips, common yams first. Very thick but small, more eating than seed however.

Gave out the last allowance of roots. Cut sugarcane. I fear the cold has much injured for seed next year. Dug only 2½ tasks—got more than 2 banks seed, 15 baskets each, & 2 of eating, 25 baskets each.

Nov. 25th.   Dug 1 acre, 2½ acres in all. 1 task of common yams left. Have 10 banks of seed, & 7 weeks' allowance, besides 1 bank for the house, dug.

Nov. 27th.   Friday. Cloudy. High wind. Cool. Finished common yams & dug brimstones, they all turn out well. Filled up the potato pen, it held all the banks I made last year. I have now to bring in the yard, to be removed when I can make the pen larger.

Nov. 29th.   The Captain came over & we rode together to see old Mr. Capers. Found the old man very low, do not think he will ever recover. Mrs. Capers fell from top to bottom of staircase the other day, & hurt herself very much. She was up. All of the old man's family are with him.

Dec. 1st.   Finished digging slips. Made 19 banks eating of 28 baskets each, & 22 of seed of 18 baskets, equal to 928 baskets in all or 9860 lbs. pr. acre. 78,880[27] in all.

[27] Pounds of potatoes.

Dec. 2nd.   Mary was confined about 5 a.m. Boy child.

Dec. 3rd.   Agricultural Society day. Gabe Capers sent me the lodge keys about 9 o'clock this morning with a message that I had to find dinner. He is mistaken however, so I sent them back to him. I suppose we will have no dinner. Which was the case. J. Edings Fripp was elected a member, so he finds next time. There were very few members out, & nothing done, not even the principal & most important business, eating & drinking.

Dec. 4th.   Friday. Got about 20 lbs. to hand cotton today & yesterday. Sent to Beaufort. Got from town 6 sacks of salt, stuff for riding skirt for Virginia, & curtains for bed & bedroom. Also 50 lbs. coffee.

    The boys went after ducks on the island, got 4, & got 3 pr. of shoes, 3 pants & 3 coats ruined. Had to send 4 hands in boat to fetch them over at 9 p.m. They left the paddling boat behind, have to send for that tomorrow. *All this* for 4 shad pole ducks[28]—

Dec. 12th.   Saturday. Clear & cold, white frost. I went to the Island (Chaplin's) with the Captain, on Tuesday morning. Wm. Adams, Jno. H. Webb,[29] T. A. Bell & Philip Webb in company. Had fair wind & made a good run down. Had not much sport. Killed nothing but coons & ducks. Jumped 2 deer, saw none myself. Had rain on us on Tuesday and Wednesday night, with heavy fogs, but we had a very good close tent. So kept dry & comparatively comfortable. Got back to Lands End at 12½ o'clock p.m. yesterday. I got home to dinner.

    Bell & Adams go home today. Webb stays on account of his wife being sick last night. I have my hands still picking cotton. They get over 20 lbs. each, but finish the field today.

    Old Mr. Capers died at 1 a.m. on Wednesday morning, & was buried on Thursday.

9th inst.

Dec. 13th.   Sunday. Sophy & I went to church. Poor sort of a funeral sermon by Johnson.

as usual

Dec. 23rd.   Mr. Johnson & Dr. Jenkins called. I had taken a ride after 11 a.m. to the store, & missed of them, as they came up one way & I went the other, not intentionally by any means.

O no, but we missed each other

[28] Possibly the red-breasted merganser, locally named the fish duck, an abundant winter visitor to the salt marshes, generally spurned by hunters because of its fishy flavor.
[29] Pvt. John H. Webb, C.S.A., died at McPhersonville, S.C., in 1862.

Dec. 25th. Friday. Christmas Day, and a very stormy day it is. Wind blew a perfect storm all day. All dined at home together except Daniel & Ernest. D. with the boys at the Captain's, & E. on the main. Gave the Negroes one of the oxen I got of Edgar Fripp last year. He was not poor, but would not, owing to inhuman treatment by my Negroes in breaking, be fit for an ox again.

So thus ends *the Merry Christmas,* 1857.

Dec. 26th. Saturday. Negroes doing nothing, & we did nothing but take a short ride. Robert went to see his wife on Jerico, & passing each other on the way. She came here.

Dec. 28th. Monday. Clear & very calm and pleasant. Last day of the Negro holiday & thanks for it. Many persons put their Negroes to work today. And I think the day is fast approaching when Negroes will only be allowed Christmas Day alone, instead of the three days.
They are now allowed every day—1868

I gave out an allowance of corn last Monday, at the request of the Negroes. Today makes the 4th allowance of slips.

Dec. 29th. The Negro holidays are over & I am truly glad. Started 5 gins.

Dec. 30th. Robert did not come home yesterday.

5 gins going. Cotton turns out about 22¾ lbs. to the 100. Which will be about 1325 to the bag of 300. 75 lbs. less than I allowed. Packed 1st bag.

Dec. 31st. Thursday. The last day of A.D. 1857.

Horse broke axle to cart, had to stop 1 gin to make new one (axle). Played billiards with W. Jenkins. He 4, I 3 games.

End of 1857.

1858-61

Jan. 1st. This [is] the commencement of the thirteenth[1] year of this journal—Clear, warm & pleasant. Sent to Beaufort in boat for things expected from town, but got nothing.

Packed 2nd bale of cotton, 300 lbs. Killed 2 hogs, making 4 this year. Played billiards with W. Jenkins.

Jan. 3rd. Sunday. Went to church. Johnson declines to take my two boys to board this year, consequently, they cannot go to his school. I have to go immediately to Beaufort & get them at school there, with Wm. Treville,[2] I suppose. I am not sorry for this. My opinion of Johnson is not *very* exalted. **He was & is a skunk**

Saw J. W. B. Pope,[3] & T. A. Coffin, the two grooms, being each lately married.[4]

19 years 1876

Jan. 4th. Went to Beaufort with the Captain, in his boat. He took up his boys to school.

I made arrangements with Wm. De Treville to take my boys to school, and with John Baker to board them. Treville charges $6 for Eugene and $10 for Dan'l. He is to prepare the latter for the military academy.

[1] Fourteenth.
[2] William J. DeTreville (1830–1897), attorney and schoolmaster. Son of Chaplin's attorney Richard DeTreville and Cornelia Matilda Joyner. In 1856, Mrs. T. A. Bell (Mary Chaplin Adams) wrote to former schoolmaster A. B. Wardlaw: "William Traville has a very good School, I think twenty-two scholars and the promise of more next quarter." After the Civil War, DeTreville was the plaintiff in a landmark case which tested the constitutionality of the Direct Tax imposed on St. Helena Parish in 1862, and the subsequent confiscations of property and resale to freedmen and others. (*De-Treville* v. *Smalls,* 98 U.S. 174.)
[3] John W. B. Pope (b. 1825), Charleston attorney. Son of Joseph James Pope and Sarah Jenkins. Brother of Joseph D. Pope.
[4] Coffin married Sarah Heyward Cruger.

Jan. 6th. Wednesday. Found muster dinner. All went off well. Great trouble, wish I could well get rid of it.

Ned Capers came home with me & stayed all night. Sent boat to Beaufort for things I expect from town, pr. st. *Everglade,*[5] & got nothing but some twine.

Packed 3rd bale cotton, 300 lbs.

Jan. 9th. Saturday. Fog, rain & wind since Thursday evening, could not take the boys up to school as I intended & wished.

Packed 4th bale cotton, 305 lbs. Hope to get five bales more of white.

Jan. 13th. Wednesday. I, fool like, send the boat off last night, about midnight, and here I find it this morning, raining like blazes, with no signs of clearing directly. Brightened up a little about 10 & I started with the boys. Had an unpleasant day but did not get wet. Got to Beaufort about 1 p.m. The boat got up about 8 in the morning. The bedding got a little wet. Saw Mrs. Baker.[6] She seems a very sociable & clever lady, & I think the boys will get along well with both her & John Baker. They will commence school tomorrow. I got home about dark. Got some things from town—Irish potatoes, shoes for boys &c.

Jan. 14th. Packed 5th bale yesterday. D. P. J. came here, *not on a visit,* but to beg garden truck.

Jan. 15th. Rogues broke my seed banks. Sam's guard, gave him thunder. Had a calf killed a night or two ago. Elimus catches it for that.

Jan. 16th. Planted oats in the yard, & set out some wild orange plants around the yard fence.

Jan. 18th. Monday. Cool. Killed 2 hogs. 7th slips.

Jan. 25th. Monday. Captain dined. I laying out flower garden for S. C. C.[7] 8th slips, rotting.

Jan. 26th. Wm. Jenkins' house at his Capers place[8] was burned down completely on Friday night last. We knew nothing of it at the time. Hear

[5] Per steamer *Everglade.*
[6] The tax collector's wife.
[7] Sophy Creighton Chaplin.
[8] Eliza Jenkins testified to a U.S. Court of Claims in 1892 that the Capers place had been given to *her* by her Uncle Ben Chaplin as a wedding gift. Hence, Dr. Jenkins had acquired the place through marriage.

that he lost not more than a bale of cotton, but his whole crop (packed) ran a very narrow chance.

Jan. 27th.   Finished ginning cotton. Commenced hauling out marsh.

Jan. 28th.   Packed 8th bale cotton (light). Spreading mud. Met Dr. R. Croft at Dr. Jenkins'.

Jan. 29th.   Packed 9th & last bale cotton. Total No. lbs. white cotton, 2582, about 65 lbs. pr. acre.
little better than last year

Jan. 30th.   Finished spreading all the mud I had out, about 10¼ acres. 13½ acres' compost for corn.
    Steamer *Edisto* came up Station for cotton. I did not send mine, wish I had.

Jan. 31st.   Sunday. Went to church. Ned Capers came home, dined & spent the night. He is just from town, & made each of us a small present, S., V. & myself.
purse to S., work box to V., forgot mine

Feb. 3rd.   Wednesday. Pleasant. Killed 5th pr. hogs.

Feb. 4th.   Went to Agricultural meeting, there were a few men out. Edings Fripp found his first & a very fine dinner.
forgot he was a member

Feb. 6th.   Sent to Beaufort. Got hoes, axes, saddle for self & side ditto for Virginia, from I. & W. Eugene came home with Frank. Treville has to attend court. Daniel did not come without my permission.
He is not so particular now. 1870

Feb. 7th.   Sunday. Sent to Beaufort for Daniel, did not wish him to stay by himself.

Feb. 9th.   Finished spreading marsh, 15½ acres in all, less than expected. Hauled out all the cotton seed, 190 baskets. Ought to go over 16 acres.

Feb. 11th.   Thursday. Cloudy all day. Listed for corn. Ed Capers came & spent the night. He comes here more frequently *now* than for many past years. Killed 11th hog.
Found out he was fool enough to be coming after Vr.,[9] but no go.

---

[9] Ned was thirty-eight; Virginia, sixteen.

Feb. 13th. Saturday. Rain all day. Cold. Ginned s[tained] cotton.

I went over to play billiards & the rain compelled me to dine with Dr. J. Dr. Croft & family were there, quite a crowd.

Feb. 15th. Monday. Gave out 11th & expect the last allowance of slip potatoes. Went to Beaufort to carry the boys back to school. They have had a week's holiday.

Sent my crop of white cotton to Beaufort, & pr. str. *Cecile* to Charleston. 9 bales.

Feb. 17th. Wednesday. Very delightful day. Dined with Ned Capers. Finished listing in cotton seed for corn, 11 acres.

Feb. 19th. Got my oxen back from the Captain, they work well and I have a plenty of it for them to do, as I have over 16 acres yet to manure.

Feb. 20th. Went to Beaufort. Got a/c sales of my cotton, sold at 40 c., better than I expected.[10] The town weight considerably overrun my weight here. The gross weight, 2697 lbs. Net proceeds, $1,038.61 cts.

Feb. 25th. Packed the yellow cotton. Dined with E. Capers. He came home with me & spent night.

Feb. 26th. Friday. Went to Beaufort. Brought the boys home with me (wrong in doing so). Got a traveling blanket for myself from town.

Webb won't send me any money. Was afraid he would trick me after getting my cotton in his hands. I'll fix him for it.

March 2nd. Tuesday. Very high wind all day. Very cold with plenty of thick ice. March is really kicking up a fuss. Winter seems to have really set in in spring.

Got a little corn land listed.

March 3rd. Ground too hard to list in the morning. Sent the boys back to Beaufort. Went to muster. Edings Fripp elected 2nd lieutenant.[11]

March 5th. Killed 13th & last hog on Wednesday. Planting oats, finished 2½ acres.

[10] The Charleston *Mercury* described the market for long-staple cotton as "healthy and steady." Forty cents a pound was a mid-range price for fine Sea Island.
[11] Pvt. Joseph Edings Fripp died at Port Royal Ferry in 1862.

March 7th.   Sunday. Went to church. Richard Johnson,[12] brother of our parson, preached a *so so* sermon. I have heard him before.

March 8th.   Sent seed to exchange with Wm. Chisolm for his. I will not plant the Fripp seed. Everyone is for planting coarse cotton, so I will not.

March 13th.   Saturday. High wind. Sent boat with std. cotton up to Beaufort to go to town. Sophy & I went over by land. Dined with Baker,[13] Mrs. B. not at home. Hands ditching corn land, finished.

March 17th.   Finished listing cotton land, don't know exactly how much, have to count it up, over 50 acres I know. Commenced tracking out corn land, tracks 3 feet today.

March 18th.   Heard of first drum fish taken today by E. Fripp's man Abel, 3.
   Tracked a small portion of corn land today at 2½ feet, rather near, but open ground.[14]

March 20th.   Finished tracking for corn & commenced planting, ground dry.

March 23rd.   Finished planting corn, 12½ of Ward & 12½ of Uncle Paul's seed.

March 25th.   Cut potatoes to plant & planted a few, red seed. Kept well. So many persons complaining of their seed rotting I was apprehensive that mine would be short.

March 26th.   Went to Beaufort and brought the boys home for the holidays. Very sorry. Trouble now for one month, & God knows where money is to come from to send them back to school.

March 27th.   Webb refuses, now that he has the *whole* proceeds of my last year's labor, to send me my money. This is too bad, I am worried. Finished planting potatoes today.

[12] Richard Johnson (1809–1873), Episcopal minister. Son of William Johnson and Elizabeth Whaley. Brother of the Rev. William, Col. Benjamin J., Dr. Joseph F. and Dr. John A. Johnson, and Sarah Johnson Verdier. Husband of Maria Smith, sister of Virginia Governor William Smith.
[13] John M. Baker, tax collector.
[14] The corn rows are being laid out close together, indicating that the ground is "strong" or fertile. The land may have just been "opened" after having "rested" for several years.

April 2nd. I drove Sophy to T. J. Fripp's to call on Mrs. Charles Fripp. We were persuaded to stay to dinner, did very well. I have 24½ acres of cotton land banked & will commence planting tomorrow, God willing.

April 5th. Monday. Ground in fine order for planting. I'm planting with 3 hands and banking with balance. The Captn. finished today I believe.

April 8th. Attended, as favor, a trial of Negroes for stealing cattle from Dr. Scott. Flogged one of Ann B. Fripp's slightly, & one of F. T. Pritchard's severely. Evidence conclusive.

April 10th. Saturday. Clear, went fishing with Captn. Took 4 in the boat, I, 2 on own line, Dan'l 1, Capt. 1—the 1st I have taken this year.

April 12th. Monday. Finished planting cotton all to ¾ acre. First planting coming up very prettily, & very regular. Seed has germinated much sooner than usual this year. My corn is also up very prettily. I plant this year 52 acres of cotton, 24¼ corn. 4½ potatoes, &c &c. Hope for good yield.

    This is about to be the end of my journal. Let me then conclude **dedicate** thus, to my children Ernest A. Chaplin, Virginia S. Chaplin, Daniel J. Chaplin, & Eugene L. Chaplin, to you all.
All dead but one,[15] & he does not want it

April 14th. Wednesday. Out fishing, caught nothing but a good wetting &c. River very rough.

April 20th. Salinas's store burned down. He lost everything & barely saved his life.[16] Took place about 2 a.m. 21st. Supposed to be the work of an incendiary, & white, but no proof of either white or black.

April 27th. Tuesday. My birthday, 36. Thought I was older, but I am not.
ought to be if I ain't

May 3rd. Monday. Sent the boys back to Beaufort to school. Wish to God I had the money to pay up.

May 5th. Wednesday. Fine morning. Shower in evening. Went to muster, paid taxes. Many men out.

---

[15] Daniel, who lived until 1924, surviving his father by thirty-four years.
[16] Salinas apparently left the Parish following the fire. He was probably related to Charleston cotton broker and auctioneer A. J. Salinas.

May 15th. Went to the main in Uncle Paul's boat. Got there about 2 p.m. and was a little put out to find Baker there. He treated us very politely & left soon after we got there. The steamer *Edisto* came up on Sunday & we went on board, Ernest & self, & lunched very heartily with Capt. Sassard.[17] Saw Dr. Lawrence Service on board. Knew him in Greenville years ago.[18] I sent my hands back on Monday, and we returned in Mother's boat on Friday 21st. Stayed in the house nearly all the time on the main, having hurt my foot badly coming downstairs on Tuesday. Saxby came down to see us on Monday. But, thank God we are all safe at home again.

July 7th. Wednesday. Peg's daughter Mary delivered of a girl child, name *Grace.*

[after this date, entries complete, but widely spaced]

Aug. 22nd. Heard today that Miss Amanda Jenkins has at last found a man to her fancy and is engaged. The happy fellow, one Tom Scriven[19] of Grahamville. So note it be.

Sept. 6th. My beautiful filly Little Dorrit[20] got fastened in the stable last night & was strangled to death by the halter getting fastened around her nose, near the nostrils. The Capt. was spending the night with us, & he heard the noise & woke me up, but before I could get to the stable & cut the rope she was dead. I would not have taken $200 for her yesterday.

On the 28 day of April, 1858, I gave to my wife, Sophy C. Chaplin, a colt, name Little Dorrit.

Poor colt. Got hung to death in stable by halter & carelessness, *when she was little over a year old & one of the handsomest colts ever seen. Was offered $250 for her the day before by Clarence Kirk,*[21] *of St. Lukes.*

Nov. 16th, 1858. Nelly confined. Girl, name Lizzie.

[17] John Sassard (b. 1810), steamboat captain and farmer, St. Helena Parish. He owned eight slaves in 1850.
[18] Chaplin's first stepfather, Rev. John Fields, had owned Chestnut Hill Plantation near Greenville, and took his adopted family there in the early 1830s. Another Greenville connection with St. Helena was established between the Croft and the Jenkinses. Mary McDowell also had relatives in Greenville, though there is no evidence that Chaplin knew them.
[19] Thomas Edward Screven, of St. Luke's Parish. Amanda was the last of the "three Misses Jenkins" to marry.
[20] Title character of the novel by Charles Dickens, published serially in 1855–56, and in a complete edition in 1857.
[21] Clarence Kirk (b. 1814). Son of James Kirk and Mary Baldwin, of St. Luke's Parish. First cousin to Dr. John William Kirk.

Martha died. Thursday 27, 1859, suddenly, disease not known.

May 17th, 1859. Bay mare Moonlight had a bay horse colt, not a single white spot on him, dark bay. Name Humphrey Clinker.[22]

July 2nd. Eliza confined. Boy, name Prince.

Sept. 14th, 1860. Elsie ″ . Boy, Herb or Will.

Feb., Thursday 2nd. Tenah delivered of a little horribility, name Morris.

Helen had a girl, Flora, Oct. 1860.

July 6th, 1861. Nelly confined of a boy, Sumter.

[22] Title character of Tobias Smollett's picaresque novel, published in 1770.

1886

January 1st, 1886.

Many eventful years have now passed since the last lines were written in this journal, nearly 28 years. During that time the War of Secession has been fought & lost, & with the cause, all of our worldly possessions, or very nearly all. We were driven from our home in St. Helena Island on the 7th day of Nov. 1860,[1] never to return to it except on a visit as strangers. On the close of the war in 1865, I mortgaged the land left me by Mother to a man from New York named Cowle,[2] for some $8000, & tried the chances at planting, but owing to the then very unsettled state of the country, & unjudicious management, I made little or no crops, & lost the land. Though I had a plenty of land, I rented, on account of the buildings, the Point Island place of Oliver Middleton.[3] We lived in the overseer's house very comfortably for about two years, then, having put up a log house at Fields Point, we moved there, and I may say, lived from hand to mouth for several years, until about 1871 or 2. Sometimes very bad off indeed. Ernest was there with us. His health was very bad. About Jan. 1872, having had the keeping of a public school at Coffin's Point on St. Helena offered to me, we moved over there and occupied the house that Cockcroft—Coffin's overseer—used to live in. It was a poor cousin's but it was a shelter & a home for many years. I taught to the best of my ability a large school for Negro children during the winter & early spring months for $60 pr. mo. but at first could get nothing but "pay certificates" which I had to dispose of at heavy loss, but we got credit at Oliver & Ward's

---

[1] 1861.
[2] William H. Cowl, of Brooklyn, New York.
[3] Oliver Hering Middleton (1798–1892), planter, St. Bartholomew's Parish. Son of Henry Middleton, Governor of South Carolina 1810–12, and Mary Helen Hering. Husband of Susan Chisolm, daughter of Robert T. Chisolm, of Edisto Island. Middleton was a neighbor of Isabella Baker's on the Combahee.

713

store for provisions &c &c on the strength of them. Coffin's Point then was owned by a Yankee named S. W. Whitwell.[4] He & wife, a confirmed cripple, lived in the *big house,* a half mile from where we lived. They had no children of their own, but had adopted a boy & girl. These people I cannot describe. They were "different from any people I had ever met with in my life." They appeared to us to turn about, to be quite clever & obliging, & then quite mean & disagreeable, but the old man was far the best of the two and often assisted us when assistance was really needed, and about 1874 or 5, in the spring, persuaded us to move up & occupy two or three rooms in their house, & when they went North, which they did every summer, we had the whole house to ourselves. We moved up therefore in June, were better sheltered, but I don't think more comfortable. I was not paid any stated sum for taking care of the premises, but I got something—what land I could plant, for one thing. Ernest also came over from the Point & lived with us the few short days he had to live & we had the satisfaction & comfort of caring for & making his last days more comfortable.

In July of that year I was offered the situation of custodian of government property on Hunting Island, North Point, where a new lighthouse was being built. I accepted of course, though I would have to stay down there nearly alone, but I thought Ernest would be able to take turns with me. He was not able to do so, & so that I could come up home when I wanted to, I got Charley Fripp[5] to go down for his grub & stay with me. My pay was $50 pr. mo. & found, or $75 & find myself.[6] I chose the latter after the first month or two. I was also allowed a cook or servant. I held the place till Dec'r., I think, or about five months, when the hands came back to work. I continued to teach in the winter, at less pay, but better paid, till 1877, when, having been appointed a trial justice by Gov. Hampton,[7] I found I could not well attend to both. I made out to live by the office & any other jobs I could pick up. Before that I was also ap-

---

[4] Samuel W. Whitwell (1816–1880).
[5] Charles Edward Fripp (1830–1906). Son of Charles E. Fripp and Mary Minott. Chaplin's second cousin, once removed, on his father's side.
[6] Chaplin received an extra $25 a month for feeding himself.
[7] Wade Hampton (1818–1902). Son of Wade Hampton II and Ann Fitzsimmons. Chaplin's schoolmate at Richland Academy in 1831. Wealthy from birth and successful at planting, in South Carolina and Mississippi, Hampton came to doubt the economic soundness of slavery. He did not favor secession, though he conceded a state's right to secede. At the start of the Civil War, he raised a cavalry unit, the Hampton Legion, which he led at First Bull Run. In the summer of 1862 he was named Brigadier General, C.S.A., and in May, 1864, upon the death of J.E.B. Stuart, he assumed command of the Cavalry Corps of Northern Virginia. After the War, he became Governor of South Carolina in the disputed election of 1876, decided in his favor by the intercession of President Rutherford B. Hayes. He served in the U.S. Senate 1890–91 and left politics upon the rise of the Populist party.

pointed notary public by Gov. Chamberlain,[8] but that paid very little. I sometimes clerked in Oliver & Ward's store, & in 1880 I got the appointment of supervisor of the census, which paid very well considering I had to hire buggy & horse. Whitwell died very suddenly in Dec'r. of this year, and then the old woman let herself loose. She immediately set to build & improve. Had the old overseer's house fixed up after a fashion, & had us moved back into it. We preferred it, as Mrs. W. had many of her relations about her by this time, & we had for some time before W.'s death been living in a small but somewhat comfortable house in the yard. We lived in this house till 1884 on what I could make in my office, & one year, about '82, Mrs. W. employed me to see after her place at a salary of $25 per month. In '84 we were both sick. I could not attend to any business. Daniel & Jim Chaplin[9] came over to see us, & insisted that we should move over to a farm Jim had near Walterboro where his father was living & where he died in the fall of '83. There was no alternative. Daniel could help us, being near him, & we could not help ourselves. In fact, I looked for nothing but death or starvation, or both. So on the 11th of October, Jim came over in a schooner & moved us bag & baggage. We had a tedious trip, having grounded on the marsh in the mouth of Coffin's Creek, & did not get over to Chapman's Fort[10] (near which Daniel spent most of the time attending to his work of shipping wood to the phosphate mines[11]) till daylight on the 13th. We stayed there till 19th Oct. & we began to improve in health from the day we went aboard the vessel. On that day we moved up to this place, & here we hope to remain to the end. I see no chances of my making anything to live on, & can only work a garden & try to raise poultry. My son, not well off himself & having a family of 4 children, has to support us entirely. God help him to be able to do so.

I find a good neighbor, & quite near, in John Witsell,[12] an oldtime friend. He & wife, an excellent lady, are the only persons Sophy & I visit. I

[8] David Henry Chamberlain (1835-1907), last Reconstruction Governor 1874-76 of South Carolina and last Republican to hold that office until 1975. Came to the state during the Civil War as a lieutenant in the 5th Massachusetts Colored Regiment (he was white). When the War ended he stayed in South Carolina and became state Attorney General in 1868. He lost the Governor's office to Wade Hampton (see note 7, p. 714) and moved to New York, where he practiced law.
[9] James H. Chaplin. Saxby's son. See Chaplin's note, Dec. 31, 1849.
[10] A small earthwork on the Ashepoo River built in 1861 as part of the coastal defenses; site of a bloody skirmish on May 26, 1864.
[11] Abundant deposits of phosphate rock were discovered in the beds of the Coosaw River in 1867. The leading promoter of using phosphates as a fertilizer, and president of S.C. Mining and Manufacturing Company, was Francis S. Holmes. A geologist and paleontologist, Holmes had compiled Chaplin's agricultural bible, *The Southern Farmer and Market Gardener*.
[12] John Witsell. See note, April 17, 1845.

have no conveyance, so I ride into the village occasionally with John, & get anything we want from there through his kindness. Dan'l & his family moved down to the pine land in the winter, & we don't see much of them. Ann[13] & her family live in D.'s house in W.[14] which enables us to get this house & farm. If I had a few hundreds of capital, I think I could make a living on this farm, but as it is, can only try to live as cheap as it is possible to do. Wood is plentiful for the cutting.

So this brings the time up to Jan. 15th, 1886. We have been here one year & 3 months, less 2 days, and the last week has been the coldest we have had, & the coldest here I am told, since 1880. The thermometer fell to 14 above 0. Weather clear till today. Our health thank the Lord has been much better than the last year of 1884. But we are both feeling the effects of age & can't stand much more thumping & tumbling about, & I pray the remainder may be passed in peace and ease. So this ends.

[13] Anne O'Hear Witsell Chaplin. John Witsell's sister and Saxby Chaplin's wife. See note, Nov. 15, 1845.
[14] Daniel's house in Walterboro.

APPENDICES

PROPERTY AND PRODUCE

NAME OF OWNER	Improved 1850	Improved 1860	Unimproved 1850	Unimproved 1860	Cash Value of Farm 1850	Cash Value of Farm 1860	Value of Farm Tools 1850	Value of Farm Tools 1860	Horses 1850	Horses 1860	Asses & Mules 1850	Asses & Mules 1860	Mulch Cows 1850	Mulch Cows 1860	Working Oxen 1850	Working Oxen 1860	Other Cattle 1850	Other Cattle 1860	Sheep 1850	Sheep 1860	Swine 1850	Swine 1860
Isabella Baker	328	—	—		4,500		100		2	—	—		10		2		10		—		10	
John M. Baker	—	100		150		3,000	75	200	3	3			6	6	2	2	15	13			20	8
C. B. Capers	—	150		120		9,000		280	—	5		2		12		4		30		20		30
C. G. Capers*	1,220		1,313		32,000		2,200		14	4	4		20	10	10		150		50		100	—
Edward M. Capers	—	250		50		10,000		600	—	4		2		12		6		30		20		15
Benjamin Chaplin, Sr.	930	140	443	20	30,000	3,000	1,600	50	12	12	8		30	8	10		100	12	50		75	8
Edwin Chaplin	250	800	50	50	5,000	6,000	250	500	4	3	6		16	6	8	2	20	14	8		30	6
John F. Chaplin, Jr.	—	200		800		9,000		440		8		1		7		5		38		4		14
John F. Chaplin, Sr.	1,035	500	360	1,000	20,000	26,000	855	1,600	8	7	2	3	30	25	5	12	180	100	32	20	39	10
Marion T. Chaplin	—	600		542		18,000		800		16		4		28		6		80		14		20
Paul Chaplin	186	500	—	580	3,500	15,000	700	400	4	3	2	4	10	12	4	6	20	40	12	33	50	40
Thomas B. Chaplin	406	300	—	106	6,000	5,000	380	300	2	4	1	2	5	10	2	4	10	18	—	20	16	15
T. A. Coffin	1,181	825	400	510	25,000	21,000	2,500	2,200	5	7	3	7	30	50	39	20	130	200	—	73	—	100
Edgar Fripp	847	700	350	300	25,000	20,000	785	650	12	9	6	7	30	20	10	10	50	60	50	52	30	40
Isaac Fripp	200	400	100	250	12,500	15,000	680	1,000	5	13	2	—	16	10	10	6	28	30	45	14	50	24
J.E.L. Fripp	222	222	24	25	5,000	6,000	200	500	3	2	1	1	9	10	2	2	10	25	11	11	35	40
J.T.E. Fripp	304	450	—	184	6,000	12,000	500	1,300	4	10	1	2	5	25	2	2	20	50	15	70	15	30
James Fripp	194	200	148	143	6,800	7,000	720	250	1	2	1	2	10	12	—	2	35	35	—		25	15
Capt. John Fripp	—	1,200		200		15,000		1,000		13		7		20		10		75		35		33
John M. Fripp	255	100	—	155	5,000	8,000	300	480	2	5	1	1	6	35	2	6	18	80	20	6	20	45
Thomas B. Fripp	201	300	—	87	5,000	7,500	280	240	2	5	—	1	10	10	2	4	10	35	18		—	6
W.O.P. Fripp	280	240	24	24	5,000	8,000	850	450	4	4	2	2	4	8	—	4	10	25	13	12	25	10
William Fripp, Sr.	1,900	2,000	1,572	1,000	30,750	50,000	1,800	1,500	16	20	2	9	20	30	15	8	150	85	15	60	101	45
William B. Fripp	250		76		7,500		600		8		2		20		8		60		40		30	
Maj. Daniel P. Jenkins	126	280	37	46	3,000	7,000	250	500	5	8	—	1	5	18	2	2		20	7	—	—	20
Capt. Daniel T. Jenkins	164	220	—	30	2,200	5,000	400	100	2	2	1	2	5	20	2	6	16	50	16		12	10
Dr. William J. Jenkins†	388	515	—	1,000	5,400	40,000	600	2,500	4	15	2	6	10	50	4	16	17	150	10	10	18	90
William A. Morcock	170	160	100	300	5,000	10,000	850	1,200	10	6	—	2	8	10	6	4	11	25	12	25	10	10
Joseph W. Perry	76		—		1,000		120		2		—		5		2		8		—		15	
J.J.T. Pope	413	1,000	205	148	25,000	25,000	1,500	1,500	8	10	4	6	16	18	6	6	45	45	20	40	47	20
Dr. M. M. Sams	121		20		2,500		400		2		1		6		2		10		—		10	
Dr. John A. P. Scott	450	570	110	80	7,000	18,000	1,600	2,000	7	7	1	2	45	45	—	10	45	105	10	45	10	40
John H. Webb	125	125	—		5,000		400		2		1		10		2		18		10		18	
Thomas G. White	—	500		110		12,000		150		4		2		10		4		48		30		18
Robert L. Baker‡	300	400	662	1,500	20,000	30,000	100	150	2	1	2	5	13	30	—		34		—		—	35
Saxby Chaplin‡	500	171	720	1,049	9,000	10,000	350	30	6	6	3	1	15		12		50		65	4	—	15

*C G Capers in 1850 also reported producing 50 pounds of cheese, 15 bushels of Irish potatoes, and 25 bushels of buckwheat

†Dr William J Jenkins in 1860 reported 12 gallons of wine

‡Reported from St Bartholomew's Parish, Colleton District

Value of Livestock (dollars)		Indian Corn, bushels		Oats, bushels		Rice, pounds		Ginned Cotton, bales of 400 lbs		Wool, pounds		Peas and Beans, bushels		Sweet Potatoes, bushels		Butter, pounds		Hay, tons		Beeswax and Honey, pounds		Value of Home Manufactures		Value of Animals Slaughtered		Slaves			
1850	1860	1850	1860	1850	1860	1850	1860	1850	1860	1850	1860	1850	1860	1850	1860	1850	1860	1850	1860	1850	1860	1850	1860	1850	1860	1845	1850	1860	1861
365		200	—	—		—		3	—	—		40		350		100	—	—		—		—		$50		14	8	—	—
585	500	250	200	—		—		4	4	—	—	50	25	200	160	—	50		2	—		—		50	$50	9	21	20	18
	1,700		460						7		60		80		600		120		6						140	42	—	37	—
3,300		1,700		100		500		50		350		150		2,000		365		2		50		—		380		—	123		
	2,100		600						15		65		120		1,000		180		7						160	—	—	29	40
2,850	1,000	1,200		—		—		156	4	—		100	20	2,500	400	350	50		2	200		—		450	40	137	133	—	—
1,250	520	150	100	40		750		8	15	—		20	40	50	400	200	50		2	—		—		100	40		—	46	51
	2,500		560						15		12		50		520		100		6						100		—	9	38
2,100	2,500	2,000	1,800	—		—		40	60	—	50	150	100	1,500	1,600	300	160	2	4	—		—		300	200	109	143	93	—
	2,800		700						35		30		200		800		160		15						80		—	57	66
1,116	2,400	800	700	—		—		8	25	30	90	70	200	800	1,200	200	150		7	100		—		100	200	34	38	75	—
550	1,200	250	500	—		—		8	7	—	60	40	60	800	800	60	200		6	—		—		75	150	67	25	30	38
2,650	2,600	2,100	2,000	200		1,200		105	60	—	140	200	75	2,000	1,160	300	400		10	200		—		400	270	133	248	253	193
3,350	3,800	1,500	1,400	—		—		55	38	—	200	300	300	3,200	2,200	220	250		13	—		—		300	320	62	122	123	—
2,100	3,000	1,000	600	—		820		33	28	100	—	180	50	1,750	400	400	100		6	150		—		300	120	61	70	80	90
1,125	1,020	650	450	40		400		14	18	30	40	50	80	1,600	1,000	250	100		2	200		—		200	250	43	47	52	56
800	6,650	500	450	—		—		15	25	—	300	100	600	900	1,000	100	150	—	8	—		—		100	150	—	32	83	44
575	780	245	400	—		250		12	13	—	—	80	20	600	400	200	100		5	50		—		80	50	26	25	43	50
	3,000		1,800						55		150		200		2,000		260		10						250	110		172	174
500	1,500	210	300	—		—		4–10	—	—		50	20	600	500	180	150		2	—		—		25	200	11	19	16	—
450	1,170	—	500	—		—		8	16	—		—	80	100	800	—	150		6	—		—		20	60	—	—	—	—
730	1,400	500	500	30		—		10	14	30	40	50	200	500	1,200	100	200		7	—		—		20	100	27	32	44	46
3,000	5,000	3,000	3,800	—		630		80	60	—	860	5,600	3,000	—		400	260	3	26	100		—		380	400	—	301	316	314
1,400		1,600		—		—		58		—		100		100		400				—		—		190					
405	1,100	800	500	—		—		10	16	—		40	100	400	350	75	100		8	—		—		25	100	16	27	50	54
600	1,200	185	600	—		—		7	20	—		75	100	600	500	100	100		4	—		—		75	50	17	19	41	—
1,000	7,000	680	2,500	—		—		18	78	—	40	100	300	1,400	1,500	180	180		2	—		—		100	480	42	60	148	155
1,400	1,500	450	450	—		600		18	15	—	25	50	50	1,000	800	400	200	3	7	50		—		95		32	31	35	18
325		200		—		—		3		—		20		300		75				80		—		35		11	—	—	—
2,150	2,700	1,500	2,200	—		300		40	45	50	150	200	200	1,500	2,000	300	250		20	—		—		180	180	91	90	122	130
500		220		—		—		7		—		50		1,500		120				—		—		50		11	20	13	—
2,100	2,140	900	1,000	180		—		25	40	—	75	300	100	500	500	250	160		20	100		—		300	180	90	100	52	—
560		350		—		—		5		25		60		650		200				—		—		100		13	30		
	1,800		470						18		100		100		480		150		6						100	—	—	37	56
550	1,800	1,400	1,400	20		68,000		—	28	—		1,311	100	750	400	250	500		8	—		—		140	150	—	—	—	—
1,896	130	800	150	400		157,000		7	2	240		350	35	400		156			1½	—		—		136	60	—	—	—	—

CHAPLIN Family

William Francis (1744–1795)
m. Martha Fripp (b. 1747)

Mary Ann (1716–1764)
m. Jonathan NORTON

Phoebe (b. 1718)
m. Joseph JENKINS

Martha (b. 1720)
m. John BARNWELL

Elizabeth
m. John EVANS (d. 1768)

William (b. 1722)
m. Sarah Saxby Reynolds

Thomas Benjamin (b. 1752)
m. Elizabeth Fripp (b. 1750)

John*
m. Ann ——— John (1682–1752)
m. Phoebe Ladson (d. 1764)

Sarah (b. 1726)
m. William FIELD

John Cato FIELD
m. Elizabeth Perry
had issue, including:

Ann (b. 1757)
m. David ADAMS

Benjamin (b. 1729)
m. 1. Sarah Ladson
   2. Eleanor Reynolds

Benjamin
m. 1. ——— Bailey
   2. Martha Reynolds

John (b. 1732)
m. Elizabeth Perry Ladson

Mary
m. William FRIPP

*John Chaplin arrived in Carolina in 1672.

Thomas (d. 1815)
m. Mary Jenkins
had issue including:

Mary Isabel (1807–1837)
m. Benjamin JENKINS

William Fripp (1767–1828)
m. 1. Catherine Toomer
had issue including:

Thomas
Saxby (1801–1873)

Edwin W. (b. 1827)
Elvira
Paul (b. 1832)
Erskine (b. 1837)
Sarah

2. Harriet Martinangel
(1796–1830)
had issue including:

James P. (1818–1865)
William F. (1820–1883)

John Fripp (1765–1817)
m. Mary Fripp

Eliza (1796–1842)
m. William B. FRIPP
(1792–1853)
Edwin (b. 1798)
m. Elizabeth _____
John Fripp (1801–1876)
m. 1. Ann Rebecca Fripp
(1804–1855)
2. Ellen Cunningham
Mary
m. William JENKINS
Hamilton F.
Charlotte
m. Isaac FRIPP

John Fripp
m. Caroline Jenkins
Marion T. (1823–1865)
m. 1. Sarah Fripp (b. 1822)
2. Ann Eliza Fripp
Edwin
Evans
Elvira (1827–1881)
m. William RABB (b. 1820)

Thomas (1768–1769)

William (1770–1818)
m. Sarah Jenkins
Thomas (1772–1855)
Elizabeth (d. 1774)
Benjamin (1776–1851)
m. Elizabeth Hann Jenkins
(1785–1867)
Sarah (1778–1816)
m. John JENKINS (1771–1822)

William S. (d. 1845)
m. Ann Fripp Jenkins
(b. 1816)
Sarah Ann (b. 1804)
m. John A. P. SCOTT
(1794–1874)

Catherine SCOTT (1822–1895)
m. Joseph D. POPE (1820–1908)
Julia SCOTT
Caroline SCOTT (b. 1837)
m. Benjamin BAILEY
William SCOTT (1840–1867)
Benjamin SCOTT (b. 1842)

Saxby (1780–1828)
m. Isabella Caroline Field
Jenkins (1785–1864)

Elizabeth Isabella (1817–1840)

Mary Louisa (1819–1828)

Thomas Benjamin (1822–1890)
m. 1. Mary Thomson
McDowell (1822–1851)
2. Sophia Creighton
(d. 1891)

Saxby (1825–1884)
m. Ann O'Hear Witsell
(1825–1915)

Ernest A. (1840–1878)
Maria Louisa (1841–1845)
Virginia Sophia (1842–1867)
m. John Wilson GLOVER
(1846–1882)
Daniel Jenkins (1843–1924)
m. Maria Louisa Chaplin
(1847–1931)
Eugene Thomas (1845–1865)
Isabella Caroline (d. 1847, infant)
Mary Frances (1849–1851)

Thomas S. (1868–1900)
Daniel J. (1870–1942)
Eugene (1872–1874)
Joseph C. (1874–1905)
m. Jessie Smith
Frederick Witsell
(1877–1955)

Frederick Saxby (1844–1850)
Caroline Isabella (1845–1935)
m. Frederick RIVERS
Maria Louisa (1842–1931)
m. Daniel J. CHAPLIN
(1843–1924)

—For issue, see above.

Archibald (1783–1849)
m. Martha Fripp (b. 1788)
had issue including:

William L. (1823–1851)
Eliza Mary (1825–1894)
m. William J. JENKINS
(1818–1883)

James Hagood (1848–1930)
m. 1. Jane D. Williams
2. Ida _____
Ann Sophia (1850–1935)
m. Henry M. NEYLE
Josephine (1853–1902)
m. Oliver P. WILLIAMS
Ruth (1855–1892)
m. Wilford BELLINGER
Florence (1852–1946)
m. Clarence ANDERSEN
Saxby (1859–1862)
Elizabeth Mary (1861–1915)
Emma George (1863–1948)
m. U. W. DAVIS
Saxby (1866–1930)
m. Pauline Sellers

Mary Rebecca
m. Benjamin ADAMS (b. 1780)
Paul Hamilton (1788–1866)

Mary Chaplin ADAMS
(1815–1890)
m. Theodore A. BELL
(1822–1882)
William ADAMS (1804–1884)
m. Elizabeth Stobo

— For issue, see above.

Benjamin ADAMS (b. 1780)
m. Mary Rebecca Chaplin
Elizabeth ADAMS

Benjamin S. (b. 1795)
m. Laura _____

Laura
Eveline
Augusta S. (1825–1852)
m. Joseph W. PERRY
(d. 1853)
Benjamin (d. 1831)

Lavinia (1802–1868)
m. 1. Robert OSWALD
2. H. D. DUNCAN

Cecilia (b. 1802)
m. William Benjamin OSWALD
Martha S. (b. 1805)
m. A. C. BAYARD

Ann OSWALD (1825–1859)
m. Richard REYNOLDS
(d. 1861)
Robert OSWALD (b. 1828)

FRIPP Family

Sarah (b. 1726)

Martha (1728–1783)
  m. Isaac WAIGHT

John (1729–1781)
  m. Elizabeth Hann

John (d. 1742) ————
  m. Sarah Frampton

John (1704–1739)
  m. Martha ————

William (1732–1794)
  m. 1. Tabitha Eddings (d. 1769)

    2. Magdalen Meggett (d.   )4)

Mary (b. 1733)
  m. John JENKINS

Elizabeth (b. 1736)

Paul (1737–1800)
  m. Amelia Reynolds (1752–1822)
  had issue including:

Martha (b. 1747)
 m. William F. CHAPLIN
John (b. 1749)
Elizabeth (b. 1750)
 m. Thomas B. CHAPLIN*
Sarah (b. 1752)
 m. 1. John EVANS
     2. _____ GRAHAM
Mary (b. 1754)
 m. John JENKINS (1750–1814)
 had issue including:

 Daniel Field JENKINS
  m. Isabella Field

William (b. 1755)
 m. Mary Chaplin

 Elizabeth (b. 1785)
 Thomas Hann (b. 1786)
 John A. (1794–1870)
  m. Mary Eddings

  Sarah (b. 1822)
   m. Marion T. CHAPLIN (1825–1865)
  Mary Julia (b. 1827)
   m. Charles TANNENT
  John Evans (1840–1918)
   m. Martha Walpole
  William Eddings (b. 1834)
   m. 1. Adeline Wescoat
       2. Alice Wescoat

 William (1788–1861)
  m. Sarah Harriet Reynolds (1797–1865)

  William Washington (1825–1885)
   m. Mary Porteous
  Alviro A. (1830–1871)
   m. Elizabeth Fripp (d. 1891)
  Clarence A. (1831–1876)†
  Phoebe Caroline (1836–1845)
  Joseph Eddings (d. 1862)
  Juliana (d. 1909)
   m. Samuel PRIOLEAU

John (b. 1757)
 m. Martha Scott

 John W. (1792–1865)
  m. 1. Caroline Chaplin (1794–1836)
      had issue including:

  Caroline (b. 1824)
   m. William CHISOLM
  Martha (1825–1900)
   m. William P. Fripp
  Elizabeth Catherine
   m. Albert CHAPLIN
  John B. (1834–1852)
  Matilda C.

Rebecca (b. 1759)
 m. James EDWARDS

      2. Elizabeth McKean (d. 1888)

  Mary (d. 1845)

 Sarah (1789–1825)
  m. Lewis R. SAMS (1784–1856)
 James (1793–1848)
  m. 1. Ann Pope (1794–1830)
      2. Mary Pope (1796–1854)
 Elizabeth Hann (1795–1831)
  m. Berners B. SAMS (1787–1855)
 William Eddings (d. 1826)
  m. Martha Edwards

  James E. Lawrence (1817–1864)
   m. Evelina Sams (1822–1861)
  William Oliver Perry (b. 1820)
   m. Thomas Ann Taylor (1826–1895)
  James Thomas E. Fripp (1822–1863)
   m. Elizabeth Amelia Fripp (1826–1867)
  Martha Ann (1824–1825)

Thomas (b. 1761)
 m. Martha Fripp (1764–1799)

 Martha (b. 1788)
  m. Archibald CHAPLIN (1783–1849)
  had issue including:
 Ann Jenkins (1793–1874)
  m. Joseph E. JENKINS (1794–1874)

  William L. (1823–1851)
  Eliza Mary (1825–1894)
   m. William J. JENKINS (1818–1883)

 Isaac K. (b. 1798)
  m. Charlotte Chaplin

  J. Edmund (d. 1862)
  George W. (1832–1862)
   m. Phoebe Morrall (d. 1862)

 David S.
  m. _____ Chaplin

  David
   m. Julia Kiddle
  Mary

Paul (1762–1810)
 m. Elizabeth Jenkins (1764–1839)
Hannah (b. 1764)
 m. Benjamin JENKINS (d. 1826)
Ann (b. 1765)
 m. Peter PERRY
Archibald (1766–1835)
 m. Elizabeth Scott (1771–1840)
Isaac (d. 1768)

 Thomas James (1808–1840)

  Thomas James

Martha (b. 1765)
 m. Thomas FRIPP
Isaac Perry (m. 1773)
 m. Mary Pope

 Eliza (1810–1860)
  m. Edgar Fripp (1806–1860)
 James (1811–1880)
  m. Caroline Eddings Sams
 Edward (1820–1842)
  m. Elizabeth Fripp
 Perry

  Eugenia (d. 1849)
  Mary Sarah (1840–1911)
   m. Clarence CHAPLIN (b. 1843)

Mary
 m. John Fripp CHAPLIN (1765–1817)
James (1777–1811)
 m. Mary _____ (1778–1817)

 Edgar (1806–1860)
  m. Eliza Fripp (1810–1860)

Thomas (1781–1837)
 m. Emmeline Jenkins
William B. (1792–1853)
 m. 1. Eliza Chaplin (1796–1842)
     had issue including:
     2. Ann F. Chaplin

 Thomas B. (1829–1862)
  m. Ellen Chisolm (d. 1895)
 John E. (1831–1906)
  m. Isabella Jenkins
 William Paul (1834–1914)
  m. Martha S. Fripp (1825–1900)

Sarah (1794–1837)
 m. Edward H. SAMS
John F.
Charles Edward (1785–1843)
 m. 1. Elizabeth M. Rivers (d. 1819)
     2. Mary Minott (1795–1860)
     had issue including:

 Elizabeth Amelia (1826–1867)
  m. James Thomas E. FRIPP (1822–1863)
 Paul Hamilton (1828–1891)
 Charles Edward (1830–1906)
  m. Harriet Ann Croskeys

*See CHAPLIN Family chart
†Clarence A. Fripp acknowledged that before
1860 he had fathered two children by his
slave and housekeeper Rachel.

JENKINS Family

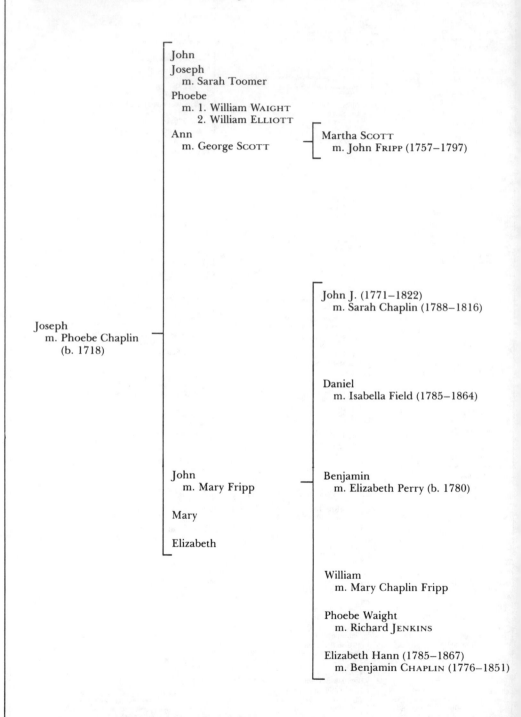

John

Joseph
    m. Sarah Toomer

Phoebe
    m. 1. William WAIGHT
         2. William ELLIOTT

Ann
    m. George SCOTT
                    Martha SCOTT
                        m. John FRIPP (1757–1797)

Joseph
    m. Phoebe Chaplin
        (b. 1718)

John J. (1771–1822)
    m. Sarah Chaplin (1788–1816)

Daniel
    m. Isabella Field (1785–1864)

John
    m. Mary Fripp
                    Benjamin
                    m. Elizabeth Perry (b. 1780)

Mary

Elizabeth

William
    m. Mary Chaplin Fripp

Phoebe Waight
    m. Richard JENKINS

Elizabeth Hann (1785–1867)
    m. Benjamin CHAPLIN (1776–1851)

William FRIPP (1788–1861)
   m. Sarah Harriet Reynolds
John FRIPP (1792–1865)
   m. 1. Caroline Chaplin (1794–1836)
      2. Elizabeth McKean (d. 1888)

Sarah
   m. Charles M. MYERS (b. 1797)

Charles Augustus MYERS (b. 1834)

Elizabeth Phoebe (b. 1803)
   m. Thomas RHODES (b. 1796)

John Jenkins RHODES (b. 1829)
Emmeline RHODES (b. 1831)
Julia RHODES
Richard Wright RHODES (b. 1834)
Frances RHODES (b. 1836)
   m. Charles Augustus MYERS

Mary (b. 1805)
   m. Joseph LEE
John
   m. Elizabeth E. Sams
Daniel T. (b. 1810)
Emmeline (b. 1812)
   m. 1. Thomas FRIPP (1781–1837)
      2. John WEBB (1811–1862)

John (d. age 12)

Benjamin
   m. Mary Isabel Chaplin (1807–1837)

Caroline (1830–1882)
   m. John Fripp CHAPLIN
Amanda (b. 1832)
   m. Thomas SCREVEN
Isabella (1833–1883)
   m. John E. FRIPP (1831–1906)

Daniel Perry (1812–1891)
   m. Anne Jenkins

seven children

Ann (b. 1816)
   m. 1. William S. CHAPLIN (d. 1845)
      2. William B. FRIPP (1792–1853)
William J. (1818–1883)
   m. Mary Eliza Chaplin
      (1825–1894)

nine children

Charlotte (1820–1892)
   m. Randall CROFT (1808–1869)

John JENKINS
Mary Caroline JENKINS (1813–1889)
   m. John F. TOWNSEND (1799–1881)
Daniel Fields JENKINS

Camilla Francine JENKINS
   m. John Wilson GLOVER (1846–1882)*

*John Wilson Glover was previously married
to Thomas B. Chaplin's daughter Virginia.

NOTE ON SELECTED SOURCES

Tombee is built upon the works of uncounted writers. The purpose of this note is to single out some books and essays whose contribution cannot be expressed adequately in a citation and to call attention to several underused sources whose obscurity strikes me as undeserved.

Many sources historians might have wished to use do not exist for antebellum Beaufort. The District's public records were sent to Columbia for safekeeping and burned in the fires which ravaged the state capital during Sherman's visit. The town library, together with collections taken from plantation Big Houses, were shipped to New York by Treasury Department agents eager to sell the captured rebel property at auction. But the plan was fiercely opposed by the Army and the northern civilian press. Declaring "we do not war on libraries," Treasury Secretary Salmon P. Chase halted the sale and ordered the books sent to Washington, to be returned to their owners when the nation was reunified. The plan proved disastrous, however. In 1865, Beaufort's books were lost in the fire that gutted the Smithsonian Institution, where they were being stored.

Yet the War, which made casualties of these fragile volumes, created a new literature that speaks eloquently of the prewar history of Beaufort and its surroundings. Of major importance are the records of the United States Direct Tax Commission for South Carolina, at the Fiscal Branch of the National Archives. Boxes of land claims and surveyors' notebooks, freedmen's petitions and tax-sale certificates, applications to redeem land and to recover the surplus proceeds from property sold and permanently lost—all are immensely useful in constructing a picture of Sea Island life *before* the Civil War. In these records are found precise measurements of

727

plantations; information on soil conditions, race relations, social alliances, and dietary habits; facts, figures, anecdotes, and a surprising diversity of outlooks. Certain aspects of family life among whites—the part played by marriage in estate formation and division, for example—are filled out by testimonies found in three volumes of cases compiled in *The United States Court of Claims for Beaufort.*

The tide of war brought northern soldiers and abolitionists to the Sea Islands and carried away the Confederates; both groups, strangers and native whites, emerged with something to tell. A strong sense of place, of a landscape that functions as a vital and enduring force in history, marks the best accounts on both sides. Northerners not only wanted to read about the novel Sea Island topography, they wanted to learn about the ways of the Negroes whose wishes would have to be considered in a reconstructed democratic society. The craving for information was partially filled by journalists who followed the northern armies into the South.

War memoirs began appearing immediately after First Bull Run. The stream of recollections continued into the early 1900s, when most Americans were not old enough to remember the War. Some who wrote at the dawn of the new century were veterans striving to preserve memories of their comrades in arms. Some had been missionaries, teachers, labor organizers—radicals in the cause of social regeneration. A few of these people were still on the job. Most helpful to me in establishing the freedmen's views of slavery and of the stewardship of their former masters were *The Letters and Diary of Laura M. Towne* (ed. by Rupert Sargent Holland: Cambridge, Mass., 1912) and *Enfranchisement and Citizenship,* by Edward L. Pierce (Boston, 1896). Towne's unedited and unscrubbed letters were an even richer source. The single most valuable abolitionist work for my purposes was the unpublished diary of William F. Allen, a Wisconsin schoolteacher who spent three war years collecting songs on St. Helena Island. (The manuscript is kept at the State Historical Society of Wisconsin, in Madison.) Allen was an empiricist in a sea of idealists. He watched; he listened; he came to the simple astonishing conclusion that race is irrelevant to understanding human nature or to measuring human potential. The discovery led him to ask: how was slavery possible? What qualities singled out some people to be masters and others to be slaves?

Willie Lee Rose made exemplary use of these and many other abolitionist sources in *Rehearsal for Reconstruction* (New York, 1964), a narrative history of the betrayal of the St. Helena freedmen.

Of the military memoirs which touch on events and people on St. Helena, the *War Letters of William T. Lusk* (New York, 1911) and *The Life of Isaac Ingalls Stevens* (Boston, 1900), by his son, Hazard Stevens, are among the most pertinent and perceptive. Lieutenant Lusk and General Stevens arrived with the invaders. Arthur W. Dimock's eyewitness account of the planters' last hours, in Katherine M. Jones's *Port Royal Under Six Flags* (New York, 1960) and John A. Johnson's recollections of life before the War, in *Beaufort and the Sea Islands: Their History and Traditions* (published serially in the *Beaufort Republican*, Beaufort, S.C., Jan. 16–July 3, 1873) are enriched by a native-born understanding of the Sea Island cultural heritage. Johnson was the man who stayed behind with Chaplin to guard the Confederate retreat from Bay Point. His story of the land confiscations and attempts at "redemption" emphasizes the sufferings of the whites.

Augustus D. Dickert's *History of Kershaw's Brigade* (Newberry, S.C., 1899) follows the movements of the cavalry units in which many Sea Island men, including Chaplin's three sons, served. It is valuable for more than its chronology and details of battles and camp life. Dickert's *History* appeared at a moment when children of the defeated Confederates were joining in organizations to memorialize the War. The mood of despair that had characterized Reconstruction—from the white perspective—had given way to new feelings. Social life had stabilized and newly invented segregation laws were fixing race relations in the old hierarchical mode. Old plantation life never seemed so perfect as it did when looked back upon from the 1890s. And its very brightest moment was the one before it ended. Dickert was steeped in this attitude—an attitude that shaped popular American ideas for sixty years.

For range and clarity, Mark M. Boatner's *The Civil War Dictionary* (New York, 1959) is an indispensable one-volume reference guide to America's bloodiest war. For rigorous accounts of any skirmish or battle, the reader should plunge into the multivolume *War of the Rebellion: A Compilation of the Official Records of the Union and Confederate Armies.* The collection could use a modern index, but once you get past the difficulties of locating your subject, you will find the firsthand accounts more stirring than any work of fiction.

The "Capture of Forts Walker and Beauregard" is told in reports from thirteen officers on both sides. Mixed with descriptions of the attack, defense, and retreat are shrewd observations of the Sea Islanders and their land.

The Autobiography of William J. Grayson (ed. by Samuel Gaillard Stoney, *South Carolina Historical and Genealogical Magazine,* vols. 48–51, 1947–50) was written in exile from Beaufort in 1862 but not published until 1947. Since then, this engrossing memoir has been mysteriously ignored by historians, perhaps because they think they know what Grayson had to say. But readers familiar with the picture of happy Negroes and kind masters pulling at the same end of the rope in *The Hireling and the Slave* will find a more sober, less ideological, and profoundly self-critical vision in Grayson's later work, written but six years after the polemical poem. The War had taught Grayson the cruel lesson that history does not necessarily proceed according to the will of people who imagine they are in control. It magnified the failings of his social class and deepened his affection for the old days—especially the years between the American Revolution and the tariff controversy, an era, he recalled, of mixed farming, freethinking, and natural abundance. Writers in the 1890s may have looked back with reverence to 1860, but Grayson did not. Against the reigning chaos and the force of disillusion, he erected a monument to a distant time in graceful, scrupulously measured prose.

A very different kind of memoir, a dissertation on cotton based on the author's observations, gave me a structure for organizing Chaplin's field routine and filled gaps in my knowledge of making a crop. Whitemarsh B. Seabrook's *A Memoir on the Origin, Cultivation and Uses of Cotton* (Charleston, S.C., 1844) is indeed autobiographical. Seabrook was an immensely successful grower of Sea Island cotton, and a renowned *thinker* on agriculture. By calling his work a memoir, he meant to convey the additional meaning of memorandum, a record to be preserved for future use. Seabrook's purpose in writing was avowedly educational. He was prodding planters to become more conscientious and observant, to standardize their procedures and share their knowledge. The content for his essay was the tenacious agricultural depression of the 1820s, '30s, and early '40s. Planting could become profitable again on a grand scale, he believed, if growers would change their habits and improve the quality of their cotton. His memoir is a repository for the techniques every grower should follow. In his time, the land of the South had not yet assumed its mystical character. The land was dirt, soil, the loose surface material of the earth in which plants grow.

An exquisite study of the planters' pastimes, and a neglected gem of American literature, is William Elliott's *Carolina Sports by Land and Water* (Charleston, S.C., 1846). Grandson and namesake of the man who had raised the first commercially successful crop of Sea Island cotton in America, Elliott was an outspoken agricultural reformer. With Seabrook, he chided planters for their laziness and lack of science. As part of a program of renewal he promoted the virtues and enjoyments of rural life—chief among them, hunting, shooting, and fishing.

Carolina Sports was roughly handled by northern reviewers— Henry David Thoreau among them—who found offensive the planters' philosophy of conquest and consumption, their aristocratic approach to the wild, and the pleasure they got from their slaves—from the lucky few who got to go on the expeditions and from the many whose labor made such activities possible. Contention over slavery was so raw at the time that reviewers missed the author's self-parody and his excellent natural history.

Thus, several of my most important sources were written by men known personally to Chaplin. He was a drinking buddy of Grayson's son William, Jr.; his brother, Saxby, was Seabrook's aide-de-camp in 1850, when Seabrook was Governor; Chaplin stayed at Elliott's hunting camp and fished with him in Port Royal Sound. Seabrook, Elliott, and Grayson shared a critique of society, though Elliott and Grayson masked it behind adulation. Troubled by the odd mix of inefficiency and greed that was sapping the planters' potential for happiness, all three men advocated reform while maintaining a self-righteous face to the outside threat of free labor and class struggle.

Much of what I know about the evolution of cotton finance, antebellum political leadership, and plantation medicine, I have learned from outstanding monographs. Three special studies, as important to me for their methods as for their results, are: Alfred Glaze Smith's *Economic Readjustment of an Old Cotton State: South Carolina, 1820–1860* (Columbia S.C., 1958), Harold S. Schultz's *Nationalism and Sectionalism in South Carolina 1852–1860* (Durham, N.C., 1950), and Todd L. Savitt's *Medicine and Slavery* (Chicago, 1978), a book about the social and environmental roots of disease in Virginia. Its insights apply with little modification to South Carolina. Besides relying heavily on these secondary sources, I have unconsciously simmered together the assumptions and findings of various distinguished scholars, notably Kenneth M. Stampp, David M. Potter, Eugene D. Genovese, and Edgar T. Thompson. Thompson's *Plantation Societies, Race Relations, and the South: The Regimentation of Populations* (Durham, N.C. 1975) is scarcely known. This is a shame. Despite its ponderous title, the book is a far-ranging, stimulating speculation on the creation of southern institutions and on the shifting adaptation of human motives to weather, soils, markets, and sources of labor.

Index

All personal names in the biography and in Chaplin's journal are listed below. Thomas B. Chaplin has no entry of his own. For an outline of his activities, the reader should consult the Table of Contents. The initials of a slave's owner follow in brackets the name of the slave. Freedmen—former slaves—are indexed without regard to status or race. Old Joe and Edward are freedmen whose surnames are not known. Free Billy was a free person of color during the slavery era. An asterisk (*) by a name calls attention to one of these possible ambiguities: Adam and Old Adam may be the same person, as may Elcy and Elsie; the entry for Charles may be a composite of two men by that name, and the entry for Mary a composite of two women; references to Mary and Little Mary may be intermingled, like references to Judy and Old Judy.

The subject listings, which follow the list of names, refer *only* to the biography. Considerations of space and the extensive distribution of subjects in the journal guided this choice. For similar reasons, entries in both name and subject listings are identified simply by page number, whether the reference is found in the text or in a note on the page.

Key to Abbreviations (listed by surname)

Personal Names

Subjects